The Routledge Handbook
of Health Tourism

The Routledge Handbook of Health Tourism provides a comprehensive and cutting-edge overview of the philosophical, conceptual and managerial issues in the field of health tourism with contributions from more than 30 expert academics and practitioners from around the world. Terms that are used frequently when defining health tourism, such as wellbeing, wellness, holistic, medical and spiritual, are analysed and explored, as is the role that health and health tourism play in quality-of-life enhancement, wellbeing, life satisfaction and happiness. An overview is provided of health tourism facilities such as thermal waters, spas, retreats and wellness hotels and the various challenges inherent in managing these profitably and sustainably. Typologies are given not only of subsectors of health tourism and related activities but also of destinations, such as natural landscapes, historic townscapes or individual resources or attractions around which whole infrastructures have been developed. Attention is paid to some of the lifestyle changes that are taking place in societies which influence consumer behaviour, motivations and demand for health tourism, including government policies, regulations and ethical considerations.

This significant volume offers the reader a comprehensive synthesis of this field, conveying the latest thinking and research. The text is international in focus, encouraging dialogue across disciplinary boundaries and areas of study and will be an invaluable resource for all those with an interest in health tourism.

Melanie Kay Smith is Associate Professor at Budapest Metropolitan University in the School of Tourism, Leisure and Hospitality. She is the co-author of the book *Health, Tourism and Hospitality: Spas, Wellness and Medical Travel* (Routledge, 2013) with Dr László Puczkó and has worked for over ten years on health tourism, including research, lecturing and the publication of several journal articles and book chapters. She has been an invited keynote speaker at many international conferences, and has undertaken health tourism consultancy work in a range of countries, including for the European Travel Commission and United Nations World Tourism Organization. She has most recently been working on Baltic health tourism and Balkan wellbeing concepts, as well as a European Cooperation in Science and Technology (COST) project on tourism, wellbeing and ecosystem services. Her most recent teaching and research focus on evidence-based healing resources and therapies.

László Puczkó is the Director of Industry Intelligence at Resources for Leisure Assets and the Head of Tourism and Leisure Knowledge Centre at the Budapest Metropolitan University (Hungary). He has been working as a travel and tourism expert in the health, wellness, medical services and spa arenas for over 20 years. He founded the Tourism Observatory for Health, Wellness and Spa in 2012. He has participated in more than a hundred projects in various fields: research, planning, product development, experience mapping and design, impact assessment and marketing. László is an internationally known and acknowledged expert; he lectures at various international professional and academic conferences and congresses. He is the (co-)author of numerous specialised books (e.g. *Health, Tourism and Hospitality* (Routledge, 2013), *Impacts of Tourism* (Häme Polytechnic, 2002)) and articles in professional journals.

The Routledge Handbook of Health Tourism

Edited by Melanie Kay Smith and
László Puczkó

LONDON AND NEW YORK

First published 2017 by Routledge

2 Park Square, Milton Park, Abingdon, Oxon OX14 4RN

605 Third Avenue, New York, NY 10017

Routledge is an imprint of the Taylor & Francis Group, an informa business

First issued in paperback 2022

British Library Cataloguing in Publication Data
A catalogue record for this book is available from the British Library

Library of Congress Cataloging in Publication Data
A catalog record for this book has been requested

ISBN 13: 978-1-138-90983-0 (hbk)
ISBN 13: 978-1-03-233980-1 (pbk)
DOI: 10.4324/9781315693774

Typeset in Bembo
by Swales & Willis, Exeter, Devon, UK

The editors would like to dedicate this book to all of the people who have helped to make their lives healthier and happier!

They would also like to thank all of the authors for their interesting chapters as well as thanking Routledge staff and especially Emma Travis and Pippa Mullins for all of their support.

Contents

Figures

Figures

Tables

Contributors

Daniel Binder, Head of Programme, MBA International Hospitality and Spa Management at FH Joanneum University of Applied Sciences, Austria

Daniel Binder is currently leading the worldwide first MBA programme focusing on hospitality and spa management. He managed several ERASMUS projects dealing with the development of learning materials and course development in spa management and health tourism. He is lecturing with a special focus on health and tourism topics like marketing, communication management, information management and new media, as well as tourism destination management. Beside his functions at the university he is working as Marketing Manager for a tourism highlight of Styria, the Birds of Prey Arena in Riegersburg. Daniel Binder is self-employed and runs a marketing agency, focusing on graphic and content development.

Robyn Bushell, Associate Professor, Institute for Culture and Society and School of Social Sciences and Psychology, Western Sydney University, Australia

Robyn Bushell teaches and researches in the field of critical heritage and tourism studies. Her research focuses on the relationship between heritage, wellbeing/quality of life and community development to deliver sustainable futures.

She authored the *Health* entry in the 2016 Routledge *Encyclopedia of Tourism* and the United Nations World Tourism Organization *Indicators of Sustainable Tourism*. She has many refereed edited books, book chapters, journal articles, commissioned reports and a number of international policy documents with a strong international network and close working relationship with lead agencies in Australia, the United Nations and the Asia Pacific Region. This includes producing the *Healthy Tourism* policy document for the Association of Southeast Asian Nations Secretariat.

Dr Paul Cleave, freelance researcher and lecturer, and honorary research fellow at the University of Exeter, UK

Paul Cleave has been researching and writing on food and tourism for over 20 years. His long-term interests in the social history of food, tourism and leisure have resulted in contributions to educational projects with the National Trust, and the use of oral histories in community support groups. This dates from the 1992 World Wildlife Summit Conference in Rio, and Paul's contribution to *Beyond the Green Horizon* (WWF UK, 1992). Recent publications include chapters in five textbooks: *Recording Leisure Lives – Holidays and Tourism in 20th Century Britain*, *Narratives of Travel and Tourism*, *Sugar Heritage and Tourism in Transition*, *Sustainable Culinary Systems*, and *The Routledge Handbook of Sustainable Food and Gastronomy*. His current research at the University of Exeter focuses on the social history of twentieth-century tourism and the evolving relationships between food, health and wellbeing in the context of tourism.

Isabelle Cloquet, Université Libre de Bruxelles, Faculté des Sciences (IGEAT-LIToTeS), Belgium

Isabelle Cloquet is a post-doctoral visiting researcher at the University of Exeter Business School. Supported by a EU-COST TObeWELL grant, her work addresses social innovation relating to health-promoting tourism experiences adapted to the needs and aspirations of the elderly. Isabelle particularly enjoys researching complex processes from a holistic and multi-disciplinary approach. Her PhD research is another example of such interest. She investigated tourism entrepreneurship and the phenomenon of destination stasis at the early stages of tourism development. Based on political economy and structure agency, her study of the case of Gabon, Central Africa, highlighted the major effects of the country's structural variables on destination shaping and growth.

Josée-Ann Cloutier, health and wellness professional, writer, environmental educator, Canada

Josée-Ann Cloutier has been researching, studying and travelling around Europe, Asia, North and Central America for the last ten years to learn and experience the various bathing and sauna traditions. She was one of the two scholarship recipients in the Master's in Wellness and Spa Service Design programme which she completed in 2015. She also won the Mary Tabacchi Scholarship in 2014 from the International Spa Association. She has trained as a massage professional and meditation instructor and has been a retreat participant and volunteer assisting with retreats for over ten years within the Shambhala Buddhist tradition. She has done research, writing and presenting on the topic of community, retreats, wellbeing, sauna bathing, water and energy conservation.

John K. Coffey, Assistant Professor of Psychology, Sewanee University, USA

John K. Coffey is an Assistant Professor at Sewanee: the University of the South, Tennessee, USA. He is the second person to earn a PhD in Positive Developmental Psychology. He earned his PhD at Claremont Graduate University and his MSW at the University of Michigan. He served on the Board of the International Positive Psychology Association as the President of the Student Division. He has authored numerous research articles and presented internationally on ways to promote wellbeing while vacationing, in close relationships, and in workplace and academic settings. John continues to consult with organisations and companies seeking to promote happiness and flourishing.

Mihály Csikszentmihályi, Professor of Psychology and Management at Claremont Graduate University, USA

Mihály Csikszentmihályi taught for 30 years at the University of Chicago, where he became Chair of the Department of Psychology. He is currently the co-director of the doctoral programme in Positive Developmental Psychology at Claremont Graduate University. He is the co-founder of the field of Positive Psychology, and the author or co-author of over 250 peer-reviewed articles and 19 books, translated into 26 (Flow), 11 (Good Business), and 9 languages (Creativity).

Maria João Ferreira Custódio, researcher, University of Algarve/International Centre of Territory and Tourism Research, Faro, Portugal

Maria João F. Custódio has been a researcher at the University of Algarve/International Centre of Territory and Tourism Research since 2000. She received her PhD in Management at the University of Exeter, Business School, in 2014. She develops applied and fundamental research in the scientific domains of management and marketing applied to tourism. Her research interests include tourism, destination branding and image, nautical tourism, tourism competitiveness, management and impacts of events on tourism.

Frederick J. DeMicco, Professor and ARAMARK Chair in the Department of Hotel, Restaurant and Institutional Management at the University of Delaware, USA

Frederick J. DeMicco is Professor and ARAMARK Endowed Chair in the Department of Hotel, Restaurant and Institutional Management at the University of Delaware, USA. He has worked in healthcare at the Massachusetts General Hospital, Boston, and also served as the Chief Dietitian and Associate Director of Dining and Technology in the Virginia Tech Dining Services for five years. He completed his PhD in Hotel, Restaurant and Institutional Management at Virginia Polytechnic Institute and State University. In 1996, he worked in Hotel Management at Walt Disney World, Florida, and obtained his Ducktorate degree from Disney University. Dr DeMicco's scholarly interests are in international strategic management, medical tourism, wine and beverage management, managerial accounting and innovation. He has authored or co-authored nearly 100 refereed articles in the area of tourism and hospitality management and he has co-authored several books, including *Restaurant Management: A Best Practices Approach* (Kendall-Hunt Publishers, 2015) and *Hospitality 2015: The Future of Hospitality and Travel* (Educational Institute of the American Hotel and Lodging Association, 2010).

Anya Diekmann, Professor in Tourism, Université libre de Bruxelles, Brussels, Belgium

Anya Diekmann is head of the tourism department at the Université Libre de Bruxelles. Her research and publications focus on cultural and social tourism, with a particular focus on social tourism systems, benefits and tourism rights. She has worked in various research projects on social tourism for governmental agencies and the International Organisation of Social Tourism and has recently participated in the COST Action TObeWELL. Amongst others, she co-edited with Scott McCabe and Lynn Minnaert the book *Social Tourism in Europe: Theory and Practice* (Channel View Publications, 2011) and with Louis Jolin, *Social Tourism: International Perspectives. The Contribution of Research* (Presses de l'Université du Québec, 2013).

Professor Sonia Ferrari, University of Calabria, Rende, Italy

Sonia Ferrari is a professor of Place Marketing and Tourism Marketing at the Department of Scienze Aziendali e Giuridiche (University of Calabria, Italy), where she has been associate professor of tourism since 2005. She has been a researcher in the same university since 1993 and has also taught management, service management, event marketing, marketing of museums and tourism management. At the same university she is President of the Tourism Science Degree Course.

Her main fields of study and research are services management, tourism marketing, place marketing, event marketing, wellness tourism, parks and natural areas marketing.

Dr Harald A. Friedl, Associate Professor, FH JOANNEUM University of Applied Sciences, Institute for Health and Tourism Management

Harald A. Friedl is a lawer and philosopher, who has worked for many years as a tour guide for ethnotourism in West Africa and Arabian countries. Since 2004, he has been a lecturer on the study program Health Management in Tourism at Bad Gleichenberg for tourism sociology, sustainable nature tourism, tourism ethics and conflict management. He has published several book chapters on health aspects in ethnotourism, peace tourism, tourism ethics and sustainability, focusing his research on the influence of cultural patterns of perception on social behaviour in the context of tourism and leisure.

Markus Frischhut, Jean Monnet Chair "European Integration & Ethics", MCI Management Center Innsbruck, Austria

Markus Frischhut has studied law in "Innsbruck and EU law at the Robert Schuman University in Strasbourg, France, with now more than 15 years of teaching and research experience. On the topic of EU cross-border healthcare, he has spoken at many international conferences (Berlin, Heidelberg, Monaco, Prague, Riga, Trento, Washington DC, to name but a few), and has published several articles, as well as a book (together with H. Stein). He has been an invited guest speaker of EU institutions, at the TAIEX event in Ankara on patient mobility (2015), and on EU law and ethics in the European Parliament, Strasbourg (2016). Furthermore, he is a member of the European Association of Health Law and the International Forum of Teachers/UNESCO Chair in Bioethics.

Warwick Frost, Associate Professor, La Trobe University, Bundoora, Victoria, Australia

Warwick Frost is a co-author of five research books: *Books and Travel: Inspiration, Quests and Transformation* (Channel View, 2012), *Commemorative Events: Memory, Identities, Conflict* (Routledge, 2013), *Explorer Travellers and Adventure Tourism* (Channel View, 2014), *Imagining the American West Through Film and Tourism* (Routledge, 2015) and *Gastronomy, Tourism and the Media* (Channel View, 2016). His research interests include heritage, events, nature-based attractions and the interaction between media, popular culture and tourism. He is a co-editor of the Routledge Advances in Events Research series; a foundation member of the organising committee of the International Tourism and Media conference series; and a member of the editorial board of the *Journal of Heritage Tourism*.

Professor Kathryn Gallagher, Seneca College, School of Fashion and Esthetics, Toronto, Canada

Kathryn Gallagher has worked in the spa industry for 28 years, beginning her career as an aesthetician, which led to management, sales, training and consulting for spa properties, before becoming a full-time professor for the two- and three-year Esthetician and Advanced Spa Therapies programme. This collected experience, along with input from various stakeholders in the spa industry, resulted in this research report and the invitation to join other leaders as a panellist at the Esthétique Spa International conference, to discuss key influences impacting the spa industry.

Monica Gilli, Sociologist of Tourism at the University of Milano-Bicocca , Italy

Monica Gilli is a sociologist of tourism at the University of Milano-Bicocca, Italy. Her research interests are: tourism as a factor in urban regeneration and local development, cultural and heritage tourism, and the relationship between tourism and identity construction. Her publications include: *Authenticity and Interpretation in Tourist Experience* (*Autenticità e interpretazione nell'esperienza turistica*: FrancoAngeli, 2009), *The Voyage Out. Sociological Studies* (*The Voyage Out. Studi sociologici*: Scriptaweb, 2012); with E. Ruspini, M. Decataldo and M. del Greco, *Tourism, Genres, Generations* (*Turismo, generi, generazioni*: Zanichelli, 2013) and *Tourism and Identity* (*Turismo e identità*: Liguori Editori, 2015).

Dina Glouberman, PhD, Co-Director Skyros Holistic Holidays, Shanklin, Isle of Wight, UK

Dina Glouberman, psychologist and humanistic psychotherapist, has been since 1979 the co-founder/director of Skyros Holistic Holidays, which has pioneered community-oriented holistic health holidays worldwide. She is also the creator of Imagework, an interactive imagery process that harnesses the imagination, and president of the International Imagework Association, as well as a specialist in burnout. She is the author of the widely translated books *Life Choices, Life Changes, The Joy of Burnout* (Skyros Books, 2010) and *You Are What You Imagine* (Watkins, 2014). Formerly lecturer at Kingston University, she is now an international trainer, coach, keynote speaker, and psychotherapist, and a member of the Board of Directors of the Association of Humanistic Psychology (Britain) (www.dinaglouberman.com; www.skyros.com; www.ahpweb.org).

Colin Michael Hall, University of Canterbury, Christchurch, New Zealand

C. Michael Hall is Professor in the Department of Management, Marketing and Entrepreneurship at the University of Canterbury, New Zealand; Docent, Department of Geography, University of Oulu, Finland, and Visiting Professor, Linnaeus University School of Business and Economics, Kalmar, Sweden. He has published widely on tourism, regional development and environmental change.

Associate Professor Dr Arnulf Hartl

Arnulf Hartl is Professor for Immunology and researcher, head of the Institute of Ecomedicine at the Paracelsus Medical University, Salzburg, Austria. His research focuses on evidence-based health tourism and the beneficial effects of nature and exercise on human physiology, immunology and psychology. He is the scientific head of Hohe Tauern Health and a member of the strategic board of the Alpine Health Region Salzburg. He earned his *venia docendi* in immunology at the Paris-Lodron University, Salzburg.

Edward H. Huijbens, Research Professor, Icelandic Tourism Research Centre, University of Akureyri, Iceland

Edward H. Huijbens is a geographer and scholar of tourism working on tourism theory, innovation, landscape perceptions, marketing strategies and health and wellbeing product development in Nordic and Arctic contexts. Edward is involved in research projects focusing on slow adventure tourism, nature perception and experiences as well as an EU COST project on Tourism, Wellbeing and Ecosystem Services. Edward has published monographs both in Iceland and internationally and co-edited four books. His latest published work focuses on the interplay of tourism and global environmental change.

Dr John S. Hull, Associate Professor, Tourism Management Department, Thompson Rivers University, Kamloops, British Columbia, Canada

John S. Hull's research focuses on tourism planning and development in peripheral regions. He has consulted for and conducted research on the health and wellness industry in a number of countries. From 2007 to 2011, he was a guest professor at the Icelandic Tourism Research Centre and was project director for a tourism strategy for Northeast Iceland focused on wellness as one of the major development themes. In 2008 he was a keynote speaker at the New Zealand Wellness Tourism Symposium and in 2011 he was a presenter at the Bali International Spa and Wellness Expo. He has published a number of articles on wellness tourism and is a case study contributor to Smith and Puczkó's *Health, Tourism and Hospitality: Spas, Wellness and Medical Travel* (Routledge, 2013). He has taught courses in spa and wellness tourism in New Zealand, Germany and Canada and is a guest professor at the University College of Southern Norway and at Harz University of Applied Sciences, Germany. He is presently researching wellness tourism and its links to mountain and Indigenous tourism in western Canada. He is co-editor of *Mountain Tourism* (CABI, 2016).

Kai Illing, Professor of Health Management in Tourism at the FH Joanneum Graz/Bad Gleichenberg (University of Applied Sciences), Austria
Kai Illing is full professor at the University of Applied Sciences in Graz/Bad Gleichenberg (Austria) in the faculty for Health Management in Tourism. Having started his career in the field of Business Administration he teaches management-related topics such as marketing, management, quality and risk management. He is freelancer at Technischer Überwachungsverein Austria and responsible for quality audits in health and leisure-related companies. He is the CEO of a consultancy dealing with the development of medical hotels.

Barbara Jongsma, Lund University, Sweden
Barbara Jongsma developed a profound interest in the human side of management and organisations during her (tourism) studies and work practice. She is therefore currently broadening her knowledge in human resources at Lund University in Sweden.

Professor Marion Joppe, University of Guelph, School of Hospitality and Tourism Management, Guelph, Canada
Marion Joppe has worked with spa organisations for over 20 years on issues of concern to them such as the professionalism of spa personnel, the adequacy of the education they receive and labour needs of the industry. The work has resulted in several reports, book chapters and journal articles. She has been an invited keynote speaker at spa industry events, but concentrates her work on the management of destinations and how spa and wellness tourism can be a powerful motivator for travel as well as a distinguishing attribute.

Dr Catherine Kelly, Senior Lecturer, University of Greenwich, London, UK
Catherine Kelly is a geographer with research interests in wellness, tourism, culture and the relationships between landscape, place, nature and wellbeing. She has worked for more than ten years in the field of wellness tourism, undertaking research, lecturing and publishing several journal articles and book chapters. She sits on the British Standards Institute for wellness, spas and tourism and also chairs the UNESCO biosphere committee for sustainable development in Brighton, with key roles in tourism and wellbeing. She is also a practitioner and works with teachers, lecturers, students and parents in educational settings delivering both indoor and outdoor wellbeing programmes and learning.

Hyelin (Lina) Kim, William F. Harrah College of Hotel Administration, University of Nevada, Las Vegas, Nevada, USA
Hyelin (Lina) Kim is Assistant Professor at William F. Harrah College of Hotel Administration at the University of Nevada, Las Vegas, USA. She received her PhD in Hospitality and Tourism Management at Virginia Tech. Her research mainly focused on senior tourist behaviour, quality-of-life research in tourism, and meeting and event management.

Dr Jinok Susanna Kim, Lecturer in Division of Tourism, College of Social Sciences, Hanyang University, Seoul, South Korea
Jinok Susanna Kim is a lecturer in the Department of Tourism at Kyung Hee University, Korea. She earned her PhD in Tourism Science at the Hanyang University, Korea. The topic of her doctoral degree thesis was 'The impact of nature-based outdoor recreation settings on the healing of tourists' attention and quality of life'. Her main research interests are health tourism, healing of tourism, wellness tourism and quality of life. Her research particularly focuses on psychological health and restorative components of environmental aspects of health tourism behaviour, and

health tourism development impacts. She has published papers on wellness tourism and the effects of forest healing programmes in the health tourism industry.

Dr Sharon Kleefield, Faculty Emeritus, Harvard Medical School, Boston, Massachusetts, USA
Sharon Kleefield was on the faculty of Harvard Medical School for 15 years. She provides International Health Care Management Education and Training programmes with faculty internationally. She also served as an Associate Professor at the University of Nice, France, for five years, teaching medical students and building a Medical and Surgical Simulation Center – the first of its kind in Europe. Dr Kleefield continues to consult and publish internationally, including for organisations and hospitals that provide services for patients who want to travel for healthcare outside their own communities. In addition to providing education and training in quality and safety related to medical travel, Dr Kleefield has worked in the following countries: Brazil, the Bahamas, China, Colombia, France, Greece, India, Italy, Portugal, Saudi Arabia, Spain, Thailand, Turkey and the UAE.

Henna Konu, Project Manager/Researcher, University of Eastern Finland, Centre for Tourism Studies, Savonlinna, Finland
Henna Konu has worked in various national and international (wellbeing) tourism research and development projects as a researcher and project manager. Her research interests are in service development, customer involvement, consumer/tourist experiences, experiential services, and wellbeing and nature tourism. Her publications include articles in several international tourism journals and she has also co-authored book chapters in international edited books in the tourism field. She is also a substitute member of the Management Committee of COST action IS1204 Tourism, Wellbeing and Ecosystem Services.

Peter Kruizinga, HZ University, the Netherlands
Peter Kruizinga is senior lecturer and researcher at the Lectorate Healthy Region at HZ University, the Netherlands and PhD candidate at Wageningen University and Research Centre. His field of research is the use of health and lifestyle in the development of coastal regions.

Associate Professor Jennifer Laing, La Trobe University, Department of Management and Marketing, Bundoora, Victoria, Australia
Jennifer Laing is a co-author of five research books: *Books and Travel: Inspiration, Quests and Transformation* (Channel View, 2012), *Commemorative Events: Memory, Identities, Conflict* (Routledge, 2013), *Explorer Travellers and Adventure Tourism* (Channel View, 2014), *Imagining the American West Through Film and Tourism* (Routledge, 2015) and *Gastronomy, Tourism and the Media* (Channel View, 2016). Her research interests include tourist narratives, rural and regional development through tourism and events and health and wellness tourism. She is a co-editor of the Routledge Advances in Events Research series; a member of the organising committee of the International Tourism and Media conference series; and a member of several editorial boards, including *Journal of Travel Research* and *Tourism Analysis*.

Dr Timothy J. Lee, Ritsumeikan Asia Pacific University (APU), Beppu, Japan
Timothy J. Lee is Professor in the Department of Hospitality and Tourism at the Ritsumeikan Asia Pacific University (APU), Japan. He is the Founding Director of the Asia Pacific Research Institute for Health-Oriented Tourism (APRI-HOT) at APU. His research interests include medical/wellness/health tourism, ethnic identity issues in the tourism industry, cultural heritage tourism and tourism development which incorporates East Asian values. He has published more than 140

research articles in academic journals, books and conferences. He is a member of the editorial board of ten leading academic journals, including *Tourism Management* and the *Journal of Travel Research*. He also acts as the Editor-in-Chief of the *International Journal of Tourism Sciences*.

Dr Courtney W. Mason, Canada Research Chair in Rural Livelihoods and Sustainable Communities, Thompson Rivers University, Kamloops, British Columbia, Canada

Courtney W. Mason's research examines how Indigenous peoples negotiate pressing health and education issues in the backdrop of enduring colonial legacies. His collaborative work with Indigenous communities identifies the impacts of being displaced from ancestral lands through the creation of parks and protected areas. His community-based research is centred on local food security and tourism development initiatives in rural and northern regions of Canada. He is the author of *Spirits of the Rockies: Reasserting an Indigenous Presence in Banff National Park* (University of Toronto Press, 2014).

Dr Scott McCabe, Professor of Marketing and Tourism, Nottingham University Business School, Nottingham, UK

Scott McCabe is editor of the *Routledge Handbook of Tourism Marketing* (2014), co-editor of *Social Tourism in Europe: Theory and Practice* (Channel View, 2012) and author of *Marketing Communications in Tourism and Hospitality* (Taylor & Francis, 2009). He has written over 50 journal articles and chapters on issues, including social tourism, tourist experience and identity, tourist motivation and stakeholder management. He has 20 years' experience as a lecturer and researcher, mainly focusing on tourism consumer behaviour and marketing. He has wide experience of managing research for the non-governmental organisation sector in UK social tourism, and has worked on numerous EU projects.

Jeremy McCarthy, Group Director of Spa for Mandarin Oriental Hotel Group and Lecturer in Spa and Hospitality Management through the University of California, USA

Jeremy McCarthy is the Group Director of Spa for Mandarin Oriental Hotel Group, leading their internationally acclaimed luxury spa and wellness division across 28 luxury hotel and resort properties and several more under development. He holds a Master of Applied Positive Psychology degree from University of Pennsylvania, USA, and has over 20 years of experience operating luxury spas in resort and hotel properties worldwide. McCarthy teaches courses in the online certification programme in Spa and Hospitality Management through the University of California, is the author of *The Psychology of Spas and Wellbeing* (2012) and hosts a blog about holistic wellbeing at http://psychologyofwellbeing.com.

Ondrej Mitas, NHTV Breda University of Applied Sciences, Academy for Tourism, Breda, the Netherlands

Ondrej Mitas is a Lecturer at the Academy for Tourism, NHTV Breda University of Applied Sciences, the Netherlands. His research interests include tourists' experiences, their emotions and their wellbeing. Specifically, he works with tourism and leisure industry partners to understand how their customers' positive emotions develop across occasions before, during and after their experiences.

Dr Jeroen Nawijn, Senior Lecturer in Tourism, NHTV Breda University of Applied Sciences, Academy for Tourism, Breda, the Netherlands

Jeroen Nawijn has published extensively on happiness and tourism. He is also interested in issues of sustainability, specifically the intention–behaviour gap in sustainable tourism, carbon labelling and decision-making processes. His most recent research focuses on touristic consumer behaviour in non-hedonic contexts, such as concentration camp memorial visits. His research has been featured extensively in newspapers and magazines worldwide.

Dr Juho Pesonen, Head of eTourism, University of Eastern Finland, Centre for Tourism Studies, Savonlinna, Finland

Juho Pesonen is the head of eTourism research at the Centre for Tourism Studies in the University of Eastern Finland. In his research Juho focuses on how information and communication technologies are changing tourism, with the emphasis on consumer behaviour. In particular, he studies market heterogeneity in wellbeing and rural tourism and the possibilities it creates for different tourism stakeholders. He has published in numerous academic journals, including the *Journal of Travel Research* and the *Journal of Travel and Tourism Marketing*.

Christina Pichler, Institute of Ecomedicine, Paracelsus Medical University, Salzburg

Christaina Pichler is a researcher and project manager at the Institute of Ecomedicine at the Paracelsus Medical University, Salzburg. Her focus is on research, project development and implementation in the field of evidence-based health tourism, urban green and blue space and indoor environmental quality. She is a member of the strategic board of the Alpine Health Region Salzburg. She graduated in Nonprofit Social and Healthcare Management with specialisations in health economics and health services research from the Management Center Innsbruck.

Dr László Puczkó, Resources for Leisure Assets, Budapest Metropolitan University, Hungary

László Puczkó is the Director of Industry Intelligence at Resources for Leisure Assets and the Head of Tourism and Leisure Knowledge Centre at the Budapest Metropolitan University, Hungary. He has been working as a travel and tourism expert in the health, wellness, medical services and spa arenas for over 20 years. He founded the Tourism Observatory for Health, Wellness and Spa in 2012. He has participated in more than 100 projects in various fields: research, planning, product development, experience mapping and design, impact assessment and marketing. László is an internationally known and acknowledged expert; he lectures at various international professional and academic conferences and congresses. He is the (co-)author of numerous specialised books (e.g. *Health, Tourism and Hospitality*: Routledge, 2013; *Impacts of Tourism*: Häme Polytechnic, 2002) and articles in professional journals. He graduated as an economist specialised in tourism at Budapest University of Economics and, following his interests in culture, arts and experiences, he also graduated from Art and Design Management of the Hungarian University of Applied Arts. Supporting his academic rigour in business and teaching, he completed his PhD in 2000. He became a Certified Management Consultant in 2003. Between 2006 and 2014 he was the president of the Association of Tourism Consultants (Hungary) and was manager at KPMG TLT (Europe, the Middle East and Africa) between 2001 and 2004.

Dr Sarah Rawlinson, Head of Department, University of Derby, Department of Hotel, Resort and Spa Management, Buxton, Derbyshire, UK

Sarah Rawlinson led the development of spa management as a subject area in higher education in the UK. The University of Derby is the world leader in spa management degrees and provides graduates to some of the most prestigious spas in the world. She has worked in education for over 20 years, including teaching, management and research, and has published several journal articles and book chapters. She has been invited to speak at international conferences, and has undertaken research on the impact of spa graduates on spa businesses and the development of curriculum, work-based learning and the different use of knowledge in the workplace. Her most recent teaching and research focus on reconfiguring tourism destinations.

David Reisman, Professor Reisman is Senior Associate at the Centre for Liberal Arts and Social Sciences, Nanyang Technological University, Singapore
David Reisman is Professor Emeritus of Economics at the University of Surrey, UK, and Senior Associate in the Centre for Liberal Arts and Social Sciences, Nanyang Technological University, Singapore. He is the author of *Health Tourism: Social Welfare Through International Trade* (Elgar, 2010), *Trade in Health: Economics, Ethics and Public Policy* (Elgar, 2014), *Health Policy: Choice, Equality and Cost* (Elgar, 2016) and a number of other books and articles. Professor Reisman received the Minerva Award for Excellence in Research on Medical Tourism from the Medical Tourism Association in 2012.

Susanna Saari, Senior Lecturer Turku University of Applied Sciences (TUAS), Faculty of Business, ICT and Chemical Engineering, Turku, Finland
Susanna Saari is co-author of *How to Develop a Competitive Health and Wellbeing Destination* (Turku University of Applied Sciences, 2014) with Donna Dvorak and Telle Tuominen. She holds an MSocSc in Leisure and Recreation studies and is a doctoral student at the University of Lapland, majoring in tourism. Her doctoral dissertation will study urban wellbeing destinations. Susanna has been the project coordinator of both the WelDest (2010–2012) and the Innovations and Learning in Spa Management (ILIS) project (2008–2010), financed by the EU and dealing with issues on health and wellness tourism destination development and spa management. Susanna is a representative of TUAS at Turku Tourism Academy as well as a board member of the Finnish Society of Tourism Research.

Gareth Shaw, Professor of Retail and Tourism Management and Associate Dean of Research at the University of Exeter Business School, UK
Gareth Shaw is Professor of Retail and Tourism Management in the University of Exeter Business School, UK. He has held numerous research grants on aspects of tourism, including a recent EU COST Action on 'Tourism, Wellbeing and Ecosystem Services'. He has co-authored a number of textbooks, including *Critical Issues in Tourism* (Wiley-Blackwell, 2002), *Tourism and Tourism Spaces* (Sage, 2004) and has co-edited *Managing Coastal Tourism Resorts: A Global Perspective, Tourism and Economic Development: European Experiences* (Channel View, 2007) and *The Rise and Fall of British Coastal Resorts* (Thomson Learning, 1996). He is currently working on innovation and knowledge transfer, tourism, wellbeing and ageing.

M. Joseph Sirgy, Department of Marketing, Pamplin College of Business, Virginia Polytechnic Institute and State University, Blacksburg, Virginia, USA
M. Joseph Sirgy is the Virginia Tech Real Estate Professor of Marketing in the Pamplin College of Business, Virginia Tech. His research interests focus on consumer self-concept, business ethics and issues related to quality of life and human wellbeing in tourism, marketing, management, real estate, urban planning, healthcare, public policy, transportation and technology.

Melanie Kay Smith, Associate Professor, Budapest Metropolitan University, School of Tourism, Leisure and Hospitality, Budapest, Hungary
Melanie Kay Smith is co-author of the book *Health, Tourism and Hospitality: Spas, Wellness and Medical Travel* (Routledge, 2013) with Dr László Puczkó. She has worked for over ten years on

health tourism, including research, lecturing and the publication of several journal articles and book chapters. She has been an invited keynote speaker at many international conferences, and has undertaken health tourism consultancy work in a range of countries, including for the European Travel Commission and United Nations World Tourism Organization. She has most recently been working on Baltic health tourism and Balkan wellbeing concepts, as well as a European Cooperation in Science and Technology (COST) project on tourism, wellbeing and ecosystem services. Her most recent teaching and research focus on evidence-based healing resources and therapies.

Professor Georg Christian Steckenbauer, Business Department, IMC University of Applied Sciences, Krems, Austria

Georg Christian Steckenbauer is Tourism Management Professor and researcher and head of research unit for the Business Department at the IMC University of Applied Sciences, Krems, Austria. His research focuses on service and experience design in tourism, tourism product development, tourism marketing and health and wellness tourism. He earned his doctorate at the Johannes Kepler University, Linz, Austria, in social sciences and economics.

Dr Ivett Sziva, Associate Professor at the Budapest Metropolitan University of Applied Sciences in Budapest, Hungary

Ivett Sziva takes part in academic and consulting research, and is mostly committed to qualitative methods. She lectures and has publications in the topic of destination management, competitiveness, health and medical tourism and e-tourism. She was recently one of the main researchers in a two-year Balkan Wellbeing project.

Alessandra Theuma, Head of Department, St Martin's Institute of Higher Education, Hamrun, Malta

Alessandra Theuma is a tourism management doctoral student at the University of Exeter in the UK. Her research interests stem from within the tourism sector: the management of firms related in the tourism sector; knowledge absorption; and tourism services purchase decisions. She has currently been working on an EU COST project on Tourism, Wellbeing and Ecosystem Services, which sees her primarily interested in exploring the impact of ageing on the consumption of tourism services.

Stephanie Tischler, IMC University of Applied Sciences, Krems, Austria

Stephanie Tischler is Tourism Management lecturer and researcher at the IMC University of Applied Sciences, Krems, Austria. Her focus is on quantitative and qualitative research methods, tourism marketing, consumer behaviour and health and sports tourism. She graduated in business administration with specialisations in tourism and leisure management, marketing science and business psychology from the Vienna University of Economics and Business.

Dr Andrzej Tucki, Assistant Professor, Department of Regional Geography and Tourism, Maria Curie-Sklodowska University, Lublin, Poland

Andrzej Tucki is co-editor of the book *The Role of Environment, Recreation and Law in People's Health* (International Scientific Association for the Support and Development of Medical Technologies, 2015) (in Polish). He has worked for over ten years on tourism geography and landscape, including research, lecturing and the publication of several journal articles. He has participated at several international conferences, visitting many european universities as an Erasmus lecturer, and undertaken tourism consultancy work in a range of cities and regions. He has most recently been working on health tourism, quality of life and senior tourism and an EU COST project on Tourism, Wellbeing and Ecosystem Services (TObeWELL).

Dr Anja Tuohino, Development Manager, University of Eastern Finland, Centre for Tourism Studies, Savonlinna, Finland

Anja Tuohino has worked in various research and development projects as a researcher and project manager since 2001. Her research has focused on wellbeing tourism development, strategic development of tourism and innovation policy. She is a member of a national wellbeing tourism strategy working group and a member of the Management Committee of COST action IS1204 Tourism, Wellbeing and Ecosystem Services. She has published academic research papers nationally and internationally. Her publications include articles in academic journals and she has co-authored several chapters in international edited books.

Telle Tuominen, Senior Lecturer, Turku University of Applied Sciences (TUAS), Faculty of Business, ICT and Chemical Engineering, Turku, Finland

Telle Tuominen is co-author of the eBook *How to Develop a Competitive Health and Wellbeing Destination* (2014) with Donna Dvorak and Susanna Saari. She has MA and MSc (Econ) degrees, and works for TUAS as senior lecturer in tourism management. Her recent research focuses on wellness destination development and wellness consumer behaviour. Telle has been responsible for several TUAS-led research and development projects and she is also a member of several steering groups of tourism development projects. Telle was actively involved in the steering groups updating the strategic programme of Finnish wellbeing tourism as well as the regional tourism strategy of Southwest Finland. She was also a core team member of the EU-financed projects Health and Wellbeing in Tourism Destination, and Innovation and Learning in Spa Management.

Muzaffer Uysal, Department of Hospitality and Tourism Management, Isenberg School of Management, Amherst, Massachusetts

Muzaffer Uysal is Professor and Chair in the Department of Hospitality and Tourism Management, Isenberg School of Management, Amherst, Massachusetts. His current research interests centre on tourism demand/supply interaction, tourism development and quality-of-life research in tourism and hospitality.

Peter Wiltshier, Senior Lecturer and Programme Leader for Travel and Tourism, Department of Hotel, Resort and Spa Management, University of Derby, UK

Peter Wiltshier is senior lecturer and programme leader for tourism management at the University of Derby in Buxton, where he aims to ensure that the public and private sector work together to develop resources and skills for communities to take charge of their own destinies. It is the pursuit of bottom-up planning and policy development that is sought. Peter is currently researching small business and lifestyles in the Peak District, as well as working with the Diocese of Derby to identify how tourism can benefit churches and through local government offices evaluating the impact of tourism on host communities. Peter supports the county, the district and parishes within Derbyshire and the Peak District in their endeavours to create a better environment for all through purposeful leisure and recreation.

Eunju Woo, Department of Tourism Administration, College of Business Administration, Kangwon National University Chuncheon, Republic of Korea

Eunju Woo is Assistant Professor in the department of Tourism Administration, Kangwon National University, Korea. She completed her PhD at Virginia Tech in 2013. Her research interests include destination marketing, tourism development and quality of life.

Preface

I have now been involved in the field of health tourism for more than ten years and it has been fascinating to increase my knowledge and understanding of this fast-changing and even faster-growing sector on an ongoing basis. Ten years ago I first came across the term 'wellness', which was not in common parlance in the UK at that time (more so in the USA). My own research had been focused on those forms of activity which are more associated with complementary and alternative therapies rather than evidence-based or medically proven treatments. Yoga, meditation and massage were the cornerstones of my work then and were an integral part of my own life too, both in terms of leisure and learning (e.g. training courses). Ten years later I find myself teaching a Master's course on evidence-based therapies and healing resources and reading numerous clinical trials about the medical evidence base for thermal waters, muds, herbs, climate therapy and ancient healing systems like Ayurveda and Chinese medicine. Some of this work suggests that much of what is offered in alternative therapies and therefore in spas and wellness centres is essentially placebo effect. This is hard to believe for someone like me, who has constantly experimented with and benefitted from all kinds of alternative therapies. I have also been lucky enough to have enjoyed robust health with almost no visits to the doctor during that time. My own holidays have often been centred around spas or retreats. I feel very lucky to have had access to the opportunities to teach, research and become a practitioner/advisor in this field. Along the way I have taught courses to students at BA and MA level about health and wellness tourism. My future teaching will include quality of life and wellbeing too. I have supervised many theses in this field. I have given keynote talks in numerous countries (thank you for the invitations!). I have been involved in a two-year project based on Balkan Wellbeing with research on health, happiness and tourism in 11 Balkan countries. As this book goes to press, a four-year EU-funded Cooperation in Science and Technology project on Tourism, Wellbeing and Ecosystem Services will end which has enabled me to gain many new insights into the importance of landscape and nature to wellbeing and tourism.

I have lived in Hungary for the past ten years, which is something of an epicentre for thermal waters and a major priority for the tourism sector here. As a result, a deeper interest in balneotherapy has developed, the results of which can be seen in one of my *Handbook* chapters here. However, in much of my writing, including this handbook, I return to my first love, which is yoga and many of the alternative therapies that can be found in retreat centres. I am the kind of person who believes in ongoing personal development: life is a perpetual journey and I believe that it is always possible to make improvements to one's own health and happiness. I constantly read books about happiness for pleasure and it is essential to remember that health and happiness need to be treated almost like a hobby and most definitely as a lifestyle in order to become a reality. In order to be truly healthy and happy, one needs to know first of all what that means (the subject of another one of my chapters in this handbook), and second, to practise it wherever possible.

We are not all lucky enough to live in a so-called 'Blue Zone' where people live the longest and possibly healthiest lives in the world, but we can always create our own Blue Zones within ourselves. This can happen in our everyday lives as well as in tourism. It has always been my personal experience that what begins as a leisure interest and an everyday passion eventually becomes part of one's personal tourism choices (e.g. for me, going to retreats or visiting spas). It is something of a cliché, but the inner journey helps to shape the outer one, whether it is life or tourism. If the inner life is a healthy, happy one, the external one will be too. And usually these positive feelings radiate to others and to the environment around us. Sustainability, ethics and wellbeing are always close to my heart, not just as global buzzwords, but as a lived reality which we can only hope may make the world a better place to live and travel in.

Melanie Kay Smith, Budapest, May 2016

Health and travel. This is the form of travel I have been involved in for over 20 years. Actually, for over 40 years. As a child, I grew up in a historic spa town (Gyula, Hungary) and I used to go and enjoy the thermal waters during my childhood years.

As a professional, I took my interest further. I visited numerous health, wellness, medical and spa destinations all around the world. I am grateful for all of these encounters since I learned so much from these visits, discussions and traditions. I learned that this industry is wonderful with rich traditions, great people, excellent resources and breath-taking sites.

I also learned that it is an industry which is so popular that there are people who want to 'own' it. And this is true not only for the industry but for academic circles. All of these, oddly, assure me that this is a really interesting and valuable branch of tourism.

During the last couple of years, working with Generation Z I had to recognise how important it would be to raise the awareness of this generation. They believe that they are super-healthy, fit and cool, and invincible. We also know that some 50 per cent of the world's population is under 30 years of age! Still, who is talking to these people? They will represent the key demand for most health services (including wellness and spa) in the coming five to ten years. Are they aware of what these services can do for them or will they look at them as lifestyle accessories? On the other hand, have we looked at what we can learn from the Blue Zone communities? What makes them live so long? How can we translate all of these traditions and rituals to our over-wired lives?

Tourism is (or mostly is) about visiting destinations which, and people who, represent different cultures, sites and traditions. Health tourism can do all of this. Culturally and geographically defined traditions, resources and destinations can make this branch of tourism really special. Certainly, health tourism can have links to heritage and cultural resources and rituals as well as to natural sites and landscapes. Of course, there are several other areas of health tourism, e.g. medical tourism based on invasive procedures that do not have much to do with local services and resources.

It can be very exciting and inspiring to work in the field of health tourism. Planning destinations, new facilities or working on policies and marketing activities can all be very rewarding. I have had the privilege to work in several countries with large numbers of great colleagues from all around the world. This is another great appeal of this industry.

I believe that sharing what I know in another way as paid work is very important. Sharing knowledge and discussing experiences both with industry representatives and with students can be very motivating and rewarding.

I have to make one resolution, however: I have to take a more active part in what I work in and know of. I thank my wonderful wife for keeping her and our spirits up!

László Puczkó, Budapest, May 2016

1

Introduction

Melanie Kay Smith and László Puczkó

Health and travel? Travelling for health? Healthy travel? The arena of health-related tourism appears to be very dynamic. Medical tourism is forecast to enjoy exponential growth. Wellness tourism is forecast to grow at an exponential rate. We can read annual trend reports and forecasts which enlist destinations and services that are expected to represent a high rate of growth or popularity every year. Industry publications and press releases are shared almost daily indicating how exceptional this industry is. Professional books and journal articles show the interest of the academic community, too.

Still, we know relatively little about this rather complex form of travel. The definition and taxonomy of health tourism are topics which are often discussed both in academic and in industry circles. It is worth noting that the UN World Tourism Organization and the European Travel Commission will soon publish their first study on this topic, titled *Exploring Health Tourism*. The editors of the handbook were co-authors of that study and learned from numerous sources how diverse and rich this industry actually is. The study suggests definitions and descriptions which the editors of this volume used as a guide for their work. Most of the chapter authors also shared similar views regarding the structure and scope of health tourism (with a few exceptions, but such debates are to be expected and encouraged, especially with authors of this calibre).

This handbook represents an important addition to existing literature in the field of health, wellness, medical, spa, wellbeing and tourism as it brings together some of the most significant authors, researchers and practitioners in the field to share their latest thoughts and most recent cutting-edge work. It is recognised that there is now a growing body of literature in this fast-growing field and that books are emerging on sub-sectors of health tourism such as wellness tourism (e.g. Voigt and Pforr, 2013), medical tourism (e.g. Connell, 2011; Lunt, Horsfall and Hanefeld, 2015), as well as more comprehensive publications encompassing all of the sectors (e.g. Smith and Puczkó, 2013). There are also numerous industry reports providing research-based studies on spas and wellness and their relationships to tourism (Global Spa Summit, 2011).

The chapters in this handbook indicate some rather important and critical aspects of the relationship between health and tourism. The authors go beyond the traditional understanding of health tourism. Many apply a wider understanding of health, which is wellbeing. Chapters explore the more holistic relationship between wellbeing, health and travel and discuss the differences and similarities between health tourism and healthy travel.

There have been few comprehensive publications which bring together such a broad spectrum of theories and research about the relationships between tourism, wellbeing and health. There have already been several studies on tourism, wellbeing, health, happiness and quality of life (e.g. Corvo, 2010; Puczkó and Smith, 2010; Nawijn, 2011; Dolnicar, Yanamandram and Cliff, 2012; Filep, 2012; Uysal, Perdue and Sirgy, 2012). It has been suggested that individual trips can create greater pre-trip than post-trip happiness (Corvo, 2010; Narwijn, 2011), that vacationers' happiness does not increase long-term wellbeing (Nawijn, 2011) and that research should perhaps focus on tourism and 'authentic happiness' rather than SWB or subjective wellbeing (Filep, 2014). It is also interesting to note that Brajša-Žganec, Lipovčan and Poljanec-Borić's (2014) research showed that residents of destinations with a higher evaluated quality of tourist offer were happier and more satisfied with their lives in general. Some of the authors in this handbook take these debates further and elaborate on them.

Numerous academic and research-based studies have attempted to define and measure wellbeing and differentiate it from quality of life, life satisfaction, happiness and other indicators of a good life. Theofilou (2013) suggests that most recent studies have failed to make a clear distinction between quality of life and wellbeing. However, when indicators are developed for wellbeing research, health is one dimension that is always included (e.g. Gross National Happiness Index, 2010; Eurofound, 2013; Gallup, 2013; Halleröd and Seldén, 2013; OECD, 2013; Human Development Index, 2014; King, Reno and Novo, 2014; Villamagna and Giesecke, 2014).

Many recent studies emphasise the importance of environmental quality for human wellbeing (e.g. Knight and Rosa, 2011; New Economics Foundation, 2012). Previous studies also suggested that nature-based experiences can improve health and wellbeing (e.g. Kaplan and Kaplan, 1989; Ulrich et al., 1991; Kaplan, 1995; Louv, 2005, 2012; Bell and Ward Thompson, 2014; Tyrväinen et al., 2014). Research has suggested that people may be at risk of losing contact with nature and developing what Louv (2005, 2012) describes as 'nature deficit disorder'. This involves an outdoor-to-indoor migration and intensive use of electronic media (Barton, 2012). Many authors in this handbook place considerable emphasis on the importance of natural landscapes as health- and wellbeing-enhancing environments in which to take holidays.

The major focus of the *Handbook* is not only on health tourism, but more the ways in which tourism can improve health and what forms of activities, experiences or environments can enhance wellbeing. There is therefore little debate about definitions of health tourism, which have been the starting point for many books in this field. It has been relatively well established that wellness tourism and medical tourism are sub-sectors of health tourism and that spa resorts, wellness hotels, retreats and hospitals are some of the contexts in which such forms of tourism take place (Smith and Puczkó, 2013). In some countries, the term 'wellness' has not always been appropriate to describe the main forms of health-related tourism that takes place there. For example, the Finnish have no word for 'wellness' and have been using the term 'wellbeing tourism' for more than ten years now, with the health-enhancing qualities of nature and landscape being a major focus (Konu, Tuhoino and Björk, 2013). Van den Eynde and Fisher (2013) examined the Australian context where wellbeing tourism is also widely used. Indeed, forms of tourism which take place in natural landscapes do not fit easily into the conventional categories of health tourism (i.e. wellness and medical tourism). However, they are becoming increasingly important for human wellbeing in the light of debates about sustainability, nature deprivation and urban stress and speed.

Smith and Puczkó (2012) suggest that different forms of tourism are likely to have different impacts on wellbeing. For example, business trips may enhance work and productivity. Going to conferences improves a sense of social wellbeing in addition to providing new professional contacts. Sun, sea and sand tourism is one of the most traditional and best-loved forms of tourism. Although there is a temptation for many tourists in this sector to engage in hedonistic activities like drinking and partying which can be detrimental to their health, there are also ample opportunities to rest offered by sun-bathing, increasing fitness through swimming and beach sports, the vitamin D benefits of the sun and social opportunities to meet others. Most tourists exaggerate their behaviour on holiday and eat, drink, party and socialise far more than at home. This can even be detrimental to health if done in excess, even though it creates a feeling of temporary wellbeing. There are debates within both psychological and tourism circles about 'hedonic' versus 'eudaimonic' paradigms of health and wellbeing (Hartwell, Hemingway, Fyall, Filimonau and Wall, 2012; McCabe and Johnson, 2012). The hedonic approach focuses on happiness and defines wellbeing in terms of pleasure attainment and the eudaimonic approach focuses on meaning and self-realisation. Voigt, Brown and Howat (2011) suggest that, in the context of wellness tourism, more hedonic wellbeing experiences might take place in a beauty spa whereas more eudaimonic experiences can be gained from spiritual retreats.

Certain forms of tourism are designed especially to improve health. In some cases, tourism is funded by governments or employers as a way of preserving or enhancing workers' health. The work of McCabe and Johnson (2012) analyses the ways in which social tourism impacts on the subjective wellbeing of participants. For example, this was the traditional function of seaside holidays for workers from industrial cities. Some trips have a primary focus on health, for example, going to medical spas or having surgery as part of medical tourism abroad. In Central and Eastern Europe and many former Soviet states, the governments fund health tourism, which mainly consists of spending several days or weeks in a medical spa or sanatorium with healing thermal waters and other therapies. Some companies may offer their employees incentive trips to spas or some form of 'occupational wellbeing'. This can include massage, personal training, nutrition, meditation and psychotherapy as well as medical assessments.

The industry still remains fragmented. There are the medical people and there are the wellness (or spa) people. The communication between the two 'sides' is developing rather slowly but it is improving. This handbook intends to build a bridge and support the communication and understanding among all those who work and research any aspect of health tourism.

Health tourism may seem to be a new form of tourism. The contrary is true. Health tourism is one of the oldest forms of tourism. Still, certain forms of health tourism have been changing and evolving, e.g. visiting retreats. Certain forms of health tourism (e.g. thermal tourism) are recently being (re)discovered in many areas of the world. This is the real reason why such health tourism forms seem to be new. They are new to a given market but can be rather traditional in other countries.

The general 'healtharisation' of the tourism and hospitality industries can lead to a wider spectrum of health and wellbeing improving services in the industry. This, however, will not make tourists staying in 'healthy' hotels health tourists, but rather health-conscious guests. The industry has not yet agreed on what a medical or wellness hotel can and should be or what a medical spa is.

We will see more diversification as well as likely standardisation running parallel. Researchers can provide a great contribution to support a better understanding of how tourism can contribute to visitors' as well as locals' wellbeing and how to incorporate wellbeing, health, wellness traditions, local assets and medical procedures into tourism products.

This handbook focuses on those forms of tourism and destinations which are especially designed to improve health (e.g. medical tourism, thermal baths, spas, holistic holidays and retreats) and those which can provide wellbeing-enhancing experiences under the right conditions and with the right management (e.g. natural landscapes). It seems to be the case that there is a growing interest in identifying which kinds of environments, landscapes, activities and experiences can contribute to enhancing human health and wellbeing.

We are grateful to all of our authors for sharing their latest insights and research with us in this handbook. It has been a pleasure and an excellent learning experience working with you all!

References

Barton, K. S. (2012) 'Colorado's millennial generation: Youth perceptions and experiences of nature', *Journal of Geography*, 111, 6.

Bell, S. and Ward Thompson, C. (2014) 'Human engagement with forest environments: Implications for physical and mental health wellbeing', in Fenning, T. (ed.) *Challenges and Opportunities for the World's Forests in the 21st Century*, Dordrecht, The Netherlands: Springer, pp. 71–92.

Brajša-Žganec, A., Lipovčan, L. K. and Poljanec-Borić, S. (2014) 'What is good for tourists should be good for residents too: The relationship between the quality of the touristic offer and subjective wellbeing of residents', *Tourism Analysis*, 19, 719–730.

Connell, J. (2011) *Medical Tourism*, Wallingford, UK: CABI.

Corvo, P. P. (2010) 'The pursuit of happiness and the globalised tourist', *Social Indicators Research*, 102, 95–97.

Dolnicar, S., Yanamandram, V. and Cliff, K. (2012) 'The contribution of vacations to quality of life', *Annals of Tourism Research*, 39(1), 59–83.

Eurofound (2013) *Third European Quality of Life Survey – Quality of Life in Europe: Subjective Wellbeing*, Luxembourg: Publications Office of the European Union.

Filep, S. (2012) 'The positive psychology and tourism', in Uysal, M., Perdue, R. and Sirgy, M. J. (eds) *Handbook of Tourism and Quality-of-Life Research: Enhancing the Lives of Tourists and Residents of Host Communities*, Dordrecht, The Netherlands: Springer, pp. 31–50.

—— (2014) 'Moving beyond subjective wellbeing: A tourism critique', *Journal of Hospitality and Tourism Research*, 38(2), 266–274.

Gallup (2013) *State of Global Wellbeing*. Available online at: http://info.healthways.com/hs-fs/hub/162029/file-1634508606-pdf/WBI2013/Gallup-Healthways_State_of_Global_Wellbeing_vFINAL.pdf (accessed 8 October 2014).

Global Spa Summit (2011) *Wellness Tourism and Medical Tourism: Where Do Spas Fit?*, New York: Global Spa Summit.

Gross National Happiness Index (2010) Available online at: http://www.grossnationalhappiness.com/survey-results/index (accessed 23 October 2015).

Halleröd, B. and Seldén, D. (2013) 'The multi-dimensional characteristics of wellbeing: How different aspects of wellbeing interact and do not interact with each other', *Social Indicators Research*, 113, 807–825.

Hartwell, H., Hemingway, A., Fyall, A., Filimonau, V. and Wall, S. (2012) 'Tourism engaging with the public health agenda – can we promote 'wellville' as a destination of choice?', *Public Health*, 126(12), 1072–1074.

Human Development Index (2014) *Sustaining Human Progress: Reducing Vulnerabilities and Building Resilience*, New York: UNDP.

Kaplan, R. and Kaplan, S. (1989) *The Experience of Nature. A Psychological Perspective*, Cambridge, UK: Cambridge University Press.

Kaplan, S. (1995) 'The restorative benefits of nature: Towards an integrative framework', *Journal of Environmental Psychology*, 15, 169–182.

King, M. F., Reno, V. F. and Novo, E. M. L. M. (2014) 'The concept, dimensions and methods of assessment of human wellbeing within a socioecological context: A literature review', *Social Indicators Research*, 116, 681–698.

Knight, K. W. and Rosa, E. A. (2011) 'The environmental efficiency of wellbeing: A cross-national analysis', *Social Science Research*, 40, 931–949.

Konu, H., Tuohino, A. and Björk, P. (2013) 'Wellbeing tourism in Finland', in Smith, M. K. and Puczkó, L. (eds) *Health, Tourism and Hospitality: Spas, Wellness and Medical Travel*, London: Routledge, pp. 345–349.

Louv, R. (2005) *Last Child in the Woods: Saving Our Children from Nature Deficit Disorder*, Chapel Hill, NC: Algonquin Books.

—— (2012) *The Nature Principle: Human Restoration and the End of Nature Deficit Disorder*, Chapel Hill, NC: Algonquin Books.

Lunt, N., Horsfall, D. and Hanefeld, J. (2015) *Handbook on Medical Tourism and Patient Mobility*, Cheltenham, UK: Edward Elgar Publishing.

McCabe, S. and Johnson, S. (2013) 'The happiness factor in tourism: Subjective well-being and social tourism', *Annals of Tourism Research*, 41, 42–65.

Nawijn, J. (2011) 'Happiness through vacationing: Just a temporary boost or long-term benefits?', *Journal of Happiness Studies*, 12(4), 651–665.

New Economics Foundation (2012) *Happy Planet Index*. Available online at: http://www.happyplanetindex.org/assets/happy-planet-index-report.pdf (accessed 20 October 2015).

OECD (2013) *Better Life Index*. Available online at: http://www.oecdbetterlifeindex.org (accessed 21 September 2015).

Puczkó, L. and Smith, M. K. (2010) 'Tourism-specific quality of life index: The Budapest model', in Budruk, M. and Philips, R. (eds) *Quality-of-Life Community Indicators for Parks, Recreation and Tourism Management*, Social Indicators Research Series 43, Dordrecht, The Netherlands: Springer, pp. 163–184.

Smith, M. K. and Puczkó, L. (2012) 'An analysis of TQoL domains from the demand side', in Uysal, M., Perdue, R. R. and Sirgy, M. J. (eds) *Handbook of Tourism and Quality-of-Life (QOL) Research: The Missing Links*, Dordrecht, The Netherlands: Springer, pp. 263–277.

—— (2013) *Health, Tourism and Hospitality: Spas, Wellness and Medical Travel*, London: Routledge.

Theofilou, P. (2013) 'Quality of life: Definition and measurement', *Europe's Journal of Psychology*, 9(1), 150–162.

Tyrväinen, L., Ojala, A., Korpela, K., Lanki, T., Tsunetsugu, Y. and Kagawa, T. (2014) 'The influence of urban green environments on stress relief measures: A field experiment', *Journal of Environmental Psychology*, 38, 1–9.

Ulrich, R. S., Simons, R. F., Losito, B. D., Fiorito, E., Miles, M. A. and Zelson, M. (1991) 'Stress recovery during exposure to natural and urban environments', *Journal of Environmental Psychology*, 11, 201–230.

Uysal, M., Perdue, R. and Sirgy, R. (2012) *Handbook of Tourism and Quality-of-Life Research: Enhancing the Lives of Tourists and Residents of Host Communities*, Dordrecht, The Netherlands: Springer.

Van den Eynde, A. and Fisher, A. (2013) 'The social construction of travelling for wellbeing in Australia', in Smith, M. K. and Puczkó, L. (eds) *Health, Tourism and Hospitality: Spas, Wellness and Medical Travel*, London: Routledge, pp. 391–395.

Villamagna, A. and Giesecke, C. (2014) 'Adapting human well-being frameworks for ecosystem service assessments across diverse landscapes', *Ecology and Society*, 19(1), 283–300.

Voigt, C. and Pforr, C. (2013) *Wellness Tourism*, London: Routledge.

Voigt, C., Brown, G. and Howat, G. (2011) 'Wellness tourists: In search of transformation', *Tourism Review*, 66(1/2), 16–30.

Part I
History and trends

This first part focuses on the factors that have shaped the development of health tourism over time, as well as analysing some of the contemporary trends which continue to influence the sector. There has always been a multi-layered usage of health resources such as spas and thermal waters, with spiritual or religious, medical and social motivations variously influencing visitors. As noted by Warwick Frost and Jennifer Laing in Chapter 2, there are different cycles and trends over time, with hot springs or thermal waters sometimes being imbued with sacred meaning, yet at other times they have taken on a more hedonistic character. It is also evident that cultures influence and re-influence each other. Eastern cultures tended to have a strong culture of bathing in springs and these traditions were re-introduced by Arabs and Turks to Europe, for example. Spa resorts and other health tourism facilities are constantly being re-invented in response to changing political and market conditions.

Changing definitions of health also impact on the usage of resources. In Chapter 3, Melanie Kay Smith discusses the contested debates that are waged around definitions of health and healthy lifestyle. Although there is often consensus during certain periods of time, these can be short-lived and therefore create trends which require rather quick responses on the part of the industry. Historically, spa resorts often served a double (if seemingly contradictory) function of both health and hedonism. Today's societies are also grappling with the dilemma of whether to choose a healthy and hopefully long life or perhaps a happier, more hedonistic but shorter one! On the other hand, studies show that healthier people tend to be happier and that happier people are usually healthier.

The third chapter in this part, by Jennifer Laing and Warwick Frost (Chapter 4), shows how such trends are also influenced by fashionistas and famous people, including royalty but also mass media celebrities. The power of cultural icons to influence large swathes of societies should not be under-estimated. Tourists often wish to emulate celebrity lives and famous individuals can become major opinion leaders and destination champions.

Overall, health tourism is influenced by numerous factors, including politics, religion, cultural traditions, social trends, mass media and technology. These change significantly over time, but societies still come back to the same questions of how to live a long, healthy and happy life – and one which is often enhanced by tourism.

2

History of spa tourism

Spirituality, rejuvenation and socialisation

Warwick Frost and Jennifer Laing

Introduction

Budapest is a city known for its spas, which take advantage of its numerous thermal springs. This spa heritage is conjured up for many by the glorious architectural exuberance of the neo-baroque Széchenyi Baths and the Seccession-style Gellért Hotel and Baths, as well as Turkish examples such as the Rudás and Király baths, dating back to the time of the Ottoman occupation. Yet it has a far older story to tell, which reaches back to the Stone Age.

Within the limits of the modern city of Budapest are the archaeological remains of the Roman city of Aquincum, capital of the province of Lower Pannonia. They include examples of public and private baths, which are a common feature of Roman settlements throughout Europe. The Romans were not however the first to exploit this natural resource and 'there is evidence that the Celts and Dacians also used these springs during the earlier Neolithic period' (Laing, Voigt and Frost, 2014: 224). During the medieval period, the current site of the Gellért Hotel and Baths was chosen as the location for a hospital, leveraging off the perceived healing properties of the waters.

As we explore in this chapter, these places can be understood as a kind of *palimpsest* or layers of cultural heritage which we call *cultural landscapes* (Frost, Laing, Reeves and Wheeler, 2012; Hardesty, 2003), comprised of layers of settlements associated with the use of thermal water for a variety of purposes, including religious rites, medicinal treatments and social encounters.

In order to understand the current state of play of contemporary spa tourism, including the development and marketing of modern spa resorts (see Chapter 3), it is important to trace its historical roots. The presence of mineral springs or sources of geothermal water led to the establishment of towns and cities that now market themselves as spa or wellness centres, as well as their rejuvenation in different periods in history, often as the result of conquest or, in more recent times, due to trends that made it fashionable to seek out spa treatments and cures. Aside from Budapest, other notable examples around the world include Bath and Cheltenham in England, Karlovy Vary (Carlsbad) in the Czech Republic, Saratoga Springs in the USA and Daylesford/Hepburn Springs in Australia.

This chapter will examine the history of spa tourism, starting from ancient times, when many travelled to or settled in places boasting hot springs and baths, a number of which were based on former sacred sites. We then trace the rise of interest in 'taking the waters' at thermal or mineral spas throughout the eighteenth and nineteenth centuries (Aron, 1999; Lempa, 2002). Beyond a Eurocentric view of spa history, we finish by exploring the role of spas or *onsen* in Japanese culture and the development of spa resorts in the New World, such as the USA, Australia and New Zealand. In doing so, we recognise that a single chapter can only provide an overview of the most important of these historical developments and that there are a number of gaps in the literature. Our conclusion thus contains recommendations for future research.

The appropriation of springs as sacred sites

The concept of a *water cult* stretches from prehistory into the early medieval period. Rivers, lakes and springs were seen as sacred and possessing magical powers. These were often the sites for religious ceremonies and offerings. Archaeologists now believe that many sword finds were the result of a long-running custom of sacrifice to the water gods – and that the story of Excalibur and the Lady of the Lake associated with the King Arthur myth is based on this practice. In Britain, the most famous of these ancient sites is the hot spring at Bath. In addition, other sacred places were associated with springs (Miles, 2005).

The Romans appropriated these sites for their own purposes. While turning them into bath houses, they still recognised their earlier religious significance and associated them with their own gods. Bath, for example, was called *Aquae Sulis*, meaning the 'Waters of the God Sul' (Miles, 2005). The Christians of the early medieval period followed the same logic. Initially, Pope Gregory ordered Augustine to destroy all pagan sites, but within a short space of time he realised that he risked alienating those he wished to convert. The policy was changed, so that sacred places were *appropriated* (Adams, 2013). Springs became holy wells, albeit still with magical healing properties. At Glastonbury, a sacred site dating way back into prehistory, a monastery was constructed, probably on the site of an ancient water shrine (Miles, 2005).

Throughout the medieval period, springs continued as sacred sites. For the common folk, they had magical healing properties and they were the sites for ongoing customs of ritual offerings such as ribbons. The main differences with earlier times were that most springs were now named for saints and their rituals incorporated those of Christianity. Even after the Reformation, the springs continued to be important to local people, albeit secularised, with local Protestant elites placing a greater emphasis on their *medicinal* rather than magical properties (Thomas, 1971).

The Romans and their legacy

Erfurt-Cooper and Cooper (2009) view the Romans as building on the traditions of using springs in the regions they conquered. Certainly, wherever they went, the Romans built bath houses which became an integral part of their culture. These were elaborate structures, with various rooms for bathing at different temperatures. Whilst having a religious element, they were widely used as a general meeting place and area for relaxation and informality.

With the decline of the Western Roman Empire, most of these baths fell into disuse. In some cases, all knowledge of these sites was lost and they have only been uncovered by accident. For example, in Braga (Portugal), the remains of a Roman bath house were discovered in 1977 when construction workers began excavating foundations for apartments (Figure 2.1). In some cases, there were surface ruins, such as Aquincum in Hungary, which was the subject of archaeological excavation in the nineteenth century. Alternatively, excavation might be prompted by a desire for loot. The Carballo bath house in Galacia was thus only rediscovered 'by two farmers in search of treasure' (Alonso-Alvarez, 2012: 18).

Figure 2.1   Archaeological remains of Roman baths at Braga, Portugal.

Source: J. Laing.

While the Western Empire declined, the Eastern Empire (Byzantium) flourished for centuries. It retained a strong culture of bathing in springs. Most importantly, through contact with adjoining cultures – particularly the Arabs and Turks – the appreciation of baths was passed on to them. When, in later centuries, the Arabs and Turks conquered parts of Europe, they reintroduced many of these customs and traditions. Accordingly, what looks today like influences simply coming from the East is in reality the result of complex processes of continual cross-fertilisation.

An intriguing example of confusion regarding this heritage comes from the town Girona in Catalonia, Spain. The Banys Àrabs (Arab Baths) (Figure 2.2) is a prominent heritage tourism site, though it is no longer a working bath house and was recently used as a backdrop for the television series *Game of Thrones*. Built in the twelfth century, its name identifies it as Arab. However, it is not, having been built by the local medieval nobility. In style and layout, it closely follows Roman design. This raises questions of whether it was based on Arab examples further south or on remaining Roman examples.

Across Europe, the remains of Roman spas existed through the medieval period. Some continued to operate, linking in with older traditions of magical springs. Others were mere ruins. It was not until the seventeenth century that a revival came. The water from springs began to be used as the basis for therapeutic treatments (*balneotherapy* or *balneology*), both for bathing in and for consuming, as part of a regime or *cure*. Royal support was also instrumental in setting the fashion for bathing, sometimes for political reasons. For example, Queen Elizabeth I 'popularised public bathing in 1571 in Britain to discourage the British from travelling to Spa in Belgium' (Smith and Puczkó, 2014: 31). The town of Spa was such a well-known resort at the time that its name was subsequently used as the nomenclature to describe all thermal resorts collectively (Smith and Puczkó, 2014; Walton, 2012). Elizabeth's actions paved the way for the rise of what was to become the most fashionable spa town of its times – Bath.

Figure 2.2   The Banys Àrabs (Arab Baths) in Girona.

Source: J. Laing.

Case study: Bath

Bath is inextricably linked with the novelist Jane Austen, despite the common perception that she disliked Bath for its shallow artificiality and the constant need to 'see and be seen'. Her characters certainly reinforce that view. For example, Austen's heroine Anne Elliot in *Persuasion* (1818) 'persisted in a very determined, though very silent, disinclination for Bath' (149) and refers to 'the white glare' (61) and 'the elegant stupidity of private parties' (189). Yet Jane herself wrote to her sister in 1799 that 'I am very happy at Bath' (quoted in Berger, 2013: 122). It was perhaps her family's permanent move to Bath that was the problem, forcing Austen to uproot herself from her beloved Hampshire countryside. She wrote almost nothing while she lived there (Berger, 2013), which contributed to the myth that Jane found Bath unsettling and brittle. Certainly Bath in Jane Austen's time was a whirl of social activity, encompassing balls, theatrical performances and concerts (Aron, 1999). Aside from the Roman Baths, there were visits to the Pump Room, to drink glasses of the mineral water, as well as the Assembly Rooms, a place for congregation and gossip, and a venue for music, card playing and dancing.

There are a number of reasons that have been advanced for Bath's reputation and fame as a spa destination in the eighteenth century. First, its waters were regarded as having medicinal properties and we can see that Austen's characters often come to Bath for that reason, rather than for socialising. Second, there was the presence of the gregarious Master of Ceremonies,

Beau Nash, who 'perhaps ensured that its frenzied gambling never became too scandalous' (Havinden, 1981: 207) and regulated social mobility and contact (Borsay, 2012; Walton, 2012). There was also the royal seal of approval, which started in 1702, when 'Queen Anne visited Bath, bringing the court, London society and a veneer of respectability with her' (Aron, 1999: 17). Third, the spa visit was a regular part of the itinerary of the Grand Tour (Borsay, 2012; Lempa, 2002) and Bath benefited from its proximity to London and 'the broader emergence of recreational travel as a pastime among the elite and upper middle class' (Borsay, 2012: 168). Fourth and perhaps foremost, was its backdrop of magnificent Regency architecture, notably the Circus (1754–1758) and the Royal Crescent (1767–1774) (Borsay, 2012; Havinden, 1981), the work of John Wood the elder and his son (John Wood the younger). The sight of these stylishly harmonious neo-classical facades is still jaw-dropping and linked with British spa heritage through its nods to Roman design, creating an image of Bath in the minds of visitors 'as a Roman city on English soil' (Haley, Snaith and Miller, 2005: 648).

The city declined as a spa resort after the Battle of Waterloo (Havinden, 1981), when visiting European spas once again became feasible. It briefly revived in the nineteenth century with the building of the Royal Baths, but was then superseded by various seaside towns in the late Victorian era (Smith and Puczkó, 2014), such as Bournemouth and Blackpool. Thankfully, despite the waning of the spas, plans to destroy the Georgian architectural heritage in the 1960s were met with protests, preserving the architectural fabric and the city is now designated as a World Heritage site (Haley et al., 2005). The closure of its municipal hot pools in 1978, due to fear of infection after a woman contracted legionnaires' disease, seemed to mark the end of Bath's grand spa reputation.

Figure 2.3 The Thermae Spa, Bath.

Source: J. Laing.

(continued)

(continued)

However these pools were eventually reopened under the brand of the *Thermae Spa* in 2006, with the help of money from the National Lottery (Laing et al., 2014).

Advertising collateral of the Thermae Spa acknowledges the spiritual history of its spring, which is described in one brochure we picked up as 'an official sacred site' and homage is paid to its Roman heritage in the naming of the Minerva Bath (Laing et al., 2014). The architecture incorporates Georgian elements, juxtaposed with glass and steel (Figure 2.3), in a fusion of old and new that is both sensitive to the past and boldly contemporary.

Europe

The eighteenth and nineteenth centuries were a golden age of spas in Europe. In nearly every country, tourist resorts grew up around springs and provided the template for later developments in specialised tourism urban landscapes. Indeed, spas set the pattern for towns built on providing leisure services for tourists attracted by nature (Borsay, 2012). While spas were attractive in general, demand ebbed and flowed and fashions and the possibilities for complementary activities and infrastructure changed over time. Consequently, many of these spa resorts were dynamic, reinventing themselves a number of times in response to changing market and political conditions (Alonso-Alvarez, 2012; Blackbourn, 2001; Brodie, 2012; Gordon, 2012).

What drove the fashion for spas has been the subject of some debate. Commonly, it is linked to changing attitudes to nature and science, associated with the more rational approach of the Age of Enlightenment. As a result there was a greater interest in the health properties of spas (Alonso-Alvarez, 2012; Aron, 1999). However, Blackbourn (2001), whilst acknowledging the new ideas of the Age of Enlightenment, argued that the eighteenth-century growth of continental spas was also driven by the fashions and needs of royal courts (Alonso-Alvarez, 2012) and by a more entrepreneurial attitude towards the commercial possibilities of leisure. Brodie (2012) and Lempa (2002) also highlight the growth of a middle class that was attracted to leisure pursuits, especially those that involved conspicuous consumption.

Paradoxically, while consuming spa water was promoted as the antidote to the problems of civilisation – nerves, stress, alcoholism and other addictions – spas were developed to provide the pleasures of that civilisation – dining, social events, gambling (Blackbourn, 2001; Walton, 2012). As Lempa (2002: 65) observes: 'A spa guest was thus pressed between dietetic prescriptions of tranquillity and rhythm, on the one hand and social incentives to find stimulation and excitement or, at least, to avoid boredom, on the other'. The fashion for royalty to holiday at spas led to a strong court culture and the idea of a season in which it was important for the elite of society to be present and to be seen. In time, a concept of *spa diplomacy* developed, in which informal and formal talks could occur in the relatively neutral space of the international spa resort.

By the nineteenth century, the market for European spas had broadened. Particularly in Germany, the *bourgeoisie* were keen to imitate the manners and customs of royalty and nobility. Accordingly, certain resorts developed to cater for this demand, whilst others struggled to retain the aura of exclusivity. Yet the presence of guests from a socially diverse background was part of its charm and provided novelty and an exotic ambience for guests, regardless of their class or ethnicity (Lempa, 2002). The development of cheap railway transport brought a flood of new customers, including large numbers of day trippers from nearby cities, with consequent criticisms that once high-class cultural enclaves were being ruined (Blackbourn, 2001).

A wide range of novelists found patronage and material in spa society. In surveying the fictional narratives of eighteenth- and nineteenth-century continental spas, Blackbourn (2001) identified a number of intriguing tropes. Spas created their own temporary societies in which social divisions were not as apparent, as the usual cues were missing or distorted. People dressed and behaved differently. Emperor Wilhelm I of Germany, for example, nearly always dressed in military uniform, except when he holidayed at the resort of Bad Ems. Introductions and assignations were less structured and formal. Consequently, spa fiction focused on the fears of such a society without the normal rules. Two types of characters regularly appeared. The first was a beautiful female, pretending to be upper class whilst trying to marry above her station. The second was the male confidence trickster, taking advantage of this social fluidity to pass himself off as aristocratic. Their targets were bored, naïve and resultantly vulnerable. Similarly, a study of eighteenth-century Scarborough identified a sexually permissive society with a high level of prostitution (Brodie, 2012).

The New World

As European settlers in the nineteenth century settled across the USA, Canada, Australia and New Zealand, they carried with them a cultural baggage that included the knowledge of trends in Europe. Paradoxically, they both appreciated and wanted to exploit nature. As their frontiers expanded, they came across a range of thermal and mineral springs. In many cases, these were already known to and used by the Indigenous people (Erfurt-Cooper and Cooper, 2009). Knowing how hot and mineral springs were valued in Europe, the settlers sought to enjoy and develop these as spa resorts. Whilst promoted as sophisticated, in contrast to Europe, the tourism that developed was broad-based and there were no royal spas. However, like their European counterparts, they served as socially sanctioned places for *courting*, giving men and women the opportunity to 'meet, socialize, play and sometimes find mates' (Aron, 1999: 26; see also Brodie, 2012). They also provided proximity to the hazards of gambling, with frequent games such as billiards or cards acting as a lure, particularly for young men (Aron, 1999).

In the USA, the two most well-known spa resorts developed in the early nineteenth century were Saratoga Springs (New York) and Hot Springs (Arkansas). Close to urban markets on the Atlantic seaboard, Saratoga Springs became arguably the pre-eminent American spa resort. Distinguished by grand hotels, it followed the European model in offering vacationers an array of gambling and social opportunities to complement the waters (Aron, 1999; Cross, 2012). Hence, many of the visitors were there 'for pleasure or fashion' (Aron, 1999: 23), rather than for recuperation. Saratoga had a miniature railroad, while another resort, Fauquier White Sulphur Springs in Virginia, staged yearly medieval festivals to keep visitors amused (Aron, 1999). Intriguingly, in 2007 Disney opened Saratoga Springs Resort in Florida, where 'the predominance of the late Victorian theme . . . suggests that the era of genteel tourism and especially the mineral springs spa holds lasting appeal' (Cross, 2012: 84).

The success of Saratoga Springs was partly due to a decision made in 1819 to separate its municipal government from the local conservative county. Further west, a different model was adopted for the Hot Springs in Arkansas. In 1832, a federal reserve was created to protect the springs. It was a federal initiative, for at that time Arkansas had not yet achieved statehood. Such an arrangement anticipated the federal declaration of Yellowstone National Park, in the territories of Montana and Wyoming in 1872 and the Hot Springs Reserve is often cited as an important milestone in the history of national parks and other protected natural areas (Frost and Hall, 2009).

Across the USA, other attempts were made to promote hot springs as tourist resorts. These met with mixed success, for often the springs were too distant from markets. Noteworthy examples include Thermopolis in Wyoming, Hot Springs in New Mexico (which changed its name to Truth or Consequences in 1950 as part of a radio promotion) and Calistoga in California's Napa Valley (an invented name combining Saratoga and California, either arising from a marketing ploy or a malapropism, depending on which story one believes).

Across the border in Canada, the builders of the Canadian Pacific Railway discovered hot springs at Banff in the Rocky Mountains. Following the example of Arkansas Hot Springs and Yellowstone, the national government acted to protect them from inappropriate development, proclaiming a reserve in 1885 and an expanded national park in 1887 (Boyd and Butler, 2009; Frost and Hall, 2009). A grand hotel was built and 'the core of the park, the Banff townsite, represented tamed nature set within British aesthetic tradition and landscape design' (Frost and Hall, 2009: 33).

New Zealand, a geologically new land, was highly thermally active. By 1888, it had 20 spa resorts, whereas in contrast Australia – much larger, but much older – had only 13 (White, 2012). In 1874, former Premier William Fox called for the thermal springs at Rotorua to be protected, specifically citing the recent US legislation to establish Yellowstone. This was probably the first example in New Zealand or Australia of the intention to duplicate the American idea of national parks. However, unlike in the USA, the Indigenous Maori were recognised as retaining ownership. Reacting to the pressure/opportunities of tourism, the solution was to create a thermal reserve, surrounded by a planned township with blocks offered on 99-year leases (Frost and Laing, 2013). A variety of European architectural styles were appropriated, with the bathhouse known as the Great South Seas Spa (now the Rotorua Museum of Art and History) built in Tudor style in 1908 and the Blue Baths (Figure 2.4) built in the 1930s in Spanish mission style (Laing et al., 2014).

In Australia, the Victorian Gold Rushes revealed numerous mineral springs. As occurred elsewhere, the settlers were led to many of these by the Indigenous people. At Hepburn Springs, Swiss-Italian miners who stayed were instrumental in developing a spa resort (White, 2012). They ran small hotels and ancillary tourist services, whereas the colonial government

Figure 2.4   The Blue Baths in Rotorua, New Zealand.

Source: J. Laing.

proclaimed the springs a reserve in 1865 and opened a railway in 1880. The government also had a role in conducting official analyses of the mineral content, providing an authoritative stamp of approval (White, 2012).

Demand for spa holidays reached a peak in the period between the two World Wars. This was an intriguing period in Australia's history. Despite the Great Depression and pressure to increase agricultural production at all costs, there was a boom in nature-based tourism. This was manifest by large increases in bushwalking, camping, scenic roadways, national parks and wild-life zoos (Frost, 2004). Spas in rural settings complemented this trend. After the Second World War, a wider range of leisure options led to a decline in spa visitation, but this has increased again in the last few decades, with redevelopments such as the Hepburn Bathhouse and Spa in Hepburn Springs and Peninsula Hot Springs at Rye on the Mornington Peninsula.

Japan

Public use of hot spring baths (*onsen*) in Japan is said to date back to the Edo Period (seventeenth to eighteenth centuries) according to Hiwasaki (2006). However, evidence of bathing in hot thermal water goes back over 2,000 years, with the Yumine *onsen* said to be 1,800 years old (Guichard-Anguis, 2011) and these places were considered to be sacred; many were graced with 'shrines or dedicated monuments to the water gods' (Serbulea and Payyappallimana, 2012: 1371). Bathing was a form of purification and a ceremony and etiquette have been developed for visiting the *onsen* which is 'unique to Japan' (Laing and Weiler, 2008: 386). Many of these *onsen* have inns (*ryokan*) attached (Laing and Weiler, 2008) which encourage visitors to stay nearby and spend longer in the region.

Japan has the greatest number of hot springs in the world, located in 3,170 areas across the country (Serbulea and Payyappallimana, 2012). This ubiquity has provided the impetus for development of therapies such as *touji* (bath cures) or *onsen ryohou* for dealing with symptoms of ill health or disease (Serbulea and Payyappallimana, 2012). This use of thermal water for medicinal or healing purposes dates back to the sixteenth century (Serbulea and Payyappallimana, 2012). Their usage was later changed to an emphasis on play and relaxation, similar to the European story. There was a similar decline in patronage in the twentieth century, with steps taken in more recent times to boost interest in visiting the *onsen*, particularly amongst younger people (Laing and Weiler, 2008). While 'there have been several rural revitalisation initiatives through decentralisation and place branding that have resulted in the revival of onsens as part of the tourism industry, they have not substantially focused on their healing aspects' (Serbulea and Payyappallimana, 2012: 1367).

Conclusion

The phenomenon of bathing in mineral springs is a global one (Walton, 2012) and thus the history of spa tourism has a tremendous reach. We have only provided a brief overview of its evolution in this chapter and more work is needed to tease out its early evolution and growth, particularly the importance of the spiritual or religious dimension in this process.

Other areas that merit further study include the history of spas in the twentieth century, 'especially post-Second World War spa histories, engaging with wide-spread decline (and revival)' (Walton, 2012: 3). We have considered Bath and Hepburn Springs in this chapter, but there are other destinations that merit closer attention in both the Old and New Worlds.

We have briefly considered the Asian history of spa tourism in the context of the Japanese *onsen*, given its longevity and importance within Japanese culture, but there are many other examples that could have been considered and are in need of further research. These include the Indian ayurvedic practices and spa tourism heritage in destinations such as Thailand, Bali and Malaysia. Other parts of the world that would benefit from research on their history of use of springs include Africa and the Middle East.

References

Adams, M. (2013) *The King in the North: The Life and Times of Oswald of Northumbria*, London: Head of Zeus.

Alonso-Alvarez, L. (2012) 'The value of water: The origins and expansion of thermal tourism in Spain, 1750–2010', *Journal of Tourism History*, 4(1), 15–34.

Aron, C. (1999) *Working at Play: A History of Vacations in the United States*, New York: Oxford University Press.

Austen, J. (1818) *Persuasion*, 1984 edition, Harmondsworth, UK: Penguin.

Berger, R. (2013) 'Hang a right at the Abbey: Jane Austen and the imagined city', in Raw, L. and Dryden, R. G. (eds) *Global Jane Austen: Pleasure, Passion and Possessiveness in the Jane Austen Community*, London: Palgrave Macmillan, pp. 119–142.

Blackbourn, D. (2001) '"Taking the waters": Meeting places of the fashionable world', in Geyer, M. H. and Paulmann, J. (eds), *The Mechanics of Internationalism: Culture, Society and Politics from the 1840s to the First World War*, Oxford, UK: Oxford University Press, pp. 435–457.

Borsay, P. (2012) 'Town or country? British spas and the urban–rural interface', *Journal of Tourism History*, 4(1), 155–169.

Boyd, S. W. and Butler, R. W. (2009) 'Tourism and the Canadian National Parks system: Protection, use and balance', in Frost, W. and Hall, C. M. (eds) *Tourism and National Parks: International Perspectives on Development, Histories and Change*, London: Routledge, pp. 102–113.

Brodie, A. (2012) 'Scarborough in the 1730s – spa, sea and sex', *Journal of Tourism History*, 4(1), 125–153.

Cross, G. (2012) 'Saratoga Springs: From genteel spa to Disneyified family resort', *Journal of Tourism History*, 4(1), 75–84.

Erfurt-Cooper, P. and Cooper, M. (2009) *Health and Wellness Tourism: Spas and Hot Springs*, Bristol, UK: Channel View.

Frost, W. (2004) 'Australia unlimited? Environmental debate in the Age of Catastrophe, 1910–1939', *Environment and History*, 10(3), 285–303.

Frost, W. and Hall, C. M. (2009) 'American invention to international concept: The spread and evolution of national parks', in Frost, W. and Hall, C. M. (eds) *Tourism and National Parks: International Perspectives on Development, Histories and Change*, London: Routledge, pp. 30–44.

Frost, W. and Laing, J. (2013) 'From Yellowstone to Australia and New Zealand: National parks 2.0', *Global Environment*, 12, 62–79.

Frost, W., Laing, J., Reeves, K. and Wheeler, F. (2012) 'A golden connection: Exploring the challenges of developing interpretation strategies for a Chinese heritage precinct on the Central Victorian Goldfields', *Historic Environment*, 24(1), 35–40.

Gordon, B. (2012) 'Reinventions of a spa town: The unique case of Vichy', *Journal of Tourism History*, 4(1), 35–55.

Guichard-Anguis, S. (2011) 'Walking through World Heritage forest in Japan: The Kumano pilgrimage', *Journal of Heritage Tourism*, 6(4), 285–295.

Haley, A. J., Snaith, T. and Miller, G. (2005) 'The social impacts of tourism: A case study of Bath, UK', *Annals of Tourism Research*, 32(3), 647–668.

Hardesty, D. L. (2003) 'Mining rushes and landscape learning in the modern world', in Rockman, M. and Steele, J. (eds) *Colonization of Unfamiliar Landscapes: The Archaeology of Adaptation*, London: Routledge, p. 81.

Havinden, M. (1981) *The Somerset Landscape*, London: Hodder and Stoughton.

Hiwasaki, L. (2006) 'Community-based tourism: A pathway to sustainability for Japan's protected areas', *Society and Natural Resources*, 19(8), 675–692.

Laing, J. and Weiler, B. (2008) 'Mind, body and spirit: Health and wellness tourism in Asia', in Cochrane, J. (ed.) *Asian Tourism: Growth and Change*, Oxford, UK: Elsevier Publishing, pp. 379–389.

Laing, J., Voigt, C. and Frost, W. (2014) 'Fantasy, authenticity and the spa tourism experience', in Voigt, C. and Pforr, C. (eds) *Wellness Tourism: A Destination Perspective*, London: Routledge, pp. 220–234.

Lempa, H. (2002) 'The spa: Emotional economy and social classes in nineteenth-century Pyrmont', *Central European History*, 35(1), 37–73.

Miles, D. (2005) *The Tribes of Britain*, London: Phoenix.

Serbulea, M. and Payyappallimana, U. (2012) 'Onsen (hot springs) in Japan – transforming terrain into healing landscapes', *Health and Place*, 18, 1366–1373.

Smith, M. and Puczkó, L. (2014) *Health, Tourism and Hospitality: Spas, Wellness and Medical Travel*, 2nd edn, London: Routledge.

Thomas, K. (1971) *Religion and the Decline of Magic*, New York: Scribner.

Walton, J. K. (2012) 'Health, sociability, politics and culture. Spas in history, spas and history: An overview', *Journal of Tourism History*, 4(1), 1–14.

White, R. (2012) 'From the majestic to the mundane: Democracy, sophistication and history among the mineral spas of Australia', *Journal of Tourism History*, 4(1), 85–108.

3

An overview of lifestyle trends and their impacts on health tourism

Melanie Kay Smith

Introduction

This chapter provides an overview of some of the main lifestyle trends in Western developed countries that influence the health tourism sectors (e.g. spas, wellness hotels, retreats, medical facilities). This includes health developments, such as the increase in life expectancy and longevity, but the parallel decrease in healthy lifestyle practices. It includes the growing obsession with food, not only in positive directions such as healthier eating and local, homegrown produce, but also the more negative sides such as anorexia and other eating disorders like orthorexia. There is a focus on the importance of exercise and fitness for both health and happiness, while recognising that moderation can be as good as, if not better than, excess. Sleep deprivation and poor sleep quality are also growing problems for many people, and research suggests that the impacts of this are significant. Emphasis is placed on the need to slow down, to be more mindful, to decrease the use of technology and to (re)connect with nature. A positive outcome of this may be greener lifestyles and more sustainable approaches to hospitality and tourism. Work plays an important role in life but can also be a major source of stress and even depression. The use of complementary and alternative therapies appears to be growing, despite a convincing lack of evidence to prove their benefits. The implications of these and other trends are then considered for the health tourism sector in terms of product and service development.

A case study is given of research undertaken in 11 Balkan countries about self-perceived health and happiness levels of a representative sample of residents of those countries. Although they were not asked specifically about health tourism, data was collected about how important travel is for health and happiness, whether they travel outside their country to improve their health and happiness and which activities make them happiest. These findings (and others like these) may have implications for leisure and tourism developments in the future.

Healthy lifestyles

The definition of health has broadened in recent years to include not only the physical body, but mental and psychological health too. There are some doubts that conventional healthcare can provide all of the tools that one might need to lead a 'holistically' healthy life. As stated by

Crowley and Lodge (2007: 30), 'Modern medicine does not concern itself with lifestyle problems'. However, the concept of healthy lifestyles in Western, developed countries is a contested one. Research studies seem to emerge every few years which contradict previous studies that had influenced lifestyle trends for years (e.g. eggs are unhealthy; wine is good for health; coffee is bad for health; chocolate boosts mood; all fats are bad, only certain fats are bad). It is difficult even to define what is meant by a healthy lifestyle. Is it one where people live a long time or where they are happy for the time that they are alive (even if it is shorter)? Clearly, a long, happy, healthy life would be optimum, but this is not easy to define and even more difficult to achieve. According to the NHS (2013), despite a continuing trend of increasing life expectancy, overall, many adult populations are less healthy than they used to be in the past. They quote a study that was based on 6,000 adults in the Netherlands aged 20–59 comparing the prevalence of risk factors for stroke, heart disease and diabetes within different generations over a period of 16 years. 'Unfavourable generation shifts' were most pronounced for overweight or obesity, as well as high blood pressure and diabetes. However, it was also reported that a decrease in smoking and improved healthcare compensated for some of these increasing risks, explaining the still-growing life expectancy.

Jaslow (2013) quotes a US study in which researchers found that almost 39 per cent of baby boomers were obese, compared to about 29 per cent of adults in the previous generation. Boomers were also more inactive, with 52 per cent of them reporting a sedentary lifestyle with no physical activity, compared with only 17.4 per cent of the previous generation. Baby boomers were also more likely to have diabetes, high blood pressure and high cholesterol than their parents. Overall, 32 per cent of adults in the previous generation reported they were in 'excellent' health, compared with only 13 per cent of baby boomers.

King et al. (2009) support this finding in another study from the United States. The purpose of their study was to compare adherence to healthy lifestyle habits in adults between 1988 and 2006. The five healthy lifestyle trends included: five fruits and vegetables per day; regular exercise 12 times per month; maintaining healthy weight (body mass index 18.5–29.9 kg/m^2); moderate alcohol consumption (up to one drink per day for women, two per day for men); and not smoking. Results from the National Health and Nutrition Examination Survey 1988–1994 were compared with results from the same survey for 2001–2006 among adults 40–74 years. Over the last 18 years, body mass index has increased from 28 per cent to 36 per cent; physical activity has decreased from 53 per cent to 43 per cent; smoking rates have not changed; eating five or more fruits and vegetables a day has decreased from 42 per cent to 26 per cent; and moderate alcohol use has increased from 26 per cent to 40 per cent. Adherence to all five healthy habits has gone from 15 per cent to 8 per cent. Overall, adherence to a healthy lifestyle pattern had decreased in three out of five healthy lifestyle habits.

It seems that there is some consensus about what constitutes a healthy lifestyle and what does not. The Harvard Health Letter (2015) quoted several studies: one large study which found that women who had six healthy lifestyle habits – not smoking, getting regular physical activity, eating a healthy diet, maintaining normal weight, drinking no more than one alcoholic drink per day and watching TV for 7 hours or less per week – were 92 per cent less likely to develop heart disease than those who did not have these lifestyle habits. Two notable studies found that the Mediterranean diet may improve cognitive function and slow the ageing process. Moderate exercise was found to be almost as beneficial as intensive exercise.

Wijnkoop et al. (2013) suggest that nutrition is undoubtedly a major modifiable determinant of disease. They give the example of how trials showed that dietary improvements were associated with between 65 and 72 per cent reduction in all-cause mortality, major cardiovascular events and stroke over the 5-year follow-up among those receiving the Mediterranean diet compared with those on the American Heart Association diet. But for many people, quick-fix, faddy diets seem a much easier solution for weight loss than a new, long-term regime of healthy eating. However, it is fairly well documented that not only do diets not work, but that more weight will ultimately be gained as a result (Roth, 2010).

On the other hand, it is equally unhealthy to be overly preoccupied by food, diet and exercise. Orthorexia nervosa (ON) is an alleged eating disorder in which the person is excessively pre-occupied with healthy food. ON entails a fixation on healthy food or a health food depend-ence. Fears and worries about health, eating and the quality of food are significant. In extreme cases, the obsessive and compulsive characteristics of ON become pathological and dominate a person's life. The pathological obsession with biologically pure food and shops which sell it leads to a special lifestyle. Orthorectic features are also related to lifestyle habits such as regular sports activity, more dietary restrictions and less alcohol intake and an inclination to per-suade others about the importance of a healthy diet (Varga et al., 2014). The National Eating Disorders Association (2016) suggest that eating disorders have grown at an unprecedented rate over the past two decades and that nearly 50 years of research confirms that anorexia nervosa has the highest mortality rate of any psychiatric disorder. A negative body image is one of the main causes of this. Roy and Payette (2012) suggest that a negative body image has been linked with an array of unhealthy physical and mental health outcomes, including emotive, anxious and depressive disorders as well as psychological distress.

The role of exercise in health can be significant, but again, it is difficult to determine how much and what kind is best. Nunan et al. (2013) cite World Health Organization recommenda-tions that all adults should aim for 30 minutes of moderate activity daily on at least 5 days over a 1-week period, with slight variants of these recommendations for children (under-5s and 5–18 years) and older adults (aged 65+). Paoli and Bianco (2015: 610) note that, although 'physical fitness' is not synonymous with 'wellness' or 'health', they conclude from a systematic review that 'beyond age, regular physical activity and a healthy lifestyle (so an increased fitness level) can help individuals in being "healthy"'. Ideally, they recommend a minimum of 60 minutes per day of physical activity. Crowley and Lodge (2007) have written popular self-help books for both men and women that advocate at least 6 days of exercise per week. They state the reason that people are so tired at the end of the day is because they do not get enough exercise. Part of this they attribute to losing touch with one's inherent and ancestral nature and the need for natural movement.

Another area of life that can positively or adversely affect health is sleep. In addition to physical activity, sleep has been shown to be a positive coping mechanism. Darling et al. (2012) quote a study of both genders that showed that subjects who slept less than 7 hours per day had a higher average body mass index and were more likely to be obese than subjects who reported getting 7 or more hours of sleep per day. In their own study, Darling et al. (2012) noted that those women who slept 7 or more hours per day perceived fewer family strains/changes, less health stress and a greater satisfaction with life. Shochat (2012) discusses the impact of lifestyle and technology trends on sleep quality, quantity and timing. Factors include excessive and constant use of technology (e.g. TV, computer, cell phone) and behavioural lifestyle factors like weight gain, insufficient exercise and consumption of caffeine, alcohol and nicotine. In addition to lifestyle changes and reduction of use of technology, especially close to bedtime or in the bedroom, Shochat (2012) suggests that exercise interventions have shown some benefits in sleep quality.

Technology use is also responsible for decreasing time spent outdoors and in nature. Richard Louv's work on nature deficit disorder (2005, 2012) suggests that human beings and especially children, have increasingly lost touch with nature and the natural environment, resulting in attention problems, obesity, anxiety and depression. In his study of human happiness, Weil (2013: 41) states that 'Not only do we suffer from nature deficit, but we are also experiencing information surfeit'. He concludes that the modern, post-industrial lifestyles that human beings have created for themselves are incompatible with their true nature, which was to thrive in natural environments and in bonded social groups.

Khoury et al. (2013) concluded from their meta-analysis of existing studies on mindfulness-based therapy that it was effective in treating psychological disorders and showed large and clinically significant effects in treating anxiety and depression. Olano et al. (2015) provided an analysis of mindfulness practices (e.g. meditation, yoga, tai chi and qi gong) based on the US National Health Interview Survey from 2002, 2007 and 2012. They concluded that around 13 per cent of all adults engaged in at least one of the practices, but that men were approximately half as likely as women to engage in any of the practices and more than three times less likely to practise yoga.

Many people are exploring alternative forms of healthcare, including treatments and therapies and many are self-diagnosing and medicating using internet sites. Studies report that over 65 per cent of Japanese, 48.5 per cent of Australian, 20–50 per cent of European, the majority (80 per cent) of the Chinese and 42.1 per cent of people from the USA used complementary and alternative medicine (CAM) in the past year (Bomar, 2013). Versnik Nowak and Hale (2012) suggest that Americans are using increasing amounts of CAM. In the USA, 38.3 per cent of adults reported using at least one of 36 types of CAM therapies in the past 12 months. The most commonly used were non-vitamin, non-mineral, natural products (17.7 per cent), deep-breathing exercises (12.7 per cent), meditation (9.4 per cent), chiropractic or osteopathic manipulation (8.6 per cent), massage therapy (8.3 per cent) and yoga (6.1 per cent). The main increases seen are for acupuncture, deep-breathing exercises, massage therapy, meditation, naturopathy and yoga. Posadzki et al. (2012) undertook research on CAM use in the UK. The three most commonly used methods of CAM were acupuncture, homeopathy and relaxation therapy. Zheng and Xue (2013) describe how one-quarter of Australians are using one of the three CAM therapies: acupuncture, chiropractic and osteopathy. Versnik Nowak and Hale (2012) cite the National Center for Complementary and Alternative Medicine, which has organised CAM therapies into five main categories:

1 alternative medical systems (e.g. acupuncture, ayurveda, homeopathy, naturopathy, traditional Chinese medicine;
2 biologically based therapies and natural products (e.g. diet-based therapies, folk medicine, multivitamin therapy);
3 manipulative and body-based therapies (e.g. chiropractic/osteopathic, massage therapy, movement therapy);
4 mind–body therapies (e.g. aromatherapy, deep breathing, reiki, meditation, tai chi, qi gong, yoga);
5 other CAM therapies (e.g. crystal therapy, light therapy, energy healing, iridology, reflexology).

Bomar (2013) suggests that the reasons for increased use of CAMs are: (1) acceleration in the cost of healthcare; (2) a desire for increased health autonomy by consumers; (3) interest in new CAM healthcare options; (4) belief in holistic values and wellness promotion; and (5) Western medicine/mainstream medicine is not completely effective in meeting consumers' body–mind–spirit needs. A large proportion of doctors in the UK seem to employ CAM, but only 10 per cent had received any training. However, White et al. (2014) suggest that, although serious

CAM-related risks are low, CAM practice is provided outside the national healthcare systems and often practised by non-regulated personnel.

It seems that conventional medicine is only one route to health. The combination of a healthy diet, regular (moderate) exercise, mindfulness practices, contact with nature, as well as some alternative and complementary therapies can afford a surer way to holistic health. The following section explores in more depth some of the ways in which happiness levels can be enhanced further, also boosting health. Davidson and Begley (2013) note that people with high levels of positive emotion tend to rate their health as better than those with low levels of positive emotion even if objectively they are no healthier. On the other hand, there is some evidence to suggest that happier people show better health outcomes and that positive thinkers may live longer.

Happy lifestyles

Happiness is almost as contentious as health in terms of agreed definitions and characteristics. Happiness is often considered to be synonymous with 'subjective wellbeing' by positive psychologists (e.g. Diener et al., 1999). Ryan and Deci (2001) suggest that conceptualisations of wellbeing originate from two different philosophical traditions – the hedonic and the eudaimonic approach. The former is associated mainly with happiness, whereas the latter includes self-actualisation and fulfilling one's potential. Helliwell and Putnam (2004) suggest that the optimum notion of happiness or living life well should include both perspectives. The World Health Organization (WHO, 1998) uses the WHO-5 scale to measure (subjective) wellbeing, which includes:

- I have felt cheerful and in good spirits.
- I have felt calm and relaxed.
- I have felt active and vigorous.
- I woke up feeling fresh and rested.
- My daily life has been filled with things that interest me.

One of the problems with undertaking research on happiness as suggested by Davidson and Begley (2013) is that researchers cannot trust respondents to tell them honestly and accurately how happy or satisfied they are. Feelings and emotions change from moment to moment depending on the weather or if people have had a bad day at work, for example. Therefore, it is always better to measure people's levels of happiness longitudinally and across multiple moments and to aggregate the data. Power (2013: 145) suggests that '"happiness" is an over-worked and ambiguous word, which, it is argued, should be restricted and only used as the label for a brief emotional state that typically lasts a few seconds or minutes'. He also argues that being (over)-optimistic can be detrimental to health; for example, older people who are pessimistic and who experience health events often do better than older people who are optimists. This might be the case if someone were over-optimistic about a disease diagnosis and failed to receive treatment as a result, for example. Weil (2013: 21) states that, 'The notion that a human being should be constantly happy is a uniquely modern, uniquely American, ultimately destructive idea'.

There is something of a consensus that happiness (as well as health and longevity) is dependent on a number of factors. These include:

- enjoyable or engaging work;
- social activities and a sense of community;
- altruism, helping others or volunteering;

- moderate exercise;
- healthy and light eating;
- enough rest and sleep (7 hours or more);
- living in the present/mindfulness practices;
- regular contact with nature and green spaces;
- spiritual or religious activities;
- slowing down, doing everything at the right speed.

(Chopra, 1993; Honoré, 2004; Haidt, 2006;
Davidson and Begley, 2013; Weil, 2013)

Chopra (1993: 249) states that 'successful aging is far more than the avoidance of disease, although that is important. It involves a lifelong commitment to oneself every day'. Health and happiness are viewed as states that require some effort to achieve. Haidt (2006) suggests that happiness comes from within and without and is about balance and adapting to different approaches at different stages of life (e.g. ancient and new, Eastern and Western). De Botton (2009) suggests that the role of work in people's lives should not be underestimated, providing not only meaning in life but a distraction from life's futility and thoughts of death. On the other hand, occupational stress is becoming a major problem for many people. Indeed, the Global Wellness Institute (GWI, 2016) recently brought out a research report which examines wellness at work and how to overcome disengagement and work-related stress.

Still, it is not enough to focus only on one's individual sense of happiness and health. At the same time as losing touch with nature, many human beings have been over-consuming the earth's resources, but Pretty (2013) demonstrates that environmental 'overshoot' has not actually increased wellbeing. The Happy Planet Index (New Economics Foundation, 2012) was one of the first wellbeing research studies to insist that it is not enough for societies to have a long life expectancy and to feel happy; they must also take some responsibility for the planet and issues of sustainability. Hence, the so-called 'happiest' countries in other surveys (e.g. Denmark in Eurofound, 2013 or Gallup, 2013) scored lower in the rankings because of their high carbon footprint. Ericson et al. (2014) insist that the trade-off between wellbeing and environment need not mean huge sacrifices. Many individuals feel that they cannot make enough difference to the planet because of the overwhelming influence of uncommitted governments and global corporations, but Colin Beaven (2009: 221) in *No Impact Man* stresses the power and responsibility of the individual: 'We cannot wait for the system to change. We individuals are the system'. Ericson et al. (2014) suggest that mindfulness can increase people's propensity to value nature and encourage sustainable behaviour. Indeed, mindfulness can have multiple benefits for healthy lifestyles.

Case study: health and happiness in the Balkan countries[1]

Research was undertaken in 2014 with a sample of the general populations of 11 Balkan countries which asked them to evaluate their levels of health and happiness. The 11 countries were: Albania, Bulgaria, Bosnia and Herzegovina, Bulgaria, Croatia, Macedonia, Montenegro, Romania, Serbia, Slovenia and Turkey. The questionnaire was undertaken in each Balkan country over the telephone with 1,000 residents who were sampled representatively in terms of gender, age, education level

(continued)

(continued)

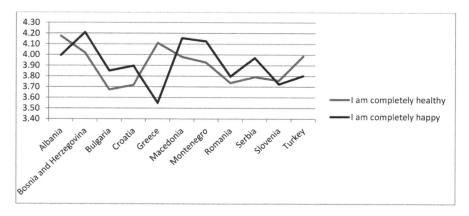

Figure 3.1   Relationship between health and happiness in the Balkans.

and place of residence (town or countryside). Respondents were asked to rank their health and happiness levels. The results were quite diverse (Figure 3.1), showing that it is perfectly possible to feel quite healthy but also very unhappy at the same time (e.g. Greece, which had exceptional political and economic circumstances at the time of the research).

In most cases, Balkan residents rate their happiness higher than their health. This is not surprising given the relatively short life expectancies in the region, the growing cost of medicines relative to salaries and the low number of doctors in many countries because of outmigration, lack of investment and incentives.

In terms of age and health, there is, not surprisingly, a steady decline in feeling completely healthy as people get older and they have more conditions which need constant attention or treatment. On the other hand, healthy living becomes more important and people make more efforts to stay healthy. In all countries, young people (15–29 years) consider themselves to be the healthiest whereas older people (60–99 years) consider themselves to be the least healthy. They have more health conditions which need constant attention, they sometimes travel elsewhere for medical treatments, healthy living is more important to them and they make more effort to keep healthy. Although not statistically significant for the overall sample, women seem to have more health problems, consider themselves less healthy and travel more for medical treatments, but healthy living is more important to them and they make more effort to keep healthy.

In terms of happiness and age, it seems that the youngest (aged 15–29) are the happiest, followed by the oldest (aged 60–69), with the middle generations, especially 40–49-year-olds, being the least happy (this is in line with theories which suggest that middle-aged people have the lowest levels of happiness, e.g. Office for National Statistics, 2016). Older people make a bit more effort to stay happy. People living in the countryside seem to be a little bit happier than those in towns. Education levels affect happiness in quite diverse ways according to each country, but there is a noticeable pattern that people with higher education are often unhappier than those with less. This could be due to unfulfilled expectations in countries that have many economic and political problems and afford few opportunities for highly educated people.

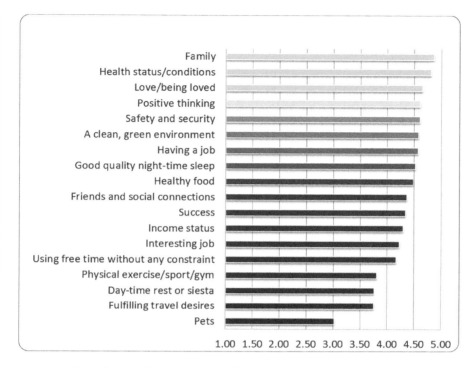

Figure 3.2 Main factors of happiness in Balkan countries.

Family, health and love are the three most important elements (Figure 3.2). This is consistent with quality of life surveys (e.g. Rahman et al., 2005). However, it is surprising that work and income do not feature as prominently as they do in some other studies. For example, Easterlin (2006) stated that, according to most research on quality of life or subjective wellbeing income, family, health and work play the most important role. Travel is the least important (along with siesta). This is also consistent with other quality-of-life studies where travel is not top of mind for respondents, but if it is mentioned by the researcher, they declare that it *is* actually important or at least the act of travelling regularly rather than individual trips (Puczkó and Smith, 2010). It also has to be remembered that in the majority of the Balkan countries salaries are very low and large numbers of local residents are unable to fulfil travel desires for financial reasons. It is therefore unsurprising that travel may not be top of mind when discussing happiness.

One interesting point should be noted about food. Those countries with a predominantly or partly Mediterranean diet (e.g. Greece, Albania, Slovenia) seem to have the longest life expectancy. Although Greeks and Slovenians have the highest levels of obesity in the Balkans (Becic, 2014), they also have the highest life expectancy (Human Development Index, 2014). As discussed earlier in the chapter, it is possible to be obese yet live a long life. During the research, some discussion took place about food that is good for mood (i.e. happiness) and food that is good for health. The two are not necessarily the same and this raises interesting questions again

(continued)

27

(continued)

about whether it is better to engage in activities that make one happy or to focus on what is supposedly healthy (assuming that this is known).

A comparison was made between which of the activities in Figure 3.3 were learnt from parents and grandparents and which ones are still practised now. The most significant findings were that in all countries the respondents are cooking and eating traditional foods in far greater numbers than those who learnt; religious activities have increased but non-religious spiritual practices have declined significantly, whereas a reverse trend can be seen in many Western European countries (in many Balkan countries, religion was often surpressed in the past, for example, during social-ist times); visits to the sea have increased in almost all countries except in those that became landlocked after the Yugoslavian war (e.g. Serbia, Macedonia); the use of spas, hammams or steam is surprisingly low considering the history of balneology in many of the Balkan countries; however, the use of natural healing resources is increasing. Natural healing resources are used mainly for health reasons (almost 50 per cent); religious activities are undertaken mainly for happiness (42 per cent); 38 per cent of people cook and eat traditional food for health reasons, 27 per cent for happiness. These findings could have useful implications for tourism product and service development, for example, showing the importance of natural healing resources, seaside, healthy gastronomy and religion.

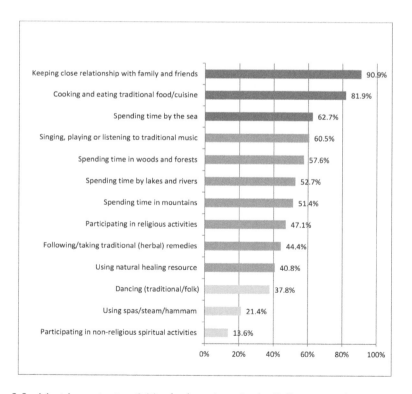

Figure 3.3 Most important activities for happiness in the Balkan countries.

Table 3.1 Lifestyle trends and health tourism products

Lifestyle trend or issue	Related heath tourism product/service
Lack of exercise	Fitness retreats; gyms and fitness classes in wellness hotels and spas
Growing obesity/unhealthy eating	Boot camps; detox clinics or spas; retreats with vegetarian, vegan, raw and/or organic food; slow food destinations
Over-use of technology	Digital detox retreats; booking into hotels with limited WiFi access, no TV, etc; visiting areas with limited access to technology (e.g. small islands, mountain villages)
Sleep deprivation/poor sleep quality	Sleep therapy clinics in spas; wellness hotels with special features for promoting sleep (e.g. special pillows, aromatherapy oils)
Occupational/work-based stress	Occupational wellness retreats; incentive spa visits
Negative body image	Psychological counselling in a retreat; beauty treatments in a spa; cosmetic surgery in a medical tourism hospital or clinic
Increasing interest in CAM	CAM therapies on spa menus; energy healing in retreats
Limited contact with nature/ unsustainable lifestyle	Eco-therapy in retreats or spas; eco-retreats; eco-villages; green spas
Need to slow down/ mindfulness	Stays in small villages or on remote islands; holistic retreats (e.g. offering meditation, yoga)
Need for spiritual activities	Spiritual ashrams or retreats; stays in monasteries; pilgrimages

Note: CAM = complementary and alternative medicine.

Leisure and lifestyle trends: implications for health tourism

Clearly, many of the lifestyle trends that have been identified in the research about health and happiness can be used to inform the health tourism sector in terms of what kinds of products to develop and which services to offer. As a summary, Table 3.1 lists the main lifestyle trends that have been discussed in this chapter so far, including measures that should or could be taken to improve health. Some suggestions are made as to how the health tourism sector has already integrated or could integrate these trends into their product and service development.

Conclusion

The main trends identified in this chapter will be elaborated on throughout this handbook. Although research shows some contradictory and confusing notions about health, there is nevertheless some consensus about what constitutes a healthy and happy life and the two are deeply connected (i.e. healthier people tend to be happier and vice versa). More holistic approaches need to be taken towards health which integrate the physical, emotional, psychological and even spiritual dimensions of life. Subsequent chapters will explore how far it is necessary to engage in tourism experiences in order to enhance health and happiness and what benefits are afforded by tourism compared to everyday life activities. Although it could be argued that tourism experiences are short-lived and contribute to happiness rather than long-term wellbeing or quality of life, healthier holidays which address some of the lifestyle issues that affect human health may have a very different impact. Although they are unlikely to cure illnesses (with the exception of surgical medical tourism in some cases), they can set the tourist on a path towards improved lifestyle and better health once back home. The educational and transformational potential of health tourism is certainly an area worthy of further investigation and will be touched upon in subsequent chapters, especially those which focus on wellness and holistic forms of tourism.

Note

1 The research quoted in this case study was financed under the Research and Technology Innovation Fund (KTIA_AIK_12-1-2013-0043) called Adaptation and ICT-supported development opportunities of regional wellbeing and wellness concepts to the Balkans.

References

Beaven, C. (2009) *No Impact Man: Saving the Planet One Family at a Time*, London: Piatkus.
Becic, S. (2014) *Balkan Health Statistics Intro*. Available online at: http://healthfitnessrevolution.com/balkan-health-statistics (accessed 9 October 2014).
Bomar, P. J. (2013) 'Comments on complementary and alternative healing modalities', *International Journal of Nursing Practice*, 19(2), 1–6.
Chopra, D. (1993) *Ageless Body, Timeless Mind*, London: Random House.
Crowley, C. and Lodge, H. S. (2007) *Younger Next Year: Live Strong, Fit and Sexy – Until You're 80 and Beyond*, New York: Workman.
Darling, C. A., Coccia, C. and Senatore, N. (2012) 'Women in midlife: Stress, health and life satisfaction', *Stress and Health*, 28, 31–40.
Davidson, R. J. and Begley, S. (2013) *The Emotional Life of Your Brain*, London: Hodder and Stoughton.
De Botton, A. (2009) *The Pleasures and Sorrows of Work*, London: Penguin Group.
Diener, E., Suh, E. M., Lucas, R. M. and Smith, H. L. (1999) 'Subjective wellbeing: Three decades of progress', *Psychological Bulletin*, 125(2), 276–302.
Easterlin, R. A. (2006) 'Life cycle happiness and its sources: Intersections of psychology, economics and demography', *Journal of Economic Psychology*, 27, 463–482.
Ericson, T., Kjonstad, B. G. and Barstad, A. (2014) 'Mindfulness and sustainability', *Ecological Economics*, 104, 73–79.
Eurofound (2013) *Third European Quality of Life Survey – Quality of Life in Europe: Subjective Wellbeing*, Luxembourg: Publications Office of the European Union.
Gallup (2013) *State of Global Wellbeing*. Available online at: http://info.healthways.com/hs-fs/hub/162029/file-1634508606-pdf/WBI2013/Gallup-Healthways_State_of_Global_Wellbeing_vFINAL.pdf (accessed 8 October 2014).
GWI (2016) *The Future of Wellness at Work*, New York: GWI.
Haidt, J. (2006) *The Happiness Hypothesis*, London: Random House.
Harvard Health Letter (2015) *The Year in Medicine*, December. Available online at: file:///F:/Health%20Tourism%20Handbook/The%20year%20in%20medicine.pdf (accessed 19 February 2016).
Helliwell, J. F. and Putnam, R. D. (2004) 'The social context of wellbeing', *Philosophical Transactions of the Royal Society of London*, 359, 1435–1446.
Honoré, C. (2004) *In Praise of Slow*, London: Orion.
Human Development Index (2014) *Sustaining Human Progress: Reducing Vulnerabilities and Building Resilience*, New York: UNDP.
Jaslow, R. (2013) 'Baby boomers unhealthier than their parents, study says', *CBS News*, 5 February. Available online at: http://www.cbsnews.com/news/baby-boomers-unhealthier-than-their-parents-generation-study-says (accessed 20 February 2016).
Khoury, B., Lecomte, T., Fortin, G., Masse, M., Therien, P., Bouchard, V., Chapleau, M., Paquin, K. and Hofmann, S. G. (2013) 'Mindfulness-based therapy: A comprehensive meta-analysis', *Clinical Psychology Review*, 33, 763–771.
King, D. E., Mainous, III, A. G., Carnemolla, M. and Everett, C. J. (2009) 'Clinical research study: Adherence to healthy lifestyle habits in US adults, 1988–2006', *American Journal of Medicine*, 122(6), 528–534.
Louv, R. (2005) *Last Child in the Woods: Saving Our Children from Nature Deficit Disorder*, London: Atlantic Books.
—— (2012) *The Nature Principle: Human Restoration and the End of Nature Deficit Disorder*. Chapel Hill, NC: Algonquin Books.
National Eating Disorders Association (NEDA) (2016) *General Statistics*. Available online at: https://www.nationaleatingdisorders.org/general-statistics (accessed 23 February 2016).
New Economics Foundation (2012) *Happy Planet Index*. Available online at: http://www.happyplanetindex.org/assets/happy-planet-index-report.pdf (accessed 24 February 2013).

NHS (2013) 'Today's adults unhealthier than their parents were', *NHS News*, 11 April. Available online at: http://www.nhs.uk/news/2013/04April/Pages/current-generation-unhealthier-than-their-parents.aspx (accessed 20 February 2016).

Nunan, D., Mahtani, K. R., Roberts, N. and Heneghan, C. (2013) 'Physical activity for the prevention and treatment of major chronic disease: An overview of systematic reviews', *Systematic Reviews*, 2, 56.

Office for National Statistics (ONS) (2016) *At What Age is Personal Well-Being the Highest?* Available online at: http://www.ons.gov.uk/ons/dcp171776_431796.pdf (accessed 2 February 2016).

Olano, H. A., Kachan, D., Tannenbaum, S. L., Mehta, A., Annane, D. and Lee, D. J. (2015) 'Engagement in mindfulness practices by U.S. adults: Sociodemographic barriers', *Journal of Alternative and Complementary Medicine*, 21(2), 100–102.

Paoli, A. and Bianco, A. (2015) 'What is fitness training? Definitions and implications: A systematic review article', *Iranian Journal Public Health*, May, 44(5), 602–614.

Posadzki, P., Alotaibi, A. and Ernst, E. (2012) 'Adverse effects of aromatherapy: A systematic review of case reports and case series', *International Journal of Risk and Safety in Medicine*, 24(3), 147–161.

Power, M. (2013) 'Well-being, quality of life and the naive pursuit of happiness', *Topoi*, 32, 145–152.

Pretty, J. (2013) 'The consumption of a finite planet: Well-being, convergence, divergence and the nascent green economy', *Environmental and Resource Economics*, 55, 475–499.

Puczkó, L. and Smith, M. K. (2010) 'Tourism-specific quality of life index: The Budapest model', in Budruk, M. and Philips, R. (eds) *Quality-of-Life Community Indicators for Parks, Recreation and Tourism Management*, Social Indicators Research Series 43, Dordrecht, The Netherlands: Springer, pp. 163–184.

Rahman, T., Mittelhammer, R. C. and Wandschneider, P. (2005) *Measuring the Quality of Life Across Countries. A Sensitivity Analysis of Well-Being Indices*, Research paper No. 2005/06, Helsinki, Finland: World Institute for Development Economics Research (WIDER) established by United Nations University (UNU).

Roth, G. (2010) *Women, Food and God: An Unexpected Path to Almost Everything*, London: Simon and Shuster.

Roy, M. and Payette, H. (2012) 'The body image construct among Western seniors: A systematic review of the literature', *Archives of Gerontology and Geriatrics*, 55(3), 505–521.

Ryan, R. M. and Deci, E. L. (2001) 'To be happy or to be self-fulfilled: A review of research on hedonic and eudaimonic well-being', in Fiske, S. (ed.) *Annual Review of Psychology*, 52, 141–166.

Shochat, T. (2012) 'Impact of lifestyle and technology developments on sleep', *Nature and Science of Sleep*, 4, 19–34.

Varga, M., Thege, B. K., Dukay-Szabó, S., Túry, F. and van Furth, E. F. (2014) 'When eating healthy is not healthy: Orthorexia nervosa and its measurement with the ORTO-15 in Hungary', *BMC Psychiatry*, 14, 59.

Versnik Nowak, A. L. and Hale, H. M. (2012) 'Prevalence of complementary and alternative medicine use among U.S. college students', *American Journal of Health Education*, 43(2), 116–126.

Weil, A. (2013) *Spontaneous Happiness: Step-by-Step to Peak Emotional Wellbeing*, London: Hodder & Stoughton.

White, A., Heather Boon, H., Terje, A., Lewith, G., Liu, J. P., Norheim, A. J., Steinsbekk, A., Yamashita, H. and Fønnebø, V. (2014) 'Reducing the risk of complementary and alternative medicine (CAM): Challenges and priorities', *European Journal of Integrative Medicine*, 6, 404–408.

WHO (1998) WHO (Five) *Wellbeing Index*. Available online at: https://www.psykiatri-regionh.dk/who-5/Documents/WHO5_English.pdf (accessed 27 August 2015).

Wijnkoop, L., Jones, P. J., Uauy, R., Segal, L. and Milner, J. R. (2013) 'Nutrition economics – food as an ally of public health', *British Journal of Nutrition*, 109, 777–784.

Zheng, Z. and Xue, C. C. L. (2013) 'Pain research in complementary and alternative medicine in Australia: A critical review', *Journal of Alternative and Complementary Medicine*, 19(2), 81–91.

4

Leading taste

The influence of trendsetters on health tourism

Jennifer Laing and Warwick Frost

Introduction

Linking the fashion designer Coco Chanel to the growth in health tourism in the early twentieth century is not intuitively obvious. Yet she played her part in the popularity of various French health resorts, placing them firmly in the public eye and making them *de rigueur* for those of a certain social status. Chanel was a woman of prodigious energy and liked to walk, ride, ski and swim, unlike the languid elegance of many of her contemporaries. This required a wardrobe that allowed women to *move*, liberating them from corsets and giving them a new streamlined silhouette (Cosgrave, 2012). Being outdoors so much, it has also been said that Chanel made the suntan fashionable for upper-class women, although Segrave (2005: 4) argues that she was only 'following an existing fad'. Her boutiques at Deauville and Biarritz became a showcase for her sportswear, which was 'perfectly suited to the relaxed, outdoor activities of a beach resort' (Cosgrave, 2012: 18).

These destinations became the rage for wealthy patrons such as Princess Victoria Eugenie of Battenberg, who could afford Chanel's exorbitant prices (Cosgrave, 2012), with Deauville referred to as the 'summer branch office of the Paris upper crust' (Charles-Roux, 1974: 74). While Chanel wasn't the first to discover these places, she added to their glamour. Biarritz, for example, was a favoured holiday spot of King Edward VII, who generally spent three weeks there every March (Plumptre, 1995). The Chanel story highlights that, while the popularity of a health tourism destination is generally the outcome of a series of factors, such as the desire of tourists to try new experiences, the availability of natural resources such as a sunny climate, thermal water or salt and various marketing campaigns and strategies, the influence of various individuals on their growth cannot be discounted.

Like the example of Chanel above, these people have a platform to lead fashion or set trends due to their status in society, as well as their own personal charisma. As *champions*, they encourage or act as 'an advocate of a particular cause or way of thinking' (Mair and Laing, 2012: 686), but also of certain places or pursuits. As *trendsetters* or *taste makers*, they 'may strongly influence aesthetic and economic identifications and practices among both consumers and producers of cultural products' (Lane, 2013: 343). They can promote particular destinations or types of tourist activities, making these people valuable sources of *image formation* (Glover, 2009). This influence, however, is normally achieved with the assistance of various types of media, including newspapers, magazines and, in more recent times, social media, as we highlight in this chapter.

What we have identified here is not unique to the health tourism sphere. In a business context, Hughes (1986) shines a spotlight on a small group of men, the *vital few*, who he argues have contributed to America's economic rise. He makes the case for adopting this approach in order to understand our history:

> To ignore the impact of individuals in our historical development would be like studying physiology without considering the actions of the organs and cells of the body and their effects on each other. We cannot assume, as many have done, that somehow or other the individuals have cancelled each other out and change has come automatically from the 'masses' and the 'forces of history'. There are no 'masses'. There are only individuals. There are no 'forces of history', only human action and the human beings involved are individuals as well as parts of society.
>
> *(Hughes, 1986: 2)*

There are similarly examples of high-profile individuals who have helped to shape public taste for certain food cultures, cuisines and destinations. Examples include Elizabeth David's role in promoting Mediterranean food after the Second World War (Chaney, 1998; Jones and Taylor, 2001) and Julia Child's popularisation of French *haute cuisine* cooking (Riley Fitch, 1997; Spitz, 2012), as well as celebrity chef Rick Stein's influence on the gastronomic development of Padstow in Cornwall (Busby, Huang and Jarman, 2012).

What is interesting in the case of health tourism and distinguishes it from these other contexts is the *range of individuals* who have had an influence on its development. These include patronage by members of the aristocracy and royalty in the eighteenth and nineteenth centuries, through to celebrity endorsement and the entrepreneurial work of industry leaders in the twentieth and twenty-first centuries. In this chapter, we consider how these people have contributed to the popularity and acceptance of health tourism and the leading of public opinion and taste, as well as destination image and branding.

The eighteenth century: aristocratic patronage and the rise of 'Beau' Nash

The eighteenth century saw a number of seaside and spa destinations become desirable places for both socialising and medical cures, particularly amongst the social elite, who led the way for others lower down the scale to follow. For example, Brighton was 'buzzing with life' (Smith, 1999: 44), even before the Prince Regent put it on the map, thanks to the many sporting activities in close proximity to the town, as well as the benefits of fresh air and sea bathing (Smith, 1999). However, it became even more fashionable in 1783 when the Prince first visited it to treat ailments linked to overeating and general excess. His time in Brighton delighted him so much that he created the oriental-style Royal Pavilion (Figure 4.1), which is still one of Brighton's premier tourist attractions. The royal presence was a magnet for aristocratic kindred spirits (Jeans, 1990) who helped to shake the town out of its torpor:

> His favourites, like the dashing horseman and driver Sir John Lade, Beau Brummell, the dandy of dandies or George Hanger, roistering and barely literate, were the types of Regency buck who might be found racing their chariots through the narrow Lanes of the town to the danger of the public in the daytime and gambling, drinking and carousing into the small hours of the morning.

Figure 4.1 The Royal Pavilion in Brighton.

Source: J. Laing.

This pattern of elite leaders of fashion giving a health resort a dashing or glamorous image can be seen right across Europe during this period. As Lempa (2002: 50) notes in relation to Pyrmont, a popular eighteenth-century spa in Germany: 'Not only the regular visits by royal guests accompanied by large entourages including various persons of high and low aristocracy, but also the visits of Prussian and Westphalian aristocrats to Pyrmont laid the foundation for its reputation'. The frisson of potentially encountering the nobility also enticed the emerging middle and upper middle class, including doctors, lawyers and merchants, to the resort town. In fact, they complained of 'boredom' when the cream of society was absent, even though direct fraternisation was limited and generally highly regulated and differences of class were acknowledged and preserved (Lempa, 2002).

It is the town of Bath where one can most clearly see the impact that a single charismatic individual can have on the image of health tourism. Its origins as a health resort reached as far back as Celtic and most notably Roman times (Figure 4.2). Richard 'Beau' Nash put it on the map as the place to see and be seen in the eighteenth century. The son of a partner in a bottle-making factory, he rose to become the 'King of Bath', managing social interactions and the gentility of proceedings as the master of ceremonies (Eglin, 2005). The curious thing about Nash is that he does not appear to have had any formal role bestowed on him by the city authorities or *corporation*, as it was known, although he was given the freedom of the city in 1716 (Eglin, 2005; Towner, 2010). The fact that visitors to Bath (the *company*) were under the *illusion* that he was entitled to use this epithet is a testament to the skill with which Nash created 'his own mythology' (Towner, 2010: 21).

Word of mouth, presumably through anecdotes in letters as well as face-to-face stories told about Beau in drawing rooms throughout England, helped his profile to grow, along with his

Figure 4.2 The Roman Baths, Bath.

Source: J. Laing.

appearance as a character in popular novels of the time, such as Fielding's *Tom Jones* (1749) (Towner, 2010). Nash can be argued to be one of the earliest exponents of what we would call today *personal branding* (Labrecque, Markos and Milne, 2011; Shepherd, 2005), inventing a persona that others wanted to believe in. Towner (2010: 21) describes him as 'a prototype of the modern celebrity – the first public figure famous for being famous'. Nash didn't shy away from his humble background, but transcended it and helped to make Bath the pre-eminent spa resort of its time. Even if one takes the position that his influence on Bath has been over-stated or is complemented by the role of other individuals such as the architect John Wood Senior (Borsay, 1989; Towner, 2010), it is difficult to argue against the *impression* he gave to those who flocked to Bath 'of his own significance' (Towner, 2010: 21).

The role of master of ceremonies appears to have been appropriated from the French grand master of ceremonies, who oversaw court ceremonies and events, which in turn originated in the Catholic Church – an example of the endless appropriation of rituals and customs through-out history (Frost and Laing, 2015a). Nash was said to have seen an opportunity after Queen Anne visited Bath in 1702, to assist a town that was 'ill-prepared to receive, house or entertain' (Eglin, 2005: 6) the top echelons of society who wanted to follow their sovereign's lead. Nash's forte was organising public entertainment such as music and balls, paid for by public subscrip-tions. He was also the champion for grand public buildings and infrastructure such as new hos-pitals (Figure 4.3) and assembly rooms (Eglin, 2005). His enduring fame rests on his ability to create alongside these social activities 'a code of conduct enjoining civil behaviour on the part of all visitors regardless of background' (Eglin, 2005: 7), subsequently adopted by other resorts in his wake, along with the appointment of their own master of ceremonies. This is an example of what Lane (2013: 343) calls *taste making*, through 'imposing a canon of rules and standards'.

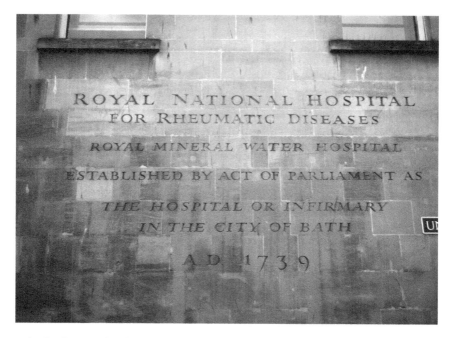

Figure 4.3   Dedication for the Royal National Hospital for Rheumatic Diseases, Bath.

Source: J. Laing.

While Bath society was on the surface egalitarian, Nash took care to ensure that status and rank were preserved, with his support of hospitals for the poor 'aimed at keeping the leisured elite away from the reality of everyday life' (Towner, 2010: 26). This was a difficult balancing act and a testament to Nash's abilities that he managed to pull it off so brilliantly.

Curiously, Nash wasn't a *habitué* of the baths, which were ostensibly the reason for the visits. He understood the importance of leisure activities to augment the health benefits of taking the waters. His first contact with newcomers generally involved visiting them at home, once they had signed in at the Assembly Rooms and taken out their subscriptions (Towner, 2010). Nash was also regularly to be found at the Pump Room in the morning, where 'newly inducted members of the Company were acquainted with the rules governing their behaviour' (Eglin, 2005: 63). At night, he presided over card playing as well as the balls, signalling the start and finish of the music and the formal bringing of partners together for the opening minuets (Eglin, 2005). Women treated him as a *confidant* and he created an environment in which they could safely enter into society and meet eligible men, without risk to their reputation (Eglin, 2005).

Gambling appeared to be the chief means of Nash's income and was the source of his eventual downfall, with the suppression of high-stakes gaming taking away his power along with his livelihood (Eglin, 2005; Towner, 2010). He died in 1761 as rumours began to circulate of the appointment of a new master of ceremonies. While Nash was given money for his funeral from the Corporation, the burial remains a mystery and a pauper's grave might be a plausible scenario (Eglin, 2005). In 1770, a stone memorial in his honour was placed in Bath Abbey. Much of Georgian Bath that we fête today was not even present when Nash died, such as the Upper Assembly Rooms (1771), the Royal Crescent (1774) and the Grand Pump Room (1799), where Nash's statue can be found. His fame continued after his death, thanks in part to the early 'celebrity biography' (Eglin, 2005) written by Oliver Goldsmith in 1762, although Bath began to wane as a 'centre of fashion', competing with newer spas and developing seaside resorts (Towner, 2010: 29). Nash's influence is still manifest in the way that tourism is conducted in modern-day Bath and its contemporary spa resort Tunbridge Wells, with stories about his life at the heart of guided tours and guidebooks (Eglin, 2005).

The nineteenth century: royalty and the continental spa holiday

In the nineteenth century, royal and aristocratic personages were still largely responsible for setting trends in health resorts, particularly in European settings. Bath was no longer a fashionable spa destination, supplanted by resorts such as Baden Baden in Germany, Karlsbad in Bohemia (now known by its Czech name of Karlovy Vary) and Nice on the Côte d'Azur in France. It was Queen Victoria who helped to make the French Riviera a popular destination for holidays, as opposed to 'a centre for convalescence' (Nelson, 2001: 2). As a widow, she visited this part of France nine times between 1882 and 1889, staying variously at Menton, Cannes, Grasse, Hyères and Nice. Other relatives from amongst the crowned heads of Europe paid her visits while she was there, including Franz Josef and Elisabeth, the Emperor and Empress of Austria, Eugénie, the former Empress of France and many of Victoria's children. Her eldest son, Bertie, then Prince of Wales and later Edward VII, also frequented the Riviera each year, although 'never in the same town as his mother' (Nelson, 2001: 45). Both Victoria and Bertie loved picturesque annual rituals such as the Battle of the Flowers and illustrations and reports of their attendance at these local festivals were now familiar to their subjects back home. The Queen wrote about these events in her journals, some of which were published after her death, while others remain in the Royal Archives. Her wistful entry on 1 May 1899, refers to 'My last charming drive in this paradise of nature, which I grieve to leave, as I get more attached to it every year' (quoted in Nelson, 2001), prescient given that this was to be her last visit to the Riviera.

The publicity that Queen Victoria garnered for the region was immeasurable. Local newspapers such as the *Menton and Monte Carlo News – A Society Journal with List of Visitors* and *L'Eclaireur de Nice* reported her activities and the visitors she received while on holiday, as did the British newspapers such as *The Times*, which carried the Court Circular, detailing the Queen's movements, as well as reports by various correspondents and sources, including Reuters. Unlike her reputation in Britain as the reclusive widowed queen, removed from her subjects, Victoria was regularly seen out and about on her Riviera holidays and enjoyed interacting with locals whom she met while riding in her pony and trap, even giving one small Dutch girl and her dog rides and inviting them to tea (Nelson, 2001). There were concerns that cancellation of her visits to France would affect the local tourism industry, which relied on the growth in visitors and media coverage that her trips engendered (Nelson, 2001). In fact, only one of her visits did not go ahead as planned, cancelled in 1900 due to concerns about her being in France during the Anglo-Boer War (Nelson, 2001). Victoria passed away the next year, aged 81.

The British were aware of the advantages that these royal visits bestowed on the various French resorts and how this might be politically or commercially manipulated. While there was an attempt to discredit the health benefits of Grasse, visited by the Queen in 1891, the correspondent was told to print a retraction, with the Queen said to have been 'furious' (Nelson, 2001) at these false allegations. There was a lot at stake for those involved in the local industry. Luxurious hotels were built to house the Queen, as well as 'the number of visitors that would surely follow if the Queen of England were to stay in their hotel' (Nelson, 2001: 94). In 1897, it was reported that 'no less than' 100 carriages gathered near the Queen's hotel in Nice to watch her depart on a daily pony cart drive (Nelson, 2001).

While Victoria did not overtly visit the Riviera for health reasons, it could be argued that she needed the peace and quiet that these holidays allowed and was keen for a 'change of air and surroundings' (Nelson, 2001: 18). Her first visit in 1882 coincided with that of her son, Prince Leopold, who suffered from haemophilia and she spent time with him, including on his birthday. Sadly, Leopold died after a fall two years later, while in Cannes. Victoria later made a pilgrimage to the site of his death on her visit to the Riviera in 1887 (Nelson, 2001). Interestingly, while she was strongly associated with the region during the latter years of her life, this link has been largely overlooked by twentieth-century studies of her reign (Nelson, 2001). The contemporary image of the French Riviera is more likely to be intertwined with that of the Grimaldi family in Monaco, notably the Hollywood actress turned princess, Grace Kelly, who married Prince Rainier in 1956.

The twentieth and twenty-first centuries: celebrity and entrepreneurial influence

In the modern era, the influence of celebrities as the new social elite has largely overtaken that of royalty, although there are exceptions that blur the boundaries, such as the late Princesses Grace and Diana and, more recently, Diana's son William and daughter-in-law Kate, the Duke and Duchess of Cambridge. Many celebrities such as actors, musicians, models and sportspeople are 'cultural icons in mass media driven societies' (Lee, Scott and Kim, 2008: 809), which leads to them becoming *opinion leaders* (Rojek, 2001; Cowen, 2002). Their every tweet is monitored and paparazzi photographers dog their heels, so that few occasions in their lives are private. Social media has helped to break down the barriers between public and private life and shown us intimate details of celebrities at work and at play, including their holiday destination choices and preferred leisure activities. Some even choose to put their whole life in the public spotlight, notably the infamous Kardashian family in their reality TV show *Meet the Kardashians* (2007–).

A celebrity's actions or behaviour might lead members of the public to emulate his or her behaviour, particularly with respect to consumption – an example of the *demonstration effect*. Those fans who follow closely (obsessively, in some cases) these people and mimic or adopt their clothes, interests and way of life or visit the places associated with them may gain *cultural capital* as a result (Busby and Meethan, 2008; Lee et al., 2008). This might be deemed to be a *parasocial relationship* (Giles, 2002; Glover, 2009; Kim, 2012), 'to which the user responds [to the celebrity] as though in a typical social relationship' (Giles, 2002: 279), even though there is no physical contact or meeting. Jackson, Payne and Stolley (2013: 125) observe that 'in our media-saturated culture, one way that Americans learn about medical tourism possibilities is through celebrities' – a quote that could also be applied to health tourism more generally. Unlike other eras considered in this chapter, it appears that no single individual celebrity stands out from the rest as a taste maker or trendsetter in terms of health tourism. Instead, a critical mass of celebrities take part in these kinds of activities and receive media exposure for doing so, such that they build awareness of and aspirations for this kind of tourism, potentially leading people to emulate their behaviour.

Popular culture can have 'a significant impact on destination image' (Mercille, 2005: 1040) and the role that celebrities can play in this process has been obvious for some time. O'Connor and O'Leary (2012) found that some visitors to regional Ireland were keen to visit places associated with former US President John F. Kennedy, while a number of visitors to Padstow in Cornwall have been found to be motivated by the presence of TV chef Rick Stein and his food-related businesses and restaurants (Busby et al., 2012). Hotels associated with famous fashion designers such as Versace and Missoni have lured visitors who are fans of the luxury brands (Dallabona, 2015). Much of this research, however, has focused on destinations associated with actors in films or a television series. For example, Lee et al. (2008) found that their Japanese respondents who had a high level of involvement with Korean celebrities were likely to report a high level of intention to visit Korea. With a boost to visitation in mind, some destinations have tried to develop tourist attractions based on their links with celebrities, such as the Errol Flynn Trail in Tasmania (Frost and Laing, 2015b), which takes visitors to see sites associated with the Hollywood actor, who was born in Hobart. There have also been a number of studies that explore celebrity *endorsement* of destinations (Van der Veen, 2008; Glover, 2009; Van der Veen and Song, 2014), in the sense of paid advertising using the celebrity as a spokesperson. Glover (2009: 21) observes that 'media reporting of celebrities using a product or brand or holidaying at a destination may be more valuable than the targeted use of celebrities in promotional materials'. Despite this, there has been a paucity of research considering the way that media exposure of celebrity holidays might act as an *organic* influence on destination image.

There are a number of destinations which boast celebrity residents or visitors. The ski town of Aspen in Colorado has been well known for its celebrity sightings over the years, as well as the island of Ibiza, the Hamptons on Long Island and, more recently, the Mexican resort of Cabo San Lucas and Italy's Lake Como. Similarly, a number of celebrities patronise spas, which appears to have led to these activities and by extension some health-related destinations becoming popular. Websites such as Citysearch and AOL and glossy magazines like *Vogue* and *Hello* publish their lists of 'Top Ten Celebrity-Frequented Spas' and feature articles which highlight the presence of celebrity guests at spa resorts, such as models Kate Moss and Naomi Campbell and former footballer David Beckham and his fashion designer wife Victoria at the Chiva-Som spa in Thailand. This may lead tourists to 'play at being royalty or a pampered celebrity, albeit for a brief period' (Laing, Voigt and Frost, 2014: 222). Some of these celebrity spa resort visits are the backdrop to a lavish wedding, which adds to the glamour and appeal of these settings (Laing and Weiler, 2008). Research is needed to examine whether there is a relationship between celebrity holidays and a subsequent increase in visitation, as well as whether celebrity involvement in spa or medi-spa treatments is associated with subsequent adoption by fans, as well as the public more generally.

There have also been a number of entrepreneurs over the past hundred years who have been instrumental in developing new spa products and health tourism markets, particularly in the USA, Asia and Australia. Examples include Elizabeth Arden – who offered the first day spa in 1910 – Red Door Salon in Manhattan (immortalised in her fragrance Red Door) – and Edmond and Deborah Szekely, who created the first destination spa in 1940 – Rancho La Puerta in Baja, California. Deborah Szekely was the founder of the Golden Door spa chain in 1959, also in California, which has become a global phenomenon (Smith and Puczkó, 2014). Like Rancho La Puerta, it was a pioneer of 'the local organic, whole foods concept' behind *spa cuisine* (Tabbachi, 2008). The following case study looks at the entrepreneurial vision of Charles Davidson, founder of Peninsula Hot Springs on the Mornington Peninsula in Victoria, Australia.

Case study: Charles Davidson and Peninsula Hot Springs, Australia

Day trippers as well as tourists head to the Mornington Peninsula to enjoy its beaches, wineries and restaurants and wellness experiences. Peninsula Hot Springs is arguably the most high-profile and iconic spa in the region, thanks to its thermal mineral water (Figure 4.4), a series of pools in

(continued)

(continued)

Figure 4.4 Hilltop bathing at Peninsula Hot Springs.

Source: Peninsula Hot Springs.

a natural setting amongst the coastal scrub and array of treatments and activities. It opened in 2005 and now averages over 1,000 visitors a day year round, attracting a variety of age groups and locals as well as domestic and international tourists (NAB, 2015).

Visitors can soak in one of a number of small public pools, as well as taking advantage of more private offerings, including spa treatments in the Spa Dreaming Centre. These treatments are often based on or associated with Indigenous practices or therapies, such as the *kodo* massage 'inspired by traditional Australian aboriginal techniques which tone and re-align energy flow' and the use of *Li'tya* (meaning 'of the earth') products, which draw on Indigenous therapies and knowledge. Demand is so high that, rather than increase their prices, there are plans to expand the facility to incorporate more pools and accommodation. The difficulty for the owners is to find an appropriate time for these works, given that Peninsula Hot Springs is currently open 7 days a week from 7.30 a.m. to 10 p.m. (NAB, 2015).

The creation and development of Peninsula Hot Springs are largely attributable to the efforts of its charismatic CEO, Charles Davidson. In an interview with us, he told how he first conceived of the concept during his time working overseas:

> This place itself was driven out of that natural hot spring experience which came out of Japan. Then deciding, getting excited about the hot water, the relaxation ability of the hot water and then starting to do research around the world about how is hot water, natural hot springs used . . . We were looking at the Peninsula and really felt that while hot water is part of it . . . you also have the food element and you had the broader environment.

Charles' influence is far deeper than just developing a popular health tourism attraction. He was also instrumental in encouraging the local health tourism providers to band together and form the Mornington Peninsula Spa Association, in order to present a strong and consistent brand to visitors, based around wellness:

> The reason was sort of deciding 'How are we going to try to pull this story together?' . . . We were being booked out and just referring people on willy-nilly. So it was easier to put it into a structure and also the idea that we work together to create a community rather than everybody being in competition. That's a pretty normal evolution I think.

Davidson is also keen that the branding of the Peninsula be *authentic* to the region: 'You can come in with billions of dollars and try to create things but really at the end of the day, it's got to be something that's from the environment – being the people and the actual space'.

His personal vision appears to have been a driver for this collaboration to occur, perhaps earlier than it would have happened organically. Davidson believes in cooperation, rather than competition, amongst the different tourism and leisure operations 'to bring business to the region' (Laing, 2009: 331), with initiatives such as the development of joint packages with other wellness providers and the accommodation sector. The media exposure that Peninsula Hot Springs receives across a wide variety of channels, including social media, but also television, radio and magazines, helps to ensure that the region as a whole benefits from high awareness of its wellness offerings. Fellow members of the Association that we interviewed acknowledged the contribution he has made to the region, with comments such as: 'he really is a force to be reckoned with and he really is passionate about this area . . . without him, I don't think we'd have half of what we've got down here' (R1) and 'You do need people like him to push. They've got the strength to push and because of the type of business he has, he has got the power there to push' (R2). Davidson is an example of a destination champion, with a successful business that is based on a philosophy of corporate social responsibility through contributing to a strong community.

Conclusion

While there have been a number of studies examining the development and marketing of health tourism-related destinations, little account has been taken to date of the role played in this process by individuals who have acted as taste makers, leaders of fashion or destination champions. This chapter has focused on examples from the eighteenth century through to the twenty-first century, to help fill this gap, using an approach similar to that used by Butler and Russell (2010) in their edited book *Giants of Tourism*. The latter make it clear that they feel that the contribution of individuals to tourism development has 'not been sufficiently promoted or studied . . . [and] individuals or entrepreneurs are often considered as outliers or anomalies and therefore discarded and the contributions ignored' (Russell and Butler, 2010: xi).

Research is therefore needed to explore this phenomenon further. This is particularly the case with respect to the potential influence of celebrities in making health tourism destinations desirable places to visit and spa visitation an important leisure and holiday activity. Studies that have considered the impact of celebrity endorsement on tourism could be adapted to examine whether this influence extends to members of the public copying the holiday behaviour of their favourite stars. Is this behaviour considered to be more persuasive than a paid endorsement in the eyes of fans? Perhaps the existence of payment to endorse an attraction or destination is irrelevant in terms of authenticity where a strong parasocial relationship has developed between the fan and the celebrity. The mere fact that a favourite celebrity has engaged in spa tourism might act as the trigger that makes a fan want to imitate or follow their lead. The potential complexity of fandom in this context needs to be teased out in future studies.

There has also been little work carried out on the role played by entrepreneurs in the development of health tourism, including the examples discussed in this chapter. As noted above, this is a gap in knowledge across tourism studies more generally, in terms of how these individuals drive innovation and its diffusion throughout broader society. Based on our analysis of some of the individuals we highlight in this chapter, it might be useful to draw upon recent research on the activities of women entrepreneurs (Hughes, Jennings, Brush, Carter and Welter, 2012), as well as studies on *social entrepreneurship*, which 'marries two distinct and ostensibly competing organizational objectives: creating social value and creating economic value' (Miller, Grimes, McMullen and Vogus, 2012: 616).

The interplay between these influential individuals and the media in contemporary times may also prove a fruitful area for research, given the evolution of social media, increasing use of technology, less central control over forms of media and greater interactivity in communication. The question remains whether this backdrop of a new digital world will lead to a diminution of their power or, alternatively, heighten their influence. It may also lead to the emergence of a new breed of taste maker in the form of bloggers, with a global following that the likes of Beau Nash could only envy.

References

Borsay, P. (1989) *The English Urban Renaissance: Culture and Society in the Provincial Town, 1660–1770*, Oxford, UK: Clarendon Press.

Busby, G. and Meethan, K. (2008) 'Cultural capital in Cornwall: Heritage and the visitor', in Payton, P. (ed.) *Cornish Studies Sixteen*, Exeter, UK: University of Exeter Press, pp. 146–166.

Busby, G., Huang, R. and Jarman, R. (2012) 'The Stein effect: An alternative film-induced tourism perspective', *International Journal of Tourism Research*, 15(6), 570–582.

Butler, R. W. and Russell, R. A. (eds) (2010) *Giants of Tourism*, Wallingford, UK: CAB International.

Chaney, L. (1998) *Elizabeth David: A Biography*, London: Macmillan.

Charles-Roux, E. (1974) *Chanel*, 1995 edition, London: Harvill.

Cosgrave, B. (2012) *Vogue on Coco Chanel*, London: Quadrille Publishing.

Cowen, T. (2002) *What Price Fame?* Cambridge, MA: Harvard University Press.

Dallabona, A. (2015) 'Luxury fashion flagship hotels and cultural opportunism: The cases of Hotel Missoni Edinburgh and Maison Moschino', *Hospitality and Society*, 5(2/3), 117–144.

Eglin, J. (2005) *The Imaginary Autocrat: Beau Nash and the Invention of Bath*, London: Profile.

Frost, W. and Laing, J. (2015a) 'Ritual structure and traditions of events', in Laing, J. and Frost, W. (eds) *Rituals and Traditional Events in a Modern World*, London: Routledge, pp. 1–19.

—— (2015b) 'On the trail of Errol Flynn: Explorations in autoethnography', *Tourism Analysis*, 20(3), 283–296.

Giles, D. C. (2002) 'Parasocial interaction: A review of the literature and a model for future research', *Media Psychology*, 4(3), 279–305.

Glover, P. (2009) 'Celebrity endorsement in tourism advertising: Effects on destination image', *Journal of Hospitality and Tourism Management*, 16(1), 16–23.

Hughes, J. R. T. (1986) *The Vital Few: The Entrepreneur and American Economic Progress*, expanded edn, Oxford, UK: Oxford University Press.

Hughes, K. D., Jennings, J. E., Brush, C., Carter, S. and Welter, F. (2012) 'Extending women's entrepreneurship research in new directions', *Entrepreneurship Theory and Practice*, 36(3), 429–442.

Jackson, K. M., Payne, L. L. and Stolley, K. S. (2013) 'Celebrity treatment: The intersection of star culture and medical tourism in American society', *Journal of American Culture*, 36(2), 124–134.

Jeans, D. N. (1990) 'Beach resort morphology in England and Australia: A review and extension', in Fabbri, P. (ed.) *Recreational Uses of Coastal Areas*, Dordrecht, The Netherlands: Springer, pp. 277–285.

Jones, S. and Taylor, B. (2001) 'Food writing and food cultures: The case of Elizabeth David and Jane Grigson', *European Journal of Cultural Studies*, 4(2), 171–188.

Kim, S. (2012) 'Audience involvement and film tourism experiences: Emotional places, emotional experiences', *Tourism Management*, 33(2), 387–396.

Labrecque, L. I., Markos, E. and Milne, G. R. (2011) 'Online personal branding: Processes, challenges and implications', *Journal of Interactive Marketing*, 25(1), 37–50.

Laing, J. (2009) 'Peninsula Hot Springs: A new spa tourism experience "down under"', in Smith, M. and Puczkó, L. (eds) *Health and Wellness Tourism*, London: Elsevier, pp. 329–333.

Laing, J. H. and Weiler, B. (2008) 'Mind, body and spirit: Health and wellness tourism in Asia', in Cochrane, J. (ed.) *Asian Tourism: Growth and Change*, Oxford, UK: Elsevier Publishing, pp. 379–389.

Laing, J., Voigt, C. and Frost, W. (2014) 'Fantasy, authenticity and the spa tourism experience', in Voigt, C. and Pforr, C. (eds) *Wellness Tourism: A Destination Perspective*, London: Routledge, pp. 220–234.

Lane, C. (2013) 'Taste makers in the "fine dining" restaurant industry: The attribution of aesthetic and economic value by gastronomic guides', *Poetics*, 41, 342–365.

Lee, S., Scott, D. and Kim, H. (2008) 'Celebrity fan involvement and destination perceptions', *Annals of Tourism Research*, 35(3), 809–832.

Lempa, H. (2002) 'The spa: Emotional economy and social classes in nineteenth-century Pyrmont', *Central European History*, 35(1), 37–73.

Mair, J. and Laing, J. (2012) 'The greening of music festivals: Motivations, barriers and outcomes. Applying the Mair and Jago model', *Journal of Sustainable Tourism*, 20(5), 683–700.

Mercille, J. (2005) 'Media effects on image: The case of Tibet', *Annals of Tourism Research*, 32(4), 1039–1055.

Miller, T. L., Grimes, M. G., McMullen, J. S. and Vogus, T. J. (2012) 'Venturing for others with heart and head: How compassion encourages social entrepreneurship', *Academy of Management Review*, 37(4), 616–640.

NAB (2015) 'Peninsula Hot Springs: In hot demand', *NAB Business Research and Insights*. Available online at: http://business.nab.com.au/peninsula-hot-springs-in-hot-demand-9239/ (accessed 2 December 2015).

Nelson, M. (2001) *Queen Victoria and the Discovery of the Riviera*, 2007 edn, New York: Tauris Parke.

O'Connor, N. and O'Leary, S. (2012) 'The importance of celebrity association in tourism destination branding: Determining the power of the JFK brand in New Ross (County Wexford, Ireland)', *European Journal of Tourism, Hospitality and Recreation*, 3(3), 87–98.

Plumptre, G. (1995) *Edward VII*, London: Pavilion.

Riley Fitch, N. (1997) *Appetite for Life: The Biography of Julia Child*, New York: First Anchor Books.

Rojek, C. (2001) *Celebrity*, London: Reaktion Books.

Russell, R. A. and Butler, R. W. (2010) 'Introduction', in Butler, R. W. and Russell, R. A. (eds) *Giants of Tourism*, Wallingford, UK: CAB International, pp. x–xvii.

Segrave, K. (2005) *Suntanning in 20th Century America*, Jefferson, NC: McFarland and Company.

Shepherd, I. D. (2005) 'From cattle and coke to Charlie: Meeting the challenge of self marketing and personal branding', *Journal of Marketing Management*, 21(5–6), 589–606.

Smith, E. A. (1999) *George IV*, New Haven, CT: Yale University Press.

Smith, M. and Puczkó, L. (2014) *Health, Tourism and Hospitality: Spas, Wellness and Medical Tourism*, 2nd edn, London: Routledge.

Spitz, B. (2012) *Dearie: The Remarkable Life of Julia Child*, New York: Alfred A. Knopf.

Tabbachi, M. (2008) 'American and European spa', in Cohen, M. and Bodeker, G. (eds) *Understanding the Global Spa Industry: Spa Management*, Oxford, UK: Elsevier, pp. 26–40.

Towner, J. (2010) 'The master of ceremonies: Beau Nash and the rise of Bath, 1700–1750', in Butler, R. W. and Russell, R. A. (eds) *Giants of Tourism*, Wallingford, UK: CAB International, pp. 18–31.

Van der Veen, R. (2008) 'Analysis of the implementation of celebrity endorsement as a destination marketing instrument', *Journal of Travel and Tourism Marketing*, 24(2–3), 213–222.

Van der Veen, R. and Song, H. (2014) 'Impact of the perceived image of celebrity endorsers on tourists' intentions to visit', *Journal of Travel Research*, 53(2), 211–224.

Part II
Happiness, wellbeing and quality of life

This part builds on some of the concepts introduced in the first part, especially the notion of happiness and how it can be differentiated from wellbeing, quality of life and life satisfaction and how it relates to health. Authors in this part also emphasise the significance of tourism in contributing to wellbeing and happiness. Ondrej Mitas, Jeroen Nawijn and Barbara Jongsma describe how happiness (or subjective wellbeing as it can be called in preference) is one of the main aims of human beings and is a major focus of positive psychology. However, they make the point that happiness is not always individual and that it can be culturally determined. It is also important to note that tourism experiences do not always have to be positive to enhance wellbeing and that holidays are not uniformly positive experiences. Even in health tourism, physical or mental pain may need to be experienced in order to create greater wellbeing long-term. It seems that tourism may have a short-term impact on wellbeing, especially if travel is frequent, but the length and type of tourism may need to be researched further in order to draw deeper conclusions.

Muzaffer Uysal, M. Joseph Sirgy, Eunju Woo and Hyelin (Lina) Kim provide a comprehensive analysis of the literature, theories and research dealing with the relationship between tourism and broader aspects of life. This includes life satisfaction in different domains and positive functioning. Again, the research is not conclusive and there is not always a positive relationship between tourism experiences and subjective wellbeing, it can very much depend on life stage, importance attributed to tourism by individuals, background experience and culture, all of which require further research. It is also noted that not all domains of life will be equally important for all tourists (e.g. for medical tourists, the health domain may be the most important at that point in time).

The third chapter by John K. Coffey and Mihály Csikszentmihályi focuses on Csikszentmihályi's famous concept of flow and the way(s) in which it can be experienced in tourism. It is suggested that tourists who engage in intrinsic or 'autotelic' activities on holiday are more likely to benefit and to be excited enough to repeat the activities after the holiday ends. Research shows that those people who experience 'flow' more regularly than others tend to display fewer physical health symptoms, less psychological distress, greater connectedness to others and they are also more likely to return to the destination and to write positive reviews. Even though flow is purportedly three times more likely to occur at work, holidays are also ideal occasions for people to engage in flow-inducing activities.

Although more research is clearly needed to support the fact that tourism and holidays impact on wellbeing in the long term, this part gives extremely useful insights in to how wellbeing can be enhanced through tourism and which activities may be the most conducive to doing so.

5

Between tourists

Tourism and happiness

Ondrej Mitas, Jeroen Nawijn and Barbara Jongsma

Happiness

Human beings wish to be happy. Most people's daily thoughts and actions have the end goal of achieving, maintaining or salvaging happiness (Tomasulo and Pawelski, 2012). Throughout history, philosophers, priests, artists and self-help authors have struggled to understand what happiness is and how people can have more of it in their lives (Tomasulo and Pawelski, 2012). This struggle has produced myriad definitions of happiness, resulting in much ambiguity and little consensus.

Research on happiness as a scientific topic, in contrast, has only become an organised collective pursuit in the past 15 years. The so-called positive psychology movement (Seligman and Csikszentmihalyi, 2000) has evolved into a substantial field of research using contemporary psychological science to understand happiness. Much like their philosophical and popular predecessors, positive psychology researchers have struggled to define happiness. A substantial majority, however, now define happiness as subjective wellbeing (Lyubomirsky, King and Diener, 2005a), a combination of cognitive and affective judgements that individuals make about the quality of their life (Diener, Suh, Lucas and Smith, 1999). We do the same in the present chapter, defining happiness as subjective wellbeing, essentially a summative judgement of how well individuals think their life is going and how good they feel most of the time (Diener et al., 1999; Veenhoven, 2009). Important in this definition is the explicit understanding that happiness is subjective and situated within the individual.

In the present chapter, we first review subjective wellbeing research in general. We argue that this literature emphasises positive emotions and thus delves into precedents and interventions of positive emotions. We then review the concurrent evolution of tourism research on individuals' positive emotions before, during and after their holiday experiences. In doing so, we explicitly focus on tourism as leisure travel, excluding travel for business, migration or medical purposes. Subsequently, we briefly review tourism research on other, less powerful aspects of subjective wellbeing. We conclude with a case study that takes an incremental step in building this knowledge and suggest further steps for future research.

The evolution of happiness research

A 2000 initiative by scholar Martin Seligman to refocus psychology from mental illness and unhappiness triggered a movement to study happiness known as *positive psychology* (Seligman and Csikszentmihalyi, 2000). Important conceptual origins of positive psychology lay in Diener's research on life satisfaction in the 1980s (Diener and Emmons, 1984). Positive psychology expanded this research domain to include positive experiences and positive character traits. Studying happiness using a scientific, social psychological approach quickly bore fruit, leading to seminal findings that happiness predicts objective wealth and health (Lyubomirsky et al., 2005a) and that positive emotions in particular are the drivers of this effect (Fredrickson, 1998, 2001). Leading happiness researchers such as Martin Seligman, Sonja Lyubomirsky and Barbara Fredrickson quickly – some would say too quickly – converted these empirical breakthroughs into self-help books for popular audiences. The enthusiasm spread to allied scientific and professional fields, including tourism. Searches of major scientific databases for 'happiness and tourism' each produce dozens of hits spanning psychology, leisure and tourism journals.

Unfortunately, despite these developments there remains much ambiguity concerning the term happiness and related concepts such as enjoyment, positive emotions, good mood, quality of life *and* wellbeing in the tourism literature. A growing majority of studies in positive psychology, however, follow the definitions within the seminal work of Diener and associates (e.g. Diener et al., 1999; Diener and Seligman, 2002). Known as the subjective wellbeing view of happiness, we take the present chapter as an opportunity to view the state of tourism research through the lens of this framework. Doing so allows us to compare and interlink the growing body of extant studies on tourists' happiness.

We choose to follow Diener and colleagues' view in place of a number of other conceptualisations of happiness, notably Seligman's theory of authentic happiness (e.g. Seligman, 2004). Advocated by Filep and Deery (2010) as applicable to tourism, the relative complexity of Seligman's theory hampers its application, especially in cross-cultural contexts. Furthermore, although both authentic happiness and subjective wellbeing theories have been criticised as ethnocentric (Christopher and Hickinbottom, 2008), we find Seligman's prescriptions for what are and are not positive character traits an especially ethnocentric endeavour not attempted by subjective wellbeing researchers.

In fact, a scientific interest in happiness is 'more of a culturally and socially motivated movement than a detached science' (Thin, 2011: 46). Criticisms of psychological conceptualisations of happiness as ethnocentric are based on their Western view of the individual (Christopher and Hickinbottom, 2008). Both subjective wellbeing and authentic happiness theories take a Western view of the individual as discrete entity for whom happiness holds value. Though happiness was equally valued by Western and Eastern samples in one study (Scollon and King, 2011), a broader view shows that cultures differ in the value they attach to individual happiness (Thin, 2011).

The authentic happiness theory of Seligman, however, takes a Western perspective on more than just the value of individual happiness, but also on what legitimate sources of positive character are. The positive character traits discussed are allegedly universal, though not ubiquitous, based on readings of prominent religious and philosophical texts from many different cultures (Seligman, 2004). Done through Western eyes, the selection and reading of these texts necessarily exclude other perspectives, most obviously those of common people, that could have turned up different "universal" traits, such as physical survival, resistance to authority or, in the case of some Easterners, material wealth (Scollon and King, 2011). Instead, Seligman's sources are limited to Western-accepted authoritative texts, taking the Western view that these and not unwritten narratives or folk wisdom (Scollon and King, 2011), are where authority resides. As Thin (2011) points out, a psychology of happiness that is not ethnocentric must look at participants from a variety of cultures in detail, rather than merely making 'occasional forays into non-western cultures' such as reading a few select authoritative texts (42). Because subjective wellbeing theory does not attempt to uncover cross-cultural universals for what humans should value, instead documenting (sometimes from very diverse samples) their own views on their happiness, it partly captures rich cultural differences in what is important in life. The theory of authentic happiness, in contrast, accommodates differences between Western and Eastern cultures, but glosses over differences between written and unwritten, formal and informal, well-known and less-well-known sources of what is important in life. We therefore continue our analysis of tourists' happiness based on the more culturally inclusive theory of subjective wellbeing.

Subjective wellbeing researchers such as Diener and colleagues eschew the term happiness on account of its ambiguity. Happiness is alternately used in popular language to describe something momentary (i.e. an emotion) and something durable (e.g. life satisfaction, spiritual fulfilment). Instead, the more precise term subjective wellbeing refers to the durable, profound, overarching sense of happiness – being happy with one's life.

Several theories have proffered explanations of what affects subjective wellbeing as an overall outcome. The most deterministic is set-point theory, which posits that subjective wellbeing is biologically and psychologically fixed and that any deviation from one's set-point is only temporary (Headey, 2010). Although it is highly plausible that some individuals are genetically more or less happy, there is much evidence that individuals' levels of subjective wellbeing are influenced by events or their own actions (Headey, 2010). Comparative views of subjective wellbeing address how individuals view their life relative to how they want their life to be (Veenhoven, 2009). For example, social comparison theory (Festinger, 1954) posits that individuals' subjective wellbeing is dependent upon the perceived quality of life of others. However, Diener et al.'s (1999) crucial insight that subjective wellbeing consists of several partly independent components has enabled far deeper insights into subjective wellbeing and how it may be increased.

Reflecting the psychological distinction between cognitive and affective functions of the mind, Diener and colleagues define subjective wellbeing as comprising (1) a cognitive component, i.e. how happy someone thinks s/he is and (2) an affective component, i.e. how happy someone generally feels. In contrast to Filep and Deery's (2010) contention, how well a person feels is not the full picture of her or his subjective wellbeing. The cognitive component is usually operationalised as life satisfaction, which in turn comprises overall and life domain aspects. While overall life satisfaction is measured by questionnaire items asking how satisfied respondents are with life and the extent to which life has met their expectations, satisfaction with life domains measure to what extent respondents are satisfied with family, health and other circumstances.

The affective component of subjective wellbeing includes positive and negative emotions and moods, each of which in turn may be assessed at long-term (trait) or short-term (state) levels. When measuring the affective component of subjective wellbeing, psychologists have emphasised emotions rather than moods, as emotions are strong, intense drivers of behaviour and memory, rather than merely colouring the background of experience, as moods do (Rosenberg, 1998). Emotions are at the very essence of decision making, while moods merely shade ambiguous decisions in a certain direction (Zeelenberg, Nelissen, Breugelmans and Pieters, 2008; in the context of holiday satisfaction, Meng, Turk and Altintas, 2012;

Sirakaya, Petrick and Choi, 2004). Regrettably, the distinction between emotions and moods rarely penetrates research of tourists' subjective wellbeing, with affect too often unintentionally operationalised as mood or, worse, a mixture of emotion, mood and cognitive variables.

Emotions may be analysed across numerous dimensions, including frequency, intensity, variety and granularity (Tugade, Fredrickson and Feldman Barrett, 2004). In subjective wellbeing, emotions are most often assessed in terms of valence – how positive or negative they feel. As positive and negative emotions are partly independent (Diener and Emmons, 1984), the most common measurement of this variable involves Likert-type ratings of how strongly participants feel each emotion in a list, such as the modified Differential Emotions Scale (mDES) (Cohn, Fredrickson, Brown, Mikels and Conway, 2009).

Trait-level emotion measurement involves asking respondents how they generally feel. State-level emotion measurement is more challenging. As emotional states change frequently, they should be measured at least daily for acceptable accuracy (Fredrickson, 2000). More frequent measurement using experience sampling (e.g. Csikszentmihalyi and Hunter, 2003) is understood as a "gold standard" for emotion measurement among psychologists, with the Day Reconstruction Method suggested as a laborious alternative (Kahneman, Kruger, Schkade, Schwarz and Stone, 2004). Positive emotions and negative emotions are then averaged across emotions and across days. The resulting positive and negative emotion indices may be treated independently (Mitas, Yarnal, Adams and Ram, 2012a), subtracted (Nawijn, 2011a) or divided (Fredrickson and Losada, 2005). In other instances, specific emotions such as joy, interest and love are addressed (Mitas, Yarnal and Chick, 2012b; Lin, Kerstetter, Nawijn and Mitas, 2014). While demanding more of analysts and readers, studies that treat specific emotions separately have the advantage of supporting much more detailed theoretical and managerial implications, as each emotion has distinct aetiology and consequences (for an excellent discussion of four positive emotions, see Fredrickson, 1998).

Thus, subjective wellbeing is usually measured using Likert-type self-response items over various time spans. These items are arranged in sub-scales that address life satisfaction, satisfaction with specific life domains, positive emotions and negative emotions. Of these components, positive emotions have demonstrated a uniquely powerful role in affecting the other components, fuelling the engine of subjective wellbeing. Interventions that increase positive emotions neutralise the physical markers of negative emotions (Fredrickson and Levenson, 1998) and contribute to increases in life satisfaction over time (Cohn et al., 2009).

Positive emotions

Positive emotion theory

The power of positive emotions is explained by the broaden-and-build theory, an evolutionary account of positive emotional function. According to Fredrickson (1998, 2001), positive emotions open the mind as an expressive, creative and problem-solving tool during moments of safety and abundance. Specifically, people in positive emotion states explore broader possibilities of thought and behaviour. Such exploration makes it easier to build skills, self-knowledge and, especially, relationships. These resources outlast the positive emotional experiences that facilitated them. Just as the self-destructive behaviours associated with mental illness self-perpetuate in a downward spiral of unhealthy coping and dysfunction, the most emotionally positive individuals continually improve their life and relationships (Diener and Seligman, 2002) in 'upward spirals' of subjective wellbeing (Fredrickson and Joiner, 2002). Pearce (2009) pointed out the potential applicability of the broaden-and-build theory to tourism contexts.

Classic studies of novice nuns linking emotions at a moment in early adulthood to life circumstances years later confirm that positive emotions lead to important, durable life outcomes (Lyubomirsky et al., 2005a). Lyubomirsky et al. synthesised over 100 studies that show effects consistent with the broaden-and-build theory. The few studies from which direction of causation may be inferred generally showed that life circumstances are shaped by subjective wellbeing components such as positive emotions, rather than success in life making people happy, as previously believed. In sum, positive emotions are key components as well as drivers of subjective wellbeing and contribute to valuable life outcomes such as health and wealth. Given the importance of positive emotions, we examine predictors and interventions related to positive emotions before bringing tourism experiences into the picture. Subsequently, we focus on positive emotions as a subjective wellbeing outcome of tourism before reviewing research linking tourism to other aspects of subjective wellbeing. This choice is motivated by the balance of findings showing myriad effects of holiday behaviours on positive emotions, with less striking effects on negative emotions, life satisfaction or other aspects of subjective wellbeing (e.g. Mitas, 2010; Lin et al., 2014).

Positive emotion predictors

As the first five years of positive psychology research brought positive emotions to the forefront, researchers have sought to uncover predictors of positive emotional experience. Findings from these efforts portray an emotionally positive person as someone outgoing, socially connected and integrated with the surrounding cultural practices. People who spend less time alone (Diener and Seligman, 2002), have higher levels of extraversion (Diener et al., 1999) and are less wealthy (Quoidbach, Dunn, Petrides and Mikolajczak, 2010) experience more positive emotions. Interindividual variation tends to be more closely related to genetic differences such as personality than to circumstantial differences such as socioeconomic status or disability (Lyubomirsky, Sheldon and Schkade, 2005b). While many of the cited studies focus on subjective wellbeing as a whole rather than isolating positive emotions, all measure positive emotionality either as a major component of or as a proxy for more general wellbeing constructs. As we will see, similar measurement challenges bracket many findings linking subjective wellbeing to tourism.

Within individuals, a landmark study by Killingsworth and Gilbert (2010) revealed attention to be a crucial predictor of positive emotions. Namely, when individuals' attention wanders from their present activities and surroundings, they report fewer positive and more negative emotions. Conversely, positive experiences coincide with attending to the present moment. This finding fits closely with outcomes of psychologists' attempts to boost individuals' positive emotions reliably and repeatedly.

Positive emotion interventions

Substantial research programmes, notably by Fredrickson and colleagues (e.g. Fredrickson, Cohn, Coffey, Pek and Finkel, 2008), Lyubomirsky and colleagues (e.g. Sheldon and Lyubomirsky, 2006) and Seligman and colleagues (e.g. Seligman, Steen, Park and Peterson, 2005), have sought to theorise, develop and test artificial sources of positive emotions (see Bolier et al., 2013, for a summary and meta-analysis). Many positive emotion interventions have had a popular self-help flavour, including counting one's blessings, writing letters of gratitude and watching comedy. Typically such interventions elevate participants' positive emotions over several occasions but eventually lose effectiveness as individuals habituate (Lyubomirsky, 2008). When viewed at a distance, these efforts evoke the insightful assertion by philosopher Thomas Aquinas that explicitly pursuing happiness is paradoxically sure to extinguish it (Haidt, 2006).

One intervention whose effectiveness remains over time – or increases, according to some studies (e.g. Brefczynski-Lewis, Lutz, Schaefer, Levinson and Davidson, 2007) – is meditation (Davidson et al., 2003). Meditation was excluded from Bolier et al.'s (2013: 16) meta-analysis of positive psychology interventions as it has been researched in 'long-standing independent research traditions for which effectiveness has already been established in several meta-analyses'. While meditation takes many different forms and processes, a shared feature is training the mind to attend to the present moment rather than to the past or future. This present-focused cognitive state is often referred to as mindfulness (Jha, Stanley, Kiyonaga, Wong and Gelfand, 2010) and, as we have seen, predicts positive emotions in daily activities (Killingsworth and Gilbert, 2010). With accumulating years of meditation experience, individuals are able to refocus their attention more efficiently to the present at a neurological level, even when not meditating (Brewer et al., 2011). Thus, seasoned meditators may be more likely to experience daily activities and life episodes as enjoyable.

Findings about the short-lived effects of most positive emotion interventions as well as the long-term effects of meditation leave much room to explain effects of people's activity choices on their positive emotions. In numerous studies 40 per cent or more of interindividual variation is unexplained (Lyubomirsky et al., 2005b). The potential of individuals' tourism behaviour choices to explain a portion of this variation makes the study of tourists' positive emotions interesting.

Tourism and subjective wellbeing

Positive emotions in tourism

Beginning with Hammitt's (1980) test of the classic recreation experience model of Knetsch and Clawson (1966), several studies have shown that people's emotions become more positive during tourism or day trip experiences (e.g. Mitas et al., 2012a; Strauss-Blasche, Ekmekcioglu and Marktl, 2000). As measurement of tourists' positive affect has suffered from ambiguity between emotions and mood as well as trait and state levels, studies touching all aspects of positive affect, not just positive emotions, are reviewed in this section.

We focus here on positive emotions instead of emotions in general. Although many of the cited studies measured negative as well as positive emotions, most findings about negative emotions during tourism experiences are unremarkable. Even under normal circumstances, 'holidays are not always uniformly happy experiences' (Kemp, Burt and Furneaux, 2008: 134). It is worth noting that negative emotions do not necessarily make a holiday undesirable or unlikely to be repeated. It is logical that a tourist upset by poor service, false portrayals in advertising or crime makes negative judgements about her or his holiday. However, negative emotions are actively sought and contextually appropriate in so-called dark tourism experiences (Buda, d'Hauteserre and Johnston, 2014), which involve attractions associated with death and suffering (Stone and Sharpley, 2008). A study by Nawijn and Fricke (2013) demonstrated that experience of some negative emotions at such a site actually predicted positive behaviour toward the attraction. Studies focusing on all other types of tourism report few differences between negative emotions on holiday and in daily life, though personality plays a role in any extant changes (Lin et al., 2014).

Several PhDs in recent years have focused on the contribution of tourism experiences to individuals' subjective wellbeing (Filep, 2009; Hagger, 2009; Mitas, 2010; de Bloom, 2012;

Nawijn, 2012). Each of these scholars has addressed positive emotions or moods as a central variable in their thesis. Furthermore, several researchers outside of the field have focused either on tourism experiences or on time away from work as a potential antecedent of positive emotions. Unfortunately, work psychologists do not always distinguish between vacation time spent at home and tourism experiences, making it difficult to apply their findings to the topic of tourism and happiness (e.g. Lounsbury and Hoopes, 1986). Other studies in work psychology as well as health psychology do address tourism experiences specifically and are integrated with relevant tourism studies below.

The overwhelming consensus is that tourists enjoy more positive emotions while on holiday than during daily life at home (Kemp et al., 2008; Mitas et al., 2012a) and that people who take holidays in a given period of time feel more positive than those who do not (Gilbert and Abdullah, 2004; Kroesen and Handy, 2014; Nawijn, Marchand, Veenhoven and Vingerhoets, 2010). Graburn (2001) theorised that tourism experiences also contribute to positive emotions shortly before and after a holiday. Empirical tests of this idea showed that positive emotions are present before, during and after a holiday (Jung and Cho, 2015), begin to rise just before a holiday and decline rapidly after (Mitas et al., 2012a). Thus, according to Mitas et al., tourists' positive emotions follow a 'peak' model, where emotions improve from baseline leading up to a holiday, are elevated during and decline after (e.g. de Bloom et al., 2010; Mitas et al., 2012a; Strauss-Blasche et al., 2000; Strauss-Blasche et al., 2004a; Strauss-Blasche, Muhry, Lehofer, Moser and Marktl, 2004b). Evidence of positive emotion decline after a holiday is especially robust, showing decline of positive emotions to baseline within days (de Bloom et al., 2010; Mitas et al., 2012a; Strauss-Blasche et al., 2004b) to weeks (McCabe and Johnson, 2013; Nawijn et al., 2010; Strauss-Blasche et al., 2000).

Interestingly, the peak model holds at various time scales, including within the holiday itself. Boosts in positive emotions during tourist experiences occur especially during the middle part of the holiday (Nawijn, 2010; Nawijn, Mitas, Lin and Kerstetter, 2013; Strauss-Blasche et al., 2004a, 2004b). An interesting counterexample to the peak model is a detailed study of volunteer tourists at sea by Coghlan and Pearce (2010), which shows more subtle patterns of day-to-day variation. Even in this study, however, the first and last days of travel showed less positive emotion. Zooming out to a time scale of years, measurements of emotions or moods are more positive closer to holidays (Chen, Lehto and Cai, 2013; Nawijn et al., 2010; Strauss-Blasche et al., 2000). Vacation frequency in one year, however, may not influence trait affect the following year (Kroesen and Handy, 2014). In an effect called the 'rosy view', tourists may predict and remember positive emotions during the holiday as stronger than they were (Kemp et al., 2008; Wirtz, Kruger, Scollon and Diener, 2003).

Several mechanisms of positive emotions in tourism experiences have been posited. Unlike in psychological studies of positive emotions, as of this writing, neither self-help interventions nor mindfulness has been examined as positive emotion sources in a tourism context. Related conceptual work (Coghlan, 2015) and exploratory experimental data on podcasting (Kang and Gretzel, 2012) exist. The bulk of tourism emotion research suggests, however, that an important mechanism of positive emotions in tourism experiences is interaction between people (Farber and Hall, 2007; Kang and Gretzel, 2012; McCabe, Joldersma and Li, 2010; Mitas, Qian, Yarnal and Kerstetter, 2011; Nawijn, 2011a; Mitas et al., 2012b; Strauss-Blasche et al., 2005). As an example of interaction between people in a tourism context, photography has been described as a tool to capture positive emotions derived from being together. People experience positive emotions when taking a photograph together, but also when they review the photograph together on the spot (Gillet, Schmitz and Mitas, 2016). Other variables related to positive emotions on holiday include lower holiday stress (Nawijn, 2011a), viewing scenery and wildlife (Farber and Hall, 2007), sunny weather (Jeuring and Peters, 2013), relaxation (Nawijn et al., 2010) and highly proximate cognitions such as goal congruence (Ma, Gao, Scott and Ding, 2013).

Several studies have analysed development of specific positive emotions in a tourism context. These include explorations of interest, warmth, amusement and the sublime (Mitas et al., 2012b), joy, love and positive surprise (Prayag, Hosany and Odeh, 2013), excitement and pleasure (Farber and Hall, 2007) and delight (Ma et al., 2013), as well as a developmental breakdown of the 19 mDES emotions (amusement, anger, awe, compassion, contempt, contentment, disgust, embarrassment, hope, fear, gratitude, guilt, interest, joy, love, pride, sadness, shame and surprise: Cohn et al., 2009) over the course of the holiday (Lin et al., 2014). These initial efforts leave much fertile ground to uncover which emotions are prominent in different holiday experiences, under different circumstances and with different consequences.

While our synthesis of research on tourists' positive emotions is driven by implications for tourists' subjective wellbeing, it is necessary to mention that positive emotions have been studied as precedents for tourism consumption behaviours. These studies generally show that positive emotions during or about a holiday affect satisfaction (del Bosque and San Martín, 2008; Lee, Manthiou, Jeong, Tang and Chiang, 2014; Song, Ahn and Lee, 2013) and revisit intention (Prayag et al., 2013; Hosany, Prayag, Deesilatham, Causevic and Odeh, 2014; see also Kim, Woo and Uysal, 2015 for a related finding). Emotions can be used as a psychographic segmentation variable (Bigne and Andreu, 2004). Consumer behaviour research on tourists' emotions is considered crucial in the contemporary 'emotion economy' in which people purchase based on their feelings (Rock, 2015).

In sum, research confirms what popular culture and tourism advertising would have us believe: tourists' experiences are rich and varied in positive emotions (Hosany and Gilbert, 2009). The findings on tourists' positive emotions represent a far more complete and coherent body of work than research on cognitive aspects of tourists' subjective wellbeing or on wellbeing in general.

Other research on tourists' subjective wellbeing

Studies of tourists' subjective wellbeing, while generally focusing on emotions, often also measured the cognitive aspect of subjective wellbeing, life satisfaction. Lounsbury and Hoopes (1986; Hoopes and Lounsbury, 1989) showed an improvement in life satisfaction after a holiday. Consistent effects have been found in older adults (Hagger, 2009), seasonal migrants (Simpson, Siguaw and Sheng, 2014) and disadvantaged families receiving a subsidised holiday as an act of charity (McCabe and Johnson, 2013).

The classic, well-designed studies of Gilbert and Abdullah (2004) as well as Chen, Petrick and Shahvali (2016) explored the tourism–life satisfaction link in more depth, distinguishing between participants who did and those who did not travel during vacation. They showed that life satisfaction is higher post-holiday and in tourists compared to non-tourists. Chen et al. (2013) found this positive effect to fade out over two months. Kroesen and Handy (2014) used a cross-lagged panel analysis to show that holiday frequency improves life satisfaction from year to year, consistent with Hagger's (2009) finding of higher life satisfaction among older tourists who travelled more frequently and anticipated doing so in the future. A number of other studies have indicated no effect on life satisfaction associated with vacations, however (Mitas, 2010; Nawijn, 2011b; Strauss-Blasche et al., 2000). Though one study indicated that recovery experiences during a recent holiday were associated with life satisfaction (Chen et al., 2016), aspects of tourists' experiences or behaviour that affect life satisfaction otherwise remain unknown.

Worth mentioning are a number of other studies from which the components making up subjective wellbeing cannot be discerned, yet clearly address outcomes related to subjective wellbeing. An early effort to link tourism and subjective wellbeing was Milman's (1998) study of older American tourists, which showed no change in an overall subjective wellbeing index between the beginning and end of a week-long organised group tour. Several subsequent studies did find positive effects of tourism experiences on subjective wellbeing. These findings occurred in populations such as mental health patients (Pols and Kroon, 2007), the general population of the Netherlands (Nawijn and Peeters, 2010) and white-collar employees in Austria (Strauss-Blasche, Reithofer, Schobersberger, Ekmekcioglu and Marktl, 2005).

Some studies also sought out predictors of subjective wellbeing in tourism experiences. Milman (1998) and later Wei and Milman (2002) positively linked the number of activities undertaken on holiday to subjective wellbeing. Risk may play a factor in this relationship, as a recent study on the island of Vanuatu showed (Filep, Klint, Whitelaw, Dominey-Howes and DeLacy, 2014). Similar studies presented findings about the positive effects of interacting with nature (Bimonte and Faralla, 2012, 2014), warm outside temperatures (Nawijn, 2010; Strauss-Blasche et al., 2005), pleasurable physical exercise (Strauss-Blasche et al., 2005; de Bloom et al., 2011) and a sense of freedom in daily activities (Strauss-Blasche et al., 2005), as well as in destination choice (Nawijn and Peeters, 2010). From the above studies, it may be concluded that activity and setting choices somehow relate to tourists' wellbeing. Longitudinal research that distinguishes between the components of subjective wellbeing is necessary to deduce the nature of this connection. The proposed effects of internet use (Jun, Hartwell and Buhalis, 2012), identifying with a destination (Üner and Armutlu, 2012) and certain motivations for going on holiday (Dann, 2012; Puczkó and Smith, 2012) also deserve empirical exploration.

A research programme by consumer psychologists at Virginia Tech has aimed to explore further how components of subjective wellbeing in the tourism domain interrelate. This research programme has produced an excellent literature review (Uysal, Sirgy, Woo and Kim, 2016) and a theoretical work (Sirgy, 2010). Noteworthy is also a massive collection of literature reviews and empirical works assembled into a *Handbook of Tourism and Quality-of-Life Research* (Uysal, Perdue and Sirgy, 2012).

Empirical studies in the Virginia Tech programme addressed the "bottom-up" theory of life satisfaction, which posits that life satisfaction arises from satisfaction with specific life domains. In line with this theory, satisfaction with: (1) tourism services on holiday (Neal, Sirgy and Uysal, 1999; replicated by Lee et al., 2014); (2) life domains that may intersect with tourism (Sirgy, Kruger, Lee and Yu, 2011); and (3) holiday experiences in general (Kim et al., 2015) had positive effects on various indices of life satisfaction. Neal, Uysal and Sirgy (2007) found this effect only for holidays of more than seven days. The indices used in these studies are questionable, as they sometimes included items measuring other constructs such as tourism experience reflection (Sirgy et al., 2011; Kim et al., 2015), rather than using complete, well-tested available instruments such as the Satisfaction With Life Scale (Pavot and Diener, 2008).

Support for the "bottom-up" theory of life satisfaction in these studies is worth noting. These studies do not, however, address how holiday experiences themselves contribute to subjective wellbeing, as only indirect effects of holiday experience variables, if measured, are analysed. As such, like early studies of tourist personality, they 'simply re-describe rather than explain' (Pearce and Packer, 2013: 402) subjective wellbeing. Similar limitations are unfortunately common to tourism research of subjective wellbeing (e.g. Strauss-Blasche et al., 2005; Simpson et al., 2014). It would be interesting to test the models developed in these studies using longitudinal research that uses precise, valid and reliable measurements of behaviour as well as subjective wellbeing.

It is also worth noting here that a portion of the work psychology literature on vacation from work and tourism effects claims to address wellbeing. Wellbeing tends to be conceptualised as stress, burnout or physical health in this literature, however (e.g. Westman and Etzion, 2002; Fritz and Sonnentag, 2006; de Bloom et al., 2009; Kühnel and Sonnentag, 2011). Though interesting, these findings are difficult to synthesise with research of subjective wellbeing and will thus not be explored further here.

Case study: the effect of holiday length and frequency

The reviewed literature shows fragmented but increasingly informative understanding of tourists' subjective wellbeing. It is now widely understood that tourists enjoy elevated positive emotions on holiday, an effect that quickly fades, while effects on negative emotions and life satisfaction are more varied. A basic question about effects of holiday behaviour on life satisfaction concerns frequency and duration of holidays. Most working individuals are granted a certain period of paid vacation time, over which they have limited choice, especially if they have children whose schooling is organised around fixed holiday periods. Nevertheless, the literature reveals little about, for example, whether to divide holiday time into several shorter holidays rather than one longer holiday when such flexibility exists. Exceptions are the findings of Neal et al. (2007) showing a positive effect of holiday duration, findings of Hagger (2009) showing a positive effect of frequency and findings of Kemp et al. (2008), Nawijn et al. (2010) and Strauss-Blasche et al. (2005) showing no effect. Puczkó and Smith (2012) suggest that frequency is important, as within tourism experiences, 'peaks of happiness can contribute to long-term satisfaction if they are repeated often enough, thereby contributing to overall wellbeing' (265). The purpose of the present case study was to examine this effect in the general population of the Netherlands.

The third author's personal social network comprised a convenience sample which was expanded using snowballing (Trochim, 2000) to a total sample of 245 adult Dutch citizens. Sample participants were contacted by email with an online survey. The survey measured their holiday frequency and duration for the past year. Specifically, participants were asked how many total days they spent on holiday in 2014 and how many times they went on holiday. An interaction of these variables represents the effect of their vacation frequency. We elected to define holidays as trips for leisure purposes with at least one night spent away from home and outside of the Netherlands. Our focus on international trips was motivated by the increasingly blurred line between commuting, leisure travel and visiting family for child care purposes within the Netherlands. For a Dutch adult, crossing a national border is much more likely to occur within the context of a leisure trip. Despite the limitation of excluding Dutch domestic tourism, we felt the clarity of definition offered by focusing on international trips was important.

Participants also indicated their emotions at the trait level using the mDES (Cohn et al., 2009), an emotion list that has worked well in previous studies of tourists' emotions, as it contains sufficient positive emotion diversity (Mitas et al., 2012a). Three changes were made to the original mDES list. First, *compassion* was removed, as it can be seen as either neutral or positive and has been difficult for some respondents to understand in our experience. Second, for the similar reason that its valence is unclear, *surprise* was divided into *positive surprise* and *negative surprise*. Finally, due to the difficulty of accurately translating *embarrassment* into Dutch, two words that could be translated as *embarrassment* were used instead of favouring one or the other. Participants' life satisfaction was measured using the well-tested Satisfaction with Life Scale (Pavot and Diener, 2008). Positive emotions, negative emotions and life satisfaction were separately modelled using linear regression models taking total days on holiday, number of holidays taken and the interaction between the two as independent variables.

Participants were slightly more educated (over 82 per cent had at least a bachelor's degree) than the general population. Just over 60 per cent of participants were women. Average age was 42.1 years, with a standard deviation of 16 years. Data of one participant were removed as a very high number of holidays in 2014 (76) suggested this item may have been misinterpreted. Regression models showed no effects of any independent variables on any subjective wellbeing outcome. Interactions as well as main effects were not significant, with no model explaining more than 3 per cent in any subjective wellbeing outcome (Tables 5.1–5.3). In subsequent models we added level of education as a second moderator variable. Level of education was also not significant in interaction with total days on holiday and variance explained was once again very low, reaching at most 7.2 per cent (Tables 5.4 and 5.5). Thus, we concluded that length and frequency of holidays do not affect subjective wellbeing. While holidays generally improve positive emotions during a tourism experience and tourism events and circumstances may affect wellbeing, how long and how often individuals travel for holidays over the course of a single year does not affect their wellbeing in the months that follow.

Table 5.1 Regression of life satisfaction on holiday frequency and total holiday duration

Coefficient	Unstandardised beta	Standard error
(Constant)	5.1567***	0.1304
Total days on holiday	0.0018	0.0036
Holiday frequency	0.0368	0.0407
Total days on holiday × Holiday frequency	0.0004	0.0011

Note: Adjusted R^2 for this model = 0.0285; significance level: $*p \leq 0.05$; $**p \leq 0.01$; $***p \leq 0.001$.

Table 5.2 Regression of positive emotions on holiday frequency and total holiday duration

Coefficient	Unstandardised beta	Standard error
(Constant)	3.6480***	0.0737
Total days on holiday	0.0020	0.0020
Holiday frequency	−0.0008	0.0228
Total days on holiday × Holiday frequency	0	0.0006

Note: Adjusted R^2 for this model = 0.0111; significance level: $* p \leq 0.05$; $** p \leq 0.01$; $***p \leq 0.001$.

Table 5.3 Regression of negative emotions on holiday frequency and total holiday duration

Coefficient	Unstandardised beta	Standard error
(Constant)	1.7492***	0.0672
Total days on holiday	−0.0005	0.0018
Holiday frequency	−0.0153	0.0211
Total days on holiday × Holiday frequency	0.0001	0.0005

Note: Adjusted R^2 for this model = 0.0052; significance level: $* p \leq 0.05$; $** p \leq 0.01$; $***p \leq 0.001$.

(continued)

O. Mitas, J. Nawijn and B. Jongsma

(continued)

Table 5.4 Regression of life satisfaction on holiday frequency, total holiday duration and education level

Coefficient	Unstandardised beta	Standard error
(Constant)	4.8914***	0.1911
Total days on holiday	0.0012	0.0037
Holiday frequency	0.0567	0.0423
Education level	0.1598	0.2039
Total days on holiday × Holiday frequency	−0.0005	0.0012
Total days on holiday × Education level	0.0071	0.0046

Note: Adjusted R^2 for this model = 0.0717; significance level: * $p \leq 0.05$; ** $p \leq 0.01$; ***$p \leq 0.001$.

Table 5.5 Regression of positive emotions on holiday frequency, total holiday duration and education level

Coefficient	Unstandardised beta	Standard error
(Constant)	3.3998***	0.1092
Total days on holiday	0.0028	0.0020
Holiday frequency	−0.0054	0.0237
Education level	0.3118**	0.1168
Total days on holiday × Holiday frequency	0.0000	0.0006
Total days on holiday × Education level	−0.0015	0.0025

Note: Adjusted R^2 for this model = 0.0496; significance level: * $p \leq 0.05$; ** $p \leq 0.01$; ***$p \leq 0.001$.

Implications of research on tourists' subjective wellbeing

Implications for tourism industry

Given the favourable behaviours that follow increases in tourists' subjective wellbeing, the travel industry would be wise to take tourists' subjective wellbeing seriously (Dolnicar, Lazarevski and Yanamandram, 2012). Unfortunately, the fragmented nature of research on tourists' subjective wellbeing in terms of sampling and measurement, as well as pervasive use of cross-sectional designs, precludes forceful recommendations from the numerous studies cited. Furthermore, we wish to avoid the rush to judgement that has discredited some findings in positive psychology (Brown, Sokal and Friedman, 2013). Thus, our recommendations are based on the emerging consensus from multiple studies done in varying contexts using valid and reliable designs and instruments. Given these qualifiers, two recommendations may be emphasised: the tourism industry should work strategically to make tourism as accessible as possible and as rich with meaningful social interaction as possible.

Given that tourism experiences generally contribute to subjective wellbeing, particularly to positive emotions, the efforts of the tourism industry to encourage people to travel for holidays are well placed. One constraint placed on holidays comes from government policy favouring economic growth over generous holiday and leave laws. Industry lobbying to ensure ample time off for travel and economic conditions that support holidays is recommended. Many countries and regions have professional associations that represent tourism businesses to the public. These associations would do well to connect with governments over vacation and economic policy.

The industry can also broaden the appeal of tourism to a substantial portion of individuals who have means to travel but lack inspiration. Familiar industry price wars, overblown advertisements and complex distribution systems do little to spur non-travellers to head out. On the other hand, creativity in product and distribution design from new industry players, large and small, is making travel not only more appealing but more varied. For example, booking a holiday package to an unknown, unspecified destination was unheard of a decade ago. Yet it has proven to be a viable business and an appealing way to go on holiday for some. Such innovation in the industry should be encouraged and celebrated.

The tourism industry also has more tools than ever to encourage social interaction, which appears to be the most important source of positive emotions on holiday. In particular, the connectivity of the present-day traveller makes it easier than ever for tourism companies to facilitate social interactions between travel partners as well as strangers. This should be further explored, keeping privacy concerns in mind. Destinations can also develop events, architecture and attractions with social interactions among tourists and between tourists and locals as a priority.

Future questions

Numerous questions about the effects of tourism on subjective wellbeing abound. Because of the financial and logistical challenges of longitudinal research, as well as short university performance review cycles, the most difficult, yet important, questions relate to the long-term interrelations between tourism and subjective wellbeing. When measured over longer time spans (five years or more), does tourism behaviour have a replicable effect on life satisfaction? Do shorter-term trajectories of emotion development change from one year to the next? Does change in life stage or family composition precipitate a change in the subjective wellbeing outcomes of tourism experiences? In sum, it is unknown to what extent tourism is a "core" or fundamentally necessary ingredient for subjective wellbeing (Dolnicar et al., 2012: 302). The role of tourism in wellbeing is also doubtless affected by the role of tourist experiences in a culture.

The documented positive emotion source of mindfulness also warrants further research. Are individuals more or less mindful on holiday? Does this affect their emotions? Are interventions in this arena warranted? If so, which work best?

Finally, from the myriad of tourism experiences offered, little is known about which varieties of tourism, transport modes, destinations, accommodations and other behavioural choices can affect tourists' subjective wellbeing. Such effects doubtless interact with variations between tourists themselves. Which holiday is best for which tourist? While algorithms to help tourists select the holiday they "want" exist, individuals are notorious for not necessarily "wanting" to make decisions that would optimise their subjective wellbeing. Personality and culture (Genç, 2012), in particular, would be interesting variables for exploring interactions between individual differences, choices of various holiday behaviours and subjective wellbeing.

References

Bigne, J. E. and Andreu, L. (2004) 'Emotions in segmentation: An empirical study', *Annals of Tourism Research*, 31(3), 682–696.

Bimonte, S. and Faralla, V. (2012) 'Tourist types and happiness: A comparative study in Maremma, Italy', *Annals of Tourism Research*, 39(4), 1929–1950.

—— (2014) 'Happiness and nature-based vacations', *Annals of Tourism Research*, 46, 176–178.

Bolier, L., Haverman, M., Westerhof, G. J., Riper, H., Smit, F. and Bohlmeijer, E. (2013) 'Positive psychology interventions: A meta-analysis of randomized controlled studies', *BMC Public Health*, 13, 119–138.

Brefczynski-Lewis, J. A., Lutz, A., Schaefer, H. S., Levinson, D. B. and Davidson, R. J. (2007) 'Neural correlates of attentional expertise in long-term meditation practitioners', *Proceedings of the National Academy of Sciences*, 104(27), 11483–11488.

Brewer, J. A., Worhunsky, P. D., Gray, J. R., Tang, Y. Y., Weber, J. and Kober, H. (2011) 'Meditation experience is associated with differences in default mode network activity and connectivity', *Proceedings of the National Academy of Sciences*, 108(50), 20254–20259.

Brown, N. J. L., Sokal, A. D. and Friedman, H. L. (2013) 'The complex dynamics of wishful thinking: The critical positivity ratio', *American Psychologist*, 68(9), 801–813.

Buda, D. M., d'Hauteserre, A. M. and Johnston, L. (2014) 'Feeling and tourism studies', *Annals of Tourism Research*, 46, 102–114.

Chen, C. and Petrick, J. F. (2013) 'Health and wellness benefits of travel experiences: A literature review', *Journal of Travel Research*, 52(6), 709–719.

Chen, C. C., Petrick, J. F. and Shahvali, M. (2016) 'Tourism experiences as a stress reliever examining the effects of tourism recovery experiences on life satisfaction', *Journal of Travel Research*, 55(2), 150–160.

Chen, Y., Lehto, X. Y. and Cai, L. (2013) 'Vacation and well-being: A study of Chinese tourists', *Annals of Tourism Research*, 42, 284–310.

Christopher, J. C. and Hickinbottom, S. (2008) 'Positive psychology, ethnocentrism and the disguised ideology of individualism', *Theory and Psychology*, 18(5), 563–589.

Coghlan, A. (2015) 'Tourism and health: Using positive psychology principles to maximise participants' wellbeing outcomes – a design concept for charity challenge tourism', *Journal of Sustainable Tourism*, 23(3), 382–400.

Coghlan, A. and Pearce, P. (2010) 'Tracking affective components of satisfaction', *Tourism and Hospitality Research*, 10(1), 42–58.

Cohn, M. A., Fredrickson, B. L., Brown, S. L., Mikels, J. A. and Conway, A. M. (2009) 'Happiness unpacked: Positive emotions increase life satisfaction by building resilience', *Emotion*, 9(3), 361–368.

Csikszentmihalyi, M. and Hunter, J. (2003) 'Happiness in everyday life: The uses of experience sampling', *Journal of Happiness Studies*, 4(2), 185–199.

Dann, G. M. (2012) 'Tourist motivation and quality-of-life: In search of the missing link', in Uysal, M., Perdue, R. and Sirgy, M. J. (eds) *Handbook of Tourism and Quality-of-Life Research*, Dordrecht, The Netherlands: Springer, pp. 233–250.

Davidson, R. J., Kabat-Zinn, J., Schumacher, J., Rosenkranz, M., Muller, D., Santorelli, S. F., Urbanowski, F., Harrington, A., Bonus, K. and Sheridan, J. F. (2003) 'Alterations in brain and immune function produced by mindfulness meditation', *Psychosomatic Medicine*, 65(4), 564–570.

de Bloom, J. D. (2012) *How Do Vacations Affect Workers' Health and Well-Being? Vacation (After-) Effects and the Role of Vacation Activities and Experiences*, Doctoral Dissertation, Radboud Universiteit Nijmegen.

de Bloom, J., Geurts, S. A., Sonnentag, S., Taris, T., de Weerth, C. and Kompier, M. A. (2011) 'How does a vacation from work affect employee health and wellbeing?', *Psychology and Health*, 26(12), 1606–1622.

de Bloom, J., Geurts, S. A., Taris, T. W., Sonnentag, S., de Weerth, C. and Kompier, M. A. (2010) 'Effects of vacation from work on health and wellbeing: Lots of fun, quickly gone', *Work and Stress*, 24(2), 196–216.

de Bloom, J., Kompier, M., Geurts, S., de Weerth, C., Taris, T. and Sonnentag, S. (2009) 'Do we recover from vacation? Meta-analysis of vacation effects on health and wellbeing', *Journal of Occupational Health*, 51(1), 13–25.

del Bosque, I. R. and San Martín, H. (2008) 'Tourist satisfaction: A cognitive-affective model', *Annals of Tourism Research*, 35(2), 551–573.

Diener, E. and Emmons, R. A. (1984) 'The independence of positive and negative affect', *Journal of Personality and Social Psychology*, 47(5), 1105–1117.

Diener, E. and Seligman, M. E. (2002) 'Very happy people', *Psychological Science*, 13(1), 81–84.

Diener, E., Suh, E. M., Lucas, R. E. and Smith, H. L. (1999) 'Subjective well-being: Three decades of progress', *Psychological Bulletin*, 125(2), 276–302.

Dolnicar, S., Lazarevski, K. and Yanamandram, V. (2012) 'Quality-of-life and travel motivations: Integrating the two concepts in the Grevillea model', in Uysal, M., Perdue, R. and Sirgy, M. J. (eds) *Handbook of Tourism and Quality-of-Life Research*, Dordrecht, The Netherlands: Springer, pp. 293–308.

Farber, M. E. and Hall, T. E. (2007) 'Emotion and environment: Visitors' extraordinary experiences along the Dalton Highway in Alaska', *Journal of Leisure Research*, 39(2), 248.

Festinger, L. (1954) 'A theory of social comparison processes', *Human Relations*, 7(2), 117–140.

Filep, S. and Deery, M. (2010) 'Towards a picture of tourists' happiness', *Tourism Analysis*, 15(4), 399–410.

Filep, S., Klint, L. M., Whitelaw, P., Dominey-Howes, D. and DeLacy, T. (2014) 'Happiness, satisfaction, and risk perception', *Tourism Review International*, 17(4), 283–298.

Fredrickson, B. L. (1998) 'What good are positive emotions?', *Review of General Psychology*, 2(3), 300–319.

—— (2000) 'Extracting meaning from past affective experiences: The importance of peaks, ends and specific emotions', *Cognition and Emotion*, 14(4), 577–606.

—— (2001) 'The role of positive emotions in positive psychology: The broaden-and-build theory of positive emotions', *American Psychologist*, 56(3), 218.

Fredrickson, B. T. and Joiner, T. (2002) 'Positive emotions trigger upward spirals toward emotional wellbeing', *Psychological Science*, 13(2), 172–175.

Fredrickson, B. L. and Levenson, R. W. (1998) 'Positive emotions speed recovery from the cardiovascular sequelae of negative emotions', *Cognition and Emotion*, 12(2), 191–220.

Fredrickson, B. L. and Losada, M. F. (2005) 'Positive affect and the complex dynamics of human flourishing', *American Psychologist*, 60(7), 678–686.

Fredrickson, B. L., Cohn, M. A., Coffey, K. A., Pek, J. and Finkel, S. M. (2008) 'Open hearts build lives: Positive emotions, induced through loving-kindness meditation, build consequential personal resources', *Journal of Personality and Social Psychology*, 95(5), 1045–1062.

Fritz, C. and Sonnentag, S. (2006) 'Recovery, well-being, and performance-related outcomes: The role of workload and vacation experiences', *Journal of Applied Psychology*, 91(4), 936.

Genç, R. (2012) 'Subjective aspects of tourists' quality-of-life (QOL)', in Uysal, M., Perdue, R. and Sirgy, M. J. (eds) *Handbook of Tourism and Quality-of-Life Research*, Dordrecht, The Netherlands: Dordrecht, pp. 149–167.

Gilbert, D. and Abdullah, J. (2004) 'Holidaytaking and the sense of well-being', *Annals of Tourism Research*, 31(1), 103–121.

Gillet, S., Schmitz, P. and Mitas, O. (2016) 'The snap-happy tourist: The effects of photographing behavior on tourists' happiness', *Journal of Hospitality and Tourism Research*, 40(1), 37–57.

Graburn, N. H. H. (2001) 'Secular ritual: A general theory of tourism', in Smith, V. L. and Brent, M. (eds) *Hosts and Guests Revisited: Tourism Issues of the 21st Century*, New York: Cognizant Communication Corporation.

Hagger, J. C. (2009) *The Impact of Tourism Experiences on Post Retirement Life Satisfaction*, Doctoral dissertation, University of South Australia.

Haidt, J. (2006) *The Happiness Hypothesis: Finding Modern Truth in Ancient Wisdom*, New York: Basic Books.

Hammitt, W. E. (1980) 'Outdoor recreation: Is it a multi-phase experience?', *Journal of Leisure Research*, 12(2), 107.

Headey, B. (2010) 'The set point theory of wellbeing has serious flaws: On the eve of a scientific revolution?', *Social Indicators Research*, 97(1), 7–21.

Hoopes, L. L. and Lounsbury, J. W. (1989) 'An investigation of life satisfaction following a vacation: A domain-specific approach', *Journal of Community Psychology*, 17(2), 129–140.

Hosany, S. and Gilbert, D. (2009) *Dimensions of Tourists' Emotional Experiences towards Hedonic Holiday Destinations*, Egham, UK: Royal Holloway University of London.

Hosany, S., Prayag, G., Deesilatham, S., Causevic, S. and Odeh, K. (2014) 'Measuring tourists' emotional experiences: Further validation of the destination emotion scale', *Journal of Travel Research*, 54(4), 482–495.

Jeuring, J. H. and Peters, K. B. (2013) 'The influence of the weather on tourist experiences: Analysing travel blog narratives', *Journal of Vacation Marketing*, 19(3), 209–219.

Jha, A. P., Stanley, E. A., Kiyonaga, A., Wong, L. and Gelfand, L. (2010) 'Examining the protective effects of mindfulness training on working memory capacity and affective experience', *Emotion*, 10(1), 54–64.

Jun, S. H., Hartwell, H. J. and Buhalis, D. (2012) 'Impacts of the internet on travel satisfaction and overall life satisfaction', in Uysal, M., Perdue, R. and Sirgy, J. (eds) *Handbook of Tourism and Quality-of-Life Research*, Dordrecht, The Netherlands: Springer, pp. 321–337,

Jung, D and Cho, M. (2015) 'A discovery of the positive travel experience in pre-trip, on-site and post-trip stage', in Griffin, K. and Joppe, M. (eds) *Tourism Travel and Research Association: Advancing Tourism Research Globally*, Whitehall, MI: Travel and Tourism Research Association, pp. 1–6.

Kahneman, D., Krueger, A. B., Schkade, D., Schwarz, N. and Stone, A. A. (2004) 'A survey method for characterizing daily life experience: The day reconstruction method', *Science*, 306(5702), 1776–1779.

Kang, M. and Gretzel, U. (2012) 'Effects of podcast tours on tourist experiences in a national park', *Tourism Management*, 33(2), 440–455.

Kemp, S., Burt, C. D. and Furneaux, L. (2008) 'A test of the peak-end rule with extended autobiographical events', *Memory and Cognition*, 36(1), 132–138.

Killingsworth, M. A. and Gilbert, D. T. (2010) 'A wandering mind is an unhappy mind', *Science*, 330(6006), 932.

Kim, H., Woo, E. and Uysal, M. (2015) 'Tourism experience and quality of life among elderly tourists', *Tourism Management*, 26, 465–476.

Knetsch, J. L. and Clawson, M. (1966) *Economics of Outdoor Recreation*, Baltimore, MD: Johns Hopkins Press.

Kroesen, M. and Handy, S. (2014) 'The influence of holiday-taking on affect and contentment', *Annals of Tourism Research*, 45, 89–101.

Kühnel, J. and Sonnentag, S. (2011) 'How long do you benefit from vacation? A closer look at the fade-out of vacation effects', *Journal of Organizational Behavior*, 32(1), 125–143.

Lee, S. A., Manthiou, A., Jeong, M., Tang, L. R. and Chiang, L. L. (2014) 'Does consumers' feeling affect their quality of life? Roles of consumption emotion and its consequences', *International Journal of Tourism Research*, 17, 409–416.

Lin, Y., Kerstetter, D., Nawijn, J. and Mitas, O. (2014) 'Changes in emotions and their interaction with personality in a vacation context', *Tourism Management*, 40, 416–424.

Lounsbury, J. W. and Hoopes, L. L. (1986) 'A vacation from work: Changes in work and nonwork outcomes', *Journal of Applied Psychology*, 71(3), 392.

Lyubomirsky, S. (2008) *The How of Happiness: A Scientific Approach to Getting the Life You Want*, New York: Penguin.

Lyubomirsky, S., King, L. and Diener, E. (2005a) 'The benefits of frequent positive affect: Does happiness lead to success?', *Psychological Bulletin*, 131(6), 803–855.

Lyubomirsky, S., Sheldon, K. M. and Schkade, D. (2005b) 'Pursuing happiness: The architecture of sustainable change', *Review of General Psychology*, 9(2), 111.

Ma, J., Gao, J., Scott, N. and Ding, P. (2013) 'Customer delight from theme park experiences: The antecedents of delight based on cognitive appraisal theory', *Annals of Tourism Research*, 42, 359–381.

McCabe, S. and Johnson, S. (2013) 'The happiness factor in tourism: Subjective wellbeing and social tourism', *Annals of Tourism Research*, 41, 42–65.

McCabe, S., Joldersma, T. and Li, C. (2010) 'Understanding the benefits of social tourism: Linking participation to subjective wellbeing and quality of life', *International Journal of Tourism Research*, 12(6), 761–773.

Meng, F., Turk, E. S. and Altintas, V. (2012) 'Tour operators' service quality and efficacy of satisfaction measurement', *Tourism Analysis*, 17(3), 325–342.

Milman, A. (1998) 'The impact of tourism and travel experience on senior travelers' psychological wellbeing', *Journal of Travel Research*, 37(2), 166–170.

Mitas, O. (2010) *Positive Emotions in Mature Adults' Leisure Travel Experiences*, Doctoral dissertation, Pennsylvania State University.

Mitas, O., Qian, X. L., Yarnal, C. and Kerstetter, D. (2011) '"The fun begins now!": Broadening and building processes in Red Hat Society participation', *Journal of Leisure Research*, 43(1), 30.

Mitas, O., Yarnal, C., Adams, R. and Ram, N. (2012a) 'Taking a "peak" at leisure travelers' positive emotions', *Leisure Sciences*, 34(2), 115–135.

Mitas, O., Yarnal, C. and Chick, G. (2012b) 'Jokes build community: Mature tourists' positive emotions', *Annals of Tourism Research*, 39(4), 1884–1905.

Nawijn, J. (2010) 'The holiday happiness curve: A preliminary investigation into mood during a holiday abroad', *International Journal of Tourism Research*, 12(3), 281–290.

—— (2011a) 'Determinants of daily happiness on vacation', *Journal of Travel Research*, 50(5), 559–566.

—— (2011b) 'Happiness through vacationing: Just a temporary boost or long-term benefits?', *Journal of Happiness Studies*, 12(4), 651–665.

—— (2012) *Leisure Travel and Happiness: An Empirical Study into the Effect of Holiday Trips on Individuals' Subjective Wellbeing*, Doctoral dissertation, Erasmus University, Rotterdam.

Nawijn, J. and Fricke, M. C. (2013) 'Visitor emotions and behavioral intentions: The case of concentration camp memorial Neuengamme', *International Journal of Tourism Research*, 17(3), 221–228.

Nawijn, J. and Peeters, P. M. (2010) 'Travelling "green": Is tourists' happiness at stake?', *Current Issues in Tourism*, 13(4), 381–392.

Nawijn, J., Marchand, M. A., Veenhoven, R. and Vingerhoets, A. J. (2010) 'Vacationers happier, but most not happier after a holiday', *Applied Research in Quality of Life*, 5(1), 35–47.

Nawijn, J., Mitas, O., Lin, Y. and Kerstetter, D. (2013) 'How do we feel on vacation? A closer look at how emotions change over the course of a trip', *Journal of Travel Research*, 52(2), 265–274.

Neal, J., Sirgy, M. J. and Uysal, M. (1999) 'The role of satisfaction with leisure travel/tourism services and experience in satisfaction with leisure life and overall life', *Journal of Business Research*, 44, 153–163.

Neal, J., Uysal, M. and Sirgy, M. J. (2007) 'Effect of tourism services on travelers' quality of life', *Journal of Travel Research*, 46, 154–163.

Pavot, W. and Diener, E. (2008) 'The Satisfaction With Life Scale and the emerging construct of life satisfaction', *Journal of Positive Psychology*, 3, 137–152.

Pearce, P. L. (2009) 'The relationship between positive psychology and tourist behavior studies', *Tourism Analysis*, 14(1), 37–48.

Pearce, P. L. and Packer, J. (2013) 'Minds on the move: New links from psychology to tourism', *Annals of Tourism Research*, 40, 386–411.

Pols, J. and Kroon, H. (2007) 'The importance of holiday trips for people with chronic mental health problems', *Psychiatric Services*, 58(2), 262–265.

Prayag, G., Hosany, S. and Odeh, K. (2013) 'The role of tourists' emotional experiences and satisfaction in understanding behavioral intentions', *Journal of Destination Marketing and Management*, 2(2), 118–127.

Puczkó, L. and Smith, M. (2012) 'An analysis of tourism QOL domains from the demand side', in Uysal, M., Perdue, R. and Sirgy, M. J. (eds) *Handbook of Tourism and Quality-of-Life Research*, Dordrecht, The Netherlands: Springer, pp. 263–277.

Quoidbach, J., Dunn, E. W., Petrides, K. V. and Mikolajczak, M. (2010) 'Money giveth, money taketh away: The dual effect of wealth on happiness', *Psychological Science*, 21(6), 756–763.

Rock, M. (2015) 'Human emotion: The one thing the Internet can't buy', *New York Times Style Magazine*, 14 October. Available online at http://www.nytimes.com/2015/10/14/t-magazine/human-emotion-the-one-thing-the-internet-cant-buy.html?_r=0 (accessed 15 October 2015).

Rosenberg, E. L. (1998) 'Levels of analysis and the organization of affect', *Review of General Psychology*, 2(3), 247–270.

Scollon, C. N. and King, L. A. (2011) 'What people really want in life and why it matters: Contributions from research on folk theories of the good life', in Biswas-Diener, R. (ed.) *Positive Psychology as Social Change*, Dordrecht, The Netherlands: Springer, pp. 1–14.

Seligman, M. E. (2004) *Authentic Happiness: Using the New Positive Psychology to Realize Your Potential for Lasting Fulfillment*, New York: Simon and Schuster.

Seligman, M. E. and Csikszentmihalyi, M. (2000) 'Positive psychology: An introduction', *American Psychologist*, 55(1), 5–14.

Seligman, M. E., Steen, T. A., Park, N. and Peterson, C. (2005) 'Positive psychology progress: Empirical validation of interventions', *American Psychologist*, 60(5), 410–421.

Sheldon, K. M. and Lyubomirsky, S. (2006) 'How to increase and sustain positive emotion: The effects of expressing gratitude and visualizing best possible selves', *Journal of Positive Psychology*, 1(2), 73–82.

Simpson, P. M., Siguaw, J. A. and Sheng, X. (2014) 'Tourists' life satisfaction at home and away: A tale of two cities', *Journal of Travel Research*, doi: 0047287514541004.

Sirakaya, E., Petrick, J. and Choi, H. S. (2004) 'The role of mood on tourism product evaluations', *Annals of Tourism Research*, 31(3), 517–539.

Sirgy, M. J. (2010) 'Toward a quality-of-life theory of leisure travel satisfaction', *Journal of Travel Research*, 49(2), 246–260.

Sirgy, M. J., Kruger, S., Lee, D. and Yu, G. B. (2011) 'How does a travel trip affect tourists' life satisfaction?', *Journal of Travel Research*, 50(3), 261–275.

Song, H. J., Ahn, Y. J. and Lee, C. K. (2013) 'Structural relationships among strategic experiential modules, emotion and satisfaction at the Expo 2012 Yeosu Korea', *International Journal of Tourism Research*, 17, 239–248.

Stone, P. and Sharpley, R. (2008) 'Consuming dark tourism: A thanatological perspective', *Annals of Tourism Research*, 35(2), 574–595.

Strauss-Blasche, G., Ekmekcioglu, C. and Marktl, W. (2000) 'Does vacation enable recuperation? Changes in well-being associated with time away from work', *Occupational Medicine*, 50(3), 167–172.

Strauss-Blasche, G., Muhry, F., Lehofer, M., Moser, M. and Marktl, W. (2004b) 'Time course of well-being after a three-week resort-based respite from occupational and domestic demands: carry-over, contrast and situation effects', *Journal of Leisure Research*, 36(3), 293.

Strauss-Blasche, G., Reithofer, B., Schobersberger, W., Ekmekcioglu, C. and Marktl, W. (2005) 'Effect of vacation on health: Moderating factors of vacation outcome', *Journal of Travel Medicine*, 12(2), 94–101.

Strauss-Blasche, G., Riedmann, B., Schobersberger, W., Ekmekcioglu, C., Riedmann, G., Waanders, R., . . . and Humpeler, E. (2004a) 'Vacation at moderate and low altitude improves perceived health in individuals with metabolic syndrome', *Journal of Travel Medicine*, 11(5), 300–306.

Thin, N. (2011) 'Socially responsible cheermongery: On the sociocultural contexts and levels of social happiness policies', in *Positive Psychology as Social Change*, Dordrecht, The Netherlands: Springer, pp. 33–49.

Tomasulo, D. J. and Pawelski, J. O. (2012) 'Happily ever after: The use of stories to promote positive interventions', *Psychology*, 3(12A), 1189–1195.

Trochim, W. M. (2000) *The Research Methods Knowledge Base*, 2nd edn, http://www.socialresearchmethods.net/kb/ (version current as of 20 October 2006).

Tugade, M. M., Fredrickson, B. L. and Feldman Barrett, L. (2004) 'Psychological resilience and positive emotional granularity: Examining the benefits of positive emotions on coping and health', *Journal of Personality*, 72(6), 1161–1190.

Üner, M. M. and Armutlu, C. (2012) 'Understanding the antecedents of destination identification: Linkage between perceived quality-of-life, self-congruity and destination identification', in Uysal, M., Perdue, R. and Sirgy, M. J. (eds) *Handbook of Tourism and Quality-of-Life Research*, Dordrecht, The Netherlands: Springer, pp. 251–261.

Uysal, M., Perdue, R. and Sirgy, J. (eds) (2012) *Handbook of Tourism and Quality-of-Life Research: Enhancing the Lives of Tourists and Residents of Host Communities*, Dordrecht, The Netherlands: Springer Science & Business Media.

Uysal, M., Sirgy, M. J., Woo, E. and Kim, H. (2016) 'Quality of life (QOL) and wellbeing research in tourism', *Tourism Management*, 53, 244–261.

Veenhoven, R. (2009) 'How do we assess how happy we are? Tenets, implications and tenability of three theories', in Dutt, A. K. and Radcliff, B. (eds) *Happiness, Economics and Politics: Towards a Multidisciplinary Approach*, Cheltenham, UK: Edward Elger Publishers, pp. 45–69.

Wei, S. and Milman, A. (2002) 'The impact of participation in activities while on vacation on seniors' psychological wellbeing: A path model application', *Journal of Hospitality and Tourism Research*, 26(2), 175–185.

Westman, M. and Etzion, D. (2002) 'The impact of short overseas business trips on job stress and burnout', *Applied Psychology*, 51(4), 582–592.

Wirtz, D., Kruger, J., Scollon, C. N. and Diener, E. (2003) 'What to do on spring break? The role of predicted, on-line, and remembered experience in future choice', *Psychological Science*, 14(5), 520–524.

Zeelenberg, M., Nelissen, R. M., Breugelmans, S. M. and Pieters, R. (2008) 'On emotion specificity in decision making: Why feeling is for doing', *Judgment and Decision Making*, 3(1), 18.

6

The impact of tourist activities on tourists' subjective wellbeing

Muzaffer Uysal, M. Joseph Sirgy, Eunju Woo
and Hyelin (Lina) Kim

Summary

In recent years there has been a heightened interest in studying the link between tourism/leisure activities and subjective wellbeing of travellers. The scholarly tourism literature is replete with studies that have demonstrated in different experience settings that the nature of trip behaviour and trip characteristics directly affects tourists, experience outcomes and subjective value of tourists' experiences. The goal of this chapter is threefold: (1) to delineate the connection between tourism activities and subjective wellbeing by reviewing the extant literature and theoretical underpinning guiding this connection; (2) to identify research method issues to spur further research; and (3) to highlight management and policy implications. The chapter concludes that the provision of quality tourism experiences should be created with the wellbeing of today's and tomorrow's travellers in mind.

Introduction

People engage and participate in tourism activities during their leisure time because tourists' experiences generate a sense of wellbeing, excitement and fulfilment of higher-order needs such as self-enrichment, personal growth and development and self-actualisation, thus contributing to quality of life. For example, Pearce (2008) conducted a study that provided evidence that holiday trips, vacation as a special form of leisure and pleasant activities contribute to individuals' happiness. Benefits induced by partaking in recreation and leisure activities are well documented in outdoor recreation- and leisure-related research (e.g. Bimonte and Faralla, 2012, 2013; Driver and Brown, 1978; Driver, Brown and Peterson, 1991; Ibrahim, 2008; Lu and Argyle, 1994). Driver et al. (1991) use the term 'benefits' broadly to mean quality of life – psychological, health, sociological, environmental and economic benefits to individual tourists.

Specifically, every leisure activity provides functional benefits (i.e. instrumental value). In addition to the functional benefits, many leisure activities are associated with terminal values – benefits related to basic needs (safety, health, economic, hedonic, escape and sensation seeking) as well as growth needs (symbolic, aesthetic, moral, mastery, relatedness and distinctiveness benefits). The central tenet implied in this view of leisure benefit is that a leisure activity contributes significantly to leisure wellbeing if it delivers not only functional benefits but also a range of other benefits related to both basic and growth needs (e.g. Bjork, 2014; Chen and Petrick, 2013; Payne, Ainsworth and Godbey, 2010; Sirgy, Uysal and Kruger, 2016; Smith and Puczkó, 2014) – the more a leisure activity delivers functional benefits plus benefits related to basic growth, the greater the likelihood that such an activity would contribute significantly to satisfaction in leisure life and subjective wellbeing (i.e. leisure wellbeing) (cf. Heo, Lee, Kim and Stebbins, 2013; Heo, Stebbins, Kim and Lee, 2012; Lee, Kruger, Whang, Uysal and Sirgy, 2014; Silverstein and Parker, 2002). However, the challenge remains to link tourism activities with leisure life and subjective wellbeing. Can tourists' subjective wellbeing be predicted through tourist behaviour, including traveller and trip characteristics, satisfaction with life domains, satisfaction with life overall and the consumption life cycle?

The scholarly tourism literature is replete with studies that have demonstrated in different experience settings that the nature of trip behaviour and trip characteristics directly affects tourists, experience outcomes and subjective value of tourist experiences (e.g. Bjork, 2014; Campos, Mendes, do Valle and Scott, 2015, 2016; Chen, Lehto and Cai, 2013; Filep, 2012; McCabe and Johnson, 2013; Nawijn, 2011a; Nawijn, Mitas, Lin and Kerstetter, 2013; Pearce, 2011; Prebensen, Chen and Uysal, 2014; Prebensen, Woo and Uysal, 2013; Richards and Wilson, 2006). Research in this area has uncovered individual differences in the way tourism affects quality of life and happiness (e.g. Bimonte and Faralla, 2012; Brajsa-Zganec, Merkas and Sverko, 2011; Brown, MacDonald and Mitchell, 2015; Chen, Fu and Lehto, 2014; Konu and Laukkanen, 2010; Malkina-Pykh and Pykh, 2014). Trip characteristics are usually captured in tourism studies by profiling both quantitative aspects of travel behaviour (e.g. number of nights spent on the trip, accommodation type selected, amount of money spent and the like) and qualitative aspects (e.g. reasons for travel, involvement, expected benefits, experiential value of trips). Thus, trip characteristics are factors that can affect quality of life either directly or indirectly. Both quantitative and qualitative characteristics of trip experiences interact to help explain how tourist satisfaction contributes to satisfaction within various life domains (social life, family life, leisure life, spiritual life, work life, etc.) and satisfaction with life in general (e.g. Dann, 2012; Kruger, 2012; Puczkó and Smith, 2012). Satisfaction with life domains and life overall is essentially what many quality-of-life researchers refer to as 'subjective wellbeing' (e.g. Sirgy, 2012).

In some studies moderator effects are hypothesised and tested. These moderators reveal conditions under which trip characteristics can strongly influence tourists' satisfaction in certain life domains and overall life satisfaction. For example, recent research shows that co-creation of experience and engagement can serve as a moderating variable between satisfaction with travel experience and outcome variables such as loyalty, intention to visit or repurchase and/or satisfaction with life overall (Matias, Kim, Uysal, Sirgy and Prebensen, 2016; Prebensen, Kim and Uysal, 2015).

Research has also investigated mediating effects. For example, Neal, Sirgy and Uysal (2004) found that satisfaction with tourism services affects travellers' overall life satisfaction mostly through the mediating effects of satisfaction with travel/tourism experiences and satisfaction with leisure life. Since travel and tourism activities usually take place during one's leisure time, one can claim that subjective wellbeing induced by participating in tourism activities is also satisfaction with leisure life. Satisfaction with leisure life (or the sense of leisure wellbeing) contributes directly to subjective wellbeing (Kruger, Sirgy, Lee and Yu, 2015; Newman, Tay and Diener, 2014).

The goal of this chapter is threefold: (1) to delineate the connection between tourism activities and subjective wellbeing by reviewing the extant literature and theoretical underpinning guiding this connection; (2) to identify measurement issues, theoretical frameworks and variables and moderating factors; and (3) to provide management, policy implications and future research directions.

Definition of subjective wellbeing

It is important that, before proceeding with an in-depth discussion, we should provide a brief discussion on definitional issues of subjective wellbeing in the broader field of quality-of-life studies. One of the commonly cited definitions of subjective wellbeing is provided by Diener, Suh, Lucas and Smith (1999). Diener and his colleagues define *subjective wellbeing* as a broad category of phenomena that includes people's emotional responses, domain satisfactions and global judgements of life satisfaction. Specifically, subjective wellbeing can be viewed as either a unidimensional or multidimensional construct. The unidimensional approach to subjective wellbeing is essentially overall life satisfaction (Sirgy, 2012). Tourists are surveyed and asked, 'How satisfied are you with your life in general?' Respondents answer this question on a ten-point rating scale varying from 'not satisfied at all' to 'very satisfied'. In contrast, the multidimensional approach to subjective wellbeing captures the construct through a composite of domain satisfaction ratings. For example, Dolnicar, Yanamandram and Cliff (2012) captured subjective wellbeing through a composite of tourists' sense of wellbeing in selected life domains such as physical health wellbeing, psychological wellbeing, social wellbeing and so on. Domain satisfaction focuses on capturing satisfaction with specific life domains such as social life, family life, work life, community life and leisure life (e.g. Genc, 2012a, 2012b; Lee and Sirgy, 1995; Sirgy, 2001). As such, subjective wellbeing can be captured through a summative or average score of satisfaction with life domains such as material life, emotional life, environmental life, family life, community life and leisure life. Even though there is a general agreement that subjective wellbeing can be captured through a composite of satisfaction with a number of life domains (Meadow and Sirgy, 2008), there is little agreement on the key domains that should be included in the measure (Sirgy, 2012).

However, the elements of how subjective wellbeing is captured depends on the research setting, culture and the study goals. For example, Kozma, Fazion, Stones and Hannah (1992), in a study of personality, indicate that subjective wellbeing is a direct function of two psychological states, one short-term and the other long-term. The short-term state is an affective state that involves positive and negative affect mostly influenced by environmental factors. The long-term state is also an affective state involving both positive and negative affect. The long-term component is dispositional and is less affected by environmental factors (cf. Lapham, Kozma and Weiss, 1996). Additionally, Simsek (2009) brings the importance of a whole-time perspective into the definition of subjective wellbeing, which defines subjective wellbeing as one's evaluation of life in both past and future time perspectives in addition to the present (510). A recent study by McCabe and Johnson (2013) revealed support that holidays offer more value than simply short-term hedonic experiences, but can contribute to longer-term broader aspects of life satisfaction and positive functioning (60).

In this chapter, we will use the following definition of subjective wellbeing: subjective wellbeing is an enduring (long-term) affective state that is made of a composite of three components: (1) actual experience of happiness or cumulative positive affect (joy, affection, pride, etc.) in salient life domains; (2) actual experience of depression or cumulative negative affect (sadness, anger, guilt, shame, anxiety, etc.) in salient life domains; and (3) evaluation of one's overall life or evaluation of salient life domains (Sirgy, 2012). The following section focuses on the link between tourism/leisure activities and subjective wellbeing.

Tourism: leisure activities and subjective wellbeing

The link between tourists' experiences and subjective wellbeing is uniquely embedded in the fully functioning tourism system. The nature of tourism research for both practical and theoretical reasons embodies the interplay of such constructs as benefits obtained from engaging in tourism activities, satisfaction induced by tourism experiences and subjective wellbeing. An underlying assumption is that tourists are consumers of different tourism and hospitality goods and services at a destination and the destination community with its different providers and stakeholders serves as a host to such consumers (Jennings and Nickerson, 2006; Pearce, Filep and Ross, 2010; Woo, Kim and Uysal, 2015).

Uysal, Perdue and Sirgy (2012) proposed that within the fully functioning tourism system we have two models that should be considered in examining tourism activities and their consequences from a systems point of view. The first model examines and explains the impact of tourist-related variables on the wellbeing of tourists. The second model examines and explains the impact of tourism-related variables on the wellbeing of residents of the host community and its stakeholders, including providers of tourism goods and services. In these two nested models of the tourism system, tourists as consumers, service providers and stakeholders are the central parts of the system, where interaction between supply and demand is reciprocal. This interaction has an effect on the total vacation experience, as simultaneous production and consumption of goods and services take place. These models are helpful in understanding how the tourism system works, what benefits it has and how resources are allocated in order to develop a successful marketing and management plan. This chapter, however, exclusively focuses on the first model, namely tourist activities and their link to wellbeing of tourists or subjective wellbeing.

A review of the extant literature on the topic reveals that researchers have employed major theoretical perspectives to explain the effect of tourism-related variables on tourists' subjective wellbeing, namely bottom-up spillover theory of life satisfaction. Bottom-up spillover theory (Diener, 1984; Diener et al., 1999; Kim, Woo and Uysal, 2015; Nimrod, 2008; Sirgy, 2002; Sirgy and Lee, 2006) asserts that overall life satisfaction is affected by satisfaction with all life domains and sub-domains in the context of a satisfaction hierarchy. Life satisfaction is considered to be at the top of a satisfaction hierarchy. For instance, overall life satisfaction is influenced by satisfaction with family, social life, leisure and recreation, health, work, finances and travel. Satisfaction with a particular life domain is influenced by lower levels of life concerns within that domain (Kruger, 2012). Satisfaction with a hospital stay or a wellness spa destination, for example, affects satisfaction with health life and community life, which in turn contributes to life satisfaction (Sirgy, Hansen and Littlefield, 1994).

A recent literature review (Uysal, Sirgy, Woo and Kim, 2015) provided a comprehensive examination of empirical studies that covered wellbeing issues from the perspective of residents and tourists. The same authors are also the authors of this particular chapter. The following discussion is drawn from that study with respect to wellbeing from the perspective of tourists. One of the general observations of the study pointed out that the contribution of vacations to life satisfaction has recently attracted substantial research (e.g. Dolnicar et al., 2012; Filep, 2012, 2014; Filep and Deery, 2010; Genc, 2012b; Nawijn, 2011a, 2011b; Nawijn and Peeters, 2010; Pearce, 2012; Sirgy, Kruger, Lee and Yu, 2011; Uner and Armutlu, 2012) and this research continues to grow (Bimonte and Faralla, 2012; Brajsa-Zganec et al., 2011; Brown et al., 2015; Chen et al., 2014; Konu and Laukkanen, 2010; Malkina-Pykh and Pykh, 2014). Richards (1999) has long argued that 'vacations can provide physical and mental rest and relaxation, they can provide the space for personal development and the pursuit of personal and social interests and they can also be used as a form of symbolic consumption, enhancing status' (189). Others (e.g. Kim,

Ritchie and McCormick, 2013; Oppermann and Cooper, 1999; Richards and Wilson, 2006) also argued that engaging in memorable and meaningful experiences such as vacations, rather than consuming material goods, can contribute significantly to subjective wellbeing.

One of the studies by Bimonte and Faralla (2012) in this area took a very different approach to examining the connection between tourist/visitor activities and life satisfaction. Instead of investigating the assumed relationship between travel experiences and personal wellbeing, they attempted to verify whether the way the trip (appreciative vs. consumptive tourist) is undertaken is positively related with individuals' (self-reported) happiness. The study found that more appreciative tourists are also happier or reported higher happiness scores than their counterparts, who are consumptive tourists visiting a natural park in Tuscany, Italy. The study supported the notion that personal satisfaction may even grow if engaged tourist activities are more appreciative in nature, such as bird watching, taking pictures or simply enjoying the outstanding scenery. Thus, practising appreciative activities as part of travel behaviour can be very beneficial for personal wellbeing. However, only a handful of studies have investigated the contribution of travel experience to tourists' subjective wellbeing. Uysal et al. (2015) found that almost 80 per cent of these studies were published since 2001, further revealing evidence for a heightened interest in this line of research.

The Uysal et al. (2015) study

The authors identified 35 studies that examined the effects of trip characteristics on tourists' subjective wellbeing directly or indirectly. To try to make sense of this literature, the study grouped these studies into three major categories: (1) studies demonstrating an effect of travel and tourism on subjective wellbeing of individual tourists; (2) the mediating mechanism between travel/tourism experience and subjective wellbeing of individual tourists; and (3) personal, situational and cultural characteristics that help further explain the link between travel/tourism experience and subjective wellbeing.

Effects of travel/tourism on the subjective wellbeing of individual tourists

The first study examining the impact of vacation experience on subjective wellbeing was conducted by Neal, Sirgy and Uysal (1999). The study revealed that satisfaction with tourism service affects tourists' overall life satisfaction. However, research has shown that the impact of tourists' perceptions of the positive impact of the tourism experience on their life satisfaction varies considerably (de Bloom et al., 2011; Dolnicar et al., 2012; Dolnicar, Lazarevski and Yanamandram, 2013). Three studies (Michalko, Kiss, Kovacs and Sulyok, 2009; Milman, 1998; Wei and Milman, 2002) did not find a positive relationship between tourism experience and subjective wellbeing. Specifically, Milman (1998) investigated the impact of tourism experience on senior tourists' psychological wellbeing. The results revealed that seniors' psychological wellbeing was not improved as a result of travel. Similarly, Michalko et al. (2009) surveyed 11,500 Hungarian tourists and found that *vacation experience* did not affect their overall life satisfaction. On the other hand, a study by Chen et al. (2014) confirmed the positive effect of satisfaction with service aspects of travel and tourism phases on global satisfaction with travel/tourism services and the direct positive effect of global satisfaction with travel/tourism experiences on travellers' subjective wellbeing (in China). Another study by Brajsa-Zganec et al. (2011) demonstrated that participation in leisure activities such as visiting friends and relatives contributes positively to subjective wellbeing of women and men, as well as people of different age groups.

Similarly, Brown et al. (2015), using longitudinal data in the UK, also demonstrated an independent and positive association of participation in sport (moderate and mild intensity), heritage and active-creative leisure activities and overall life satisfaction.

Mediating mechanism between travel/tourism experience and subjective wellbeing of individual tourists

Neal et al. (1999) were able to demonstrate that the effect of travel/tourism experience on life satisfaction occurs through a series of mediation effects. Specifically, they were able to demonstrate the following mediation effects:

- satisfaction with pre-trip services, en route services, destination services and return services influence satisfaction with travel/tourism services in general;
- satisfaction with travel/tourism services in general (in addition to trip reflections related to perceived freedom, involvement, arousal, mastery and spontaneity) influences satisfaction with travel/tourism experiences in general;
- satisfaction with travel/tourism experiences in general (in addition to satisfaction with leisure experiences at home) influences satisfaction with leisure life in general; and
- satisfaction with leisure life in general (in addition to satisfaction in non-leisure life domains such as family, job, health, etc.) influences satisfaction with life in general.

Another study by Chen, Ye, Chen and Tung (2010) also examined if satisfaction-with-event would mediate the relationship between flow and life satisfaction based on the bottom-up theory. The results using structural equation modelling indicated a statistically significant support for the mediation effect of satisfaction-with-event levels between flow and life satisfaction. In addition, satisfaction-with-event positively predicted life satisfaction, thus revealing further support for the bottom-up theory.

Furthermore, Sirgy et al. (2011) were able to demonstrate that tourists' positive and negative memories generated from the most recent trip influence satisfaction in 13 life domains (e.g. social life, leisure life, family life, cultural life, health and safety, love life, work life, spiritual life, travel life, arts and culture, culinary life and financial life), which in turn influence their overall life satisfaction.

Personal, situational and cultural characteristics that help further explain the link between travel/tourism experience and subjective wellbeing

Most of the reviewed studies reported in the Uysal et al. (2015) study have focused on one population group to examine the effect of tourism experience on their overall life satisfaction, with the exception of two studies, namely, Gilbert and Abdullah (2004) and Nawijn, Marchand, Veenhoven and Vingerhoets (2010). Gilbert and Abdullah (2004) compared two groups: holiday-taking group and non-holiday-taking group. The results indicated that the holiday-taking group had an increased sense of wellbeing prior to and after their trip experience compared to the non-holiday-taking group. Similarly, Nawijn et al. (2010) compared vacationers' and non-vacationers' overall life satisfaction. Consistent with the findings of Gilbert and Abdullah (2004), they also found that vacationers had a higher degree of pre-trip happiness compared to non-vacationers. Two studies examined moderating effects of the relationship between tourism experience and tourists' subjective wellbeing (Neal, Uysal and Sirgy, 2007; Strauss-Blasche, Ekmekcioglu and Marktl, 2000). Neal et al. (2007) built on their previous research (Neal et al.,

1999), investigating the moderation effect of length of stay. The study found that satisfaction with trip services affects satisfaction in leisure life domain and this relationship is more evident for tourists who have extended their stays compared to tourists with shorter stays.

Dolnicar et al. (2012, 2013) argued that vacation experience is not important to everyone. The impact of vacation experience on tourists' subjective wellbeing may depend on life stage and other background variables that may influence the degree of importance of travel.

A recent study by Peters and Schuckert (2014) attempted to establish a relationship between lifestyle in tourism and subjective wellbeing. It appears that those who would like to engage in certain activities in tourism entrepreneurship as a matter of personal choice believe that entrepreneurship growth would also enhance their wellbeing and thus enhance their life satisfaction. As such, the study emphasises the need for a balance between enterprise growth and work–life balance, implying that this is an area ripe for further research where there is a high degree of reliance on small, independent enterprises.

Based on the reviewed studies, the Uysal et al. (2015) study drew two key conclusions. First, tourism experiences and activities affect tourists' overall life satisfaction. In general, vacation experience appears to have the potential to lead to hedonic and enduring consumption experiences influencing tourists' wellbeing. Hedonic consumption may have a short-term effect on tourists' subjective wellbeing, whereas enduring life-changing consumption experiences could have long-term effects on subjective wellbeing. Second, the impact of vacation experience on subjective wellbeing may depend on different stages in life and other background variables that may influence the degree of importance of travel. Tourist trips contribute to positive affect in many life domains, such as leisure life, social life, family life, work life, spiritual life, culinary life, marital life, cultural life, to name a few. Such tourist experiences contributing to satisfaction in various life domains also contribute to overall life satisfaction. What is most interesting is the finding that the sense of wellbeing is significantly increased in planning and anticipating the trip, perhaps equally so to the actual experiences during the trip. Extended stays seem to further accentuate the positive affect and sense of wellbeing than short stays. Future research may investigate the moderation effects of other institutional-type variables such as trips where the tourists have to travel short versus long distances to reach the destination, trips of different types (cruise trips versus beach trips), trips designed for different population groups (families versus couples), among others. Research may also focus on cultural moderators such as trips in which the tourist destination is culturally proximal or distal to the tourists. Also, climatic conditions such as trips to the tropics versus more temperate climates may be used as moderators affecting quality of trip experience. Other moderators may include demographics such as differences in gender, age, income level and marital status. One can also investigate the moderation effects of personality factors such as novelty seeking, allocentrism and openness to experience.

Research method issues

The Uysal et al. (2015) review paper indicated that the general unit of analysis of the vast majority of studies is an individual level but shows definitional variations depending on the study context. Specifically, the majority of the reviewed studies used a general adult population; however, a number of studies focused on different target groups such as employees (de Bloom et al., 2010, 2011; Hoopes and Lounsbury, 1989; Lounsbury and Hoopes, 1986; Strauss-Blasche et al., 2000), patients (Coyle, Lesnik-Emas and Kinney, 1994; Hunter-Jones, 2003; Mactavish, Mackay, Iwasaki and Betteridge, 2007; Pols and Kroon, 2007), seniors (Heo et al., 2012; Kim et al., 2015; Lee and Tideswell, 2005; Milman, 1998; Wei and Milman, 2002; Woo, Kim and Uysal, 2014), the youth market (Eusebio and Carneiro, 2014) and low-income tourists

(McCabe, Joldersma and Li, 2010). For example, Lounsbury and Hoopes (1986) targeted 128 employees to complete a survey questionnaire capturing the interrelationships among vacation satisfaction, job satisfaction and life satisfaction. Hunter-Jones (2003) interviewed 16 patients and found that holiday taking affects patients' personal health, social effectiveness, personal identity and regaining independence. Lee and Tideswell (2005) examined travel behaviour of senior Koreans, documenting the fact that tourism experiences serve to increase wellbeing.

The majority of the reviewed papers used the survey method such as mail or online survey. However, some of these studies employed either qualitative methods (e.g. Coyle et al., 1994; Dolnicar et al., 2012; Hunter-Jones, 2003; Mactavish et al., 2007; Pols and Kroon, 2007; Sirgy et al., 2011) or secondary data with mixed methods for data collection (Nawijn and Veenhoven, 2011). For example, although in a different context of health and travel, Pols and Kroon (2007) collected observations on two trips along with in-depth interviews with 11 travellers and 4 psychiatric nurses to investigate the effect of vacation experience on subjective wellbeing. In contrast, Nawijn and Veenhoven (2011) used data from the German Socio-Economic Panel Study – a large national consumer panel – to investigate the effect of leisure activities on happiness.

Several studies have employed longitudinal research design. That is, tourists' subjective wellbeing was measured before the trip, during the trip and after the trip (de Bloom et al., 2010, 2011) and their level of subjective wellbeing was compared before, during and after. However, the majority of the studies investigated tourists' subjective wellbeing after their trip experience. Seven studies measured tourists' quality of life before and after the trip (Fritz and Sonnentag, 2006; Gilbert and Abdullah, 2004; Hoopes and Lounsbury, 1989; Lounsbury and Hoopes, 1986; McCabe et al., 2010; Milman, 1998; Strauss-Blasche et al., 2000) and only one study measured subjective wellbeing during and after the trip experience (Pols and Kroon, 2007).

The authors concluded that ideal studies capturing tourists' subjective wellbeing are those employing longitudinal research designs (better than cross-sectional designs). Longitudinal studies are better equipped to capture the full range of tourist experience – before, during and after the trip. Furthermore, longitudinal studies also make it possible to infer causality whereas cross-sectional studies may be limiting in making causality inferences. With respect to sampling techniques, probabilistic sampling techniques are more effective (compared to non-probabilistic techniques) to ensure sample representativeness of the population at large. As such, future research in this area should be encouraged to use more longitudinal designs with probabilistic sampling techniques.

The authors also reported that all of the 35 studies covered used subjective indicators to measure tourists' subjective wellbeing. However, most of these studies employed different constructs and measures of subjective wellbeing. For instance, Fritz and Sonnentag (2006) used 12 health complaint items and 16 burnout items to measure tourists' overall wellbeing. Wei and Milman (2002) used 24 affect and experience items to capture seniors' overall wellbeing.

The authors recommend that researchers in this area should use well-established constructs and measures of subjective wellbeing. The measures should have demonstrated construct validity. For example, one can argue that the subjective wellbeing measures used by Fritz and Sonnentag (2006) and Wei and Milman (2002) are not constructs and measures of subjective wellbeing that are well accepted by the larger quality of life research community.

Conclusion and future research

As individuals seek more meaningful and memorable tourism experiences, it is safe to assume that travellers are likely to be more active and engage in their pursuit of happiness. It is apparent from the preceding discussion that there is enough empirical evidence to conclude that tourist activities and engagement in leisure are likely to contribute meaningfully and significantly to feelings of wellbeing and life satisfaction. Thus, it is important to note that subjective wellbeing concepts are embedded in the very definition of tourism behaviour. As McCabe and Johnson (2013) concluded, tourism has the potential to link to key aspects that lead to subjective wellbeing, particularly the development aspects of self and eudaimonia (61).

We know from the review of literature that quality of life in tourism is customarily captured using subjective indicators (i.e. expressive and mental). Subjective indicators capture experiences that are important to the individual that tap into affective experiences and satisfaction in various life domains and life satisfaction at large. In this vein, providers of goods and services, from which tourists derive some level of satisfaction, have a major role as facilitators to influence the consumption setting in which experiences are created and behavioural outcomes are influenced. We need to investigate and experiment with instrumental and maintenance aspects of tourism activities that are staged and managed by providers of goods and services. These aspects can serve as moderating factors to help us better explain the link between satisfaction with these goods and services and tourists' subjective wellbeing.

As Uysal et al. (2015) reported, most studies in this area have employed subjective indicators to capture quality of life of tourists. In contrast, objective indicators focus on social indicators such as income, physical health and standard of living. The latter indicators are defined and quantified without relying on tourists' perceptions or judgement. Yet, from a practical point of view, studies relying on objective indicators could help better monitor and measure structural and physical changes over time and how visitors and providers may respond to such changes. Both subjective and objective measures should be used and may complement each other in the assessment of human wellbeing (Bimonte and Faralla, 2012). Given that each approach has its strengths and weaknesses, there seems to be a need to conjoin objective and subjective indicators in future tourism studies to better capture quality of life of tourists. We wholeheartedly encourage researchers to conduct research in this area.

To define and measure subjective wellbeing of tourists, various studies have articulated different life domains varying by population group and context. In identifying pertinent life domains in tourism studies, there has to be a mechanism to capture the relative importance of these life domains. Life domains are not all equally important for tourists and the importance of each life domain varies across people and contexts. Future research should focus on articulating pertinent life domains by population group and setting. For example, the pertinent life domains of tourists experiencing wildlife tourism may be different from tourists going on a cruise. The salient life domains of the former group may involve spiritual and cultural life, whereas the latter group may involve social, leisure and culinary life. When medical tourists decide to travel they might consider their health life domain as most important and this affects their overall life satisfaction (Cohen, 2012), whereas adventure tourists may consider leisure life as most important. It would be useful for researchers to develop conceptualisations and measures of quality of life for tourists that can address these nuances of complexity. Doing so should enhance the predictiveness of the subjective wellbeing measures in empirical research. These assertions imply that research in this area should be contextualised to reflect the uniqueness of the setting in which tourism activities take place. The selection of life domains should reflect the current and growth needs of tourist participants and their personal goals. In addition, more studies, both cross-sectional and longitudinal, are needed to further examine how the sense of wellbeing in different life domains may vary depending on differences in personality, situation and culture.

There is also limited research on international comparative analysis and cross-cultural studies that examine the role of different life domains and demographic variates in examining quality of life and life satisfaction issues (e.g. Iwasaki, 2007; Liang, Yamashita and Brown, 2013; Spiers and Walker, 2009; Wang and Wong, 2014). There is a need for cross-cultural tourism studies that can examine the influence of different cultural and natural attractions in different destinations on life satisfaction and subjective wellbeing of travellers.

In general, to fully appreciate and understand the assumed links between tourism activities and subjective wellbeing, we need to focus both on basic and growth needs of participants as consumers of tourism goods and services. Thus, we need to do a better job identifying both tangible and intangible benefits of tourism and investigate their effects on the wellbeing of participants. The question that needs to be addressed is, if tangible and intangible benefits of tourism activities contribute equally, indirectly or collectively to subjective wellbeing of participants, then what is the variance that could be explained by each and what is the role of providers in meeting these variations in management outcomes such as loyalty and personal outcomes such as service satisfaction? The provision of quality tourism experiences should be created with the wellbeing of today's and tomorrow's travellers in mind so that tourist experiences and the value of such experiences can heighten subjective wellbeing.

References

Bimonte, S. and Faralla, V. (2012) 'Tourist types and happiness: A comparative study in Maremma, Italy', *Annals of Tourism Research*, 39(4), 1929–1950.

——. (2013) 'Happiness and outdoor vacations: Appreciative versus consumptive tourists', *Journal of Travel Research*, DOI: 10.1177/0047287513513171.

Bjork, P. (2014) 'Tourist experience value: Tourist experience and life satisfaction', in N. Prebensen, J. Chen and M. Uysal (eds) *Creating Experience Value in Tourism*, CABI, UK, pp. 22–32.

Brajsa-Zganec, A., Merkas, M. and Sverko, I. (2011) 'Quality of life and leisure activities: How do leisure activities contribute to subjective wellbeing?', *Social Indicators Research*, 102, 81–91.

Brown, J.J., MacDonald, R. and Mitchell, R. (2015) 'Are people who participate in cultural activities more satisfied with life?', *Social Indicators Journal*, 135–146.

Campos, A. C., Mendes, J., do Valle, P. O. and Scott, N. (2015) 'Co-creation of tourist experiences: A literature review', *Current Issues in Tourism*, 1–32, DOI:10.1080/13683500.2015.1081158.

——. (2016) 'Co-creation experiences: Attention and memorability', *Journal of Travel and Tourism Marketing*, 1–28, DOI:10.1080/10548408.2015.1118424.

Chen, C. and Petrick, J. F. (2013) 'Health and wellness benefits of travel experiences: A literature review', *Journal of Travel Research*, 52(6), 709–719.

Chen, L. H., Ye, Y.-C., Chen, M.-Y. and Tung, I.-W. (2010) 'Alegria! Flow in leisure and life satisfaction: The mediating role of event satisfaction using data from acrobatics show', *Social Indicators Research*, 99, 301–313.

Chen, Y., Fu, X. and Lehto, Y. (2014) 'Chinese tourist vacation satisfaction and subjective wellbeing', *Applied Research Quality Life*, DOI: 10.1007s11482-014-9354-y.

Chen, Y., Lehto, X. and Cai, L. (2013) 'Vacation and wellbeing: A study of Chinese tourists', *Annals of Tourism Research*, 42, 284–310.

Cohen, E. (2012) 'Medical travel and the quality of life', in M. Uysal, R. Perdue and M. J. Sirgy (eds) *Handbook of Tourism and Quality-of-Life Research: Enhancing the Lives of Tourists and Residents of Host Communities*, Dordrecht, The Netherlands: Springer, pp. 169–192.

Coyle, C. P., Lesnik-Emas, S. and Kinney, W. B. (1994) 'Predicting life satisfaction among adults with spinal cord injuries', *Rehabilitation Psychology*, 39(2), 95–112.

Dann, M. S. G. (2012) 'Tourist motivation and quality of life: In search of the Missing Link', in M. Uysal, R. Perdue and M. J. Sirgy (eds) *Handbook of Tourism and Quality-of-Life Research: Enhancing the Lives of Tourists and Residents of Host Communities*, Springer, Dordrecht, The Netherlands, pp. 233–250.

de Bloom, J., Geurts, S. A. E., Sonnentag, S., Taris, T. W., de Weerth, C. and Kompier, M. A. J. (2011) 'How does a vacation from work affect employee health and wellbeing?', *Psychology and Health*, 26(12), 1606–1622.

de Bloom, J., Geurts, S. A. E., Taris, T. W., Sonnentag, S., de Weerth, C. and Kompier, M. A. J. (2010) 'Effects of vacation from work on health and wellbeing: Lots of fun, quickly gone', *Work and Stress: An International Journal of Work, Health and Organizations*, 24(2), 196–216.

Diener, E. (1984) 'Subjective wellbeing', *Psychological Bulletin*, 95(3), 542–575.

Diener, E., Suh, E. M., Lucas, R. E. and Smith, H. L. (1999) 'Subjective wellbeing: Three decades of progress', *Psychological Bulletin*, 125(2), 276–300.

Dolnicar, S., Lazarevski, K. and Yanamandram, V. (2013) 'Quality of life and tourism: A conceptual framework and novel segmentation base', *Journal of Business Research*, 66, 724–729.

Dolnicar, S., Yanamandram, V. and Cliff, K. (2012) 'The contribution of vacations to quality of life', *Annals of Tourism Research*, 39(1), 59–83.

Driver, B. L. and Brown, P. J. (1978) 'The opportunity spectrum concept and behavioral information in outdoor recreation resource supply inventories: A rationale', in H. G. Lund et al. (eds) *Integrated Inventories of Renewable Natural Resources: General Technical Report RM-55*, Tucson, AZ: USDA: Forest Service, pp. 24–31.

Driver, B. L., Brown, P. J. and Peterson, G. L. (1991) *Benefits of Leisure*, State College, PA, US: Venture Publishing.

Eusebio, C. and Carneiro, M. J. (2014) 'The impact of tourism on quality of life: A segmentation analysis of the youth market', *Tourism Analysis*, 19(6), 741–758.

Filep, S. (2012) 'The positive psychology and tourism', in M. Uysal, R. Perdue and M. J. Sirgy (eds) *Handbook of Tourism and Quality-of-Life Research: Enhancing the Lives of Tourists and Residents of Host Communities*, Dordrecht, The Netherlands: Springer, pp. 31–50.

——. (2014) 'Moving beyond subjective wellbeing: A tourism critique', *Journal of Hospitality and Tourism Research*, 38(2), 266–274.

Filep, S. and Deery, P. (2010) 'Towards a picture of tourists' happiness', *Tourism Analysis*, 15(4), 399–410.

Fritz, C. and Sonnentag, S. (2006) 'Recovery, wellbeing and performance-related outcomes: The role of workload and vacation experiences', *Journal of Applied Psychology*, 91(4), 936–945.

Genc, R. (2012a) 'Tourist consumption behavior of quality of life', in M. Uysal, R. Perdue and M. J. Sirgy (eds) *Handbook of Tourism and Quality-of-Life Research: Enhancing the Lives of Tourists and Residents of Host Communities*, Dordrecht, The Netherlands: Springer, pp. 135–148.

——. (2012b) 'Subjective aspects of tourists' quality of life', in M. Uysal, R. Perdue and M. J. Sirgy (eds) *Handbook of Tourism and Quality-of-Life Research: Enhancing the Lives of Tourists and Residents of Host Communities*, Dordrecht, The Netherlands: Springer, pp. 149–167.

Gilbert, D. and Abdullah, J. (2004) 'Holiday taking and the sense of wellbeing', *Annals of Tourism Research*, 13(1), 103–121.

Heo, J., Lee, I., Kim, J. and Stebbins, R. (2012) 'Understanding the relationships among central characteristics of serious leisure: An empirical study of older adults in competitive sports', *Journal of Leisure Research*, 44(4), 450–462.

Heo, J., Stebbins, R. A., Kim, J. and Lee, I. (2013) 'Serious leisure, life satisfaction and health of older adults', *Leisure Sciences*, 35(1), 16–32.

Hoopes, L. L. and Lounsbury, J. W. (1989) 'An investigation of life satisfaction following a vacation: A domain-specific approach', *Journal of Community Psychology*, 17, 129–140.

Hunter-Jones, P. (2003) 'The perceived effects of holiday-taking upon the health and wellbeing of patients treated for cancer', *International Journal of Tourism Research*, 5, 183–196.

Ibrahim, H. (2008) *Outdoor Recreation: Enrichment for Lifespan* (3rd edition), Urbana-Champaign, IL: Sagamore Publishing.

Iwasaki, Y. (2007) 'Leisure and quality of life in an international and multicultural context: What are major pathways linking leisure to quality of life?', *Social Indicators Research*, 82(2), 233–264.

Jennings, G. and Nickerson, P. N. (2006) *Quality Tourism Experiences*, London: Elsevier.

Kim, H. L., Woo, E. J. and Uysal, M. (2015) 'Tourism experience and quality of life among elderly tourists', *Tourism Management*, 46, 465–476.

Kim, J., Ritchie, J. R. B. and McCormick, B. (2013) 'Development of a scale to measure memorable tourism experiences', *Journal of Travel Research*, 51(1), 12–25.

Konu, H. and Laukkanen, T. (2010) 'Predictors of tourists' wellbeing holiday intentions in Finland', *Journal of Hospitality and Tourism Management*, 17, 144–149.

Kozma, A., Fazio, R. D., Stones, M. J. and Hannah, T. E. (1992) 'Long- and short-term affective states in happiness: Age and sex comparison', *Social Indicator Research*, 27(3), 293–309.

Kruger, P. S. (2012) 'Perceptions of tourism impacts and satisfaction with particular life domains', in M. Uysal, R. Perdue and M. J. Sirgy (eds) *Handbook of Tourism and Quality-of-Life Research: Enhancing the Lives of Tourists and Residents of Host Communities*, Dordrecht, The Netherlands: Springer, pp. 279–292.

Kruger, S., Sirgy, M. J., Lee, D. J. and Yu, G. (2015) 'Does life satisfaction of tourists increase if they set travel goals that have high positive valence?', *Tourism Analysis*, 20(2), 173–188.

Lapham, E. V., Kozma, C. and Weiss, J. O. (1996) 'Genetic discrimination: Perspectives of consumers', *Science*, 274(5287), 621–624.

Lee, D. J., Kruger, S., Whang, M. J., Uysal, M. and Sirgy, M. J. (2014) 'Validating a customer wellbeing index related to natural wildlife tourism', *Tourism Management*, 45, 171–180.

Lee, D. J. and Sirgy, M. J. (1995) 'Determinants of involvement in the consumer/marketing life domain in relation to quality of life: A theoretical model and research agenda', *Development in Quality of Life Studies in Marketing*, 13–18.

Lee, S. H. and Tideswell, C. (2005) 'Understanding attitudes towards leisure travel and the constraints faced by senior Koreans', *Journal of Vacation Marketing*, 11(3), 249–263.

Liang, J., Yamashita, T. and Brown, J. S. (2013) 'Leisure satisfaction and quality of life in China, Japan and South Korea: A comparative study using Asia Barometer 2006', *Journal of Happiness Studies*, 14(3), 753–769.

Lounsbury, J. W. and Hoopes, L. L. (1986) 'A vacation from work: Changes in work and non-work outcomes', *Journal of Applied Psychology*, 71(3), 392–401.

Lu, L. and Argyle, M. (1994) 'Leisure satisfaction and happiness as a function of leisure activity', *Kaohsiung Journal of Medical Sciences*, 10, 89–96.

Mactavish, J. B., Mackay, K. J., Iwasaki, Y. and Betteridge, D. (2007) 'Family caregivers of individuals with intellectual disability: Perspectives on life quality and the role of vacations', *Journal of Leisure Research*, 39(1), 127–155.

Malkina-Pykh, I. G. and Pykh, Y. A. (2014) 'Subjective wellbeing and personality: Implications for wellness tourism', *WIT Transactions on Ecology and the Environment*, 187, 51–62.

Matias, E., Kim, L., Uysal, M., Sirgy, J. and Prebensen, N. (2016) 'The effect of co-creation experience on outcome variable', *Annals of Tourism Research*, 57, 62–75.

McCabe, S. and Johnson, S. (2013) 'The happiness factor in tourism: Subjective wellbeing and social tourism', *Annals of Tourism Research*, 41, 42–65.

McCabe, S., Joldersma, T. and Li, C. (2010) 'Understanding the benefits of social tourism: Linking participation to subjective wellbeing and quality of life', *International Journal of Tourism Research*, 12, 761–773.

Meadow, H. L. and Sirgy, M. J. (2008) 'Developing a measure that captures elderly's wellbeing in local marketplace transactions', *Applied Research in Quality of Life*, 3(1), 63–80.

Michalko, G., Kiss, K., Kovacs, B. and Sulyok, J. (2009) 'The impact of tourism on subjective quality of life among Hungarian population', *Hungarian Geographical Bulletin*, 58(2), 121–136.

Milman, A. (1998) 'The impact of tourism and travel experience on senior travellers' psychological wellbeing', *Journal of Travel Research*, 37, 166–170.

Nawijn, J. (2011a) 'Determinants of daily happiness on vacation', *Journal of Travel Research*, 50(5), 559–566.

——. (2011b) 'Happiness through vacationing: Just a temporary boost or long-term benefits?', *Journal of Happiness Studies*, 12(4), 651–665.

Nawijn, J., Marchand, M. A., Veenhoven, R. and Vingerhoets, A. J. (2010) 'Vacationers happier, but most not happier after a holiday', *Applied Research in Quality of Life*, 5(1), 35–47.

Nawijn, J., Mitas, O., Lin, Y. and Kerstetter, D. (2013) How do we feel on vacation? A closer look at how emotions change over the course of a trip', *Journal of Travel Research*, 52(2), 265–274.

Nawijn, J. and Peeters, P. M. (2010) 'Travelling "green": Is tourists' happiness at stake?', *Current Issues in Tourism*, 13(4), 381–392.

Nawijn, J. and Veenhoven, R. (2011) 'The effect of leisure activities on life satisfaction: The importance of holiday trip', in I. Brdar (eds) *The Human Pursuit of Wellbeing: A Cultural Approach*, Dordrecht, The Netherlands: Springer Science, pp. 39–53.

Neal, J., Sirgy, M. J. and Uysal, M. (1999) 'The role of satisfaction with leisure travel/tourism services and experience in satisfaction with leisure life and overall life', *Journal of Business Research*, 44, 153–163.

——. (2004) 'Measuring the effect of tourism services on travellers' quality of life: Further validation', *Social Indicators Research*, 69(3), 243–277.

Neal, J. D., Uysal, M. and Sirgy, M. J. (2007) 'The effect of tourism services on travellers' quality of life', *Journal of Travel Research*, 46, 154–163.

Newman, D. B., Tay, L. and Diener. E. (2014) 'Leisure and subjective wellbeing: A model of psychological mechanisms as mediating factors', *Journal of Happiness Studies*, 15(3), 555–578.

Nimrod, G. (2008) 'Retirement and tourism themes in retirees' narratives', *Annals of Tourism Research*, 35(4), 859–878.

Oppermann, M. and Cooper, M. (1999) 'Outbound travel and quality of life: The effect of airline price wars', *Journal of Business Research*, 44(3), 179–188.

Payne, L., Ainsworth, B. and Godbey, G. (2010) *Leisure, Health and Wellness: Making the Connections*, State College, PA: Venture Publishing.

Pearce, P. (2008) 'The relationship between positive psychology and tourist behavior studies', *Tourism Analysis*, 1491, 37–48.

———. (2011) *Tourist Behavior and the Contemporary World*, Bristol, UK: Channel View Publications.

———. (2012) 'Relationships and the tourism experience: Challenges for quality of assessments', in M. Uysal, R. Perdue and M. J. Sirgy (eds) *Handbook of Tourism and Quality-of-Life Research: Enhancing the Lives of Tourists and Residents of Host Communities*, Dordrecht, The Netherlands: Springer, pp. 9–29.

Pearce, P., Filep, S. and Ross, G. (2010) *Tourists, Tourism and the Good Life*, London: Routledge.

Peters, M. and Schuckert, S. (2014) 'Tourism entrepreneurs' perception of quality of life: An explorative study', *Tourism Analysis*, 19(6), 731–740.

Pols, J. and Kroon, H. (2007) 'The importance of holiday trips for people with chronic mental health problems', *Psychiatric Services*, 58(2), 262–265.

Puczkó, L. and Smith, M. (2012) 'An analysis of QOL domains from the demand side', in M. Uysal, R. Perdue and M. J. Sirgy (eds) *Handbook of Tourism and Quality-of-Life Research: Enhancing the Lives of Tourists and Residents of Host Communities*, Dordrecht, The Netherlands: Springer, pp. 263–278.

Prebensen, N., Chen, J. and Uysal, M. (eds) (2014) *Creating Experience Value in Tourism*, London: CABI.

Prebensen, N., Kim, H. and Uysal, M. (2015) 'Co-creation as moderator between the experience value and satisfaction relationship', *Journal of Travel Research*, DOI: 10.11770047287515583359.

Prebensen, N., Woo, E. and Uysal, M. (2013) 'Experience value: Antecedents and consequences', *Current Issues in Tourism*, 16(7–8), 1–15.

Richards, G. (1999) 'Vacations and the quality of life: Patterns and structures', *Journal of Business Research*, 44, 189–198.

Richards, G. and Wilson, J. (2006) 'Developing creativity in tourist experiences: A solution to the serial reproduction of culture', *Tourism Management*, 26(6), 1209–1223.

Silverstein, M. and Parker, M. G. (2002) 'Leisure activities and quality of life among the oldest old in Sweden', *Research on Aging*, 24(5), 528–547.

Simsek, O. F. (2009) 'Happiness revisited: Ontological wellbeing as a theory-based construct of subjective wellbeing', *Journal of Happiness Studies*, 10, 505–522.

Sirgy, J., Uysal, M. and Kruger, S. (2016) *Leisure Wellbeing: Towards an Integrated Model*, unpublished manuscript, Blacksburg, VA: Virginia Tech, p. 32.

Sirgy, M. J. (2001) *Handbook of Quality-of-Life Research: An Ethical Marketing Perspective*, Dordrecht, The Netherlands: Springer.

———. (2002) *The Psychology of Quality of Life*, Dordrecht, The Netherlands: Kluwer Academic.

———. (2012) *The Psychology of Quality of Life: Hedonic Wellbeing, Life Satisfaction and Eudaimonia*, New York: Springer.

Sirgy, M. J., Hansen, D. E. and Littlefield, J. E. (1994) 'Does hospital satisfaction affect life satisfaction?', *Journal of Macromarketing*, 14(2), 36–46.

Sirgy, M.J., Kruger, S., Lee, D. and Yu, G. B. (2011) 'How does a travel trip affect tourists' life satisfaction?', *Journal of Travel Research*, 50(3), 261–275.

Sirgy, M. J. and Lee, D. J. (2006) 'Macro measures of consumer wellbeing (CWB): A critical analysis and a research agenda', *Journal of Macromarketing*, 26(1), 27–44.

Smith, M. K. and Puczkó, L. (2014) *Health, Tourism and Hospitality: Spas, Wellness and Medical Travel*, London: Routledge.

Spiers, A. and Walker, G. J. (2009) 'The effects of ethnicity and leisure satisfaction on happiness, peacefulness and quality of life', *Leisure Sciences*, 31, 84–99.

Strauss-Blasche, G., Ekmekcioglu, C. and Marktl, W. (2000) 'Does vacation enable recuperation? Changes in wellbeing associated with time away from work', *Occupational Medicine*, 50(3), 167–172.

Uner, M. and Armutlu, C. (2012) 'Understanding the antecedents of destination identification, linkage between perceived quality of life, self-congruity and destination identification', in M. Uysal, R. Perdue and M. J. Sirgy (eds) *Handbook of Tourism and Quality-of-Life Research: Enhancing the Lives of Tourists and Residents of Host Communities*, Dordrecht, The Netherlands: Springer, pp. 251–277.

Uysal, M., Perdue, R. and Sirgy, R. (2012) *Handbook of Tourism and Quality of Life Research: Enhancing the Lives of Tourists and Residents of Host Communities*, Dordrecht, The Netherlands: Springer.

Uysal, M., Sirgy, J., Woo, E. and Kim, L. (2015) 'Quality of life (QOL) and wellbeing research in tourism', *Tourism Management*, DOI:10.1016/j.tourman.2015.07.013.

Wang, M. and Wong, M. C. (2014) 'Leisure and happiness: Evidence from international survey data', *Journal of Happiness Studies*, 15(1), 85–118.

Wei, S. and Milman, A. (2002) 'The impact of participation in activities while on vacation on seniors' psychological wellbeing: A path model application', *Journal of Hospitality and Tourism Research*, 26(2), 175–185.

Woo, E., Kim, H. and Uysal, M. (2014) 'A measure of quality of life in elderly tourists', *Applied Research in Quality of life*, DOI 10.1007/s11482-014-9355-x.

——. (2015) 'Life satisfaction and support for tourism development', *Annals of Tourism Research*, 50, 84–97.

7

Finding flow during a vacation

Using optimal experiences to improve health

John K. Coffey and Mihály Csikszentmihályi

Introduction

In this chapter, we provide a vignette to highlight a few of the ways that one might experience flow (i.e. optimal experience) while on vacation. Flow experiences occur when you become fully and energetically absorbed in an activity such that the activity is rewarding in and of itself, regardless of the extrinsic outcomes. These flow experiences are so rewarding that time flies by and at the end we want to do them again, which is likely to result in travellers who are feeling healthy and excited to return to a particular destination where they enjoy and experience flow often. Knowing that people vacation for a wide range of reasons, we highlight how flow might be experienced during a range of activities such as fitness, leisure, relaxation, socialisation and intimacy. We detail the conditions of a flow experience and the numerous benefits. Despite these benefits, the tourism industry and tourists may often overlook or unintentionally add barriers to such flow experiences. Thus, we explain conditions and barriers to flow while vacationing. In addition, we offer recommendations about how the tourism industry might seek to promote more flow.

Pat and Ariel arrived at their resort in Arenal, Costa Rica, shortly after their friends Tyrone and Lyndsay. All four of them met up for dinner and drinks. Although the food was delicious, none of them really noticed, as they were too lost in a conversation that flowed non-stop. The couples caught each other up and talked about their plans for the vacation. Before anyone realised it, four hours had passed and the couples decided to call it an evening. As Pat cooked up breakfast the next morning, Ariel hummed her favourite tunes and danced around as she got ready. Pat was taking extra time to make his special French toast from scratch, so she read the local paper.

The time passed so quickly that they nearly did not leave enough time for the morning hike they planned. Rather than skip the hike, they decided to do a shorter, but more challenging hike near the base of the Arenal volcano. As recreational hikers, they had been looking forward to the hike, which turned out to be a good balance for their level of fitness and experience. As the more experienced hiker, Ariel added an extra challenge by finding and pointing out a number of different trees and animals she had read about on the flight to Costa Rica. Over lunch, they decided that they had enjoyed the hike so much that they would do a slightly more challenging one tomorrow.

After lunch, Pat met up with Tyrone to go try a local golf course. Pat was a skilled golfer, so he appreciated the challenge presented by a new course. Pat started to feel like he was in the zone, as he seemed to take the round shot by shot. Each shot dictated the adjustments he made for the next. After a few holes, Tyrone gave him some feedback about his putting and Pat made it a goal to use the tips throughout the rest of the round. Although Pat felt totally in control, the round of golf flew by.

While Pat golfed, Ariel spent her afternoon doing some reading by the pool with Lyndsay. She started by reading more about Costa Rican culture and wildlife before switching over to a murder mystery by her favourite author. Ariel lost herself in the reading as she tried to piece together the details of the murder as she read. She hardly noticed any of the children playing noisily in the pool. On the drive back from the golf course, Pat decided he wanted to get back into golfing more often, so he called his local course and booked a tee time.

Both Pat and Ariel were feeling energised after their afternoons. They went into the city and had a romantic dinner where they caught each other up on their afternoons. Both of them enjoyed brushing up on their Spanish by reading the menus and ordering in Spanish. Ariel took the time to explain to Pat about all the different cultural origins of the foods they were eating. They reflected further on how the whole day seemed just to fly by in a fantastic way and that, despite all the things they had done, they still felt revitalised.

After dinner, the couple headed back to their hotel room for a deeply intimate session. The two took their time and completely lost themselves in the experience. Afterwards, Pat wondered out loud, 'What is it about vacation sex?' Ariel offered a warm smile and a shrug to indicate she was wondering the same thing. The couple agreed that they would also need to add more vacation sex to their schedule before they nodded off together. The next morning, they woke up, made good on the previous night's commitment by having another great intimacy session and noted how refreshed they felt and excited they were to start the day's adventures.

In this vignette, we highlight a few of ways that one might experience flow while on vacation. Flow occurs when you become fully and energetically absorbed in an activity such that the activity is rewarding in and of itself, regardless of the extrinsic outcomes (Csikszentmihalyi, 1990, 1997; Nakamura and Csikszentmihalyi, 2009). In other words, these experiences are so rewarding that we want to do them again, which is likely to result in travellers who are feeling healthy, energised and excited to return. Furthermore, flow is a universal experience found across cultures, contexts and activity type (e.g. Csikszentmihalyi, 1990; Della Fave and Massimini, 1988). Despite these benefits and range of activities where flow can occur, the tourism industry and tourists may often overlook or unintentionally add barriers to such flow experiences.

Flow occurs in a wide range of activities (Csikszentmihalyi, 1997; Nakamura and Csikszentmihalyi, 2009), including those leisure activities common to vacations (e.g. hiking, sex, conversation with friends, eating) or during daily maintenance activities (e.g. driving between destinations, cleaning, organising) and during work (Csikszentmihalyi, 1997, 2003; Della Fave and Massimini, 1988; Graham, 2008; Lefevre, 1988). Flow experiences are often described using colloquial terms such as 'in the zone', 'on fire', 'focused', 'in the groove' or 'tuned in'. In this chapter, we will highlight the different ways in which vacations are primed for many flow experiences that can improve health and provide other lasting consequences. To do so, we will first explore the characteristics and conditions of flow experiences. We highlight some physical and mental benefits of flow. All of this will build up to ways to promote flow by dealing with common barriers to flow while on vacation.

Conditions of flow experiences

The roots of flow research were established as Csikszentmihalyi (1975/2000) studied creativity and began to notice some people would be completely absorbed in what they were doing, so much so that they might disregard things like fatigue or hunger. These experiences seemed to be intrinsic or 'autotelic' activities – activities that are their own reward (i.e. *auto* = self, *telos* = goal) – with little concern for extrinsic rewards (Nakamura and Csikszentmihalyi, 2009). As we examine the vignette above, we see how Pat and Ariel were experiencing different conditions for entering flow.

A first condition of flow involves a perceived balance between one's skill and the challenge of the activity, which should stretch or push the person, but not overmatch his or her skills (Figure 7.1). If challenges dramatically exceed skills (relative to each individual), people are likely to experience anxiety rather than flow; conversely, when skills exceed challenges, people experience boredom (see Csikszentmihalyi, 1997; Massimini and Carli, 1988). Above we see that the hike challenged Pat and Ariel, but Ariel, being the more experienced hiker (who might have not been as challenged as Pat) added to her challenge by pointing out Costa Rican wildlife (see Figure 7.2 for a visual representation of the balance of skill and challenge during their hike). Challenge and skill are unique to each person, so there are numerous other ways in which Ariel might have added challenge. To avoid falling into the bored region of Figure 7.2, Ariel added cognitive challenge by pointing things out; conversely, she might have added challenge by carrying all the supplies or hiking at a faster pace (both add to the physical challenge). We saw other instances of this balance as Pat was challenged by a new golf course and the couple challenged themselves when they used their Spanish skills to order dinner. Had they been required to use their Spanish skills more frequently, they might have felt overmatched. Thus, there is a constant striving for a balance between challenge and skill of an experience.

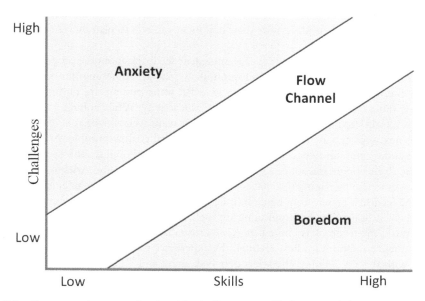

Figure 7.1 Flow experiences maintained in similar range of balance and skill.

Source: Adapted from Csikszentmihalyi (1990: 74).

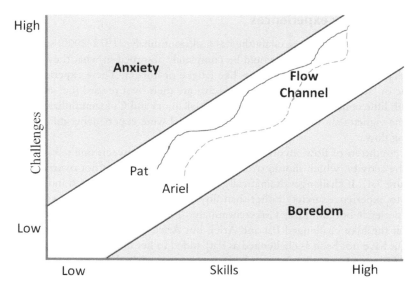

Figure 7.2 Individual pathways within the Challenge-Skill Model often vary. Here we highlight how Ariel was experiencing less challenge on the hike than Pat.

Source: Adapted from Csikszentmihalyi (1990: 74).

Another condition for entering flow is the presence of clear proximal goals (Nakamura and Csikszentmihalyi, 2009). In the vignette above, we can see some of the goals of Pat and Ariel. For example, Ariel reads a book about Costa Rica to learn about the culture, before switching to a book she reads for pleasure. In the latter case, the goal is to solve the murder mystery by reading further into the book. Pat's goal in golf, like most sports, is to hit each shot to the best of his abilities. Alternatively, musicians strive to move seamlessly from one chord to the next and chess players use their opponent's moves to plan their next set of moves (e.g. Csikszentmihalyi, 1990).

A final condition for a flow experience is immediate feedback about the progress one is making towards the goal (Nakamura and Csikszentmihalyi, 2009). Sometimes the feedback is from someone else, as was the case when Tyrone gave Pat some putting tips during their game of golf. Other times the feedback is more inherent to the activity. While golfing, Pat gets immediate feedback from each shot as he has to reassess what went well and what he might change to ensure his next shot gets as close to his target (i.e. proximal goal) as possible. As Ariel reads her book, the author presents new details that might confirm her thoughts about what will happen next or the author might introduce a new twist in the plot that requires Ariel to re-evaluate her predictions (and also increasing the challenge). During intimacy (or even an engrossing conversation), the feedback comes from being in tune with the way the couple is responding to what each of them is doing (or communicating through body movements, moaning or words). As with the goals, the feedback is immediate (Csikszentmihalyi, 1975/2000, 1986).

When these conditions for flow are met, the experience seamlessly unfolds from moment to moment with the six defining characteristics (Nakamura and Csikszentmihalyi, 2009). As we will highlight, vacations are primed to meet these characteristics.

One characteristic is an intense, present-focused concentration only on the activity (Massimini and Carli, 1988). We see this concentration alluded to throughout the vignette, but one example is during the first night's dinner when the couples hardly notice the food, because they are lost in the conversation with each other. We also see this complete involvement in the intimacy session when Pat and Ariel are only concentrating on each other. As the couple expressed their appreciation for the intimate interlude, they might have been also alluding to the fact that they were not worried about potential barriers to flow more common to daily life, such as getting enough sleep before work or their children interrupting them.

A second characteristic is that action and awareness merge such that the feedback is used strategically to take the next step towards the goal. In these situations, people describe having no room for thinking about anything else while feedback is used to improve continuously (Csikszentmihalyi, 1990; Nakamura and Csikszentmihalyi, 2009); for example, Pat's focus during the golf game where each shot dictates the next or Ariel reading by the pool where she does not notice the noisy children playing all around her. The latter case mimics that of athletes who describe times when they are not even aware of thousands of people in the crowd cheering for or against them.

Two of the next characteristics involve a freedom from worry about failure and a lack of self-consciousness (i.e. awareness of oneself as a social actor; Massimini and Carli, 1988; Nakamura and Csikszentmihalyi, 2009). Both of these elements are easier to accomplish during leisure while on a vacation as many of the outside stressors (or distractors) of day-to-day life may be less salient. As the couple has set time aside for each of the activities and left some flexibility in their schedule, they are not preoccupied with getting to the next thing (e.g. failure to finish on time) or worried about being judged or evaluated. When they got lost in the first morning's activities, they simply adjusted the length of their hike to a shorter but challenging hike that then still helped them to get in their fitness for the day. Pat was not worried about his final golf score or being judged by Tyrone or other golfers (as he might be at his country club), but just about getting better. When Tyrone gave him some putting tips, he used the feedback to improve his game. During the dinner on the first night, no one was worried about getting home to the kids or being judged by their friends (whereas they might worry more with work colleagues).

A distortion in the way time seems to be passing is another characteristic of flow (Nakamura and Csikszentmihalyi, 2009). As such, individuals usually describe that time has slowed down as they are completely in control and focused, but afterwards might be surprised by how quickly time had passed (Csikszentmihalyi, 1990; Massimini and Carli, 1988). In our vignette, we see time flying by during the first night's dinner. Similarly, we see time passed by faster than expected during maintenance-type activities as the couple got ready on the first morning, but not in a way that they felt rushed, as Pat and Ariel were just engrossed in what they were doing. A morning routine free from worry, such that time can just pass by as the individual focuses on the things he or she wants to do (e.g. make special French toast) is probably less common when not on vacation, as people need to get to work or drive their children to their commitments (e.g. school, soccer).

When all these characteristics come together, the experience becomes autotelic. A day such as the one described in the vignette might be described as an autotelic day or even be building towards an autotelic vacation. Certainly, people have experienced vacations that seem to flow by and they come to an end faster than they expected. Such a vacation might be much more rewarding than one that is more extrinsically motivated or filled with barriers towards experiencing flow (Csikszentmihalyi and Coffey, 2016).

Consequences of flow

Taking a vacation is linked to a range of psychological and physiological benefits such as better health, better relationships, higher positive affect, higher job satisfaction, higher work satisfaction and feeling revitalised (de Bloom et al., 2010, 2011; Lounsbury and Hoopes, 1986;

Westman and Eden, 1997; for a review, see Chen and Petrick, 2013). We believe that the more people engage in intrinsically motivated activities conducive to flow during a vacation, the more likely they are to benefit from the vacation (Csikszentmihalyi and Coffey, 2016). Although studies examining flow while on vacation are limited, we highlight here the ways that flow might help explain the benefits of tourism.

Given the range of ways that people experience flow, there are many potential benefits to these activities that might be easier to devote time to during a vacation. As mentioned, flow occurs during leisure activities, maintenance activities and work (e.g. Csikszentmihalyi, 1990, 2003; Graham, 2008; Lefevre, 1988; Massimini and Carli, 1988). As this chapter focuses on health tourism, we will focus on the first two, leisure and maintenance, with the idea that the consequences will have carryover upon returning home and to work. For example, getting in flow while making breakfast, catching up with your friends, playing a game of tennis or reading a good book are all useful in one way or another. Specifically, playing tennis will help with improving cardiovascular and physical fitness, while reading a book might help with cognitive efficiency and becoming immersed in conversation with friends will strengthen those social relationships. All of these can build towards a greater work–life balance. Thus, the range of ways to experience flow and the subsequent benefits from these activities are all just a starting point for why we should strive to experience flow while on vacation.

As highlighted above, a primary benefit of experiencing flow is that it is intrinsically rewarding (Csikszentmihalyi, 1997). That is to say, after people experience flow, we are excited to repeat the activity, which also tends to foster growth of skills over time (Nakamura and Csikszentmihalyi, 2009). Thus, the rewarding nature of flow experiences while on vacation is likely to inspire people to pursue them more after their vacation ends. In other words, flow experiences on vacation might carry over and result in similar healthy experiences after the vacation. In our vignette above, we saw how flow experiences during hiking, sex and golf led to the desire to repeat those experiences. Although the intrinsic reward and personal growth are enough, people also experience other benefits from flow.

Flow also has direct and indirect physiological and psychological benefits (e.g. Coffey, Wray-Lake, Mashek and Branand, 2015; De Manzano, Theorell, Harmat and Ullén, 2010; Keller, Bless, Blomann and Kleinböhl, 2011; Nakamuka and Csikszentmihalyi, 2009). For example, my colleagues and I found that college sophomores who reported higher levels of student engagement were associated with fewer visits to the doctor, higher achievement and more college success (e.g. better grades) and less psychological distress than those who reported lower levels of engagement (Study 1: Coffey et al., 2015). In a second study using American adults, we also found that higher levels of flow predicted fewer physical health symptoms and less psychological distress than those reporting lower levels of flow (Study 2: Coffey et al., 2015). Others have highlighted how flow is associated with adaptive physiological responses (e.g. De Manzano et al., 2010; Keller et al., 2011). Thus, a vacation filled with flow experiences might help a person return to work in a healthier state.

Furthermore, flow has been associated with higher levels of commitment, achievement (Carli, Delle Fave and Massimini, 1988; Massimini and Carli, 1988), cognitive engagement (Basom and Frase, 2004) and self-esteem (Rathunde, 1988). Teachers who experienced more flow had students who were more cognitively engaged and experienced more flow (Bakker, 2005; Basom and Frase, 2004). Therefore, those who experience more flow during a vacation might return to work in a revitalised state that could result in higher levels of focus and achievement that extend to co-workers or employees.

Flow has the potential to build stronger relationships in a wide range of ways. A vast array of research has highlighted the centrality of relationships on psychological and physiological health (e.g. Coffey et al., 2015; Ryan and Deci, 2000; Zhao et al., 2015). As far as romantic relationships, one study found that being highly engaged in an activity with their partner was associated with higher levels of closeness to their partner and relationship satisfaction in both leisure and maintenance activities (Graham, 2008). Other research has found that flow is associated with feelings of connectedness to others (Study 2: Coffey et al., 2015). Benefits of flow can also extend to other family relationships. For example, adolescents who perceived their family environment as highly conducive to flow experiences reported higher levels of positive affect, sociability, activation, cognitive efficiency and motivation than peers who reported their family context was less conducive to flow experiences. Furthermore, these adolescents reported higher self-esteem when with their family (Rathunde, 1988).

Flow has other potential benefits upon returning to work. Although no such research examining how flow on vacations translates to work-related outcomes, other research suggests there are potential benefits that extend to work after a vacation. Research has shown that adults are three times more likely to experience flow at work than in leisure (e.g. Lefevre, 1988). This association suggests that those who can experience more flow during leisure might be more likely to experience flow at work (e.g. developing an autotelic personality). Experiencing flow at work is important because it is associated with positive outcomes such as higher work satisfaction (e.g. Bryce and Haworth, 2002), harmonious passion and less burnout (Lavigne, Forest and Crevier-Braud, 2012).

Measuring flow

The ideal way to measure flow experiences is to use the experience sampling method (ESM), as it allows for naturalistic and online or active data collection (Csikszentmihalyi and Larson, 1987; Hektner, Schmidt and Csikszentmihalyi, 2006). In modern times, ESM is conducted by having people carry a smartphone that will randomly signal them a certain amount of times throughout a day (e.g. four to six times). When signalled, people can complete a brief report on aspects of their current activity that usually include balance of skill and challenge, intrinsic motivation, concentration, motivation and affective states (for a more complete review of ESM, see Hektner et al., 2006). People can also report on other factors that might be associated with flow, such as their physical and psychological health. In order to keep the ESM responses short, other variables might be measured before and after the vacation. ESM is preferred, because it eliminates the need for retroactive reporting that might involve bias in remembering the vacation (for an example, see Wirtz, Chi-yue, Diener and Oishi, 2009; Wirtz, Kruger, Scollon and Diener, 2003). Although concerns have been expressed about the disruptive nature of ESM, this has rarely been reported as problematic. (For a more complete review of other ways to measure flow, see Nakamura and Csikszentmihalyi, 2009, and for other ideas about using ESM on vacation, see Csikszentmihalyi and Coffey, 2016.)

Recommendations for the tourism industry

As the tourism industry often strives to promote happiness and wellbeing, finding ways to promote flow experiences is likely to motivate people to want to return to a destination and to write positive reviews. Thus, these organisations often provide opportunities for flow (e.g. countless brochures about activities, guided tours, fitness centres), but also have some built-in barriers to flow experiences that could be removed.

Common barriers to flow experiences are things that evoke negative emotions, such as anger and frustration. Any reasonable steps that can be taken to simplify processes and minimise frustration may result in higher levels of flow. For example, something as simple as a person getting extremely frustrated by a complex or time-consuming check-in process might then mean the individual has trouble getting into pleasure reading. Many places have taken great steps to eliminate barriers that might cause frustrations. For example, some companies will pick people up at their hotels to take them on tour, which can help eliminate the stress of finding transportation and navigating a foreign area. If people are travelling in a cramped or uncomfortable way (e.g. a long ride in a full bus), it might leave them too stiff to hike in the way that they normally would.

Eliminating potential distractions that might require shifting of cognitive resources from one activity to another or result in feeling self-conscious could also limit flow experiences. Digital devices and screen time are potential distractors that might take away from a flow experience. Checking email in the digital age could easily pull someone out of the focus of whatever the person is currently doing. Similarly, providing settings that reduce self-conscious feelings should also help. Thus, tour guides or fitness instructors might be careful to provide feedback in a non-judgemental way. Doing this will also reduce chances that someone is worried about a specific outcome or failing.

Opting to provide access to activities that require a balance of skill and challenge, rather than more passive activities, might also be useful. For example, watching television is not conducive to flow experiences, whereas reading, socialising and hobbies are all more likely to result in flow experiences (Cskiszentmihalyi, 2003; Massimini and Carli, 1988). Thus, removing distracting televisions from social areas (e.g. restaurants), providing complimentary books for reading (rather than movies) and even keeping televisions out of rooms with beds are all ways to steer people subtly towards flow activities. Just imagine, a couple realises they will not be able to watch some television – this shifts their attention to each other and opts for another intimate session.

Certainly, doing some of these suggestions may seem impractical (e.g. making buses less cramped) or likely to upset some tourists (e.g. removing televisions from certain areas). Thus, to be really sure about the best ways to promote flow, people in the tourism industry should partner with researchers to determine what will work best for their venue, but here we pose some broad suggestions. If the goal is to promote a healthy tourism experience, sending the right message to patrons might mitigate certain confusion or frustration with things like removing televisions from certain areas or rooms or restricting access to email. We see tourists as much more likely to appreciate getting in extra time trying new things, spending time with family, spending time on things they cannot do at home, rather than regretting that they missed an episode of their favourite show. Simply put, tourists leave saying things like, 'That was a beautiful hike' or 'That was such a fun day', rather than statements like, 'I am so glad I got to watch that sitcom'.

Summary

A vacation filled with flow experiences (i.e. an autotelic vacation) has the potential to offer lasting psychological and physiological benefits that extend long after the vacation has ended. In this chapter, we provided a vignette to highlight just some of the numerous ways that one might experience flow while on vacation. Furthermore, we have illustrated the different ways that these flow experiences are directly and indirectly related to health.

That said, flow experiences remain under-studied while on vacation. Considering the research that suggests flow is less likely to happen in day-to-day leisure than it is in maintenance activities or at work (Csikszentmihalyi, 1975), we think that intrinsically motivated vacations (where potential barriers are minimised) might be an exception. As the research here is limited, we also suspect that vacations with more flow experiences are likely to have longer-term benefits than more extrinsically motivated vacations. For example, people who are passionate about being active might plan vacations filled with physical activities, such as hiking, that could lead to improved cardiovascular health, especially if the tourists continue to hike upon their return home.

More research is needed to test ideas about different types of vacations and flow experiences. This research will help to determine if there are effective ways to reduce barriers to flow experiences while on vacation. For example, in the digital age, many employees might feel obligated to stay connected to work by frequently checking their email. Even though this might seem proactive, it has a strong potential to limit the chances of flow occurring. Specifically, reading email will instantly shift focus away from the current activities; the emails might also require extra attention, be upsetting or make individuals feel self-conscious that they are not currently at work to deal with potential problems. Thus, interventions or strategies (e.g. not checking email or limiting checking email to once a day) need to be tested to see if they can improve chances of flow and health experiences.

In conclusion, an autotelic vacation is one where people will likely feel completely involved in the moment. More importantly, these vacations can improve health in a wide range of ways, while allowing people to customise their vacations to those things that they are drawn towards and motivated to experience.

References

Bakker, A. B. (2005) 'Flow among music teachers and their students: The crossover of peak experiences', *Journal of Vocational Behavior*, 66(1), 26–44, doi: 10.1016/j.jvb.2003.11.001.

Basom, M. R. and Frase, L. (2004) 'Creating optimal work environments: Exploring teacher flow experiences', *Mentoring and Tutoring: Partnership in Learning*, 12(2), 241–258.

Bryce, J. and Haworth, J. (2002) 'Wellbeing and flow in sample of male and female office workers', *Leisure Studies*, 21(3–4), 249–263.

Carli, M., Delle Fave, A. and Massimini, F. (1988) 'The quality of experience in the flow channels: Comparison of Italian and US students', in M. Csikszentmihalyi, I. S. Csikszentmihalyi, M. Csikszentmihalyi and I. S. Csikszentmihalyi (eds) *Optimal Experience: Psychological Studies of Flow in Consciousness*, New York: Cambridge University Press, pp. 193–213.

Chen, C. C. and Petrick, J. F. (2013) 'Health and wellness benefits of travel experiences: A literature review', *Journal of Travel Research*, 52(6), 709–719, doi: 10.1177/0047287513496477.

Coffey, J. K., Wray-Lake, L., Mashek, D. and Branand, B. (2015) 'A longitudinal examination of a multidimensional wellbeing model in college and community samples', *Journal of Happiness Studies*, doi 10.1007/s10902-014-9590-8.

Csikszentmihalyi, M. (1975) 'Play and intrinsic rewards', *Journal of Humanistic Psychology*, 15(3), 41–63.

——. (1975/2000) *Beyond Boredom and Anxiety*, San Francisco, CA: Jossey-Bass.

——. (1986) 'L'Insegnamento e la trasmissione dei memi', in F. Massimini and P. Inghilleri (eds) *L'Esperienza quotidiana*, Milan, Italy: Franco Angeli.

——. (1990) *Flow: The Psychology of Optimal Experience*, New York: Harper Perennial Modern Classics.

——. (1997) *Finding Flow: The Psychology of Engagement With Everyday Life*, New York: Basic Books.

——. (2003) *Good Business: Flow, Leadership and the Making of Meaning*, New York: Viking.

Csikszentmihalyi, M. and Coffey, J. K. (2016) 'Why do we travel? A positive psychological model for travel motivation', in S. Filep, J. Laing and M. Csikszentmihalyi (eds) *Positive Tourism*, London: Routledge Publishing.

Csikszentmihalyi, M. and Larson, R. (1987) 'Validity and reliability of the experience-sampling method', *Journal of Nervous and Mental Disease*, 175(9), 526–536, doi: 10.1097/00005053-198709000-00004.

de Bloom, J., Geurts, S. A. E., Sonnentag, S., Taris, T., de Weerth, C. and Michiel A. J. Kompier (2011) 'How does a vacation from work affect employee health and wellbeing?', *Psychology and Health*, 26(12), 1606–1622, doi: 10.1080/08870446.2010.546860.

de Bloom, J., Geurts, S. A. E., Toon, W. T., Sonnentag, S., de Weerth, C. and Kompier, M. A. J. (2010) 'Effects of vacation from work on health and wellbeing: Lots of fun, quickly gone', *Work and Stress*, 24(2), 196–216, doi: 10.1080/02678373.2010.493385.

Della Fave, A. and Massimini, F. (1988) 'Modernization and the changing contexts of flow in work and leisure', in M. Csikszentmihalyi, I. S. Csikszentmihalyi, M. Csikszentmihalyi and I. S. Csikszentmihalyi (eds) *Optimal Experience: Psychological Studies of Flow in Consciousness*, New York: Cambridge University Press, pp. 193–213.

de Manzano, Ö., Theorell, T., Harmat, L. and Ullén, F. (2010) 'The psychophysiology of flow during piano playing', *Emotion*, 10(3), 301, doi: 10.1037/a0018432.

Graham, J. M. (2008) 'Self-expansion and flow in couples' momentary experiences: An experience sampling study', *Journal of Personality and Social Psychology*, 95(3), 679–694, doi: 10.1037/0022-3514.95.3.679.

Hektner, J., Schmidt, J. and Csikszentmihalyi, M. (2006) *Experience Sampling: Measuring the Quality of Everyday Life*, Thousand Oaks, CA: Sage Publications.

Keller, J., Bless, H., Blomann, F. and Kleinböhl, D. (2011) 'Physiological aspects of flow experiences: Skills–demand-compatibility effects on heart rate variability and salivary cortisol', *Journal of Experimental Social Psychology*, 47(4), 849–852, doi: 10.1016/j.jesp.2011.02.004.

Lavigne, G., Forest, J. and Crevier-Braud, L. (2012) 'Passion at work and burnout: A two-study test of the mediating role of flow experiences', *European Journal of Work and Organizational Psychology*, 21, 518–546.

LeFevre, J. (1988) 'Flow and the quality of experience during work and leisure', in M. Csikszentmihalyi and I. S. Csikszentmihalyi (eds) *Optimal Experience: Psychological Studies of Flow in Consciousness*, New York: Cambridge University Press, pp. 307–318.

Lounsbury, J. W. and Hoopes, L. L. (1986) 'A vacation from work: Changes in work and nonwork outcomes', *Journal of Applied Psychology*, 71(3), 392–401, doi: 10.1037/0021-9010.71.3.392.

Massimini, F. and Carli, M. (1988) 'The systematic assessment of flow in daily experience', in M. Csikszentmihalyi and I. S. Csikszentmihalyi (eds) *Optimal Experience: Psychological Studies of Flow in Consciousness*, New York: Cambridge University Press, pp. 266–287.

Nakamura, J. and Csikszentmihalyi, M. (2009) 'Flow theory and research', in S. J. Lopez, C. R. Snyder, S. J. Lopez and C. R. Snyder (eds) *Oxford Handbook of Positive Psychology* (2nd ed.), New York: Oxford University Press, pp. 195–206.

Rathunde, K. (1988) 'Optimal experience and the family context', in M. Csikszentmihalyi and I. S. Csikszentmihalyi (eds) *Optimal Experience: Psychological Studies of Flow in Consciousness*, New York: Cambridge University Press, pp. 342–363.

Ryan, R. and Deci, E. (2000) 'Self-determination theory and the facilitation of intrinsic motivation, social development and wellbeing', *American Psychologist*, 55(1), 68–78, doi: 10.1037/0003-066X.55.1.68.

Westman, M. and Eden, D. (1997) 'Effects of a respite from work on burnout: Vacation relief and fade out', *Journal of Applied Psychology*, 82(4), 516–527.

Wirtz, D., Chi-yue, C., Diener, E. and Oishi, S. (2009) 'What constitutes a good life? Cultural differences in the role of positive and negative affect in subjective wellbeing', *Journal of Personality*, 77(4), 1167–1196, doi: 10.1111/j.1467-6494.2009.00578.x.

Wirtz, D., Kruger, J., Scollon, C. N. and Diener, E. (2003) 'What to do on spring break? The role of predicted, on-line and remembered experience in future choice', *Psychological Science*, 14(5), 520–524, doi: 10.1111/1467-9280.03455.

Zhao, W., Young, R. E., Breslow, L., Michel, N. M., Flett, G. L. and Goldberg, J. O. (2015) 'Attachment style, relationship factors and mental health stigma among adolescents', *Canadian Journal of Behavioural Science / Revue Canadienne Des Sciences Du Comportement*, 47(4), 263–271, doi: 10.1037/cbs0000018.

Part III
Health, tourism and society

This part examines broader issues of health in society and how tourism can play a role in contributing to these. Robyn Bushell begins in Chapter 8 by analysing the interactions between tourism and the health of a place and its people. She argues that there is a need for 'healthy tourism' which improves health benefits for local people in a destination and not just for 'health tourism' which benefits tourists. There are close connections with principles of sustainable and ethical tourism and the issues are especially pertinent for developing countries. This chapter has some elements in common with Colin Michael Hall's chapter in Part V (Chapter 16), which also considers tourism's relationship to issues of safety and wellbeing as well as illness in destinations.

Anya Diekmann and Scott McCabe discuss the various ways in which tourism can contribute to the social, mental and physical wellbeing of certain target groups in society, especially the most deprived (e.g. families, the elderly and people with disabilities [Chapter 9]). Although such forms of tourism may not be described as 'health tourism' *per se*, they can offer a break from the rigours and hardships of everyday life which can ultimately contribute to better health. The authors emphasise that social tourism has a relatively long history in many countries and has long been recognised as an important aspect of life, but it has been relatively under-researched.

Gareth Shaw and his co-authors focus specifically on older tourists in the light of research about ageing populations and their health and wellbeing needs, which can also include travel (Chapter 10). In many developed countries, retired and senior citizens tend to have more leisure time and purchasing power, as well as better healthcare than the generations before. It seems that holidays can increase levels of subjective wellbeing and overall life satisfaction, especially if several activities are included. Life-course analysis research is quoted, which emphasises the importance of transitions over the course of people's lives and the way that patterns of holiday taking and types of activities change over time.

This part overall shows that there is a strong relationship between tourism and the wellbeing of societies. If it is planned and managed well, it can enhance the lives of residents as well as improving the life satisfaction and giving positive meaning to the lives of specific segments of (travelling) populations too.

8

Healthy tourism

Robyn Bushell

> Health outcomes . . . are only partly a consequence of activity within the health sector as narrowly defined. More important determinants of health status of a population relate to combinations of geography, history and culture and to the activities of the public and private sectors which condition food production and distribution, availability of cash income, education, water supply and sewage disposal, housing, policing of motor vehicles and many other factors.
>
> *(Taylor, 1994)*

This chapter explores the interactions of tourism with the health of people and place and the concept of 'healthy tourism' developed as a framework to realign the health–tourism relationship into a more positive one. It considers the role tourism can play to improve the health benefits of local people and places, not just the health of the visitor, thus it is not a form of health tourism. It ties conceptually to ideals of sustainable tourism.

A case study of Ha Long Bay, Vietnam, demonstrates the intersections of healthy places with 'healthy tourism'. This is an example of a destination enjoying considerable success in terms of growth in visitation, but where pressure from tourism is placing the health of the ecosystem and humans at risk. It demonstrates the need for 'healthy tourism' as a socially and environmentally responsible approach to tourism planning. This requires mechanisms that enable and encourage the public and private sectors of tourism and health to work together to improve the safety, health and wellbeing of local people, the natural environment and travellers (Bushell and Powis, 2009).

Unprecedented levels of global travel, especially to developing countries, have major implications for the tourism system. The interconnectedness of the economic wellbeing of tourism and the integrity and health of the natural environment and the people, particularly those from developing countries, for whom tourism represents an important tool for community development, deserves to be better understood. A more ethical framework for tourism planning has been developed to address this need. 'Healthy tourism' grew out of a World Health Organization (WHO) initiative seeking to improve the quality of life of local communities.

This requires a more collaborative approach to tourism planning and explicit management of the interrelationships between tourism and human health, environmental management, natural and cultural heritage and sustainable development. This is achieved by drawing together the expertise of the public- and private-sector professionals across tourism, health, environment and community development.

The ecological and social effects of tourism have been widely documented, though the health consequences are often overlooked. For example, marine biodiversity in small island nations significantly influences both human health and the local economy in numerous ways (Bapoo-Dundoo, 2001; McElroy, 2003; Task Force on Small States, 2000) and is directly affected by tourism. Inadequate tourism planning and control may be associated with water pollution from hotels, condominiums, pleasure craft and cruise ship waste water; coastal siltation caused by soil erosion from the removal of mangroves and improper landscaping, often associated with hotel, resort and marina developments; physical damage to coral reefs due to trampling from snorkelling and diving, collecting shells for souvenirs, boat moorings and anchors, sandmining and dredging; over-fishing for recreational fishing as a tourist attraction and excessive fishing to supply hotels and resorts (Conlin and Baum, 1995; McElroy, 2003; Sinha and Bushell, 2002). The consequent health effects include huge decreases in the fish catch (up to 50 per cent reported in the Caribbean: United Nations Environment Programme, 1999), causing decreases in income for fishers and for other families' budgets due to the need to buy more expensive sources of meat and protein (mostly imported). This in turn can lead to reduced nutrition and increased cholesterol intakes, resulting in increased heart disease, imposing pressure and costs on local health services. Heavy demands on scarce water supplies have direct consequences on local agriculture affecting the diets and wellbeing of local people. The ecological changes also cause a decrease in the scenic qualities in coastal places as well as depleting marine life. These can lead to downturns in tourism and hence a decrease in economic wellbeing. Biodiversity conservation, health and wellbeing of locals and the tourism economy are inextricably linked. The cycle can degrade increasingly over time or, with careful planning and monitoring, sustainable tourism development can serve to protect environmental and human wellbeing.

Other common health effects related to tourism in developing nations may include costs to family and community life associated with the introduction of gambling; organised prostitution and the associated communicable diseases; increased alcohol consumption; smoking; changing dietary patterns with the introduction of imported and fast foods; and family unit dislocation when young parents leave their family and village to work in resorts (Bapoo-Dundoo, 2001; Bushell and Staiff, 2001; Mastny, 2001).

Added to this, the economic benefit, the reason for pursuing tourism development, is often confined to a very small proportion of the local populations (Akama and Kieti, 2007; Mastny, 2001). Experience suggests that at the local or microeconomic level tourism does not always yield the anticipated returns due to establishment and maintenance costs of essential infrastructure, particularly roads, airports, docks, public transport, utilities, including enhanced water supply, sewerage, facilities such as communication systems and visitor service centres, all needed to attract tourism investment (Kennedy, 2002; Manning and Prieur, 1998). Often the economic 'trickle down' to the wider community is very limited because of internal, external and invisible leakage through foreign and non-local investment, employment of non-locals and the purchasing of non-local goods and services (Bapoo-Dundoo, 2001; Mastny, 2001; Task Force on Small States, 2000). Governments in developing nations are pouring money into tourism development in a bid to attract investors and diversify their economies (United Nations Conference on Trade and Development, 2001). In gross economic terms tourism investments pay off; however, according to World Bank studies, the average internal leakage for most developing countries is estimated at 55 per cent of gross tourism earnings (Ngone, 2001). A principal export in 83 per cent of developing countries (Richardson, 2010), tourism can place significant financial burden on local authorities (DANTE, 2002) if not strategic. This can divert scarce resources from local needs such as health and education.

The 'healthy tourism' concept

The WHO recognised the need for mechanisms and indicators within tourism planning and operations to promote the health, safety and wellbeing in rapidly growing destinations in developing countries (Bushell and Staiff, 2001).

While continuing to have a primary interest in the treatment and prevention of illness and equity in access to safe food, water and air, the WHO has been pursuing a more holistic view of health and wellbeing. This has encompassed the inclusion of tourism-related issues since the 1990s, when the Rio Earth Summit and subsequent meetings paid particular attention to the health and environmental problems of the most vulnerable.

As part of the United Nations (UN)-wide recognition for new and effective approaches in managing complex development issues, the WHO developed a regional policy framework, *New Horizons in Health*. The purpose was to aid governments and communities in developing new strategies and actions as a sustainable basis for health; to place an emphasis on disease prevention rather than cure; and to encourage community participation as well as intersectoral cooperation. *New Horizons in Health* gave rise to a range of strategies which were formulated across Asia and the Pacific. These include the use of 'healthy settings', such as Healthy Schools, Healthy Workplaces, Healthy Markets, Healthy Hospitals and Healthy Cities (Powis, 1999).

A WHO meeting of Pacific Health Ministers in Fiji in 1995 resulted in the Yanuca Declaration for Health in the Pacific in the 21st Century, leading to the creation of the Healthy Islands concept. It reflected a desire to seek Pacific solutions to Pacific problems. The Healthy Islands concept involved continuously identifying and resolving priority issues related to health, development and wellbeing and enabling these issues to be addressed in partnerships between communities, organisations and agencies at local, national and regional levels (Powis, 1999).

The need for more sustainable tourism practice was one such priority issue, identified along with food importation, tobacco advertising, waste management and resource exploitation as a powerful external influence with health-related consequences for small islands (Ritchie, Sparks and Rotem, 2000). As discussed above, tourism places undue pressure on small island environments. It also adds significantly to the problem of food importation. Additionally, because a large proportion of the economy is accounted for by exports and imports (some 112 per cent of gross domestic product (GDP) in the Pacific nations), even minor disruptions in world markets, including fluctuations in demand and/or prices for services like tourism, can have a major impact on the local economy. In Fiji, for example, at that time, tourism was the single most important export commodity, accounting for 26.3 per cent of export goods and services (followed by sugar at 11.9 per cent) in 1997 (Task Force on Small States, 2000). Since the 2006 coup this has fallen, but remains at 13.7 per cent of GDP compared to 3.1 per cent as the world average (World Travel and Tourism Council, 2015). A similar situation continues in most Pacific Island nations. With this reliance on tourism, any change affects the entire population. Any tourism-related impacts are significant.

'Healthy tourism' was developed in 2000–2001 with the WHO Pacific Regional Office and the WHO Collaborating Centre at the University of Western Sydney, Australia, as a component of the Healthy Islands strategy. Based on the ethic that tourism should be a tool for community development, quality of life and health benefits should be built into the goals and objectives of tourism planning (Bushell and Staiff, 2001), supporting the principles of sustainable tourism in *Agenda 21 for the Travel and Tourism Industry* (World Tourism Organization, 1996).

'Healthy tourism' provides a framework for the WHO and the tourism industry to work collaboratively with tourism destination governments, tourism associations and local communities to promote health and wellbeing.

Important health issues relate to the significant role tourism plays in levels of lifestyle illnesses, including those that relate to diet, smoking, alcohol and occupational health and safety and the transmission of communicable diseases. Specific issues include food safety, HIV/AIDS, water quality and the numerous epidemics that have arisen since work began on the concept, such as severe acute respiratory syndrome (SARS), that have spread rapidly because of the vast numbers daily of people travelling worldwide. Early-warning systems on disease outbreaks, the implementation of international health and safety regulations, timely and transparent health and safety information and services for travellers and tour organisations and the appropriate training of staff in the tourism industry are important aspects.

In 2006 the lead UN agencies concerned with tourism set up the *Marrakech Task Force for Sustainable Tourism Development*. Following a three-year review of practices, policies and programmes worldwide, they concluded:

> Tourism policy development requires a strategy that integrates strategies for sustainable development . . . At the national and regional level, policy makers should seek to adopt tourism policies that promote and protect the country as a tourism destination.
>
> *(United Nations Environment Programme, 2009: i)*

This includes protecting health and safety at destinations.

Healthy and responsible tourism

'Healthy tourism' is integral to sustainable tourism, with an explicit focus on policies and processes designed to ensure the management of resources in such a way that the health outcomes for the visitor, the community and the environment are fully integrated and considered by the appropriate authorities.

The tourism sector has endorsed the principle of sustainable tourism, yielding numerous international charters, declarations and codes, including health. The risks posed to the industry, tourists and local communities arising from emerging and re-emerging diseases are significant but remain poorly managed (World Health Organization, 2009). The health impacts of climate change on water and vector-borne diseases such as malaria and dengue have heightened the need to place health more centrally within the sustainable tourism discourse (Bushell and Staiff, 2001). The devastating effects and very rapid global spread of SARS, bird flu, swine flu and, more recently, the Ebola virus and now the mosquito-borne Zika virus are constant reminders of the significant overlaps between health and travel, with consequences for the health of people and the financial viability of tourism in entire destinations.

Responding to health impacts on tourism in the Association of Southeast Asian Nations (ASEAN) region

The swine flu (H1N1) crisis mobilised the Emerging Infectious Diseases Programme within ASEAN in 2008 to examine the health–tourism interface.

Representatives from the Ministries of Health and Tourism with partner organisations identified factors contributing to the emergence and re-emergence of infectious diseases. These included:

- rapid increases in travel;
- population growth and urbanisation leading to overcrowding and unhygienic conditions, lack of clean water and adequate sanitation;
- substantial increases in international trade, mass distribution of food and unhygienic food preparation practices;
- increased exposure of humans to disease vectors and reservoirs in nature;
- alterations to the environment and climatic change;
- traveller susceptibility to illness and the high potential of travellers to carry diseases;
- travel creating enabling environments for infection;
- discrepancies in knowledge, beliefs and behaviour in relation to health and safety standards amongst some travellers as well as those working in tourism;
- inadequate public programmes for healthy travel.

They acknowledged the need to develop policy to improve the safety, health and wellbeing of travellers and local people in tourism destinations (ASEAN, 2008).

One outcome of this regional workshop was to commission further 'healthy tourism' research to explore health issues in tourism destinations; to further develop the 'healthy tourism' concept; and to propose strategic solutions at a regional level. The project involved the ten ASEAN member states (Brunei, Cambodia, Darussalam, Indonesia, Lao PDR, Malaysia, Myanmar, the Philippines, Singapore, Thailand and Vietnam), ASEAN Plus Three Countries (China, Japan and the Republic of Korea) and partner organisations including the UN System Influenza Coordination; UN World Tourism Organization; International Organization for Migration; Joint UN Programme on HIV/AIDS; and Kenan Institute Asia with funding from the Australian government, AusAID.

Emerging architecture of 'healthy tourism'

The research comprised tourism and health data surveys, site visits and consultative meetings with national and local stakeholders in both the public and private sectors in each of the ten member states nominated, pilot tourism destinations. Information was collated on local populations, health services, facilities, health priorities, burden of disease data, existing prevention and health promotion strategies, links to tourism and local environmental health issues. Existing guidelines, regulations, training, accreditation and any health- and tourism-related initiatives or collaboration were also systematised. Site visits enabled field observations and discussions about tourism in each place and planned developments. Analysis identified key local and generic issues, priorities, gaps and best practices. Following analysis a second regional workshop facilitated the development of consensus amongst the ASEAN Health and Tourism Ministries for a 'Healthy Tourism' Strategic Framework and 'Healthy Tourism' Work Plan.

Common areas where health burdens and tourism intersected included: water- and food-borne diseases, sexually transmitted diseases, particularly HIV, respiratory diseases such as influenza (including H1N1) and vector-borne diseases, including malaria and dengue fever. Despite the obvious link to health problems, there was no evidence in any of the countries of any work being undertaken to assess, mitigate or adapt to the impacts of climate change on health and tourism. Also significant in terms of burden of disease were the non-communicable diseases, including diabetes, cancer and mental health problems. These non-communicable diseases represent lifestyle illnesses that are the major causes of morbidity and mortality in developed and increasingly also in developing nations.

The existence of a rapidly developing health/medical tourism industry was also noted as offering opportunities to healthy tourism strategies.

A working definition of 'healthy tourism' was agreed:

> 'Healthy Tourism' is a commitment to responsible tourism planning, development and operations which has as its vision the protection and promotion of the health of the tourist and host communities by working in ways which embrace open communication, effective collaboration and engagement between all stakeholders.
>
> *(Bushell and Powis, 2009)*

Other than Singapore, which was exemplary in its standards and management of tourism within a broader framework of wellbeing, there was evidence of a number of good practices throughout the remainder of the region with potential to be further developed, but these were overshadowed in most of the countries by:

- poor planning and fragmentation of effort;
- lack of awareness of the relationship between health and tourism;
- lack of effective standards and enforcement;
- lack of collaboration between stakeholders;
- poor training of operators/tourism staff.

Hence the emerging elements identified were: commitment, collaboration, community engagement, communication and capacity building. These serve as the foundation architecture upon which the concept is built:

- Commitment: establishing a health ethic that identifies health protection and health promotion for both the visitor and community built into the goals and objectives of tourism planning and operations.
- Collaboration: establishing working relationships between key stakeholders. Opportunities for collaboration range from networking, information sharing to active coordination, joint activities and shared resources.
- Community engagement: providing opportunities for the community to engage in the process of setting a shared vision and goals for future tourism; to empower the community to take a lead role and active participation in decision making, implementation and the evaluation of tourism activities where health and wellbeing benefits can be realised.
- Communication: the development of a range of strategies to promote the health and wellbeing of tourists and the community. Building trust, transparency and being inclusive with all stakeholders, particularly those with a stake in health protection, promotion and tourism and keeping stakeholders informed and engaged is key.
- Capacity building: addressing the need to provide financial, human and institutional resources to implement 'healthy tourism'. This includes developing community and workforces by building individual skills, enhancing community engagement, developing organisational leadership, governance and management and, at the highest level, addressing the need for changes in legislation, policy and resourcing.

A 'healthy tourism' approach needs to address all these issues within a local context. This will be explored using a case study drawn from an iconic tourism destination in Vietnam.

Case study: Ha Long Bay, Vietnam

Ha Long Bay was the selected 'healthy tourism' pilot site in Vietnam and illustrates the types of health problems associated with tourism, even when it sits within a protected area with a plan of management.

Located off the northeast coast of Vietnam in Quang Ninh Province, Ha Long Bay has over 1,600 limestone karst islands and islets, of which 775 are included in a 434 km^2 core zone of a World Heritage site (Haynes, 2008). Most international visitors to Vietnam visit Ha Long Bay, ranked third after Ha Noi and Ho Chi Minh City by visitor numbers. Most tourism activities concentrate in a relatively small area within the World Heritage site, namely Thien Cung, Dau Go and Sung Sot cave sites and recreation/landing sites of Ti Top and Soi Sim islands (Haynes, 2008).

Tourism creates significant economic benefit for local people, providing work in hotels, restaurants, travel agencies, boats and souvenir shops. Fishermen provide seafood and tour guide services for tourists. Tourism has grown rapidly in Quang Ninh Province due to the inscription of Ha Long Bay on the World Heritage list in 1994. In 2001 Ha Long Bay received 1.97 million visitors, including 679,555 international arrivals. There has been a massive growth, with 4.2 million visitors in 2008, including 2.35 million international visitors. International numbers for all Vietnam had increased to 7.944 million in 2015 (Ministry of Culture, Sports and Tourism, 2015) and Ha Long Bay remains one of the most-visited destinations. This is an unsustainable rate of growth. Numbers might have been even higher, but SARS and the bird flu epidemic caused decreased visitation between 2003 and 2005 (Quang Ninh Administration of Culture, Sports and Tourism, 2009). The Vietnamese government has made a significant investment in tourism in the last 15 years, increasing the number of hotels, restaurants, attractions, entertainment, administration and promotion abroad. But many worry that there is increasing visitor concern about degradation to the site itself, particularly water pollution and this is negatively impacting heritage values and may lead to a decline in tourism.

The average length of stay in Ha Long is quite short, about 1.5 days. Most come on package tours. The main attraction is to visit Ha Long Bay by boat. About 50 per cent of overnight visitors are foreigners staying either on boats or in hotels. The major source markets for international visitors are from within Asia, particularly China. In 2009 there were a total of 74 hotels with 8,437 rooms and 15,087 beds; ten were rated as 4–5 star, each with around 200 rooms and 20 at 3 star, each with around 50 rooms. There are also many small guest houses supplying 3,644 rooms. The city had 111 restaurants and many small cafes (Quang Ninh Administration of Culture, Sports and Tourism, 2009). These numbers continue to grow to service the growing visitor numbers.

In relation to quality assurance procedures, all tourist boats must have a licence issued by the provincial government. The number of licences was restricted to 400 local boats: 100 with 40–50 overnight berths and 300 day-tour-only boats. In addition there were up to 400 international cruise ships per year; the majority visited for one day/night and carried a total of 167,300 passengers in 2008 (Quang Ninh Administration of Culture, Sports and Tourism, 2009). Despite the licensing system, the activity is affecting the integrity of the site, yet the number of boats and licences has increased to meet the continually growing demand.

The Transport Department and Tourism Department jointly manage licensing of boat operators and training with regard to boat safety and customer relations. Food safety and quality assurance

(continued)

(continued)

problems are well documented and have concerned the Vietnam National Administration of Tourism (Haynes, 2008). In response to these concerns, a Circular (88/TT-BVHTTDL), issued by the Vietnam Ministry of Culture, Sport and Tourism in 2008, stipulated that all 1–5-star hotels in Vietnam must obtain a food safety licence (Quang Ninh Administration of Culture, Sports and Tourism, 2009). The issue of food safety directly affects visitor wellbeing, yet was not required for boats or restaurants. Cruise ships, which are not local, operate outside this system. Hotels do have food hygiene training.

Health impacts linked to tourism

The growth of tourism has created jobs and population growth, with many moving into the city for work. But also due to tourism, the prices for food, accommodation and general goods in Ha Long are more expensive than in other localities in the province. This affects wellbeing in numerous ways, especially for those in the lower socio-economic groups, pushing poverty deeper into the local community despite the successful economic growth.

The UNESCO World Heritage State of Conservation report (World Heritage Committee, 2009: 57) identified population growth, increased tourism pressure, urbanisation and the absence of an integrated planning approach as the main threats to the site and integrity of its outstanding universal value. As tourism has developed, the visited grottos are overcrowded during high season, with a negative impact on the visitor experience and causing damage to caves, a major concern to visitors and regular topic on tourism-related web blog sites (Haynes, 2008). Crowding and inappropriate development around the area detract from the World Heritage values.

The economic activities associated with tourism involving land reclamation, transport, residential development, dredging of the shipping channel and related port development create a range of environmental problems. These include significant loss of mangrove habitat that provides a natural mitigation system. These activities collectively greatly reduce water quality, degrade the underwaterscape and cause loss of biodiversity, especially coral reefs and seagrass beds. Increasing numbers of tourist boats increase pollution through fuel leaks, oil spills, bilge discharge, exhaust fumes, human waste, rubbish and stirring up sediment in the relatively shallow waters of the bay (Haynes, 2008). Cigarette butts were identified as a problem to the island ecology surrounding the sites (Hamilton-Smith, 2007, cited in Haynes, 2008: 28). The State of Conservation report also noted over-exploitation of the marine resources to supply the tourism trade, inadequate waste management systems, low levels of awareness and illegal settlement as major challenges (World Heritage Committee, 2009). The development of Tuan Chau International Tourist Resort with a causeway to the mainland, just outside the core zone, is a theme park-style resort with condominium upmarket accommodation, casino and amusement activities which will further detract from World Heritage values and adds potential for further water pollution and health risks if waste is not well managed.

Water pollution from the boats, hotels, restaurants and urban development is the major health issue. Seafood is the main source of protein in the local diet. Direct health consequences include food-borne disease from the polluted waters, particularly hepatitis B and gastroenteritis; also, the availability of fish, with loss of mangroves (nursery for fish hatching) and over-fishing to meet tourism demand. An increased incidence of non-communicable causes of heart disease can be linked to changes in diet and cancer (unspecified) linked to pollutants in the environment. Car accidents directly relate to huge increases in tourism-related traffic. These tourism-linked health issues are the most prevalent causes of morbidity and mortality. HIV/AIDS and bird flu are also significant in the burden of disease. The increase in HIV/AIDS shows correlations with increases in tourism (Bushell and Powis, 2009).

This case study and the policy discussions within the ASEAN based on our research demonstrated how 'healthy tourism' could provide a strategic framework to deal with local public and environmental health issues and ensure ongoing value of tourism-led economies such as Ha Long Bay. A work plan was designed to identify actions and responsible parties across all levels of governance, including a significant role for the ASEAN in supporting member countries in the delivery of their actions.

The provision of training courses and a 'healthy tourism' accreditation system (especially for tour boats, hotels and restaurants in the case of Ha Long Bay) relating to waste management procedures to avoid water pollution, food safety, hygiene and food handling are all critical entry points and issues to protect the health of local people, visitors and the marine environment. But the key to the success of the 'healthy tourism' Strategic Framework is multiple stakeholder actions, including government at national and local levels, private sectors, non-governmental organisations and community, enabling 'healthy tourism' to become an effective management tool for the protection and development of healthy people and healthy places.

The government bodies need to review policy and legislation to ensure that compatible outcomes are feasible. Our research revealed that many different policies are at cross-purposes and that they mitigate against some of the desirable outcomes. Planning processes also require revision to ensure intersectoral collaboration and involvement in tourism planning. Most agencies not directly involved in tourism operations have no voice in tourism planning despite the potential for benefits and despite the numerous negative impacts directly related to tourism that these departments deal with, such as the health and environmental management issues noted in the case study.

The private sector, in particular tourism business, together with various non-governmental organisations, has an important role to play in education and raising awareness about tourism in the local community. The tourism industry has an ethical responsibility as part of good business practice to identify training needs of managers and employees and to raise an awareness of all the issues within their control (or influence) that affect the health and wellbeing of the wider community. Industry leaders are encouraged to devise accreditation procedures to ensure compliance with regulations and legislation. Research shows accreditation systems imposed on industry have limited effect. Systems owned by the sector and designed in a way that works for the industry are more likely to enjoy genuine uptake and effect. Equally, there should be incentives for operators whereby they are acknowledged and promoted to the visitor for contributing to the 'healthy tourism' approach. This is a useful marketing tool but also a means to enable visitors to identify and select ethical operations. This increases the incentive to be compliant and proactive. Industry should also be required to adhere to the 'polluter pays' principle and take responsibility for the various environmental management issues surrounding the operation of their businesses and not pass these on to local people and places through reduced environmental quality.

Community groups need to be encouraged and willing to become fully informed about tourism developments, to have input into the planning stages and to actively assist in monitoring and assessing the various impacts on the local community and their local environments.

Equally, the visitor has a role to play in 'healthy tourism' outcomes. Educational programmes can raise visitor awareness, encouraging more appropriate, socially and environmentally responsible behaviours. This can include adopting a 'stay another day ethic' to contribute to the local economy and the 'user pays' ethic in relation to community and public resources. Such approaches make visitors aware of the role of tourism and paying for the privilege of sharing special places with local people. Such taxes should be directly applied to monitoring and restoring damage caused by visitors, such as the impacts on water quality and the grottoes in the case of Ha Long Bay, and in time for better management and avoidance of problems and health consequences.

Conclusion

'Healthy tourism' represents an attitudinal shift. It provides a framework for tourism to work collaboratively across agencies and others to promote health and wellbeing of the local population and tourists. It encourages integrated tourism planning processes. The framework assists those responsible for tourism to develop an understanding of the interrelationships between tourism and health. It also assists in the development of strategies for capacity building. Rather than simply focus on dealing with issues or preventing health problems, it should bring health promotion and safety into tourism operations. It identifies the need for appropriate authorities to provide incentives to operators to develop sound practices.

There are many ways tourism and individual businesses can make a positive contribution to healthy living conditions, healthy work places and healthy families. This can include the absence of malnutrition and poverty; care for the environment; provision of adequate water and sanitation; developing positive attitudes; providing access to healthcare and education; the conservation of natural and cultural heritage; respecting family and community values; instituting community support systems, both informal and formal; supporting human rights – for women, children, disabled, ethnic minorities, migrants; encouraging political stability, access to justice, law and order; freedom of citizens; freedom of media; recognition of rights and responsibilities; employment opportunity; reducing reliance on imports; support of traditional industries, particularly agriculture; providing good working conditions; equitable distribution of wealth; recreation and leisure opportunities; access to sporting facilities; and access to public lands (Bushell and Staiff, 2001). As such, 'healthy tourism' is an ethical approach to tourism planning. It can deliver tangible benefits to all and move beyond the boundaries of usual thinking that the only benefits are economic and that stakeholders are those involved in the business of tourism.

Success comes from thinking outside the box, collaboration and cross-sectoral dialogue amongst government agencies and businesses. Developing appropriate indicators to measure progress of any new approach and providing evidence of the effectiveness of the process itself is important. This might include evidence of intersectoral collaboration; the monitoring, reporting and discussion of standards for water, sanitation, food safety, hygiene, waste management, road safety and their effectiveness in enforcement and prevention; researching broader issues of cultural change and gender issues; together with health-promoting initiatives relating to diet, exercise, smoking and alcohol consumption. 'Healthy tourism' becomes an entry point for health promotion. A 'healthy tourism' approach should be designed to integrate existing strategies, regulations, policies and guidelines. It should not reinvent them.

The case study highlighted the need to build capacity within both the health and tourism sectors, public and private. The research confirmed the need to place 'health' within the discourse and practices of sustainable tourism and to explore practical ways to protect and promote health by developing an understanding of the interrelationships between health and tourism.

Ensuring sound management systems, integrated processes, adequate environmental and public health infrastructure and services, appropriate training, business incentives and measurable and recognisable outcomes will foster industry, community and visitor support.

'As human populations and economies grow it has become increasingly impossible to improve one's own wellbeing without affecting others' (Prescott-Allen, 2001). Importantly, the 'healthy tourism' approach is intended to ensure that quality-of-life benefits flow to the most needy local people.

References

Akama, J. S. and Kieti, D. (2007) 'Tourism and socio-economic development in developing countries: A case study of Mombasa Resort in Kenya', *Journal of Sustainable Tourism*, 15(6), 735–748.

ASEAN (2008) *Record of Meeting. ASEAN Plus Three Workshop on 'Healthy Tourism'*, Bangkok, Thailand, 17–18 September 2008.

Bapoo-Dundoo, P. (2001) *Lessons Learned from GEF/SGP Funded Community-Based Tourism. SIDS IYE Regional Meeting*, Seychelles: UNEP-WTO.

Bushell, R. and Powis, B. (2009) *'Healthy Tourism' Report*, Jakarta, Indonesia: ASEAN Secretariat on Emerging Infectious Diseases.

Bushell, R. and Staiff, R. (2001) *Development of a Conceptual Framework for 'Healthy Tourism' in the Pacific Region*, Sydney: Western Pacific Regional Office of the World Health Organization and the UWS WHO Collaborating Centre for Environmental Health.

Conlin, M. C. and Baum, T. (eds) (1995) *Island Tourism: Management Principles and Practice*, New York: John Wiley.

DANTE (Die Arbeitsgemeinschaft für Nachhalfige Tourismus Entiwcklung) (2002) *Red Card for Tourism?* Basel, Switzerland: The NGO Network for Sustainable Tourism Development Working Group.

Haynes, M. (2008) *Current Tourism Status in Ha Long Bay and Recommendations for Visitor Management Strategy*, Commissioned report, Ha Noi, Gland, Switzerland, IUCN in collaboration with IUCN Viet Nam.

Kennedy, A. (2002) 'Mad and bad in Byron. Byron Bay has become too popular for its own good', *Sydney Morning Herald*, April 1, Sydney, 17.

Manning, E. D. and Prieur, S. (1998) *Governance for Tourism. Centre for a Sustainable Future*, Toronto, Canada: Foundation for International Training.

Mastny, L. (2001) *Travelling Light: New Paths for International Tourism*, WorldWatch Paper 159, Washington, DC: Worldwatch Institute.

McElroy, J. L. (2003) 'Tourism development in small islands across the world', *Geografisker Annaler*, 85B(4), 231–242.

Ministry of Culture, Sports and Tourism (2015) *National Tourism Statistics*, Hanoi: Vietnam National Administration of Tourism.

Ngone, A. (2001) *Challenges Facing the Tourism Industry in Small Island Developing Nations*, SIDS IYE Regional Meeting, Scychelles: UNEP-WTO.

Powis, B. (1999) *Healthy Islands: Policy, Practice and Problem Solving. A Brief History*, Hawkesbury: WHO Collaborating Centre, University of Western Sydney.

Prescott-Allen, R. (2001) *The Wellbeing of Nations: A Country-by-Country Index of Quality of Life*, Washington DC: Island Press.

Quang Ninh Administration of Culture, Sports and Tourism (2009) *'Healthy Tourism' Survey Response*, unpublished. ASEAN.

Richardson, R. B. (2010) *The Contribution of Tourism to Economic Growth and Food Security*, Mali: Report for USAID.

Ritchie, J., Sparks, M. and Rotem, A. (2000) *Regional Guidelines*, Sydney: University of New South Wales.

Sinha, C. and Bushell, R. (2002) 'Understanding the linkage between biodiversity and tourism: A study of ecotourism in a coastal village in Fiji', *Pacific Tourism Review*, 6, 35–50.

Task Force on Small States (TFSS) (2000) *Small States: Meeting Challenges in the Global Economy*, London: Commonwealth Secretariat and World Bank.

Taylor, R. (1994) *Pacific 2010: The Future, a Matter of Choice. National Centre for Development Studies*, Canberra: Australian National University, p. 23.

United Nations Conference on Trade and Development (2001) *Tourism and Development in the Least Developed Countries*, Geneva, Switzerland: UNCTAD, http://unctad.org/en/Docs/poldcm64.en.pdf.

United Nations Environment Programme (1999) *Environmental Outlooks for the Island Countries of the Caribbean, Indian Ocean and South Pacific*, Nairobi, Kenya: UNEP.

—— (2009) *A Three Year Journey for Sustainable Tourism*, Paris: UNEP.

World Health Organization (2009) *International Travel and Health*, Geneva, Switzerland: WHO.

World Heritage Committee (2009) *State of Conservation of World Heritage Properties Inscribed on the World Heritage List*, WHC-09/33.COM/7, Paris: UNESCO.

World Tourism Organization (1996) *Agenda 21 for the Travel and Tourism Industry: Towards Environmentally Sustainable Development*, Madrid, Spain: WTO, WTTC and Earth Council.

World Travel and Tourism Council (WTTC) (2015) *Travel and Tourism Economic Impact 2015*, London: WTTC.

9

Social tourism and health

Anya Diekmann and Scott McCabe

Introduction

In recent years social tourism has gained much attention from policy makers, stakeholder organisations, the European Commission (EC) and researchers within the tourism social science academy. Against the backdrop of the global economic crisis following 2007 and its enduring effects on the global economy, the discourse around social tourism emanating from a range of stakeholders, including academicians, policy makers and practitioners, has developed into a renewed understanding of social tourism's role in modern society.

This marked a transition from a focus on definitions of social tourism and a desire to map variations in meaning and applications of the concept across differing systems, practices and policies, mostly in various European country contexts. Recent research is characterised by a shift to a more sociopolitical approach linking the benefits of tourism, its impact on health and wellbeing and the relational differences in access to participation together with considerations of the consequences of these inequalities (see Eusébio et al., 2015; Komppula et al., 2016). This shift has been favoured by the increasing public and policy interest in health and wellbeing and the ever-growing appeal for a more social and inclusive Europe. A recognition of (social) tourism as a significant contributor to quality-of-life issues and in particular health as a component of wellbeing has led to reflections on the future of social tourism and its position within the broader tourism economy and system in many European countries (Minnaert et al., 2009).

The specific links between social tourism and health have, however, only recently begun to emerge and much further research is necessary to expand the empirical research base (Ferrer et al., 2015). This chapter aims to set the scene for this debate. After briefly reviewing the definition(s) of social tourism, the chapter aims to highlight the recent growth of social tourism research as well as related issues by critiquing the recent literature exploring health, tourism and quality of life/wellbeing. We conclude with a discussion of how these concepts can contribute to a redefinition of social tourism in a post-crisis European society of the future.

Social tourism, underpinning values and health

There is a myriad of definitions and understandings of the term social tourism depending on the country and the system in which it evolved (ISTO (BITS, 2003); Minnaert et al., 2007,

2009; McCabe et al., 2012; Diekmann and Jolin, 2013; etc.). The first definitions came with the institutionalisation of social tourism as part of the European welfare system after the Second World War, with holidays being organised for workers by trade unions or organisations connected to them. One of the forefathers of social tourism, Hunziker (1951) defined social tourism as 'the relationships and phenomena in the field of tourism resulting from participation in travel by economically weak or otherwise disadvantaged elements in society' (1). His peer and co-founder of the Bureau International du Tourisme Social (BITS)[1] Haulot (1982: 208) declares that 'Social tourism . . . finds justification in that its individual and collective objectives are consistent with the view that all measures taken by modern society should ensure more justice, more dignity and improved enjoyment of life for all citizens'. Haulot thus proposes the links between participation in tourism and the role of the state in advancing the dignity and wellbeing of all its citizens, also linking social tourism to modernity (Minnaert et al., 2012: xxx). Therefore the emphasis placed either in theorising social tourism or in policy making and practical initiatives is a sense of social justice and fair access to tourism opportunities regardless of means or status in society. An underpinning social welfare orientation together with an emphasis on citizens/consumers is what characterises the difference between social tourism and market-based tourism and other issues around social consequences of tourism.

Current definitions highlight the role that social tourism plays in stimulating participation and fostering social inclusion in holiday participation and to understanding the circumstances that constrain different groups from being able to fully engage in tourism. This key value is based on a fundamental idea that 'having a break' from daily life (and problems) contributes to the social, mental and physical wellbeing of all individuals and subsequently contributes to 'good' health. While in the beginning the focus was on low-income groups, social tourism is now understood in a more holistic framework and expressed as 'tourism for all', reflecting both an inclusionary agenda and the ethics underpinning important consumption opportunities, such as defined by Minnaert et al. (2007), as: 'tourism with an added moral value, of which the primary aim is to benefit either the host or the visitor in the tourism exchange' (7). These ethical values behind social tourism not only concern travellers/tourists, but extend to host communities and are close to the definition of the International Organisation for Social Tourism (ISTO). Yet the research surrounding the health effects of tourism is at best described as inconclusive and in some respects, this has negatively affected the case for social tourism in those (Western European) countries such as the UK which do not have well-embedded national systems of social tourism provision, since there has been a reluctance to create new policy or provision.

The values attached to these conceptions have guided social tourism policies in different European countries in terms of the measures established to provide access to participation. However, the various schemes in place tend to be piecemeal and the ideal of 'inclusion' is often sacrificed to enable a particular focus on segmented target groups. Indeed, while the underlying tone of social tourism is inclusionary, in reality most policies and interventions are directed towards specific target groups, for which positive health outcomes are not necessarily the main rationale for provision, such as those designed to encourage participation amongst young people which may be directed more towards experiential and learning goals. The segmented approach to social tourism implementation was embedded (perhaps enforced) through the EC preparatory action CALYPSO in 2009. However, it could be perceived as antagonistic to focus on target groups when the core values are inclusivity, social cohesion and tourism for all. From a practitioner perspective, such a segmented approach is of course justified as it calls for adapted tourism products and programmes. Indeed, targeting specific publics is considered useful to maximise available opportunities, since different target groups have different needs and opportunities for going on holidays. Yet one consequence seems to have been an inability to develop systematic research on the relationships between tourism participation and positive outcomes across a range of domains, including, but not exclusively, health.

For example, the EC is interested in understanding and determining the economic benefits from social tourism for the host regions – lowering seasonality, extending employment opportunities in peripheral economies, generating spending and local tax revenue and others. Yet there has not been an ability to generate comparable and compatible evidence to date. Despite this, a great deal of research has emerged in recent years, which both contributes to more general knowledge development regarding tourism's role in individual's lives and serves to broaden the level of interest in social tourism as a field of investigation. Research in social tourism has influenced recent research on the psychological and physiological effects of tourism on consumers, for example, which we consider in the following section.

Social tourism research and policy context

Social tourism has been on the political agenda of the social democratic countries of Europe since the 1980s when Haulot (1982) argued that tourism provision for the weaker social groups should be considered a welfare issue and therefore a governmental responsibility. In some countries as a consequence, social tourism has been subjected to research for some time, such as France (e.g. Lanquar and Raynouard, 1994; Chauvin, 2002). This has been notably due to a very active and important social tourism sector and research has focused on the social economy context in particular (Caire, 2002, 2007, 2012). Around the same time, under the impulse of social tourism stakeholders such as the Family Holiday Association, the ISTO, trade unions and local governments research was funded and initiated in various countries in Europe, mostly at the same time as the launching of the preparatory action of CALYPSO of the EC. Much of this research only touched upon the health-related issues amongst a wider range of issues.

Topics varied largely from employment in the sector, to more conceptual research on the benefits of social tourism, on the beneficiaries of the policies, the structural systems that existed and so on. As aforementioned and compared to other areas of tourism, social tourism is characterised by its national differences. It is not similar, for instance, to cultural or sustainable tourism, concepts that can be implemented with the public and private tourism sector only. In contrast, social tourism depends on a range of different stakeholders such as trade unions, health insurance associations, charities and of course governmental agencies. Each country involved in provision of services has different systems and policies, with some providing direct support to individuals (*aide à la personne*) and others supporting social tourism structures, such as accommodation centres (*aide à la pierre*). Still others have a mixture of different systems, including the commercial tourism sector as accommodation provider (Diekmann and McCabe, 2011).

This particular context is reflected in social tourism research for it is mainly nationally based. However, since its slow start in 2007, there has been a rapid increase in publications. Alongside the national research for social tourism stakeholders in different countries, ISTO also initiated a research platform[2] aiming at fostering exchange and debate among scholars working in different countries on their particular national context and organising an international conference every second year.

As explained above, target groups gained momentum through the publication of several books and papers focusing on families (e.g. Lehto et al., 2012; Schänzel et al., 2012; Such and Kay, 2012; Schänzel and Yeoman, 2015), elderly people (e.g. Leroux, 2010; Ahn and Janke, 2011; Nimrod and Rotem, 2012; Eusebio et al., 2013; Berninin and Cracolici, 2015) and people with disabilities (e.g. Buhalis and Darcy, 2011; Ferrer and Sanz, 2013). Particularly the elderly are a key focus for growing scholarly interest all over Europe. This development is, amongst others, connected to the growth of this segment as a whole and the associated societal changes as well, more pragmatically, the growing interest of the EC (and the accompanying research funds). Moreover researchers are looking increasingly into the benefits on social and mental health (see section below). Not only tourism scholars, but other disciplines, notably health sciences (medicine and psychology) became interested in the impact of travelling on senior citizens (see section below).

However, while research delivers increasingly empirical evidence of the benefits of tourism, in many European countries, the provision of social tourism is questioned by governments and funding schemes are cut or at least threatened. The main arguments refer to a very competitive commercial tourism market. That assertion is however built on the outdated concept of social tourism structures providing services mainly for workers (the creation of formal social tourism structures after the introduction of paid holidays: Minnaert et al., 2012; Diekmann, 2013; McCabe and Diekmann, 2015). These redundant considerations do not take into account deep social changes in European society and the emergence of 'new' groups (or individuals) in societies that are threatened by exclusion. Funding schemes have not yet adapted to the redefinition of social tourism characterised by participation and inclusion. By looking into the rights to tourism and the benefits for social and mental health and thus indirectly at the contribution of holidays to better quality of life, research becomes a political tool (maybe more than in other areas of tourism research).

However, even today, social tourism is not a key issue in tourism research. In 2014, a researcher initiated a discussion on Trinet[3] by asking the meaning of social tourism. Although since 2007, research (and with it, publications) into social tourism has significantly increased, the definitions posted by tourism academics had little bearing on the definitions of social tourism discussed in the previous section of this chapter. The suggestions covered community-based, sustainable and welfare tourism. Another misinterpretation of the term followed shortly in the international press when Europe's ministers debated immigration issues in Brussels. The journalists used the term social tourism for describing migrants allegedly aiming to benefit from European's social welfare systems.

These examples highlight the little existing knowledge on social tourism and with it the still too limited publications on the matter. It is clear that there is still much work to be done even in the tourism social science academy to widen knowledge and understanding of tourism as a social force and in particular social tourism, let alone in the wider business market for tourism and amongst policy circles.

Social tourism and health

As mentioned above, research on social tourism and health is not yet very widespread. One reason might be found in the inherent link between the two. Indeed, since the informal beginnings of social tourism movements back in the nineteenth century, the link with health has been a central principle. The fundamental idea of sending children of impoverished families to the seaside was to improve their health. Since the late eighteenth century when it was declared that the seaside atmosphere could contribute to an improvement in a range of health issues, which incidentally were largely attributable to the poor-quality conditions of urban environments, there has been a steady link between social tourism and health (Beckerson and Walton, 2005: 55). Others started organising excursions in the alps and nature hikes aimed at providing factory workers with fresh air (Baumgartner, 2012) or allowing young mothers to spend a couple of weeks in holiday centres to recover from giving birth, which was specifically intended to enforce their good health (Carpenter, 2001). Many more examples, highlighting the close connection with health as the ultimate aim for a break, could be cited throughout social tourism history. Moreover, since their development from the eighteenth century onwards, thermal and cure destinations mostly provided accommodation for the treatment of disadvantaged people, such as the Hôpital de Vichy in France (Gordon, 2012). However, the extent to which modern spa and wellness facilities remain accessible for people from disadvantaged backgrounds is a moot point.

Even without significant research in the second half of the twentieth century, evidencing the link between health and social tourism, the positive impact of holidays on social and mental health and wellbeing was common knowledge (Hobson and Dietrich, 1995). In a recent literature review on the health and wellness outcomes of tourism, Chen and Petrick (2013) noted a broad range of approaches that have been applied to understand the links between tourism and health and this perhaps underlines why there has been only partial progress in making systematic knowledge claims. They tackled research which has asserted links between holiday taking and quality of life, health, stress reduction, active life and healthy lifestyle, highlighting however a significant gap in research, as most studies had focused on the positive outcomes of travel associated with wellbeing and quality of life with relatively fewer focusing on the effects on mental and physical health. Only a number of negative consequences associated with 'leisure sickness' have been researched so far.

In the English-speaking context, there has been intermittent interest in research on social tourism since the 1970s, from a range of sources, including the trade unions. The English Tourist Board/Trades Union Congress report in 1976 initiated a conversation generated from the then English Tourism Board, which touched upon health benefits associated with holidays for English working people. This interest in social tourism issues extended to a focus on disability rights and accessibility (English Tourism Council, 2000), which in some form remains a key pillar of the work of the now Visit England in their business support function (www.visitengland.com/biz/advice-and-support/businesses/providing-access-all). A specific early study was commissioned by the Local Government Authority in 2001 that focused primarily on health outcomes from tourism. Of a survey of 271 doctors (general practitioners), this survey found that: 90 per cent thought that most types of holiday had some benefit to health and wellbeing, particularly those with some form of engagement (physical, social or intellectual); 89 per cent believed that holidays helped alleviate depression, stress-related illness, alcohol and drug dependency and insomnia; 59 per cent believed that not taking holidays negatively affects family health; and 65 per cent felt that non-participation could have a negative effect on individual health.

Yet apart from some specific interventions from academics touching on the health issues in the context of research in disadvantage and culture and practice around holiday making (cf. Richards, 1999; Smith and Hughes, 1999), it is only much more recently that research in health in English-language publishing has begun to emerge. Minnaert et al. (2009) linked potential health outcomes to social tourism initiatives and social policy for example and McCabe (2009) also found that mental health in particular was often cited as a beneficial outcome of social tourism programmes. Yet tourism opportunities for most people provide an important outlet for leisure and recuperation from stresses associated with work and pressures of daily life. In this perspective a number of studies have found possible relationships between health-related concepts. Quinn et al. (2008), for example, explored the wellbeing of children in low-income families that participated in social tourism programmes and found improvements. Bergier et al. (2010) connected social tourism with improved self-reported health as well as social and personal factors amongst disabled people who attested to improvements in health condition and increased efficiency and physical capacity following participation in tourism, leisure and sport activities. McCabe and Johnson (2013) assessed changes in subjective wellbeing assessments amongst low-income families prior to and after a social tourism intervention. This study concluded that the social/relational aspects of wellbeing and those linked to personal resources and psychological flourishing, associated with good mental health were significantly improved after a holiday.

Thus social tourism has been identified as a possible source of intervention in social and health programmes. In the context of elderly people, a number of studies have reported improvements in perceived health conditions (PriceWaterHouseCoopers, 2004; de Aguiar et al., 2012) and their physical activity increased during their holiday (Paulo et al., 2004; IMSERSO, 2011). A recent study aimed to specifically address the links between social tourism and active ageing, by examining older people's participation in tourism to self-reported global health states (Ferrer et al., 2015). This study found links through a structural equation modelling technique that suggested that healthy people are more active and are more likely to want to participate in tourism and conversely that tourism participation contributed to positive health assessments and active ageing. Social tourism has also been linked with improvements of tourists' perceptions of self-sufficiency, independence, security and capacity. Furthermore, people with disabilities see holidays as an opportunity to recognise themselves as 'able' persons (Blichfeldt and Nicolaisen, 2011). Finally, tourism contributes to feelings of citizenship (EESC, 2006) and Minnaert et al. (2009) argued that social inclusion outcomes held one of the greatest areas of potential for social tourism programmes. Social isolation is a key issue for older people and is linked to mental health issues (IMSERSO, 2011; de Aguiar et al., 2012).

There is a growing set of examples of research undertaken by medical sciences researchers which have highlighted the contribution of holidays to physiological health. These studies go beyond the context of social tourism and have assessed the links between participation in tourism generally and health outcomes. Gump and Matthews (2000), for example, examined health and wellbeing on holiday and on return to work and found marginal improvements in self-reported health. Wei and Milman (2002) found positive wellbeing outcomes from travel amongst older people. Engaging with distractive activities eliminating or lowering external stress factors during holidays has proven to be particularly positive for mental and physical health (Luminet, 2008). Westman and Etzion (2001) found out that holidays reduce the risk of burnout and absenteeism, even after a short break and that they could help in reducing chronic pain (Strauss-Balsche et al., 2002).

Social tourism research *per se* has focused much more consistently on the leisure aspects of initiatives rather than health aspects, although many practitioners and academics agree that tourism has 'restorative' capabilities if provided at the right time and if individuals and families are provided with the right levels of support and the right types of holidays to meet their needs. 'Changing the setting' or 'having a break' is believed to help people to move on with their lives, leading to potential transformations in outlook or behaviours. As intermediaries for social tourism provision, health insurance organisations were originally and obviously remain, best placed to develop specific health-related tourism products. For instance, the Catholic insurance organisation in Belgium supports many tours each year to the pilgrimage destination at Lourdes in France for people suffering from various physical health issues and disabilities. This linking of health, pilgrimage and tourism is an important additional dimension to the wellness tourism field. What is important to underline is that social tourism is not health tourism but aims at a holistic and rounded sense of personal health and wellbeing, the complete person, through fostering mental and physical wellbeing together.

Conclusions

The chapter has aimed to highlight the connection between health and social tourism, in particular to understand the issues which have led to the rather fragmented nature of the research in this area. While health and wellness are important motivators for much tourism within the market-based tourism system, there remains a significant minority of the population of European countries which cannot access tourism for many different reasons. Barriers to access exist at different levels but financial constraints are consistently the most important factor. This is important, since wellness tourism products and services tend to focus on the luxury market, thereby working to further exclude many already disadvantaged people. Accessibility barriers are not only financial, however, but also include mobility and competence issues.

The need for additional support for people with fragile or complex issues is a further factor to be considered. Therefore a more comprehensive system of support is required as opposed to purely financial assistance if social tourism is to truly contribute to improved health and wellbeing outcomes. From an economic perspective it is clear from some important analysis of the senior tourism programmes in place in Spain and Portugal that social tourism has an important role to play as an economic stimulus to the economies in the low season. These include the health and wellness sector. There is, furthermore, tentative evidence to suggest that improved health and wellbeing can lead to indirect contributions to society through reduced public spending on health and social support. The study by Eusébio and colleagues (2015) specifically asked respondents to estimate the reduction in healthcare costs attributable to the outcomes of the holiday. The study found significant savings were identified.

From a human and social perspective, we propose that much further and detailed research is required to develop deeper understanding of the links between health and tourism participation. Clearly there is a need for balanced research in this regard. Not all tourism activity produces positive health outcomes. Much tourism is driven by primarily hedonic motives and individuals generally wish to relax and enjoy their travel experiences. This can lead to negative health consequences, such as inactivity, over-indulgence in food and drink, engagement in risky behaviours and increased stress associated with travel, which are just some of the range of factors that may impact on health. Yet we would argue that these more negative consequences are largely an issue for the market-based tourism system and that social tourism initiatives tend to focus on people in circumstances and with issues that are driven by motives based on 'recovery' rather than pure hedonism. Whilst escapism may be a critical motive, the focus for many social tourism beneficiaries is on broadening horizons and seeing problems in a different light.

Finally, in developed societies tourism is not a privilege, but can be considered as a social right (see McCabe and Diekmann, 2015). Indeed a regular annual break can provide benefits in many different ways but in particular, mental health. It is imperative that further research is undertaken with a multidisciplinary focus on the physical and mental health outcomes associated with a range of tourism contexts and that research should seek to be integrative and cut across different social tourism segment groups. However, the over-riding importance is that research is able to relate to and inform policy development in health, social policy and tourism so that findings can be transferred between policy areas, which may well lead to a more integrated approach to social tourism in the future.

Case study: BEST project (Bien-être, Emploi, Santé, Tourisme social)

In the framework of the social innovation research programme Germaine Tillion of the Walloon region (Belgium), two Belgian universities (Université Libre de Bruxelles and Louvain-La-Neuve) collaborated in a 3-year multidisciplinary research project on the impacts of tourism on the

(continued)

(continued)

wellbeing of senior citizens. First, the project aimed to understand the relationship between holiday taking and seniors' wellbeing, in terms of mental and physical health. Second, it sought to discover how senior holidays can be beneficial to the local economy. The project therefore extends recent studies that have demonstrated the positive effects of holidays on quality of life and wellbeing among different population groups.

In partnership with the social tourism provider Énéo, a division of the Christian health insurance organisation, two researchers participated in an organised trip for seniors in June 2015. The 1-week stay took place in a hotel in Mariakerke, a small seaside resort on the Belgian coast. A total of 77 seniors took part in the trip experience. The average age was 78 and most of the participants were over 80 years old. During the trip, several optional activities such as excursions, sports and games were included in the programme.

In order to analyse the seniors' tourist experience, a participant observation method was selected. Researchers were introduced to the tourist group on the first day. Interactions between participants and researchers occurred during meals, excursions or unplanned meetings inside and outside the hotel during the trip. In addition, semi-structured interviews with participants were conducted on a voluntary and anonymous basis. Interviews addressed various issues such as motivations, expectations and experiences. In total, eight interviews with 15 participants were conducted.

Based on observations and interviews made during this trip, interim conclusions regarding the relationship between holiday taking and seniors' health are:

- Social interactions with relatives or new people affect seniors' social health perceptions. Furthermore, feelings of loneliness were reduced during the trip.
- The break from daily routines seems to have positive effects on perceived mental health. Opportunities to forget worries arise from the trip.
- There is little evidence of direct effects on physical health. Nevertheless, many participants explained the need to be active in their daily life to feel physically well. In this regard, the trip provided many opportunities to be active.
- The pre-trip experience was different for all the participants. Participants identified varying levels of stress prior to the holiday. Nevertheless, a common experience of the pre-trip period seemed to be a form of self-projection and individual involvement which positively affected mental and social health.
- Given the high average age of the group, the accompanying team of volunteers and a nurse played an important role in seniors' feelings of security and wellbeing during the trip.
- Some activities such as games and excursions were perceived as opportunities of learning or thinking and therefore were valued by participants as affecting positively their cognitive health.

Notes

1 Since 2012, International Organisation of Social Tourism (ISTO).
2 The Alliance on Training and Research in Social and Fair Tourism was officially launched in 2010 and is one of the key networks of ISTO (http://www.oits-isto.org/oits/public/section.jsf?id=181).
3 Tourism Research Network with around 2,000 members worldwide hosted by the University of Hawaii.

References

Ahn, Y.-J. and Janke, M. C. (2011) 'Motivations and benefits of the travel experiences of older adults', *Educational Gerontology*, 37(8), 653–673.

Baumgartner, C. (2012) 'Social tourism and sustainability', in McCabe, S., Minnaert, L. and Diekmann, A. (eds) *Social Tourism in Europe: Theory and Practice*, Bristol, UK: Channel View, pp. 166–177.

Beckerson, J. and Walton, J. (2005) 'Selling air: Marketing the intangible at British resorts', in Walton, J. (ed.) *Histories of Tourism: Representation, Identity and Conflict*, Bristol, UK: Channel View, pp. 55–70.

Bergier, B., Bergier, J. and Kubińska, Z. (2010) 'Environmental determinants of participation in tourism and recreation of people with varying degrees of disability', *Journal of Toxicology and Environmental Health*, 73(17–18), 1134–1140.

Berninin, C. and Cracolici, M. F. (2015) 'Demographic change, tourism expediture and life cycle behaviour', *Tourism Management*, 45, 191–205.

BITS (2003) *Statutes*, Brussels: BITS.

Blichfeldt, B. A. and Nicolaisen, J. (2011) 'Disabled travel: Not easy, but doable', *Current Issues in Tourism*, 14 (1), 79–102.

Buhalis, D. and Darcy, S. (2011) *Accessible Tourism: Concepts and Issues*, Bristol, UK: Channel View.

Caire, G. (2002) *Economie de la protection sociale*, Paris: Bréal, p. 240.

—— (2007) 'Les associations françaises de tourisme: de l'impulsion d'un marché de masse aux difficultés d'un "autre" tourisme', in Dusset, A. and Lauzanas, J. M. (dir.) *L'économie sociale entre informel et formel: Paradoxes et innovations*, Rennes, France: Presses Universitaires de Rennes, pp. 129–150.

—— (2012) 'Social tourism and social economy', in McCabe, S., Minnaert, L. and Diekmann, A. (eds) *Social Tourism in Europe: Theory and Practice*, Bristol, UK: Channel View, pp. 73–88.

Carpenter, K. M. N. (2001) '"For mothers only": Mothers' convalescent homes and modernizing maternal ideology in 1950s West Germany', *Journal of Social History*, 34(4), 865–893.

Chauvin, J. (2002) *Le tourisme social et associatif en France*, Paris: L'Harmattan, p. 176.

Chen, C-C. and Petrick, J. F. (2013) 'Health and wellness benefits of travel experiences: A literature review', *Journal of Travel Research*, 52(6), 709–719.

de Aguiar, M. C., Aibéo, M. J., Kastenhols, E. and Dourado, H. M. (2012) *Social Tourism Programmes: Report I*, Portugal: Universidade de Aveiro and Fundación INATEL.

Diekmann, A. (2013) 'Le droit aux vacances: Concept fondateur du tourisme social', *Cahier Espaces*, 310: 70–74.

Diekmann, A. and Jolin, L. (eds) (2013) *Regards croisés sur le tourisme social dans le monde: l'apport de la recherche*, Quebec, Canada: Presses de l'Université du Québec.

Diekmann, A. and McCabe, S. (2011) 'Systems of social tourism in the European Union: A comparative study', *Current Issues in Tourism*, 14(5), 417–430.

EESC (2006) *Opinion of the Economic and Social Committee on Social Tourism in Europe*, Brussels, Belgium: European Economic and Social Committee.

English Tourism Council (2000) *Just What the Doctor Ordered: The Health Benefits of Holidays, Research and Intelligence, GP Omnibus 2000*, London: English Tourism Council.

English Tourist Board/Trades Union Congress (1976) *Holidays: The Social Need*, London: English Tourist Board.

Eusebio, C., Carneiro, J. M., Kastenholz, E. and Alvelos, H. (2013) 'The socioeconomic impacts of INATEL social tourism programs for the senior market', in Diekmann, A. and Jolin, L. (eds) *Regards croisés sur le tourisme social dans le monde*, Quebec, Canada: Presses de l'Université du Québec, pp. 197–214.

—— (2015) 'Social tourism programmes for the senior market: A benefit segmentation analysis', *Journal of Tourism and Cultural Change*, pp. 1–21.

Ferrer, J. and Sanz M. (2013) 'Accessible social tourism: A new concept for developing social tourism policy in Europe', in Diekmann, A. and Jolin, L. (dir.) *Regards croisés sur le tourisme social dans le monde*, Quebec, Canada: Presses de l'Université du Québec, pp. 13–28.

Ferrer, J. G., Ferri, M., Ferrandis, E. D., McCabe, S. and Garcia, J. S. (2015) 'Social tourism and healthy aging', *International Journal of Tourism Research*, DOI: 10.1002/jtr.2048.

Gordon, B. (2012) 'Reinventions of a spa town: The unique case of Vichy', *Journal of Tourism History*, 4(1), 35–55.

Gump, B. B. and Matthews, K. A. (2000) 'Are vacations good for your health? The 9-year mortality experience after the multiple risk factor intervention trial', *Psychosomatic Medicine*, 62, 608–612.

Haulot, A. (1982) 'Social tourism: Current dimensions of future developments', *Journal of Travel Research*, 20–40.

Hobson, J. S. P. and Dietrich, U. C. (1995) 'Tourism, health and quality of life', *Journal of Travel and Tourism Marketing*, 3(4), 21–38.

Hunziker, W. (1951) *Social Tourism: Its Nature and Problems. No Place*, Bern: International Tourists Alliance Scientific Commission.

IMSERSO (2011) *Social Tourism Inquiry*, http://nationbuilder.s3.amazonaws.com/appgonsocialtourism/pages/23/attachments/original/IMSERSO_-_SOCIAL_TOURISM_INQUIRY.pdf?1314889620 (accessed 23 December 2012).

Komppula, R., Ilves, R. and Airey, D. (2016) 'Social holidays as a tourist experience in Finland', *Tourism Management*, 52, 521–532.

Lanquar, R. and Raynouard, Y. (1994) *Le tourisme social et associatif*, QSJ n°1725, Paris: PUF.

Lehto, X. Y., Lin, Y.-C., Chen, Y. and Choi, S. (2012) 'Family vacation activities and family cohesion', *Journal of Travel and Tourism Marketing*, 29, 835–850.

Leroux, E. (2010) 'Comportement des seniors et tourisme: l'effet modérateur de la variable santé', *Gérontologie et Société*, 135, 153–166.

Luminet, O. (2008) *Psychologie des émotions. Confrontation et évitement*, Brussels, Belgium: De Boeck.

McCabe, S. (2009) '"Who needs a holiday?" Evaluating social tourism', *Annals of Tourism Research*, 36(4), 667–688.

McCabe, S. and Diekmann, A. (2015) 'The rights to tourism: Reflections on social tourism and human rights', *Tourism Travel Research*, 40(2), 194–204.

McCabe, S. and Johnson, S. (2013) 'The happiness factor in tourism: Subjective wellbeing and social tourism', *Annals of Tourism Research*, 41, 42–65.

McCabe, S., Minnaert, L. and Diekmann, A. (dir.) (2012) *Social Tourism in Europe: Theory and Practice*, Bristol, UK: Channel View

Minnaert, L., Diekmann, A. and McCabe, S. (2012) 'Defining social tourism and its historical context', in McCabe, S., Minnaert, L. and Diekmann, A. (eds) *Social Tourism in Europe: Theory and Practice*, Bristol, UK: Channel View, pp. 18–31.

Minnaert, L., Maitland, R. and Miller, G. (2007) 'Social tourism and its ethical foundations', *Tourism, Culture and Communication*, 7, 7–17.

—— (2009) 'Tourism and social policy: The value of social tourism', *Annals of Tourism Research*, 36(2), 316–334.

Nimrod, G. and Rotem, A. (2012) 'An exploration of the innovation theory of successful ageing among older tourists', *International Journal of Tourism Research*, 12, pp. 65–78. doi: 10.1002/jtr.739.

Paulo, P., Carrasco, M., Cabezas, M., Gac, H., Hoyl, T., Duery, P., Petersen, K. and Dussaillant, K. (2004) 'Impacto biomédico de los viajes en adultos mayores chilenos', *Revista Médica Chile*, 132, 573–578.

PriceWaterhouseCoopers (2004) *Estudio sobre el programa de vacaciones para mayores del IMSERSO*, PriceWaterhouseCoopers.

Quinn, B., Griffin, K. A. and Stacey, J. (2008) *Poverty, Social Exclusion and Holidaying: Towards Developing Policy in Ireland*, Dublin, Ireland: Combat Poverty Agency.

Richards, G. (1999) 'Vacations and the quality of life: Patterns and structures', *Journal of Business Research*, 44, 189–198.

Schänzel, H. and Yeoman, I. (2015) 'The future of family tourism', *Tourism Recreation Research*, 39(3), 343–360.

Schänzel, H., Yeoman, I. and Backer, E. (2012) *Family Tourism Multidisciplinary Perspectives*, Bristol, UK: Channel View.

Smith, V. and Hughes, H. (1999) 'Disadvantaged families and the meaning of the holiday', *International Journal of Tourism Research*, 1(2), 123–133.

Strauss-Blasche, G., Ekmekcioglu, C. and Marktl, W. (2002) 'Moderating effects of vacation on reactions to work and domestic stress', *Leisure Sciences*, 24(2), 237–249.

Such, E. and Kay, T. (2012) 'The family factor in social tourism', in McCabe, S., Minnaert, L. and Diekmann, A. (eds) *Social Tourism in Europe: Theory and Practice*, Bristol, UK: Channel View, pp. 126–141.

Wei, S. and Milman, A. (2002) 'The impact of participation in activities while on vacation on seniors' psychological wellbeing: A path model application', *Journal of Hospitality and Tourism Research*, 26(2), 175–185.

Westman, M. and Etzion, D. (2001) 'The impact of vacation and job stress on burnout and absenteeism', *Psychology and Health*, 16, 595–606.

10

A life-course analysis of older tourists and their changing patterns of holiday behaviour

Gareth Shaw, Isabelle Cloquet, Paul Cleave, Andrzej Tucki, Maria João F. Custódio and Alessandra Theuma

Introduction

The population of many Western economies is ageing, as illustrated within the EU, where currently 17 per cent of the population is over 65. Moreover, the demographic old-age dependency ratio is projected to rise from the current 28 per cent to 50 per cent by 2060 (European Commission, 2015). There are two dimensions to these trends. The first is that tourists over 65 are playing an increasingly important role within the tourism industry. The second is that tourism is more and more considered for its wellbeing benefits and consequently as a strategy for relieving pressures on healthcare public spending. The chapter aims to gain deeper knowledge on both phenomena by looking into elderly people's travelling behaviours pre- and post-retirement and their meaning in terms of a sense of a wellbeing.

Within ageing societies like South Korea, the USA and Europe, the senior market has been recognised as critical in overcoming issues of seasonality, providing an important part of off-peak demand (Borges Tiago, de Almeida Couto, Gomes Borges Tiago and Costa Dias Faria, 2016; Kim, Woo and Uysal, 2015; Lee and Tideswell, 2005). Moreover, many retired citizens have both purchasing power and certainly more leisure time available than other market segments. To illustrate this, during the financial crisis between 2006 and 2011, the senior age group was a significant contributor to the tourism sector's revival in Europe. During this period they spent 33 per cent more on tourism in 2011 than in 2006, with 10 per cent more of this age group (over 65) participating in tourism and travel. Even taking account of the growth of this group by 6 per cent over that period, it still represents a clear net gain (Demunter, 2012). According to a number of authors the current seniors group are more self-confident and fun loving than their parents (Hawes, 2004; Horx, 2003). More recent research by Borges Tiago et al. (2016) has developed these ideas further through an examination of the tourism behaviour of the 'baby boomers' generation, that is, people born between approximately 1946 and 1965. Compared to the generation before, this so-called 'mature and silent generation', the 'baby boomers' have had on the whole better healthcare and are able to and want to undertake more holidays, being able to travel more later in life. According to Sharpley and Stone (2012: 14), there is "an array of choices from which to select packaged vacations and typical destinations, whilst aiming for new experiences – or at least customized ones'.

In contrast to this view, the age dependency within the EU is expected to greatly increase the public spend on healthcare, presenting long-term challenges (European Commission, 2015). Some of the main factors affecting older people include decreased mental and physical activity, as well as problems of isolation. The challenge in this context is thus developing strategies that act on these factors and thereby keep older people in good health. Tourism is being presented as having a role to play in helping maintain and even increase the physical, mental and relational wellbeing of older people. Recent research has argued that tourism has positive impacts, offering a variety of opportunities to engage or re-engage in activities that can contribute to health and wellbeing (Nimrod and Rotem, 2010). Moreover, there is a range of emerging evidence suggesting that engaging in new experiences, feeling a sense of being away, as well as connecting with various ecosystems and environments are associated with psychological, cognitive and social benefits (Rose, 2012).

In addition, Dolnicar, Yanamandram and Cliff (2012), who explored people's satisfaction with life domains and corroborated previous findings on the contribution of holidays to people's quality of life, highlighted that holidays tend to mean different things to different individuals at different stages of their life. It is this particular observation that is addressed in this chapter by exploring changes in travel behaviour over the (later) life time and their implications in terms of wellbeing. It does so through the lens of life-course analysis that focuses attention on individual experiences of transitions. Most of the studies today have tended to be very cross-sectional in nature and have neglected the changes related to different generational groups, as pointed out, for example, by Borges Tiago et al. (2016). The chapter begins with a critical examination of the extant literature on the relations between tourism and wellbeing. The first section ends by introducing the conceptual framework adopted for the purpose of this study. The following section introduces the concept and application of life-course analysis in the understanding of tourist behaviour. Finally, the chapter presents and discusses some initial findings from a case study of older tourists within the UK regarding changes in patterns of behaviour and feelings of wellbeing over their life-course.

Tourism and wellbeing: issues arising from multiple constructs and measures

There is a multiplicity of constructs related to the notion of wellbeing. Among the most frequently used in the literature are those of subjective wellbeing, life satisfaction, quality of life, happiness, welfare and flourishing. Often used as synonyms, these concepts have slight differences which can be summarised as follows. Subjective wellbeing integrates emotional (i.e. positive and negative affects) and cognitive components (i.e. individual's judgement of one's life and life domains), whereas life satisfaction and quality of life tend to include cognitive elements only (see Diener, Suh, Lucas and Smith, 1999; Dolnicar et al., 2012; Schimmack, 2008). Welfare tends to adopt an 'objective' perspective, contrasting with the subjective approach of the other concepts. Happiness tends to be used both to refer to the affective dimension of wellbeing and as a synonym of subjective wellbeing (see Nawijn, 2011; Nawijn, Marchand, Veenhoven and Vingerhoets, 2010). The notion of flourishing adds a long-term perspective to the aforementioned approaches; it combines positive emotions with the fulfilment of aspects of human potential, including a sense of meaning/purpose in life, engagement/involvement in life, positive relationships and achievement (see Filep, 2014; Filep and Deery, 2010; Friedman and Kern, 2014; Kler and Tribe, 2012).

All of these constructs have been used to varying degrees within the context of tourism. There has been a noticeable predominance of subjective wellbeing (Gilbert and Abdullah,

2004; McCabe and Johnson, 2013) and of measures of affective and/or cognitive components (Dolnicar et al., 2012). A primary source of information on an individual's subjective experience has thus been the person's self-reported feelings and judgement. In their review paper, Chen and Petrick (2013) identified 27 papers, the vast majority of which adopted a subjective approach, with subjective wellbeing and quality of life being central constructs. Only three studies utilised physiological measures of health in an attempt at gaining some objectivity. Interestingly, of these only two confirmed the positive importance of holidays on health, namely Toda et al.'s (2004) study in Japan of females and Tarumi, Hagihara and Moimoto's (1998) study of 551 employees, again undertaken in Japan (see Chen and Petrick, 2013).

Based on the evidence found in the papers they reviewed, the authors (Chen and Petrick, 2013) constructed an overview of levels of 'life satisfaction' at four different strategic stages in the life cycle of the holiday, distinguishing between anticipation (before the holiday), experience (during the holiday), beneficial (towards the end and just after the holiday) and fade out in the post-holiday phase. Of course, such a perspective, although interesting, is based on a variety of studies using different measures and as such it is difficult to compare across these various stages.

Tourism, wellbeing and the elderly: a behaviour-centred analytical framework

There is an increasing range of literature relating to understanding and improving ageing and the health and wellbeing of older people. Such literature is characterised by its interdisciplinary nature. The links between research in social gerontology and tourism and leisure studies are relatively new but are increasing rapidly. Much of the work has related to aspects of leisure and ageing, although more recently the focus on tourism has developed. Within both contexts the links with social gerontology have been via aspects of active ageing, subjective wellbeing, along with theories relating to engagement/activation, disengagement and continuity (see Nimrod, 2008).

The emphasis on ideas of responsible or active ageing followed the report of the World Health Organization (2002) which highlighted the goals of maintaining a degree of independence and autonomy of older people. The latter is the ability to control and make personal decisions whilst the former concerns being able to perform these findings. In this context the term 'active ageing' relates to the engagement with various physical and mental activities. Such ideas of responsible ageing have emerged from social gerontology (Davey, 2002; for reviews, see Franklin and Tate, 2009; Katz, 2013). As Seitsamo (2007: 11) explains, such approaches are based 'on the maintenance of health through lifestyle choices that encapsulate aspects of personal wellbeing'. The active ageing approach certainly points to the influence that the nature of holidays may have on the way that health and wellbeing are enhanced.

Clearly intersecting in many respects with the general notions of active ageing is research on the importance of both 'green' and 'blue' spaces on wellbeing, notably via the notions of therapeutic landscapes (Gesler, 1991) and of restorative environments (Kaplan and Kaplan, 1989). The relationships between landscapes and health-promoting products and feelings of wellbeing have been reviewed by a number of authors. One example is Morris' (2003) wide-ranging review of open spaces, health and wellbeing. The author identified five key ways in which such beneficial effects occur: enhanced personal skills, increased physical activity, enhanced mental and spiritual health, sensory and aesthetic awareness and ability to assert personal control along with increasing awareness of personal wellbeing. Others have undertaken more systematic reviews of the health-promoting aspects of different environments, with Abraham and Sommerhalder and Abel (2010) examining landscape types and their impacts on health. They concluded there was a requirement to understand the needs of different social or user groups and their relationships with different landscapes. This is certainly the case with regard to older tourists, as explored by Sugiyama and Thompson (2007). In this study they point to the dilemma of outdoor recreation for older people along with opportunities if physical barriers can be overcome. They also point to the relatively little research in this area, despite its significance in the active ageing agenda (see also the review by Wahl and Weisman, 2003).

The focus on older people and holidays may be viewed from the perspective of subjective wellbeing and/or quality of life. Studies in this area have also showed a number of interesting findings. Early work by Milman (1998) found that the experience of the holiday and the levels of activity undertaken had no measurable effect on the feelings and perceptions of wellbeing. He concluded that this may have been due to the relatively small sample of just 124 respondents and their rather homogeneous characteristics. Following this study Wei and Milman (2002) undertook further work on a larger sample of 300 senior tourists and found evidence of those involved in more activities whilst on holiday appeared to benefit more in terms of their sense of wellbeing. Using a structural equation modelling approach based on a sample of 208 Koreans aged between 55 and 64, Kim et al. (2015) found that leisure life satisfaction and satisfaction with travel experience are significant predictors of quality of life.

The problems with these studies are not only differences in measurement terms but also the different types of holidays being undertaken. For example, Milman (1998) and Wei and Milman (2002) focused on older tourists on escorted tours, which was also the case in Kim et al.'s (2015) research. Gilbert and Abdullah (2004) argued that other factors also hindered such studies, including the timing of when measurements of satisfaction took place. Their work went on to compare two groups of seniors, those taking holidays and those not. They concluded that the former had increased levels of subjective wellbeing compared to the latter group.

A further important issue – yet not derived from the literature on the elderly – concerns the relationship between subjective wellbeing gained on holidays and its potential to spill over into overall life satisfaction. Early work by Neal, Sirgy and Uysal (1999) highlighted a spillover link between satisfaction with travel/tourism services on satisfaction with travel/tourism experiences and in turn through to general life satisfaction. Interestingly, the authors' findings did not support the hypothesis of a significant predictive relationship between satisfaction with travel/tourism experiences and satisfaction with leisure life. This further supports the idea of direct effects of holidays on life satisfaction. The effect of length of stay has also received attention, with most studies finding no significant correlation with affective components of wellbeing (e.g. Nawijn et al., 2010) or satisfaction with life (Neal, Uysal and Sirgy, 2007). However, Neal et al. (2007) found some indication of a moderating effect of length of stay on the relationship between satisfaction with leisure life and satisfaction with life in general. Sirgy, Kruger, Lee and Yu (2011) drew attention to two key issues in their research, the first being the limited understanding we have on the nature of spillover between holiday satisfaction and overall life satisfaction. The second, based on their empirical study in South Africa, was that positive affect derived from holidays has positive effects on satisfaction with most life domains, but, interestingly, not with regard to health and safety and self.

A final area of literature relates to the ideas of changing leisure and holiday behaviour of older tourists. Nimrod (2008: 859) provides a partial review of studies examining 'tourism in later life', and in doing so she fits her study around theories drawn from social gerontology. She explores a number of propositions relating to tourism during the retirement phase. These are summarised below and their relationship to broader theories is indicated.

- The centrality of tourism in retirement: this follows work by Weiss (2005), arguing that more opportunities are available post-retirement. Other studies by Gibson (2002) and Statts and Pierfelice (2003) support the views of the increased importance of tourism post-retirement. Nimrod (2008) found evidence that, along with increased opportunities, older tourists had to think more about navigating constraints.
- Post-retirement tourism becomes a compensation for other losses following retirement and helps retired people to preserve pre-retirement roles (e.g. work-related roles). In a broader context these ideas are reviewed by Wang, Henkens and van Solinge (2011), who also view retirement in terms of 'a challenge to personal wellbeing'. The development and application of continuity theory by Atchley (1999) see this in terms of an adaptive strategy for dealing with issues related to getting older, mainly in the retirement stage of their life-course.
- During later stages of retirement researchers have highlighted the need to develop negotiating strategies to overcome increasing constraints related to ageing (Blazey, 1992; Hubbard and Mannell, 2007). Nimrod (2008) points out that these negotiating strategies can be viewed in terms of the selective optimisation and compensation model (as presented by Baltes and Carstensen, 1996). This simply sees successful ageing as merely making the best of possible opportunities by adapting to conditions.

This chapter builds on Nimrod's findings and theories by adopting a life-course analysis approach. Indeed, although Nimrod's work highlights the ideas of different life phases, these are unfortunately not fully developed in this context. It is worth mentioning that in a small number of cases tourism researchers have used the notion of life-course as a means of suggesting changes over time. For example, Gibson and Yannakis (2002) have examined tourist roles (in terms of particular preferences for holidays) and the needs of tourists over their life-course. In some respects they, along with other researchers, confuse and mix life-course and family life-cycle models which, as we will explain later, are different approaches. In the case of their study it was a kind of cross-sectional study of life-stages rather than the life-course this chapter is proposing.

Moreover and following Filep's (2014) argument that subjective wellbeing fails to capture the powerful meaning that some holiday experiences may have for tourists, the chapter examines wellbeing from a broader perspective. Drawing on the work of Allardt (1999), the notion of wellbeing will be defined here in terms of:

- having – which highlights such things as standard of living;
- loving – which emphasises the sense of togetherness and community;
- being – which relates to the need for social identity.

In all three aspects, wellbeing can be classified as either objective or subjective in nature. These three components will be examined as regards how they relate to holiday taking and ageing.

Life-course analysis in the context of tourism

The concept of life-course was developed during the 1970s as a means of examining patterns of work and family organisation at different times (Hareven, 1978). In its basic format life-course is a synthesis of two different models that record human activity over time. The first are developmental models which are normally based upon physiological and psychological stages occurring between birth and death. The second are life-cycle models that function by examining the normative stages through which individuals pass; this normally includes the family unit.

The idea of life-course shifts the emphasis to the individual but uses the ages at which significant events occur as markers and in this context it highlights differences to traditional studies using life-cycles. According to Elder (1978: 17), this approach views the family 'as a setting of mutually contingent individuals' careers, whose dynamics shape the family as a unit'. In contrast, the notion of life-cycle has been criticised for ignoring individual experiences and for focusing too closely on periods of stability rather than transitions (Hareven, 1978: xiii). The idea of using biographical approaches within tourism studies has been highlighted by Sedgley (2007), although this has not extended into the notion of life-course, as we argue here.

Hareven's (1978) work has been much more focused on the application of life-course to broad historical periods. In this context she has identified some essential features of life-course, namely: the timing and synchronisation of transitions (these include movements of individuals within the family in terms of employment, education and in our case, the transition to retirement); the impact of historical processes on the timing of individual transitions (again, in our case this would cover the changes in transport innovations as, for example, the innovation of low-cost airlines); the cumulative impact of earlier transitions (in our case this may include the types of earlier patterns of holiday taking such as package holidays).

The approach to life-course in this chapter follows that taken by Bailey, Shaw, Alexander and Nell (2010) in their study of changes in consumer behaviour in the face of the retail innovation of the supermarket. They claimed that 'in the absence of longitudinal data, recall methodologies are the only techniques available that provide access to historical information' (1499). This is in spite of the problems of remembering past events related to, in our case, the practice of holiday taking of individuals within a family setting.

The methodologies used around life-course in this chapter extend and develop Bailey et al.'s (2010) study. We have utilised two main methods of data collection. The first is the development of a biographical survey designed to capture fundamental information such as occupations, changes in residence, number of holidays taken at different time periods and types of holidays (including destinations), main activities whilst on holiday and feelings of subjective wellbeing. All these data were collected over the life-course which in this case started with the initial marriage and followed through until retirement into old age. Our objective was to look at key transitions across the life-course which included marriage, birth of children, holidays taken with young children and older ones, then holidays taken when children had left home and then holidays following retirement of either one or both partners. Other significant transitions were also recorded, including moving house, changing jobs, illness and loss of a partner either through divorce or death. This biological questionnaire on average took 30–40 minutes to complete and was undertaken face to face. It was normally completed by both partners if they were available.

The second stage of the life-course involved more traditional oral history. This has the advantage of gathering more life-course information which addresses particular areas of transition and can focus more on experimental aspects of holiday taking; it also provides rich contextual narratives (Bailey et al., 2010; Nell et al., 2009; Witkowski and Jones, 2006). In the oral histories emphasis was directed towards the major transitions between pre- and post-retirement holiday activities. The oral histories varied in length and in detail, with the longest taking up to 3 hours and the shortest just 1 hour and were all recorded. In a few instances the respondents produced a diary of all the major holidays, with dates and locations.

This is an on-going larger project being undertaken in the UK, Poland, Malta and Portugal using this common methodology. In this chapter we report some initial results from a small number of respondents in the UK. The ultimate target is to complete 40 biographical questionnaires and ten oral histories in each of the survey countries. The data collection is time consuming given the time for both collecting and transcribing the oral histories. In this chapter we utilise just one oral history to illustrate the technique and draw on narratives given in a number of the biographical questionnaires or oral histories.

There are issues associated with using history in this context and these should be noted. First, it should be recognised that people plot their participation in holiday taking often in a way that may exaggerate aspects rather than merely reporting past actions. Second, oral history is historically contingent and tends to communicate self-referentially, to create and maintain a sense of coherence and identity. Given the unique experience of the individual, there is a degree of partiality in which past events are woven into life stories, in this case about particular experiences on holiday. As Bailey et al. (2010: 1500) note, 'we also believe that oral history is corrigible and that memories are more or less accurate in terms of the recall of dates, times, events, places and personal reactions'. In this study the oral histories were checked with the biographical questionnaire to obtain some measure of at least consistency.

Life-course results of pre- and post-retirement holiday behaviour

Our small empirical study based on the UK is framed within the theories discussed earlier, particularly continuity theory and the ideas of the centrality of tourism (Weiss, 2005), notions of increased opportunity (Nimrod, 2008), increased constraints (Blazey, 1992) and negotiating mechanisms (Hubbard and Mannell, 2007). In addition, we record the importance that participants attribute to holidays in terms of meaning and general sense of wellbeing. Figure 10.1 presents the life-course of a husband and wife who undertook both the biographical questionnaire and the oral history. As can be seen, there are significant phases in the life-course of this couple, starting with their marriage in 1961 and their honeymoon to Austria on a package holiday (Table 10.1). This was their first use of package holidays but was something they returned to as a usual form of holiday taking after retirement in the late 1990s. During the mid and late 1960s and into the 1970s, holidays were taken locally in Scotland following the birth of their children. During this pre-retirement phase the main change came in the 1980s with three trips to Canada – visiting friends and relatives. House and job moves limited holidays after this. However, following retirement we see a major increase in holidays abroad, giving evidence of the increased centrality of holidays in the early phases of retirement. Figure 10.1 does not record all their trips and during this period they holiday more and more frequently, taking both long-stay and numerous short breaks.

Later phases of retirement highlight a further transition in their life-course due to illness of the male. This change in the 'having' component of wellbeing increases constraints inevitably – as Blazey (1992) suggests – but the change does not prevent the couple from taking holidays. Instead, the couple enters a stage of using negotiating mechanisms (Hubbard and Mannell, 2007). These take two forms; using local coach operators with couriers that pick them up from home and take them to destinations in Europe and as the male became frailer, they still used coach holidays but more as short breaks within the UK, which became more frequent, making multiple trips.

Further evidence of negotiating mechanisms came from Ann (64) and William (75) who completed a biographical questionnaire and an oral history (Table 10.1). In the words of Ann:

> We do less sightseeing now; with John in a wheelchair it depends how far I can push him. We go off for the day, we go on trips. When we were in Budapest we'd go off after breakfast, we are slow, we don't rush. I can't do what I used to. It's not the barriers to taking a holiday, it's the barriers what we can do when we get there. When we go on cruises they have trips that are organized or graded according to activities.

(Interview EX/2)

119

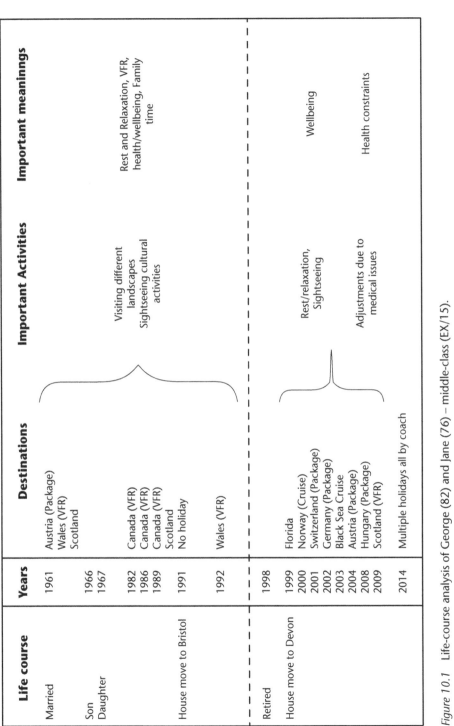

Figure 10.1 Life-course analysis of George (82) and Jane (76) – middle-class (EX/15).

Table 10.1 Characteristics of survey respondents

Code number	Respondents
EX/1	Jane (65) was a teacher and retired at 62, whilst her husband John (68) was a mechanical engineer and retired at 61. They had two children (now in their early to mid-30s) and they always tended to holiday abroad prior to retirement, mainly on camping holidays
EX/2	Ann (64) was an administrator in local government whilst her husband William (75) was a computer consultant. Before retirement he didn't take many holidays and they had no children – he took early retirement at 60
EX/3	Cathy (64) is semi-retired and a teacher; her husband Simon (66) recently retired as a local farmer. They have two children and when the children were young family holidays were taken in Cornwall, then later in France
EX/15	Jane (76) was a financial analyst and before retirement was working freelance; her husband George (82) was a retired heating engineer. On retirement they moved to Devon. They have two children and took mainly local holidays when the children were younger

Source: Authors' interview data.

The ideas about the anticipation of retirement to allow more time for holidays is illustrated by Jane (63) and John (68). As Jane explained, 'We just kept wanting to be retired, we were satisfied with our standard of living, but we were not doing what we wanted to due to work stresses'. John went on to explain that, after retirement, 'These things changed, types of destinations, more time and more frequent holidays. We can travel all year round and go away whenever we like'. Further on in the interview he explained that in retirement, 'We're not going away for family, [but] we do like a bit of adventure and excitement. Travel is good for my health' (EX/1). For this couple retirement and the related changes in terms of 'having' more time and less stressful lives, had brought a sense of freedom epitomised by more experiences of holidays.

In terms of their satisfaction with life, they were very satisfied and strongly agreed with the statement 'Travel and tourism are good for my health and physical wellbeing'. These notions of wellbeing were also confirmed by Cathy (64) and Simon (66), who were semi-retired. They believed tourism was 'very good for everybody' but they also recognised the issue of health and holidays, stating, 'Of course illness stymies everything, you just don't know what lies ahead'; their solution – 'get as many holidays as you can'. They also saw holidays as a potential antidote for the loss of status following retirement (i.e. a change in 'being'), with Cathy stating, 'When people retire they don't have that prestige, they're not an important person' (EX/6). Tourism was viewed as a means of escaping these feelings of lost positions.

These narratives are of course part of a larger study and are used to reflect parts of the life-course, in this case post-retirement. The full life-course data maps our pre- and post-retirement, as shown in Figure 10.1. This gives some clear ideas about how holiday making changes over time both in narratives but also in quantitative terms from the closed quotations in the biographical questionnaire, which have not been utilised in this small-scale study.

Concluding discussion

With its life-course approach, this chapter has attempted to draw attention to a number of important transitions in the life of older tourists and their meaning in terms of tourist behaviour and wellbeing. Although this study is still in its initial phase, the chapter represents the first, but important, step in developing these life-course techniques and also developing a comparative study across parts of the EU. Initial results give some support for the key ideas regarding the growing importance of tourism following retirement along with the anticipation of what it brings in terms of holiday taking. They also tend to corroborate Nimrod's (2008) findings, showing strong levels in continuity of holiday activities across the life-course. Although continuity patterns were illustrated here by just one case study, other narratives from the biographical questionnaire point out similar activities pre- and post-retirement at least in the earlier years of retirement. What does change following retirement (income and health permitting) is the increased frequency of holidays.

The initial results also allow for two additional observations. First, retirement involves important changes in at least two components of wellbeing, as defined by Allardt (1999). Retirement is associated with 'having' more time and more freedom (as the children left home and work-related stress is gone) but also with 'being' deprived of a social status and identity. Our initial results tend to indicate that holidays are used as a strategy to cope with and give positive meaning to, these changes.

Second, the results point to another important transition in the life of senior tourists, pertaining to health and capabilities. This transition and its effect on tourist behaviours and wellbeing have received only limited attention within the tourism literature. Laslett (1996, as cited in Boyes, 2013: 646) suggests that the main criterion used to distinguish stages in later life is the level of autonomy. What he coined as the 'Fourth Age' is a phase characterised by dependence and decrepitude, contrasting with the 'Third Age' stage 'when people [are] socially connected with family and friendship networks and when they [can] fulfil their personal goals, dreams and life plans' (Boyes, 2013: 646). This transition is most certainly at the core of current public health policies like active ageing. Our initial results tend to highlight that tourism plays an important part in coping with emotional and physical aspects of the transition between these two life stages, with some interview participants adapting their travelling behaviour by making use of a range of negotiating strategies (e.g. short-distance coach tours but multiplying experiences).

Undoubtedly, both observations deserve further research in order to gain a fuller understanding of what these transitional phases imply in terms of 'having', 'loving' and 'being' and how – and to what extent – tourism is and can be, used as a tool for enhancing wellbeing in later life.

References

Abraham, A., Sommerhalder, K. and Abel, T. (2010) 'Landscape and wellbeing: A scoping study on the health-promoting impact of outdoor environments', *International Journal of Public Health*, 55(1), 59–69.

Allardt, E. (1999) 'Philosophical and sociological debate on good life and its relevance to health research', *Journal of Social Medicine*, 36, 203–212.

Atchley, R. C. (1999) *Continuity and Adaptation in Aging: Creating Positive Experiences*, Baltimore, MD: Johns Hopkins University Press.

Bailey, A. R., Shaw, G., Alexander, A. and Nell, D. (2010) 'Consumer behaviour and the life course: Shopper reactions to self-service grocery shops and supermarkets', *Environment and Planning A*, 42, 1496–1512.

Baltes, M. and Carstensen, L. L. (1996) 'The process of successful ageing', *Ageing and Society*, 16(4), 397–422.

Blazey, M. (1992) 'Travel and retirement status', *Annals of Tourism Research*, 19, 771–783.

Borges Tiago, M. T. P. M., de Almeida Couto, J. P., Gomes Borges Tiago, F. and Costa Dias Faria, S. M. (2016) 'Baby boomers turning grey: European profiles', *Tourism Management*, 54, 13–22.

Boyes, M. (2013) 'Outdoor adventure and successful ageing', *Ageing and Society*, 33, 644–665.

Chen, C. C. and Petrick, J. F. (2013) 'Health and wellness benefits of travel experiences: A literature review', *Journal of Travel Research*, 52(6), 709–719.

Davey, J. A. (2002) 'Active ageing and education in mid and later life', *Ageing and Society*, 22, 95–113.

Demunter, C. (2012) *Europeans Age 65+ Spend a Third More on Tourism: Ageing and Tourism in the EU, Eurostat 43/2010*, Brussels, Belgium: EU.

Diener, E., Suh, E., Lucas, R. and Smith, H. (1999) 'Subjective wellbeing: Three decades of progress', *Psychological Bulletin*, 125, 276–302.

Dolnicar, S., Yanamandram, V. and Cliff, K. (2012) 'The contribution of vacations to quality of life', *Annals of Tourism Research*, 39, 59–83.

Elder, G. H. (1978) 'Family history and life course', in Hareven, T. K. (ed.) *Transitions: The Family and the Life Course in Historical Perspective, Studies in Social Discontinuity*, New York: Academic Press, 17–64.

European Commission (2015) *The 2015 Ageing Report. Economic and Budgetary Projections for the 28 EU Member States (2013–2060)*, Brussels, Belgium: Directorate-General for Economic and Financial Affairs.

Filep, S. (2014) 'Moving beyond subjective wellbeing: A tourism critique', *Journal of Hospitality and Tourism Research*, 38, 266–274.

Filep, S. and Deery, M. (2010) 'Towards a picture of tourists' happiness', *Tourism Analysis*, 15, 399–410.

Franklin, N. C. and Tate, C. A. (2009) 'Lifestyles and successful ageing: An overview', *American Journal of Lifestyle Medicine*, Jan–Feb, 6–11.

Friedman, H. S. and Kern, M. L. (2014) 'Personality, wellbeing and health', *Annual Review of Psychology*, 65, 719–742.

Gesler, W. M. (1991) *The Cultural Geography of Health Care*, Pittsburgh, PA: University of Pittsburgh Press.

Gibson, H. (2002) 'Busy travelers: Leisure-travel patterns and meanings in later life', *World Leisure*, 44(2), 11–20.

Gibson, H. and Yannakis, A. (2002) 'Tourist roles. Needs and the life course', *Annals of Tourism Research*, 29(2), 358–383.

Gilbert, D. and Abdullah, J. (2004) 'Holiday taking and the sense of wellbeing', *Annals of Tourism Research*, 31(1), 103–121.

Hareven, T. K. (ed.) (1978) *Transitions: The Family and the Life Course in Historical Perspective, Studies in Social Discontinuity*, New York: Academic Press.

Hawes, D. K. (2004) 'Travel-related lifestyle profiles of older women', in Pizam, A. and Mansfield, Y. (eds) *Consumer Behaviour in Travel and Tourism*, London: Haworth, 19–21.

Horx, M. (2003) *Future Fitness*, 5th ed. Frankfurt, Germany: Eichborn.

Hubbard, J. and Mannell, R. (2007) 'Testing competing models of leisure constraint negotiation process in corporate employee recreation selling', *Leisure Sciences*, 23(3), 145–163.

Kaplan, R. and Kaplan, S. (1989) *The Experience of Nature: A Psychological Perspective*, New York: Cambridge University Press.

Katz, S. (2013) 'Active and successful ageing: Lifestyle as a gerontological idea', *Recherches Sociologiques et Antropologiques*, 44(1), 33–49.

Kim, H., Woo, E. and Uysal, M. (2015) 'Tourism experience and quality of life among elderly tourists', *Tourism Management*, 46, 465–476.

Kler, B. V. K. and Tribe, J. (2012) 'Flourishing through scuba: Understanding the pursuit of dive experiences', *Tourism in Marine Environments*, 8(1/2), 19–32.

Lee, S. H. and Tideswell, C. (2005) 'Understanding attitudes towards leisure travel and the constraints faced by senior Koreans', *Journal of Vacation Marketing*, 11(3), 249–263.

McCabe, S. and Johnson, S. (2013) 'The happiness factor in tourism: Subjective wellbeing and social tourism', *Annals of Tourism Research*, 41, 42–65.

Milman, A. (1998) 'The impact of tourism and travel experience on senior travellers' psychological wellbeing', *Journal of Travel Research*, 37(2), 166–170.

Morris, N. (2003) *Health, Wellbeing and Open Space: Literature Review Open Space: Research Centre for Inclusive Access to Outdoor Environments*, Edinburgh, UK: Heriot-Watt University.

Nawijn, J. (2011) 'Happiness through vacationing: Just a temporary boost or long-term benefits?', *Journal of Happiness Studies*, 12, 651–665.

Nawijn, J., Marchand, M. A., Veenhoven, R. and Vingerhoets, A. J. (2010) 'Vacationers happier, but most not happier after a holiday', *Applied Research in Quality of Life*, 5, 35–47.

Neal, J. D., Sirgy, M. J. and Uysal, M. (1999) 'The role of satisfaction with leisure travel/tourism services and experience in satisfaction with leisure life and overall life', *Journal of Business Research*, 44, 153–163.

Neal, J. D., Uysal, M. and Sirgy, M. J. (2007) 'The effect of tourism services on travelers' quality of life', *Journal of Travel Research*, 46(2), 154–163.

Nell, D., Alexander, A., Shaw, G. and Bailey, A. (2009) 'Investigating shopper narratives of the supermarket in postwar England, 1945–1975', *Oral History Journal*, 37, 61–73.

Nimrod, G. (2008) 'Retirement and tourism themes in retirees' narratives', *Annals of Tourism Research*, 35(4), 859–878.

Nimrod, G. and Rotem, A. (2010) 'Between relaxation and excitement: Activities and benefits gained in retirees' tourism', *International Journal of Tourism Research*, 12, 65–78.

Rose, E. (2012) 'Encountering place: A psychoanalytic approach for understanding how therapeutic landscapes benefit health and wellbeing', *Health and Place*, 18(6), 1381–1387.

Schimmack, U. (2008) 'The structure of subjective wellbeing', in Eid, M. and Larsen, R. J. (eds) *The Science of Subjective Wellbeing*, New York: Guilford Press, 97–123.

Sedgley, D. (2007) 'The contribution of biographical research in understanding older women's leisure', in Ateljevic, I., Pritchard, A. and Morgan, N. (eds) *The Critical Turn in Tourism Studies: Innovative Research Methodologies*, Oxford, UK: Elsevier, 331–347.

Seitsamo, J. (2007) *Retirement Transition and Wellbeing: A 16 Year Long Study*, People at Work Research Report 76, Helsinki, Finland: Dept. of Social Policy, University of Helsinki.

Sharpley, R. and Stone, P. K. (eds) (2012) *Contemporary Tourist Experience: Concepts and Consequences*, London: Routledge.

Sirgy, J., Kruger, P. S., Lee, D.-J. and Yu, G. B. (2011) 'How does a travel trip affect tourists' life satisfaction?', *Journal of Travel Research*, 50(3), 261–275.

Statts, S. and Pierfelice, L. (2003) 'Travel: A long-range goal of retired women', *Journal of Psychology*, 137, 483–494.

Sugiyama, T. and Thompson C. W. (2007) 'Older people's health, outdoor activity and supportiveness of neighborhood environments', *Landscape and Urban Planning*, 83(2–3), 168–175.

Tarumi, K., Hagihara, A. and Morimoto, K. (1998) 'An investigation into the effects of vacations on the health status in male white-collar workers', *Environmental Health and Preventive Medicine*, 3, 23–30.

Toda, M., Makino, H., Kobayashi, H., Nagasawa, S., Kitamura, K. and Morimoto, K. (2004) 'Medical assessment of the health effects of short leisure trips', *Archives and Environment Health*, 59(12), 717–724.

Wahl, H. W. and Weisman, G. D. (2003) 'Environmental gerontology at the beginning of the new millennium: Reflections on its historical, empirical and theoretical development', *The Gerontologist*, 43(5), 616–627.

Wang, M., Henkens, K. and van Solinge, H. (2011) 'Retirement adjustment: A review of theoretical and empirical advancements', *American Psychologist*, 66(3), 204–213.

Wei, S. and Milman, A. (2002) 'The impact of participation in activities while on vacation on seniors' psychological wellbeing: A path model application', *Journal of Hospitality and Tourism Research*, 26(2), 175–185.

Weiss, R. (2005) *The Experience of Retirement*, Ithaca, NY: Cornell University Press.

Witkowski, T. and Jones, D. G. B. (2006) 'Qualitative historical research in marketing', in Belk, R. (ed.) *Handbook of Qualitative Research Methods in Marketing*, Cheltenham, UK: Edward Elgar, 70–82.

World Health Organization (2002) *Active Aging. A Policy Framework*, Madrid, Spain: WHO, p. 59.

Part IV
Holistic wellbeing

This part focuses on those forms of health tourism which offer holistic health and wellbeing activities and aim for a balance of body, mind and spirit. Some of the activities may be water-based (e.g. spas) but many of them are not (e.g. retreats, yoga). None of them are purely physical in their aims or impacts. Jeremy McCarthy examines spa treatments and how the healing power of touch can induce not only physical but also strong psychological and emotional responses (Chapter 11). Human contact is identified in research as being extremely important to both human and animal wellbeing. In addition, energy healing can also be used for healing (e.g. reiki or craniosacral therapy). Although the evidence is sometimes scarce for such alternative modes of therapy, this chapter emphasises the importance of the placebo effect which can even out-perform conventional medicine. In addition to their numerous benefits (placebo or medically proven), spas can also offer a sanctuary from the demands of a fast-paced and technologically driven world where sacred moments of reflection are rare.

Catherine Kelly and Melanie Kay Smith turn their attention to retreats which offer non-water-based activities which go beyond rest and relaxation (still important benefits) and aim to offer self-development and even transformation (Chapter 12). The chapter considers how different stages of life, especially mid-life and gender affect the need to retreat. Middle-aged women still tend to be the main segment for all forms of health tourism, therefore the chapter focuses in more depth on middle-aged women. The chapter overall questions why it is necessary to retreat, including the desire to slow down, to become more mindful and to (re)discover the true or authentic self (rather than a 'social' or 'ideal' self).

Whereas Kelly and Smith place their emphasis on the individual and his or her needs, Dina Glouberman and Josée-Ann Cloutier emphasise the importance of community for health (Chapter 13). Going back to Ancient Greek concepts of 'holism', they argue that community plays a central role in wellbeing, as well as the crises or 'turning points' which force individuals to change. The latter process should, they argue, take place in a supportive, communal environment such as on a holistic holiday. This is especially important in this age of increased physical and mental isolation.

The final chapter in this part, by Melanie Kay Smith and Ivett Sziva, examines the healing power of yoga, a holistic practice which often begins with physical aims and benefits, but leads to greater spiritual and transformational ones (Chapter 14). Although there is more evidence-based research on the medical benefits of yoga, it is argued that true transformation includes a changing of values, emotions, relationships and spiritual connections to oneself, others and the universe. Holidays can intensify yoga practice and reinforce its importance back home.

Overall, this part shows that holistic health is dependent on a number of factors which need ideally to be balanced to create optimum wellbeing: individual and collective or communal self; body, mind and spirit; physical and psychological or emotional dimensions; rest and relaxation alongside self-development – to name but a few.

11

The psychology of spa
The science of 'holistic' wellbeing

Jeremy McCarthy

The International Spa Association (ISPA) has defined spas as 'places devoted to enhancing overall wellbeing through a variety of professional services that encourage the renewal of mind, body and spirit' (ISPA, 2006). The spa industry's promotion of 'holistic' healing across 'mind, body and spirit' is ubiquitous, but is typically mentioned without definition, detail or support from scientific study. Scientific research on spa services is scant and the majority of studies that have been done are based on the physical effects of therapeutic treatments on clinical populations. This gives us some insight into the effectiveness of spa treatments as a form of physical therapy, but does little to attest to the ability of a spa to impact diverse populations, even healthy ones, across mind, body and spirit. To truly validate this claim we need to review the literature from the field of psychology and see if contained within, we can find some of the keys to how a spa might have a healing effect on the mental and spiritual domains.

For the most part, spa treatments appear to be primarily physical in nature: massage is a physical manipulation of the tissues of the body; facials and skincare include more superficial treatments for the skin, one of the most important organs of the body; hydrotherapy involves using heat, water and steam to loosen up body tissues and improve circulation. What do any of these physical therapies have to do with mind and spirit?

Many spa advocates claim that spa therapies somehow enhance the connection between mind and body in healing and some bodywork techniques have evolved to address this relationship specifically. Rolfing and the Trager method are two examples of bodywork therapies that work on 'the correlation between manipulation of the body and the releasing of deep emotions' (Wisneski and Anderson, 2005: 151).

This kind of language seems to reflect at least the intentions of the spa industry, with most spa therapies being designed with the goal of not only creating healthy physiological changes in the body, but also bringing mental relaxation and psychological harmony. The mental and physical natures of these therapies 'are intimately intertwined and often overlap' (Kendall-Reed and Reed, 2004: 123), suggesting that there may be more to the spa experience than can be easily detected by only examining the physical realm. In this chapter, I explore some of the relevant constructs from the field of psychology that can help to explain or enhance the psychological impact of the spa experience.

The effect of person

Some of the most interesting findings from the relatively new field of positive psychology have been summed up by the simple statement, 'other people matter' (Peterson, 2006). In medicine, the influence of the doctor on his patient has been recognised since the time of Hippocrates and is often cited as one of the greatest drawbacks to the 'disappearance of the family physician' (Anderson and Gantt, 1966: 181). Researchers have also cited that there are 'many other examples of assuaging influence of one person on another' (Anderson and Gantt, 1966: 181) and studies on 'social support' have found the mitigating effect of good relationships with other people on the harmful effects of stress (Acuna and Bruner, 2002). One way that spas provide healing across mind, body and spirit is by the presence of a nurturing therapist.

The importance of the therapist in the spa setting can be easily noted by considering the difficulty for someone to get as much enjoyment out of massaging her own muscles as she does when the therapy is being done by someone else. The touch of another person can be healing in a way that a person touching herself cannot achieve, much in the way that a person cannot tickle herself (Sapolsky, 2004: 336). The touch and nurturing care of another person are important mechanisms in the subjective benefits of a visit to a spa.

Most people are aware of the famous psychological conditioning experiments involving Pavlov's dog. By associating a bell with food, a dog would learn to salivate at the sound of the bell. Similar experiments have been done with flashing lights and electric shock, showing that the dog's fear reactions (heart rate, etc.) would amp up as soon as the light flashed. The 'effect of person' describes the calming effect observed in these kind of studies when a researcher remains in the room with the dog (Anderson and Gantt, 1966; Lynch, 2000). The dog's heart rate did not go up as quickly and returned to normal much sooner whenever there was a person in the room.

In the case of a spa experience, the client may see some benefit from simply being in the room with a nurturing therapist and this effect might begin before the therapist has even set her hands on him. Some of the 'energy' spa treatments, such as reiki, therapeutic touch and craniosacral, are deeply rooted in this philosophy.

There is some limited research suggesting the presence of a person can have 'marked effects on the heart rate of another person' (Whitehorn, Kaufman and Thomas, 1935, as cited in Gantt, Newton, Royer and Stephens, 1966: 31). And studies have shown the positive effects of 'contact comfort' of another person on stress levels (Bridger and Birns, 1963; Geer and Turteltaub, 1967; Jones, 1924; Schachter, 1959, as cited in Gattozzi, 1971: 181). Darwin once described a heart patient with an irregular pulse rate which 'invariably became regular as soon as my Father entered the room' (1955, as cited in Gantt et al., 1966: 32). Another doctor wrote of his amazement as a dying patient's heart rate and heart rhythm changed 'just as soon as a nurse began to hold his hand shortly before his death' (213). What amazed him was that his patient was in a deep coma and should have been completely unaware of the presence of the nurse.

From as far back as 2,000 years ago, doctors have documented cardiac reactions to brief, transient human interactions. Sometimes these effects can be negative, as in the increased heart rate and blood pressure caused by the stress of being evaluated by a doctor (known as 'white-coat hypertension'; Lynch, 2000: 217). Heart rate studies of psychotherapy sessions have shown a concomitant 'cardiac relationship' between the patient and the therapist when they were communicating well (218). The 'effect of person' could explain why different styles of psychotherapy all seem to have similar positive results, regardless of the specific techniques being used (Luborsky, 1975, as cited in Prochaska, Norcross and DiClemente, 1994). 'The quality of the relationship' seems to matter more than the technique employed by the therapist

(Shannon, 2002). And military specialists since the Second World War have observed the importance of relationships in helping soldiers cope with battle stress. This phenomenon has been replicated in laboratory settings, where experiments have shown that people prefer not to be alone when confronting a stressful situation (Lynch, 2000).

The power of touch

In the spa setting, not only do people benefit from the presence of another person, whose role is to nurture and care for them, but those benefits are deepened because they are transmitted through touch. Those same studies on 'effect of person' show that the relaxation effect on dogs is greatly enhanced when the dog is being petted by a human being. Even when the dog is aware of an impending electrical shock, the gentle petting of a researcher can help the dog's heart rate go *down* rather than up (Lynch, 2000). Pavlov called this a 'social reflex', noting that different dogs had different reactions to different researchers, depending on the specific relationship the dog had with each individual (Pavlov, 1928, as cited in Gantt et al., 1966: 18). Other research has shown changes in heart rate and behaviour in dairy cows influenced by human stroking of the skin (Schmied, Waiblinger, Scharl, Leisch and Bovin, 2007).

One study found that having pets was one of the strongest predictors of survival one year after release from a coronary care unit (Lynch, 2000: 240), presumably due to the companionship, sense of purpose and affectionate touch that pets provide. Another study showed that small children were more likely to smile and reach for live animals (i.e. the family pet) than they were a mechanised version of the animal (Kidd and Kidd, 1987). Psychologists (who are notorious for stressing out mice and rats in lab experiments) have found that handling rats when the rats are young makes them more resilient to stress as they grow older (Meaney, Aitken, Bhatnager, van Berkel and Sapolsky, 1988, as cited in Sapolsky, 2004). In the wild, a follow-up study showed that rats that are licked and groomed by their mothers are also better able to withstand the effects of stress as they get older (Liu et al., 1997, as cited in Sapolsky, 2004).

Even Darwin, in his work on the evolution of the animal kingdom, found that touch had a powerful influence. Certain animals had a 'strong desire to touch the beloved person . . . Dogs and cats manifestly take pleasure in rubbing against their master and in being rubbed . . . Monkeys delight in fondling and in being fondled' (1955, as cited in Gantt et al., 1966: 32). He described human expressions of affection as being innate 'insofar as it depends on the pleasure derived from contact with the beloved person'.

While research on humans is not as easy to find, there are studies in the literature of the importance of touch to newborns and childhood development. Touch is the first of the senses to develop (and it lasts 'even after seeing and hearing begin to fade'; Field, 1994: 8). Cases of 'psychosocial dwarfism' are found in institutionalised children who have all their physiological needs met and yet find their growth stunted due to the lack of a loving caretaker (Field, 1994; Harrington, 2002).

Studies in Uganda show that the way parents carry their children helps them to develop and learn to walk more quickly and parents massaging their infants brings the parents and children closer together in a way that few other activities can. Touch not only helps with growth and development, but also gives reassurance and self-esteem (Field, 1994). 'A child's first emotional bonds are built from physical contact, laying the foundation for further emotional and intellectual development' (9).

One study showed that hand holding helped to calm the nerves of people anticipating an electric shock. The effect was greatest when the person was holding his or her spouse's hand, but even holding a stranger's hand was more calming than no hand holding whatsoever (Coan, Schaefer and Davidson, 2006). Other research on couples showed how positive physical contact lowered their cortisol and heart rate responses to stress, while verbal social support did not (Ditzen et al., 2007). Another study done with married couples showed that 'warm touch' behaviours between spouses had beneficial effects on many stress-related health systems, including blood pressure and levels of cortisol and oxytocin (Holt-Lunstad, Birmingham and Light, 2008).

Oxytocin, which is 'released in the brain in response to social contact, especially skin-to-skin touch' is a hormone-like substance that seems to provide the biochemical basis for love emotions (Insel, 1997, as cited in Peterson, 2006: 249). Oxytocin may be one of the mechanisms behind how touch reduces not only the heart rate, but also levels of hormones such as cortisol that are associated with the stress response (Ditzen et al., 2007). As one expert on touch therapies said, 'Given that most diseases are exacerbated by stress and that massage therapy alleviates stress, receiving massages should probably be high on the health priority list, along with diet and exercise' (Field, 1996: 320).

This research suggests that some of the benefits of massage therapies may come simply from the body's physiological reaction to human touch. The power of touch to heal is not a new phenomenon of the modern spa industry. Stories of healers using the 'laying on of hands' are found in most religious texts from across cultures and throughout recorded history (Field, 1994). It has been said to be 'one of the oldest and most persistent treatments, still used today'. References to the 'royal touch', in which a king or other person of power heals by touching, can be found from as far back as 300 BC (Shapiro and Shapiro, 1997: 17).

Studies have shown that superficial touch is almost as effective as deep-tissue massage in relieving pain as compared to a control group, suggesting that much of the benefits of massage could come simply from touch. This could be attributed to the placebo effect, with the superficial touch giving the client a greater expectation that a treatment is occurring as compared to a no-treatment control group. But it could also be an indication of the oxytocin-producing, stress-relieving effects of light touch that has been shown in numerous studies. The release of oxytocin is facilitated by touch and this hormone has been shown to increase pain threshold, relieve pain, induce physical relaxation and lower blood pressure (Law et al., 2008).

One study attempted to compare massage and simple touch on the ability to enhance mood and reduce pain in advanced-stage cancer patients. Patients in both the massage and the touch groups showed improvement in both mood and pain levels, showing that the benefits may have come less from the physical manipulation of the body tissues and more from the attention and touch of a nurturing therapist (Kutner et al., 2008). Even in psychological therapies, where touch has traditionally been taboo – a violation of the boundaries of trust between the patient and the therapist – it is becoming more accepted to recognise touch as an effective therapy for 'promoting, nurturing and enhancing emotional expression' (LaTorre, 2005: 185).

The effects of people and touch become even more relevant for people who are experiencing or recovering from heart problems. Dr James J. Lynch, who has done substantial research on 'the medical consequences of loneliness', said that 'the importance of human touch in such circumstances ought not to be minimised: human contact can serve as one of the primary healing agents for the injured heart' (Lynch, 2000: 221). Research showed that the simple touch of a nurse taking a palpated pulse reading was enough to reduce dangerous arrhythmias in patients with heart problems (232).

'Although touch is an effective healing agent,' said one researcher, 'it is under-utilized by healing practitioners, from neurologists to social workers and has been generally ignored by institutions and neglected by researchers' (Field, 1994: 16). As medical technologies become more high-tech rather than high-touch, people will need a place to go for the nurturing comfort of touch that is disappearing in other areas of society. 'Laying-on of hands is not merely folklore or mysticism,' said another researcher in the same department (Field, 1994). 'Reinstituting the backrub as standard hospital procedure could balance the introduction of the computerized axial tomography scanner' (17). Spas play an important role in society as a healing institution where the benefits of touch are still cherished and applied.

Energy work

Some spa practitioners claim that the healing power of touch comes, not so much from the physical manipulation of the tissues in the body, but from the facilitating of the flow of energy. Some spa therapies, collectively referred to as 'energy work', have evolved to focus more on a healing and nurturing touch than on the deep manipulation of body tissues. An example of this is a technique known as therapeutic touch, in which the practitioner places the hands on 'or slightly above' an injured area to 'feel' the problem and 'send healing energy' to the site (Newman and Miller, 2006: 11). The philosophy of therapeutic touch is that healing is 'a natural human ability' and occurs when there is a 'balanced, even flow of energy within a person and between the person and the environment' (Bonadonna, 2002: 233). Research is limited on these kinds of spa therapies, although they have been shown to reduce anxiety and 'people commonly report feelings of relaxation, lightness, tingling or heaviness' (235).

Shiatsu, which is commonly found on spa massage menus, is a holistic healthcare method originating in Japan that is based on using 'Oriental energetic diagnosis and body energy techniques to correct imbalances in the body and focuses on the whole person (mind, body and spirit as an interconnected whole)' (Long, 2008: 921). Shiatsu treatment consists of gentle pressure to 'energy channels' that are believed to exist along the surface of the body (922). Studies showed that consumers of shiatsu treatments would try it first 'out of curiosity' but repeat clients were seeking 'to maintain health' and they perceived the treatment to be successful in helping them. Clients of an experimental shiatsu programme were found to show reduced medical symptoms and greater uptake of healthy lifestyle behaviours that they attributed to their treatments (Long, 2008).

Reiki is another energy treatment of Japanese origin that is popular in spas. Reiki means 'universal (rei) life force energy (ki)' (Honervogt, 1998, as cited in LaTorre, 2005: 184). In reiki, the therapist places her hands over the body but there is no actual massage. If the therapist touches the patient at all, it is very light (Johnson and Redman, 2008). Reiki is said to 'rebalance the vibrational field within mind and body although there is no agreed-upon theory on how it works or basic understanding for the mechanism of its actions' (LaTorre, 2005: 184). Reiki is thought to be beneficial for clients 'who are anxious, stressed, depressed or in chronic pain' (Nield-Anderson and Ameling, 2001, as cited in LaTorre, 2005: 185). Reiki has even been suggested as a possible enhancement to traditional psychotherapy treatments since the gentle touch of reiki can help build a safe relationship between the client and therapist and can model a healthy, calming behaviour that clients can consider for reducing stress even when they are at home (LaTorre, 2005).

Another example of an energy-based spa modality is craniosacral therapy, which is said to be 'useful for alleviation of pain from accidents, for stress-related symptoms, for sensory disorders and to promote overall health' (Wisneski and Anderson, 2005: 150). The energy flow being treated in craniosacral is even more literal as this treatment works on releasing the 'restrictions in the craniosacral hydraulic system of the body' that are thought to prevent the central nervous system from working properly. The treatment is performed while the therapist gently holds the client's head '"listening" to the rhythms as the body moves' (Johnson and Redman, 2008: 222). Craniosacral quite literally works on the connection between the mind and the body.

The mechanisms behind energy treatments are not completely understood and warrant a certain amount of scepticism, but they have shown some significant results as a method of reducing anxiety, reducing pain, speeding healing and for a variety of clinical conditions (Phalen, 1998). It seems that at least some of the results of these kinds of treatments come from helping the patient to relax and allowing the body's own healing mechanisms to come into play.

Intention and the placebo effect

Intention plays a role in some of the energy work of spa therapies, where it is believed that the 'focusing of consciousness' of the therapist directs the energy of the body to facilitate healing (Bonadonna, 2002). Intention is also meaningful to spa customers because they may begin to see benefits simply from selecting the intention to visit a spa and taking steps for their own wellbeing.

The expectation that a customer has when visiting a spa can have a significant impact on the outcome of the experience. One study on using tai chi for stress relief showed the impact of participant expectations. The researchers compared tai chi, walking, meditation and book reading (control group) as different methods for alleviating stress (Jin, 1992). All of these methods were found to help alleviate the stress response in the participants. Tai chi had a greater calming effect on state anxiety than the book reading, but this effect disappeared when they controlled for the expectations of the participants. In other words, they could not tell if the tai chi was actually more beneficial for relieving stress or if it was simply attributed to the participants' belief that it would be more beneficial.

The 'power of intention' has been popularised by many modern-day 'self-help' healers such as Wayne Dyer (2004), Deepak Chopra (2003) and Rhonda Byrne in the best-selling book, *The Secret* (2006). But the ability of belief, intention and mental focus to have an impact in reality is not just new-age mumbo jumbo. Rather, it is grounded in hard scientific research. In actuality, it may be the *most researched* healing method in all of science: the placebo effect. The placebo effect is a physiological improvement that comes from an 'inert' treatment and has been described as 'the only treatment common to all societies and cultures . . . its effectiveness has been attested to, without exception, for more than two millennia' (Shapiro and Shapiro, 1997: 1).

The effectiveness and persistence of many ancient, alternative and Indigenous healing methods (often the staples of a typical spa menu) are commonly attributed to the placebo effect. Some would say that 'placebos were the dominant treatment in preliterate cultures' (Shapiro and Shapiro, 1997: 3). Belief in magic 'played the dominant role in medicine from prehistory well through the Middle Ages' (Kradin, 2008: 25). Using the 'perceived power of the Healer' and other amulets and potions, shamans or medicine men played an exalted role in society (35). These rituals were all useful in creating positive expectations in those who were seeking a cure. Historically, spa-like temples were centres for religious rituals, bathing therapies and other healing treatments 'where sick patients were encouraged to partake in activities designed to soothe mind and body' (39). Testimonials from the period suggest that patients responded well to these treatments and spas continue to pay homage to this shamanic healing practice today.

Complementary and alternative medicine practices in general are often attributed to the placebo effect. Some would say that alternative medicine is defined as medicine that works primarily through a placebo response. If it was shown to have mechanisms for healing that were scientifically identified in random controlled trials to be effective, it would no longer be considered 'alternative' (Kradin, 2008). This does not mean that these kinds of healing therapies should be discarded. While 'the incredible power of positive placebo responses' has been 'undervalued' in American medicine (Phalen, 1998: 87), the healing effects of alternative medicines are documented enough to suggest that if they are all attributable to the placebo response, then *all* healers should learn more about how to generate these effects in their patients (Bootzin and Caspi, 2002).

The research on placebo effects has shown that these effects are far from being inconsequential. Researchers use terms like 'relatively large' and 'robust' to quantify both the size of effects attributed to placebo and the consistency with which such effects are found. In some cases, the placebo effects have even been larger than the effects of the actual medical treatments to which they were compared (Wampold, Imel and Minami, 2007: 402). Studies on a variety of symptoms across hundreds of patients found that placebos provided a 35 per cent improvement on average (Beecher, 1955, as cited in Shapiro and Shapiro, 1997). These findings suggest that, in some cases, patients could avoid costly and potentially risky healthcare procedures if they could tap into the mechanisms behind the placebo effect and use it to 'augment healing and promote wellness' (Wampold et al., 2007: 403). The placebo effect draws upon 'the innate ability of the body to heal itself spontaneously' according to the 'fundamental biological principle of homeostasis that is believed to exist in all living beings' (Bootzin and Caspi, 2002: 125). Sometimes the best treatment is 'no treatment' because the simpler treatments do 'no harm to patients and let nature heal' (Shapiro and Shapiro, 1997: 59).

'Placebo' comes from the Latin verb *placare*, which means 'to please' (Rajagopal, 2006), and is a name given to any medicine 'adopted more to please than to benefit the patient' (attributed to *Fox's New Medical Dictionary*, 1803, as cited in Shapiro and Shapiro, 1997: 29). The paradox of the placebo effect is that if a placebo is, by definition, 'inert', then there should be no such thing as a 'placebo effect'. This confusion has plagued medical practitioners for centuries (Price, Finniss and Benedetti, 2008). In a conference on the placebo effect hosted by the National Institutes of Health, they gave the health benefits of these 'inert' treatments 'new legitimacy' and described them as 'real and significant, not make believe; an emperor *with* clothes' (Kleinman, Guess and Wilentz, 2002: 1).

Hope and the placebo effect

Some theories suggest that what drives the healing effect is any action 'performed by the Healer that imbues the Patient with hope' (Kleinman et al., 2002: 8). 'Generation of hope, a shared belief system and an emotionally charged, confiding relationship' are the common factors found in healing encounters from a variety of settings and cultures (Frank, 1961, as cited in Shannon, 2002: 4). Hope is instilled in distressed patients when they have a sense that they are in the hands of 'an expert clinician' and that they are given an acceptable explanation of their diagnosis and treatment 'even if it is a "myth"' (Bootzin and Caspi, 2002: 117). One explanation for the placebo effect is the reduction of stress, which interferes with the body's own ability to heal itself (Kradin, 2008). Creating meaningful settings and treatments makes clients feel cared for and gives them a sense of control over their own illness and symptoms. Spas have always emphasised the importance of ritual and this ritual of interaction between the healer and patient can instill hope and affect health and wellbeing.

For spas, legitimacy and authenticity in their treatments, which can help generate trust and belief in the healing abilities of spas, can be a self-fulfilling prophecy that can lead to real physiological results for their clients. Spas sometimes do better than other healing institutions at telling the stories and the history behind their treatments. These stories add meaning to the experience that can have a direct impact on the outcome of the treatment. Some have suggested, for example, that the reason chiropractors do better than medical doctors at treating low-back pain is not due to the treatment itself, but rather due to an increased sense of meaning and hope given to the patient (Moerman, 2002).

This is not to say that spa treatments are 'inert' or do not have real physiological value. But we should not discount the ways the mind can influence healing through the release of endorphins and neurotransmitters that reduce pain and improve nervous system functioning (Rajagopal, 2006: 186). Even when 'real' scientifically validated medical treatments are being administered, their ability to heal or reduce pain is heightened when the treatment is administered in view of the patient, due to the higher expectations of the patient (Price et al., 2008).

Today, physicians recognise the importance of the healing effect of the mind, not only from the standpoint of having to control for it in medical research, but also for the value of the effect itself as an aid for real healing (Wampold et al., 2007). While the mechanisms behind it are still unclear, research has shown that a majority of diseases can be improved simply by the power of the mind believing in the treatment.

I am not suggesting that a spa is *only* a placebo and no other benefit may be gained from it. But spas improve wellbeing in many ways and one of them is by engaging their customers in a ritual that is performed for their own good. Simply having the right intentions and a place to go to focus on their own wellbeing can have a powerful effect. Spas help people to benefit from the mind's powerful healing properties, even when we do not fully understand them.

The effect of time and mindfulness

A visit to a spa usually consists of a certain amount of time just being in a quiet space, enjoying the experiences one is having or reflecting on whatever is on the mind at the moment. Often the hour that a person spends in a spa treatment is the only hour of waking time the individual may have being disconnected from technology, separated from the noise of urbanisation and disconnected from the demands of a fast-paced world. Technology has helped us to become so connected that we have lost the space and, more importantly, the time to disconnect, sit, breathe, relax and reflect.

George Prochnik, the author of *In Pursuit of Silence: Listening for Meaning in a World of Noise* (2010a), writes and speaks about the scarcity of silence 'in a world of diminishing natural retreats and amplifying electronic escapes'. Spas are one of the last havens of tranquility left in our culture and, as Prochnik said, 'evidence for the benefits of silence continues to mount' (2010b).

A quiet, tranquil space to escape to can provide the right setting for a meditation practice. Herbert Benson, associate professor of medicine at the Mind/Body Medical Institute at Harvard Medical School, has been a pioneer in research on relaxation. Benson learned 'that meditation and other modalities induced beneficial physiological responses. For example, subjects in a meditation group consumed 17% less oxygen, had lower heart and respiratory rates and had lower blood pressure than did control subjects' (Wisneski and Anderson, 2005: 120). Research has found real physiological changes to brain tissues in experienced meditators, particularly in the prefrontal cortex where positive emotions reside (Vaillant, 2008).

Yoga practice, another common offering of the spa world, also begins with concentration on breathing to quiet the mind. When the mind is quiet, the release of cortisol, our stress hormone, decreases (Kendall-Reed and Reed, 2004). One study of long-term yoga practice on women over 45 showed that the more yoga people do, the healthier they are (Moliver et al., 2011).

Researchers and medical practitioners are beginning to recognise relaxation as a critical element to the healing process. Put simply, conventional medicine is more effective on relaxed patients.

Dr Benson identified the 'relaxation response', describing the body's physiological response to relaxation that facilitated healing. He encouraged people to practise slow, deep breathing to elicit this state of relaxation as a part of a healing process he called 'wellness remembered' (Newman and Miller, 2006: 48). A lot of the spa's emphasis on stress relief could be attached to the aforementioned belief that the body's ability to heal itself can be facilitated by simply relaxing the mind and body and allowing them to do their work.

Jon Kabat-Zinn believes meditation training can help people to stimulate their own self-healing capabilities. The mindfulness-based meditation involves 'developing a keen sense of moment-to-moment awareness by observing thoughts and sensations' (Wisneski and Anderson, 2005: 120). He found the training was beneficial for medical patients in reducing pain and anxiety. Spending time sitting in silence helps people to 'listen more carefully' to 'the messages from [their] own body and mind and feelings'. Kabat-Zinn calls this 'mobilizing the inner resources of the patient for healing' (1994: 192).

The most powerful benefits from visiting a spa may come simply from being in a safe space, separated from the interruptions of noise and technology, where a person can become present and tune into the thoughts in his or her own head. Personally, I find I have the greatest flashes of inspiration and insight while I am lying on a massage table. Solutions appear for problems that have been lingering, ideas come without thinking and stress dissipates into the silence. The scarcity of silence, time and space for reflection in our culture makes these moments sacred. Spas give us that time and space to tap into our spiritual side and reflect on what is important.

Conclusion

There is an important place for the science of psychology in the world of spas. This chapter only gives a few examples of how spas can benefit greatly from studying and applying what the scientific literature yields to improve the impact they have on their clients' wellbeing. Spa consumers benefit when the science of wellbeing is applied in a holistic way, helping them to reduce stress, improve health and increase their overall satisfaction with life.

In a world where there is a growing appreciation for more holistic approaches to health and where time, touch and silence are all becoming increasingly scarce, spas may hold the keys to some of the biggest health problems of the future. The medical side is already realising this and we are seeing an influx of spa influence, on service, therapy and design, in conventional healthcare settings (as I like to call it, the 'spaification' of the modern medical centre). But the spa industry needs to take ownership of this as well and become more scientific in its approach.

Reading spa menus today, it is easy to find descriptive statements such as 'soothes the mind and the body' or 'relaxes your mind, body and spirit'. Some of this can be dismissed as hyperbole, an exaggerated claim for the sake of marketing the spa. But looking at some of the related research from the field of psychology, we can see that spas may indeed have the power to make good on these claims.

That being said, it is important to note that the research on spa experiences is very limited. In this chapter, I have taken great liberties to draw conclusions based on scant research and anecdotes from a handful of health professionals. In order to truly validate the promise of spas, spa professionals need to push for a more scientific approach to their offering, familiarising themselves with the research that does exist and avoiding claims that they cannot substantiate with evidence.

But, in a very general way, the winds of psychology seem to be moving in a way that is favourable to spas. There is a growing awareness of the importance of rest and recovery, of the value of meditative and mindful experiences and of the need for positive emotional experiences: all pillars of what spas have to offer.

References

Acuna, L. L. and Bruner, C. (2002) 'El efecto de las personas sobre la salud', *Revista Mexicana de Psicologia*, 19(2), 115–124.

Anderson, S. and Gantt, W. H. (1966) 'The effect of person on cardiac and motor responsivity to shock in dogs', *Conditional Reflex*, 1(3), 181–189.

Bonadonna, J. R. (2002) 'Therapeutic touch' in Shannon, S. (ed.) *Handbook of Complementary and Alternative Therapies in Mental Health*, San Diego, CA: Academic Press, pp. 231–248.

Bootzin, R. R. and Caspi, O. (2002) 'Explanatory mechanisms for placebo effects: Cognition, personality and social learning', in Guess, H. A., Kleinman, A., Kusek, J. W. and Engel, L. W. (eds) *The Science of the Placebo: Toward an Interdisciplinary Research Agenda*, London: BMJ Books, pp. 108–132.

Byrne, R. (2006) *The Secret*, New York: Atria Books.

Chopra, D. (2003) *The Spontaneous Fulfillment of Desire: Harnessing the Infinite Power of Coincidence*, New York: Crown Publishing.

Coan, J. A., Schaefer, H. S. and Davidson, R. J. (2006) 'Lending a hand: Social regulation of the neural response to threat', *Psychological Science*, 17(12), 1032–1039.

Ditzen, B., Neumann, I. D., Bodenmann, G., von Dawans, B., Turner, R. A., Ehlert, U. and Heinrichs, M. (2007) 'Effects of different kinds of couple interaction on cortisol and heart rate responses to stress in women', *Psychoneuroendocrinology*, 32, 565–574.

Dyer, W. W. (2004) *The Power of Intention*, Carlsbad, CA: Hay House.

Field, T. M. (1994) Touch hunger, in Goodman, J. D. and Nusbaum, H. C. (eds) *The Development of Speech Perception*, Cambridge, MA: The MIT Press.

Field, T. M. (1996) 'Touch therapies for pain management and stress reduction', in Resnick, R. J. and Rozensky, R. H. (eds) *Health Psychology Through the Life Span: Practice and Research Opportunities*, Washington, DC: American Psychological Association, pp. 313–321.

Gantt, W. H., Newton, J. E. O., Royer, F. L. and Stephens, J. H. (1966) 'Effect of person', *Conditional Reflex*, 1(1), 18–35.

Gattozzi, R. (1971) 'The effect of person on a conditioned emotional response of schizophrenic and normal subjects', *Conditional Reflex*, 6(4), 181–190.

Harrington, A. (2002) '"Seeing" the placebo effect: Historical legacies and present opportunities', in Guess, H. A., Kleinman, A., Kusek, J. W. and Engel, L. E. (eds) *The Science of Placebo: Toward an Interdisciplinary Research Agenda*, London: BMJ Books.

Holt-Lunstad, J., Birmingham, W. A. and Light, K. C. (2008) 'The influence of a "warm touch" support enhancement intervention among married couples on ambulatory blood pressure, oxytocin, alpha amylase and cortisol', *Psychosomatic Medicine*, 9, 976–985.

International Spa Association (2006) *Types of Spas*, http://www.experienceispa.com/spa-goers/spa-101/types-of-spas (accessed 9 May 2009).

Jin, P. (1992) 'Efficacy of tai chi, brisk walking, meditation and reading in reducing mental and emotional stress', *Journal of Psychosomatic Research*, 36(4), 361–370.

Johnson, E. M. and Redman, B. M. (2008) *Spa: A Comprehensive Introduction*, Lansing, MI: The American Hotel and Lodging Educational Institute.

Kabat-Zinn, J. (1994) *Wherever You Go There You Are: Mindfulness Meditation in Everyday Life*, New York: Hyperion.

Kendall-Reed, P. and Reed, S. (2004) *The Complete Doctor's Stress Solution: Understanding, Treating and Preventing Stress and Stress-Related Illnesses*, Toronto, Ontario, Canada: Robert Rose.

Kidd, A. H. and Kidd, R. M. (1987) 'Reactions of infants and toddlers to live and toy animals', *Psychological Reports*, 61, 455–464.

Kleinman, A., Guess, H. A. and Wilentz, J. S. (2002) 'An overview', in Guess, H. A., Kleinman, A., Kusek, J. W. and Engel, L. E. (eds) *The Science of Placebo: Toward an Interdisciplinary Research Agenda*, London: BMJ Books, pp. 1–32.

Kradin, R. (2008) *The Placebo Response and the Power of Unconscious Healing*, New York: Routledge.

Kutner, J. S., Smith, M. C., Corbin, L., Hemphill, L., Benton, K., Mellis, B. K., Beaty, B., Felton, S., Yamashita, T. E., Bryant, L. L. and Fairclough, D. L. (2008) 'Massage therapy versus simple touch to improve pain and mood in patients with advanced cancer: A randomized trial', *Annals of Internal Medicine*, 149, 369–379.

LaTorre, M. A. (2005) 'The use of reiki in psychotherapy', *Perspectives in Psychiatric Care*, 41(4), 184–187.

Law, L. A. F., Evans, S., Knudtson, J., Nus, S., Scholl, K. and Sluka, K. A. (2008) 'Massage reduces pain perception and hyperalgesia in experimental muscle pain: A randomized, controlled trial', *Journal of Pain*, 9(8), 714–721.

Long, A. F. (2008) 'The effectiveness of shiatsu: Findings from a cross-European, prospective observational study', *Journal of Alternative and Complementary Medicine*, 14(8), 921–930.

Lynch, J. J. (2000) *A Cry Unheard: New Insights into the Medical Consequences of Loneliness*, Baltimore, MD: Bancroft Press.

Moerman, D. E. (2002) 'Explanatory mechanisms for placebo effects: Cultural influences and the meaning response', in Guess, H. A., Kleinman, A., Kusek, J. W. and Engel, L. (eds) *The Science of Placebo: Toward an Interdisciplinary Research Agenda*, London: BMJ Books, pp. 77–107.

Moliver, N., Mika, E. M., Chartrand, M. S., Burrus, S. W., Haussmann, R. E. and Khalsa, S. B. (2011) 'Increased hatha yoga experience predicts lower BMI and reduced medication use in women over 45', *International Journal of Yoga*, 4, 77–86.

Newman, R. B. and Miller, R. L. (2006) *Calm Healing: Methods for a New Era of Medicine*, Berkeley, CA: North Atlantic Books.

Peterson, C. (2006) *A Primer in Positive Psychology*, New York: Oxford University Press.

Phalen, K. F. (1998) *Integrative Medicine: Achieving Wellness Through the Best of Eastern and Western Medical Practices*, Boston, MA: Journey Editions.

Price, D. D., Finniss, D. G. and Benedetti, F. (2008) 'A comprehensive review of the placebo effect: Recent advances and current thought', *Annual Review of Psychology*, 59, 565–590.

Prochaska, J. O., Norcross, J. C. and DiClemente, C. C. (1994) *Changing for Good: A Revolutionary Six-Stage Program for Overcoming Bad Habits and Moving Your Life Positively Forward*, New York: HarperCollins.

Prochnik, G. (2010a) *In Pursuit of Silence: Listening for Meaning in a World of Noise*, New York: Doubleday.

—— (2010b) 'Now don't hear this', *New York Times*, 1 May 2010, http://www.nytimes.com/2010/05/02/opinion/02prochnik.html?src=tptw (accessed 26 December, 2011).

Rajagopal, S. (2006) 'The placebo effect', *Pschiatric Bulletin*, 30, 185–188.

Sapolsky, R. (2004) *Why Zebras Don't Get Ulcers*, New York: Owl Books.

Schmied, C., Waiblinger, S., Scharl, T., Leisch, F. and Bovin, X. (2007) 'Stroking of different body regions by a human: Effects on behavior and heart rate of dairy cows', *Applied Animal and Behavior Science*, 109, 25–38.

Shannon, S. M. D. (2002) 'Introduction: The emerging paradigm', in Shannon, S. (ed.) *Handbook of Complementary and Alternative Therapies in Mental Health*, San Diego, CA: Academic Press, pp. 3–20.

Shapiro, A. K. and Shapiro, E. (1997) *The Powerful Placebo: From Ancient Priest to Modern Physician*, Baltimore, MD: Johns Hopkins University Press.

Vaillant, G. (2008) *Spiritual Evolution: A Scientific Defense of Faith*, New York: Broadway Books.

Wampold, B. E., Imel, Z. E. and Minami, T. (2007) 'The placebo effect: "Relatively large" and "robust" enough to survive another assault', *Journal of Clinical Psychology*, Apr 63(4), 401–403.

Wisneski, L. A. and Anderson, L. (2005) *The Scientific Basis of Integrative Medicine*, Boca Raton, FL: CRC Press.

12

Journeys of the self

The need to retreat

Catherine Kelly and Melanie Kay Smith

Introduction

In 2006, the authors of this chapter wrote a paper about holistic tourism and edited a special edition of a tourism journal (Smith and Kelly, 2006) to collate research on an emerging sector now well known as 'wellness tourism'. At the time, the authors chose to focus on the term 'holistic tourism' to reflect a preference for exploring tourism spaces that tried to engage with the whole self and the balance of body, mind and spirit. A distinction was made between those forms of tourism that take place in thermal or healing waters (e.g. hot springs and spas) and those that usually take place in (holistic) retreats and are generally not water-based. The former (i.e. health tourism using water) tends to be based more on curative treatments for the body, whereas the latter (i.e. retreat tourism) tends to be based more on preventive therapies for the mind and spirit. Self-development is also a major focus of this form of tourism. Subsequent publications (e.g. Bushell and Sheldon, 2009; Erfurt-Cooper and Cooper, 2009; Smith and Puczkó, 2009, 2013; Kelly, 2012; Voigt and Pforr, 2013) have made this distinction much clearer. For example, Voigt, Brown and Howat's (2011) wellness tourism research makes the distinction between beauty spas, lifestyle resorts and spiritual retreats, but there have still been relatively few publications that have focused exclusively on retreat-based tourism (with the exception of Lea, 2008; Heintzmann, 2013; Fu, Tanyatanaboon and Lehto, 2015). Along with Dina Glouberman and Josée-Ann Cloutier's contribution to this handbook (Chapter 13), this chapter provides a re-visitation of retreat-based tourism. However, as a complement to Glouberman and Cloutier's chapter, which focuses on the importance of communities for holistic wellbeing, this chapter explores the idea of how individual selves negotiate their everyday lives in conjunction with the idea of retreating for various purposes at different stages in their lives.

Women, in particular, are focused on as key participants in this form of tourism, especially middle-aged women. Research has shown that the majority of spa and wellness consumers and tourists are women, e.g. ISPA (2011) showed that around 78 per cent of visitors are women in US spas and with an average age of 45 (Smith and Puczkó, 2009, 2013). Kelly's (2012) research, based on several retreats, showed that 88 per cent of retreat visitors were female. The age range varied, but a relatively high number tends to be between 35 and 55. As suggested by Gray (2002), women are more open to discussing their feelings and emotions in a public forum, according to popular psychological research. The Retreat Company (2013) represents at least 500 retreat centres in the UK and Europe and reported that their most popular requests are for yoga holidays. Gerritsma (2008) analysed yoga in the Netherlands and showed that on average yoga practitioners are about 80 per cent women and 20 per cent men. This confirmed the study of Lehto, Brown, Chen and Morrison (2006) and is also confirmed by Smith and Sziva in this handbook (Chapter 14). Women's identities, family responsibilities and physical bodies are scrutinised by others and by themselves on an ongoing basis according to objectification theory (Mask, Blanchard and Baker, 2014). Fullagar and O'Brien (2014) suggest that women aged 35–44 in Australia make the most use of online access to psychologists and psycho-therapists. A recent study showed that, although women are generally happier and more satisfied than men, they also report higher levels of anxiety (Office for National Statistics, 2016). Engagement with holistic retreats for spiritual or psychological respite/reflection allow women space, time and support to cope with their everyday lives, their self-perceptions and anxiety levels. A case study of a women's retreat is presented in the latter part of the chapter to illustrate how this works in practice.

The growing need to retreat

One question that needs to be considered in the context of wellness or wellbeing is whether (and if so, why?) it is actually necessary to retreat from everyday life in order to enhance a sense of self. Optimum wellbeing should ideally be possible in the context of everyday life – in leisure rather than tourism – but there are several reasons why retreating may sometimes be desirable. Contemporary capitalist societies encourage a culture of instant gratification. Unfortunately, the result of instant gratification, over-consumption and increasing speed has not been a very happy one, with growing rates of obesity in most Western countries, high levels of depression and suicide, even in some of the supposed 'happiest' countries and a lingering sense that 'there must be more to life than this'. One principle that has been proved time and again is the fact that money does not buy happiness, at least, after a certain point. The Easterlin paradox has been debated in wellbeing circles for three decades and consensus was reached that increased material gains do not necessarily equate to increased wellbeing or happiness, especially after a certain level of income has been attained (Easterlin, 1974; Knight and Rosa, 2011). The exact level has not been agreed, but the principle still holds. It is often assumed that reducing consumption would lead to a decrease in quality of life or wellbeing, but this need not be the case (it should be noted here that quality of life and wellbeing are often seen as synonymous terms and that happiness is often considered to be synonymous with subjective wellbeing, e.g. Theofilou, 2013).

The cult of speed has engulfed societies to such an extent that the intervention of a whole movement was needed to counter it, the so-called 'Slow Movement'. The author of *In Praise of Slow*, Carl Honoré (2004) encouraged this movement in response to his own horror that his life had become one big 'soundbite'. Another 'counter-movement' (at least, in holistic circles) could be considered to have taken place with the publication of Erkhart Tolle's (1999) *The Power of Now*, which was published even earlier. This involves being fully present in the moment (arguably an early reference to a form of mindfulness) and very much 'here'. Kabat-Zinn (1994: 3) defines mindfulness as:

waking up and living in harmony with oneself and the world. It has to do with examining who we are, with questioning our view of the world and our place in it and with cultivating some appreciation for the fullness of each moment we are alive. Most of all, it has to do with being in touch.

Smalley and Winston (2010: xvi) state that 'Mindfulness may be thought of as a state of consciousness, one characterized by attention to present experience with a stance of open curiosity. It is quality of attention that can be brought to any experience'. Ericson, Kjonstad and Barstad (2014) argue that mindfulness has positive effects on both wellbeing and empathy and quote studies where mindfulness increased happiness and where happier people live more sustainably and with greater ecological awareness. Lewis-Smith, Diedrichs, Rumsey and Harcourt (2016) discuss how mindfulness has also been successful in improving the body image and problems of disordered eating among middle-aged women.

Gretchen Rubin (2013) conducted an interesting experiment to enhance her sense of happiness at home by truly appreciating what was already around her, arguably, a form of mindfulness. The last words of the book were 'Now is now. *Here* is my treasure' (Rubin, 2013: 253). Her experiment did not involve travel outside of her own city (New York), despite acknowledging that 'people who travel to new places and try new things are happier than those who stick only to the familiar' (Rubin, 2013: 219), but it did involve what might be described as 'staycation' experiences such as visiting new places within the city and appreciating them fully. This book raises the questions how far people may find what they are looking for within their home environment and how far it is necessary or desirable to travel. An interesting question to pose might be how much the everyday 'here' is lived or perhaps even tolerated, with the forward anticipation of being 'there' or away. Ouellette, Kaplan and Kaplan (2005) explored the motivation of 'being away' as one facet of spiritual retreat tourism and found it to be significant in a deeper experience for the visitor. Corvo (2011) also observes that it is a fragile, unsatisfied self that often waits all year for a holiday and focuses on it with great expectations and hope. Narwijn (2011) and Corvo (2011) even suggest that individual trips can create greater pre-trip than post-trip happiness.

Being aware, being present and engaged with the self are important elements, arguably, of holistic retreat tourists. Often, new participants in mindfulness practices find that an appetite for self-reflection and review happens and these needs can often be met through holistic or spiritual retreats. Tolle (2004: 271) states that 'your entire life journey ultimately consists of the step you are taking at this moment', so moving and being fully present in the moment are by no means incompatible. Mindfulness does not mean a literal standing still, but a state of being where awareness and presence are needed. During times of stillness and appreciation, the biggest changes may take place (e.g. during meditation, but also perhaps while travelling or being out of one's everyday environment and perspective). However, Tolle (2004) also suggests that many people feel more alive when they travel to foreign places or countries because this 'experiencing' or 'being' takes up more of their consciousness than thinking; they become more present. Some however, are still possessed by internal dialogue or constant 'mental chattering': 'they haven't really gone anywhere . . . only their body is travelling, while they remain where they have always been: in their head' (Tolle, 2004: 239). Therein lie some of the complexities of 'here versus there', being really present and variances within individual propensities for travel-prompted reflection or transformation. As suggested by Alain de Botton (2002), in *The Art of Travel*, one of the barriers to the enjoyment of travel is the fact that people cannot easily escape from themselves and their persistent worries. However, retreating may be one of the ways in which they can confront their worries in an alternative setting and learn how to deal with them better in everyday life when they return. A process of transformation may also begin to take place.

Wellness tourism and transformation

Reisinger (2013, 2015) argues that tourism offers rich transformational experiences. She suggests that:

> Travel can offer physical, psychological, cognitive affective and spiritual experiences that can change one's assumptions, expectations, world views and fundamental structures of the self. Travel can offer a journey to a new awareness, development and growth. This journey creates new meaning, offers fulfilment of unsatisfied needs and develops new authentic experiences.
>
> *(Reisinger, 2015: 5)*

Transformation is described as 'an inner journey' and part of a broader process of social change. This includes self-actualisation, being true to one's own nature and being authentic. However, she also argues that some types of tourism lead to transformation whereas others do not. For example, wellness tourism 'embraces the self and enhances the well-being of the individual, group and community' (Reisinger, 2013: 223). Reisinger's earlier work (Steiner and Reisinger, 2006) had suggested that wellness tourism is partly based on getting in touch with what is inside and outside us and on 'letting be' when encountering and dealing with the world. Smith (2013) outlines the potentially transformative power of wellness tourism in terms of physical, emotional/psychological, existential, spiritual, social, cultural and environmental dimensions.

Little (2012) also notes that health and wellness tourism is 'transformational' – taking people from one state of mind or bodily appearance to another, generally a positive one they are more happy and content with. She notes that there is a 'growing aspect of tourism emerging around exercise, healthy eating and bodily size and shape' (Little, 2012: 259). Fitness and weight loss holidays highlight modern ideas of the healthy body and the appropriate sizing of the body and the responsibilities people are taking for their own healthy bodies. Indeed, 'fitness retreats' often framed as 'bootcamps' use phrases such as 'journey to the more impressive you' (No. 1 Bootcamp, Ibiza, online 2015).

Little (2015) also explores the role of nature as an actor participating in this process of the transformative self, as does Lea (2008) in her exploration of 'retreating to nature'. These spaces often form important aspects of retreat destination decision making and Ouellette et al. (2005) further note that 'beauty' is an important factor in repeat visitation to the retreat in their research. So it can be argued that the individual self – gender, life-cycle stage, parenting, responsibilities, career changes, illness or even more abstract existential crises – all play a role in this transformational-reflective process, whilst the external environment and nature are also important for supporting and nurturing this process.

Travel and the self

Travel can be posed as both a means of escaping from one's self and reality or indeed as a means of finding it. Gazley and Watling (2015) disagree with the idea that tourists somehow 'find themselves' when travelling, but argue instead that self is created using symbolic products and experiences when abroad. The 'tourist' self is not considered to be a fixed entity. They define 'self' using the work of James (1950) and Blummer (1969), who divided the self into four: the material self, social self, spiritual self and pure ego. Tolle (1999) suggests that it is the 'ego' that watches and judges the 'true' self. Subsequent studies concur that self is indeed multi-faceted, e.g. Sirgy and Su (2000), who use four dimensions to explain and predict behaviour: actual self-image (how people actually see themselves); ideal self (how they would like to see themselves);

social self (how they think others see them); and ideal social self (how they would like others to see them). Gazley and Watling's (2015) findings support previous literature that how one sees one's 'ideal self' and 'social self' will have an impact on consumption-buying decisions.

However, holistic or transformational literature might argue that there is a 'true' or 'authentic' self (Reisinger, 2013). Smith (2013: 62) describes how 'Travel becomes truly transformative because it not only reveals a true or authentic self, but maybe a new and more adventurous self who may never had existed had the individual not travelled'.

Important here also is Ning Wang's conceptualisations of tourism and 'existential authenticity' (1999), which is in opposition to ideas of authenticity focused on objects or experiences – instead Wang considers the notion of tourist travel being driven by the search for 'the authentic self' or true self, which is relevant for many forms of wellness and holistic tourism.

Part of the true self may reside in the 'spiritual self', which is often explored in the context of retreats. Moal-Ulvoas and Taylor (2014: 454) note the importance of self in their definition of spirituality 'Spirituality is [thus] concerned with understanding reality in a broad sense and includes understanding one's self, other human beings or alterity and the sacred'. Although spiritual development is seen as a lifelong process, it is well documented that spirituality tends to grow in later life. Moal-Ulvoas and Taylor (2014) researched how spirituality can motivate older adults to travel and results in knowing the self better, giving global meaning to their lives, better understanding of others and connecting more closely with nature.

All of the above may cause us to question the different senses of self that individuals may experience at different ages and life stages and to consider how this may impact upon their behaviour and activities. The average age of wellness tourists (including those who go to spas, retreats or for medical tourism) is around 45 or middle age (Smith and Puczkó, 2013). It is no coincidence that this is the average age, as several studies suggest, that middle-aged people have the lowest levels of happiness, with the so-called 'U-bend' of life reaching its lowest point in the mid-40s or early 50s (*The Economist*, 2010; Office for National Statistics, 2016). Robinson and Wright (2013: 408) describe midlife crises (usually occuring between 40 and 49) as the presence of strong negative emotions and major changes 'not just a time of internal crisis but also a time of external transition . . . it centres on major, tangible changes in life structure, as well as challenges and changes to identity and affect'. Whatever happens, the journey continues and there is no choice but to continue with it. As stated by Shafak (2010: 343), 'Little by little, one turns forty, fifty and sixty and, with each major decade, feels more complete. You need to keep walking, though there's no place to arrive at'. Finding ways to do this while experiencing the maximum levels of happiness possible is one of life's biggest challenges.

Tolle (2004: 115) suggests that it comes from the power of now, stating that 'Being one with life is being one with NOW. You then realize that you don't live your life, but life lives you. Life is the dancer and you are the dance'. Most human beings need a helping hand at one time or another to achieve this, even temporarily. This may come from psychotherapy or counselling, from spiritual practices or from wellness activities. The following section provides a brief overview of how retreats may provide the space and activities to nurture and develop the self through its life journey. However, long-term benefits are only really possible with regular practice of what is learnt there and that may be the critical difference between wellness tourism, everyday life and long-term benefits.

Holistic retreats and tourism

Lea (2008) suggests that there is a long history of removing oneself from everyday life in order to rest and recuperate; however, escapism is only one part of the experience in retreat tourism

(Smith, 2013). Connections with the self and nature are all part of the therapeutic process, but these may be negative and uncomfortable, however healing they become ultimately (Lea, 2008). Indeed, Reisinger (2013, 2015) emphasises the challenges of transformation in terms of feelings of insecurity, risk or even trauma. Retreats technically offer 'safe' spaces in which to develop the self, but self-development is not always a comfortable process, just as a pilgrimage is not an easy route to spirituality. Indeed, as suggested by Heintzmann (2013), some tourists visit retreat centres to deal with or overcome negative or life events, such as serious illnesses, relationship break-ups or the death of a loved one. Even the names of many retreat centres reflect the emphasis on restoration/the self, including Restival, an eco-tent detox retreat in the Sahara desert in Morocco and Reclaim Your Self, a yoga holiday company offering luxury yurt-based yoga holidays in Mongolia.

Retreats can be defined as places for quiet reflection and rejuvenation, an opportunity to regain good health and/or a time for spiritual reassessment and renewal, either alone or in a group (Retreats Online, 2007, cited in Kelly, 2010). Unpicking this definition, it is apparent that the concept of 'retreat' may mean a physical place or an opportunity or moment in time for rest, reflection or self-improvement of some sort. An immense variety of retreat options exist, some driven by spiritual organisations, others by tourism-led motives and the term itself borrowed often in different contexts making a comprehensive typology difficult. However, examining the current offering in Table 12.1 suggests a typology of retreats from the provision/supply side.

It is possible to classify retreats in many ways – based on the place, the environment, the activities, the spiritual emphasis and so on. What is clear from the literature and the actual holidays on offer to visitors is that the range, content and purpose are quite immense. Retreats Online (2007), for example, classify retreats by location, by date and by 'activity' – the latter uses categories such as 'personal/creative', 'spiritual', 'outdoor', 'yoga' and so on, led by market preferences perhaps. Specialist retreats offering nutritional advice are very current, as are fitness weight loss 'camps'. Many appeal to the solo traveller and as such, the 'self' is therefore the critical element, whether for psychological or physical respite or improvement. Descriptors of going 'off grid' or to 'secluded boltholes' are common, emphasising displacement from the everyday stresses of modern life. For this chapter, the main interest lies in spiritual, religious, mind-based and holistic body–mind–spirit retreats and their visitor experiences and motivations. Table 12.1 offers a wider contextualisation of the way in which the sector itself liberally uses the term 'retreat'.

Of the limited amount of academic research on retreats, much of the work centres on the visitors and their engagement with different activities and motivations. Fu et al.'s (2015) study of online reviews of retreat guests revealed that many of them were driven to visit retreats because of physical, work or existential challenges. Four major themes of perceived changes were identified, including bodily change, emotional change, attitudinal change and skill change. Their cluster analysis of retreat activities identified three types of visitors: i.e. physical and psychological balance seeker; bodily therapeutic seeker; and spiritual enhancement seeker. Overall, they concluded that a transformative experience may be intentionally sought by guests but can only be facilitated through co-creative processes, including carefully designed programmes and tailored activities coupled with conducive settings and service delivery. However, they emphasise that only a longitudinal study could test whether there is a long-term transformative effect after guests return home.

In other research on retreat visitors, Kelly (2012) noted that the rest/relaxation factor was the main motivator, with social and spiritual reasons coming in strongly, but to a much lesser degree. Supporting this, a typology of visitors classified these retreat tourists into learners, exploratory dabblers, reinforcers and spiritualists. All have varying reasons for coming on retreats and with

Table 12.1 A typology of retreats

Category	Emphasis	Examples
Spiritual	Spiritually informed spaces and practices, e.g. ashrams Practices: silent/other meditation, personal reflection	Buddhist retreat centres, ashrams, e.g. Rivendale, Gaia House, UK
Religious	Spaces owned and/or run by religious communities Practices: prayer, reflection	Monasteries, convents and other religious settings offering residential retreats to visitors
Yoga retreats	Specifically advertised as 'yoga retreats' Practices: yoga-dominated holidays offering different types of yoga (ashtanga, hatha, etc.)	Purpose-built centres, or temporary settings hired overseas by yoga teachers to offer their everyday clients a yoga-based holiday
Health retreats	Permanent or temporary settings offering health improvement retreats Practices: often based on certain nutritional activities such as juicing, fasting, healthy diet or aimed at certain ailments (e.g. asthma, obesity, and so on)	Explore Raw, UK company running retreats in Portugal, and many others with various combinations of nutrition/place offerings
Fitness retreats	Aimed at short-term motivation and supported programmes for kickstarting physical exercise Practices: scheduled programmes of running, and indoor/outdoor classes and challenges, usually involves nutrition and dietary programme aimed at weight loss	'Bootcamps' for weekend or weeklong stays in the UK or overseas. Some focus on certain activities, such as running, e.g. GI Jane camps, UK Often celebrity-endorsed Wild Fitness, Zanzibar
Mind-based retreats	Offering retreats emphasising rest, relaxation and reflection outside of spiritual/religious contexts Practices: meditation, mindfulness, counselling	Permanent or temporary retreat spaces hired by practitioners abroad, e.g. Wildnerness Minds – mindfulness in nature; Corejourneys, everyday and outdoor/retreat wellbeing: both UK Vipassana meditation centres, India
Body–mind–spirit	Usually permanent retreat centres, established to offer a holistic provision of activities that help revive the physical, spiritual and the psychological self (yoga, meditation, nutrition, exercise, groupwork)	Skyros, Greece, Cortijo Romero, Spain, Kamalaya Wellness Sanctuary, Thailand
Miscellaneous	Place-defined retreats, e.g. eco-retreats in rainforests, deserts or other unsual locations, where the environment itself contributes strongly to the experience	e.g. Negev desert eco-retreat, Tailwind Jungle Lodge, Mexico, Wind, Sand and Stars silent retreat, Sinai desert, Egypt

different levels of experience in common retreat practices such as yoga, meditation, tai chi and so on. Notions of the reflective self and transformation were very evident in this research, where participants spoke about going away to feel better and returning home as new and 'better' versions of themselves. Personal growth, enlightenment, new-found understandings of practices, of themselves and of others were discussed by retreat participants, reflecting other research noted above by Lea (2009), Little (2012) and Reisinger (2013).

Women's need to retreat

Kelly (2012) notes that the lens through which a person sees his/her own sense of self and life purpose in a home setting can be blurred by the everyday routines of work, childcare, commuting and other duties. This lens is clearer when individuals take themselves to a chosen retreat location with the purposeful decision of engaging with a particular practice, guru or even just to rest. Corvo (2011) suggests that holidays have strong symbolic values for individuals and can serve to recoup lost identities. For women there are changes in physical appearance with age and childbirth and objectification theory posits that women are generally socialised to adopt a 'body-as-object' perspective of their physical self. This is reinforced by the media, which values women mainly for their visual and sexual appeal (Mask et al., 2014). Lewis-Smith et al. (2016) suggest that body dissatisfaction and disordered eating are prevalent among women in midlife and often have adverse and long-term impacts on both physical and psychological quality of life. Post-childbirth women engage in multi-tasking and 'juggling' as attempts are made by many to hold on to old identities and hard-won careers as well as take on new self-identities as mothers. Fullagar and O'Brien (2014) suggest that many women find themselves in a feminised carer role which is constantly 'other-orientated'. They describe 'the challenges women face in overcoming gendered constraints that impede their exploration of different relations to self and how leisure practices are an important domain of capabilities' (Fullagar and O'Brien, 2014: 120). They also suggest that, rather than becoming the object of medical intervention when and if depressed, women could learn to understand themselves and engage in more affective transformations through self-care practices. There can be a silencing, a privatised isolation of women as they take on these new and different roles. Many find themselves constantly tired as they attempt to run families and homes, support partners and children, with very little physical or emotional time left for themselves.

Robinson and Wright (2013) suggest that women's midlife crises (if they happen) tend to centre more around problems with family and relationships, whereas men's include more work and career problems. A growing awareness of mortality and ageing, often engendered by bereavement, can also contribute to crisis episodes. Darling, Coccia and Senatore (2012) mention some of the other stressors that can lower women's life satisfaction in midlife, such as symptoms of menopause and hormone changes, sleep disturbances, reduced energy levels, body fat re-distribution and weight gain.

As discussed earlier, it is no surprise that it is women and especially middle-aged women, who make up the largest proportion of wellness tourists. Again, research shows that different motivations exist around specific types of wellness tourism. Voigt et al. (2011), for example, discuss the beauty spa tourist, the lifestyle resort tourist and the spiritual retreat tourist as three quite separate entities. Women are attracted to all of these and they all offer different forms of respite for the female body, mind and spirit.

Wellness tourism is often overtly multi-sensuous and explicitly an embodied experience (Lea, 2008). Thinking about tourism as being constructed in a 'multi-sensuous way' (Haldrup, 2004) makes it easier to view the intersections between tourists' embodied experiences and the spaces they are situated in (Edensor, 2000). Retreats are very much female, embodied spaces, where women can engage in social, spiritual or physical practices that collectively encourage holistic wellbeing outside their everyday contexts. Going back to 1996, Kinnaird and Hall (95) observed that whether we examine divisions of labour, the social construction of landscape, how societies construct the cultural 'other' or the realities of the experiences of tourist and hosts, it is possible to examine the issues of relationships, differences and inequalities resulting from tourism-related processes in terms of gender relations. This therefore allows us to differentiate to a certain extent between women's and men's construction, consumption and experiences of tourism. Retreats as sites of tourism are female-dominated (Kelly, 2010, 2012) and as such are interesting spaces within which to observe how women rest, reflect and connect with the self and others.

Despite the tendency to assume that male appeals are universal appeals, research suggests that female and male perceptions and experiences of space differ substantially. Women are more concerned usually with the quality of the tourism experience and the process, while men are more oriented towards the activity and the visit (Pritchard and Morgan, 2000). Furthermore, Shields (1991) argues that any examination of space must explore its emotional geography. This term, arguably, is central to place and space of retreat tourism, in so far as the creation of 'emotional communities' is critical for a deep, fulfilling experience for many visitors, especially women (see Chapter 13). It can be suggested therefore that holistic tourism in forms such as retreats set themselves apart from traditional gendered power relations inherent in much of the tourism sector. Swain (1995) states that men's capacity to control women's sense of security and self-worth has been central to the evolution of tourism politics. Holistic tourism retreats, in contrast, often enable women to reinforce, rediscover and reflect on their self-worth. Unlike family holidays, where a mother usually makes decisions that prioritise the children's or whole family's preferences, retreat breaks are usually taken by solo women and allow a woman to choose just for herself, a diminishing action for many women in today's society that ironically sells the myth of 'having it all'.

For women, the sense of an informal, albeit temporary, sense of community, in the form of other guests, instructors and support staff, helps to create a sense of safety and sharing. This is crucial in the nature of activities where life crises, uncertainty or identity challenges prompt women literally to retreat from their everyday lives. Motivations for women to go on holistic holidays include the need to overcome loss of emotional ties, demonstrate women's abilities, establish independence, escape from domesticity and the comfort in doing something alone (Kinnaird and Hall, 1996). In addition, there is a desire for connection with other women, the voyage of inner journeys, escapism from gendered responsibilities (young children and/or elderly parents) and the draw of a place that is peaceful, safe and beautiful. Kelly (2012) notes the three elements of 'the place', 'the activities' and the 'intangible retreat experience' for retreat visitors. The latter, intangible experiences, often centre around friendships made, problems shared or lightened or a positive energy that is created through a mix of like-minded people doing something fulfilling.

Unlike many male-oriented activities, where patriarchal 'mastery' of a landscape (mountain-eering, for example or other adventure sports) is embedded in a sense of performance or competition (even with the self), the female-dominated activities of many retreat centres are inward looking and focus on working with the body/mind. Yoga, for example, often means rethinking or unlearning traditional physical instructions. Rowling (2005), commenting on a women-only yoga retreat, observed that she had gained insight into how to 'work *with* my body as a woman, rather than against it'. She notes the special dynamic created by women-only audiences, where instructors concur that there is no external spirit of competition, only inwardly directed competition in relation to self-work. This retreat work of offering women an understanding of their body and its specific needs during the transitional periods of life (pregnancy, motherhood, menopause) allow women to be better armed psychologically for the transformations they face.

Male and female differences of perception towards these activities can be noticed. Indeed, Onaro et al.'s (2015) research using the extensive US National Health Interview Survey 2002, 2007 and 2012 showed that men were half as likely as women to engage in meditation as well as mind–body exercise activities containing a mindfulness element (e.g. yoga, tai chi, qigong). In fact, they were three times less likely to practise yoga. Blowhard (2005) cites sources which suggest that yoga creates a state of vulnerability, especially emotional vulnerability and that women tend to be more comfortable with this than men. He also quotes one online male yoga webchat participant who announced:

> as far as getting in touch with my inner-whatever, that's the opposite of that I want to do with my free time. I want to do something that gets me outside and engaged in the world. Introspection has its place, but inherently its a private and unstructured activity, rather than social and directed – at least it is for me.

It can be seen from this section that retreats can serve multiple purposes depending on the needs of a particular individual at a given time in his or her life. It seems that men are far less likely to partake of the experiences and activities offered by retreats and that women and especially middle-aged women, tend to be the core market. Therefore, the following case study gives an example of a women-only retreat in the UK which serves this important and growing market.

Case study: Breathing Space, Norfolk

Breathing Space . . . for Women is a retreat centre based in the Norfolk Broads in the east of the UK. The name was coined by one of the authors of this chapter (Kelly). It was set up just over 10 years ago by its founder, a woman on her own who had moved from London to escape the stresses of the city, in a small barn conversion. Over time the concept grew and Breathing Space now resides in a beautiful historic country manor house surrounded by lovely grounds and retreat spaces outside in nature. It is close to both the inland waterways of the Norfolk Broads as well as the coast, just 1 km away. It is promoted as 'the place for women on their own or with friends to come and relax, just "Breathe" and feel the stresses of everyday life fall away, re-charge, re-energise and feel uplifted' (Breathing Space, 2016). The founder says her motivation for starting the retreat was 'to share the experience of living the Norfolk country life by the sea and to share the fun and freedom' (personal interview, 2016). At the time she was living alone in her barn conversion and thought male guests might be intimidating in a small space, but as it turns out women-only retreats have become a strong niche market. It is not only the visitors to retreats who seek these emotional geographies of safety and connection, but their owners too in many cases. Kelly's (2010) work on retreat operators notes the lifestyle and the altruistic motivations of many retreat operators and this case study supports these ideas.

The founder notes that 'women feel free to be more themselves and more comfortable not having men around . . . they can connect with each other and there is no need to impress'. This supports research mentioned earlier about women's need for community and the freedom to be themselves or indeed, their 'authentic selves'. Success, says the founder of Breathing Space, is 'creating a loving and nurturing environment, a feeling of community and family'.

The motivations to set up this retreat centre and its criteria for success are mirrored in the views of the guests who stay there. Unlike retreat centres that offer pre-determined programmes of activities (such as Skyros or Cortijo Romero in Spain), guests at Breathing Space are encouraged to choose what they would like to do from a wide range of possible offerings (see breathingspacenorfolk.com) and this makes for a restful and bespoke experience. Visitors are offered do-it-yourself programmes for taking advantage of various holistic therapies, engaging with nature, walks or other

(continued)

(continued)

outdoor activities. Meditation, yoga, nutrition, massage and beauty treatments as well as many other spiritual therapies are on offer, given by in-house and also local community-based practitioners. Breathing Space is one of only a few retreat centres that are strongly embedded in their local community and have won awards for Community Impacts in Tourism. 'Community', therefore, is something which is practised and created for guests within the retreat space but also for locals as a place to gather, plan and share ideas. Many women practitioners of alternative or complementary therapies who live locally are employed by Breathing Space to deliver treatments as requested by guests. In addition, the centre draws high-profile speakers/performers and guests alike.

Groups of women friends and relatives are also catered for, especially for celebrations – a move away from traditional hen-party hedonism. The food on offer is locally sourced and organic where possible and the founder is trained in nutrition. In addition, aromatherapy organic products for the bathroom and face/body creams are produced by the founder's own family, Sorrells Naturally and guests who use these products during their stay can purchase some to take home.

Many of the guest comments or visitor testimonials on TripAdvisor (2015–2016) give a good indication of the motivations for going to a retreat and the benefits that can be gained from the experience:

> Whatever rest means for you, this place has it all: gorgeous surroundings, nurturing food, truly kind people, restorative therapies, lovely nature reserves right nearby, the beach.

> As a busy working Mum and nurse I spend a lot of time looking after other people. It was such a lovely experience to be looked after myself!

> A place that worked miracles on me. I ran to Mags and team in the midst of a personal crisis. I was welcomed with open arms, nurtured and respected.

> The 'family' at Breathing Space are wonderful and a sense of calm envelops you as you walk through the door.

(Visitor testimonials, TripAdvisor, 2015–2016)

The coast, the Broads and an onsite lake: therapeutic landscapes for everyone

The female visitors to Breathing Space meet many of the characteristics described in previous research. Nurturing, connections and support are paramount. Women requiring rest and peace or at a crossroads can find a fulfilling retreat experience offered by other women, who themselves have had similar 'journeys of the self'.

Conclusion

This chapter suggests that everyday life may not always afford individuals enough opportunities to resolve some of life's challenges, especially at particular moments or stages in life (e.g. crisis, middle age). Journeys of the self may need to be taken in alternative locations to home, especially in retreat centres, many of which are purposely designed with self-development and transformation in mind. In cultures where speed, materialism, instant gratification and over-consumption have become key characteristics, retreats can offer a range of mindful practices which bring individuals back to the 'here and now' and to a more existentially authentic sense of self – a 'true self', rather than one driven by ego, the 'social self' or the 'ideal self'. Women, particularly middle-aged women, are especially drawn to retreat activities and experiences and they tend to constitute one of the main markets for this form of tourism. This is even more likely to be the case if the retreat focuses on yoga. The case study in this chapter illustrated some of the benefits of women-only retreat centres, which can provide supportive, nurturing, restorative experiences for women who may have lost touch with elements of their self and identity in everyday life. Retreats offer individuals the opportunity to reconnect with themselves in the company of like-minded others, with the inner and outer selves, body, mind and spirit combining together in a healing and holistic experience.

References

Blowhard, M. (2005) *Yoga Notes*, 2Blowhards Blog, http://www.2blowhards.com/archives/002149.html (accessed 16 February 2016).

Blummer, H. (1969) *Symbolic Interaction*, Englewood Cliffs, NJ: Prentice Hall.

Breathing Space (2016) *Breathing Space for Women*, www.breathingspacenorfolk.com (accessed January 2016).

Bushell, R. and Sheldon, P. J. (2009) *Wellness and Tourism: Mind, Body, Spirit, Place*, New York: Cognizant.

Corvo, P. P. (2011) 'The pursuit of happiness and the globalised tourist', *Social Indicators Research*, 102, 95–97.

Darling, C. A., Coccia, C. and Senatore, N. (2012) 'Women in midlife: Stress, health and life satisfaction', *Stress and Health*, 28, 31–40.

De Botton, A. (2002) *The Art of Travel*, London: Hamish Hamilton.

Easterlin, R. A. (1974) 'Does economic growth improve the human lot? Some empirical evidence', in David, P. A. and Reder, M. W. (eds) *Nations and Households in Economic Growth: Essays in Honour of Moses Abramowitz*, New York: Academic Press, pp. 89–125.

Edensor, T. (2000) 'Staging tourism: Tourists as performers', *Annals of Tourism Research*, 27(2), 322–344.

Erfurt-Cooper, P. and Cooper, M. (2009) *Health and Wellness Tourism: Spas and Hot Springs*, Clevedon, UK: Channel View.

Ericson, T., Kjonstad, B. G. and Barstad, A. (2014) 'Mindfulness and sustainability', *Ecological Economics*, 104, 73–79.

Fu, X., Tanyatanaboon, M. and Lehto, X. Y. (2015) 'Conceptualizing transformative guest experience at retreat centres', *International Journal of Hospitality Management*, 49, 83–92.

Fullagar, S. and O'Brien, W. (2014) 'Social recovery and the move beyond deficit models of depression: A feminist analysis of mid-life women's self-care practices', *Social Science and Medicine*, 117, 116–124.

Gazley, A. and Watling, L. (2015) 'Me, my tourist self and I: The symbolic consumption of travel', *Journal of Travel and Tourism Marketing*, 32, 639–655.

Gerritsma, R. (2008) 'The growing yoga community in the Netherlands: How yoga is becoming a lifestyle product including tourism activities', in Smith, M. K. and Puczkó, L. (eds) *Health and Wellness Tourism*, Oxford, UK: Butterworth Heinemann, pp. 361–365.

Gray, J. (2002) *Men Are from Mars, Women Are from Venus: How to Get What You Want in Your Relationships*, London: HarperCollins.

Haldrup, M. (2004) 'Laid-back mobilities: Second-home holidays in time and space', *Tourism Geographies*, 6(4), 434–454.

Heintzmann, P. (2013) 'Retreat tourism', in Reisinger, Y. (ed.) *Transformational Tourism Tourist Perspectives*, Wallingford: CABI, pp. 68–81.

Honoré, C. (2004) *In Praise of Slow*, London: Orion.

ISPA (2011) http://www.spalietuva.lt/wp-content/uploads/2011/04/ISPA-US-Spa-Industry-Study-2011-FINAL-260911-online.pdf (accessed 2 March 2013).

James, W. (1950) *The Principles of Psychology*, New York: Dover Publications.

Kabat-Zinn, J. (1994) *Wherever You Go, There You Are: Mindfulness Meditation for Everyday Life*, London: Piatkus.

Kelly, C. (2010) 'Analysing wellness tourism provision: A retreat operator's study', *Journal of Hospitality and Tourism Management*, 17(1), 108–116.

—— (2012) 'Wellness tourism: Retreat visitor motivations and experiences', *Tourism Recreation Research*, 37(3), 205–213.

Kinnaird, V. and Hall, D. (1996) 'Understanding tourism processes: A gender-aware framework', *Tourism Management*, 17(2), 95–102.

Knight, K. W. and Rosa, E. A. (2011) 'The environmental efficiency of well-being: A cross-national analysis', *Social Science Research*, 40, 931–949.

Lea, J. (2008) 'Retreating to nature: Rethinking "therapeutic landscapes"', *Area*, 40(1), 90–98.

—— (2009) 'Becoming skilled: The cultural and corporeal geographies of teaching and learning Thai yoga massage', *Geoforum*, 40(3), 465–474.

Lehto, X., Brown, S., Chen, Y. and Morrison, A. M. (2006) 'Yoga tourism as a niche within the wellness sector', *Journal of Tourism Recreation Research*, 31(1), 25–36.

Lewis-Smith, H., Diedrichs, P. C., Rumsey, N. and Harcourt, D. (2016) 'A systematic review of interventions on body image and disordered eating outcomes among women in midlife', *International Journal of Eating Disorders*, 49(1), 5–18.

Little, J. (2012) 'Transformational tourism, nature and wellbeing: new perspectives on fitness and the body', *Sociologia Ruralis*, 52(3), pp. 257–271.

—— (2015) 'Nature, wellbeing and the transformational self', *Geographical Journal*, 181(2), 121–128.

Mask, L., Blanchard, C. M. and Baker, A. (2014) 'Do portrayals of women in action convey another ideal that women with little self-determination feel obligated to live up to? Viewing effects on body image evaluations and eating behaviors', *Appetite*, 83, 277–286.

Moal-Ulvoas, G. and Taylor, V. A. (2014) 'The spiritual benefits of travel for senior tourists', *Journal of Consumer Behaviour*, 13, 453–462.

Narwijn, J. (2011) 'Happiness through vacationing: Just a temporary boost or long-term benefits?', *Journal of Happiness Studies*, 12, 651–665.

No.1 Bootcamp, Ibiza, online (2015) http://www.no1bootcamp.com/index.php?page=abroad (accessed 26 July 2016).

Office for National Statistics (ONS) (2016) *At What Age Is Personal Well-Being the Highest?* http://www.ons.gov.uk/ons/dcp171776_431796.pdf (accessed 2 February 2016).

Onaro, H. A., Kachan, D., Tannenbaum, S. L., Mehta, A., Annane, D. and Lee, D. J. (2015) 'Engagement in mindfulness practices by U.S. adults: Sociodemographic barriers', *Journal of Alternative and Complementary Medicine,* 21(2), 100–102.

Ouellette, P., Kaplan, R. and Kaplan, S. (2005) 'The monastery as a restorative environment', *Journal of Environmental Psychology*, 25(2), 175–188.

Pritchard, A. and Morgan, N. J. (2000) 'Privileging the male gaze: Gendered tourism landscapes', *Annals of Tourism Research*, 27(4), 884–905.

Retreat Finder (2013) http://www.retreatfinder.com (accessed 3 March 2013).

Retreats Online (2007) *Directory of Retreats*, www.retreatsonline.com (accessed February 2016).

Reisinger, Y. (2013) *Transformational Tourism: Tourist Perspectives*, Wallingford, UK: CABI.

—— (2015) *Transformational Tourism: Host Perspectives*, Wallingford, UK: CABI.

Robinson, O. C. and Wright, G. R. T. (2013) 'The prevalence, types and perceived outcomes of crisis episodes in early adulthood and midlife: A structured retrospective-autobiographical study', *International Journal of Behavioral Development*, 37(5), 407–416.

Rowling, D. (2005) 'In the company of women', *Yoga Journal*, www.yogajournal.com/travel/275.cfm (accessed January 2016).

Rubin, G. (2013) *Happier at Home*, London: Hodder & Stoughton.

Shafak, E. (2010) *The Forty Rules of Love*, London: Penguin.

Shields, R. (1991) *Places on the Margin: Alternative Geographies of Modernity*, London: Routledge.

Sirgy, M. J. and Su, C. (2000) 'Destination image, self-congruity, and travel behavior: Toward an integrative model', *Journal of Travel Research*, 38(4), 340–352.

Smalley, S. L. and Winston, D. (2010) *Fully Present: The Science, Art and Practice of Mindfulness*, Philadelphia, PA: Da Capo Press.

Smith, M. K. (2013) 'Wellness tourism and its transformational practices', in Reisinger, Y. (ed.) *Transformational Tourism Tourist Perspectives*, Wallingford, UK: CABI, pp. 55–67.

Smith, M. and Kelly, C. (2006) 'Journeys of the self: The rise of the wellness tourism sector', *Journal of Tourism and Recreation Research*, 31(1), 15–25.

Smith, M. K. and Puczkó, L. (2009) *Health and Wellness Tourism*, Oxford, UK: Butterworth Heinemann, Elsevier.

—— (2013) *Health, Tourism and Hospitality: Spas, Wellness and Medical Travel*, London: Routledge.

Steiner, C. and Reisinger, Y. (2006) 'Ringing the fourfold: A philosophical framework for thinking about wellness tourism', *Journal of Tourism Recreation Research*, 31(1), 5–14.

Swain, M. (1995) 'Gender in tourism', *Annals of Tourism Research*, 22(2), 247–266.

The Economist (2010) *The U-Bend of Life*, 16 December, http://www.economist.com/node/17722567 (accessed 26 August 2015).

Theofilou, P. (2013) 'Quality of life: Definition and measurement', *Europe's Journal of Psychology*, 9(1), 150–162.

The Retreat Company (2013) http://www.theretreatcompany.com (accessed 3 March 2013).

Tolle, E. (1999) *The Power of Now: A Guide to Spiritual Enlightenment*, London: Hodder & Stoughton.

—— (2004) *A New Earth: Awakening to Your Life's Purpose*, New York: Plume.

Voigt, C. and Pforr, C. (2013) *Wellness Tourism*, London: Routledge.

Voigt, C., Brown, G. and Howat, G. (2011) 'Wellness tourists: In search of transformation', *Tourism Review*, 66(1/2), 16–30.

Wang, N. (1999) 'Rethinking authenticity in tourism experience', *Annals of Tourism Research*, 26(2), 49–370.

13

Community as holistic healer on health holiday retreats

The case of Skyros

Dina Glouberman and Josée-Ann Cloutier

The dialogue between the conventional view that a health holiday is one that offers visitors a form of luxury spa with healthy food or no food, physical treatments, classes and exercises, thermal baths and the like, and a more niche view that health can best be promoted in holiday community retreats that enable participants to go inward as well as outward, revise their lives as well as exercise their bodies, is one that has not yet been sufficiently aired in the literature on health tourism.

And yet, the increasing awareness that illness and early mortality can be psychologically precipitated, for example, by unresolved loss, loneliness, powerlessness, depression, anxiety or burnout and, more generally, that the body does not function out of context of the mind and emotion, draws us to an inescapable conclusion that promoting health with physical means alone will not be sufficient.

A holistic approach, which by definition works towards the health of the whole person, would seem therefore to make more sense. Further, an approach that takes account of the way that crises and turning points can lead to illness or health depending on the choices made can show why health-promoting holidays can be so powerful at certain life junctures.

Kelly (2012: 208) mentions that:

> retreats provoke their visitors to reflect upon themselves, before and after their holi-
> day . . . to contextualize who they are, often, in relation to where they are in their lives and
> where they would like to be. Individuals can use this touristic experience to ask questions
> of themselves that do not usually arise in mass tourism contexts.

Today, retreats and health holidays have been crafted to meet specific outcomes and needs and are increasingly becoming more attractive and appealing as demand increases within the wellness industry. The 2014 Wellness trends indicate that wellness retreats and holidays are on the rise (Trends Report, 2014) and 'specialty wellness retreats' that are tailored to specific goals and interests are again on the trends list in 2015 (Top Wellness Spa Travel Trends for 2015, 2015).

Retreats are a growing form of holiday and vacation time and are intended to relax and replenish personal health and development. The understanding of retreat is no longer associated with traditional spiritual and religious contexts alone but includes many types of holidays and getaways. Both urban retreats and destination spas offer more integrative wellness-oriented experiences. They accommodate a diverse range of interests, needs, styles and demographics and as a result, there are different retreat types addressing various needs, such as spiritual, lifestyle, holistic, eco, work, writing, art, detox, cancer, weight loss and more (Cloutier, 2015). Online platforms make them easier to access and find organised by location, date and type. For example, Retreats Online classifies retreats as 'yoga, spiritual-religious, health-wellness, personal creativity, destination-getaway, outdoor-adventure, business executive and meeting space' (Yoga Retreats on Retreats Online, 2014).

Looking at current trends within the health, wellness and spa sector, wellness holidays and retreats are growing due to the 'wellness-minded consumer', with wellness tourism defined as 'travel associated with the pursuit of maintaining or enhancing one's personal well-being' (Global Spa and Wellness Economy Monitor, 2014: v). The Global Spa and Wellness Economy Monitor report (2014) indicates that the wellness tourism economy was $494 billion in 2013, a 12.7 per cent increase from 2012. Retreats listed under lodging represented $103.6 billion.

Thus, retreats and holidays provide opportunities to replenish people's lives that may be neglected due to social forces and challenges such as the increase of speed and technology and the decrease in community support which together result in heightened disconnection and stress. It is suggested here that there is a growing longing and search for community and belonging which community-oriented holidays and retreats can address.

While there is a commonly held illusion that, due to the advancement of technology and especially online networking, people are more connected than ever, a study which compared the happiness effects of real and online friends found that the number of real-life friends is positively correlated with subjective wellbeing and the size of online networks is largely uncorrelated with subjective wellbeing (Helliwell and Huang, 2013).

A sense of community and belonging is the main lens examined in this chapter as a health outcome. Zygmunt Bauman (2001) discusses how a consumer-based worldview influences human bonds, thus pointing to the challenge and difficulty: 'Perceiving the world, complete with its inhabitants, as a pool of consumer items, makes the negotiation of lasting human bonds exceedingly hard' (Beilharz and Bauman, 2001: 165). Peter Block (2014) goes on to say that community goes against individualism and that the fear embedded in our modern culture makes community more of a longing than reality.

As a result, retreats, health holidays and other wellness-oriented environments can help counteract harmful social habits and the ill effects of isolation by creating temporary places, activities and structures that re-instill a sense of place by training to engage and interact more meaningfully (Cloutier, 2015). For example, Detox Retreats (Digital Detox, 2014) have gained popularity for people needing to 'disconnect to reconnect' and to 'create balance in the digital age'. Creating opportunities for community and connection to arise in a real way is not only a need but a necessity for individual and collective health.

It is important to explore the modern relevance of the ancient Greek approach to holistic health, which offers a comprehensive notion of health and emphasises the importance of a healthy community as well as the relevance of crisis in illness and health. The role of community in promoting holistic health and the psychological and psychiatric traditions of creating community, is also drawn out. The particular contribution of humanistic psychology to an understanding of how communication structures create healthy groups and communities, as well as its emphasis on evolution and development through life, is further discussed.

A case study of Skyros Holistic Holidays, co-founded and co-directed by Glouberman and researched by Smith and Puczkó (2013) and Cloutier (2015), brings together these strands of holism, community, communication, evolution and crisis. Skyros Holistic Holidays is a groundbreaking trendsetting holiday which has been operating and expanding since 1979. It offers a model of how a holistic healing community holiday can be created through a series of communication structures, as well as a background set of values and intentions and how this can have a profound effect on participants' lives. Skyros Holidays is recently including the natural environment and ecological concerns more directly. Recommendations for health holidays based on a holistic approach are suggested.

Ancient Greek holistic health

Notions of health today range from the conventional medical model which is oriented towards curing individual diseases and usually focuses on a particular area of the body, to community-based approaches like that of the Ottawa Charter of the World Health Organization, which views 'health promotion' as a health strategy that aims to develop communities to create supportive environments for health and endeavours to build healthy public policy (Public Health Agency of Canada, 1986).

This approach is not in fact new, but is very clearly expressed in ancient Greek philosophy. Socrates (circa 470–399 BC) warned against treating only one part of the body 'for the part can never be well unless the whole is well' (Jowett, 1892). Likewise, Hippocrates (circa 460–370 BC), who has been referred to as the 'father of modern medicine', espoused an approach that saw the role of the doctor as assisting the natural healing process and that took account not only of internal states, but also of the patient's physical and social context.

Health consisted of a balance in mind, emotion, body and spirit within a healthy physical and social environment. Even the way the wind blew was relevant to the patient's state. Similarly, the Greek *polis* or city-state was intended to be a training in the kind of political participation that was essential for health. Against this background, the Olympics historically included not only physical prowess but also poetry and philosophy (Andricopoulos, 2015).

Another important concept in Hippocratic medicine was that of a crisis, a point in the progression of disease at which either the illness would begin to triumph and the patient would succumb to death or the opposite would occur and natural processes would make the patient recover (Garrison, 1966). Illness, therefore, was an upset in the equilibrium and balance of the person and had to do with external events as well as the person's way of life, with the natural and social environment as much as what happened inside the body. Crisis or turning points could be particularly crucial in the treatment of illness.

Against this background, health promotion needs to be seen as a broad-based approach that transforms the entire community and environment rather than seeking to fix particular symptoms in the body of an individual and that is best targeted at particular crisis points when it would have the most effect.

While Hippocrates' concept of crisis was particular to illness, the concept is in fact relevant to critical moments in life, when the choices a person makes are crucial to determining whether that person will become ill, mentally or physically or healthy. Burnout is a good illustration of this process (Glouberman, 2007).

It is worth noting that many traditional societies have had a similar holistic approach to health. Ancient healing traditions, as far back as 5,000 years ago in India and China, stressed living a healthy way of life in harmony with nature. Similarly, from an Indigenous perspective, holistic healthcare is an integrative approach that seeks to balance the mind, body and spirit with community and environment (National Aboriginal Health Association, 2011).

Social isolation and health

The reality is that, in industrialised societies, many of the social supports that promote health are absent, leaving individuals at risk. Indeed, social isolation, as measured by social disconnectedness (physical separation from others) and perceived isolation (feelings of loneliness and lack of social support) is rapidly increasing to the point of becoming an epidemic. A study conducted in Bhutan, for example, demonstrated that the rapid social transformation and transition into faster and busier lives created greater isolation and detachment from community as a consequence (Ura et al., 2012).

Loneliness and social isolation are harmful to physical and mental health: lacking social connections exceeds the impact of well-known risk factors such as smoking 15 cigarettes a day (Holt-Lunstad and Layton, 2010). Thus physically, among other findings, it has been shown to increase the risk of high blood pressure (Hawkley et al., 2010) and of the onset of disability (Lund et al., 2010). From a mental health perspective, lonely individuals are more prone to depression (Cacioppo et al., 2006; Green et al., 1992) and at greater risk of cognitive decline (James et al., 2011). One study concludes lonely people have a 64 per cent increased chance of developing clinical dementia (Holwerda et al., 2012). Loneliness and low social interaction are also predictive of suicide in older age (O'Connell et al., 2004). More generally, social isolation has been found to be associated with a higher risk of death in older people regardless of whether they consider themselves lonely and this relationship was independent of demographic factors and baseline health (English Longitudinal Study of Ageing, 2012).

Long- and short-term communities in relation to health

Against this background, community and a sense of community become crucial to health. Sense of community, defined by McMillan and Chavis (1986: 9), is 'a feeling that members have of belonging, a feeling that members matter to one another and to the group and a shared faith that members' needs will be met through their commitment to be together'. An extensive analysis by the Gross National Happiness Index found that those who feel a sense of belonging tend to lead happier and healthier lives and create more stable communities and a more supportive society (Zavaleta, 2007).

The Gross National Happiness Index defines the notion of belonging or social identity as a central aspect to wellbeing. 'It is the strong and positive membership in families, communities or groups that ensures an individual's sense of belonging' (Ura et al., 2012). Social networks and friendships not only have an impact on reducing the risk of mortality or developing certain diseases, but also help individuals to recover when they do fall ill (Marmot, 2010).

Some societies seem to promote community health and wellbeing much more than others. The Japanese prefecture of Okinawa, Japan, is an outstanding example of a health-promoting environment. Elderly Okinawans have among the lowest mortality rates in the world from a multitude of chronic diseases of ageing and as a result enjoy not only what may be the world's longest life expectancy but the world's longest health expectancy.

The Okinawa Centenarian Study is an ongoing population-based study of centenarians and other selected elderly in Okinawa that began in 1975. A combination of health- and longevity-promoting factors emerged, such as diet, a slower pace of life, engaging in activities such as meditation and tai chi, along with a network of social support reducing stress, loneliness and isolation (Okinawa Centenarian Study: Centenarians, 2007).

Similarly, Dan Buettner, American explorer and author, studied a number of communities such as Sardinia in Italy, Ikaria in Greece and Okinawa in Japan, which he called the Blue Zones. He looked specifically at how the community itself supported good health, finding that in these communities people have a sense of purpose, take time each day to relax, belong to some faith-based community, put loved ones first and have healthy social networks (Buettner, 2009).

Communities may be long-term or short-term. Long term communities range from traditional naturally occurring social communities to consciously created communities with an inspiring ideology like the Israeli kibbutz, the Buddhist Plum Village Monastery of Thich Nhat Hanh and eco-village communities such as Findhorn in Scotland. Short-term communities can be a byproduct of an institution, with temporary members such as university education, or they can be intentionally created with a guiding ideology. Some have been modelled after long-term communities, such as, for example, summer camps for children inspired by the principles of the kibbutz (Habodror, 2013).

Some short-term communities specifically geared to promote health, like the therapeutic communities set up in hospitals and prisons or in small homes for the mentally, emotionally or physically challenged, are oriented towards specific populations with well-defined challenges or problems. Equally they may be, as is the particular focus of this chapter, retreats or holidays intended for the general public. The lessons to be learned from the therapeutic communities for specific populations can certainly be applied with modifications to creating communities for the general public.

Therapeutic communities

The concept of therapeutic community, which was aimed at the promotion of mental and emotional health, emerged in 1940 when the problems of war neurosis brought about an awareness of the possibilities of community treatment. It involved creating a social structure in a hospital or elsewhere which differed from that of the outside world, but was specifically geared towards having a therapeutic impact on the patients.

This was a participative, group-based approach to long-term mental illness, personality disorders and drug addiction based on milieu therapy principles. These included group psychotherapy as well as practical activities. While therapeutic communities were originally residential, the principle was later applied to day units.

Dr Maxwell Jones was a key figure in setting up therapeutic communities such as the ones in Henderson Hospital in Sutton, Surrey and later in Dingleton Hospital in Melrose, Scotland. His view was that the lessons of therapeutic community could and should be taken out of the hospital and used to transform families and other social systems.

To his way of thinking and working, every social interaction or crisis presented a 'living–learning situation' which provided the grist for the therapeutic mill and the opportunity for changing and learning how to continue to transform (Bloom, 1997).

He believed that a key aspect of a therapeutic community was to achieve consensus and commitment by members of the community and that this could only be done if traditional authoritarian leadership and hierarchy were replaced with a dynamic and co-creative process of directing and moving responsible people towards a common goal.

The core principles of the therapeutic communities are as follows:

- The total social organisation in which the patient is involved – and not only the relationship with the doctor – affects the therapeutic outcome, indeed is a vital force for maximising therapeutic effects.
- This social organisation needs to be democratised, such that there are meetings allowing for patients to give opinions which get communicated to the staff or, even further, that group decisions are made by consensus between staff and patients.
- All relationships are regarded as potentially therapeutic.
- The qualitative atmosphere of the social environment, referred to as the 'emotional climate', is regarded as therapeutic.
- A high value is placed on communication, which is crucial for morale and has therapeutic effects for staff and patients.

(Rappaport, 2000)

Humanistic psychology, community and communication

While Maxwell Jones was himself a doctor and his work evolved out of the psychiatric and psychodynamic tradition, the therapeutic community concepts fit in very well with those of humanistic psychology. Humanistic psychology is a psychological perspective which rose to prominence in the mid twentieth century in response to the limitations of Sigmund Freud's psychoanalytic theory and B. F. Skinner's behaviourism. Considered a 'third force', this approach emphasised individuals' inherent drive towards self-actualisation, the process of realising and expressing one's own capabilities and creativity.

Like other approaches emphasised in this chapter, it moved away from a medical model to a democratic and holistic one, in this case based on fostering communication, creativity and personal development throughout life for everyone, through self-exploration and group work as much as through professional consultation.

The underlying assumptions were that we are constantly evolving beings, that we need to take a holistic approach to being human, that self-exploration, creativity, free will, authenticity and positive human potential were important for everyone and that self-development could be done in an essentially democratic way through self-exploration and group work as much as through professional consultation.

One of the focuses of the movement was on creating healthy groups and communities where people could be authentically themselves. To this end, a number of different methods emerged, including psychodrama, gestalt, encounter, breathwork and dance therapy, which helped people in a group or community to become open and intimate with each other quickly, as well as to explore issues in more dramatic ways. These methods tended to utilise movement, drama, imagination and other verbal and non-verbal ways to open up, shed light upon and often resolve issues that had not responded to highly professionalised and verbally based therapies like psychoanalysis. Open and honest communication was considered key to creating honest, loving groups that could be a crucible for healthy personal development and transformation (House et al., 2013).

Interdependence

A key underpinning in many of the approaches described so far is interdependence, in the sense that health emerges in the context of a community and a natural environment, rather than being a matter of the individual alone, as in the medical model.

The South Africans use the word *ubuntu* to express the concept that 'I am because you are' or that a person is a person because of other people and that a universal bond connects and defines us as humans. Similarly, much of Buddhist thought is based on interdependence or, as Zen monk Thich Nhat Hanh calls it, interbeing (Hanh, 2003).

Dr Martin Luther King, Jr. explains interdependence thus:

> It really boils down to this: that all life is interrelated. We are all caught in an inescapable network of mutuality, tied together into a single garment of destiny. Whatever affects one directly, affects all indirectly. We are made to live together because of the interrelated structure of reality . . . Before you finish eating breakfast in the morning, you've depended on more than half the world. This is the way our universe is structured, this is its interrelated quality. We aren't going to have peace on Earth until we recognize the basic fact of the interrelated structure of all reality.

> *(King, 1967)*

Community provides the opportunity to develop this sense that 'self' and 'other' are connected and interdependent rather than fundamentally separate. This understanding, as it becomes more and more deeply felt, provides a ground for greater healing and wellbeing.

It is important to note that the community that people participate in directly, as in a holiday retreat, is usually found within the context of a larger community, such as, for example, the staff, the local community and indeed, the natural environment. The larger community needs to be included in some way in the smaller one. To create such strong boundaries that the members of the smaller community overlook the welfare of the surrounding community and environment would not only underline some of the worst aspects of tourism, but also be deleterious to the sense of the interrelationship of life that the holiday is intended to foster.

Turning points and health

The final strand of this discussion about the relationship between health and holistic holiday communities has to do with the importance of turning points and crises in people's lives and the consequent significance of health-promoting holidays at these crucial times.

As Gerald Caplan (1964), who is considered the father of modern crisis intervention theory, pointed out, a crisis is provoked when individuals face a problem for which they appear not to have an immediate solution and that is for a time insurmountable by utilising their usual methods of problem solving. This creates an imbalance, which, as we have seen in the work of Hippocrates, is dangerous to health. A period of upset and tension follows during which they make many attempts at the solution of the problem. Eventually, some kind of adaptation and equilibrium is achieved which may leave the person in a better or worse condition than prior to the crisis.

It is during this time of crisis when the individual is trying to solve the problem that the individual is most in need of help and most amenable to help. The choices the person makes at this juncture will be crucial in determining his or her future personality and future health. As in Hippocrates' view of crisis in illness, there is a juncture when the individual is most vulnerable and unstable and the direction the person takes is most crucial. In fact, Caplan believed that our personality is based on the solutions we reach in these crisis moments (Caplan, 1964). For example, if a young boy is bullied on the playground and runs away, refusing to go back to school, he is more likely to flee from difficult situations in future, whereas if he stays and confronts the bullies, courage in facing difficulties will become part of his personality repertoire. This said, these solutions need not be figured out alone. The young boy is not in a vacuum and, with the support of the community, both the bullied and the perpetrator can be helped to make better choices for a healthier future.

Glouberman (2007), taking a similar approach to burnout, demonstrates that people come to a point when their heart goes out of a situation about which they were formerly whole-hearted. This may be because the situation has changed and is no longer good for them, but it may also be because they have themselves evolved and need to step into a bigger picture. The choices they make at this time are crucial. If at that moment they step back, consider their relationship to the situation and decide to change the situation, to leave the situation or to stay but change their attitude, all is well and they will move toward rebalancing and health. But if they do not consider what is happening and drive themselves forward compulsively in the old direction, they are likely to burn out. The burnout then has a large number of physical and emotional health consequences.

Thus moments of crisis can become turning points in people's lives. But turning points do not happen once or twice in a lifetime, nor are they only the result of a crisis, but are a normal part of a creative life. As evolving beings, in order to be healthy, we need to keep developing our understandings of ourselves and the world and be open to the transformations that may ensue.

This is particularly so because change is a constant reality of life and learning how to move with change is key. If a reaction is fear-based, decisions taken are not adaptive in the current reality and the likelihood is that there is a contraction, anxiety, depression, illness or hopelessness which can create patterns restricting future choices.

It is at turning point moments that people tend to seek out help to guide themselves and this is a point when people may look for and find a health-promoting holiday or retreat to help them on their way. Having access to a supportive friend, caregiver, partner or a community and lessening the stress of going through hardships and challenges alone, has a tremendous impact in moving through and forward. The individualist model of a culture that values independence over community is thus challenged.

By providing environments with tools to facilitate safe spaces for working with fear and turning points, participants have an opportunity during these vulnerable moments to step through their fear into a bigger picture.

Case study: Skyros Holidays – the lessons gleaned from Ancient Greek holistic health

In creating a health-promoting community for a short-term holiday retreat, the lessons gleaned from therapeutic communities, humanistic psychology, spiritual philosophies of interdependence and crisis theory are crucial building blocks.

The case study here is of Skyros Holidays, founded in 1979 by the co-author of this chapter, American psychologist Dr Dina Glouberman, along with her then-husband, Greek historian Dr Yannis Andricopoulos. These holidays were pioneering and trendsetting in their field and as such can be of immense interest to those looking for new approaches to health tourism.

Without formal quantitative research, with the exception of written or oral questionnaires and some surveys, this account relies rather heavily on a description of the founding theories and practices and on the participant and press comments. Thus the case study is more in the tradition

(continued)

(continued)

of qualitative research and participant observation, some of which was undertaken over several years. These give a good anecdotal picture, which however would need to be supplemented by more research. Further, press reviews such as those which refer to Skyros as 'The first and still the best alternative holiday' (*The Guardian*, 2008) or 'One of the world's best holidays' (*The Sunday Times*, 2010) are evidence of the generally accepted power and importance of this holiday model.

The Skyros Centre, in Skyros Village, Skyros Island, Greece, when it started in the summer of 1979, was comprised of two 2-week sessions of a personal development holiday community. In 1984, Atsitsa, housed in houses and huts in the Skyros Island pine forest by the sea, was founded as a holistic holiday community. Skyros Holidays eventually expanded in terms of programme and location. It became a holistic holiday with a wide range of courses, still held primarily in these two bases on Skyros Island but also offering sessions all around the world, including in Thailand, Cambodia, Morocco, Cuba, Trinidad and Tobago and throughout Europe. As of 2016 there are eight locations worldwide. Sessions outside of Greece are housed mainly in hotels.

Over the 37-year span, there have been about 20,000 Skyros Holiday participants. The vast majority of Skyros participants are single or at least travelling solo, though there are always a few couples and some families during school holidays.

The statistics for 2015 indicate that, while participants range in age from 5 to 85, approximately 60 per cent are aged 40–60 and the female-to-male ratio is 3:1. Participants' occupations include teaching, social work, managerial positions, writing, IT and retirees. They are predominantly British, but come from all over Europe, as well as from Africa, Asia, North America, South America and Australia.

Informal surveys indicate that participants are typically successful in their field and with a much higher proportion of self-employed people than in the general population. They are likely to be left or liberal in their politics and unconventional in their lifestyle.

A large majority come to Skyros for the first time when they are facing burnout, a crisis or a life change. This, as we have seen, is a crucial moment for achieving life change. After the first time, they often return regularly and many view it as their regular holiday home. Thus in 2015, 53 per cent were returning participants, which, among other things, indicates a high level of guest satisfaction.

The Skyros community

Despite the expansion of Skyros Holidays, the community focus has remained more or less constant, with variations based on adaptation to particular environments and situations. The principles that support a community environment at Skyros include: symbolic community, courses, natural environment and holiday atmosphere.

Symbolic community

A healthy community life, long- or short-term, which promotes belonging, interdependence, authenticity and empowerment, has already been shown to be an important building block of a holistic health-promoting life.

The theoretical contribution of Skyros here is the concept of 'symbolic community', i.e. an educational experience of community that can potentially carry over into one's personal life thereafter. This is certainly the most crucial and life-changing aspect of Skyros Holidays. The creation of a community atmosphere had a number of challenges to consider.

First, given that people who came to Skyros are typically single and are often self-employed, living on their own and coming from an individualistic culture, it can be expected that they might find it challenging to live in a shared and communal atmosphere. Few will have known each other before the beginning of the session, yet they need to pull together into a community where there is trust, openness, intimacy and authenticity. The community experience needs to be robust enough to weather differences and disagreements and yet would begin and end in the space of a week or two.

To set the conditions for this community to arise, people are encouraged to let go of their regular reference points for interaction and communication and become actively engaged in their own unique way, knowing that they have a voice and place in this short-term community life. The methods developed in the humanistic psychology movement are ideal for achieving this and the background of the therapeutic community and of other short-term communities gives a theoretical framework for it.

The term 'participant' here, rather than client or customer or guest or holiday maker, is relevant. Each person of the holiday community not only participates in community life, but is also involved in the co-creation of that particular 1-week or 2-week community. Even criticism is seen as helpful if it is used positively to help move the community for the benefit of everyone; thus there is a motto, 'No complaints without suggestions'.

In this way, interdependence, democracy and empowerment are fostered. And indeed, especially in the early days of Skyros, the evolution of the present programme depended on the interventions of the succeeding communities. In this sense, it resembled the ancient Greek view of the *polis* or city state, whose job was not merely to govern, but to be an educational experience for the citizens who were involved in the process.

Second, this community needs to have important differences from the traditional naturally occurring communities. These traditional communities offer people a sense of being cared for and belonging, which is why there is a yearning to go back to them. But they also tend to have fairly high levels of social control and role expectations which can be damaging, particularly for the kind of unconventional people drawn to Skyros.

This is because one's sense of belonging to one's community, which is absolutely crucial to identity formation, becomes dependent on a level of conformity which may not be possible or desirable for people who are different in a variety of ways, whether politically, sexually, socially, emotionally or spiritually. Being different can then lead to being discriminated against, bullied or gossiped about, or simply gaining the identity of being an outsider who cannot trust or be trusted, by one's community.

Indeed, many have escaped to the freedom of city life for just this reason. Yet anonymous city life, with its potential for alienation and disconnection, can be isolating for those yearning for more human connection and acceptance for who they are.

The symbolic community created in the Skyros Holidays addresses this dilemma by supporting both individuality and connectedness. Participants are to be accepted as they themselves want to be and become, rather than in terms of their conformity to the expectation of others. In this sense, the community is referred to not only as a symbolic community but also as a 'soul community' (Glouberman, 2007), because it supports people on their deepest, most authentic level.

Third, the community needed to be effective as a learning community for everyone involved. The teaching and administrative staff, as well as the local community, all need to be benefitting

(continued)

(continued)

and not just the participants. This would make it a democratic and dynamic evolving environment, the importance of which was emphasised by Maxwell Jones in creating therapeutic communities.

In order to do this, methods derived from the humanistic psychology groupwork as well as from the therapeutic communities were adapted to the holiday situation. A programme was created with an interlocking set of communication structures, which included:

- meetings with the whole community, including two or three community meetings[1] and daily get-togethers at breakfast called *demos* (Greek for 'the people');[2]
- smaller group meetings: besides the course groups, there are also *oekos* (Greek for 'home') or home groups, for sharing each day,[3] and the 'work groups', where people chopped vegetables or swept or watered plants or made some contribution to the community;[4]
- one-to-one meetings, called 'co-listening', where participants take turns sharing and listening;[5]
- staff meetings that are for support and learning as well as running the community. In this way, staff as well as participants participate in the learning experience in the community and indeed, tend to feel that Skyros is as life-changing for them as for the participants;[6]
- drop-in courses, parties and social activities that include everyone who wanted to participate.

A sense of co-creation emerges through group retreat structures in which participants contribute to shaping their physical living environment by engaging in activities related to upkeep, preparing for meals and decorating for celebratory events and tending to the emotional atmosphere by sharing, participating, connecting and opening to others and their experience (Cloutier, 2015). Essentially participants have a voice that influences the shaping and experience of community life.

Courses

To bring mind, emotion, body and spirit in alignment with each other and to help people to evaluate where they are and find a new way forward, there is a wide range of courses which include all levels from spirit to psyche to body, from life choices, writing, art, music, yoga, t'ai chi and meditation to trapeze, windsurfing, comedy improvisation, dance and many others. This range is unparalleled and is one of the groundbreaking aspects of the experience.

All the courses, besides teaching a specific skill, are aimed at the development of the whole person and give confidence for life. Jennie Dempster of *Red Magazine* (2008) called it a 'you-can-do-anything atmosphere'. Many of these courses are particularly potent at a time of crisis, which is when many people will seek out this type of holiday.

The world-class quality of the team of facilitators and tutors is also rather unique. The Writers Lab in particular has attracted world-famous writers as facilitators.

Environment

Holistic health includes a sense of balance not only with the social environment but also the physical environment. The locations of Skyros Holidays were chosen for their natural beauty, as in Greece or Thailand or in some cases, for their cultural interest, as in Cuba. They range from village locations to more rural locations to big-city locations. In general they are also places with much sunshine, both for holiday pleasure and for the healing power of the sun. Of course, connection and community can arise in any environment, but a beautiful and warm environment can bring people together in a pleasurable way.

The Skyros Island Holidays in particular have close contact with the local community. An exchange of benefits occurs, with learning opportunities for both participants and villagers. Skyros Holidays also supports a variety of projects in the local community with fundraisers that bring together Skyros participants with local villagers.

Recently, the difficult financial environment of Greece has inspired the creation of a fund-raising mechanism called The Auction of Promises, where participants offer services and products which others bid for and significant sums of money are raised which have funded the heating in the schools and the health centre in the winter as well as supporting a number of health-related causes.

Holiday atmosphere

Skyros Holidays could be termed a retreat holiday because the emphasis is that this is not only an opportunity to step back from life, gain skills and revision life, but also a good old-fashioned enjoyable holiday. People enjoy beach time, parties, celebrations, meals out together and all the fun of a traditional holiday, but with people with whom a deeper connection is formed. Activities may be suggested or facilitated by participants, not just by staff. The last evening is traditionally a soirée or cabaret, where people present skits, songs, readings, dance, some of which was learned or produced in the classes and some based on participants' talents and expertise.

Thus the holiday atmosphere includes light-hearted fun along with deeper intentions, both supporting each other. One of the most common comments people make is that they laughed more than they had in years or that it was the best holiday they'd ever had. As comedian Arthur Smith wrote, 'The laughter echoed around the town' (*The Stage*, 2010).

New developments

From April, 2016, Skyros Holidays began a new ecotourism holiday in Grande Riviere, Trinidad, where the local community has been heavily involved in the conservation of the leatherback turtles that nest there and lay eggs in large numbers. Participants have the opportunity to combine taking courses with living alongside these ancient turtles nesting on the beach in front of the hotel.

Outcomes

Over these years, thousands of people from all over the world have come to Skyros Holidays, a large proportion of whom were facing crises or turning points in their lives and indeed, a large proportion of whom came away feeling that they had created a better present and future for themselves. In one survey, over 80 per cent report that the Skyros experience had a lasting positive effect on their lives. Poet Hugo Williams called them: 'Holidays to take home with you' (*Times Literary Supplement*, 1993).

It is interesting to note that, in the feedback forms given out to participants, not only are the responses positive, but their descriptions of the benefits are similar whichever centre they have gone to or course they have attended.

(continued)

(continued)

Thus, for example, in the Atsitsa forms:

> It's like being in a wonderful bubble with human connections: creativity, calmness and huge fun can flourish. Thank you.

> A week to remember forever – maybe difficult to explain that to my friends back home – but this is a personal journey which will always be in my heart.

> I've had another unique experience for which I am very grateful. The way Skyros does it reconnecting people with themselves and each other is very important and has my full respect. Western civilisation needs more of this.

Or Skyros Centre:

> To create a sense of community in two weeks where people are honest and prepared to bare their souls takes a special kind of magic.

> A totally different experience for me. Enlightening, refreshing and enough memories for a lifetime.

> Such a wonderful community spirit. A wealth of characters and shared experiences – never to be forgotten.

This attests to the power of the overall experience and particularly of the community, as a context for the holiday experience and holiday effect.

Anecdotally, participants talk of the many different ways in which Skyros was a turning point in their lives. Although a great many changes happen in the courses, there are even more that come as a result of the relationships formed in the community.

Perhaps one of the most striking is Jimmy Carr, a prominent comedian, who came to Skyros and was so funny in the cabaret that people suggested he become a stand-up comedian. As he put it, 'I have had one life-changing holiday – on the Greek island of Skyros. People kept saying that I was really funny and ought to be a comedian, so I thought I'd give it a go' (*The Sunday Times*, 2010). He is now a hugely successful television personality.

Recently, one of the administrative staff who was facing her own turning point sat on the beach with a participant who is an educator and consultant and together they discussed possible careers for the staff member; they agreed that a degree in Psychology was a way forward and she immediately applied for the Psychology degree while still in Skyros and is now completing it and about to go on to postgraduate work.

Many attest to the power of the relationships formed which last long after the holiday; as Anne Roper put it, 'I made bonds that will last a lifetime' (*Sunday Independent*, 1999).

Holistic health and healing in community-oriented holidays

In conclusion, it is important for those seeking health holidays or group retreats as well as for the holiday operators who offer them to take into account a great deal more than any one dimension of health. Promotion of health and healing in the field of health tourism needs to focus also on mental, emotional, creative and spiritual aspects alongside the physical. These include the relationship to the community created on the holiday, as well as to the local community and the ecological environment.

The search for connection and belonging in today's world is heightened due to the prevalence of isolation and loneliness, overstimulation by too much information, distractions, technology and speed, the high degree of burnout and the increasingly common tendency to make a series of career and personal life changes. The creation of a healthy community atmosphere is therefore more crucial than ever and can potentially promote healing and enhance health on holidays and group retreats.

Since the understanding of empowerment, interdependence and democracy is an important part of creating a healthy community, the holiday or retreat programme requires participant input and contribution to each other and to the whole. Participants at Skyros, for example, step out of an individualistic social construct into a short-term symbolic collectivist environment that values the individual as a participant in the creative process of the holiday and not merely as a guest. This approach has been shown to have far-reaching positive effects on participants' lives and wellbeing.

As outlined in this chapter, highlighting the community view and approach to health and healing is not new; many spiritual traditions and cultures recognise and honour relationships and community as central to wellbeing. From the historical roots of ancient Greece's Hippocrates and Socrates to modern therapeutic communities emerging from hospital environments, there is a great deal of evidence that this particular strand of holistic approach is needed and necessary in a world that is becoming increasingly fragmented.

Coming back to balance requires us to bring all the pieces that make up being human together. Creating environments for people to experience and reconnect to the areas that make them whole is the invitation, challenge and potential that wellness-oriented holidays and retreat operators have to offer, as is illustrated at Skyros.

Furthermore, since crisis and turning points are an important time for significant healthy change, health-oriented holidays are ideal for these crucial times. Participants in such a situation may require support to evaluate their present situation, distinguish between what is life enhancing and what needs to be let go of and find inspiration, a vision and, in some cases, a plan.

These objectives can be expressed by creating communication structures that enhance belonging, authenticity, self-empowerment and personal or spiritual development and by having a daily programme with a variety of courses to address the needs of mind, body, emotion and spirit, as well as time to participate in the community, to socialise, to reflect or meditate and to explore the natural environment. This programme should also have a good relationship to the surrounding local community that is enhancing for participants and for locals.

Such an experience would help work towards the health of the whole person and the empowerment of individuals to take healthy steps forward in their lives when they return home, while having a positive impact on their own communities.

Notes

1 People are greeted the first evening or morning with a community meeting, where they are encouraged to get to know each other, integrate, learn about Skyros, each other and themselves. There are also one or two other community meetings within the programme, where people are encouraged to air issues and plan together. These meetings have often had a lasting effect on the Skyros structure, particularly in the early days of Skyros. The methods used derive from humanistic psychology and therapeutic communities.
2 The daily breakfast *demos* meetings are more like the oral newspaper to share, inform and communicate.
3 The *oekos* groups ran for half an hour every weekday and the format is that each person shares for about 3 minutes and then there is group feedback and discussion. These were especially important in those holidays where people did not have a main course group to feel part of.

4 The 'work groups' are intended to foster a sense of belonging by encouraging participants to contribute to the community rather than being passive guests. They became shorter and more symbolic as the years went on. Where the holiday takes place in hotels around the world, rather than on home ground in Skyros, they are difficult to maintain.

5 'Co-listening' developed as a one-to-one communication practice, where people take turns talking and listening. Thus the first speaker deeply focuses, lets go of mental plans and basically thinks out loud and the second person listens with full focus and they then switch roles. They reflect back to each other afterwards, but with no advice, interpretation, criticism or approval. This highly focused format enables people to think in a creative way and often to resolve their own difficulties (Glouberman, 2002).

6 The staff meetings are notable for their emphasis on personal support as well as cooperative planning. There is a framework of the five Ps: personals (a chance for each person to check in and say how s/he is doing), practicals, participants (a discussion of any issues arising with participants), programme and process (any issues arising among the staff).

References

Andricopoulos, Y. (2015) 'An ethical philosophy', *Skyros Holidays*, http://www.skyros.com/philosophy_holism.htm (accessed 7 April 2015).

Beilharz, P. and Bauman, Z. (2001) 'Liquid modernity', *Contemporary Sociology*, doi:10.2307/3089803.

Block, P. (2014) 'Community has a job to do deepening community', *Tamarack: An Institute for Community Engagement*, http://deepeningcommunity.ca/blogs/peter-block/community-has-job-do (accessed 15 January 2015).

Bloom, S. L. (1997) *Creating Sanctuary: Toward the Evolution of Sane Societies*, http://www.sanctuaryweb.com/TheSanctuaryModel/HistoryoftheSanctuaryModel/MaxwellJones.aspx (accessed 15 June 2015).

Buettner, D. (2009) *The Blue Zones: Lessons for Living Longer from the People Who've Lived the Longest*, Washington, DC: National Geographic.

Cacioppo, J. T., Hughes, M. E., Waite, L. J., Hawkley, L. C. and Thisted, R. A. (2006) 'Loneliness as a specific risk factor for depressive symptoms: Cross-sectional and longitudinal analyses', *Psychology and Aging*, 21(1), 140–151.

Caplan, G. (1964) *Principles of Preventive Psychiatry*, New York: Basic Books.

Cloutier, J. (2015) *The Significance of Community in Wellness Service Design: The Case of Retreats* (Master's thesis, University of Tartu, Estonia), http://dspace.ut.ee/bitstream/handle/10062/49423/cloutier_josee-ann.pdf (accessed 10 March 2016).

Digital Detox (2014) *Disconnect to Reconnect*, http://digitaldetox.org/ (accessed 29 December 2014).

English Longitudinal Study of Ageing (2012) http://www.elsa-project.ac.uk (accessed 5 June 2015).

Garrison, F. H. (1966) *History of Medicine*, Philadelphia, PA: W.B. Saunders.

Global Spa and Wellness Economy Monitor (2014) http://www.globalwellnesssummit.com/images/stories/gsws2014/pdf/GWI_Global_Spa_and_Wellness_Economy_Monitor_Full_Report_Final.pdf.pagespeed.ce.Ty_aHJE2Ym.pdf (accessed 23 April 2015).

Glouberman, D. (2002) *Joy of Burnout*, Isle of Wight: Skyros Books.

Green, B. H., Copeland, J. R., Dewey, M. E., Shamra, V., Saunders, P. A., Davidson, I. A., Sullivan, C. and McWilliam, C. (1992) 'Risk factors for depression in elderly people: A prospective study', *Acta Psychiatriatrica Scandinavica*, 86(3), 213–217.

Habodror (2013) http://habodror.org.uk (accessed 15 June 2015).

Hanh, T. N. (2003) *Interbeing: Commentaries on the Tiep Hien Precepts*, Berkeley, CA: Full Circle Publishing.

Hawkley, L. C., Thisted, R. A., Masi, C. M. and Cacioppo, J. T. (2010) 'Loneliness predicts increased blood pressure: Five-year cross-lagged analyses in middle-aged and older adults', *Psychology and Aging*, 25(1), 132–141.

Helliwell, J. F. and Huang, H. (2013) 'Comparing the happiness effects of real and on-line friends', *PloS One*, 8(9), e72754. doi:10.1371/journal.pone.0072754.

Holt-Lunstad, J. and Layton, J. B. (2010) 'Social relationships and mortality risk: A meta-analytic review', *PLoS Medicine*, 7(7), http://www.plosmedicine.org/article/info%3Adoi%2F10.1371%2Fjournal.pmed.1000316 (accessed 2 June 2015).

Holwerda, T. J., Deeg, D., Beekman, A., van Tilburg, T. G., Stek, M. L., Jonker, C. and Schoevers, R. (2012) 'Research paper: Feelings of loneliness, but not social isolation, predict dementia onset: Results from the Amsterdam Study of the Elderly (AMSTEL)', *Journal of Neurology, Neurosurgery and Psychiatry*, http://jnnp.bmj.com/content/early/2012/11/06/jnnp-2012-302755 (accessed 12 June 2015).

House, R., Kalisch, D. and Maidman, J. (eds) (2013) *The Future of Humanistic Psychology*, Ross on Wye, UK: PCCS Books.

James, B. D., Wilson, R. S., Barnes, L. L. and Bennett, D. A. (2011) 'Late-life social activity and cognitive decline in old age', *Journal of the International Neuropsychological Society*, 17(6), 998–1005.

Jowett, B. (1892) *Plato Charmides* (Chapters 154–160), http://pages.ucsd.edu/~dkjordan/arch/greeks/PlatoCharmides.html (accessed 5 May 2015).

Kelly, C. (2012) 'Wellness tourism: Retreat visitor motivations and experiences', *Tourism Recreation Research*, 37(3), 205–213.

King, M. L. (1967) 'Only in the darkness can you see the stars', *The Book Haven, Stanford University*, http://bookhaven.stanford.edu/2012/01/martin-luther-king-on-his-day-only-in-the-darkness-can-you-see-the-stars/ (accessed 1 March 2015).

Lund, R., Nilsson, C. J. and Avlund, K. (2010) 'Can the higher risk of disability onset among older people who live alone be alleviated by strong social relations? A longitudinal study of non-disabled men and women', *Age and Ageing*, 39(3), 319–326.

Marmot, M. (2010) *Fair Society, Healthy Lives, the Marmot Review* (The Marmot Review: London), http://www.instituteofhealthequity.org/projects/fair-society-healthy-lives-the-marmot-review (accessed 12 June 2015).

McMillan, D. W. and Chavis, D. M. (1986) 'Sense of community: A definition and theory', *Journal of Community Psychology*, 14, 6–23. doi: 10.1002/1520-6629(198601)14:1<6::AID-JCOP2290140103>3.0.CO;2-I.

National Aboriginal Health Association (2011) *Holistic Health and Traditional Knowledge*, http://www.naho.ca/blog/2011/07/25/holistic-health-and-traditional-knowledge/ (accessed 4 March 2015).

O'Connell, H., Chin, A., Cunningham, C. and Lawlor, B. (2004) 'Recent developments: Suicide in older people', *British Medical Journal*, 29, 895–899.

Okinawa Centenarian Study: Centenarians (2007) http://www.okicent.org/cent.html (accessed 16 April 2015).

Public Health Agency of Canada (1986) *Ottawa Charter for Health Promotion: An International Conference on Health Promotion*, http://www.phac-aspc.gc.ca/ph-sp/docs/charter-chartre/index-eng.php (accessed 13 February 2015).

Rappaport, R. (2000) *Community as Doctor*, Hove, UK: Routledge Psychology Press.

Red Magazine (2008) *Skyros, Press*, https://www.skyros.com/about/press/ (accessed 5 June, 2015).

Smith, M. K. and Puczkó, L. (2013) *Health Tourism and Hospitality: Spas, Wellness and Medical Travel*, 2nd edn. London: Routledge.

Sunday Independent (10 January 1999) *Skyros, Press*, https://www.skyros.com/about/press/ (accessed 5 June 2015).

The Guardian (2008) *Skyros, Press*, https://www.skyros.com/about/press/ (accessed 5 June 2015).

The Stage (4 November 2010) *Skyros, Press*, https://www.skyros.com/about/press/ (accessed 5 June 2015).

The Sunday Times (2010) *Skyros, Press*, https://www.skyros.com/about/press/ (accessed 5 June 2015).

Times Literary Supplement (1993) *Skyros, Press*, https://www.skyros.com/about/press/ (accessed 5 June 2015).

Top Wellness Spa Travel Trends for 2015 (2015) http://www.healthandfitnesstravel.com/blog/top-wellness-spa-travel-trends-for-2015 (accessed 29 December 2014).

Trends Report (2014) *Wellness Retreats Rise . . . and Urbanize Spafinder Wellness 365*, http://www.spafinder.ca/trends/2014/wellness-retreats-rise-urbanize.htm (accessed 29 December 2014).

Ura, K., Alkire, S., Zangmo, T. and Wandi, K. (2012) *An Extensive Analysis of GNH Index*, http://www.grossnationalhappiness.com/wp-content/uploads/2012/10/An%20Extensive%20Analysis%20of%20GNH%20Index.pdf (accessed 6 March 2015).

Yoga Retreats on Retreats Online, a Worldwide Directory (2014) http://www.retreatsonline.com/site/yoga.html (accessed 29 December 2014).

Zavaleta, D. (2007) 'The ability to go about without shame: A proposal for international comparable indicators on shame and humiliation', *Oxford Development Studies*, 35(4), 405–430.

14

Yoga, transformation and tourism

Melanie Kay Smith and Ivett Sziva

Introduction

This chapter will examine the relationship between yoga, transformation and tourism, building on the work of Reisinger (2013, 2015) and Ponder and Holladay (2013). It is based on the idea that yoga is a practice which can gradually change the the life of human beings and possibly communities too. It may start with the physical body as a series of postures, but mental and spiritual transformation can follow, especially with regular practice. Even medical science has tentatively started to recognise the health benefits of yoga, e.g. for back pain, anxiety, depression, hypertension and asthma (Verrastro, 2014), but more especially as an adjunct to mitigate some medical conditions (Büssing et al., 2012). The concept of transformational tourism will be used, as defined by Reisinger (2013, 2015), where travel has the potential to contribute to a return to the existentially authentic self. This includes addressing the fundamental question(s) about meaning of life and embracing a less materialistic, more spiritual path. Yoga can arguably pave the way for such a transformation. It will be argued that for those who practise yoga this process starts even before travel takes place, but that the practice of yoga engenders a desire to intensify practice in alternative settings and maybe more 'authentic' ones (for example, in India), for longer periods and with like-minded communities. Ponder and Holladay (2013: 101) suggest that the development of yogic activities and spaces can lead to the creation of communities or tribes, who then seek yogic experiences in other places, e.g. through tourism. Yoga has the capacity to transform lives within both leisure and tourism contexts and can even become a vehicle for societal changes. As stated by Garrett (2001: 337), yoga 'contains a potential for ethical development, for the transformation of self beyond ego towards responsibility for others'.

The role of yoga in transformation

This chapter places yoga in the context of the so-called 'transformation economy'. Pine and Gilmore (1999) suggested that transformations are the next stage after experiences in the progression of economic value. In a more recent interview, Joeseph Pine (interviewed by Summers, 2012) emphasises that the healthcare industry in particular is very much focused on transformation and ideally, transformation should be sustained long-term. People are becoming more focused on self-development or transformation not only in their everyday lives, but also on holiday. Indeed, it may be more likely on a holiday that time and space are taken to reflect on life's meaning and issues that need addressing to enhance everyday life. Pine was asked by Summers (2012) whether transformation could be instantaneous and he agreed that in some cases it could. A tourism 'moment' may lead to an epiphany which changes a life. As stated by Reisinger (2015: 5), 'Travel can offer a journey to a new awareness, development and growth. This journey creates new meaning, offers fulfilment of unsatisfied needs and develops new authentic experiences'.

Reisinger (2013: 22) develops the work of Mezirow (2000), discussing how the major outcome of transformation is 'a change in one's values, beliefs and assumptions through which personal perceptions and experiences are mediated and made sense of'. She also describes, in accordance with Mezirow, how personal transformation often begins with a 'disorientating dilemma' such as a stressful life event which disrupts the order of one's life. Many people may turn to yoga or meditation or visit a retreat away from their normal place of residence as a result of stress and thus the transformational path can begin. Reisinger (2015) states that experiencing transcendence or spiritual healing of some kind can lead an individual to travel outside the ordinary confines of the body. Lea's (2008: 95) research in a yoga retreat extends this point, suggesting that part of the therapeutic potential of the retreat focused on how 'taking the body away from the "everyday" opened up attention to the body itself, foregrounding its connection to the world'.

Although yoga is often viewed as a purely physical activity in some Western countries, it has also been considered a spiritual healing tradition for centuries in India. Gerritsma's (2008) research conducted amongst 101 yoga and Pilates students in Amsterdam revealed that 75 per cent joined the classes for relaxation reasons, 42 per cent to get more energy, 24 per cent for better respiration and 9 per cent to meditate. The respondents considered yoga/Pilates mainly as a way of taking care of their body (marked 68 times) and also their mind (marked 43 times). Although many Westerners firstly view yoga as a fitness or exercise regime, they are often surprised by the mental, psychological and spiritual transformations which take place with regular practice. Ponder and Holladay (2013: 101) suggest that yoga goes beyond health: 'Yoga shifts mindsets and alters thoughts on health while creating understanding that personal and social issues are related which empowers change in existence'. Luskin (2004) discusses how the full transformative powers of practices like yoga have rarely been examined because the emphasis is on proving the physical benefits (e.g. blood pressure, breathing capacity, impact on stress and depression). He describes this as 'translation' rather than 'transformation' and that the long-term evolution of the individual should also be observed (e.g. in terms of values, emotions, relationships). It is clear that experiences are not enough; it is also necessary to engage in self-developmental challenges. For example, yoga takes many years of dedicated practice to have an intense transformational effect (e.g. where a whole lifestyle and outlook is transformed, not just creating a better body shape or temporary mental calm). The results may well be worth it, as described by Ponder and Holladay (2013: 102):

> Master yogis represent individuals who have become self-actualized through an experiential sojourn of self. This transformation through yoga allows one to become renewed, invigorated and spiritual as a constant state of being.

All of this may be difficult to achieve on holiday, but doing yoga for the first time in a spa or retreat may set the individual on a life journey and subsequent trips to yoga retreats or similar can intensify the practice. Reisinger (2013) quotes Clark (1991), who identified three major outcomes of transformation:

1   psychological (a change in understanding of self);
2   convictional (a revision of one's belief systems);
3   behavioural (changes in one's lifestyle).

Heelas and Woodward (2005: 27) analyse the growing significance of spiritual and holistic practices like yoga, stating that 'Holistic milieu activities facilitate the convergence of the spiritual path and the *personal* path'. They argue that such activities enable people to become themselves. Reisinger (2013: 30) suggests that 'Transformational experience represents a return to our existentially authentic selves in intimate relation to the world'. She mentions certain forms of yoga as being part of this experience, as it can affect the 'psychological, emotional and spiritual wellbeing of individuals and communities' (Reisinger, 2015: 10). Yoga has the power to transform one's sense and perception of self, whole lifestyle and philosophy of life with regular practice. Travel may not provide this regular practice, but it can first introduce the traveller to the practice; second, yoga is easy to practise anywhere, it does not require special equipment, so it can easily be practised on holiday; third, holidays may provide more time and a greater sense of relaxation which allow the practice to deepen, especially if the traveller spends time in a retreat or spa which offers yoga. Finally, in extreme cases, the traveller may connect to a destination so well that s/he decides to remain there indefinitely and even train to become a yoga teacher (e.g. in places like Rishikesh, Goa or Byron Bay).

The meaning of yoga is 'union', which can mean union of the mind, body and spirit with God or the universe. Iyengar (1999: xiii) defines yoga as 'a disciplinary art which develops the faculties of the body, mind and intellect. Its purpose is to refine man. It is a commitment to a life's pattern and a way towards right living'. Sri Swami Satchidananda (1999: xii) calls yoga the science of the mind. It is an integral process which takes into consideration all the aspects of an individual: physical, emotional, mental, intellectual and social, which basically means the entire life of a person. Swami Vishnu-Devananda (1988: ix) suggests that a positive future for all human beings lies in the health of the mind and changes within themselves:

> The world crisis is but a reflection of the chaotic state of the collective consciousness. The most positive action we can perform to contribute to the momentous task of bringing our planet back into balance is to start changing ourselves.

This, he believes, can be achieved through (Sivananda) yoga. Suggested lifestyle changes within the Sivananda yoga system include proper exercise, proper breathing, proper diet, proper relaxation, positive thinking and meditation. Reisinger (2013) also emphasises that transformation is about multiple aspects of life at different levels. Lifestyle changes that have been learnt about while on a yoga holiday or similar can be integrated into everyday life back home. Yoga starts with the self but can lead to greater benefits for communities and society. Transformation and transcendence can become eventual outcomes of the yoga journey, as suggested by Garrett (2001: 335), who describes how yoga tries to:

> change people for their own good and for the good of their society . . . Some of their practitioners call them 'spiritual', while others describe them more prosaically as 'working on myself', but both these descriptions refer to the transformative potential of ritual, to take people beyond their current selves and towards a differently imagined future.

Numerous studies have emerged in recent years that emphasise the health benefits of yoga. There are too many to review here (i.e. a search using keywords 'yoga' and 'health' from the last five years generates around 3,200 peer-reviewed journal articles); however, systematic reviews can provide some useful summaries. Several studies have been undertaken on the benefits of yoga for diabetes, multiple sclerosis, depression and anxiety, stress, hypertension, spinal pain, cancer and many forms of chronic pain. Park et al. (2015) use a systematic analysis of studies about yoga to confirm that many people turn to yoga for relief of health conditions. The authors also reviewed the factors associated with yoga practice and summarised the following: the majority of studies report more women doing yoga than men; more white people practise yoga than those from ethnic minorities; there tend to be higher numbers of middle-aged people practising yoga due to the onset of health issues in later life; higher education and income levels of practitioners are noted in many of the studies reviewed. Yoga practitioners are reported to be more spiritual, but not necessarily more religious; they tend to cope with stress better and be more mindful (especially with more advanced practice). Lower rates of smoking and healthier diets than in non-yoga practitioners were also observed.

Some studies have also started to focus on different types of yoga and the relative benefits of each type. In a review of 465 articles, Elwy et al. (2014) note, for example, that 28 per cent of studies focus on hatha yoga, followed by 9 per cent on Iyengar yoga. Their systematic review also includes the results of several studies in 30 countries which focused on the outcomes of yoga: 40 per cent mention physiological outcomes such as heart rate, blood pressure or hormone levels; 26 per cent include physical functioning such as chronic pain and arthritis; 25 per cent look at mental and emotional health outcomes, including depression, anxiety and stress; 8 per cent assessed cognitive and perceptual outcomes, such as concentration, attention and memory; 6 per cent focused on general wellbeing, such as quality of life or mindfulness; and 3 per cent included workplace experience such as employee satisfaction and fatigue. Cramer et al.'s (2016) meta-analysis of 301 controlled trials of yoga from 1975 to 2014 concluded that, as a form of healthcare and exercise, yoga is safe and seemingly beneficial.

On the other hand, Verrastro (2014) warns that some yoga can pose health risks for individuals with certain conditions and Luskin (2004) reminds us that not all transformational experiences, including those in the context of yoga, are always positive or good for health. They can even make health worse. Lea (2008) notes that the process of unlocking and releasing emotions that comes through yoga and retreat experiences can be temporarily physically and mentally uncomfortable. The healing 'journey' does not always feel positive, which echoes Reisinger's (2013, 2015) discussions of transformation involving risk, uncertainty, fear and loss. Although the research on the benefits of yoga can be inconsistent, inconclusive and sometimes confusing (e.g. yoga practitioners sometimes report more health problems than non-practitioners, but this can be because people with health problems are more likely to turn to yoga), on the whole, far more positive benefits seem to be reported than negative ones, especially if yoga is practised regularly and long-term.

The growth of yoga tourism

Yoga could be described as a sub-sector of health or wellness tourism but also of spiritual tourism (Smith and Kelly, 2006; Smith and Puczkó, 2009, 2013; Voigt et al., 2011). Ponder and Holladay (2013: 105) suggest that 'What is right to health, what is whole to spirituality, yoga tourism instils all of these into a being'. Yoga tourists are a sub-sector of wellness tourists in that true yoga enthusiasts do not see yoga as a fitness or exercise programme, but rather as a spiritual path which aims to balance body, mind and soul. Yoga tourists may be seen as being similar to 'seekers', as characterised by Yiannakis and Gibson (1992: 291), who seek 'spiritual and/or personal knowledge to better understand self and meaning of life'.

Yoga is often offered within retreat centres. The Retreat Company (2013) represents at least 500 retreat centres in the UK and continental Europe. They report that currently their most popular requests are for yoga holidays. Those who practise yoga regularly may be more inclined to engage in yoga tourism. As stated by Ponder and Holladay (2013: 103), 'At some point of practising, yogis develop desire to experience other yoga environments'. However, Kelly's (2012) research shows that, although 14 per cent of retreat visitors practise activities like yoga, tai chi and meditation every day, 20 per cent had never done them before. The same research based on several retreats showed that 88 per cent of retreat visitors were female. The age range varied, but a higher number tended to be older (35–55). Voigt et al. (2010) show that spiritual retreats in Australia tend to attract the highest proportion of visitors over the age of 55 (38 per cent) and the highest percentage of males (26 per cent) of all wellness facilities in Australia. Yoga tourists tend to be mainly female, professional, well educated and aged 35–54 (Lehto et al., 2006), and although more women than men tend to practise yoga, there are large numbers of male yoga teachers and spiritual gurus. Gerritsma (2008) analysed yoga in the Netherlands and showed that on average yoga practitioners are about 80 per cent women and 20 per cent men, where more dynamic forms of yoga (e.g. Ashtanga) attract a higher percentage of men. Ali-Knight (2009) showed that yoga tourists are a distinctive segment motivated primarily (sometimes only) by their interest in yoga (i.e. yoga tourism is a quest in itself).

Aggarwal et al. (2008) researched the experiences of yoga tourists in Rishikesh, which is seen to be the yoga capital of India. They showed that yoga tourists were motivated by the spiritual nature of the destination. They were not looking for luxury but to make life simpler and to meet spiritual goals and gain peace of mind. Maddox (2015) focuses on those tourists who want to study yoga at the 'source' of its origins and traditions. They are concerned not only with the authenticity of the practice itself, but also with their own sense of self and identity. She gives the example of Ashtanga yoga in Mysore, India, stating that 'not only are Westerners in search of an objectively authentic yoga in Mysore, they also pursue an existential authenticity that is largely defined within the binary of Indian asceticism versus Western consumption' (Maddox, 2015: 334). This experience cannot easily be replicated in one's own home town or country; however, it is also suggested by Maddox (2015) that what exists in India is (also) subject to dynamic forces of change and that Western variations of yoga are often no more 'fraudulent' than their counterparts in India. If yoga is viewed as culturally flexible, it can be enjoyed in various locations in the world (e.g. retreats) without concerns that it is a 'lesser' form of yoga than that which exists at the 'source' (i.e. India).

It is common in Western countries and in retreats run by Western practitioners (i.e. those offering yoga holidays rather than more spiritual ashrams) that yoga is packaged with a number of different activities. For example, BookYogaRetreats (2016) claims to be the world's leading online yoga company and its website offers vacation packages of 2,344 organisers in 250 destinations. This includes 3,428 yoga retreats, yoga holidays and yoga teacher trainings (Table 14.1). Yoga is packaged with spas, massage, meditation, weight loss, vegetarian and vegan diets, detoxification, walking, beaches, surfing and a range of complementary and alternative therapies such as Ayurveda and reiki. They offer around 20 different forms of yoga, but as seen also in Elwy et al.'s (2014) study, hatha yoga is the most popular. The website states that holidays listed under 'General Yoga' are also most likely to be hatha yoga. This is already a sophisticated offer compared to studies undertaken ten years ago, e.g. Smith

Table 14.1 Types of yoga offered by BookYogaRetreats (2016)

• Anusara 75	• Dynamic 257
• Ashtanga 703	• General (usually Hatha) 1,201
• Ayurveda 404	• Integral 102
• Bikram/hot yoga 64	• Jivamukti 17
• Hatha 1,575	• Kripalu 23
• Iyengar 246	• Kriya 145
• Kundalini 290	• Nidra 264
• Tantra 121	• Power 231
• Vinyasa 1,253	• Restorative 688
• Yin 592	• Sivananda 179

and Kelly's (2006) analysis of 500 retreats, where yoga retreats usually just mentioned 'yoga' rather than a range of different types (with the exception perhaps of Sivananda yoga retreats, which have been offering teacher training for many years). Smith and Kelly's experiences within holistic retreats like Skyros did, however, suggest that some visitors were already starting to insist on certain types of yoga more than ten years ago (Smith and Kelly, 2006). One participant insisted on Ashtanga yoga during a week in Skyros because that was advertised in the brochure and she would not be placated with hatha yoga instead (participant observation in Skyros holistic holiday retreat, 2002).

Yoga holidays and retreats are offered in more than 80 countries. The top five countries include India, which is described as follows: 'As the cradle of yoga, India has served for over 4,000 years as the land of transformation to yogis of all over the world who travel to South Asia in quest of themselves' (BookYogaRetreats, 2016). It seems that yoga is considered to be a path which enables people to transform themselves or at least, to get to know themselves better. India is followed by Thailand, Indonesia, Costa Rica and Spain. Yoga retreats are offered for couples and families, as well as individuals. More retreats are offered for women than men, but this is consistent with past studies, as discussed earlier in the chapter. One of the main aims is to enhance and change people's lives:

> Our passion is to enrich people's lives. We believe that a yoga travel experience is a lifetime memory that increases happiness and personal growth. That is why we want more and more people to experience an eye-opening yoga journey.
>
> *(BookYogaRetreats, 2016)*

Following on from Gerritsma's (2008) research on yoga in Amsterdam, the authors of this chapter decided to undertake a similar study in their city of residence, Budapest in Hungary, to examine the relationship between yoga as leisure and yoga tourism. This includes the types of yoga practised, the motivations for practising yoga, regularity of practice, the benefits derived and the propensity to engage in yoga tourism. Although the research does not yet give significant insights into the long-term transformational benefits of yoga and more especially, yoga tourism, it gives an indication that yoga is an increasingly popular leisure activity and that its benefits are more multi-faceted than purely physical. Restrictions on disposable income in countries like Hungary (where a salary is one-fifth or one-sixth of the Dutch or British equivalent, for example) mean that yoga practitioners may not be financially able to visit retreats outside Hungary for tourism purposes despite the desire to do so.

Case study: yoga, leisure and tourism in Budapest, Hungary

The following section presents research on yoga practice in Budapest, Hungary. In 2012, questionnaires were undertaken with 201 yoga practitioners in Budapest to ask about their motivations for doing yoga, the impacts and benefits and their propensity to travel to do yoga (Sziva et al., 2013). A follow-up study with 98 practitioners was undertaken in 2015 in conjunction with Orbán (2015). Yoga is a relatively new leisure activity in Hungary compared to many other European countries. However, it is growing rapidly and the number of yoga centres is increasing all the time. This is particularly true of the capital city, Budapest, where the research was undertaken. According to research by GFK (2012), health and body–mind–spirit balance is important for 41 per cent of Hungarians, mainly for those in the highest social categories and the well educated, but also for young people. Thirty-nine per cent use some kind of alternative therapy service (e.g. bio-, energy- or mind-based treatments). Six per cent do meditation; 5 per cent take part in personality improvement training; 5 per cent in mind-control training; and 4 per cent of the total population do yoga regularly (several times weekly or monthly).

A questionnaire with closed-ended questions was distributed to yoga practitioners in Budapest. Some difficulties arose when attempting to undertake research in yoga centres due to the lack of free access to classes and practitioners and the lack of time before or after classes. Therefore the majority of the questionnaires were undertaken at a yoga festival (the Uj Élet Jóga Fesztivál or New Life Yoga Festival) in May 2012. This event, which took place in a central city location, was a 'showcase' for eight different types of yoga, with the objective of promoting yoga and healthy lifestyle (e.g. nutrition, massage). Around 150 people participated in the festival and the yoga classes offered. To supplement this sample, questionnaires were also distributed electronically using the same questionnaire between May and July 2012. A snowball sampling approach was taken using known yoga practitioners and community websites. This additional research phase resulted in a total of 201 valid questionnaires.

Eighty-nine per cent of yoga practitioners were women, which reflects similar studies mentioned earlier (e.g. Lehto et al., 2006; Gerritsma, 2008). The majority (40 per cent) were aged 30–39, which also corresponds with other studies (e.g. Lehto et al., 2006; Kelly, 2012). Seventy-three per cent of them were in permanent employment, while the second largest group was that of students (14 per cent). A high number of the respondents (58.2 per cent) evaluated their health state as average, 38.8 per cent as good and only 3 per cent as bad. Half of the respondents never tried smoking, 23 per cent gave it up and only 5.5 per cent smoke regularly. The majority of the respondents take care of their diet: 30 per cent are interested in special diets, e.g. Ayurveda, Paleo. There are a relatively high number of vegetarians (20 per cent), bio-food consumers (13 per cent – many of whom are vegetarian too) and those interested in detoxification (17.8 per cent). It could be seen from the BookYogaRetreats (2016) website that yoga is frequently packaged with special diets, especially vegetarian, vegan and detoxification programmes.

One of the most important motivations for practising yoga is balance, which gained the highest score on the Likert scale of 1–5 (4.44). The philosophical and spiritual experience of yoga is important for half of the respondents (reaching an average of 3.5 on the Likert scale). It is interesting to note that exercise is a less important motivation than achieving balance, calm or stress relief. This means that yoga has already been recognised as a practice which is not only based on physical fitness. However, Figure 14.1 shows that physical fitness is the first benefit that is noticed

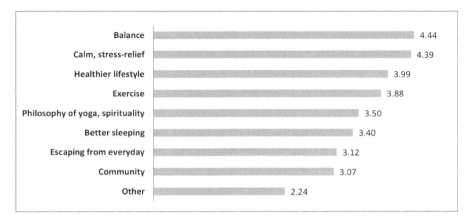

Figure 14.1 Motivations for practising yoga (1 = no importance; 5 = very important).

by practitioners, suggesting that the effects can be felt on the physical body more quickly or easily than they are felt in the mind or spirit. Elwy et al.'s (2014) review also suggested that 25 per cent of studies focused on the stress-relief benefits of yoga.

The most important impact of doing yoga is fitness and calm (measuring 4.11 and 4.06 respectively on a Likert-scale of 1–5). Other important impacts are self-understanding and improving concentration (average of 3.86 and 3.8). Self-understanding is arguably one of the first stages of transformation. Healthier nutrition, accepting one's own body and the spiritual experience are important for half of the respondents. Socialising and community involvement seem to be of relatively little importance, which implies that yoga is seen more as a personal development practice.

In all, 40.8 per cent of the respondents had already travelled with the objective of doing yoga. It should be highlighted that those practising regularly (daily, weekly) are those who are most likely to participate in yoga holidays and are mainly in the age groups of 30–39 and 40–49

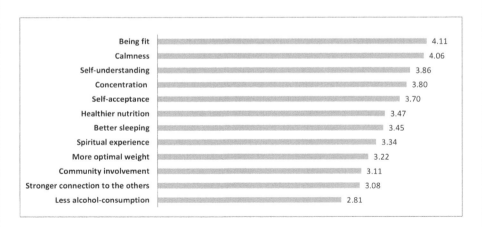

Figure 14.2 The impacts of practising yoga (1 = no importance; 5 = very important).

(continued)

(continued)

(this is consistent with other studies of yoga tourism and retreats, e.g. Lehto et al. (2006), Voigt et al. (2010) and Kelly (2012)). A total of 63.6 per cent of male respondents have participated in yoga holidays (although the rate of men doing yoga in this sample was only 11 per cent). The tendency to go on a yoga holiday is higher amongst those practitioners for whom self-understanding and spirituality are important. This suggests that holidays are used as a way of intensifying self-development and not only fitness. Respondents spend an average of five days on a yoga holiday, but with a high variation (1–30 days). A total of 47.2 per cent selected a yoga camp in a forest as the preferred destination for their yoga holiday, followed by yoga festivals (13.8 per cent) and retreats (10.6 per cent). These categories were suggested to them in the questionnaire (i.e. they were pre-set) but an 'Other' option was also available. It should be noted that there are not many retreat options in Hungary. For example, BookYogaRetreats (2016) only lists one retreat in Hungary but 345 in Spain! Community involvement and stronger connections to others are not (yet) such an important motivation or benefit, as suggested by Ponder and Holladay (2013). According to Hofstede (2016), Hungary is an individualist society, which means there is a high preference for a loosely knit social framework in which individuals are expected to take care of themselves and their immediate families only. This may have had some bearing on these results.

Domestic destinations (in Hungary) were visited by 61 per cent, while India is the second most frequently chosen destination (10.2 per cent), followed by Western European destinations (Figure 14.3). This shows that, when given the chance, yoga tourists would like to study yoga at the 'source' of its origins and traditions, as suggested by Maddox (2015). It should be noted that the salaries in Hungary are much lower than their Western European counterparts (sometimes as little as one-sixth); therefore overseas and long-haul travel is relatively expensive for Hungarians. Some recent studies (e.g. OECD, 2012) also show that Hungarians currently have the lowest amount of disposable income to travel in the EU.

In 2015, similar research was undertaken using the same questionnaire which was distributed using some of the same websites and social media channels. However, this time, no questionnaires were distributed at the Yoga Festival, so only 98 responses were received. Data was also collected using secondary sources of information, such as websites of yoga centres. Out of 88 yoga centres in Budapest, 20 websites were content-analysed. These were identified via Google

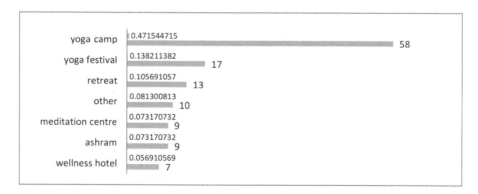

Figure 14.3 The preferred locations for yoga holidays.

and were selected using systematic sampling (every fourth website was selected). The most popular form of yoga seems to be pregnancy yoga (60 per cent of centres offer this type) followed by hatha (50 per cent), spinal (45 per cent) and mummy–baby yoga (40 per cent). Analyses of yoga retreats or holidays would most likely not include so many entries for pregnancy or mummy–baby yoga because of travelling restrictions and challenges. Workshops (e.g. half day or full day) are the most important complementary offers (65 per cent of them offer this service), followed by meditation (50 per cent) and yoga camps (40 per cent).

In the 2015 questionnaires, 77 per cent of respondents were women, so it seems that the number of men doing yoga may have increased since 2012. In all, 45.9 per cent were aged 30–39, slightly more than in the 2012 sample; 38.8 per cent were younger (19–29 years old). As in the previous research, the number of respondents aged 40 and above is much lower. This might be explained by the fact that many women (or men) are having children later and are unable to frequent yoga centres as often as younger, childless people. In terms of health status, 78 per cent claimed to feel healthy or very healthy, which is much higher than in the previous sample (38.8 per cent) and 16 per cent are vegetarians (20 per cent last time).

In terms of types of yoga practised, in 2015 hatha yoga played the most important role (45.9 per cent of the answers), followed by Ashtanga (23.5 per cent), Bikram (6.1 per cent), spinal (5.1 per cent) and karma (5.1 per cent) (Figure 14.4). Other types included Sivananda, Iyengar, Kundalini and mixed types of yoga. A total of 59.2 per cent of respondents practise yoga several times weekly, followed by 22.4 per cent who do yoga daily.

The most important sites for practising yoga are: yoga centres (47.6 per cent of the answers), followed by doing yoga at home (29.2 per cent) and outdoors (13.7 per cent).

In 2015 balance was the most important motivation (4.59 on a Likert scale of 1–5), followed by calm (4.47) and a healthier lifestyle (3.72); being in a strong community is less important (2.73 in 2015, compared to 3.07 in 2012). Calmness and being fit were the most important impacts of doing yoga (similar to 2012, with a slightly higher average of 4.3 for calmness and 4.23 for being fit), followed by self-acceptance (which was rated lower in 2012) and self-understanding (3.76).

In 2015, 35 per cent of the respondents travelled with the special purpose of doing yoga. The lower rate of tourists can perhaps be explained by the fact that the 2015 sample was collected

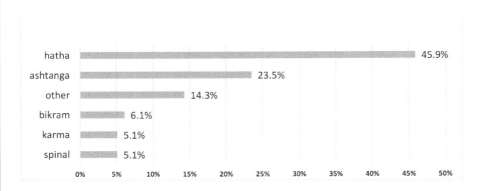

Figure 14.4   Types of yoga practised in Budapest.

(continued)

(continued)

in yoga centres in the city centre which focus mainly on daily yoga instead of yoga holidays and yoga camps. The majority of the tourists are hatha and Ashtanga practitioners. A total of 51.4 per cent of the yoga tourists are aged 30–39 years and 80 per cent of them are female (again, consistent with other studies). As in the previous study, the tendency to go on a yoga holiday is higher amongst those practitioners for whom spirituality is important. The average length of stay on yoga vacations was seven days (only five days in 2012). Yoga camps were the most popular (39.4 per cent), followed by yoga festivals (19.7 per cent), ashrams (10.6 per cent) and retreats (7 per cent). In all, 63.3 per cent are domestic trips (i.e. in Hungary), but India (10.2 per cent) and Northern Europe (4.1 per cent) were also mentioned. These numbers are very similar to last time.

Practising yoga is becoming more and more popular in Hungary and seems to be part of a growing wellness or holistic trend. This research shows that for the majority of yoga practitioners it has become a lifestyle with regular practice leading to stress relief, calmness and self-understanding, as well as many other impacts. Spirituality is also important for many of the respondents and it seems that those who equate yoga with spirituality are more likely to travel (suggesting that yoga has gone beyond a mere fitness regime). Although physical fitness is the first impact or benefit noted by practitioners, other mental, emotional or spiritual benefits follow close behind. Community and social benefits are not as important for Hungarian respondents. This might be partly due to the high level of individualism in Hungary (Hofstede, 2016). It can also be the case that it is mainly during retreats or yoga holidays that practitioners start to bond with one another and develop a sense of community (see Chapter 13). Although the development of yoga holidays is in its relative infancy in Hungary, many respondents had been or were enthusiastic about going on yoga holidays and a third (2015) to a half (2012) had already been on one. As mentioned earlier, financial factors are much more likely to inhibit travel propensity than lack of motivation.

Conclusions

This chapter has suggested that yoga has the power to transform people's lives beyond the physical body and personal fitness and that yoga holidays or retreats can help to intensify practice and to set participants on the path to greater self-development or even transformation. Although the primary data does not suggest much evidence for enhancing social or community connections, other retreat research (e.g. Chapter 13) emphasises the importance of community for retreat participants and yoga retreats are no exception. The research in Budapest discussed here is based only on the self-perceptions of yoga practitioners, but there are many more studies emerging which give more objective evidence for the health benefits of yoga, for example, as summarised by Cramer et al. (2016), Elwy et al. (2014) and Park et al. (2015). Although some of the studies are inconclusive or inconsistent, there is evidence to suggest that yoga has many positive physical and mental benefits. However, as suggested by Luskin (2004), the true transformative powers of practices like yoga go way beyond the physical body and there is a need for more longitudinal research that takes into consideration emotions, values and relationships too. Yoga does not provide immediate transformation of an individual and certainly, even less, a society. However, a yoga class during one's leisure time or a yoga holiday, even with no prior knowledge of yoga, can provide the moment of epiphany when a person embarks on a yoga journey which eventually changes his or her life forever.

References

Aggarwal, A. K., Guglani, M. and Goel, R. K. (2008) 'Spiritual and Yoga Tourism: A Case Study on Experience of Foreign Tourists Visiting Rishikesh India', Conference on Tourism in India – Challenges Ahead, IIMK, 15–17 May.

Ali-Knight, J. (2009) 'Yoga Tourism', in Bushell, R. and Sheldon, P. J. (eds) *Wellness and Tourism: Mind, Body, Spirit, Place*. New York: Cognizant Communication, pp. 84–98.

BookYogaRetreats (2016) *Yoga Retreats and Vacations*, https://www.bookyogaretreats.com (accessed 4 February 2016).

Büssing, A., Michalsen, A., Khalsa, S. B. S., Telles, S. and Sherman, K. J. (2012) 'Effects of Yoga on Mental and Physical Health: A Short Summary of Reviews', *Evidence-Based Complementary and Alternative Medicine*, Article ID 165410, doi: 10.1155/2012/165410.

Clark, C. M. (1991) *The Restructuring of Meaning: An Analysis of the Impact of Context on Transformational Learning*, Unpublished doctoral dissertation, University of Georgia, Athens.

Cramer, H., Ward, L., Steel, A., Lauche, R., Dobos, G. and Zhang, Y. (2016) 'Prevalence, Patterns and Predictors of Yoga Use', *American Journal of Preventative Medicine*, 50(2), 230–235.

Elwy, A. R., Groessl, E. J., Eisen, S. V., Riley, K. E., Maiya, M., Lee, J. P., Sarkin, A. and Park, C. L. (2014) 'A Systematic Scoping Review of Yoga Intervention Components and Study Quality', *American Journal of Preventative Medicine*, 47(2), 220–232.

Garrett, C. (2001) 'Transcendental Meditation, Reiki and Yoga: Suffering, Ritual and Self-Transformation', *Journal of Contemporary Religion*, 16(3), 329–342.

Gerritsma, R. (2008) 'The Growing Yoga Community in the Netherlands: How Yoga Is Becoming a Lifestyle Product Including Tourism Activities', in Smith, M. K. and Puczkó, L. (eds) *Health and Wellness Tourism*, Oxford, UK: Butterworth Heinemann, pp. 361–365.

GFK (2012) *Egészséggazdasági Monitor, Kutatási Jelentés*, Budapest, Hungary: GFK.

Heelas, P. and Woodward, L. (2005) *The Spiritual Revolution: Why Religion Is Giving Way to Spirituality (Religion and Spirituality in the Modern World)*, Oxford, UK: Blackwell Publishing.

Hofstede, G. (2016) *The Hofstede Centre: Hungary*, http://geert-hofstede.com/hungary.html (accessed 6 February 2016).

Iyengar, B. K. S. (1999) *The Art of Yoga*, New Delhi, India: HarperCollins.

Kelly, C. (2012) 'Wellness Tourism: Retreat Visitor Motivations and Experiences', *Tourism Recreation Research*, 37(3), 205–213.

Lea, J. (2008) 'Retreating to Nature: Rethinking "Therapeutic Landscapes"', *Area*, 40(1), 90–98.

Lehto, X., Brown, S., Chen, Y. and Morrison, A. M. (2006) 'Yoga Tourism as a Niche Within the Wellness Sector', *Journal of Tourism Recreation Research*, 31(1), 25–36.

Luskin, F. (2004) 'Transformative Practices for Integrating Mind–Body–Spirit', *Journal of Alternative and Complementary Medicine*, 10(1), 15–23.

Maddox, C. B. (2015) 'Studying at the Source: Ashtanga Yoga Tourism and the Search for Authenticity in Mysore, India', *Journal of Tourism and Cultural Change*, 13(4), 330–343.

Mezirow, J. (2000) *Learning as Transformation: Critical Perspectives on a Theory in Progress*, San Francisco, CA: Jossey Bass.

OECD (2012) Better Life Index, http://www.oecdbetterlifeindex.org/countries/hungary (accessed 6 May 2013).

Orbán, E. (2015) *Spiritual Travel and the Role of Yoga in Tourism*, BA thesis, Budapest Metropolitan University of Applied Sciences.

Park, C. L., Braun, T. and Siegel, T. (2015) 'Who Practices Yoga? A Systematic Review of Demographic, Health-related and Psychosocial Factors Associated with Yoga Practice', *Journal of Behavioral Medicine*, 38, 460–471.

Pine, B. J. II and Gilmore, J. H. (1999) *The Experience Economy*, Cambridge, MA: Harvard Business School Press.

Ponder, L. M. and Holladay, P. J. (2013) 'The Transformative Power of Yoga Tourism', in Reisinger, Y. (ed.) *Transformational Tourism: Tourist Perspectives*. Wallingford, UK: CABI, pp. 98–108.

Reisinger, Y. (2013) *Transformational Tourism: Tourist Perspectives*, Wallingford, UK: CABI.

——. (2015) *Transformational Tourism: Host Perspectives*, Wallingford, UK: CABI.

Smith, M. K. and Kelly, C. (2006) 'Holistic Tourism: Journeys of the Self?', *Journal of Tourism and Recreation Research*, 31(1), 15–24.

Smith, M. K. and Puczkó, L. (2009) *Health and Wellness Tourism*, Oxford, UK: Butterworth Heinemann: Elsevier.

——. (2013) *Health, Tourism and Hospitality: Spas, Wellness and Medical Travel*, London: Routledge.

Sri Swami Satchidananda (1999) *The Yoga Sutras of Patanjali*. Buckingham, UK: Integral Yoga Publications.

Summers, D. (2012) 'Personal Transformation in the Experience Economy: An Interview with B. Joseph Pine II', *American Management Association*, Fall, MWORLD.

Swami Vishnu-Devananda (1988) *The Complete Illustrated Book of Yoga*, New York: Julian Press.

Sziva, I., Kulcsár, N. and Smith, M. K. (2013) 'The Propensity for Yoga Practitioners to Become Tourists: A Case Study of Budapest', in Smith, M. K. and Puczkó, L. (eds) *Health, Tourism and Hospitality: Spas, Wellness and Medical Travel*, pp. 435–441.

The Retreat Company (2013) http://www.theretreatcompany.com (accessed 3 March 2013).

Verrastro, G. (2014) 'Yoga as Therapy: When Is It Helpful?', *Journal of Family Practice*, 63(9), E1–E6.

Voigt, C., Brown, G. and Howat, G. (2011) 'Wellness Tourists: In Search of Transformation', *Tourism Review*, 66(1/2), 16–30.

Voigt, C., Laing, J., Wray, M., Brown, G., Howat, G., Weiler, B. and Trembath, R. (2010) *Health Tourism in Australia: Supply, Demand and Opportunities*, http://www.crctourism.com.au/wms/upload/resources/WellnessTourism_Ind%20Summary%20WEB%20(2).pdf (accessed 22 February 2013).

Yiannakis, A. and Gibson, H. (1992) 'Roles Tourists Play', *Annals of Tourism Research*, 27(1), 132–147.

Yoga Magazine (2013) *Variety Is the Spice of Yoga*, February, pp. 64–71.

Glossary of terms

Some of the types of yoga mentioned in this report have been defined according to *Yoga Magazine* (2013) as follows:

Ashtanga: goes back to the ancient principles of yoga sage Pantanjali. Sometimes called power yoga, it was introduced to the West in the 1970s by Sri Krishna Pattabhi Jois. It combines dynamic (*ujjayi*) breathing with a series of strong, fast, flowing movements.

Bikram yoga: consists of a series of 26 energetic postures performed in very high temperatures (around 100°C/40°F) designed to stretch muscles further and expel toxins. Founder Bikram Choudhoury, who has a college in the USA.

Hatha yoga: although often described as the yoga of physical exercise, hatha follows the classical yoga theory of learning how to control the body so it can absorb the universal life-force energy (*prana*). In Sanskrit *ha* means sun and *tha* means moon.

Iyengar yoga: was developed by B. K. S. Iyengar in India. He introduced a systematic, disciplined approach to align mind, body and spirit through *asanas*, *pranayama* and meditation. Very popular in the West.

Karma yoga: takes the path of selfless action, working for others in the hope of gaining spiritual and healing powers.

Kundalini yoga: is an ancient, mystical branch of yoga. Movement, breathing, sound, chanting and meditation are used to activate the kundalini – a spiritual healing energy – and guide it through seven major energy centres in the body. The kundalini cleanses and purifies the *chakras*, dispelling negative thoughts, emotions and disease.

Sivananda yoga: combines 12 basic poses, plus salute to the sun, breathing and meditation to open the *chakras*. It is one of the best-known yoga systems in the West and was introduced in the 1950s by Swami Vishnu Devananda.

Part V
Medical tourism
Ethics, regulation and policy

This part looks at the rather complex issues of ethics, regulation and policy in medical tourism. International medical tourists visit a country to have medical treatments because of a number of factors such as preferable prices, instant availability of medical treatments or branded physicians. They probably would not consider some very critical parameters such as liability issues, regulative measures or infection risks.

David Reisman raises the question about the fundaments of ethics in cross-border healthcare (Chapter 15). Ethical considerations can and do influence what one may consider ethical or unethical, especially in relation to such highly sensitive topics as health or medical status. While morals can be looked at as being absolute and unquestionable, certain moral norms can actually limit or shape what cross-border healthcare provision and demand could or should actually provide.

Medical tourism can have certain externalities. One of these unwanted impacts is the biosecurity risk. As Colin Michael Hall discusses in Chapter 16, medical tourists travel across borders and so too can infectious diseases such as antibiotic-resistant bacteria or nosocomial infections. This risk is not only relevant to medical tourists who stay on various hospital wards but also to any other form of health tourism. The potential transfer of biological material by medical tourists either into the host or back to the home destination can be serious in the case of intercontinental medical travel. It is also important to note that hospital accreditation schemes and safety measures can vary greatly according to national and local regulations.

Reproductive care has a very special status in medical tourism given its extremely sensitive nature. Markus Frischhut looks at the legal and ethical considerations and related legislation of cross-border reproductive care in Chapter 17. Legal systems and regulations about reproductive care differ greatly country by country. This is one of the reasons why travellers seek care in another country, i.e. a certain treatment may not be legal or could be unregulated in the home country. The cases used to illustrate the various situations are actual cases from the European Court of Justice's practice.

Beauty treatments and massages are now basic services in any spa or wellness centre or spa hotel. Kathryn Gallagher and Marion Joppe discuss how the rapid development of the sector and the growing overlap between the medical sector and spas may not be paired with the necessary improvement and knowledge of therapeutic staff (Chapter 18). Spa trade in terms of personnel tends to represent an unregulated market which calls for more training and education for aestheticians in particular, since they are responsible for delivering the treatments.

Overall, this part makes the point that medical tourism needs to be more closely regulated and monitored than some other forms of tourism if it is to provide maximum benefits and minimal risks to patients as well as residents in host destinations.

15

The ethics of medical travel

David Reisman

Ethics is the domain of right conduct. It is a normative constraint and the binding *ought-to-be*. It is the moral constitution which cannot be bought and sold like indulgences at the margin. This chapter is about good and evil, deontology and consequentialism, virtue and vice, duty and expediency, equity and efficiency, procedure and endstate. The rules can be broken. The violators can experience social and psychological sanctions. Broken or not, they are still the rules. They are the guidelines and the map. We can depart from the path but we do so at our peril.

Ethics lays down tramlines for the cross-border transmission of medical care. Even when services, patients, professionals and capital have become integrated into the worldwide economic net, still there are fundamental notions of personhood and obligation which cannot be trampled underfoot in the scramble for profit and dividend. The first section, 'The ethical constraint', establishes the foundations, the fulcrum, the Archimedean point upon which the prison is built. The second section, 'Final services', says what is ethical and unethical about services which are delivered down a broadband link and about customers who go abroad to shop. The third section, 'Intermediate inputs', shows that moral norms limit the freedom of practitioners and investors to reap gains from trade through globalisation and comparative advantage.

The ethical constraint

One source of morals is absolute and unquestionable. The other is relative and contingent. Both are external to the individual. A single individual alone cannot choose his norms[1] as if they were wine and textiles in a street bazaar.

An absolutist or universalist stance relates to bedrock principles which emanate from unquestionable authority. The normative code is as eternal as the differential calculus, as immutable as the second law of thermodynamics. It is always and everywhere the same. When God gave the Ten Commandments to Moses he made it a divine edict that 'You shall not kill'. Hippocrates, who among doctors holds a quasi-theocratic mandate, specified that the practitioner must never 'give a woman an abortive remedy' or 'give a deadly drug to anybody if asked for it'. The Koran enjoins Muslims to abstain from gambling, alcohol, lending at interest and pork which it makes not *halal* but *haram*. A free market in abortion and euthanasia is ruled out by transcendent morals. Like them or loathe them, the client and the doctor are obliged to conform.

Standards transcend desires. One man's meat is another man's meat. Preferences and emotions do not vitiate the interpersonal and intertemporal wall of steel.

Locke derived obligation from the law of nature: 'And reason, which is that law, teaches all mankind who will but consult it that, being all equal and independent, no one ought to harm another in his life, health, liberty or possessions' (Locke, 1993 [1689]: 263–264). Locke saw *oughtness* as the negative duty not to inflict harm rather than the positive duty spontaneously to enhance the wellbeing of the generalised other. The felt desire to do good (benevolence) and the altruistic alleviation of non-ego distress (beneficence) were superstructure but not foundation. Explicit was abstention. *Laissez-faire*. We keep our hands to ourselves.

It was freedom *from* and not freedom *to* that was explicitly encoded in the natural order. Nature was the *suprema lex*. As the US Declaration of Independence put it: 'We hold these truths to be self-evident, that all men are created equal; that they are endowed, by their Creator, with certain unalienable rights; that among these are life, liberty and the pursuit of happiness' (United States Congress, 1800 [1776]: 5). If it is self-evident, then no further justification is required.

The natural order is not invented or created. Constant and not negotiable, it is the same at all times in all places. The World Health Organization made it clear that no state could ever have a mandate to curtail what is encoded in the very essence of the species being: 'The enjoyment of the highest attainable standard of health is one of the fundamental rights of every human being without distinction of race, religion, political belief, economic or social condition' (World Health Organization, 1962 [1946]: 1). The passport is issued to all citizens who are inscribed in *Homo sapiens*. No other qualifications are required.

It is in the nature of *Homo sapiens* to be responsive and alert. Aware that the Hobbesian war of each against all is an ever-present threat to peaceful coexistence, concerned because in the veil of unknowledge no one can foresee his own future stake, it is inherent in the logic of the situation that social actors, rational, intelligent and analytical, will gravitate to the Golden Rule. The categorical imperative as defined by Kant is a moral law that derives respect for persons from the unanimous wish to enjoy *as much* and *as good* in return: 'Act in such a way that you always treat humanity, whether in your own person or in the person of any other, never simply as a means, but always at the same time as an end' (Kant, 1961 [1785]: 86). If everyone stole or told lies, human interdependence would become impossible. Intrinsic values stem not from revelation but from the thinking person's recognition that inperiod selfishness, partiality or bias are a threat not just to health but to survival itself.

The absolutes of nature, revelation and Socratic truth are one source of ethical commitment. Society *sui generis* is another. Internalised standards, shared mores and common conventions add up to mutual constraint by consent and consensus. Durkheim makes explicit that Rousseau's 'general will' is nothing but the encompassing We that conditions and situates the lonely I: 'We may say that what is moral is everything that is a source of solidarity, everything that forces man to take account of other people' (Durkheim, 1984 [1893]: 331). Ethics would disappear if the authority of the cultural community were to wither away. Freedom of choice exists within the boundaries of the social order. Absolute absolutes are not the *sine qua non*. Relative absolutes are more than enough to legitimate the moral code.

T. H. Marshall, like Durkheim, believed that ethical constraint was inseparable from belonging and solidarity. Citizenship, he said, is 'a status bestowed on those who are full members of a community' (Marshall, 1992 [1950]: 18). All the team players enjoy full membership in the club. In exchange they must replicate the duties which are the concomitant of their rights: 'Your body is part of the national capital and must be looked after and sickness causes a loss of national income, in addition to being liable to spread' (Marshall, 1981 [1965]: 91). Your nation gifts you the clinics. You in return must not smoke or drink. To demand the categorical imperative you must supply the categorical imperative. An apple a day is the social contract. It is *as if* the market economist's *quid pro quo*.

Adam Smith was a market economist who believed in the power of money-mediated exchange. Commercialisation delivers the goods. Privatisation is the invisible hand. Importantly, he was also a sociological libertarian who believed that background ethics were essential if self-interest is to be kept within accepted boundaries:

> When the happiness or misery of others depends in any respect upon our conduct, we dare not, as self-love might suggest to us, prefer the interest of one to that of many. The man within immediately calls to us, that we value ourselves too much and other people too little and that, by doing so, we render ourselves the proper object of the contempt and indignation of our brethren.
>
> *(Smith, 1966 [1759]: 194)*

Market capitalism will only succeed if it is practised under the umbrella of self-policing ideals. Individualism is collectivism by consent. There is no other way.

James Buchanan too was an ethical relativist who regarded the common benchmark as the precondition for factored-down exchange. Sceptical about revelation but optimistic about consensus, Buchanan stated that there was in his opinion no 'higher form of truth' accessible only to 'those who hold the sacred keys' (Buchanan, 1999: Vol. XVII, 168). Precisely because 'no man's values are better than any other man's' (Buchanan, 1999: Vol. I, 431), no totalitarian scale can ever be invoked: 'Values are widely acknowledged to be derived from individuals and there are not absolutes. God has been dead for a century' (Buchanan, 1999: Vol. XVII, 168). There is no God. There are no great books. There is only agreement. Without the multiperiod constitutionalism of rules-utilitarianism, transcending the immediacy and isolation of the case-by-case and the hedonic, neither society nor exchange would last very long.

It is a consensus held up by its own bootstraps. Although moral absolutists are reluctant to derive *what ought to be* from the empiricists' *what is* or to say that 'the good' and 'the right' are no more than acculturated habits, customs and traditions, still moral relativists will insist that obligation is not invented but inherited. Shared norms are all that protects the going concern from cacophony, anarchy and in the end the Leviathan enforcer who makes the hospitals open on time. Consensus in that sense legitimates itself. Agreement *per se* is more important than the precise rules that keep Hobbes from the door.

Thus our constitution might converge on the welfare state because of a visceral reaction that human beings have a hard-wired requirement to be integrated in past-dominated, future-oriented social organisms. Cocoons provide an outlet for what Titmuss calls 'creative altruism' – 'creative in the sense that the self is realized with the help of anonymous others' (Titmuss, 1970: 212). To be *I* it is necessary to be *We*. That is why caring human beings with a 'biological need to help' donate their blood to unknown strangers. Wanting to become fully themselves, they are 'denying the Hobbesian thesis that men are devoid of any distinctively moral sense' (Titmuss, 1970: 198, 239). They are seeking to declare that sympathy and self-sacrifice are as much a part of their body and psyche as the self-seeking 'propensity to truck, barter and exchange' which makes the market go round.

Our constitution might converge on the welfare state. Alternatively, our constitution might converge on the maximum feasible devolution of decision making to the unique one-off because only the patient can say where it hurts and by how much. Because of information asymmetry, John Stuart Mill said, it is essential for decision making to be returned to individuals from the doctors and the leaders who so often appear sanctimonious and priggish:

> The only purpose for which power can be rightfully exercised over any member of a civilized community, against his will, is to prevent harm to others. His own good, either physical or moral, is not a sufficient warrant . . . Over himself, over his own body and mind, the individual is sovereign.
>
> *(Mill, 1974 [1859]: 68–69)*

Only the individual can know her perception of beauty when she presents for cosmetic surgery. Only the individual can decide if a debased and undignified quality of life warrants euthanasia in Zurich. The nation is made up of intimate choices like these. The *summum bonum* can only be built up from the desires and inclinations, the expected gratifications and utilitarian consequences of the constituent parts: 'It is the greatest happiness of the greatest number that is the measure of right and wrong' (Bentham, 1988 [1776]: 3). Autonomy reveals the preferences. Paternalists suffer from an information deficit.

Yet Mill's escape clause, 'to prevent harm to others', is in truth an open door. There are ethical spillovers when rich and poor, black and white, do not experience the social conditioning engineered by a one-class National Health Service hospital. There are economic spillovers where a botched implant, an infected transfusion or a rejected organ transplanted abroad have to be put right at a social cost at home. The patient as an individual does not bear the full burden of these externalities. The result is that citizens often empanel the judges and the politicians to serve as their philosopher-rulers where otherwise the optimum identified by the consensus would not be attained. Even individualism might generate a groundswell for laws and lawmakers whom the people trust to fill in the gaps.

Final services

Medical services can cross the borders. Even if demand and supply are situated in different jurisdictions, the international division of labour de*nation*alises the public goods. The press and the web diffuse information about health and illness. Knowledge of medical innovations and impending epidemics becomes common property for all. AIDS, malaria and Ebola are borderless threats that promote a worldwide 'spirit of Dunkirk', collective action and perceived cooperation. It is organic solidarity in the sense of Durkheim: 'In a world of shared global problems, the moral imperatives of addressing these problems also bring mutual benefits' (Yach and Bettcher, 1998: 741). It may be an ethical argument for freedom of trade. The exchange of superfluities makes the interdependent one.

Know-how crosses the borders. Even medical treatments get on a plane. Some services cannot. The dentist and the patient must be in the same space if a tooth is to be extracted. Others can. Back-office functions such as the transcription of notes or call centres that make appointments can be outsourced. Pharmaceutical trials can be offshored to human guinea pigs abroad. Helplines that give general advice and laboratories that process X-rays can be situated in India or the Philippines. Surgeons using a da Vinci machine and a fibreoptic cable can deliver a triple bypass in a country that has no high-value-added doctoring of its own. Saving a human life is supremely ethical. Absolutely or relatively, medical travel satisfies the meta-ethic of medicine itself.

Just as the service can cross the borders, so the patients themselves can go abroad for care. The price may be lower and the quality better. The queue for hernia repair may be shorter. Long-stay facilities may have a higher professional-to-patient ratio. Price and quality aside, there is also the differentiation of service. Patients go abroad for non-Western specialities like Ayurveda, meditation, yoga and traditional Chinese medicine. They go abroad because their world-view and language are different. The ethical norm of respect for persons suggests that felt wellbeing would rise if the patient and the practitioner were given the freedom to tailor-make their mutually satisfactory package.

There is a hidden text in the doctor–patient relationship. Korean doctors tell the patient what has to be done. They do not share Westerners' concern with individualism, choice and self-centred medicine. Western doctors make the consultation two-way. Korean doctors socialised into Korean expectations do not. A Korean doctor who is not authoritative or assertive will be called 'stupid' (Lee et al., 2010: 109) by patients used to something else. Medical travel gives patients the freedom to see professionals who share their cultural baggage.

The globe is a kaleidoscope of heterogeneities. Concepts of *ansai*, tranquillity, harmony, community, family, filial piety, altruism, compassion, equality, fate, non-confrontational subordination, reincarnation, the unity of all things, the anonymous stranger, the Good Samaritan all impact upon the medical encounter. Precisely because the sub-cultures are not all the same, travel allows the citizen domiciled in one country to seek out a doctor resident in a different country who understands that medicine, because it is person-centred, must always be relative and specific.

'Stupid' doctors and the karma of kismet are cultural proclivities which a multi-flowered society will often pass through on the principle of tolerant coexistence. More difficult will be the twilight interventions that the national consensus and its responsive state decree must be outlawed because they offend against the relative values of time and place. Embryonic stem cells, semi-trialled pharmaceuticals, designer babies, gender reassignment, female genital mutilation, the purchase of sperm and eggs, the artificial insemination of a postmenopausal woman or a same-sex couple are some of the services which have become international tradeables precisely because they are illegal in the country where the would-be consumer happens to hang his hat.

Thus the would-be consumer, paralysed and in pain, might want to have a say in when his dying stops, where and how his death takes place. Sedation and the withholding of fluids are common. Assisted suicide at the request of sick people or their family exposes the doctor and the relatives to a charge of manslaughter. Such a ban is in keeping with the absolute code which says that the body was created by God and is God's alone to destroy. It is at variance with libertarian relativism which says that only each Adam can know when it is in his best interest to call it a day. So long as there is no coercion, blackmail or third-party cost, respect for persons means that suicide, like wine and textiles, is a shopping-trolley choice.

So is abortion. Absolutists say that an unborn fetus is a credible person with a natural right to life. Relativists say that the destruction of potential is a threat to growth in a country experiencing a manpower shortage. The absolutists and the relativists make common cause in opposing abortion. They are sharply critical of resentful non-conformists who defy natural and man-made law by escaping into imports and shopping abroad. The road to Hobbes, if not to Hell, is paved with selfish Indonesians seeking their terminations in Singapore, conscienceless Irish sailing into international waters in order to desecrate the Book and war-zone rape victims whose mental or physical health may be at risk. Don't they know what would happen if everyone exercised their individual right to opt out of social control?

Surrogacy is another service which is delivered in the twilight zone that straddles the frontiers. The gestational surrogate in the South is paid less than in the North but more than she would have earned in subsistence agriculture. The status of women is raised when she contributes towards her children's schooling and her sister's dowry. In exchange for her willingness to rent herself out, the couple in the North gets a child which they will not cherish the less because of the commodification that surrounded its birth. If the exchange is 'bi-laterally voluntary and informed' (Friedman, 1962: 13), neither the surrogate nor the couple might regard it as exploitation by consent rather just another dyadic swap.

If there is no victim, then the consensus might be that it should be allowed. Yet emotions run high where childbearing, foreigners and race are concerned. White people are using brown people to buy a family. The First World is stealing from the Third World. The price is too low because the slumdogs are too desperate to refuse. Xenophobia and sympathy run high but still the ethical position is complex. The consensus might be that in an ideal world women would enjoy equal status and that economic deprivation would not exist. In favour of growth, trickle down, aid for development and social reform, the consensus is nonetheless obliged to start from here. If we believe that it is ethical to buy and sell, then we might have no choice but to condone surrogacy so long as it is out of sight, out of mind far away in Mumbai.

The same ethical issues arise in connection with the market for body parts. Kidneys, corneas, hearts and livers have an economic value. Organs transplanted from an unrelated donor may save the life of the recipient while providing the living merchant with much needed income. Provided that both parties are aware of the risks and benefits, Mill's ethics would preclude an appeal to the Nuremberg Code or the Declaration of Istanbul. All that is happening is that the two parties are concluding a mutually advantageous swap.

Some who use the absolute standard do not see it that way. Scheper-Hughes writes of 'the howl of the hungry wolf at the door' which leaves the donors easy prey to 'the despicable greed of organ brokers' (Scheper-Hughes, 2011: 63). She condemns the trade as 'neo-cannibalism', 'bio-terrorism', 'biopiracy', 'body theft', 'crimes against humanity'. Her attack, however, is more on the choices that are the forbidden fruit of poverty than it is on the choices that free people freely make. She is invoking the Kantian standard of respect for persons to say that each body is an integral whole, each body owner an end that can never be a means. The social consensus might, however, be that even starving people have a natural or a citizenship right to give their informed consent.

It would not be informed consent if there had been coercion. No one would call it ethical if the organ had been extricated from a corpse in the hospital morgue or from powerless orphans and the mentally retarded or from a third party who had been kidnapped and drugged or from a prisoner of conscience shot to order. Nor would it be informed consent if there had been deception. It cannot be ethical if the donor had been promised lifetime medical aftercare that was never followed up or if clinical trials were continued (the case of the Tuskeegee syphilis patients) even after a cure had been found. The grey area is where the kidney proletariat knows precisely what they are doing but that they have no choice. A Kantian viewpoint would be that it is unethical for any human being to be so vulnerable that he or she is forced by economics to accept so degrading a deal.

The consensus may despise the traffickers, the brokers, the bullies and the crooks who may be getting the lion's share of the fee, but at least the donor gets some money and the beneficiary gets the organ. Since there is a worldwide shortage of body parts, it cannot be entirely unethical when someone somewhere is able to purchase an extension of his lease.

Looking at the suicides, the abortions, the surrogates and organs, what is clear is that an improvement in welfare is being made because of the difference in the ethical endowment. Absolute ethics do not leave room for trade-creating dissensus. Relative morals do. A human being sentenced to death in one jurisdiction can enjoy a reprieve through an imported service bought over from another. When in Rome, do as the Romans do. Medical travel is ethical arbitrage which allows minorities to travel to Rome for the alcohol, oral contraceptives and *in vitro* fertilisation which are banned at home in line with a conceptual referendum in which the winner takes all.

Medical travel, Pennings writes, is a plus-sum compromise. 'External tolerance' respects the median viewpoint at home but, bypassing the law, also gives the fringes and the minorities the chance to breathe:

> The purpose of national regulation should not be to prevent those who disagree to perform certain acts or make use of certain interventions or services. Prohibitive laws can only determine which services are available on the territory. As such, the law expresses the moral values of the majority within a community; nothing more, nothing less . . . Allowing people to look abroad demonstrates the absolute minimum of respect for their moral autonomy.
>
> *(Pennings, 2004: 2691)*

It is the minimum. It is not the maximum. There is still more that a liberal democracy can do to protect a minority which can be as large as 49 per cent from the tyranny of a majority which can be just-past-the-post. Rather than forcing dissenters into temporary emigration, there must be an argument for a multiple-stream system within a single country itself. Even minorities have rights. Where there is a conflict of ethics, doctors can opt out of procedures to which they object but the marginalised opt in to interventions without having to rebel against the central value system by means of going abroad.

An example would be the management of gender selection. Instead of amniocentesis followed by abortion in a foreign clinic, the state could protect the social interest in a balanced population through paired licences for parents who want a boy or a girl. The licences issued, it would not violate the social consensus for parents to be permitted to select a second child of a different gender: 'Family balancing is intuitively accepted by a majority of the population' (Pennings, 1996: 2339).

Pennings, adopting a relativist standard, treats medical travel as the 'absolute minimum'. Others, refusing to tolerate the intolerable, see it as a pact with the Devil. If murder is always and everywhere an infringement of Locke's natural law, then abortion cannot be made legitimate merely by relocating the violation to a foreign country. Absolutists say that ethics is conformity to an invariant rule. If it is morally wrong for a Hindu to eat a beefsteak in India, then it is morally wrong to do so in Rome merely because the Romans live by Mill and not by the Book.

The Book aside, citizenship does presuppose Durkheim's common ground as well as Mill's freedom of choice. Some observers believe there is something lacking in a society that gives its citizens a mandate to violate core standards of right and wrong. Describing medical travel as 'circumvention tourism' (Cohen, 2012: 1309), Cohen objects that the social ethic is not a buffet from which malintegrated nationals can select whichever constraint they feel in the mood to accept:

> In terms of most of the perquisites of citizenship and our home country's obligations to us as citizens, we carry our citizenship abroad with us when we travel . . . Home countries have a strong argument for criminalizing the activities abroad of their citizens in abortion or assisted suicide to the same extent they would if the activity took place at home.
>
> *(Cohen, 2015: 355, 356)*

Cohen is not evaluating the abortions and the suicides *per se*. He is simply defending the common baggage against the corrosive of anomic corner cutting that eats away at the social binding. Yet there is a worm in the apple. Necessary though it may be, extra-territorial legislation may not be enforceable. Absolute or relative, the law discredits itself where medical travellers call it an ass and do what they please.

Can all young women be examined gynaecologically in the customs shed for evidence of a possible abortion? Can accompanying relatives be prosecuted for aiding and abetting where the final act at Dignitas is perfectly legal in Switzerland? Can a newborn infant be left either stateless or Indian where a birth mediated by a surrogate may not be repatriated like a Barbie doll to the buyer's home country? Can a doctor be asked to release confidential information to policemen and spies from a different jurisdiction? Can public hospitals at home refuse corrective care for illegal interventions badly executed abroad? It is neither cost-effective nor Kantian to micro-manage the globe. If, however, the law is not enforced, then the law is toothless. It is just for show.

Intermediate inputs

Wine and textiles are crossing the international frontiers. So are healthcare professionals and medically relevant investments. Trade is trade. Sentimentalists may be giving in to the medical mystique to treat medical inputs as, ethically speaking, a thing apart.

Commodities in boxes move from low-cost to high-return markets. Medical practitioners migrate too. Disproportionately the displacement is from South to North. It is a logical choice. Pay is higher. Facilities are better. Children's life chances are brighter. The philosophical issue is the loss to the country of origin. Professionals trained at national expense in Malawi become a costless externality in Manchester. Citizens left behind, most of all outside the capital, cannot find a physician. Reverse foreign aid means that the richer countries are under less pressure to put resources into their own medical schools. That is what happens when nations open up to the world. The First World brings in human capital from the Third. The Third World bleeds human capital to the First. It is certainly unequal. But is it inequitable as well?

The debate is an ethical minefield. Individualists would say that the nation does not own its citizens. So long as they have covered the full costs of their education and not defaulted on the five-years' public service in deprived areas that in some countries is the bond for their scholarship or loan, medical professionals have a free person's right to self-selected mobility. Communitarians would be more conservative. The ethical counterpart of socialisation is economic and political patriotism. Citizens pay their taxes and do their military service. They also stay in their own country to assist their fellow-citizens to reach the vanguard's own high educational and income level. It is the great chain of being. The children of Shakespeare look after the children of Churchill. That is why the White Cliffs do not speak French, Spanish or German.

Communitarians therefore call upon the state to regulate the flow:

> When they accept the privilege of a medical education, medical and nursing students enter implicitly into a covenant with society to use their knowledge for the benefit of the sick. By entering into this covenant they become stewards rather than proprietors of the knowledge they acquire . . . Stewardship is a better metaphor than proprietorship for medical knowledge and skill.
>
> *(Pellegrino, 1999: 251)*

The state can tax foreign earnings at a punitive rate. It can deny passport renewal to nationals who spend too long abroad. It can instruct foreign polities to limit the supply of work-permits. It can renegotiate the European Union's commitment to unimpeded mobility. In the limit it can build a Berlin Wall to keep its stewards in Bulawayo and not in Rome where anything goes.

Economic growth can defuse some, at least, of the philosophical tensions. At home, more resources for more clinics will increase the demand for professionals. It will retain them through more jobs and higher pay. Internationally, the law of one price suggests that at some point the terms and conditions will converge. The economic incentive to join the brain drain will then become less. Worldwide affluence does not resolve the ethical conflict between the individualists and the communitarians. Still less does it reconcile the absolute and relative ethics upon which they build. What it does is to take poverty out of the equation. It is hard to focus on moral philosophy when rain is coming through the roof and the children do not have enough to eat.

Capital, like labour, is crossing the borders. Savings go into paper portfolios or foreign direct investments. Both vehicles make possible the building of medical centres and the transfer of technology. When a hospital multinational penetrates a new market it brings in managerial expertise, skilled professionals, patented drugs and high-quality equipment. It creates employment. It unleashes a regional multiplier. It trains locals in computing, credit card billing bookkeeping and five-star hotel and catering as well as high-end proficiencies in radiography and physiotherapy.

Ethically speaking, if the moral imperative of medicine is to make sick people well, then the training and the treating cannot be other than ethical. The downside is inequality. The privileged will no longer travel abroad for their scans and operations but the deprived will be no better placed to access the diagnosis and attention that they require. The imbalance will actually be aggravated if manpower relocates to expensive international hospitals in urban areas. If capacity becomes an international tradeable, the quantity available for the home country's public patients is reduced. Competition with the invisible export pushes up the price.

Cosmetic surgery crowds out the well-baby clinics and the immunisation campaigns. Local people become a footnote in the scramble for value-added leveraged on the tertiary sector. The neglect is a political as well as a business failure. Poverty and not internationalisation is the real access barrier. It is not so much the multinational enclave that is starving the left-behind as it is the absence of pro-poor insurance and public assistance schemes. The redistribution of purchasing power would make charity pariahs into paying customers for whom even profit-seeking businesses would have to compete.

Capital comes in. Interest, profits and dividends flow out. Local entrepreneurs who cannot match the multinationals' standards will be competed away or taken over. Subsidies will be skewed towards export-intensive hospitals which bring in foreign currency. Labour laws and union exemptions will be changed in response to a threat from footloose enterprise. International investors may nudge domestic policies in a direction that the host country's citizens would not endorse. Absolutes are fudged. Consensus is ignored. What remains is a state-of-the-art corporation that spins money from foreigners and the local élite. The love of money is the root of all evil. Yet most nations, like most people, seem determined to have more and more.

Ethics is not yet on the endangered species list. It might still happen. Medical travel challenges the solidaristic nation building of a national health service. In its place it puts value for money and the mercantilisation of a merit good. It is consumer sovereignty and business profits all the way to the bank. Community and nationhood can be trampled underfoot in the stampede. As Sandel says: 'There are some things money can't buy, but these days, not many. Today, almost everything is up for sale . . . Markets – and market values – have come to govern our lives' (Sandel, 2012: 3, 5).

Medical tourism cannot be blamed for that. Nor is it right to run together the criticism of medical tourism with an attack on materialism, globalisation, capitalism, inequality, the damage done by foreigners or the North–South divide. There is more to human life than medical tourism alone. Medical travel does not exist in a sociopolitical vacuum. Medical travel is a part of the wider debate about the impact of internationalisation on the moral constraint.

Note

1 The pronouns 'his' and 'he' in this chapter are of course generic, and cover both genders.

References

Bentham, J. (1988 [1776]) *A Fragment on Government*, Cambridge, UK: Cambridge University Press.
Buchanan, J. M. (1999) *The Collected Works of James Buchanan*, Indianapolis, IN: Liberty Press, Vols. I, XVII.
Cohen, I. G. (2012) 'Circumvention tourism', *Cornell Law Review*, 97, 1309–1398.
——. (2015) 'Medical tourism for services illegal in patients' home country', in Lunt, N., Horsfall, D. and Hanefeld, J. (eds) *Handbook on Medical Tourism and Patient Mobility*, Cheltenham, UK: Elgar, pp. 350–359.
Durkheim, E. (1984 [1893]) *The Division of Labor in Society*, transl. by W. D. Halls, New York: The Free Press.
Friedman, M. (1962) *Capitalism and Freedom*, Chicago, IL: University of Chicago Press.
Kant, I. (1961 [1785]) *Groundwork of the Metaphysic of Morals*, transl. by H. J. Paton, in Paton, H. J. (ed.) *The Moral Law*, London: Hutchinson, pp. 53–148.
Lee, Y., Kearns, R. A. and Friesen, W. (2010) 'Seeking affective health care: Korean immigrants' use of homeland medical services', *Health and Place*, 16, 108–115.
Locke, J. (1993 [1689]) *Second Treatise on Civil Government*, in Wootton, D. (ed.) *John Locke: Political Writings*, Harmondsworth, UK: Penguin Books.
Marshall, T. H. (1981 [1965]) 'The right to welfare', *Sociological Review*, 13, reprinted in his *The Right to Welfare and Other Essays*, London: Heinemann Educational Books, pp. 83–94.
——. (1992 [1950]) *Citizenship and Social Class*, London: Pluto Press.
Mill, J. S. (1974 [1859]) *On Liberty*, Himmelfarb, G. (ed.), Harmondsworth, UK: Penguin Books.
Pellegrino, E. D. (1999) 'The commodification of medical and health care: The moral consequences of a paradigm shift from a professional to a market ethic', *Journal of Medicine and Philosophy*, 24, 243–266.
Pennings, G. (1996) 'Ethics of sex selection for family balancing', *Human Reproduction*, 11, 2339–2343.
——. (2004) 'Legal harmonization and reproductive tourism in Europe', *Human Reproduction*, 19, 2689–2694.
Sandel, M. J. (2012) *What Money Can't Buy: The Moral Limits of Markets*, New York: Farrar, Straus and Giroux.
Scheper-Hughes, N. (2011) 'Mr. Tati's holiday and João's safari – seeing the world through transplant tourism', *Body and Society*, 17(2/3), 55–92.
Smith, A. (1966 [1759]) *The Theory of Moral Sentiments*, New York: Augustus M. Kelley.
Titmuss, R. M. (1970) *The Gift Relationship: From Human Blood to Social Policy*, London: George Allen and Unwin.
United States Congress (1800 [1776]) *A Declaration by the Representatives of the United States of America*, reprinted in *The Constitutions of the Sixteen States which Compose the Confederated Republic of America*, Newburgh, UK: David Denniston.
World Health Organization (1962 [1946]) *Constitution of the World Health Organization*, in WHO, *Basic Documents*, Geneva, Switzerland: WHO, pp. 1–18.
Yach, D. and Bettcher, D. (1998) 'The globalization of public health, II: The convergence of self-interest and altruism', *American Journal of Public Health*, 80, 738–741.

16

The environmental externalities of medical and health tourism

Implications for global public health

Colin Michael Hall

Introduction

Much of the literature on health and medical tourism in the tourism literature tends to emphasise the potential value to consumers of medical tourism as well as the associated value to (primarily) private healthcare operators and destinations (Musa, Thirumoorthi and Doshi, 2012; Wang, 2012; Medina-Muñoz and Medina-Muñoz, 2013; Alberti, Giusti, Papa and Pizzurno, 2014; Alén, De Carlos and Domínguez, 2014; Woo and Schwartz, 2014; Johnson and Garman, 2015; Wu, Li and Li, 2016). In the medical literature the value drive has been more critically assessed, in part because of concerns over the implications for the patient when things go wrong, but also because of the implications for state-funded public health systems, especially those geared towards a model of universal health (Hall, 2011; Barros, 2015). Nevertheless, there appear to be significant academic and policy divides between countries that primarily embrace private health models and those with stronger publicly provided health systems, especially regarding the ethics and equity of medical and health tourism (Hall, 2012a; Ormond, 2015). However, a key issue in considering medical and health tourism is where the externalities lie, the nature of those externalities and over what timeframe they should be considered in policy making. This chapter therefore seeks to address these questions in the context of the wider health implications of medical tourism and how these should be considered at a time of increasing concerns as to the physical and economic capacities of health systems to respond to disease threats.

Framing medical and health tourism

The issue of medical and health tourism, especially in the form of international tourism, needs to be understood in the context of the globalisation of healthcare and how public health is understood (Collier and Lakoff, 2008; Jönsson, 2014; Reubi, Herrick and Brown, 2015). This means moving beyond focusing on patient mobility and how that may be enhanced to a more critical understanding of the shaping of public health policy and the social construction of the body, illness and disease (Farmer, Kleinman, Kim and Basilico, 2013; Whitmarsh, 2013) and within which tourism and medical and health tourism are strongly implicated (Hall, 2011).

Medical and health tourism presents a major paradox. On the one hand medical and health tourism, including commercially oriented wellbeing, is the epitome of the neoliberal model of consumer responsibility and the marketisation of health (Hall, 2015a), including the externalisation of individual and private risks to the public health sector. However, at the same time and especially following the Ebola outbreak in West Africa in 2014–2015 (WHO Ebola Response Team, 2014), in order to combat the spread of disease and viruses many countries and regions have introduced biosecurity strategies to enhance their economic and health security and reassure the public on occasion of major pandemics. Despite claims as to the borderless nature of a globalised world (Institute of Medicine, 2010), 'Amid an effectively global, interconnected and highly networked economy, health scares reassert the validity of borders: prosperity is equated with security, which decodes to border control for health' (Hooker, 2008: 127). This paradox is even more surprising given the 'lack of attention to the contradictions and implications of the international marketisation of health services by which citizens and residents of a country engage in medical services in other national jurisdictions and then return' (Hall, 2015a: 194).

The public health risks of medical and health tourism

Health risk is intrinsic to human mobility, yet medical and health tourism more so. As Hall (2012b: 207) argued,

> medical tourism is intrinsically different with respect to increasing biosecurity risk because individuals who engage in medical tourism are deliberately travelling to a medical environment and engaging in medical practices that expose them to pathogens and microbiologic fauna and flora that are qualitatively different from those found in their home environment.

Yet medical and health tourism is not treated in the same way as other biosecurity risks or even recognised as a biosecurity issue. Tourism is a significant pathway for the introduction of diseases and species, with tourism infrastructure, especially transport and the tourists being the vectors. There is a clear and unequivocal relationship between the extent of international trade, including tourism and the number of invasive alien species in a country (Westphal, Browne, Mackinnon and Noble, 2008). Medical tourism is therefore a potentially significant component of tourism's broader role in biological exchange (Hall, 2015a, 2015b). However, the scale and environment of cross-border medical treatment create a significant public health challenge.

Scale

Scale is important because of the extent of international mobility by individuals for medical and health reasons as well as the speed at which international travel now occurs. This is of direct relevance to medical and health tourism, for example, because international air arrivals transport antibiotic-resistant bacteria (ABRB) between different regions at a much faster rate and at a greater rate than at any other time in the antibiotic era (Hall, 2015a, 2015b).

Environment

The environment is relevant because of the specific medical environments to which individuals are located for treatment or participation in medical and health tourism (Table 16.1). In the case of the environment, two key issues can be identified with respect to the potential transfer of biological material by medical and health tourists. First is the risk of nosocomial infections, also referred to as 'hospital-' or 'healthcare-acquired' or 'associated' infections (Leahy, 2008; Reed, 2008; Allegranzi et al., 2011; Hall and James, 2011; Franck et al., 2015; Ling, Apisarnthanarak and Madriaga, 2015; Zingg et al., 2015), as a result of medical tourism, that act to transfer pathogens and immunologic sequelae between the health environments of the destination and tourist home country. For example, in the European Union alone, the number of healthcare-associated infections (HCAIs) is estimated at 4.544 million annually, leading directly to around 37,000 deaths and 16 million extra days of hospital stay (Zingg et al., 2015). According to a 2011 World Health Organization (WHO) meta-analysis, pooled HCAI prevalence in mixed patient populations was 7.6 per cent in high-income countries. Although there is scant data available in developing countries, it appears that HCAI incidence is higher than in developed countries. On the limited quality literature available, hospital-wide prevalence of HCAI varied from 5.7 per cent to 19.1 per cent, with a pooled prevalence of 10.1 per cent (WHO, 2011). Surgical site infection is the most surveyed and most frequent type of infection in low- and middle-income countries, with incidence rates ranging from 1.2 to 23.6 per 100 surgical procedures and a pooled incidence of 11.8 per cent. In contrast, surgical site infection rates vary between 1.2 per cent and 5.2 per cent in developed countries (WHO, 2011).

Also note that medical tourists can bring in bacteria or viruses which can be infectious to the host community or to the medical tourism facility and its staff.

Table 16.1 Factors predisposing to increased risk of infection and carriage of antibiotic-resistant bacterial organisms in medical tourists

Facilities

- Hospital accreditation varies greatly within and between some countries, providing variable levels of oversight for institutional infection control and antimicrobial use
- Medical tourists may undergo procedures in unlicensed settings, occasionally using unproven and experimental techniques
- Tourists may transit through multiple health and hospitality facilities in a short space of time in which there are different degrees of infection control
- Confined spaces and limited facilities of transport vehicles used for transfer may make some regular infection control practices impossible
- Barriers, including language and differing clinical practices, may limit the scope of information exchanged between patient and medical service provider

Patients

- Medical tourists undergoing solid-organ transplant or cancer therapy acquire the additional risk factor of immunosuppression while abroad, while intensive care units traditionally have high rates of multi-resistant organisms
- Medical tourism packages are frequently combined with a vacation, putting patients at risk for exposure to a broader range of community pathogens

Sources: Rogers et al. (2011); Hall and James (2011); Hall (2012b, 2015a).

Second, the growth of ABRB (Hawkey and Jones, 2009; Davies and Davies, 2010; Kumarasamy et al., 2010; Spellberg, Bartlett and Gilbert, 2013; Barlam and Gupta, 2015; Price, Koch and Hungate, 2015): travel, including medical tourism, is identified as 'a key feature of the international spread of these highly resistant bacteria within health care facilities' (Barlam and Gupta, 2015: 13). Importantly, it is not just the immediate medical and health environment that provides a potential source of ABRB (Rogers, Aminzadeh, Hayashi and Paterson, 2011), but other aspects of the destination that tourists may encounter, such as the food (Price et al., 2015) and the waters in which they go swimming (Leonard, Zhang, Balfour, Garside and Gaze, 2015).

ABRB transfer in the hospital environment can be an issue at the destination or on return (Kumarasamy et al., 2010). For example, an outbreak of carbapenem-resistant *Klebsiella pneumoniae* at the US National Institutes of Health Clinical Center resulted in 18 infections and 11 deaths more than three weeks after the index patient was discharged.

The Gram-negative bacteria *K. pneumoniae* is a major cause of nosocomial infections, primarily among immunocompromised patients and the ability of the organism to colonise patients in the hospital contributed to the ongoing outbreak (Snitkin et al., 2012). There is also a substantial body of evidence demonstrating that international tourists can become asymptomatically colonised with resistant pathogens. In a German study by Lübbert et al. (2015), 255 international travellers were studied for faecal colonisation with ABRB Enterobacteriaceae before and after travel to one of 53 different countries (mostly in Asia, Africa and South America). Extended-spectrum beta-lactamase (ESBL)-producing *Escherichia coli* and *K. pneumoniae* were present in 6.8 per cent of study volunteers pre-travel but post-travel, 30.4 per cent were colonised with ESBL *E. coli* and 8.6 per cent were colonised with ESBL *K. pneumoniae*. Travellers to India and South-East Asia were found to have the highest acquisition rates for those ABRB bacteria. Although half the individuals had a clinical bout of gastroenteritis associated with the travel, the rest were totally asymptomatic. No carbapenem-resistant Enterobacteriaceae were detected. The Enterobacteriaceae persistence rate after six months was 8.6 per cent (Lübbert et al., 2015). Such was the extent of Enterobacteriaceae persistence that the authors recommended that active surveillance and contact isolation precautions may be required at admission to medical facilities for patients who have travelled to India and South-East Asia in the previous six months.

In a study conducted in the Netherlands of 122 travellers with a similar pre- and post-travel design by von Wintersdorff et al. (2014), ESBL Enterobacteriaceae was found to have increased from 9 per cent pre-travel to 33.6 per cent post-travel, while quinolone-resistance genes qnrB and qnrS increased from 6.6 per cent and 8.2 per cent pre-travel to 36.9 per cent and 55.7 per cent post-travel, respectively. Again, travel to South-East Asia and the Indian subcontinent was associated with the highest acquisition rates. In a study of the role of international travel in the spread of methicillin-resistant *Staphylococcus aureus* (MRSA), Zhou, Wilder-Smith and Hsu (2014: 276) reported:

> Repatriation of patients from foreign hospitals or returning of patients who traveled for medical tourism has further fostered the emergence and spread of multidrug-resistant bacteria, including MRSA, from countries where multidrug-resistant organisms are endemic and noted that the Dutch had reported an overall MRSA carriage rate of 2.7% in repatriates from foreign hospitals, a rate which was higher than that among Dutch hospitals.

Response

Although there is no specific data on international patients in the WHO (2011) data, there is limited information on the HCAI rates for some of the countries that actively promote medical tourism. According to WHO, the prevalence of HCAI, 1995–2010, in Thailand was 6.5 per cent, in Cuba 7.3 per cent, in Brazil 14 per cent, in Malaysia 14 per cent and in Morocco 17.8 per cent. However, some of these figures do compare favourably with developed countries over the same period, including, for example, Switzerland (8.8 per cent), the UK (9 per cent), Canada (11.6 per cent) and New Zealand (12 per cent) (WHO, 2011). However, the picture is even more complicated as nosocomial infections and other complications are often under-reported, while if the patients are international and have returned home their HCAI may not even be recorded (Hall, 2015a).

In reviewing the limited literature on return medical tourists, Hall (2015a) noted that medical tourists represent only a small percentage of reported ill post-travel patients (0.1–0.5 per cent). However, as Hall and James (2011) suggested, even if these small percentages, which are much lower than those of HCAI reported in the international literature (WHO, 2011), were to be extrapolated as a percentage of the global international medical travel and tourism market, the potential consequences with respect to the spread of pathogens and drug-resistant bacteria are substantial.

Several responses to the threat posed by medical and health tourism in relation to the spread of antibiotic resistance as well as disease in general can be identified. One clear response would be to deter engagement in risky medical practices overseas. This could be done by the development of promotional and social marketing campaigns that focus on the reasons why people engage in medical tourism and their perceptions of its benefits. An associated response is the development of a much better understanding by public health authorities of the health implications of the medical tourism market and their associated attitudes and behaviours. This may also be important for a more thorough economic assessment of waiting times for 'elective' and 'minor' surgery in which delays encourage people to seek treatments offshore. Hospitals can also improve medical practices to deal with risks associated with return medical tourists (Rogers et al., 2011), but essential to this process is the gaining of adequate information about where the patient has been when travelling and the treatment that the patient sought. Such information needs to be integrated into any patient information system. However, such measures only reflect the extent to which the public health service incurs the cost of private medical travel decisions, especially if resistant bacteria or a disease is introduced into a community and/or health setting. Hall (2015a) also suggests:

> Biosecurity practices arguably also need to be specifically developed for medical tourists upon both exit and entry into a country as well as appropriate profiling, risk management and surveillance and monitoring strategies being established. A number of developed countries have elements of such a system in place, but many of the countries that are most active in promoting medical tourism do not.

(Hall, 2015a: 199–200)

A stronger international regulatory system to manage medical tourism would be one valuable contribution to reducing the public health threats posed by medical and health tourism (Cohen, 2011), while improvements to national policy measures (Lunt, Mannion and Exworthy, 2013), including having medical treatment or health tourism listed on arrival and departure cards, may also be significant for the development of appropriate international policy and regulatory frameworks in the longer term (Hall, 2015a) (Table 16.2).

Table 16.2 Biosecurity stages and medical tourism policy

Technical response	Behavioural response
Pre-border	
• Identifying threats to public health posed by medical and health tourism • Profiling and modelling the characteristics of damaging or potentially damaging organisms and vectors • Identifying controls for selected organisms • Analysing and predicting risk pathways • Identifying and collating databases and expertise • Developing information systems • Developing standards and compliance validation methodologies • Auditing compliance with standards	• Analysis of public attitudes and perceptions of biosecurity risks posed by medical and health tourism • Development of educational and social marketing programmes for tourists as to risks of offshore medical treatment
Border	
• Developing improved systems, including sampling methodologies, and technologies for intercepting unwanted organisms • Inclusion of medical/health treatment category in visitor arrival declarations • Developing border containment methodologies according to entry standards	• Developing profiles of non-compliance behaviour • Border-located social marketing and education integrated with final opportunities for declaration of engaging in medical tourism • Clear arrival and customs declaration procedures
Post-border (medical and health facilities)	
• International travel of patients for prior 12 months needs to be recorded on health care contact • Active surveillance and contact isolation precautions may be required at admission for patients who have travelled to high-risk destinations and/or been a medical tourist • Screening needs to customised to the receiving facility • All receiving facilities must have a readily accessible infection prevention policy defining at-risk patients, screening procedures, and pre-emptive isolation criteria	• Social marketing and education campaign to encourage compliance on information provision

Sources: Rogers et al. (2011); Hall (2015a); Lübbert et al. (2015).

Case study: NDM-1

Muir and Weinbren (2010) reported the case of a dialysis patient who had visited and dialysed in India 18 months previously and who had acquired a highly resistant *Escherichia coli* organism. The organism was found to be a New Delhi metallo-β-lactamase (NDM-1) producer, acquisition of which is strongly associated with medical contact in Pakistan or India. This enzyme confers resistance to all known antibiotics except polymyxins and, sometimes, tigecycline. Spread of resistance is thought to occur by plasmid-mediated transfer. This case raised a number of important issues, particularly concerning renal dialysis patients who dialyse in countries where carbapenemase-producing bacteria are common (India, Pakistan, the USA, Israel, Greece,

Turkey) while on holiday or during return visits to family. According to Muir and Weinbren (2010: 240), 'these patients may use or be admitted to, a number of healthcare facilities within a short period of time. All these factors could facilitate rapid spread of NDM-1 with potentially serious consequences'. In addition to concerns over the spread of ABRB, such cases also incur substantial costs with respect to the need for deep cleaning of potentially affected areas as well as patient screening and room controls. The potential dangers of outsourcing medical procedures offshore as part of attempts to improve health service economy and efficiency were indicated in Kumarasamy et al.'s (2010: 6) observation:

> It is disturbing, in context, to read calls in the popular press for UK patients to opt for correc-tive surgery in India with the aim of saving the NHS money. As our data show, such a pro-posal might ultimately cost the NHS substantially more than the short-term saving and we would strongly advise against such proposals. The potential for wider international spread of producers and for NDM-1-encoding plasmids to become endemic worldwide, are clear and frightening.

The NDM-1 case also created much controversy because of its affects on perceptions of Indian medical services, even though the review of NDM-1 by Kumarasamy et al. (2010) concluded that several of the UK source patients had undergone elective, including cosmetic, surgery while visiting India or Pakistan. India also provides cosmetic surgery for other Europeans and Americans and NDM-1 will likely spread worldwide. The association of NDM-1 with New Delhi (because the Swedish patient of Indian origin who had travelled to New Delhi and picked up the infection in which the drug-resistant strain was first identified there: Yong et al., 2009) was widely criticised in India by media and public officials (Pandey, 2010). Although the lead author was based in India, the Kumarasamy et al. (2010) study was described by the officials of the Indian health indus-try as 'malicious propaganda' and as a 'conspiracy' by members of the Indian parliament who also associated it with the activities of multi-national pharmaceutical companies (Pandey, 2010). Nevertheless, Indian Ministry of Health officials were reported as saying, 'We strongly refute the naming of this enzyme as New Delhi metallo beta lactamase . . . We also refute that hospitals in India are not safe for treatment, including medical tourism' (in Pandey, 2010).

Conclusions

This chapter has suggested that medical and health tourism has significant negative externalities, the cost and implications of which are often carried by the public health service. These exter-nalities are only likely to get worse as a result of growing resistance to antibiotics. Many of these negative aspects of medical and health tourism are downplayed in the tourism literature that tends to focus on individual, business and destination value creation. In contrast, the medical literature is more circumspect with the implications of cross–border medical and health mobil-ity. These differences also reflect broader issues with respect to how medical and health tourism is framed and understood.

Of particular importance for understanding the public health implications of medical and health tourism is the need to understand the spaces and time within which mobility is located. This refers both to the capacity of medical and health tourists to travel quickly as well as the health and medical environments. As a result of shifts in mobility in space and time, medical and health tourists potentially become significant vectors not only of disease but also of antibiotic resistance. Examples of the implications of this were shown from the medical literature.

Biotic transfer is not a significant issue for tourism studies in general or medical and health tourism in particular (Hall, 2015a, 2015b). However, it is one of the major environmental and public health challenges facing the world today and is integral to any understanding of wellbeing. Research on medical and health tourism by those in tourism studies needs to move beyond its narrowly defined neoliberal focus on individual value and the marketisation of health to one that is more inclusive of community and public wellbeing. From a more critical perspective medical and health tourism is therefore not just an issue of ethics and equity at a personal level, as important as they are, but also of global environmental and public health.

References

Alberti, F. G., Giusti, J. D., Papa, F. and Pizzurno, E. (2014) 'Competitiveness policies for medical tourism clusters: Government initiatives in Thailand', *International Journal of Economic Policy in Emerging Economies*, 7(3), 281–309.

Alén, E., De Carlos, P. and Domínguez, T. (2014) 'An analysis of differentiation strategies for Galician thermal centres', *Current Issues in Tourism*, 17(6), 499–517.

Allegranzi, B., Nejad, S., Combescure, C., Graafmans, W., Attar, H., Donaldson, L. and Didier, D. (2011) 'Burden of endemic health-care-associated infection in developing countries: Systematic review and meta-analysis', *The Lancet*, 377(9761), 228–241.

Barlam, T. F. and Gupta, K. (2015) 'Antibiotic resistance spreads internationally across borders', *Journal of Law, Medicine and Ethics*, 43(S3), 12–16.

Barros, P. B. (2015) 'Health systems and medical tourism', in Lunt, N., Horsfall, D. and Hanefeld, J. (eds) *Handbook on Medical Tourism and Patient Mobility*, Cheltenham, UK: Edward Elgar, pp. 71–81.

Cohen, I. G. (2011) 'Medical tourism, access to health care and global justice', *Virginia Journal of International Law*, 52, 1–56.

Collier, S. and Lakoff, A. (eds) (2008) *Biosecurity Interventions: Global Health and Security in Question*, New York: Columbia University Press.

Davies, J. and Davies, D. (2010) 'Origins and evolution of antibiotic resistance', *Microbiology and Molecular Biology Reviews*, 74(3), 417–433.

Farmer, P., Kleinman, A., Kim, J. and Basilico, M. (2013) *Reimaging Global Health: An Introduction*, Berkeley, CA: University of California Press.

Franck, K. T., Nielsen, R. T., Holzknecht, B. J., Ersbøll, A. K., Fischer, T. K. and Böttiger, B. (2015) 'Norovirus genotypes in hospital settings – differences between nosocomial and community-acquired infections', *Journal of Infectious Diseases*, 212(6), 881–888.

Hall, C. M. (2011) 'Health and medical tourism: Kill or cure for global public health?', *Tourism Review*, 66, 4–15.

——. (ed.) (2012a) *Medical Tourism: The Ethics, Regulation and Marketing of Health Mobility*, London: Routledge.

——. (2012b) 'The contested futures and spaces of medical tourism', in Hall, C. M. (ed.) *Medical Tourism: The Ethics, Regulation and Marketing of Health Mobility*, London: Routledge, pp. 203–216.

——. (2015a) 'The coming perfect storm: Medical tourism as a biosecurity issue', in Lunt, N., Horsfall, D. and Hanefeld, J. (eds) *Handbook on Medical Tourism and Patient Mobility*, Cheltenham, UK: Edward Elgar, pp. 193–206.

——. (2015b) 'Tourism and biological exchange and invasions: A missing dimension in sustainable tourism?', *Tourism Recreation Research*, 40(1), 81–94.

Hall, C. M. and James, M. (2011) 'Medical tourism: Emerging biosecurity and nosocomial issues', *Tourism Review*, 66, 118–126.

Hawkey, P. M. and Jones, A. (2009) 'The changing epidemiology of resistance', *Journal of Antimicrobial Chemotherapy*, 64(Suppl. 1), i3–i10.

Hooker, C. (2008) 'SARS as a "health scare"', in Ali, S. H. and Keil, R. (eds) *Networked Disease: Emerging Infections in the Global City*, Chichester, UK: Wiley-Blackwell, pp. 123–137.

Institute of Medicine (2010) *Infectious Disease Movement in a Borderless World*, Washington, DC: The National Academies Press.

Johnson, T. J. and Garman, A. N. (2015) 'Travelling for value: Global drivers of change in the tertiary and quarternary markets', in Lunt, N., Horsfall, D. and Hanefeld, J. (eds) *Handbook on Medical Tourism and Patient Mobility*, Cheltenham, UK: Edward Elgar, pp. 57–70.

Jönsson, K. (2014) 'Legitimation challenges in global health governance: The case of non-communicable diseases', *Globalizations*, 11(3), 301–314.

Kumarasamy, K. K., Toleman, M., Walsh, T., Bagaria, J., Butt, F., Balakrishnan, R., Chaudhary, U., Doumith, M., Giske, G., Irfan, S., Krishnan, P., Kumar, A., Maharjan, S., Mushtaq, S., Noorie, T., Paterson, D., Pearson, A., Perry, C., Pike, R., Rao, B., Ray, U., Sarma, J., Sharma, M., Sheridan, E., Thirunarayan, M., Turton, J., Upadhyay, S., Warner, M., Welfare, W., Livermore, D. and Woodford, N. (2010) 'Emergence of a new antibiotic resistance mechanism in India, Pakistan and the UK: A molecular, biological and epidemiological study', *The Lancet Infectious Diseases*, 10(9), 597–602.

Leahy, A. L. (2008) 'Medical tourism: The impact of travel to foreign countries for healthcare', *Surgeon*, 6(5), 260–261.

Leonard, A. F., Zhang, L., Balfour, A. J., Garside, R. and Gaze, W. H. (2015) 'Human recreational exposure to antibiotic resistant bacteria in coastal bathing waters', *Environment International*, 82(September), 92–100.

Ling, M. L., Apisarnthanarak, A. and Madriaga, G. (2015) 'Systematic literature review and meta-analysis of the burden of healthcare-associated infections (HAI) in Southeast Asia', *Clinical Infectious Diseases*, 60(11), 1690–1699.

Lübbert, C., Straube, L., Stein, C., Makarewicz, O., Schubert, S., Mössner, J., Pletz, M. W. and Rodloff, A. C. (2015) 'Colonization with extended-spectrum beta-lactamase producing and carbapenemase-producing Enterobacteriaceae in international travelers returning to Germany', *International Journal of Medical Microbiology*, 305(1), 148–156.

Lunt, N. T., Mannion, R. and Exworthy, M. (2013) 'A framework for exploring the policy implications of UK medical tourism and international patient flows', *Social Policy and Administration*, 47(1), 1–25.

Medina-Muñoz, D. R. and Medina-Muñoz, R. D. (2013) 'Critical issues in health and wellness tourism: An exploratory study of visitors to wellness centres on Gran Canaria', *Current Issues in Tourism*, 16(5), 415–435.

Muir, A. and Weinbren, M. J. (2010) 'New Delhi metallo-β-lactamase: A cautionary tale', *Journal of Hospital Infection*, 75(3), 239–240.

Musa, G., Thirumoorthi, T. and Doshi, D. (2012) 'Travel behaviour among inbound medical tourists in Kuala Lumpur', *Current Issues in Tourism*, 15(6), 525–543.

Ormond, M. (2015) 'What's where? Why there? And why care? A geography of responsibility in medical tourism', in Lunt, N., Horsfall, D. and Hanefeld, J. (eds) *Handbook on Medical Tourism and Patient Mobility*, Cheltenham, UK: Edward Elgar, pp. 123–132.

Pandey, G. (2010) 'India rejects UK scientists' "superbug" claim', *BBC News South Asia*, 12 August, http://www.bbc.co.uk/news/world-south-asia-10954890 (accessed 1 April 2013).

Price, L. B., Koch, B. J. and Hungate, B. A. (2015) 'Ominous projections for global antibiotic use in food-animal production', *Proceedings of the National Academy of Sciences*, 112(18), 5554–5555.

Reed, C. M. (2008) 'Medical tourism', *Medical Clinics of North America*, 92(6), 1433–1446.

Reubi, D., Herrick, C. and Brown, T. (2015) 'The politics of non-communicable diseases in the global South', *Health and Place*, doi: 10.1016/j.healthplace.2015.09.001.

Rogers, B. A., Aminzadeh, Z., Hayashi, Y. and Paterson, D. L. (2011) 'Country-to-country transfer of patients and the risk of multi-resistant bacterial infection', *Clinical Infectious Diseases*, 53(1), 49–56.

Snitkin, E. S., Zelazny, A. M., Thomas, P. J., Stock, F., Henderson, D. K., Palmore, T. N. and Segre, J. A. (2012) 'Tracking a hospital outbreak of carbapenem-resistant *Klebsiella pneumoniae* with whole-genome sequencing', *Science Translational Medicine*, 4(148), 148ra116.

Spellberg, B., Bartlett, J. and Gilbert, D. (2013) 'The future of antibiotics and resistance', *New England Journal of Medicine*, 368(4), 299–302.

von Wintersdorff, C. J., Penders, J., Stobberingh, E. E., Lashof, A. M. O., Hoebe, C. J., Savelkoul, P. H. and Wolffs, P. F. (2014) 'High rates of antibiotic drug resistance gene acquisition after international travel, the Netherlands', *Emerging Infectious Diseases*, 20(4), 649–657.

Wang, H. Y. (2012) 'Value as a medical tourism driver', *Managing Service Quality: An International Journal*, 22(5), 465–491.

Westphal, M. I., Browne, M., Mackinnon, K. and Noble, I. (2008) 'The link between international trade and the global distribution of invasive alien species', *Biological Invasions*, 10, 319–398.

Whitmarsh, I. (2013) 'The ascetic subject of compliance: The turn to chronic diseases in global health', in Biehl, J. and Petryna, A. (eds) *When People Come First: Critical Global Studies in Global Health*, Princeton, NJ: Princeton University Press, pp. 302–324.

WHO (2011) *Report on the Burden of Endemic Health Care-Associated Infection Worldwide: A Systematic Review of the Literature*, Geneva, Switzerland: WHO.

WHO Ebola Response Team (2014) 'Ebola virus disease in West Africa – the first 9 months of the epidemic and forward projections', *New England Journal of Medicine*, 371(16), 1481–1495.

Woo, E. and Schwartz, Z. (2014) 'Towards assessing the knowledge gap in medical tourism', *Journal of Quality Assurance in Hospitality and Tourism*, 15(2), 213–226.

Wu, H. C., Li, T. and Li, M. Y. (2016) 'A study of behavioral intentions, patient satisfaction, perceived value, patient trust and experiential quality for medical tourists', *Journal of Quality Assurance in Hospitality and Tourism*, 17(2), 114–150.

Yong, D., Toleman, M. A., Giske, C. G., Cho, H. S., Sundman, K., Lee, K. and Walsh, T. R. (2009) 'Characterization of a new metallo-betalactamase gene, blaNDM-1 and a novel erythromycin esterase gene carried on a unique genetic structure in *Klebsiella pneumoniae* sequence type 14 from India', *Antimicrobial Agents and Chemotherapy*, 53(12), 5046–5054.

Zhou, Y. P., Wilder-Smith, A. and Hsu, L. Y. (2014) 'The role of international travel in the spread of methicillin-resistant *Staphylococcus aureus*', *Journal of Travel Medicine*, 21(4), 272–281.

Zingg, W., Holmes, A., Dettenkofer, M., Goetting, T., Secci, F., Clack, L., Allegranzi, B., Magiorakos, A. P. and Pittet, D. (2015) 'Hospital organisation, management and structure for prevention of health-care-associated infection: A systematic review and expert consensus', *The Lancet Infectious Diseases*, 15(2), 212–224.

17

Legal and ethical issues of cross-border reproductive care from an EU perspective

Markus Frischhut

The notion of health tourism has been very well illustrated by Hall (2013: 12), who positioned fertility tourism (together with stem cell tourism, transplant tourism and abortion tourism) at the periphery of health and, as a more narrow concept (Smith and Puczkó, 2014), of medical tourism.

These four forms of health tourism might be illegal in their home country, but legal elsewhere, which can lead to the phenomenon of circumvention tourism, as described by Cohen (2012, 2015a, 2015b). Therefore, in this context, this contribution covers what I call the constructive form of fertility treatment and not destructive ones, such as abortion, female genital mutilation (FGM) and euthanasia, although some emphasise the parallels of both forms (Mulligan, 2015).

While cross-border reproductive care sometimes is related to touristic reasons (in terms of stress reduction), this cannot be seen as the primary motivation (Culley et al., 2011). In addition, the term fertility tourism can be seen as entailing a negative connotation (Pennings et al., 2008; Shenfield et al., 2010; Hudson and Culley, 2011), that is why in the following, reference will be made to cross-border reproductive care.

For both cross-border healthcare in general, as well as for cross-border reproductive care, getting reliable data remains a challenge. Nevertheless, Shenfield and others have described a 'considerable flow' (2010: 1367) of patients seeking reproductive care, mainly for legal reasons (Storrow, 2013: 128). Culley and others have estimated 'that there could be 24–30,000 cycles of cross-border treatment, involving 11–14,000 patients in Europe annually' (2011: 2373).

Different reasons have been evoked for seeking cross-border reproductive care (Pennings et al., 2008, 2009; Culley et al., 2011), which to some extent correspond with those invoked for cross-border healthcare in the European Union (EU) (EC, 2007, 2015). People travel because of both medical as well as 'social infertility', such as in the case of single people, same-sex relationships or those carrying genes for disease or disability (Mutcherson, 2013: 150); donor shortage can also be seen as a specific reason for cross-border reproductive care (Turkmendag, 2013). Within the 28 member states (MS) of the EU, we can observe discrepancy not only in costs (Connolly et al., 2010), but also in different legal settings (MPI, 2005; Pennings et al., 2008; EP, 2010, 2013a; Shenfield et al., 2010; Flatscher-Thöni and Voithofer, 2015), also called 'legal mosaicism' (Pennings, 2009). Popular destinations in the EU seem to be Spain and the Czech Republic (Culley et al., 2011).

However, reproductive care issues can not only arise when travelling to another country, they can also occur in one country (home country) only, including situations of travelling within the latter. Destination countries can be clustered into the EU (including 28 MS), the Council of Europe (CoE; including 47 MS) or even beyond.

This phenomenon of cross-border reproductive care raises a number of sensitive (*Der Spiegel*, 2015) and cutting-edge problems, both from a legal as well as from an ethical (Deonandan et al., 2012; Shalev and Werner-Felmayer, 2012; Whittaker, 2012) perspective. The objective of this contribution is to tackle some of them by means of a case study which entails five examples of assisted reproductive technology (ART), that is to say, in the field of in vitro fertilisation (IVF) and/or surrogacy (Shalev and Werner-Felmayer, 2012; Flatscher-Thöni and Voithofer, 2015; WHO, 2015), all examples – except the last one – based on real court cases.

Before having a look at the case study, the following limitations should be emphasised. This contribution only covers some of the issues that can arise, mainly based on selected cases, as decided by different national or European courts; therefore, other important aspects such as concerns of commodification which touch upon both ethical (Sandel, 2010: 99–102) and legal issues (e.g. Directive 2004/23/EC, 18th recital) cannot be covered in detail. For the sake of clarity, a lot of statements are simplified and the author tried to resist the temptation of addressing more theoretical issues. Last but not least, this contribution was completed in August 2015 (with some minor updates in the meantime).

Case study: five examples of IVF and/or surrogacy

Ms Alpha was employed in Austria. In the course of attempted IVF and after hormone treatment lasting for about 1½ months, a follicular puncture (i.e. homologous) was carried out on her on 8 March 2005. Two days later (i.e. on 10 March 2005), the ova taken from her were fertilised with her partner's sperm cells (i.e. homologue insemination). On this day, Ms Alpha was dismissed by her employer, which means that in vitro fertilised ova already existed on that date of dismissal. Three days later (i.e. 13 March 2005), two fertilised ova were transferred into her uterus (Court of Justice [ECJ], *Mayr*, 2008: 16–21).

Due to an earlier cancer disease, Ms Beta, a German woman, is not able to produce egg cells on her own. Therefore, eggs of a Spanish woman have been fertilised with her husband's sperm (i.e. homologue insemination) and the embryo transferred into her uterus. Unfortunately, also after this egg cell donation, her wish for a child did not come true. At least, she wanted to deduct the cost of the medical treatment from her German income tax as an extraordinary burden, but this was refused by the German tax authorities, who argued that this is illegal according to German law (FG Berlin-Brandenburg, 2015).

Ms Gamma, who works in the UK, entered into a surrogacy agreement to have a baby. The agreement was in compliance with the relevant national law. The sperm was provided by her partner (i.e. homologue insemination), but the egg was not hers and at no material time was she herself pregnant. As a commissioning mother, she was not granted maternity leave or maternity pay, because those rights rest with the child's birth mother. Within an hour of the birth, Ms Gamma began to mother and breastfeed the child and she continued breastfeeding the child for 3 months. Ms Gamma and her partner were granted full and permanent parental responsibility for the child and were therefore treated in law as the parents of that child (ECJ, *D*, 2014: 17–26).

In Ireland, pregnant employees are entitled to maternity leave, while surrogacy is unregulated. Ms Delta has a rare condition which has the effect that, although she has healthy ovaries and is fertile, she has no uterus and cannot support a pregnancy. Ms Delta and her husband opted for surrogacy and turned to a specialist agency in California (USA), where the law provides for detailed regulation of surrogate pregnancies and births. IVF treatment took place in Ireland, with egg transfer to the surrogate mother occurring in California. The child, born in California, is the genetic child of Ms Delta and her husband, having been created from their gametes (i.e. homologue). As a matter of Californian law, Ms Delta and her husband are considered the baby's parents and the surrogate mother is not identified on the child's birth certificate. Ms Delta, with the help of her husband, has been taking care of the child since the birth. One month after the birth, the three of them returned to Ireland. Similarly to Ms Gamma, she was refused maternity leave (ECJ, *Z*, 2014: 25–44).

Last but not least, we can consider the example of Ms Epsilon, who opted for reproductive treatment in another EU MS, which is considered to be an infringement according to criminal law in her home country.

The examples of these five women have several elements in common, while certain decisive elements differ. Therefore, the following overview (Table 17.1) will help to depict better both the similarities as well as the differences and will identify the main questions at hand.

As mentioned above, all those examples concern cutting-edge problems from both a legal as well as from an ethical perspective.

This is also true for the first example, the example of Ms Alpha. The ECJ acknowledged that 'artificial fertilisation and viable cells treatment is a very sensitive social issue in many Member States, marked by their multiple traditions and value systems'. Consequently, the Court emphasised that it 'is *not* called upon . . . to broach questions of a medical or *ethical* nature, but must *restrict itself* to a *legal* interpretation of the relevant provisions' (ECJ, *Mayr*, 2008: 38; emphases added). This statement reveals two important findings about the EU's approach to reproductive care. First, the ECJ accepted that not only legal, but also ethical, issues play a role in this context. Second, in line with the general motto of the EU, also in the field of reproductive care, the EU is 'united in diversity'. The latter is stressed by the ECJ, as it is basically up to the MS to take a decision in this sensitive field, which can be based upon their respective – more liberal or more conservative – value system. Consequently, those decisions are to be taken not only at a national (and not at an EU) level, but, in addition, they should be taken by citizens or their representatives and not primarily by courts. Nevertheless, deciding such a case based on legal (and not on ethical) considerations, of course, can result in a decision of ethical issues in an indirect way (i.e. by legal interpretation).

Following those guiding principles, the solution to the example of Ms Alpha is a very technical one, not touching upon a lot of interesting questions, which one could have thought of. The fertilisation of the ova was not taken as the moment of beginning of pregnancy, as before their transfer into the uterus of the woman concerned, those ova can be kept for a period of up to 10 years, which would result in a long period of protection against dismissal, even if the transfer is postponed or definitively abandoned (ECJ, *Mayr*, 2008: 42). Consequently, Ms Alpha was not protected against dismissal in the same way as pregnant workers and workers who have recently given birth or who are breastfeeding (Directive 92/85/EEC). Nevertheless, the ECJ left open

Table 17.1 Overview problems and questions of the case study

Example	Country/ countries	Reproductive element	Problem	Question
Ms Alpha	Austria	IVF: her ova, partner's sperm, transferred into her uterus	Dismissal from work	What counts as beginning of pregnancy: fertilisation of ova, or transfer into uterus?
Ms Beta	Germany/ Spain	IVF: third woman's eggs, husband's sperm, transferred into her uterus	• Factual: she is unable to produce eggs • Legal: refusal of deduction of costs from her income tax	What counts, the law of Spain (legal) or the law of Germany (illegal)?
Ms Gamma	UK	Surrogacy contract (compliant with UK law); partner's sperm; third woman's eggs	No maternity leave or pay	• Right to maternity leave for commissioning mother according to Directive 92/85/EEC (protection of pregnant workers)? • Refusal to provide maternity leave for commissioning mother as discrimination on grounds of sex according to Directive 2006/54/EC (equal treatment of men and women)?
Ms Delta	Ireland / USA (California)	Surrogacy contract (her egg; husband's sperm)	• Factual: she has healthy ovaries and is fertile, but has no uterus • Legal: no maternity leave or pay	• Same question as above • Refusal to provide maternity leave for commissioning mother as discrimination on grounds of disability according to Dir 2000/78/EC
Ms Epsilon	Two EU MS	Reproductive treatment	Illegal under criminal law of home country	Consequences for woman and husband/partner

the possibility that Ms Alpha could be protected under the principle of equal treatment for men and women as regards working conditions (Directive 76/207/EEC), if it was established that the dismissal is essentially based on the fact that the woman has undergone IVF treatment. However, in the end, this protection against discrimination was not granted by the Austrian Supreme Court (OGH, *Mayr*, 2008).

Unlike in the example of Ms Alpha, in the example of Ms Beta, IVF treatment did not concern her ova, but those of a third woman (from Spain), while in both examples the sperm was provided by the partner or husband. In addition, this example was not about labour law, but about tax law, therefore again not about a question relating to the treatment itself, but rather about related issues, such as deduction from income tax.

Basically, the core question of this example was whether the law of the home country (illegal under German criminal law) or the law of the country of treatment (legal according to Spanish law) prevails. The German Fiscal Court Berlin-Brandenburg opted for the local German law (2015: 17–18). If German criminal law takes the decision that ova donation is illegal, it would encounter the coherence of the German legal system, if such illegal treatment could be deducted from income tax. This is also true for an example as the one of Ms Beta, as she was seeking egg donation not for vanity reasons (Sandel, 2010: 99, 2012: 8 and 71), but because of her inability to produce an egg, due to her previous cancer. In another case, decided by the German Federal Fiscal Court, tax deduction of medical costs was granted in the case of sperm donation, as this was legal according to German law (BFH, 2010: 21). In summary, we can conclude that, according to German law, egg donation is seen as more problematic than sperm donation.

In practical terms, this means that seeking treatment in another MS of the EU does not have the effect of circumventing German law (prohibition of ova donation). Unlike the example of Ms Alpha (IVF in Austria), the example of Ms Beta covered two EU MS. In many cases (of the fundamental freedoms, see below), EU law is applicable if it involves at least two MS. In the case of EU directives and regulations, EU law can also apply even in purely internal situations.

Another difference between the first example and this one lies in the fact that the first one was decided by the ECJ and the second one by a German court, which nevertheless also addressed the role of EU law; this means in practical terms that in either situation, EU law can be applicable. However, also this case can be seen as an example of a court avoiding the more interesting question that would arise (i.e. is German criminal law prohibiting egg cell donation against the EU's free movement of goods or services?), as, according to the German court's opinion, not enough arguments with regard to EU law have been provided by Ms Beta (FG Berlin-Brandenburg, 2015: 20).

After those two examples of IVF, let us turn to the two examples of surrogacy, decided by the ECJ in two different judgements, both on the same day, i.e. the examples of Ms Gamma and Ms Delta. In both cases, the sperm originated from the husband, respectively the partner, while in Ms Gamma's case a third woman's egg was used, whereas in the case of Ms Delta it was her own. Both cases were similar as regards the question of whether a commissioning mother has a right to maternity leave, respectively maternity payment.

In both cases the ECJ decided that a commissioning mother has no right to maternity leave (or pay), even if she breastfeeds the child (as was the case in the example of Ms Gamma). This was confirmed both on the basis of protection of pregnant workers (Directive 92/85/EEC), as well as from the perspective of non-discrimination on grounds of sex (Directive 2006/54/EC); i.e. the same two directives as in the case of Ms Alpha.

Still, the example of Ms Delta was different compared to that of Ms Gamma, as Ms Delta had no uterus (although healthy ovaries) and therefore the question arose of whether the refusal to grant her maternity leave could be seen as discrimination on grounds of disability (Directive 2000/78/EC). In the end, this claim was also rejected, which leads to the conclusion that all cases mentioned so far have not ultimately been successful. Therefore, it seemed not to make a difference that Ms Gamma entered a surrogacy contract in the UK and in compliance with UK law, while in the example of Ms Delta, surrogacy was unregulated in Ireland and another (third) country (i.e. USA, California) was involved. As already stated above, in the case of harmonisation of national law by means of directives or regulations, a cross-border effect (i.e. two EU MS involved) is not necessary.

Comparing this case to the tax law example of Ms Beta displays that, in both examples, the treatment was legal in the country of treatment (i.e. Spain in the case of Ms Beta, the

USA in the case of Ms Delta), although it was illegal (Ms Beta) or unregulated (Ms Delta) in the home country.

This solution of these examples (Alpha to Delta) based on real court cases (Table 17.2) still leaves open one question mentioned in the introduction, i.e. the phenomenon of circumvention tourism. In the example of Ms Beta, the German court refused to assess the German criminal law (i.e. prohibition of egg donation) in the light of EU law, based on the statement that Ms Beta should have provided more arguments in that regard. Maybe the German court's approach was too restrictive (i.e. refusal to assess the case in the light of EU law), while in

Table 17.2 Overview solution to the five case study examples

Examples	Country/ countries	Reproductive element	Solution
Ms Alpha	Austria	IVF: her ova, partner's sperm, transferred into her uterus	• Beginning of pregnancy in terms of Directive 92/85/EEC (protection of pregnant workers): transfer into uterus (not already fertilisation of ova) • No right against dismissal according to Directive 92/85/EEC • But possible protection according to Directive 76/207/EEC (now Directive 2006/54/EC; equal treatment of men and women) (ECJ, *Mayr*, 2008) • In the end no protection granted (OGH, *Mayr*, 2008)
Ms Beta	Germany/ Spain	IVF: third woman's eggs, husband's sperm, transferred into her uterus	• Focus on German law (home country), not on Spanish law (country of treatment); tax law in line with criminal law • Against German law, no deduction from income tax (FG Berlin-Brandenburg, 2015) • However, in the case of male infertility, in line with German law, deduction from income tax accepted (BFH, 2010)
Ms Gamma	UK	Surrogacy contract (compliant with UK law); partner's sperm; third woman's eggs	• No right to maternity leave for commissioning mother according to Directive 92/85/EEC (protection of pregnant workers), even if she breastfeeds the baby • Also no discrimination according to Directive 2006/54/EC (equal treatment of men and women)? (ECJ, *D*, 2014)
Ms Delta	Ireland/USA (California)	Surrogacy contract (her egg; husband's sperm)	• No discrimination according to Directive 2006/54/EC (as above) • In case of a commissioning mother without a uterus, also no discrimination according to Directive 2000/78/EC (disability) (ECJ, *Z*, 2014)
Ms Epsilon	Two EU MS	Reproductive treatment	Still to be discussed

another case (Court of Appeal, *Diane Blood*, 1997: 39–71) a court was more willing to take into account EU law; i.e. the case of a British woman relying on Community (now EU) law in order to export the sperm of her dead husband without his written consent. In this case, Ms Blood was finally permitted to receive the fertilisation treatment she sought in Belgium (Hervey, 1998: 207).

Still the question is left open of how, at a European (rather than at a national) level, the ECJ would deal with other issues of reproductive care, including the phenomenon of circumvention tourism.

In a similar way as already indicated above, at EU level one has to differentiate between harmonisation of national law based on EU directives and regulations (called positive integration) on the one side and the application of the EU's fundamental freedoms, in order to circumvent national law on the other (called negative integration).

To start with the first one, the answer is quite simple. According to EU rules on patient mobility (Directive 2011/24/EU), it is not only up to each home country (called MS of affiliation) to define the national health basket (Art. 7 para. 1), but additionally the Directive respects the 'fundamental ethical choices of Member States' (7th recital) in that regard. This notion of non-interference has been inserted by the European Parliament, in order to avoid a situation where 'ethically controversial medical "services" like euthanasia, DNA-testing or IVF maybe have to be financed by the Member States' (EP, 2009; Hoof and Pennings, 2012: 194).

Although this is a rather undefined term, it is nevertheless clear that in this case it is basically upon the MS to clarify the concrete content of this term (Frischhut, 2015). The fact that those patients' rights in cross-border healthcare – especially (but not only) related to reimbursement of costs – will not apply in the case of cross-border reproductive care, finds its confirmation in statistics; according the Shenfield and others, 'patients who sought treatment outside their country were poorly reimbursed' (i.e. only 13.4 per cent received partial and 3.8 per cent total reimbursement; Shenfield et al., 2010; Culley et al., 2011).

For the second way of applying EU law, that is to say, negative integration (or the application of the EU's fundamental freedoms), the answer is more sophisticated. In this context, courts do not apply rather precise rules (such as in the case of directives or regulations), but broader principles, which makes it more difficult to predict the final outcome of a case.

In our case of cross-border reproductive care, most cases would either fall within the free movement of goods (Art. 34–36 TFEU) or within the freedom of services (Art. 56–57, 62 TFEU). The import or export of sperm, such as in the case of Diane Blood, can either fall under free movement of goods or freedom of services, depending on which one is more pertinent in a particular case; i.e. not choosing the one which 'is entirely secondary in relation to the other and may be attached to it' (ECJ, *Omega*, 2004: 26).

Those principles can be explained by reference to the case of Diane Blood, mentioned above (export of sperm of dead husband):

> *first*, the court or decision-taker must consider whether the challenged actions or decisions are an *infringement of* the relevant *cross-border rights* of the affected [EU] citizen *and then* whether they are *justified* by the *legitimate requirements* of the state whose actions or decisions are challenged.
> *(Court of Appeal, Diane Blood, 1997: 47; emphases added).*

Consequently, Ms Blood 'has the right to be treated in Belgium with her husband's sperm [first step] unless there are good public policy reasons for not allowing this to happen [second step]' (Court of Appeal, *Diane Blood*, 1997: 70).

Therefore, in the end it comes down to a balance of those two principles, so to say, in an Aristotelean sense of the golden mean (Megone, 2012). In the case of Diane Blood, the relevant authority 'must balance [the objects of the legislation, which clearly attach great importance to consent] against Mrs Blood's cross-border rights as a [EU] citizen' (Court of Appeal, *Diane Blood*, 1997: 61).

The final outcome when applying those principles of the fundamental freedoms to reproductive care is sometimes difficult to predict; in addition, Hervey (1998) provides an excellent analysis in that regard. Therefore, in the following, this chapter aims to take a slightly different approach.

As already mentioned above, the ECJ (as the EU Court in Luxembourg) tries to avoid 'questions of a medical or ethical nature' and restricts itself 'to a legal interpretation of the relevant provisions' (ECJ, *Mayr*, 2008: 38). Therefore, the ECJ, similar to other courts, tends to answer only those questions necessary for the solution of the case to be decided, not touching upon related issues. In some of the above-mentioned examples of the case study, more statements could have been given as regards (cross-border) reproductive care. Therefore, in the following, reference will also be made to the case law of the European Court of Human Rights (ECtHR), that is to say, the Court of the CoE in Strasbourg. Not only does the ECJ regularly refer to ECtHR judgements (N.B. the only court apart from itself), but in the context of the EU's fundamental rights, the European Convention for the Protection of Human Rights and Fundamental Freedoms (ECHR) of the CoE is also attributed a prominent role (in Art. 6 of the Treaty on European Union (TEU)).

The ECtHR had to deal with several cases, in the field of both IVF and surrogacy. The following cases will help to shed light not only on reproductive care (both at home and if done cross-border), but also on the question of circumvention tourism.

An analysis of the case law of both Luxembourg and Strasbourg reveals similar underlying principles, although one should not forget that the aforementioned EU's fundamental freedoms guarantee economic rights, whereas the ECHR is about human rights. Granting MS a wide margin of appreciation in those sensitive fields is true for both courts, as it is for a balance of interests, which must be secured.

The ECtHR puts it as follows:

> since the use of IVF treatment gives rise to *sensitive moral and ethical issues* against a background of *fast-moving medical and scientific developments* and since the questions raised by the case touch on areas where there is *no clear common ground* amongst the member States, the Court considers that the margin of appreciation to be afforded to the respondent State must be a *wide* one.
>
> *(ECtHR, Evans, 2007: 81; emphases added)*

In order to establish whether there is a common ground amongst the MS, the ECtHR always not only analyses the relevant law amongst the 47 countries, but also takes into account relevant international agreements or soft law.

However, this margin of appreciation will be restricted if 'a particularly important facet of an individual's existence or identity is at stake' (ECtHR, *Evans*, 2007: 77), as we will see for the cases on surrogacy.

What also holds true for both courts is the fact that, even if MS enjoy a broad margin of appreciation, nevertheless, national law may not be inconsistent in itself, as regards the legitimate objective pursued.

- For example, the forfeiture 'of inflatable dolls which were clearly of a sexual nature and other erotic articles' imported from Germany by the UK authorities has been seen to be inconsistent with public morality, 'where the same goods may be manufactured freely on its territory' (ECJ, *Conegate*, 1986: 2 and 20).
- This is also shown by another example of the ECtHR in the context of preimplantation genetic diagnosis (PGD): in this case, two Italians who were healthy carriers of cystic fibrosis complained that they had no access to PGD for the purposes of selecting an embryo (i.e. homologous) that was unaffected by the disease. In the end, Italian legislation was judged to be inconsistent, because '[o]n the one hand it bans implantation limited to those embryos unaffected by the disease of which the applicants are healthy carriers, while on the other hand it allows the applicants to abort a foetus affected by the disease' (ECtHR, *Costa and Pavan*, 2012: 3, 57).

In terms of IVF entailing ova or sperm donation (i.e. heterologous ART), the relevant Austrian law at the time (now: FMedRÄG, 2015) was seen as not violating the ECHR, as 'the field of artificial procreation is developing particularly fast' and it is 'therefore understandable that the States find it necessary to act with particular caution'; however, at the same time this leads to an obligation to keep the national law under constant review (ECtHR, *S.H.*, 2011: 103, 117–118). Another case also concerned access to IVF by artificial insemination (i.e. homologous), although not in general, but in the particular situation where the husband was in prison (ECtHR, *Dickson*, 2007).

Another Romanian case did not concern access to IVF, but transfer of frozen embryos, not cross-border (such as in the case of Diane Blood), but within Romania (ECtHR, *Knecht*, 2012). Those embryos had been deposited in a private clinic, but due to criminal investigations launched against the clinic, they had to be transferred to a public clinic. Although in the end there was no violation of the ECHR (because the Romanian authorities had acknowledged those rights), the lesson learned is that IVF can be problematic in a clinic, which raises concerns about its credentials.

Another case concerned alleged possibility of making use of embryos obtained from IVF for the purpose of donating them to scientific research – a sensitive topic, which has two cases from Luxembourg as counterparts (ECJ, *Brüstle*, 2011; ECJ, *International Stem Cell Corporation*, 2014; both on the question of patentability of human embryonic stem cells). The Court found no violation of Art. 8 ECHR, as this case 'does not concern prospective parenthood', the invoked right 'is not one of the core rights' in that regard and the broad margin of discretion in such a sensitive area has not been overstepped (ECtHR, *Parrillo*, 2015: 174, 197).

The last case to be mentioned here in the context of IVF is different, because it not only concerned a vertical situation between the state and an individual on disputed issues of IVF, but rather a horizontal situation between two individuals (ECtHR, *Evans*, 2007: 73). After suffering from ovarian cancer (cf. the case of Ms Beta, above), Ms Evans and her partner jointly (i.e. homologous) created several embryos before her ovaries were finally removed. When their relationship ended, her former partner withdrew his consent for the embryos to be used, not wanting to be the genetic father of his ex-partner's child; i.e. the 'right not to become a genetic parent' (Cohen, 2008). Assessing the same British provisions as in the case of Diane Blood, the ECtHR not only stated that the embryos did not benefit from the right to life (ECtHR, *Evans*, 2007: 54–56), but that the decision of the national law to attribute greater weight to the ex-husband's decision not to become a genetic parent prevails over the woman's wish for a genetically related child (ECtHR, *Evans*, 2007: 90).

Table 17.3 Overview of European Court of Human Rights (ECtHR) case law on cross-border reproductive care

	Situation/case	Vertical/ horizontal	At home or abroad	Violation (Art. 8 ECHR)
IVF	No access to ova/sperm donation in general (*S.H.*)	Vertical	At home (Austria)	No violation
	No access to IVF in case of imprisonment (*Dickson*)		At home (UK)	Violation
	PGD (*Costa and Pavan*)	Vertical	At home (Italy)	Violation (inconsistency)
	Seizure of embryos (*Knecht*)	Vertical	At home (Romania)	No violation
	Seizure of embryos (*Nedescu*)		At home (Romania)	Pending
	Withdrawal of consent by partner (*Evans*)	Horizontal	At home (UK)	No violation
	Embryo donation and scientific research (*Parrillo*)	Vertical	At home (Italy)	No violation
Surrogacy	No recognition of birth certificate (*Labassee, Mennesson, Foulon and Bouvet*)	Vertical	Abroad (USA/France, India/France)	• Parents: no violation • Child(ren): violation
	No recognition of birth certificate (*Laborie*)		Abroad (Ukraine/ France)	Pending
	Denial of arrival (*D and others*)	Vertical	Abroad (Ukraine/ Belgium)	No violation
	Taking away child from parents (*Paradiso and Campanelli*)	Vertical	Abroad (Russia/Italy)	Violation

Note: ECHR, European Convention for the Protection of Human Rights and Fundamental Freedoms; IVF, in vitro fertilisation; PGD, preimplantation genetic diagnosis.

All those cases concerning IVF were mainly about the right to private and family life (Art. 8 ECHR) and were related to one country, i.e. the home country, as can also be seen from Table 17.3.

In the S.H. case, the ECtHR positively acknowledged the fact that, although heterologous IVF was illegal in Austria, there was no prohibition from seeking such treatment abroad (ECtHR, *S.H.*, 2011: 114). This can be seen as a safety valve (see below) for those not agreeing with the current opinion of a majority in a field of changing attitudes, based on the idea of 'moral pluralism' (Pennings, 2002; critical: Storrow, 2010).

This attitude of (the democratic majority of) a country as regards reproductive care or ART can be expressed in different ways, with criminal law definitely being the strongest form, as has also been acknowledged in the case of Ms Beta (FG Berlin-Brandenburg, 2015: 18), where criminal law played an indirect role (leading to refusal of deduction from income tax). However, criminal law can also play a direct role in terms of cross-border reproductive care.

Reproductive care can be treated in the following way (N.B. non-exhaustive categorisation):

1 In the strongest form, it can be illegal both at home as well as abroad, i.e. applying both territorially and extraterritorially (Hoof and Pennings, 2012).
2 The relevant treatment can still be illegal at home, while there is no prosecution when returning back home; however, the law can impose other problems, such as no recognition

of babies born from surrogacy (for some French cases in this context, see below). This can be called a 'soft form' of extraterritoriality.

3   If criminal law does not apply in an extraterritorial way, i.e. only illegal territorially, then this can be seen as a safety valve, as it is not prohibited to seek this treatment elsewhere (cf. Pennings, 2005; Pennings et al., 2008; Shenfield et al., 2010; Hoof and Pennings, 2011; Mutcherson, 2013).

4   Certain types of treatment can finally remain unregulated; that was the case for surrogacy in Ireland (Ms Delta). Other disadvantages can result in no reimbursement of costs of treatment, as described by Shenfield and others (2010), if the treatment is not covered by the national health basket, to name but a few examples.

5   Still, although certain types of treatment might be legal, different disadvantages may occur in other respects.

- Sandel (2008) mentions two decisions of the Bush administration not to finance research in the context of human embryonic stem cells (2008).
- Concerning providers, Hervey (1998) mentions more or less stringent licensing requirements, which have to be met by the providers of reproductive treatment.
- Treatment might be legal, that is to say it can be performed, but it is not part of the national health basket, i.e. no reimbursement is granted. This could be the case for alternative care (e.g. acupuncture).

6   Last but not least, treatment can be legal, with full or partial reimbursement of costs of treatment granted.

Whenever treatment is illegal (i.e. the still unsolved question of the example of Ms Epsilon), this might lead to the already-mentioned phenomenon of circumvention tourism.

While it was already mentioned that the ECtHR cases on IVF concerned the home country only, the cases concerning surrogacy always involved two countries, with basically citizens from EU countries (i.e. France, Belgium or Italy) travelling to the Ukraine, Russia, India or the USA (Table 17.3).

As mentioned in the (non-exhaustive) categorisation above, a 'soft form' of extraterritoriality can be seen in the lack of recognition of babies born from surrogacy, as happened in two leading cases from France.

In both cases, two French couples have been unable to have a child of their own due to the woman's infertility. Finally, they each used the sperm of the husband and an egg from a donor with a view to implanting the fertilised embryos in the uterus of another woman. This was done in the USA (in Minnesota and California), where each entered into gestational surrogacy contracts (ECtHR, *Labassee*, 2014; ECtHR, *Mennesson*, 2014). In both cases, legal recognition was refused by the French authorities to the parent–child relationships (i.e. birth certificate), which had been legally established in the USA, arguing that this would be against the *ordre public français* (ECtHR, *Labassee*, 2014).

From an ethical perspective, surrogacy could be seen as more of a problem than IVF. First, the consent of the surrogate mother to give away the child might be tainted and second, this might be seen as degrading (Sandel, 2010), that is to say, against human dignity. The latter is not only enshrined as one of the EU's values (Art. 2 TEU), but in addition can be seen as the cornerstone of the EU's Charter of Fundamental Rights (Art. 1 CFR: 'Human dignity is inviolable. It must be respected and protected'). This understanding of human dignity has been traced back to Kant and the idea that humans should be treated as subjects and not as mere objects (Borowsky, 2014: 96; Frischhut, 2015: 566–567).

Consequently, one could assume that if MS are free to prohibit heterologous IVF (ECtHR, *S.H.*, 2011), this should *a fortiori* be true for surrogacy. However, this is not true. As already mentioned, the wide margin of appreciation countries enjoy in sensitive moral and ethical issues will be restricted 'where a particularly important facet of an individual's existence or identity is at stake' (ECtHR, *Mennesson*, 2014: 77). The ECtHR states that there 'is no consensus in Europe on the lawfulness of surrogacy arrangements or the legal recognition of the relationship between intended parents and children thus conceived abroad'; in addition, 'whenever the situation of a child is in issue, the best interests of that child are *paramount*' (ECtHR, *Mennesson*, 2014: 78, 81; emphasis added). That is why it has been unanimously held in both cases that, with regard to the right to private and family life (Art. 8 ECHR), the right to family life of the parents has not been violated, while the right to private life of the children born out of this surrogacy situation has been violated.

In another surrogacy case taking place in the Ukraine, Belgium refused to authorise the arrival on its territory of a child born in the Ukraine from a surrogate pregnancy. However, in this case the ECtHR acknowledged that Belgium acted within its broad margin of discretion (ECtHR, *D*, 2014). Although the refusal to issue a travel document amounts to interference to the above-mentioned right to private and family life (Art. 8 ECHR), it is pursuing legitimate aims such as the objective of 'preventing criminal offences and in particular of combating trafficking in human beings' and 'the aim of protecting the rights of other persons, in this case those of the surrogate mother and also, to some extent, of the child' (ECtHR, *D*, 2014: 52–53). Therefore, the ECHR 'cannot require States Parties to authorise the entry into their territory of children born to a surrogate mother without prior legal verifications on the part of the national authorities' (ECtHR, *D*, 2014: 52–59).

In the last case to be covered here, a couple opted for a gestational surrogacy arrangement with a clinic in Moscow. After they requested the authorities in Italy to register the child's birth certificate, they were placed under investigation for 'misrepresentation of civil status', because they illegally brought the child to Italy. As revealed by a DNA test, contrary to what the parents had submitted, there was no genetic link between the father and the child (therefore, heterologous). The child was removed from the parents and contact was forbidden. Although the need to put an end to this illegal situation was acknowledged, the Court concluded that no fair balance has been struck in this case, arguing *inter alia* with the already-mentioned identity of the child and the fact that it had no official existence for more than two years. Nevertheless, as the child had developed emotional ties with the foster family, this judgement did not require an obligation of Italy to return the child to the intended parents (ECtHR, *Paradiso and Campanelli*, 2015). (Those cases decided by the ECtHR on both IVF and/or surrogacy are summarised in Table 17.3).

As we have seen, reproductive treatment can conflict with all fields of law (labour law, tax law, social security law, private law, criminal law, etc.), even challenging the Roman law principle *mater semper certa est*. This contribution has only depicted some issues in an inductive – therefore not exhaustive – way that can emerge either within one country or cross-border. In either situation, in addition to national law, both EU law (positive and negative integration) as well as the law of the CoE (especially the ECtHR case law) has to be taken into account. Reproductive care touches upon legal and ethical issues, where the latter sometimes 'only' leads to the result that MS enjoy a bigger margin of appreciation.

Some findings can be summarised in the following way:

- First of all, not only from a medical (Shalev and Werner-Felmayer, 2012), but also from a legal perspective, sperm donation is seen as less of a problem than ova donation, similar to homologous ways of IVF in relation to heterologous ones.
- The courts also tend to take into account soft law, trying to help a European consensus to emerge (ECtHR, *S.H.*, 2011: 96) in this field.

- Although different value systems have been emphasised (ECJ, *Mayr*, 2008: 38), the EU's values – as seen in the light of its human rights – can be the starting point for a process leading to more 'unity than diversity'.
- Nevertheless, it is beyond doubt that (cross-border) reproductive treatment still faces a high level of uncertainty.

What practical recommendations can be concluded?

- Given this uncertainty, awareness of the legal principles described in this contribution is of utmost importance. As we have seen (for both the EU and the CoE), these principles are developed bottom-up by means of cases referred to the courts, rather than top-down by legislation.
- If individuals want to argue against national legislation, inconsistencies can be an important counter-argument. The same holds true for an emerging consensus amongst CoE MS, which places the home country within a minority situation. Although this might be difficult to assess, the question has to be raised of whether a balanced solution has been struck by national legislation.
- Keeping in mind the high level of uncertainty, checking the credentials of a potential provider (clinic) can be advisable.
- From the providers' perspective, documents aiming at high-quality (Frischhut and Fahy, 2016) and safe reproductive treatment should serve as a guideline (Shenfield et al., 2011).

For research, reproductive treatment will remain an interesting field, both from a legal and ethical perspective, trying to catch up with new technological developments.

The question of admissibility of extraterritorial law in the context of circumvention tourism (Ms Epsilon) is difficult to answer. As hopefully depicted in the categorisation above, the more intense the reaction of a country, the more this could be a problem under EU law or the ECHR. However, we have also seen an exception to this statement: where different interests (such as those of the child in the case of surrogacy) have to be taken into account, MS are not free to extend their attitude beyond their borders. Although not decided so far, it is very likely that extraterritorial law against the destructive practice of FGM would be in line with the law of the EU (EP, 2013b) and the CoE.

Finally it remains to be seen if the voices calling for harmonisation, e.g. by means of an ART convention (Flatscher-Thöni and Voithofer, 2015), at international (Deech, 2003) or even at global (Shalev and Werner-Felmayer, 2012) level, will be heard. Depending on the content of such norms, the EU might lack competence in that field (critical for other reasons: Pennings, 2005).

References

Borowsky, M. (2014) 'Titel I Würde des Menschen', in J. Meyer (ed.) *Charta der Grundrechte der Europäischen Union*, 4th edition, Baden-Baden, Germany: Nomos, pp. 94–106.

Bundesfinanzhof (BFH, Federal Fiscal Court) judgment of 16.12.2010, VI R 43/10.

Charter of Fundamental Rights of the European Union (CFR), consolidated version: O.J. 2016 C 202, 389–405.

Cohen, G. I. (2008) 'The right not to be a genetic parent?', *Southern California Law Review*, 81, 1115–1196.

——. (2012) 'Circumvention tourism', *Cornell Law Review*, 97, 1309–1398.

——. (2015a) 'Medical tourism for services illegal in patient's home country', in N. Lunt, D. Horsfall and J. Hanefeld (eds) *Handbook on Medical Tourism and Patient Mobility*, Cheltenham, UK: Edward Elgar Publishing, pp. 350–359.

——. (2015b) *Patients with Passports: Medical Tourism, Law and Ethics*, Oxford, UK: Oxford University Press.

Connolly, M. P., Hoorens, S. and Chambers, G. M. (2010) 'The costs and consequences of assisted reproductive technology: An economic perspective', *Human Reproduction Update*, 16(6), 603–613.

Convention for the Protection of Human Rights and Fundamental Freedoms, CETS No.: 005.

Council Directive 76/207/EEC of 9 February 1976 on the implementation of the principle of equal
treatment for men and women as regards access to employment, vocational training and promotion
and working conditions, O.J. 1976 L 39, p. 40, repealed by O.J. 2006 L 204, p. 23 (= Directive
2006/54/EC).

Council Directive 92/85/EEC of 19 October 1992 on the introduction of measures to encourage
improvements in the safety and health at work of pregnant workers and workers who have recently
given birth or are breastfeeding, O.J. 192 L 348, p. 1, amended by O.J. 2014 L 65, p. 1.

Council Directive 2000/78/EC of 27 November 2000 establishing a general framework for equal treatment in employment and occupation, O.J. 2000 L 303, p. 16 (not amended).

Court of Appeal of England and Wales, ex parte *Diane Blood*, 6.2.1997, [1997] EWCA Civ 4003.

Culley, L., Hudson, N., Rapport, F., Blyth, E., Norton, W. and Pacey, A. A. (2011) 'Crossing borders
for fertility treatment: Motivations, destinations and outcomes of UK fertility travellers', *Human
Reproduction*, 26(9), 2373–2381.

Deech, R. (2003) 'Reproductive tourism in Europe: Infertility and human rights', *Global Governance*, 9(4),
425–432.

Deonandan, R., Green, S. and van Beinum, A. (2012) 'Ethical concerns for maternal surrogacy and
reproductive tourism', *Journal of Medical Ethics*, 38(12), 742–745.

Der Spiegel (2015) *Designer Domenico Dolce: "Es tut mir so leid"*, Monday 17 August. *Der Spiegel Online*, http://www.
spiegel.de/panorama/leute/domenico-dolce-entschuldigt-sich-fuer-umstrittene-kommentare-a-1048405.
html (accessed 17 August 2015).

Directive 2004/23/EC of the European Parliament and of the Council of 31 March 2004 on setting
standards of quality and safety for the donation, procurement, testing, processing, preservation, storage and distribution of human tissues and cells, O.J. 2004 L 102, p. 48, amended by O.J. 2009 L
188, p. 14.

Directive 2006/54/EC of the European Parliament and of the Council of 5 July 2006 on the implementation
of the principle of equal opportunities and equal treatment of men and women in matters of employment
and occupation (recast), O.J. 2006 L 204, p. 23 (not amended).

Directive 2011/24/EU of the European Parliament and of the Council of 9 March 2011 on the application
of patients' rights in cross-border healthcare, O.J. 2011 L 88, p. 45, amended by O.J. 2013 L 353, p. 8.

ECJ judgment in *Brüstle*, C-34/10, EU:C:2011:669.

ECJ judgment in *Conegate*, 121/85, EU:C:1986:114.

ECJ judgment in *D*, C-167/12, EU:C:2014:169.

ECJ judgment in *International Stem Cell Corporation*, C-364/13, EU:C:2014:2451.

ECJ judgment in *Mayr*, C-506/06, EU:C:2008:119.

ECJ judgment in *Omega*, C-36/02, EU:C:2004:614.

ECJ judgment in *Z*, C-363/12, EU:C:2014:159.

ECtHR judgment (2nd Section) in *Costa and Pavan v. Italy*, 28.8.2012, no. 54270/10.

ECtHR judgment (2nd Section) in *D. and Others v. Belgium*, 8.7.2014, no. 29176/13.

ECtHR judgment (2nd Section) in *Paradiso and Campanelli v. Italy*, 27.1.2015, no. 25358/12.

ECtHR judgment (3rd Section) in *Knecht v. Romania*, 2.10.2012, no. 10048/10.

ECtHR judgment (5th Section) in *Foulon and Bouvet v. France*, 21.7.2016, no. 9063/14 and 10410/14.

ECtHR judgment (5th Section) in *Labassee v. France*, 26.6.2014, no. 65941/11.

ECtHR judgment (5th Section) in *Mennesson v. France*, 26.6.2014, no. 65192/11.

ECtHR judgment (Grand Chamber) in *Dickson v. United Kingdom*, 4.12.2007, no. 44362/04.

ECtHR judgment (Grand Chamber) in *Evans v. United Kingdom*, 10.4.2007, no. 6339/05.

ECtHR judgment (Grand Chamber) in *Parrillo v. Italy*, 27.8.2015, no. 46470/11.

ECtHR judgment (Grand Chamber) in *S.H. and Others v. Austria*, 3.11.2011, no. 57813/00.

European Commission (EC, 2007) *Cross-border Health Services in the EU – Analytical Report: Flash
Eurobarometer 210*, Brussels, Belgium: EU.

European Commission (EC, 2015) *Patients' Rights in Cross-border Healthcare in the European Union: Report:
Special Eurobarometer 425*, Brussels, Belgium: EU.

European Parliament (EP, 2009), Committee on the Environment, Public Health and Food Safety (2009)
*Report of 3 April 2009 on the Proposal for a Directive of the European Parliament and of the Council on the
Application of Patients' Rights in Cross-border Healthcare*, A6-0233/2009.

European Parliament (EP, 2010), Directorate-General for Internal Policies, Policy Department C (2010) *Recognition of Parental Responsibility: Biological Parenthood v. Legal Parenthood, i.e. Mutual Recognition of Surrogacy Agreements: What Is the Current Situation in the MS? Need for EU Action?*, PE 432.738, http://www.europarl.europa.eu/thinktank/de/document.html?reference=IPOL-JURI_NT% 282010%29432738 (accessed 17 August 2015).

European Parliament (EP, 2013a), Directorate-General for Internal Policies, Policy Department C (2013) *A Comparative Study on the Regime of Surrogacy in EU Member States*, PE 474.403, http://www. europarl.europa.eu/thinktank/en/document.html?reference=IPOL-JURI_ET%282013%29474403 (accessed 17 August 2015).

European Parliament (EP, 2013b) *Resolution of 14 June 2012 on Ending Female Genital Mutilation*, O.J. 2013 C 332E, p. 87.

Finanzgericht (FG, Fiscal Court) Berlin-Brandenburg judgment of 11.2.2015, 2 K 2323/12.

Flatscher-Thöni, M. and Voithofer, C. (2015) 'Should reproductive medicine be harmonized within Europe?', *European Journal of Health Law*, 22(1), 61–74.

FMedRÄG (2015) *Bundesgesetz, mit dem das Fortpflanzungsmedizingesetz, das Allgemeine Bürgerliche Gesetzbuch, das Gentechnikgesetz und das IVF-Fonds-Gesetz geändert werden*. BGBl. Nr. I 35/2015 (Fortpflanzungsmedizinrechts-Änderungsgesetz 2015).

Frischhut, M. (2015) '"EU": Short for "Ethical" Union? The role of ethics in European Union law', *Heidelberg Journal of International Law*, 75(3), 531–577.

Frischhut, M. and Fahy, N. (2016) 'Patient mobility in times of austerity: A legal and policy analysis of the Petru case', *European Journal of Health Law*, 23(1), 36–60.

Hall, C. M. (2013) 'Medical and health tourism: The development and implications of medical mobility', in C. M. Hall (ed.) *Medical Tourism. The Ethics, Regulation and Marketing of Health Mobility*, Abingdon, Oxon: Routledge, pp. 3–27.

Hervey, T. K. (1998) 'Buy baby: The European Union and regulation of human reproduction', *Oxford Journal of Legal Studies*, 18(2), 207–233.

Hoof, W. v. and Pennings, G. (2011) 'Extraterritoriality for cross-border reproductive care: Should states act against citizens travelling abroad for illegal infertility treatment?', *Reproductive Biomedicine Online*, 23(5), 546–554.

———. (2012) 'Extraterritorial Laws for cross-border reproductive care: The issue of legal diversity', *European Journal of Health Law*, 19(2), 187–200.

Hudson, N. and Culley, L. (2011) 'Assisted reproductive travel: UK patient trajectories', *Reproductive Biomedicine Online*, 23(5), 573–581.

Max-Planck-Institut für ausländisches und internationales Strafrecht (MPI, 2005) Max-Planck-Datenbank zu den rechtlichen Regelungen zur Fortpflanzungsmedizin in europäischen Ländern, *MPI*, https:// meddb.mpicc.de (accessed 5 August 2015).

Megone, C. (2012) 'Aristotelian ethics', in R.F. Chadwick (ed.) *Encyclopedia of Applied Ethics*, 2nd edition, London: Academic Press, pp. 189–204.

Mulligan, A. (2015) 'The right to travel for abortion services: A case study in Irish "cross-border reproductive care"', *European Journal of Health Law*, 22(3), 239–266.

Mutcherson, K. M. (2013) 'Open fertility borders: Defending access to cross-border fertility care in the United States', in G.I. Cohen (ed.) *The Globalization of Health Care: Legal and Ethical Issues*, Oxford, UK: Oxford University Press, pp. 148–163.

Oberster Gerichtshof (OGH, Austrian Supreme Court) judgment in *Mayr*, 16.6.2008, 8 Ob A 27/08s.

Pennings, G. (2002) 'Reproductive tourism as moral pluralism in motion', *Journal of Medical Ethics*, 28(6), 337–341.

———. (2005) 'Legal harmonization and reproductive tourism in Europe', *Reproductive Health Matters*, 13(25), 1–9.

———. (2009) 'International evolution of legislation and guidelines in medically assisted reproduction', *Reproductive Biomedicine Online*, 18(2), 15–18.

Pennings, G., Autin, C., Decleer, W., Delbaere, A., Delbeke, L., Delvigne, A., Neubourg, D. de, Devroey, P., Dhont, M., D'Hooghe, T., Gordts, S., Lejeune, B., Nijs, M., Pauwels, P., Perrad, B., Pirard, C. and Vandekerckhove, F. (2009) 'Cross-border reproductive care in Belgium', *Human Reproduction*, 24(12), 3108–3118.

Pennings, G., Wert, G. de, Shenfield, F., Cohen, J., Tarlatzis, B. and Devroey, P. (2008) 'ESHRE Task Force on Ethics and Law 15: Cross-border reproductive care', *Human Reproduction*, 23(10), 2182–2184.

Sandel, M. J. (2008) *Plädoyer gegen die Perfektion: Ethik im Zeitalter der genetischen Technik. Mit einem Vorwort von Jürgen Habermas*, Berlin, Germany: Berlin University Press.

——. (2010) *Justice: What's the Right Thing to Do?*, New York: Farrar, Straus and Giroux.

——. (2012) *What Money Can't Buy: The Moral Limits of Markets*, New York: Farrar, Straus and Giroux.

Shalev, C. and Werner-Felmayer, G. (2012) 'Patterns of globalized reproduction: Egg cells regulation in Israel and Austria', *Israel Journal of Health Policy Research*, 1(1), 1–12.

Shenfield, F., Mouzon, J. de, Pennings, G., Ferraretti, A. P., Andersen, A. N., Wert, G. de and Goossens, V. (2010) 'Cross border reproductive care in six European countries', *Human Reproduction*, 25(6), 1361–1368.

Shenfield, F., Pennings, G., Mouzon, J. de, Ferraretti, A. P. and Goossens, V. (2011) 'ESHRE's good practice guide for cross-border reproductive care for centers and practitioners', *Human Reproduction*, 26(7), 1625–1627.

Smith, M. K. and Puczkó, L. (eds) (2014) *Health, Tourism and Hospitality: Spas, Wellness and Medical Travel*, 2nd edition, Abingdon, Oxon: Routledge.

Storrow, R. F. (2010) 'The pluralism problem in cross-border reproductive care', *Human Reproduction*, 25(12), 2939–2943.

—— (2013) 'The proportionality problem in cross-border reproductive care', in G. I. Cohen (ed.) *The Globalization of Health Care: Legal and Ethical Issues*, Oxford, UK: Oxford University Press, pp. 125–147.

Treaty on European Union (TEU); consolidated version: O.J. 2016 C 202, pp. 1–45.

Treaty on the Functioning of the European Union (TFEU); consolidated version: O.J. 2016 C 202, pp. 47–199.

Turkmendag, I. (2013) 'When sperm cannot travel: Experiences of UK fertility patients seeking treatment abroad', in M. L. Flear, A.-M. Farrell, T. Hervey, and T. Murphy (eds) *European Law and New Health Technologies*, Oxford, UK: Oxford University Press, pp. 362–380.

Whittaker, A. (2012) 'Cross-border assisted reproductive care: Global quests for a child', in J. R. Hodges, L. Turner and A. M. Kimball (eds) *Risks and Challenges in Medical Tourism: Understanding the Global Market for Health Services*, Santa Barbara, California: Praeger, pp. 167–186.

World Health Organization (WHO, 2015) *Gender and Genetics*, http://www.who.int/genomics/gender/en/index6.html (accessed 18 August 2015).

18

The need to professionalise aestheticians

Kathryn Gallagher and Marion Joppe

Twenty years ago, the term 'spa industry' did not exist in North America. The word 'spa' has been in existence since the Roman era; however, it has been the ageing of the largest percentage of the North American population (otherwise referred to by marketers as baby boomers) along with advances in science and technology that has created a US$14.7 billion spa industry (International Spa Association, 2014) focused on beauty, wellness and preserving youth. The skin care and hair salon business model offering aesthetic services such as facials, manicures and pedicures has evolved into multiple business models that include day spas, hotel/resort spas, wellness spas and medical spas, i.e. a significant percentage of skin care and hair salon treatments are very much linked to travel demand. In addition, the range of services offered has proliferated from traditional beauty treatments and massage services to holistic and medical treatments.

The growth has been significant. The global spa industry has been on an upward trajectory, growing from $60 billion in 2007 to $94 billion in 2013 – even across long global recession years (Global Wellness Summit, 2015). According to the International Spa Association (2014), there was a 387 per cent increase in US spa establishments between 1999 and 2013. In Canada, the last research conducted in 2006 of the Canadian spa sector supported the trend found in the USA: the Canadian spa industry generated just over $1 billion in revenue in 2005, with just under half being generated in the province of Ontario (Canadian Tourism Commission, 2006). A significant area of growth has been medical spas or medi-spas, with revenues in the USA expected to hit $3.6 billion by 2016 or annual growth of 18 per cent per year (LaRosa, 2013). Ageing baby boomers are fuelling this continued growth.

The growth in all these types of spa facilities increases the need to hire more aestheticians, as they tend to make up the highest percentage of spa employees. The Compensation Supplement from the 2014 US Spa Industry Study shows that aestheticians make up 65 per cent of the people employed full time in spas (International Spa Association, 2014). Although no similar study has been undertaken in Canada, a labour market needs assessment conducted in Ontario confirms that aestheticians far outnumber any other spa position, including registered massage therapists (Joppe, 2007: 8–9).

So what's the problem?

According to Larry H. Oskin, the PR Chairperson at the time of the International Medical Spa Association, 'the crossover between medical spas and day spas is blurring' (Spa Inc., 2010/2011). Indeed, many people are unwittingly put at risk, since high-tech, high-risk treatments such as cosmetic laser hair removal and laser skin rejuvenation can be found not just in so-called 'medical spas' but also day spas, hotel/resort and destination spas, nail and hair salons and even people's residences. The number of incorrectly administered treatments that have resulted in injuries is high. The Canadian Dermatology Association found that, '73% of dermatologists surveyed have treated patients for burns, scars or other wounds sustained after seeking laser treatments' (Sourtzis, 2012). It is the people who are performing the treatment that pose the biggest concern, not only for medical professionals like dermatologists, but also for spa owners/operators and the public who frequent spas. On a municipal level, Toronto Public Health's inspection unit created a website called BodySafe after an investigation by the *Toronto Star* and Ryerson University detailed public health violations inside aesthetics studios, tattoo parlours, barber shops and electrolysis clinics. They found lax enforcement among repeat offenders to be a serious health risk for the public because many of the establishments perform invasive procedures that break the skin. Risks range from minor skin infections to blood-borne diseases such as hepatitis and HIV (Cribb, 2014).

Hammes and Karsai (2013) conducted the first study of its kind in Germany on exposure to risks that includes treatment errors resulting from lasers and energy-based devices by medical laypersons (of which 51.2 per cent were cosmetologists or aestheticians). Fifty patients affected by treatment errors were examined and consistencies were found in the type of complications that occurred. They ranged from pigmentation changes to scars, textural changes and incorrect information relayed to clients receiving the treatment. The biggest problem is the treatment of pigmented lesions of uncertain benign/malignant nature. Without proper medical training, an accurate diagnosis cannot be conducted and, if left undetected, the lesion might continue to grow or metastasise.

In Canada, Galt (2010) reports dermatologists treating patients with complications from laser hair removal machines that include permanent disfigurement, skin discolouration and burns. He describes the lack of regulation in Canada and the increase in risk when people with no medical training are administering the treatment. Similarly, Numeroff (2008–2009) writes in the American *Journal of Law and Policy* about the lack of regulation in the USA for both cosmetic laser devices and people performing the treatment. The issue of inconsistent regulations from state to state creates confusion in both the clinical delivery and legal application of the proper standard of care.

Health Canada also regulates the manufacture, sale and quality of lasers in the market, but does not regulate who is using them. The only safety mechanism in place is a guide for owners and operators posted on its website. Also posted is a document titled, 'Health Canada Buyer Beware of Laser Treatments', that outlines the potential risks involved with cosmetic laser treatments (Health Canada, 2006). This notification could inform the public, if people were to take the time to look up risks identified by Health Canada; however, there seems to be an expectation that the public, without any specific knowledge about techniques or equipment for laser treatments, can judge the ability of the operator and suitability of the laser machine (Kelsall, 2010).

The question in all cases is whether the use of cosmetic laser machines is a medical procedure involving a medical device or a low-risk operation not requiring medical knowledge. Doctors argue that it not only has to do with how the machine is used but what potential contra-indications the client might have that only an experienced healthcare professional would be able to detect. The Canadian Dermatology Association (2012) takes the strong position that individuals must consult with a physician prior to undergoing laser and other energy-based treatments in order to detect possible skin cancers or other contra-indications and that either physicians or trained personnel working under the direct supervision of a physician should perform these treatments.

Baldas (2009) raises concerns with unregulated personnel in the *New York Law Journal* related to malpractice lawsuits that are on the rise for medical spas over treatments gone wrong and suggests that these will continue to rise because of the rapid growth of medical spas, the frequency of people undergoing non-surgical cosmetic procedures and weak regulation. Similarly, Jill Goldsmith, a Phoenix, Arizona lawyer in the USA says, 'Both mom-and-pops and chain companies have sprung up around the country in the past few years, creating a new billion-dollar industry and litigation hot spot' (Firm, 2009). This has led, in turn, to some states now passing Bills that require medical spa facilities to employ a medical director (SkinInc, 2013) and/or require that each medical spa employ a physician, a physician's assistant or an advanced practice registered nurse to perform all cosmetic medical procedures (State of Connecticut, 2014). In Canada, physicians are not required by law to oversee medical spa facilities, therefore it becomes the responsibility of the public to ask if the spa does so, whether that medical director conducts an initial consultation, who will perform the treatment and what are his/her qualifications? Concerns with unregulated personnel surfaced when questions asked following the death of a woman in Quebec at a wellness spa included: 'Were the people who worked there trained to know what to look for in terms of vital signs? Did they take an adequate health history? And what were their procedures in the event that something goes wrong?' (Priest and Russsell Brunet, 2011).

A case of weak oversight

In Canada, the federal government plays a role in occupational health and safety issues by coordinating the Workplace Hazardous Materials Information System under the auspices of Health Canada. This department also monitors workplace radiation exposure and regulates laser devices under the Radiation Emitting Devices Act, the Medical Devices Regulations and the Food and Drugs Act. These Acts and Regulations ensure that laser systems sold in Canada are safe and effective when used for their licensed medical purposes by trained professionals according to the manufacturers' directions (Health Canada, 2011). They do not, however, regulate who uses the machines once they have passed inspection.

At the provincial level, for example in Ontario, the Ministry of Health and Long-Term Care has regulations under the Infection Prevention and Control Unit of the Public Health Division for Personal Service Settings. There are 36 public health units in Ontario that are responsible for conducting health inspections annually or more frequently if the business failed compliance during previous inspections. According to one health inspector in Toronto, there are approximately 3,500 businesses offering hair, aesthetics and nail services and ten inspectors to conduct inspections. If a business requires only one visit, that would be 350 inspections per year, 6.7 per week, or more if it did not pass inspection and requires more visits, and that in a province twice the size of Germany, Austria and Switzerland combined! Guidelines pertaining to the cleaning, disinfection and sterilisation of equipment, instruments and supplies to minimalise the risk of contracting blood-borne and other types of infections for both clients and personal service workers during the delivery of such services are provided by BodySafe (City of Toronto, 2015). Adherence to these guidelines is based on what the service provider says when asked questions by the health inspector, but inspectors do not see what happens when they are not there, nor are they allowed to conduct a 'secret shopper' type of inspection. It would be in the hands of service providers to follow infection prevention and control practices and it appears there is no guarantee that they will do so.

Training and education of aestheticians

Since education is controlled at the provincial level in Canada and the state level in the USA, this chapter deals with the situation in one province – Ontario – to illustrate the problems encountered with aestheticians providing cosmetic medical procedures across North America, but in many ways also worldwide.

The Ontario Ministry of Training, Colleges and Universities (MTCU) is responsible for the administration of laws relating to post-secondary education and skills training. An approved programme standard for all aesthetician programmes of instruction leading to a College Diploma delivered by Colleges of Applied Arts and Technology was last updated in 2007. The standards were developed to create a greater degree of consistency for college programming across the province to help ensure graduates have the skills to be job-ready. A combination of vocational standards, essential employability skills and a 'general education' requirement outline the essential skills and knowledge a student must reliably demonstrate in order to graduate from the programme (Ministry of Training, Colleges and Universities, 2007).

Although these guidelines state that regular reviews of the vocational learning outcomes for this programme are conducted to ensure the Esthetician Program Standard remains appropriate and relevant to the needs of students and employers across the province of Ontario, the standards are now at least 8 years old and rapid changes as well as growth in the spa industry have likely rendered these standards at best incomplete and at worst obsolete. For example, medical spas and the advanced treatments offered by these facilities were not identified; however both private and community colleges are training students to perform them.

In 2010, a Private Career College Esthetician Subject Specific Standard was created and states, 'The duration of a credential leading to a Diploma 1 credential will not be less than 1,000 hours' (Ministry of Training, Colleges and Universities, 2010). However, it appears that programmes being offered are less than that. For example, 940 is the total number of hours the National Association of Career Colleges has in a programme that includes *both* basic and advanced aesthetics (National Association of Career Colleges, 2014). This standard also includes a critical point directed at aesthetician graduates, stating they, 'will refrain from performing controlled acts which are restricted/prohibited as per current legislation on Regulated Health Professions' (Ministry of Training, Colleges and Universities, 2010).

On 13 August 2010, the MTCU released a document under Superintendent Policy #6 of the Private Career Colleges Act, 2005, stating that an example of a controlled act includes 'injections of Botox and fillers, electrodesiccation, laser treatments and/or mesotherapy' and

> only a person who is authorized under the Regulated Health Professions Act, 1991 (RHPA) (Service Ontario, 2014), to perform a controlled act, such as a doctor or a registered nurse may perform a controlled act in the course of providing healthcare services to an individual in Ontario.

The policy also states that, 'Program(s) in the Esthetics field do not provide the necessary competence nor does the completion of the program legally authorize students to perform a controlled act'. The issue of who can perform a controlled act, such as injections or laser treatments, becomes grey when they also state, 'the controlled acts may also be delegated to a person by an individual who is authorized to perform the act' (Ministry of Training, Colleges and Universities, 2010) or Controlled Acts Restricted 27b under the RHPA (Service Ontario, 2014). If a person performs a controlled act without proper authorisation or delegation of authority, that person is in contravention of the RHPA and guilty of an offence under the Act. Subsequently, it would be up to the regulated health practitioner (e.g. physician or nurse) authorised under the RHPA to decide under his or her scope of practice whether s/he feels a controlled act should be delegated to an aesthetician. This also puts the responsibility on the party with the authority if anything should go wrong with the administration of the treatment. This policy also includes a disclaimer for students enrolled in an aesthetician programme at a Private Career College to sign. The legality of this policy pertaining to the RHPA should also include a policy and disclaimer under the Ontario Colleges of Applied Arts and Technology Act, 2002, but none can be found.

While the MTCU has placed a focus on creating an Esthetician Program Standard, they leave the programme structure, creation of the curriculum and delivery methods up to the individual colleges. The Ministry does not take responsibility for reviewing the credentials of instructors or monitoring and evaluating the level of expertise in the classroom.

As a result, education for aestheticians is inconsistent, not only because of the variability in classroom instruction, but programmes offered in aesthetics could also range from 6 months at a private college to 2 years at a community college. In fact, the MTCU and the Ontario College of Trades (2013) do not recognise aestheticians as a compulsory or apprenticeable trade and therefore they cannot be members of the Ontario College of Trades. This means education in aesthetics is not a requirement, nor are they required to have a licence in Ontario. Education or training requirements are left solely to the business that hires them.

There is a significant gap between no post-secondary education (non-recognised-type apprenticeships) and 2-year diploma programmes offered at community colleges. Ontario does provide government oversight via the MTCU at the education level by creating standards and approving programmes at registered private and public community colleges, but does not conduct audits to ensure safe, ethical and competent practice once students graduate. Lack of regulation also leads to individuals creating their own job titles, such as 'medical aesthetician', but these are not recognised credentials. No specific accreditation is required for aestheticians to work in medical spas either. Training to perform treatments such as laser, intense pulsed light (IPL), radiofrequency, chemical peels and other forms of high-tech, high-risk treatments also lack consistency. On one hand, courses in the field of medical aesthetics are being added to existing aesthetician programmes offered at public and private colleges or as post-graduate studies after an aesthetician certification or diploma from an approved college has been completed. On the other hand, courses in the field of medical aesthetics could be one day or a weekend offered by a supplier selling the machines or spa owners/managers offering training on site. Some spa owners express frustration hiring aestheticians because of the inconsistency in the quality of education and, as a result, skill levels are not meeting their standards (Joppe, 2007: 24). Ontario is not alone. In British Columbia, a Personal Services Industry Labour Market Research Report was conducted in 2009 and results from the survey confirm the frustration of owners and managers as well as of the employees themselves (Stewart and MacRae, 2009).

Possible approaches to professionalisation

Finding a solution to the rising threat of improperly or poorly trained aestheticians performing advanced cosmetic medical procedures on the public could range from doing nothing to stringent government regulations. In the absence of a regulatory authority, both industry and educational institutions have taken steps to reduce the threat.

Spa associations in Canada have created standards that give quality spas the opportunity to distinguish themselves from substandard establishments. For example, the Spa Industry Association of Canada (SIAC) is this country's only national spa industry association. It is a not-for-profit organisation consisting of members committed to upholding the highest standards of practice, along with a code of ethics set out by the Association. Two sets of standards and practices have been created: one is for medical spas and related establishments, the other is for all other types of spa businesses. In addition to these standards, SIAC created a Quality Assurance Program that would further allow members the opportunity to earn the distinctive Quality Assurance Approved designation through an assessment conducted by independent third-party assessors specially trained in the industry. The programme is designed to demonstrate to consumers which spas exceed industry standards and best practices (Spa Industry Association of Canada, 2015).

Similar to SIAC, the Association Québécoise des Spas (AQS) in the province of Quebec, in partnership with Spa Relais Santé and working jointly with the Bureau de Normalisation du Québec (BNQ) and Tourisme Québec, created the BNQ Spa Standard (Bureau de Normalisation du Québec, 2011) that addresses customer service for spas in Quebec. This standard defines what a 'spa' is and aims to assure a level of quality in services, products, training, equipment, hygiene and safety. In Quebec, like many other places in the world without legislation, the official classification of 'spa' is confusing. The objective of associations like SIAC and AQS is to create a distinction between substandard establishments calling themselves a spa versus establishments that offer quality services and effectively trained personnel and represent 'spas' in the true sense of the word (Bureau de Normalisation du Québec, 2011). It is important to note that the applications of both standards mentioned are on a voluntary basis. The Quality Assurance Program offered by SIAC does not provide automatic renewal of certification; therefore a spa must re-qualify once its term expires to maintain designation. In Quebec, establishments are not required to respect the BNQ Spa Standard, but are strongly advised to do so to assure a level of quality acceptable to their clientele and also to their personnel.

Some educational institutions (both private and public) have applied for and achieved international accreditation from the Comité International d'Esthétique et de Cosmétologie (CIDESCO), an international beauty therapy association based in Zurich, Switzerland. It requires a school to follow the CIDESCO training programme and to provide a training period of at least 1,200 hours. Students are then eligible to undergo practical and theoretical examinations by CIDESCO-certified examiners and are awarded a CIDESCO diploma (CIDESCO, 2015).

In spite of these measures, no standard of practice exists for aestheticians performing services and hence there is no enforcement to protect the public. The question of whether the regulation of aestheticians would help to create unified standards that apply to all who seek to practise as an aesthetician and therefore reduce the possibility of causing injury to clients appears to be gaining support. Results from surveys conducted across Canada suggest that stakeholders (aestheticians, educators and employers) feel a governing body should exist to improve consistency in education, competency and accountability. The form of regulation preferred by respondents was clearly self-regulation (Gallagher, 2015; Stewart and MacRae, 2009).

The main reason governments might regulate professions is due to the need to protect the public. Balthazard (2008) argues that self-regulation is the preferred approach to regulating the practice of professionals because it gives the government at the ministerial level some control over the practice of a profession, while delegating the implementation of setting the actual standard and enforcing the rules to professional associations. Randall (2000) further explains that the self-regulatory model also puts in place a complaint, investigative and discipline system allowing the public to raise concerns about services to professional providers. This is the approach taken for Ontario's health professions, for example, whereby every health profession has its own profession-specific Act which establishes a regulatory college responsible for governing the profession to ensure the public is protected (College of Homeopaths of Ontario, 2015).

The process of an unregulated trade becoming a recognised and regulated profession with a high level of autonomy is a lengthy undertaking. In many cases the decision to pursue self-regulation begins with a voluntary association of like-minded practitioners who are interested in enhancing the credibility and status of their profession. Through a gradual process of development and maturation, this body creates standards of practice, codes of conduct, professional ethics, educational standards for entrance to practice, a mindset of public service, a profession-specific language and a solid knowledge base. Eventually, the profession reaches the point on the professionalisation path where, in order to enhance credibility and develop autonomy, a form of regulation and self-governance is sought.

Conclusion

The continued growth of the spa industry and related businesses, inconsistent educational requirements and lack of regulation will likely increase the risk of harm and therefore necessary steps need to be taken to protect the public. The Canadian spa industry faced the most serious form of harm in 2011 when a 35-year-old woman in Quebec went to a spa for a reported natural therapy treatment and died. It prompted Louis Francescutti, a University of Alberta professor of emergency medicine and public health, to release a statement saying the spa industry needs to be regulated and that 'just because a spa service is offered doesn't mean it's safe' (Priest and Russell Brunet, 2011). As a result of this death, three people were charged with negligence causing death and negligence causing injuries (CBC News Montreal, 2012).

The research revealed that, while the spa industry has experienced significant growth and trends indicate that this growth will continue, the profession of aestheticians is at a crossroad. Demand for hiring aestheticians will continue in order to provide the services spas are offering; however, skill and competency are being questioned more frequently by employers and as a result of complaints from the public. The fact that anyone can call him- or herself an aesthetician or medical aesthetician and perform risky treatments on the public using machines that are not regulated is distinctly worrisome. The research suggests that the public needs protection, which is the basis for regulation and what will motivate the government to regulate a profession.

The scope and practice of aestheticians have advanced from salons and day spas offering traditional services such as facials, manicures, pedicures, waxing and makeup, to holistic spas, wellness centres and medical spas offering clinical-type treatments. The concern with all these types of businesses is the growing trend for high-tech treatments where neither the aesthetician nor the machine being used is regulated. Education and training are critical components of the quality and consistency of how well aestheticians are trained to perform the wide range of services that spas and related businesses offer, but creating a distinction between those who meet the criteria that a government-appointed regulatory body would establish and those that do not would be the next step in the evolution of the spa industry and the aestheticians who work in it.

The status of self-regulation has wider implications. Aestheticians would benefit by gaining recognised credentials, thereby achieving title protection and becoming true professionals. It would be the first step to achieving professional status and advance the profession forward in terms of legitimacy and further research in the field of aesthetics. It does not mean those who have not met the prerequisites for the occupation cannot practise it; rather, they cannot use the reserved title to describe themselves (Balthazard, 2008: 11). A practical implication of title protection may result in higher wages for aestheticians due to the restrictions associated with it. Drawbacks may include increased education and reporting requirements, registration fees, increased rules and accountability and the potential for reduced employment opportunities from businesses not wanting to hire title-protected aestheticians and pay the higher wages that would be expected.

The industry would benefit from the creation of standards and accountability that would no longer be the sole responsibility of businesses, but the aesthetician professional. A formal complaints process would allow the public to raise concerns about an individual. Currently, the only real option for a consumer is to file a complaint with the Better Business Bureau against the business. It would provide the industry with efficient statistical tracking of aestheticians and the businesses they work in, providing all spa industry stakeholders and potential developers with current and accurate information for benchmarking and strategic business planning. Finally, the overall satisfaction rate of clients would be improved as a result of the quality of treatment they receive and reduced probability they would be harmed due to incompetence. On the other hand, employers may experience an inflation of wages and prices due to this professional title and the increased qualifications it brings.

Developing a case for the professionalisation of aestheticians will not only require convincing aestheticians and all spa industry stakeholders that both the profession and the industry would benefit from regulation, but also the necessity of working together to present to the government a clear and consistent definition of the profession's scope of practice and potential risk of harm to the public. The spa industry has progressed significantly in the past 24 years with the establishment of the International Spa Association, which represents health and wellness facilities and its providers in over 70 countries and Canada's national association SIAC, now in its eighteenth year. They both have established a code of ethics along with standards and practices for members to commit to maintaining or exceeding. Moreover, developing bodies of research are also being made available through the associations as well as other reputable sources such as the Global Wellness Summit, which provides portals to help people explore the medical evidence that exists for spa and wellness therapies (Global Wellness Summit, 2015). Aestheticians as a profession may be the next significant step the spa industry takes to distinguish itself further from substandard business establishments usurping the label of 'spa' and protecting the public from reckless or incompetent aesthetic practitioners.

References

Baldas, T. (2009) 'Medical spas are the new litigation hot spot, attorneys say', *New York Law Journal*, 242 (48), 2.th

Balthazard, C. (2008) *What Does It Mean to Be Regulated?* http://www.hrpa.ca/RegulationandHRDesignations/Documents/ProfessionalSelfRegulationandtheHumanResourcesManagementProfessioninOntario August2008.pdf (accessed 15 January 2015).

Bureau de Normalisation du Québec (2011) *Standard BNQ 9700-040,* http://www.spasrelaissante.com/wp-content/uploads/2012/03/NormeSpa_BNQ-9700040_en.pdf (accessed 2 February 2015).

Canadian Dermatology Association (2012) *Canadian Dermatology Association Position Statement Use of Lasers,* http://www.dermatology.ca/wp-content/uploads/2013/09/CDA-Position-Statement-on-the-Use-of-Lasers-Jan-2012.pdf (accessed 1 October 2015).

Canadian Tourism Commission (2006) *2006 Canadian Spa Sector Profile,* http://en-corporate.canada.travel/sites/default/files/pdf/Research/Product-knowledge/Spa/2006_Canadian_Spa_Sector_Profile_eng.pdf (accessed 10 October 2014).

CBC News Montreal (2012) *3 Arrests Made In Spa Therapy Deaths,* http://www.cbc.ca/news/canada/montreal/3-arrests-made-in-spa-therapy-deaths-1.1223964 (accessed 25 January 2015).

CIDESCO (2015) http://cidesco.com/profile/ (accessed 3 February 2015).

City of Toronto (2015) *Body Safe Inspection Program,* http://www1.toronto.ca/wps/portal/contentonly?vgnextoid=b079fbb199b62410VgnVCM10000071d60f89RCRD (accessed 27 January 2015).

College of Homeopaths of Ontario (2015) http://www.collegeofhomeopaths.on.ca/pages/regulation. html (accessed 15 January 2015).

Cribb, R. (2014) *Manicure, Spa and Tattoo Health Violations Disclosed*, http://www.thestar.com/news/world/ 2014/09/12/manicure_spa_and_tattoo_health_violations_disclosed.html (accessed 18 December 2014).

Firm, W. L. (2009) *Lawsuits from Medi-Spa Treatments on the Rise*, http://www.legalpad.com/2009/09/ lawsuits_from_medi-spa_treatments_on_the_rise.html (accessed 10 January 2015).

Gallagher, K. A. (2015) *Government Recognition of Estheticians As a Profession*, Guelph, Ontario: University of Guelph, Masters of Business Administration.

Galt, V. (2010) 'Laser hair removal a risky business in need of regulation, experts say', *Canadian Medical Association Journal*, 182(8), 755–756.

Global Wellness Summit (2015) http://www.globalwellnesssummit.com/ (accessed 7 December 2014).

Hammes, S. and Karsai, S. (2013) 'Treatment errors resulting from use of lasers and IPL by medical laypersons: Results of a nationwide survey', *Journal of the German Society of Dermatology*, 149–156.

Health Canada (2006) *Cosmetic Laser Treatments*, http://www.hc-sc.gc.ca/hl-vs/iyh-vsv/med/laser-eng. php (accessed 27 January 2015).

—— (2011) *Retrieved from Laser Hair Removal – Safety Guidelines for Facility Owners and Operators*, http://www.hc-sc.gc.ca/ewhsemt/pubs/radiation/epilation-laser-hair_removal/index-eng.php (accessed 17 October).

International Spa Association (2014) *ISPA 2014 U.S. Spa Industry Study*. Lexington, KY: International Spa Association (accessed 9 December 2014).

Joppe, M. (2007) *Ontario Health and Wellness/Spa Industry Labour Market Needs Assessment*, Guelph, Ontario: University of Guelph, School of Hospitality and Tourism Management, Premier Spas of Ontario.

Kelsall, D. (2010) 'Laser hair removal: No training required?', *Canadian Medical Association Journal*, 182(8).

LaRosa, J. (2013) *PR Web. Retrieved from $1.9 Billion Medical Spas Market Poised For Growth*, http://www. prweb.com/releases/2013/1/prweb10363396.htm (accessed 14 December 2014).

Ministry of Training, Colleges and Universities (2007) *Esthetician Program Standard*, http://www.tcu.gov. on.ca/pepg/audiences/colleges/progstan/aa/esthetic.pdf (accessed 28 January 2015).

—— (2010) *Superintendent's Policy Directive #6*, http://www.tcu.gov.on.ca/pepg/audiences/pcc/reference/ PolicyDirective6V1_3.pdf (accessed 28 January 2015).

National Association of Career Colleges (2014) *Esthetics*, http://nacc.ca/about-nacc/nacc-curriculum/ esthetics/ (accessed 28 January 2015).

Numeroff, L. (2008–2009) *Playing Doctor: The Dangerous Medi-Spa Game with the Rules*, http://heinonline. org (accessed 5 January 2015).

Ontario College of Trades (2013) *Trades in Ontario*, http://www.collegeoftrades.ca/about/trades-in-ontario (accessed 29 January 2015).

Priest, L. and Russell Brunet, J. (2011) *Spas Need Regulation, Doctor Says After Death of Quebec Woman*, http://www.theglobeandmail.com/life/health-and-fitness/spas-need-regulation-doctor-says-after-death-of-quebec-woman/article588888/ (accessed 25 January 2015).

Randall, G. E. (2000) *Understanding Professional Self-Regulation*, http://www.collegeofparamedics.sk.ca/ docs/about-us/understanding-prof-self-regulation.pdf (accessed 15 January 2015).

Service Ontario (2014) *Regulated Health Professions Act, 1991*, http://www.e-laws.gov.on.ca/html/statutes/ english/elaws_statutes_91r18_e.htm (accessed 29 January 2015).

SkinInc (2013) *CT Passes Bill Requiring Medical Spas to Employ a Medical Director*, http://www.skininc.com/ spabusiness/regulations/CT-Passes-Bill-Requiring-Medical-Spas-to-Employ-a-Medical-Director-213138551.html (accessed 12 January 2015).

Sourtzis, L. (2012) *W5 Investigation: The Painful Side to Laser Skin Treatments*, http://www.ctvnews.ca/ w5-investigation-the-painful-side-to-laser-skin-treatments-1.759779 (accessed 16 December 2014).

Spa Inc. (2010/2011) *Medi Spa 101*, http://www.spainc.ca/spa-business-strategies/medi-spa-101.php (accessed 7 December 2014).

Spa Industry Association of Canada (2015) http://www.spaindustry.ca/about/standardsandpractices (accessed 8 December 2014).

State of Connecticut (2014) *Senate Bill Connecticut*, http://www.cga.ct.gov/2014/fc/2014SB-00418-R000428-FC.htm (accessed 12 January 2015).

Stewart, H. and MacRae, I. (2009) *Personal Services Industry Labour Market Report*, Estheticians and Spa Professionals Association British Columbia, http://espabc.com/wp-content/uploads/2014/07/Personal-Services-Industry-Labour-Market-Report.pdf (accessed 30 January 2015).

Part VI
Medical tourism
Products and services

This part focuses on some very different but very much related topics in the field of medical tourism. Medical tourism has many facets, arenas and products. The four chapters highlight how diverse medical tourism can be, which leaves readers with the understanding of both development opportunities as well as certain challenges.

In Chapter 19 Sharon Kleefield raises a rather difficult question, i.e. how to choose a hospital for treatment? Is hospital accreditation enough to ensure the expected service quality and safety? Patients or potential medical tourists, however, have limited knowledge, understanding or comparative information when learning about a certain hospital's accreditation. Would establishing an initial set of safety 'markers' that are cross-cultural and evidence-based help such difficult decisions?

There are some less widely accepted international standards and criteria for hospitals and clinics. Kai Illing introduces a recommended system for what he calls medical hotels (Chapter 20). There are a few countries where such a designation exists, but in most countries they do not understand or register this type of hotel. Illing suggests that the level or degree of medicalisation of the hotel and its relationship with the clinical partners can make all the difference.

Hospitality and medical services do not necessarily seem to be very close or closely related. However, Frederick J. DeMicco argues that the so-called H2H (Hospitality Bridging Healthcare) approach can mean a more effective approach in service design and provision in healthcare (Chapter 21). Perhaps unexpectedly, he refers to the philosophy of Disney theme parks when he lays the foundations for the H2H concept. Such arguments can inspire a more customer-oriented service concept in hospitals.

Balneotherapy may not be in the mainstream of medical tourism. However, many countries would argue otherwise. Melanie Kay Smith and László Puczkó look at what balneotherapy actually is and how such therapy has been used by medical professionals in several countries (Chapter 22). Balneotherapy, however, faces challenges as an evidence-based approach. The market is very fragmented, clinical trials may not follow similar steps to pharmaceutical companies and therefore many physicians as well as insurance companies find it difficult to accept it as an actual medical therapy.

Overall, this part demonstrates the factors that may be used to define and shape medical tourism products and services and to make them more available to, and more attractive for, potential patients or guests.

19

Choosing the good hospital

Helping medical tourists make informed decisions

Sharon Kleefield

Introduction

This chapter focuses on the number one issue of concern for medical tourism: quality, safety and potential harm for patients who travel abroad for treatment. While medical tourists seek shorter waiting times and lower costs abroad, we have limited knowledge about the factors that determine their decisions regarding quality and safety. As the number of medical tourists continues to increase and the availability of surgical and experimental treatments increases in more and more countries, limited studies from telephone interviews suggest that medical tourists choose destination hospitals based on proximity to home, affordability, physician experience and training, advertising and testimonials on social media. Although there is some indication that hospital accreditation may also influence the decision-making process, the level of healthcare understanding necessary to make an informed decision and what constitutes 'informed' are yet to be standardised in this evolving industry (Crooks et al., 2010). Hospital providers and facilitators may offer a range of unverified claims about the quality of care and expected outcomes; however, the medical tourist is unable to assess and compare international hospitals for quality and safety. Other than accreditation, which is voluntary, there are no international regulatory standards for this industry. Hospitals that advertise themselves as 'centres of excellence' should provide evidence that they are knowledgeable and responsible for promoting safety and reducing preventable harm for their patients and staff. Currently, this obligation is 'marketed' but not sufficiently substantiated.

Closing this quality chasm for the medical tourism industry will be addressed here with a modest proposal for establishing an initial set of safety 'markers' that are cross-cultural and evidence-based. While accreditation sets the necessary basic standards, there is a need to meet the quality concerns with these 'markers'. With evidence from landmark studies during the 1990s in the USA and onward internationally, we've learned to identify and measure quality and safety risks in the hospital, in particular, with proven strategies to reduce preventable harm for patients. These will be identified in this chapter with the intent of informing medical tourists and those who assist them in medical travel about how to compare hospitals based on more specific measures.

Personal experience

As a faculty member of Harvard Medical School for 15 years, I served as the Director of International Health Care Quality Programs and our mission was to establish long-term collaborations with international hospitals to continuously improve the delivery of patient care. In this capacity I provided training, education and design of hospital quality systems in more than 12 countries.

Early entries into medical tourism began in 2004–2005. While working in a private hospital in Bangalore, India, I had the opportunity to interview three patients who had come for procedures from the USA and UK. This hospital became an early hub for medical tourism, providing direct marketing and communication with patients abroad and later with medical travel companies in India. The hospital had a dedicated, well-managed office for international patients that provided direct communication between patients and physicians. Physicians were transparent about their particular specialty training and the volume of patients treated for specific procedures. The hospital was clean, equipment and operating theatres were new and the staff were eager to care for all patients, local and international.

At this hospital, which was newly designed in 2003, six large suites were dedicated to international patients, with nurses and ancillary staff specifically focused on service and patient satisfaction. The suites were equivalent to four- or five-star hotels with all amenities. The first patient I interviewed, Jane, was a 24-year-old dancer from Britain who had injured her knee in a minor car accident that prevented her from dancing – threatening both her current livelihood and her advancement to a career as a professional dancer. The waitlist for the procedure at the NHS was several months, but waiting several months would risk her position in the dance troupe. When I saw her, she was out of bed, doing her post-op exercises with the physical therapist, and stated that she had no pain in her knee just 2 days post-surgery. She had a big smile on her face and thanked everyone for their 'brilliant' care. Her surgery appeared to have been a success. The surgeon encouraged her to continue physical therapy when she returned home, but did not rush her out of the hospital, as they had started her on specific exercises to strengthen the muscles around her knee.

The suite next door was occupied by two middle-aged women from the USA, Jill and Mary. Jill had been a waitress at the same Kansas City restaurant for 29 years, a career she enjoyed and relied upon. She had no other means of income and was underinsured, making a hip procedure unaffordable in the USA. She could not continue to work with her increasing hip pain. This hospital offered her an affordable hip-resurfacing procedure that was affordable at one-tenth the cost of the procedure offered in the USA. This would be a less invasive approach to a complete hip replacement, with shorter recovery time. Hip resurfacing is typically not performed in the USA. The day after surgery, Jill reported that she had little to no pain and that she was sure that she would be able to resume her waitress job. While describing her stay at this hospital, her tears of gratitude were obvious, as were her optimistic feelings that she would be able to return to work. While staying in the suite with her sister for the 5 days, Mary decided to have a minor cosmetic procedure on her eyelids. This, too, was very affordable and went well. She was thrilled to 'look younger' and recommended this procedure to her friends.

This hospital had just received the third Joint Commission International (JCI) accreditation in all of India. For these patients and many who followed, the quality and safety of care were presented as evidence of the hospital's continued success. Patients were able to speak with the Indian physicians prior to travel and this hospital also required evidence of a follow-up plan when the patient returned home so that any problems could be properly addressed. All patient records were available electronically, allowing for appropriate screening and identification of pre-existing and post-treatment risks before and after surgery.

After my visit to Bangalore, I also visited Bumrungrad International Hospital, a multi-specialty hospital in Bangkok, Thailand, whose medical staff included more than 200 US Board Certified physicians. This hospital treated the largest number of medical tourists and had already received the first JCI accreditation. In 2007, it reported 520,000 foreign patients, including 55,000 from the USA and 190 countries. The facility was welcoming and patients were guided by trained personnel who provided specific directions and support throughout their care process. The first floor had several restaurants offering both Western and Asian food. I sat in the lobby and watched the international traffic of people in many different kinds of dress, from Asian and African countries. While sitting with my coffee, a middle-aged man sat down next to me wearing a Boston Red Sox (my home team!) baseball cap. We chatted and I asked him what he was doing so far from home. John said that he had come for a knee replacement. He was an underinsured private contractor who could not afford to have this procedure in the USA. He also said that his brother had come to Bumrungrad for the same procedure a year ago and was doing well. He was optimistic that he, too, would be walking out with a painless new knee. Compared to the new hospital in Bangalore, these international patients had somewhat less elaborate rooms; however, the occupancy was consistently near 100 per cent and there was a continuous flow of foreign patients (Bumrungrad International Hospital, 2015).

It was these early interviews that first enlightened me about the possible advantages of medical tourism. Fancy new facilities designed to provide all the amenities of the finest hotels with high-tech medicine at lower costs could be available to the medical consumer, thus positioning health services within the global marketplace (Turner, 2011). The term 'touristification' of healthcare is now associated with the business and commerce of tourism and linking it to the transnational provision of high-technology-led expert medical treatment (Botterill et al., 2013). Patients, as medical tourists, become tourist consumers – now having a variety of healthcare systems and cultures to choose from (Botterill et al., 2013).

These example hospitals have a significant number of foreign-educated physicians who would be qualified to practise in the USA. Bumrungrad International Hospital is an example of what is considered a reputable medical facility, comparable to 'the best' in industrial countries (Mattoo and Rathindran, 2006). This hospital has maintained international accreditation for more than 10 years and tracks success rates in specific surgeries that are comparable to the USA. It is also comparable in its low rate of surgical site infections, medication errors and high patient satisfaction (Bumrungrad International Hospital, 2015).

The new landscape of medical tourism

By 2006 an estimated 150,000 Americans travelled to India and Latin America for cosmetic surgery and dentistry. Thailand and Singapore became early healthcare destinations for other procedures. By 2007, the number of US medical travellers increased to 300,000, including patients seeking more advanced procedures, such as joint replacement; cardiac, spine and bariatric surgeries; liposuction; breast augmentation; and regenerative therapies such as experimental stem cell treatments and fertility treatments, including in vitro fertilisation (IVF) and surrogacy. By 2009, India, Thailand and Singapore served a majority of medical tourists in Asia. More recent reports extrapolate that more than 3 million patients will travel overseas for treatment, representing a growth rate of 20–30 per cent, with a market size predicted to be US$100 billion (Frost & Sullivan, 2012).

It is estimated that as many as 7 million patients seek healthcare outside their home country annually (Woodman, 2014). More than 50 countries, including the USA, Central and South America, Asia, Africa and Eastern Europe, are providing care to medical travellers. Currently, the Malaysian government is aggressively promoting its medical tourism through its Ministry of Tourism, hoping to make Malaysia an international hub for healthcare. Both Penang and Kuala Lumpur are advertising low-cost cosmetic, dental and dermatology procedures. Many of their physicians have postgraduate training in the UK or the USA and several of their hospitals have JCI accreditation.

India has been aggressively promoting itself as an international healthcare destination with high-tech cardiac and orthopaedic procedures at one-tenth the cost of the USA. The Indian government is planning to launch a single-window portal listing hospitals with accreditation to promote medical tourism as the destination of choice as well as to address patients' concerns directly (BusLine, 2016). The Korean government is also promoting its growing medical tourism industry, seeking to compete with other Asian countries. The United Arab Emirates is expanding its Health Care City and forming international partnerships, hoping to become a hub for inbound medical tourists and to reduce the costly outbound travel by its own citizens. Partnering with Western universities and clinics alludes to co-branding for quality, but typically is marketed too broadly (Cohen, 2015; Runnels and Carrera, 2012). A recent article in *International Living* listed '4 countries with the best healthcare in the world' – Colombia, Costa Rica, Panama and Malaysia. No measures of quality were referenced (*International Living*, 2016).

More than 50 countries currently offer a variety of established and experimental treatments to international patients, including the European Union Directive that allows EU residents to seek healthcare within its member countries with limited restrictions. Germany is attracting foreign patients from Russia and Central European countries. Jordan is a popular destination for Middle Eastern and North African medical tourists because of its sophisticated infrastructure and low costs. Cuba offers medical treatment for nearby countries. Barbados is known for fertility treatments and Panama offers orthopaedic surgery, dental care and cardiac surgery. Costa Rica offers advanced and affordable dental treatment; it also offers the controversial 'liberation' therapy to treat multiple sclerosis. Mexico attracts at least 1 million Californians for dental and medical care and cheaper prescription drugs (Lunt et al., 2011). Brazil has long provided affordable plastic surgery by experienced physicians (NaRonong and NaRanong, 2011).

The total number of medical tourists is difficult to ascertain, but the estimated number in 2013 was greater than 7 million across 11 countries and the USA. Top destinations in 2013 were Thailand, the USA, Malaysia, Europe, Singapore, Mexico and India. Major procedures include cardiac, hip/knee, eye and spinal surgeries, IVF, gastric bypass, dental implants and full face lift. Some experimental procedures are also performed, such as stem cell or other regenerative medical treatments (Woodman, 2014); however, these treatments carry considerable risks and questionable outcomes and lack US Food and Drug Administration approval (Mattoo and Rathindran, 2006).

The business case

Medical tourism offers business opportunities for entrepreneurs and governments to increase revenues from tourism. For example, Thailand made an early entry into medical tourism when the government launched a campaign to promote it as the 'medical hub of Asia', advertising high-tech, high-quality and lower-cost medical care. Bumrungrad International Hospital has generated an estimated US$2 billion in medical tourism, or 0.4 per cent of their GDP, showing that these efforts have paid off for the Thai government (Lunt and Mannion, 2014). Limited by its own population to finance what is needed for high-tech medical care, Malaysia established the government–industry partnership under the Ministry of Health, increasing the number of international patients with a target of 1 million medical tourists. The Indian government adopted a policy in 2002 to support medical tourism by subsidising the effort through tax and land concessions, duty and tax concessions on various imports and special M visas for medical tourists. With the growing medical tourism industry, the global patient and the physician are no longer restricted by geographical boundaries or local restrictions (Labonte, 2013). There are approximately 11,000 medical tourism brokers and facilitator companies who advertise their services on the internet and social media (Lunt et al., 2010; Turner, 2007).

Facilitator companies are 'mediators' between hospitals or clinics and medical tourists, but the service and advice they provide remain unregulated, so it is difficult to verify what they advertise and how they manage referrals. Facilitators provide information on locations and costs and many actually arrange the 'package' for care, including flights, visas, hotels and physician/ hospital referrals. They are likely to receive a monetary return from specific referrals. The consumer may not have this knowledge and its potential conflict of interest for facilitators. Facilitators often have built-in clauses for contracting services that do not take responsibility for patient outcomes and protect them from malpractice (Snyder et al., 2011).

Choosing an international hospital

Little is known about how patients actually utilise these resources to decide on where to travel, but two recent studies conducted via telephone interviews provide some insight. Telephone interviews were conducted with 32 Canadians who travelled abroad for care. The goal of the study was to understand better why they travelled, how they understood the risks and how they gathered information from other patients who travelled abroad. Crooks et al. (2010) conclude that we have much to learn about patients' experiences as medical tourists, specifically how they access and evaluate information from sources before deciding where to travel (Crooks and Snyder, 2010; Lunt et al., 2011). Lunt et al. suggest this gap in understanding and identifies patient decision making as a priority for medical tourism research, especially related to continuity of care, patient health and safety and the commodification of care. 'We have very limited knowledge about the process of patients' medical travel from start to completion' (Lunt et al., 2010).

Canadians, for example, use facilitators for arranging travel, visas, hotels and referrals to international hospitals. While the number of Canadian medical tourists is small compared to other countries, they do travel for dental and cosmetic surgery that is typically not covered by their healthcare system; they also travel for orthopaedic procedures because of long waiting times and ineligibility due to age.

In choosing a destination, several patients said that the major deciding factor was the reputation of the surgeon whom they had found online and/or through social networks (Hohm and Snyder, 2015). Length of stay and time to recuperate were also factors influencing their choice. As affordability was a factor, neither the USA nor the UK were viable options. Anecdotal reports from other medical tourists, such as testimonials and support from family members, were also factors in choosing the destination. Their local family physician did not typically provide advice and often was not asked for an opinion, as many patients anticipated that the general practitioner would not be supportive about them leaving their own communities. There were a few physicians who offered to speak directly with the surgeon abroad and who said they would provide follow-up care if needed. Participants stated that medical tourism facilitators and clinics abroad provided most of the support in their decision making. Some had direct communication with the surgeon via phone or email, where they could ask questions about the potential risks of the surgery, likely outcomes and if they were appropriate candidates for the procedure.

While waiting time was part of their decision to go abroad, the availability of certain procedures was more important for those who sought alternative procedures, such as hip resurfacing, an alternative to a total hip replacement or a vertical sleeve gastrectomy, a form of gastric bypass surgery. All participants expected that the surgery would improve their quality of life. The specific destination was less important than what they understood to be the expertise of the surgeon and reputation of the facility.

The Canadians who were interviewed (Penney et al., 2011) highlighted issues similar to other medical tourists who are exposed to the same internet sites, advertisements and testimonials, regardless of specific regulatory or legal issues within their home country. This study of 32 Canadian medical tourists who sought surgery abroad confirms other accounts of medical tourism that attribute its growth to the influence of the internet (and social media) in connecting appropriate expectations and needs. Information from other medical tourists also influenced these decisions, although there is limited reporting regarding effectiveness and outcomes, both short- and long-term (Penney et al., 2011; Turner, 2013a).

A similar study of medical tourists (Ozan-Rafferty et al., 2014) who travelled to Turkey is another example of how the internet is used to access information. Turkey has invested significant resources to become a 'hub' for international patients. The study included 36 medical tourists from 13 different countries who had 47 procedures in Turkey between 2007 and 2012. They were predominantly from the USA and Europe and decided on treatment in Turkey because of lower costs and availability of treatment options.

Like the Canadian study, patient reports via the internet, blogs and other discussion posts provided limited information on patients' experiences when travelling abroad for care. Turkey was reported as a top destination between 2008 and 2011. These patient narratives reported satisfaction with their outcomes of care in Turkey (75 per cent). The few negative reports included postoperative infections, negative outcomes after IVF and unsuccessful hair transplants. Most of the feedback about the physicians was positive and noted that follow-up was available via email, Skype or telephone. Facilitators provided the necessary logistics of travel. Hospital accreditation was mentioned, but did not appear to be a significant factor in their decision making. It was not clear that they understood that some facilitator companies may have had a financial incentive for these referrals (Erdogan et al., 2012; Ozan-Rafferty et al., 2014).

Both studies of patient narratives, albeit limited, identify the main pathways for learning about medical tourism as 'word-of-mouth', internet searches, media stories and direct hospital-to-patient advertising (Hohm and Snyder, 2015). Medical tourism facilitators often emphasise the benefits of such travel while there is little to no information on comparative quality, safety and risks. There are thousands of websites with very attractive pictures, personal testimonials, credentials of physicians and their experience. Common to most websites is the lack of discussion regarding safety and risks of procedures, while some minimise potential questions about the quality of care at a particular facility. Clinical outcomes are presented with very general descriptions. Due to privacy issues for the specifics of care, there is little public clinical information about postoperative complications, lapses in safety, infection and any questionable professional or business practices.

The importance of informed consent: a first principle of medical treatment

Informed consent is a first principle of the ethics of medicine. The principle of consent was already evident during Greek and Roman civilisations, with evidence that the doctor's intervention had to be, in some way, first approved by the patient. Plato had foreseen the problems, the procedures and the modes of information that are at the root of the modern principle of informed consent: the only guarantee for the patient should be derived from a fundamental principle of medicine at all times: 'In disease, focus on two aims, to improve and not to cause damage' (Plato, law IV). The Hippocratic oath suggests the awareness of precautions and preventive information. From the Hippocratic oath, the relationship between the doctor and patient was based upon two criteria: by the professional duty of the physician to do what is best for the patient and the duty of the patient to completely understand and consent to the physician's decisions and interventions. The obligation and certainty that the physician acted in the interest of the patient's best interests have been passed down for centuries as the ethical standard that bestows professional authority upon physicians.

During the twentieth century, informed consent was defined by more specific criteria: the fundamental autonomy of the patient to decide, as part of one's personal rights and also the essential objective element of having information necessary for consent to a medical intervention. A truly informed consent is said to be given based upon a clear articulation and understanding of the facts, implications and consequences of a medical intervention. To give an informed consent means that the individual has and understands all the relevant facts – possible complications, potential risks and benefits, duration and cost of treatment, as well as expected outcomes and follow-up. In providing informed consent, a patient agrees and gives explicit and written permission to an intervention (Satyanarayana, 2008). Patients have the moral right to an informed decision when choosing their care, whether at home or abroad (Beauchamp and Childress, 2001; Faden et al., 1986). Physicians (and hospitals) have the moral obligation to provide such information as the foundation for their trust and mutual agreement.

In the UK, Malaysia and Singapore, informed consent for medical procedures requires proof of the current standard of care locally. This is referred to as 'sufficient consent'. Medicine in the USA, Australia and Canada takes a more patient-focused approach, requiring doctors to disclose significant risks and benefits to the individual patient. In some of the Mediterranean and Arab countries, informed consent is approached more on the context of the delivery of information, with the emphasis more on who is saying it and where, when and how it is being said, rather than what is said, which is relatively more important in Western countries. 'Optimal' establishment of an informed consent requires an understanding of relevant cultural or other individual factors of the patient; however, the moral and technical requirements for informed consent should rest on the Western definition. With no regulatory oversight internationally, the requirements for an informed consent should have the same ethical conviction and requirement as defined by the World Health Organization (www.who.int/).

The medical professionals at the World Bank's Health Services Department developed the following criteria for choosing surgical procedures abroad: (1) only surgery for a non-acute condition; (2) the patient is able to travel without major pain; (3) the surgery is commonly performed with acceptable volumes, with minimal rates of postoperative complications; (4) the surgery requires minimal follow-up treatment on site; (5) the surgery requires minimal laboratory and pathology reports; and (6) the surgery results in minimal post-procedure immobility. In applying these criteria, medical tourists could initially understand their general risks and benefits for the most commonly performed procedures (Agency for Health Care Quality, 2012) and communicate to surgeons abroad as to their expectations for quality and outcomes.

Quality and safety risks for medical tourists

The Economist Intelligence Unit published its first study on the medical tourism market, *Traveling for Health* (EIU, 2011). The report highlights the fact that developing markets are becoming more 'pronounced' because of the continued rise of medical costs in the USA and Europe and the increasing number of 'baby boomers' moving toward retirement age, causing additional strain on healthcare systems in the West; however, identifying hospitals and physicians who provide the best care remains challenging (Connell, 2013).

What are the risks faced by medical tourists and what information do we have on comparative quality and safety of facilities and providers abroad (Greenfield and Pawsey, 2014)? In the USA, there are many regulatory mechanisms designed to protect patients in the healthcare setting. The USA requires accreditation for all hospitals, certification and professional self-regulation of physicians, nurses and other ancillary staff. Malpractice suits are reported in a National Malpractice Database that is accessible publicly; a government agency, the Department of Health and Human Services, requires hospitals to report a robust list of quality measures that are used for payment. The 'overabundance' of required reporting has led to improvement across the best hospitals.

As Lunt et al. (2011) reported, evidence of clinical outcomes for medical tourists is sparse and reports are difficult to verify. Turner observes that without data, there is no viable way to track the movement of patients, clinical outcomes, surgical complications, infections and other hospital-related events. There is no information, for example, on improperly performed procedures, disease transmission and spread of infections from inbound and outbound medical travellers. When medical tourists return home with less than satisfactory outcomes, that knowledge is not available unless through testimonials and social media (Turner, 2007, 2013b).

Many destination countries have infectious diseases of global concern, such as tuberculosis, polio, malaria and other mosquito-borne infections. Medical tourists can be exposed to circulating infectious diseases as soon as they come in contact with other patients and staff in the hospital. There are also nosocomial infections – hospital-acquired infections (HAIs) – from contaminated water, food, devices (catheters and ventilators) and contact with healthcare team members who may be delinquent in required hand hygiene practices. In developed countries, including the USA, urinary tract infections are the most common HAIs. In the USA, the annual costs of the major HAIs in hospitals (central line-associated blood stream infections, ventilator-associated pneumonia, surgical site infections and catheter-associated urinary tract infections) totalled $9.8 billion – a significant cost to the healthcare budget (Zimlichman et al., 2013).

On average, 10–15 per cent of all hospitalised patients in lower-income countries will acquire HAIs. Blood safety presents additional risks, with 39 of the 164 countries responding to a 2008 World Health Organization (WHO) survey on blood safety (www.who.int/), indicating that they do not follow the WHO guidelines for screening donated blood for HIV, hepatitis B and C and syphilis. Rates of HAIs in developing countries are recognised to be higher than those in developed countries (Allegranzi et al., 2011).

One identifying marker of a good-quality hospital is a JCI accreditation or an equivalent accreditation identified by the International Society for Quality in Healthcare. Another marker is foreign-trained physicians who have been deemed qualified to practise in the USA or UK. A third is that the hospital engages in collaborations with prestigious US medical centres (Cohen, 2015). While these considerations can identify positive characteristics of a hospital, there is limited available evidence that these are correlated with the best patient outcomes. Quality of care remains the most frequently cited concern for medical travel abroad. The medical tourist typically has this information, if guided properly, but too often these data are under-reported by hospitals and by specific procedures (Cohen, 2015; Lunt et al., 2010: 11; Snyder et al., 2011; Turner, 2011). Patients may not know what questions to ask regarding their exposure to risk and safety in a foreign country, for example infections, especially across many different cultures and local professional variations in comparable standards of care.

The influence of regulation of healthcare quality in the USA

Ernest Codman, a Boston surgeon in the 1930s, dedicated his medical career to the systematic and comprehensive study of 'end results' – the assessment of patient outcomes of surgery in American and later in Canadian hospitals – which eventually led to the standards and establishment of what is now the Joint Commission. It was his work that established an initial system to track the outcomes of patient treatments and to identify the clinical problems as the foundation for improving the care of future patients. He believed that this information should be made public so that patients could be guided in their choice of physicians and hospitals. He recorded diagnostic and treatment errors and linked these errors to needed quality improvements (Millenson, 2000).

Codman established the American College of Surgeons (ACS), where his 'end result' approach was developed by the ACS as the Minimum Standard for Hospitals – a one-page set of requirements based on which the ACS began on-site inspections of hospitals. Codman's initiatives and the ACS led directly to the standardised assessment of outcomes of surgery in US hospitals. In 1950, the American College of Physicians, the American Hospital Association, the American Medical Association and the Canadian Medical Association joined with the ACS as corporate members to create the Joint Commission, an independent, not-for-profit organisation in Chicago, Illinois, whose primary purpose was to provide the standards for hospital quality (JCI, 2014).

In 1965 the US federal government required all hospitals to have Joint Commission accreditation in order to be approved for reimbursement for patient services. The Joint Commission was an outgrowth of the work of Ernest Codman, promoting hospital quality improvement based on outcomes management in patient care. The JCI was established in 1998 as a private, not-for-profit affiliate of the Joint Commission. Through voluntary international accreditation, the JCI extends its mission to help improve the quality of patient care internationally. The JCI accreditation is considered a 'seal of approval' for medical travellers and a marker for quality. A total of 815 healthcare organisations have JCI accreditation across 100 countries. Accreditation serves as evidence that a hospital can meet high standards for the structure and processes of managing care.

Hospital quality beyond accreditation

In 1980, Dr Avedis Donabedian defined quality of care as 'that kind of care which is expected to maximize an inclusive measure of patient welfare, after one has taken account of the balance of expected gains and losses that attend the process of care in all its parts' (Donabedian, 2005). In 1984, the American Medical Association defined quality of care as that 'which consistently contributes to the improvement or maintenance of quality and/or duration of life' (Caper, 1988). One of the most widely cited definitions of quality was formulated by the Institute of Medicine in 1990 as the 'degree to which health services for patients increase the likelihood of desired health outcomes and are consistent with the current professional knowledge' (Kohn and Donaldson, 2000).

Healthcare professionals tend to define quality as the attributes and results of medical intervention – the technical definition of 'doing the right thing right'. This constitutes making the right professional/technical decisions about care for each patient and doing it with the right skill, judgement and timeliness of execution (Blumenthal, 1996). One important change beyond the more technical definition is the growing recognition that treatment should be responsive to the preferences and values of individual patients/consumers of healthcare services and that their opinions about care are important indicators for quality. 'Desired health outcomes' include the extent to which it meets the 'expectations' of patients (Kohn and Donaldson, 2000). Patients and consumers are more interested now in the quality and safety of care when choosing a hospital.

Evidence from the early 1991 Harvard Medical Practice Study was a landmark study of medical injury in the US (Brennan et al., 1991). The study was the first review of 30,121 randomly selected medical records from 51 randomly selected acute care hospitals in New York state. The results from this study were revealing: it showed that adverse events occurred in 4 per cent of hospitalisations, and 27.6 per cent of those adverse events were due to negligence. The study estimated that, among the 2,671,863 patients discharged from New York hospitals in 1984, there were 98,609 adverse events involving substandard management of patient care. Surgical wound infections accounted for nearly half of all surgical adverse events. Drug complications accounted for additional adverse events, including known and unknown allergies, wrong dosages, wrong drug or multiple drug interactions. This study revealed that most adverse events were preventable; however, errors in hospital care appeared much more common than was originally thought. The occurrence of such adverse events was a result of the interaction of the patient, the patient's disease and a complicated, highly technical system of medical care and patient management by physicians and other support personnel (Brennan et al., 1991; Leape, 1994; Leape et al., 1991).

To err is human

Following the Medical Practice Study, the Institute of Medicine, an advisory group to the US Department of Health and Human Services, published the report '*To Err is Human: Building a Safer Health Care System*' (Kohn and Donaldson, 2000). This report precipitated major public health concerns because of the estimated 4 per cent of hospital deaths in the USA that resulted from preventable medical errors, including:

- foreign objects retained after surgery (e.g. sponges, small instruments);
- trauma and falls;
- collapsed lung due to a medical treatment;
- breathing failure after surgery;
- postoperative pulmonary embolism/deep-vein thrombosis (dangerous blood clot);
- wound reopening post-surgery; wound infections;
- accidental cuts or tears linked to medical treatment.

The more common preventable errors included post-surgical infections due to poor cleanliness, HAIs due to poor hygiene practices and errors in drug management.

The publication of *Making Health Care Safer II* (Agency for Health Care Quality, 2012) provides evidence-based patient safety practices that are strongly encouraged if hospitals are committed to significant reductions in preventable harm to patients. These practices, if universally implemented, have been shown to reduce preventable errors, are measurable at the point of care and are closely linked to clinical outcomes (CDC, 2015; De Vrieset al., 2010; Haynes et al., 2009; Reames et al., 2015).

Since the Institute of Medicine report and the continued research by the USA and other countries, we have a pathway for providing an initial set of 'markers' for reducing errors and preventing harm in hospitals. Leaders in the medical tourism industry should apply the existing evidence for creating highly reliable hospital systems that minimise preventable harm for all patients and in particular for medical tourists. For those hospitals looking to become 'hubs' for medical tourism, the 'markers' shown in Table 19.1 are consistent with those identified in *Making Health Care Safe II* and provide an international strategy for promoting and competing for the best and cost-effective care. They are targeted at specific hospital practices that have been associated with reducing preventable harm and achieving good patient outcomes. Successful implementation and surveillance of these markers would encourage international hospitals to improve their organisational norms and standards of care.

Encouraging international hospitals to track these 'markers' and share these publicly will result in better-informed choices for medical tourists and facilitators and further the industry to better serve its diverse patient populations. Moving beyond choice of hospitals via the internet, social media and testimonials, the medical tourist deserves to understand and ask the questions regarding what to expect from care received. The Cleveland Clinic, with hospitals in the USA and abroad, is one of the best examples of an organisation that is committed to sharing quality data 'with the world'. Their goal is to make the principle of transparency a

Table 19.1 International 'markers' for reducing preventable harm in hospitals

What to ask?	Criteria	Suggested answer
1) Does the hospital have current accreditation?	Accreditation by ISQUA-listed organisations	At least one successful survey
2) Does the hospital staff employ WHO guidelines for hand hygiene?	Staff are trained and utilise WHO or CDC guidelines	Evidence of hand hygiene >75% before patient contact and >75% after patient contact
3) Does the hospital staff practise universal precautions?	Staff applies 'standard precautions', using appropriate protective equipment for anyone who comes in contact with pathogens, blood- and air-borne; aseptic techniques are employed	Low rate of specific hospital-associated infections
4) Does the hospital staff use preoperative and anaesthesia surgical checklists?	Use of WHO or SURPASS written checklists	Evidence of 100% compliance with checklists for all surgical patients
5) Does the hospital staff use urinary catheter insertion and removal protocols and checklists?	Use of checklists equivalent to international practice	Evidence of catheter-associated urinary tract infection rate <5%
6) Does the hospital staff use interventions to reduce surgical site infections?	Surgical site infections defined by CDC criteria and tracked appropriately	Evidence of surgical site infection rate <2%
7) Does the hospital staff appropriately administer prophylactic antibiotics before and after surgery, based on international guidelines?	Prophylactic antibiotics are given to surgical patients 1 hour prior to incision time and discontinued within 24 hours after initial completion of surgery	Evidence of 100% of appropriate surgical patients receiving antibiotics

(continued)

Table 19.1 (continued)

What to ask?	Criteria	Suggested answer
8) Does the hospital adhere to blood safety and screening, both in their own blood bank or from other source?	Blood is screened for HIV, hepatitis B and C and syphilis, etc.	Evidence of 100% screening of all blood products
9) Does the hospital monitor unplanned returns to the operating theatre within 24 hours after the initial surgery?	Documentation of all returns to the operating theatre within 24 hours of initial surgery	Evidence of the percentage of unplanned returns of <0.01%
10) Does the hospital staff assess and document those patients who may be at risk of falling during their hospitalisation?	Identification of patients at risk for falls; risk scoring methodology is documented	Evidence of low patient fall rate (defined by total number of patient days as a denominator)
11) Does the hospital track known preventable medication errors?	Tracking of compounding, dispensing, administration and monitoring by staff	Low rate of medication errors: drug–drug interactions, known allergies, known look-alike drugs, storage and packaging; no expired drugs; no hazardous abbreviation of drug name and dosages

* Data are collected and stratified by only the cohort of medical tourists and by procedure, using ICD-9/10 or specific procedure codes, with sufficient volumes of these patients.

ISQUA, International Society for Quality in Healthcare; WHO, World Health Organization; CDC, Centers for Disease Control and Prevention; SURPASS, Surgical Patient Safety System; HIV, human immunodeficiency virus.

practical reality and a worldwide source for learning, both by the hospitals and by the patients they serve. Patients are encouraged to be part of these efforts by asking questions and sharing their concerns. Their Patient Safety Program reports on good hand hygiene practice, HAIs, completeness of medical record keeping, reducing risk of patient harm from falls and patient satisfaction (Cleveland Clinic, 2016).

A modest proposal for a deeply personal activity

A colleague taught me that practising medicine is the most intimate of professions. It remains so when practised anywhere in the world. The medical tourist, when choosing a hospital in a different country and different culture, depends on the expertise and established best practices of the hospital staff and physicians. As a global consumer of healthcare, medical tourists seek information, guidance and reassurance that their care will meet 'best practices' and they will not come by harm. As patients, they want to know that they will be treated with dignity, compassion and exemplary standards of care with good outcomes. In this chapter I identified landmark studies from the past two decades that inform the practice of medicine as to how to protect patients from preventable harm and risk. There continues to be substantial progress in awareness and efforts to employ established strategies for quality and safety improvement. The opportunity in the medical tourism industry lies in helping international hospitals adopt and benchmark best practices, thus reinforcing quality and safety for all medical tourists (Bergs et al., 2014; KPMG International Cooperative, 2011).

With no regulatory oversight of quality or common safety practices, medical tourists are only able to make partially informed decisions about choosing the right hospital for their treatment. A recent study identified a set of global measures of hospital quality. These hospital measures, extracted from administrative data of 6.5 million patient discharges, are aligned with these encouraged 'markers': blood incompatibility, patient falls, catheter-associated urinary tract infection, unexpected deaths of low-mortality diagnoses, HAIs, including surgical site infections. The conclusion from this study was that these measures could be used to help determine whether hospitals are meeting a minimum level of safe care (Perla et al., 2015). The publication of *Making Health Care Safer II* (Shekelle et al., 2013) provides a list of similar safety practices and, if implemented, could significantly improve patient care internationally. These practices have been documented by earlier studies presented in this chapter, providing strong evidence for their effectiveness in reducing preventable harm at the point of care.

Adding to these safety practices, a medical outcomes study identified the importance of patient evaluations as an important 'marker' for quality, as these reflect the patient's own perceptions of care, in addition to clinical outcomes (Tarlov et al., 1989; Weldring and Smith, 2013). The relevance to medical tourism is the need to understand better and include the patients' perspective and assessment of their hospital care. Patient satisfaction surveys are an international tool for measuring patient experience and all hospitals should be encouraged to measure and report patient satisfaction. With basic statistical analysis these data would provide an additional 'generic' patient perspective along with the intervention-specific outcomes (Black, 2013).

The quality 'markers' presented in this chapter reflect the last decade of research that identified specific strategies for reducing preventable harm for hospitalised patients. The medical tourism industry, including those companies who arrange and refer patients to particular hospitals, must be 'strongly urged' to move this industry in the direction of maximising safety and quality of care internationally. The individual medical tourist must also be proactive and informed as to what questions to ask regarding a hospital's best practices of care as reflected by these 'markers'. This is a modest but important beginning to address the quality concerns of the industry and most of all to improve and protect patient safety internationally. Exercising the right to an 'informed consent' remains a basic ethical principle for all patients when seeking care. It is the responsibility of the medical tourism industry to understand and incorporate the evidence on preventing patient harm and to guide the medical tourist in choosing a hospital that can meet these modest but critical quality 'markers'. This commitment by the industry will help to improve global patient quality and safety and address the absence of information about comparative quality. Safety is an aspiration as well as a requirement to improve the quality of care for all patients. Patients believe in this aspiration as they give us their trust and accept risks and benefits in their pursuit of healthcare as medical tourists (Vincent and Amalberti, 2016).

References

Agency for Health Care Quality (2012) *Inpatient Quality Indicators*, Rockville, MD: US Department of Health and Human Services.

Allegranzi, B., Bagheri, N., Combescure, C., et al. (2011) 'Burden of endemic health-care-related infection in developing countries: Systematic review and meta-analysis', *The Lancet*, 377, 228–241.

Beauchamp, T. L. and Childress J. F. (2001) *Principles of Biomedical Ethics*, Oxford, UK: Oxford University Press.

Bergs, J., Hellings, J., Cleemput, I., et al. (2014) 'Systematic review and meta-analysis of the effect of the World Health Organization surgical safety checklist on postoperative complications', *British Journal of Surgery*, 101(3), 150–158.

Black, N. (2013) 'Patient reported outcome measures could help transform health care', *BMJ*, 346.

Blumenthal, D. (1996) 'Quality of care – what is it?', *New England Journal of Medicine*, 335, 889–891.

S. Kleefield

Botterill, D., Pennings, G. and Mainil, T. (eds) (2013) *Medical Tourism and Transnational Health Care*, New York, NY: Palgrave Macmillan, pp. 1–9.

Brennan, T. A., Leape, L. L., Laird, N., et al. (1991) 'Incidence of adverse events and negligence in hospitalized patients: Results from the Harvard Medical Practice Study I', *New England Journal of Medicine*, 324, 371–376.

Bumrungrad International Hospital, https://Brumrungrad.com (accessed 7 November 2015).

BusLine (2016) *Time of India*, www.thehindubusinessline.com, 13 January.

Caper, P. (1988) 'The definition of quality', *Health Affairs*, 7, 49–61.

Centers for Disease Control and Prevention (CDC) (2015) *National Healthcare Safety Network: Surgical Site Infection (SSI) Event*, http://www.cdc.gov/homeandrecreationalsafety/ (accessed 23 February 2016).

Cleveland Clinic (2016) *Patient Safety Program*, Quality and Patient Safety Institute, Cleveland, OH: Outcomes Books.

Cohen, I. G. (2015) *Patients with Passports*, Oxford, UK: Oxford University Press, pp. 41–77.

Connell, J. (2013) 'Contemporary medical tourism: Conceptualization, culture and commodification', *Tourism Management*, 34, 1–13.

Crooks, V. A., Kingsbury, P., Snyder, J., et al. (2010) 'What is known about the patient's experience of medical tourism? A scoping review', *BMC Health Services Research*, 10, 266.

Crooks, V. A. and Snyder, J. (2010) 'Regulating medical tourism', *Lancet*, 376, 1465–1467.

De Vries, E. N., Prins, H. A., Crolla, R., et al. (2010) 'SURPASS Collaborative Group, effect of a comprehensive surgical safety system on patient outcomes', *New England Journal of Medicine*, 363(20), 1928–1937.

Donabedian, A. (1980) *Explorations in Quality Assessment and Monitoring, Vol. 1, The Definition of Quality and Approaches to Its Assessment*, Ann Arbor, MI: Health Administration Press.

——. (2005) 'Evaluating the quality of medical care', *Milbank Quarterly*, 83(4), 691–729.

EIU (2011) *Traveling for Health*, London: Economist Intelligence Unit.

Erdogan, S., Yilmaz, E. and Isletmecilgi, T. (2012) 'Medical tourism: An assessment on Turkey', *Joint Conference of the 11th International Conference of Asia*, Istanbul, Turkey.

Faden, R., Beauchamp, T. and King, N. M. P. (1986) *A History and Theory of Informed Consent*, New York: Oxford University Press.

Frost & Sullivan (2012) *Rising Middle Income, Medical Tourism Create Impact for APAC Healthcare Market*, http://www.frost.com/prod/servlet/press-release.pag?docid=254506089 (accessed 14 May 2016).

Greenfield, D. and Pawsey, M. (2014) 'Medical tourism raises questions that highlight the need for care and caution', *Medical Journal of Australia*, 201(10), 568–569.

Haynes, A. B., Weiser, T. G., Berry, W. R., et al. (2009) 'Safe Surgery Saves Lives Study Group. A surgical safety checklist to reduce morbidity and mortality in a global population', *New England Journal of Medicine*, 360(5), 491–499.

Hohm, C. and Snyder, J. (2015) 'It was the best decision of my life: A thematic content analysis of former medical tourists' patient testimonials', *BMC Medical Ethics*, 16, 8.

International Living (2016) http://internationalliving.com/author/iladmin/ (accessed 9 July 2016).

Joint Commission International (2014) *Accredited Health Care Organizations*, www.jointcommissioninternational.org (accessed 24 February 2016).

Kohn, L. and Donaldson, M. (eds) (2000) *To Err Is Human: Building a Safer Health Care System*, Institute of Medicine, Washington, DC: National Academy Press.

KPMG International Cooperative (2011) 'Medical tourism gaining momentum', *Issues Monitor*, 7, 1–13.

Labonte, R. (2013) 'Overview: Medical tourism today: What, who, why and where? Travelling well: Essays in medical tourism', in *Transdisciplinary Studies in Population Health Series*, Ottawa, Canada: Institute of Population Health: University of Ottawa, pp. 6–12.

Leape, L. L. (1994) 'Error in medicine', *JAMA*, 272, 1851.

Leape, L. L., Brennan, T. A., Laird, N., et al. (1991) 'The nature of adverse events in hospitalized patients: Results from the Harvard Medical Practice Study II', *New England Journal of Medicine*, 1324, 377–384.

Lunt, N. and Carrera, P. (2011) 'Systematic review of websites for prospective medical tourists', *Tourism Review*, 66, 57–67.

Lunt, L. and Mannion, R. (2014) 'Patient mobility in the global marketplace: A multidisciplinary perspective', *International Journal of Health Policy and Management*, 2(4), 155–157.

Lunt, N., Hardey, M. and Mannion, R. (2010) 'Nip, tuck and click: Medical tourism and the emergence of web-based health information', *Open Medical Informatics Journal*, 4, 1–11.

Lunt, N., Machin, L., Green, S., et al. (2011) 'Are there implications for quality of care for patients who participate in international medical tourism?', *Expert Review of Pharmacoeconomics and Outcomes Research*, 11(2), 133.

Mattoo, A. and Rathindran, R. (2006) 'How health insurance inhibits trade in health care', *Health Affairs*, 25(2), 358–368.

Millenson, W. (2000) *Ernest Amory Codman: The End Result of a Life in Medicine*, Philadelphia, PA: WB Saunders.

NaRonong, A. and NaRanong, V. (2011) 'The effect of medical tourism: Thailand's experience', *Bulletin of the WHO*, 89, 336–344.

Ozan-Rafferty, M., Johnson, J., Shah, G., et al. (2014) 'In the words of the medical tourist: An analysis of internet narratives by health travelers to Turkey', *Journal of Medical Internet Research*, 16(2), 43.

Penney, K., Snyder, J., Crooks, V., et al. (2011) 'Risk communication and informed consent in the medical tourism industry: A thematic content analysis of Canadian broker websites', *BMC Medical Ethics*, 12, 1–11.

Perla, R. J., Hohmann, S. F. and Annis, K. (2015) 'Whole-patient measure of safety: Using administrative data to assess the probability of highly undesirable events during hospitalization', *Journal of Healthcare Quarterly*, 35(5), 20–31.

Reames, B. N., Krell, R. W., Campbell, D. A., et al. (2015) 'A checklist-based intervention to improve surgical outcomes in Michigan: Evaluation of the Keystone Surgery program', *JAMA Surgery*, 150(3), 208–215.

Runnels, V. and Carrera, P. M. (2012) 'Why do patients engage in medical tourism?', *Maturitas*, 73, 300–304.

Satyanarayana, K. H. (2008) 'Informed consent: An ethical obligation or legal compulsion?', *Journal of Cutaneous and Aesthetic Surgery*, 1(1), 33–35.

Shekelle, P. G., Wachter, R. M., Pronovost, P. J., et al. (2013) 'Making health care safe II: An updated critical anlysis of the evidence for patient safety practices', *Comparative Effectiveness Review*, 211, AHRQ Publication no 13, Rockville, MD: Agency for Healthcare Research and Quality.

Snyder, J., Crooks, V. A., Kingsbury, P., et al. (2011) 'The patient's physician one-step removed: The evolving roles of medical tourism facilitators', *Journal of Medical Ethics*, 9, 530–534.

Tarlov, A. R., Ware, J. E., Greenfield, S., et al. (1989) 'The Medical Outcomes Study, an application of methods for monitoring the results of medical care', *JAMA*, 262(7), 925–930.

Turner, L. (2007) 'First world health care at third world prices: Globalization, bioethics and medical tourism', *BioSocieties*, 2, 303–325.

——. (2011) 'Quality in health care and globalization of health services: Accreditation and regulatory oversight of medical tourism companies', *International Journal of Quality in Healthcare*, 23(1), 1–7.

——. (2013a) 'Ethical dimensions of global healthcare', *Cambridge Quarterly of Healthcare Ethics*, 22(2), 170–180.

——. (2013b) 'Canadian medical travel companies and the globalization of health care', in Botterill, D., Pennings, G. and Mainil, T. (eds) *Medical Tourism and Transnational Health Care*, New York: Palgrave Macmillan, pp. 151–178.

Vincent, C. and Amalberti, R. (2016) *Progress and Challenges for Patient Safety*, London: Springer Science and Business Media.

Weldring, T. and Smith, S. (2013) 'Patient-reported outcomes (PROs) and patient-reported outcome measures (PROMs)', *Health Services Insights*, 6, 61–68.

Woodman, J. (2014) *Patients Beyond Borders*, Chapel Hill: Healthy Travel Media.

Zimlichman, E., Henderson, D., Tamir, O., et al. (2013) 'Health care-associated infections, a meta-analysis of costs and financial impact on the US health care system', *JAMA Internal Medicine*, 173(22), 2039–2046.

20

Medical hotels

An approach to sustainable health in the leisure industry

Kai Illing

Introduction

The history of people who set out on a journey in search of health is very old (Smith and Puczkó, 2014: 29). The term 'medical tourism', which involves the specific consumption of medical services, describes this segment of the market. Crooks et al. (2010: 266) defines the term as follows: 'Medical tourism is understood as travel abroad with the intention of obtaining non-emergent medical services'. This definition fails to highlight that a large part of academic research concentrates on a type of medical tourism that takes place in hospitals. Such research frequently overlooks the fact that hotels can also be the destination of medical tourists. In the broadest sense, a medical hotel offers travellers not only board and lodging in a convenient hotel atmosphere, but also medical care. Thus, two totally different types of establishment try to attract guests from abroad.

Illing (2009) authored one of the first publications to examine the health tourism market with a focus on European countries. However, this study treats the topic in a broader sense and includes elements that touch upon health but have no direct link to medical services. Connell (2013) focuses on medical tourism, providing an overview of the international state of the research and calls for further research, so that the terminology, as well as the motives and consumption patterns of the guests, can be described and defined more clearly. Heung et al. (2011) stress that success in this market segment requires strategic planning and a professional coordination of hospitals, medical travel organisers and various management topics.

The specific topic of medical hotels has been intensively discussed in several studies by Han (2013), Han et al. (2015) and Illing (2014). Illing attempts to delimit related facilities and to describe the different customer groups of this market.

Han (2013) and Han and Hwang (2013) examine which aspects prior to a stay in a medical hotel are of importance so that it is booked and the stay is ultimately also felt to be rewarding. The 'guest patient' places special importance on what he[1] calls personal security. This includes aspects such as confidentiality, discretion and security. This last term relates particularly to the feeling of security in relation to therapeutic processes, trust in the good results of these interventions and trust in medical emergency measures. These results indicate that medical marketing can also be designated as trust marketing, i.e. every facility that advertises its services should place a particular emphasis on trust in precisely this sense. At this point it should also be mentioned that certificates acquired in the sector of quality management can contribute to building trust, although this aspect is highly disputed in academia (Ilkay and Aslan, 2012). Beladi et al. (2015) show that the growing market segment of medical tourism increases wages in the healthcare sector and can encourage good professionals to migrate abroad.

The present study begins with selected theoretical aspects. The second section distinguishes between various types of facility, namely normal hotels, medical hotels and hospitals. The third section examines what people do in a typical facility, while the fourth section attempts to provide a differentiated view of the target groups and distinguishes them on the basis of their state of health. The fifth section describes the various ways in which a medical hotel can develop its medical expertise, while the next section discusses aspects of profitability in connection with various guest groups and the last section deals with selected management aspects.

The services offered by medical hotels are directed just as much to guests with specific indications or conditions as to healthy guests who are nevertheless health-oriented. Medical hotels thus address a particular customer group which may consequently be called guest patients or therapy guests.

This chapter pursues a practice-oriented approach, as the author acts as an advisor to various medical hotels and is also involved in their development. Reference is also made to a medical hotel project on Cyprus, for which the author serves as international coordinator.

From a regular hotel to a medical hotel

Medical hotels have so far been largely ignored by tourism research. However, Han (2013), Han et al. (2015), Smith and Puczkó (2014) and Illing (2014) have sought to examine this market segment. Zygourakis et al. (2014) are of the opinion that hospitals can learn from hotels because the latter can look back on many years of learning how to offer excellent service to their guests. It may be added at this point that hotels can also learn from hospitals on topics ranging from specialist medical expertise to hygiene, emergency management and more.

It is not so easy to distinguish between regular hotels and medical hotels because the boundaries are fluid. All wellness and spa hotels are concerned with health and wellbeing to some extent (e.g. with the use of curative waters) and can thus, at least in a rudimentary sense, be viewed as facilities with a health-promoting offer. After all, wellness hotels also employ some staff who are trained in scientific healthcare.

However, the focus of a medical hotel differs from that of a spa or wellness hotel:

- Medical doctors play a greater role in medical hotels as part of the staff.
- A professional case history and diagnosis play a greater role in developing the correct form of treatment.
- They have a more extensive range of medical equipment.
- Their nutrition concept seeks to realise the fundamentals of scientific healthcare.
- One particularly important point in this connection is that the increasing degree of medicalisation is also associated with a voluntary surrender of the guest patient's independence. After all, the doctor tells the guest patients what to eat, how to structure their leisure time and what things they must avoid.

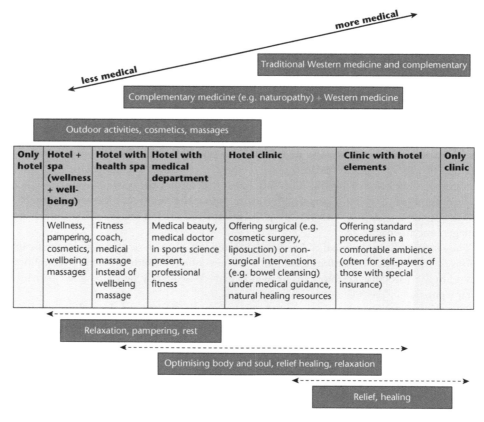

Figure 20.1   Hotels and clinics and the medical continuum.

The delimitation between a medical hotel and a hospital is equally fluid, but clear differences are also apparent:

- The health status of the patients is usually worse in hospitals than in medical hotels.
- The treatment costs in hospitals are frequently borne by the social insurance agencies, whereas guest patients in medical hotels usually pay out of their own pockets.
- A hospital concentrates on healing, whereas pampering and luxury play an equally important role in a medical hotel.
- The guest patients in a medical hotel frequently take advantage of various opportunities to get to know the local region and its attractions as regards landscape and cultural amenities. Hospital patients do this rather less, as they are frequently not in a position to do so. However, international patients in hospitals do tend to make use of tourist programmes (Yu et al., 2012: 82).

These distinctions make it clear that it is important to make a careful delimitation between hotels and hospitals. Figure 20.1 attempts to distinguish these two types of facility. The facilities shown on the left are less medically oriented, whereas those on the right tend to offer clinical equipment.

Figure 20.1 shows that very diverse types of facility are found on the continuum between hotels and hospitals, all of them being concerned to some extent with the topic of health. It is important to mention that there are not that many medical hotels in Europe. The few examples tend to focus on natural healing resources, e.g. thermal water or medical mud (e.g. Danubius Health Spa Hotels).

Health-related processes

One difference between wellness or spa hotels and medical hotels is that the guest patient in the latter type of establishment has a clearer idea of what he intends to achieve. The guest of a holiday hotel is generally seeking recreation. In contrast, the guest patient of a medical hotel has either a specific illness which he attempts to alleviate or at least a clear idea of what he would like to do for his health.

For a better understanding of these guests, a distinction should be made between what guest patients do in medical hotels and what they hope to achieve thereby. Table 20.1 shows that the same motives may be associated with very diverse measures or very diverse motives may be associated with the same measure. It is naturally also conceivable that the guest patient may do many different things and simultaneously try to achieve diverse goals.

It is advisable for medical hotels to observe a careful balance between measures (interventions, treatment) on the one hand and motives on the other, so that the desired goals can be achieved by suitable interventions. The word 'suitable' in this context refers to achieving optimal success in the form expected by the guest patient without neglecting the financial dimension (turnover). The turnover or profitability of a medical hotel depends very much on what the patients wish to achieve and what means they use to reach this goal. For example, a guest patient may try to lose weight in very diverse ways: he can minimise his costs by hiking a lot and eating little, but he can also undergo liposuction or gastric reduction in a luxury resort. The latter two would doubtless be expensive variants, but would pursue the same goal. Many goals in the sector of health tourism may be achieved in highly diverse ways and the two central aims of a medical hotel will have to be achieved by finding a balance between healing and profitability.

Various sources have examined the motives of medical tourists (e.g. Medical Tourism Association, 2010). Kucukusta and Guillet (2014) emphasise that price level, therapist qualification, a high level of privacy, a full range of spa facilities and branded spa products are of principal interest to spa-goers. Yu et al. (2012: 82) come to the following conclusions: 'The respondents travelled overseas for weight loss or bariatric treatment (32%) orthopaedic (22%), cosmetic (12%), spinal (2%) and other services (32%) and 83% of them travelled with a companion'. Intelligent Spas (2005) noted that the consumption of spa services by women and men differs significantly. The motivation of spa and wellness guests in hotels has been a frequent subject of scientific research (Lohmann and Schmücker, 2015). Thus Illing (2009: 56) noted the various motives of guests in spa and wellness hotels, namely (1) relief from diseases; (2) body styling; (3) youthfulness; (4) physical performance; (5) romantic reasons; and (6) psychological balance.

Table 20.1 Measures and motives for patients in medical hotels

	What he/she does		*What he/she wants to achieve*
Guest patient	Hiking		Acquire an attractive body
	Liposuction		Avoid social exclusion due to obesity
	Bariatric treatments		Be fitter for the tennis club

Table 20.2 What people do in a medical hotel

Type of process			Explanations
Treatment	Medical treatment (often with diagnosis and case history) Non-medical treatment (e.g. cosmetic procedure)	Non-surgical treatment Surgical treatment	Guest patient tends to be passive Treatment site often in therapy centre Therapist/physician present and leader of the process Methods and goals usually defined
Movement	Medical approaches (e.g. coach advises in fitness studio) Walking in the woods, biking		Guest patient active or movement-oriented Treatment site within or outside the regular/medical spa Therapist/physician also as adviser Methods and goals also defined
Relaxation/ leisure	Reading, sleeping, relaxing, listening to music, etc.	Guided by coach (therapist) Not guided by coach (therapist)	Guest patient tends to be passive Goals only generally defined Therapist may be process leader
Intake	Nutrition Healing ambience, inhalations Wrappings Ideas, stimulations and solutions to psychological problems	Either therapeutic or non-therapeutic	Guest patient receives healthy substances as well as stimulation

Whereas research into the goals (motives) of guest patients is a frequent topic, there has been less focus on the preceding step, namely the instruments used to attain these goals. Smith and Puczkó (2014: 110) link health and wellness products to the motives of typical user groups. Table 20.2 attempts to show a differentiated picture of typical processes in medical hotels, omitting eating and sleeping as the core services of any hotel.

This overview leaves enough room for a differentiation between medical hotels and conventional spa and wellness facilities. All four process types (treatment, movement, relaxation/leisure, intake) can essentially be interpreted or offered in a medical context. What is done gives no indication as to what the patients may wish to achieve. This topic also plays a role in the marketing (Frederick and Gan, 2015; Hallem and Barth, 2011; Martin et al., 2015) or even in the designation of the medical hotel: should the offered services be highlighted or rather what can be attained? Two examples illustrate this tricky question: Ayurveda Clinic stresses the offer, while Relief Medical Hotel stresses the goal.

The Weldest project (Dvorak et al., 2014; Illing et al., 2014) attempted to identify the consumption preferences of guests in 'health and well-being destinations', whereby the regional reference played a major role in this project because the enquiries took place in European tourist regions with a strong link to the topic of health. In the first instance, the general goals shown in Figure 20.2 can be identified.

It is striking that the top response was a general goal to improve health, with the importance of the natural environment at a close second. Those who clicked the uppermost bar were led in the online survey to a further question which aimed to elicit a more specific response. The results are shown in Figure 20.3 (Illing et al., 2014: 59).

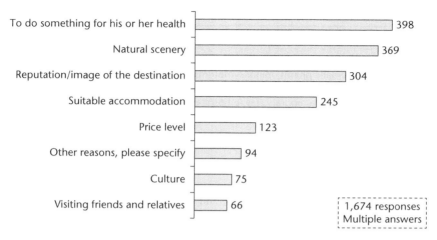

Figure 20.2 The overall reason to come to a health and wellbeing destination.
Source: Illing (2014: 58).

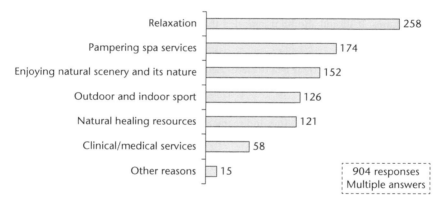

Figure 20.3 Specification of the term 'health'.
Source: Illing et al. (2014: 59).

In a regional context, relaxation and pampering played an important role together with an enjoyment of natural surroundings. Medical hotels should take this information into account, especially at the planning stage (facilities offered, location), as well as the fact that their medical services will be offered in an ecologically intact environment.

Target groups classified according to their health status

The target groups of a medical hotel may be classified based on various viewpoints. The differentiating features may be origin, income, intentions, health status or many others. Cohen (2008: 227) suggests the following groups: (1) medicated tourists, who need treatment due to injury; (2) medical tourists proper, who visit a country specifically but not exclusively in order to undergo medical treatment; (3) vocational patients, whose main motive is to undergo medical treatment, but who are also interested in typical tourist activities either before or after their

K. Illing

Table 20.3 Health status of guest patients and their suitability for medical hotels

Group	State of health	Suitability for medical hotel
Group 1	No symptoms, healthy	Suitable
Group 2	Brief symptomatic phases, minor symptoms	Very suitable
Group 3	Lengthier and recurrent problems, chronic in some cases	Very suitable
Group 4	Needing surgery, temporary stay in hospital	Medical hotel can offer pre- and post-care to patients not requiring nursing care
Group 5	Serious and recurrent illnesses, long-term stay and treatment in hospital	Not suitable

hospital stay, such as visiting local attractions; and (4) mere tourists who do not use medical services of any kind. Han and Hwang (2013: 101) examine the very strong dependence of the origin of the guest patient on the use of the medical services of a medical hotel, the importance of various parts of the building (guest rooms, restaurant, therapy area, etc.), as well as the guest's decision-making process up to the decision for or against a medical hotel. The practical consequence for the local hotelier is that he should study the national characteristics of his guests in detail and thus adapt the building design and (medical) services to the expectations typical of various cultures. It should also be mentioned that the hotel component (hospitality product) plays an extremely important role, in addition to the therapeutic aspects.

The guest groups who are treated in a medical hotel are quite diverse and follow the scheme outlined in Table 20.3, with their health status being the focal point of the discussion.

Explanations

Group 1, healthy people, are welcome and many activities are offered to maintain their healthy lifestyle. Guest groups 1 and 2 are capable of moving around freely and do not require physical or mental assistance. Group 2 is the largest one requiring treatment. Guests from this group suffer periodically from unspecific or specific conditions related to the most common lifestyle diseases. People in the third group suffer from chronic diseases. They require recurrent coaching by doctors to book medical packages. Members of group 4 are welcome if they are able to travel and are not handicapped. Soft rehabilitation treatments are then offered in the field of pre- or post-care. Cooperation with a (private) clinic can be organised. Group 5 is not treated in the hotel, as patients in this group need clinical or even intensive care.

Regarding the distribution of guests in a medical hotel, it appears to be extremely important to classify them on the basis of their health status. After all, it is important to prevent potentially conflicting guest groups from encountering each other. Hence, it seems to be inadvisable to mix patients with serious physical conditions with others who are healthy and may therefore have little understanding for the first group. Care should also be taken when mixing social classes or diverse cultures (Box 20.1).

Box 20.1   Target groups in a southern European medical hotel

A medical hotel specialises in groups 1–3 (see Table 20.3). Quite a few guests come with specific prior conditions and seek a way to manage their health problems via the facility's particular dietary offer. This is helped by the climate, as well as the psychological support offered by warmth and sun. A mixture of diverse groups within the health sector can function well. One group follows a rigorous diet, whereas the other guests are also very health-aware but are free to choose their own food and leisure programme. There is a specific treatment centre with a doctor and necessary medical personnel for the guest patients who are on a diet. There is a medical spa for the other guests which offers various treatments under the professional supervision of cosmeticians and medical masseurs; it can also be freely utilised without consulting a doctor.

Differentiation on the basis of the offer's degree of medicalisation

It is worth taking a special look at the degree of medicalisation of a medical hotel. This should be a particularly important point, as it is ultimately the proportion of medical services that distinguishes a medical hotel from a normal, wellness or spa hotel. The following discussion will consequently focus on various hotel sectors and their ability to offer health-promoting treatments.

The medical spa and fitness sector will naturally focus particularly on medicalisation. The first yardstick is whether doctors are part of the personnel. Another indication is whether the treatments offered are preceded by detailed diagnoses and case histories. Equally important are the inventory of medical equipment and the therapeutic infrastructures. Thus, a pool with a movable floor offers significantly greater scope for orthopaedic treatments than one without this feature. In the beauty and cosmetics sector, dermatologically tested cosmetics may well be offered instead of normal ones. In the sphere of medical beauty, a thorough skin analysis can be carried out by a dermatologist before the cosmetic treatment begins. Thus, the personnel may be extended by adding masseurs. Curative and medical masseurs have more skills than regular ones, although these distinctions can vary greatly between different countries.

Guest rooms may be equipped with alarms designed to summon staff or with beds with adjustable height. Mattress quality can also vary greatly. Bathtubs may be equipped with access aids and anti-slip features. Other features may include a low-radiation environment (e.g. no WLAN) or one with a reduced-dust internal atmosphere and the bathtub may be supplied with curative water, which can convince the guest of the hotel's competence in the health sector.

Food and drink

Another distinction may be drawn on the basis of the degree to which a doctor prescribes what the guest patient may eat. The most medicalised version permits neither an à la carte menu nor a buffet, but prescribes a limited range of foods, i.e. the guest patients eat only what the doctor has prescribed for them. A milder version would allow the guest patient to choose between various foods while nevertheless adhering to a rigorous diet. An even milder form allows a buffet with various sections arranged according to the various stages or forms of a diet, providing detailed information about calorie counts and contents. Normal buffets have a less medically oriented composition, although salads play an important part and specific foods are available, such as sweet dishes containing stevia instead of sugar.

Design and atmosphere

Establishments that endeavour to assume a medical character can express this by adopting a white, hospital-style design in the therapy area and by having the therapists wear white coats. In contrast, warm earthy colours will be preferred for a wellness facility.

Other areas

Other hotel areas have so far been less emphasised for health-promoting measures. These include features designed to stimulate healthy behaviour, such as inviting stairwells that encourage people not to use the lift or incentive models that reimburse guests who succeed in losing a certain amount of weight (e.g. 3 kg in two weeks).

Making guest rooms bookable

Some medical hotels make booking a room dependent on how the medical package is booked by the guest. A hotel that forces co-travelling partners also to book such a package is particularly restrictive. Other establishments require only one guest from each couple to book a medical package. Some medical hotels do not have this requirement and the use of their medical infrastructure is voluntary for their guest patients. Ordinary hotels do not link the option of booking a room to the use of additional services. In contrast, hospitals only admit patients requiring treatment or who have been referred by a doctor.

Profitability and guest groups

The financial aspects of the spa and wellness hotels are shown in detail in Illing (2009). However, the cost and sales structures of medical hotels still await thorough study.

It may be summed up in brief that the greater the proportion of guest patients who make use of medical services, the higher the sales. The price analysis in Figure 20.5 shows that medical services can lead to a considerable increase in sales. The left part of the diagram shows the standard price (rack rate) of hotels with spa and wellness services, without considering sales associated with treatments. The right-hand arrow (broken line) shows the total sales achievable by the additional provision of health-oriented or medical services. It must naturally be noted at this point that a medical hotel has much higher personnel costs due to the presence of doctors and therapists. It can be seen that medical services can increase sales by about 100 per cent or even more. If a medical hotel also makes the use of medical services mandatory, it can be regarded as extraordinarily attractive from a sales point of view. Surgical interventions also drive prices up. These may well involve cosmetic surgery. In contrast, other hotels may decide to forgo invasive measures.

He patient mix plays a crucial role regarding revenues. Some 50–80 per cent of the guests in leading hotels pay for their stay themselves. A further 10 per cent or so can come from travel organisers with a programme designed for health-oriented guests (e.g. FIT-Reisen, TUI Vital). Another approach is to conclude contracts with companies who send their management staff for prevention and check-up stays. Hotels can also cooperate with hospitals or special clinics, which send their patients to them for pre- or post-care. Finally, outpatients who live locally may visit the establishment on a self-pay or health insurance basis.

Hospitals or special clinics depend strongly on the social insurance market and the associated modes of payment (e.g. rates per diem) and avoid making offers for the self-pay market. However, some curative and rehabilitation clinics remain loyal to the social insurance market while simultaneously creating additional offers for self-payers (Table 20.4).

Case study: Thalassa LIFE Medical Hotel

Plans have been finalised to set up the first medical hotel on Cyprus. The provisional opening date is 2018.The idea behind the Thalassa LIFE Medical Hotel is to create a unique medical resort offering a variety of services in the sectors of healing, prevention and wellbeing. The hotel aims to become one of the hotspots of international medical tourism and will target those who are in need of preventive care. Thalassa LIFE aims to provide a comforting yet stimulating atmosphere where guests can heal their bodies and minds, and reconnect their daily lives with their true purposes through a wide range of medical and holistic methods. To achieve this, the establishment must focus on offering a highly effective treatment portfolio based on Western medicine and naturopathy and a skilled medical staff with expertise in preventive medicine. The Thalassa LIFE spa concept aims to achieve purification and alleviation, whereby purification includes both physical and mental cleansing. The detoxification process will relieve the effects of substances harmful to the body. Purification is a precondition for relief and healing. Relief aims to free guests from the burdens of their lifestyle diseases.

The spa in the Thalassa LIFE Medical Hotel will be subdivided into two different parts. First, the Medical Department will comprise all medical units and medical treatment rooms. The head physician and team will offer various state-of-the-art medical treatments. Second, the Wellbeing Area will offer a variety of modern relaxing and beauty treatments.

Figure 20.4 shows the structure of the medical concept. The instruments (shown on the left side) are designed to achieve specific goals (shown on the right side). These comprise both wellbeing (right top) and medical (right bottom) goals (Potamitis and Illing, 2015: 33).

The provisional aim is to achieve a balance between wellbeing and medical treatment, although it should be stressed that the medical component is to be at the centre of the project.

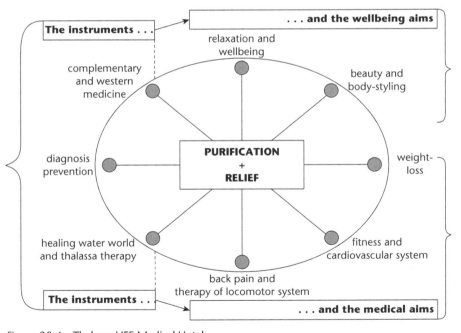

Figure 20.4   Thalassa LIFE Medical Hotel.
Source: Potamitis and Illing (2015: 33).

In summary, the sales of a medical hotel depend on the following factors: (1) their general price level; (2) their capacity utilisation; and (3) the proportion of their guests who make use of a wide range of expensive treatment options.

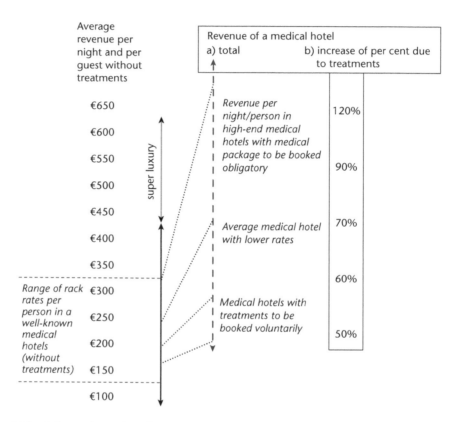

Figure 20.5 Sales analysis of medical hotels.

Source: Illing (2014).

Table 20.4 Cooperation between medical hotels and clinical partners

The following example illustrates the cooperation with clinical partners. Close to a medical hotel is a private in vitro fertilisation (IVF) clinic which has no beds and sends its patients to stay overnight in a nearby hotel with no special health orientation. The medical hotel offers customised services for the pre- and post-care of these patients:

1 A medical doctor/nurse is continuously on call in the hotel.
2 The medical hotel offers complementary treatments (acupuncture, healing herbs, etc.).
3 A shuttle service is offered by car between the hotel and private clinic.
4 A hotline is available to the doctor.
5 Very quick emergency help is available (clinic in the capital).
6 The medical hotel has extensive expertise in the field of IVF, as its staff includes gynaecologists.

This offer convinces the private clinic, which then sends its patients to the medical hotel in the future.

Location, size and type of establishment

Location

The natural surroundings of medical hotels and their health-promoting potential play an important role. In this context, a distinction can be made between objective and subjective features. A typical objective feature is measurably good air (e.g. low dust content), which may even satisfy the requirements of a resort with a curative climate. Typical subjective features would be the closeness of woods, lakes or the sea, which convey the feeling of being in healthy surroundings. Unlike for clinical establishments, the natural environment plays a major role for health hotels. Outdoor activities that take natural remedies into account, such as a healing climate, play a greater role in medical hotels than in clinical establishments. Curative waters may play an important role in the treatment concept.

Size of establishment

Various aspects may be considered as regards the size of the hotel. It is now widely accepted that larger units can be operated more cost-effectively: 100 rooms or more are desirable. On the other hand, small units with 60–80 rooms should be the goal in a medical context, as they alone guarantee the necessary intimacy, familiarity, discretion and individualised services. However, it is important to mention that modern rehabilitation clinics often have 200–300 rooms, a situation which need not contradict the above-mentioned considerations. Small health hotels impress with discretion, more personnel-intensive care and customised treatments, which consequently lead to expensive treatment prices. In contrast, rehabilitation clinics, which have to get by with low rates, attempt to insure their profitability with high patient numbers. It should be noted at this point that the daily care rates in rehabilitation clinics can be exceeded fourfold by the sales achieved by medical hotels. In summary, the generous size of the hotel infrastructure (large hotel rooms, attractive pools and many other features), as well as their personnel-intensive individual service have their price and ultimately address a clientele who find the consumption of such services important and are willing to pay for them accordingly.

Various target groups

It should further be noted that diverse target groups should not be arbitrarily mixed. It is highly problematic for a medical hotel to accommodate conference guests and bus groups with no health orientation as well. It should be considered that guests in health or medical hotels are sometimes sick or infirm and wish to be treated in a discreet manner. A large number of guests who have no interest in health will be unwilling to show the necessary consideration. Even if the hotel exclusively accommodates health guests, there are enough differences within this target group to give rise to dissatisfaction. Thus, operators should even consider whether healthy guests should be treated in the same establishment as guests with infirmities or injuries.

Organisational form

Hotels which consider wellness as an exclusive business field in addition to board and lodging can be part of either a hotel chain or individual establishments. Hotels offering higher levels of medicalisation are often in the latter category. As a rule, hotel chains tend not to offer medical services, due to a lack of relevant experience. However, normal holiday hotels often request that successful medical hotels make their concept available, for instance in the form of a franchise. This shows that hotels are in fact seeking successful concepts and regard health as a profitable business field.

Table 20.5 Delimitation of various types of establishment

	Spa and wellness hotel	Medical hotel	Hospital (special clinic)
Location	Frequently in attractive surroundings	Frequently in attractive surroundings	Many special clinics in conurbations are also located in attractive surroundings
Voluntary stay	Treatments are booked on a voluntary basis	Mix of voluntary stay and doctor's orders	Treatment due to advice/order of doctor or healthcare fund due to sickness
Aim	Wellness, non-specific recovery	Maintenance and improvement of the state of health and wellness	Relief of suffering and/or return to health
Payment	Self-payment	Mostly self-payment	Costs usually reimbursed (proportionately) by social insurer
Customer	Healthy	Healthy and sick	Sick
Personnel	Few doctors and therapists	High proportion of doctors and therapists	High proportion of doctors and therapists
Profit aim	Yes	Yes	Care mandate often more important than profit aim
Medical focus	None	Western medicine mixed with naturopathy	Centred on Western medicine
Health aim	Recovery, wellness and primary prevention	Primary and secondary prevention	Prevention, cure and rehabilitation
Process management	Guests determines what they do	Guest patient partially autonomous and partially dependent on doctor's orders	Patient defers to the doctor's orders
Rooms and ambience	Comfortable, sometimes luxurious	Mixes a pleasant ambience with medical functionality	More practical and functional
Diagnosis	Rarely	Yes	Very complex
Inclusion of natural surroundings (e.g. outdoor fitness)	Often	Often	Less common
Inclusion of pampering and wellbeing services	Often	Less often	None

Depending on the relevant national regulations pertaining to company law, medical hotels may adopt a legal form specifically designed for clinical establishments, such as an outpatient or special clinic. This can involve the introduction of special regulations, namely that nursing services must be available around the clock or that specific emergency equipment must be in place (e.g. emergency bell).

Conclusion

The precise differentiation of an establishment in the continuum from hotels to hospitals shows that such distinctions may be both very subtle and very clear (Table 20.5). Experience shows that, when planning new medical hotels, great emphasis should be placed on the degree of medicalisation of interest to various target groups. Even small changes can lead to the establishment becoming a spa and wellness hotel against the wishes of the top management or moving in the other direction and becoming a clinical establishment. Frequently, only minor adjustments are required for the establishment to move in one direction or the other.

Table 20.6 shows that it is often possible to make a very clear differentiation between establishments. Further studies are needed to obtain more in-depth information. These should include studies in the sectors of consumer research (consumer preferences), economics (cost and sales structures in medical hotels) and scientific healthcare (success of selected naturopathic treatments often offered in hotels). Further research sectors should include quality management, where direct efficacy with a view to better business success requires further study.

Note

1 The pronoun 'he' in this chapter is of course generic and covers both genders.

References

Beladi, H., Chao, C. C., Shan, E. M. and Hollas, D. (2015) 'Medical tourism and health worker migration in developing countries', *Economic Modelling*, 46, 391–396.
Cohen, E. (2008) 'Medical tourism in Thailand', in Cohen, E. (ed.) *Explorations in Thai Tourism*. Bingley, UK: Emerald, pp. 225–255.
Connell, J. (2013) 'Contemporary medical tourism: Conceptualisation, culture and commodification', *Tourism Management*, 34, 1–13.
Crooks, V., Kingsbury, P., Snyder, J. and Johnston, R. (2010) 'What is known about the patient's experience of medical tourism? A scoping review', *BMC Health Services Research*, 10, http://bmchealthservres.biomedcentral.com/articles/10.1186/1472-6963-10-266 (accessed 14 January 2016).
Dvorak, D., Saari, S. and Tuominen, T. (2014) *Developing a Competitive Health and Well-being Destination*, http://weldest.blogspot.co.at/ (accessed 18 September 2015).
Frederick, J. R. and Gan, L. L. (2015) 'East–West differences among medical tourism facilitators' websites', *Journal of Destination Marketing and Management*, http://dx.doi.org/10.1016/j.jdmm.2015.03.002i. (accessed 23 February 2016).
Hallem, Y. and Barth, I. (2011) 'Customer-perceived value of medical tourism: An exploratory study – the case of cosmetic surgery in Tunisia', *Journal of Hospitality and Tourism Management*, 18, 121–129.
Han, H. (2013) 'The healthcare hotel: Distinctive attributes for international medical travelers', *Tourism Management*, 36, 257–268.
Han, H. and Hwang, J. (2013) 'Multi-dimensions of the perceived benefits in a medical hotel and their roles in international travelers' decision-making process', *International Journal of Hospitality Management*, 35, 100–108.
Han, H., Kim, Y., Kim, C. and Ham, S. (2015) 'Medical hotels in the growing healthcare business industry: Impact of international travelers' perceived outcomes', *Journal of Business Research*, http://dx.doi.org/10.1016/j.jbusres (accessed 15 Januray 2015).
Heung, V. C. S., Kucukusta, D. and Song, H. (2011) 'Medical tourism development in Hong Kong: An assessment of the barriers', *Tourism Management*, 32, 995–1005.

Ilkay, M. and Aslan, E. (2012) 'The effect of the ISO 9001 quality management system on the performance of SMEs', *International Journal of Quality and Reliability Management*, 29(7), 753–777.

Illing, K. (2009) *Gesundheitstourismus und Spa-Management*, Munich, Germany: Oldenbourg.

——. (2014) *Angebot im Gesundheitstourismus*, Bremen, Germany: Apollon Hochschule für Gesundheitswirtschaft.

Illing, K., Binder, D., Neuhold, B. and Auer, M. (2014) *Weldest – Health and Well-being in Tourism Destination*, Research Report, http://weldest.blogspot.co.at/ (accessed 18 September 2015).

Intelligent Spas (2005) *Female Versus Male Spa Consumers – Survey of Behaviours, Expectations, Preferences and Predictions*, Singapore: Intelligent Spas.

Kucukusta, D. and Guillet, B. (2014) 'Measuring spa goers' preferences: A conjoint analysis approach', *International Journal of Hospitality Management*, 41, 115–124.

Lohmann, M. and Schmücker, D. (2015) 'Nachfrage nach gesundheitsorientierten Urlaubsformen in Deutschland', *Zeitschrift für Tourismuswissenschaft*, 7(1), 5–18.

Martin, D., Rosenbaum, M. and Ham, S. (2015) 'Marketing tourism and hospitality products worldwide: Introduction to the special issue', *Journal of Business Research*, http://dx.doi.org/10.1016/j.busres.2015.01.008.

Medical Tourism Association (2010) 'Patient survey – Bumrungrad International', *Medical Tourism*, 14, 22–25.

Potamitis, S. and Illing, K. (2015) *Thalassa LIFE Medical Hotel – Business Plan*. Version 5.3, July. Governor's Beach, Cyprus.

Smith, M. and Puczkó, L. (2014) *Health, Tourism and Hospitality. Spas, Wellness and Medical Travel*, London: Routledge.

Yu, J., Yun, K. and Tae, G. (2012) 'A cross-cultural study of perceptions of medical tourism among Chinese, Japanese and Korean tourists in Korea', *Tourism Management*, 33, 80–88.

Zygourakis, C., Rolston, J., Treadway, J., Chang, S. and Michel, K. (2014) 'What do hotels and hospitals have in common? How we can learn from the hotel industry to take better care of patients', *Surgical Neurology International*, 5(2), 49–53.

21

A Disney strategic approach to patient/guest services in Hospitality Bridging Healthcare (H2H) and medical tourism and wellness

Frederick J. DeMicco

Introduction

The author spent a part of his career working at Disney World in Orlando at the Contemporary Hotel and Wilderness Lodge Resort. This chapter will examine the guest services, management and leadership principles from Disney and Disney University that could be applied to a medical tourism healthcare environment. The author completed the Disney Traditions I and II classes required of all Disney employees and completed his *Ducktorate* degree at Disney University. The question was asked there of us: who is Disney's competition? The answer is not Universal Studios or others, but Disney takes a wider view and looks at 'any competition that the customer compares us to'. This could be Lexus, Costco or Amazon – where they may witness a high level of service and an 'over the top' experience. Therefore, it is critical that throughout the systems model service processes that all points of service contact are at a high level of guest experience.

In the book *If Disney Ran Your Hospital* (Lee, 2004), there is the statement: 'In the battle for the supremacy of perceptions in the patient's mind, our competition is anyone the patient compares us to. Unfortunately they do not compare us to other hospitals.' According to a Gallup survey the four top drivers of patient satisfaction included: nurses anticipated patients' needs, the staff and department worked together as a team, staff responded with care and compassion and the staff advised patients if there were going to be delays (Gallup Organization, 1999).

In a Press Ganey Associates patient satisfaction report (2003), top drivers for patient satisfaction included: how well the staff worked together to care for patients; overall cheerfulness of the hospital; responses to concerns or complaints made during the patient stay; amount of attention paid to patients' personal and special needs; nurses kept patient informed; nurses' attitudes towards patient requests; and skill and friendliness of the nurses. However, hospitals spend much of their time on the clinical outcomes, but less on how the patient judges the outcomes. The patient therefore is evaluating the total experience of the healthcare facility (not solely the clinical medical experience).

From a patient services perspective, focus on improving outcomes and perceptions is important (Lee, 2004). This includes focusing on outcomes such as team responsibility, eliminating carelessness, stressing what the medical team should be doing and process mapping. Focusing on improving perceptions includes: focus on personal responsibility; being tuned into patient perceptions; improvement of staff behaviours and attitudes; stressing what staff should be saying; seeking to impact impressions and best possible thinking.

At Disney employees are referred to as cast members and all customers are referred to as guests. The Disney strategy is to teach cast members what to say to make the best positive impression. Structured scripting for cast member and guest interactions does this. Healthcare can also follow these practices towards higher guest satisfaction and loyalty levels. It is about managing the moments of truth between guest and cast member interactions to create a powerful positive impression. If Disney ran your hospital, nurses, for example, would begin to believe that they are judged not so much against the standard of other nurses, but against the standards set by the nicest people providing services anywhere. The same goes for the food service staff, housekeepers and doctors (Lee, 2004).

During the Disney Traditions mandatory training programmes, the four most important areas in order that Disney stresses are: (1) safety; (2) courtesy; (3) show; and (4) efficiency. The safety as number one aligns well with hospitals, but the other areas particularly related to patient satisfaction (e.g. courtesy) are not clearly defined and thus not carried out in service delivery.

This is why Disney places courtesy higher than efficiency.

The often-used 1 to 5 rating scale for guest satisfaction

Many hospitality and healthcare facilities use a Likert scale of 1 to 5 to assess patient satisfaction with their hospital visit. So everything above a 4 was considered that the patient was satisfied. But at Disney, they do not show guest satisfaction scores; they only show cast members the percentage of guests giving 5s to satisfaction (the top score for 'Excellent'). The reason is that only scores of 5 are linked to loyalty and thus the likelihood to return again as a guest. In fact, a guest who gives a 4 score is about six times more likely to defect than a customer who gives a score of 5 or excellent. Therefore there is about a sixfold increase in customer loyalty between scores of 4 and 5 (Lee, 2004). Disney is interested in the percentage of guests giving a score of 5. Thus Disney is measuring loyalty (and likelihood to return) and loyalty, not purely satisfaction, is the most important factor needed to protect the organisation against future competition in a complex market.

An example of this is hotel staff cleaning all guests' windshields in the parking lot and placing a note on the windshield saying, clean windshields on us – have a great day. If you do something special for guests, they will remember this and if you do not do something memorable, they will not remember their stay, as it is just another night in a hotel. This experience generates a buzz or story for others to tell, building loyalty. A person who is 'satisfied' has no story to tell as everything went as expected. It is the unexpected service experience that generates a memorable story. For every loyal guest there is usually a memorable story (Lee, 2004).

Getting customers to return is the key to a profitable and long-lasting business. Unfortunately hospitals cannot bank on getting guests to return because of 'better prices' or a convenient location, coupons and the like: to get guests to become loyal and sing the praises of the healthcare facility comes from compassion shown by the staff. In a pyramid-type model, at the base is competence, as healthcare and hotel staff (we can refer to them as *Hospitelity* cast members) are hired for their expertise and competence. The next level of the pyramid is courtesy. It may be referred to as service excellence. At the top of the hospitelity pyramid we have compassion, which is the emotional level of caring. While courtesy in the middle of the pyramid may get you a service score of 4, it is compassion that gets a 5 or very satisfied rating in the patient evaluation (adapted from Lee, 2004). Over the years, the Gallup and Press Ganey surveys that include questions with the words concern or compassion and care in them have the highest correlation with overall satisfaction and loyalty. The writers of the survey may question how compassion is measured, but it is the patient who 'gets it' and knows what compassion feels like.

So in addition to hiring/selecting employees who demonstrate true compassion, along with considering 'cleaning the windshield' so to speak, to create the memorable story which can lead to more loyal or at least patients who sing the praises of the facility, according to Lee (2004) there is nothing quite as powerful in patient satisfaction scores as a phone call placed to the home of a discharged patient. If it comes from the nurse or doctor, this is a powerful message of compassion and concern.

Say 'yes' to patient/guests

Disney empowers cast members to say yes to solve a problem for the guest. Setting this type of service structure does what it takes to serve the guest and is practised successfully by the service culture of Marriott. This culture follows the mantra, if you take care of your employees they will take care of the customer/guest. This 'guest-first' structure helps to shape and drive a culture of compassion (for patient/guests). It is not possible to practise this level of service compassion if making guest decisions in real time is mired in many layers of bureaucracy, giving rise to slow and ineffective service.

When I worked at Disney World in the hotels, Disney was 'decentralised' to an extent where employees could move around the park to meet service peak time demands. For example, breakfast in the hotels was very busy (especially with Disney character breakfasts) and lighter during the lunchtime, whereas in the parks, lunch was an extremely busy time. Therefore employees could shift over to the parks from the hotels to meet this demand crunch at peak times. This team structure helped to make sure guests were taken care of during the busy service times.

Management can also be a barrier to service excellence and saying yes to the guest. Do employees need management's support to treat people nicely or to show compassion in a hospital waiting room? Do we need top management's support to give more authority to frontline people?

But do employees need to be able to solve problems and have the power and support of management for service recovery, which is a true test of decentralising (Lee, 2004)?

Write an effective service script for cast members

A service script provides a structured response for the employee in the service encounter in the system. Service scripts or storyboards provide a structured framework of what is expected in the service performance. It is not a rote-memorised script, but allows the cast member to tailor the service responds to the situation and still get the message of care and compassion across to the patient or guest. When I worked at Wilderness Lodge, on some days I had to do two costume changes (uniforms) based on my work placement.

Each place or department in the hotel has different service scripts. For example, while at Disney's Wilderness Lodge, valets would always greet car occupants at the porte-cochère as they drove up to check into the resort. They had structured storyboards for greeting. While it is not exactly a script, it is four things or service points that needed to take place during the service encounter. Give a big over-the-top welcome (big smile) to the Wilderness Lodge. Second, notice the licence plate and say something about the state or weather back home, for example, the Red Sox are awesome this year (if from a New England state). Wave and speak immediately to any children in the car and finally, notice anything interesting on the luggage rack or bumper stickers, decals, etc. to make conversation with the guests. It is a unique script – no rote for the cast member, but it has structure at the point of contact. Most directors of acting would say adhering to the intent of the scene is much more important than adhering to the actual words of the script (Lee, 2004). In essence, the service script does not change, but the words expressed will be based on the four key components listed above.

In selection of employees in the hiring practice, Disney auditions for talent instead of skills *per se* to perform roles rather than just jobs. In the healthcare setting, managers need to audition for the talent required in the role they will play – again, trying to exude compassion for the patient, which is more critical than the skills needed for the task (which often can be trained). In the restaurant setting you hear the saying 'hire the smile' or 'hire friendly – I cannot teach happy'.

Today an increasing number of businesses are moving away from the traditional commodity, goods and service model but are becoming more experience-driven. B. Joseph Pine II and James H. Gilmore first introduced 'The Experience Economy' in 1999. What many hospitals fail to realise is that patients are also customers/guests and these patients/guests are charged for the wellbeing they get by being engaged in an experience economy (Pine and Gilmore, 2011). Healthcare institutions are expected to offer travel, lodging, dining, transportation, spa care and even fitness classes in order to cater to their patients' needs. The goal for the process of the medical care is evolving from transactional care to a transformational experience in which customers/patients receive health benefits, not limited to medical care.

The goal of Hospitality Bridging Healthcare (H2H): excellent care

What are the key components for a profound healthcare experience? When it comes to medical tourism, the success of medical care obviously is one crucial determinant. Unfortunately, the patients and customers will not give credit to the well-done treatment coming with unpleasant customer service as excellent source of care. Moreover, as one of the most distinctive icons in the service industry, Disney has provided a convincing list summarised by Dr Fred Lee in his book *If Disney Ran Your Hospital*: initiative, teamwork, empathy, courtesy and communication (Lee, 2004). Based on the Disney model, six major factors should be considered necessary for realisation of excellent care in medical care settings (Mengyu, 2015) (Figure 21.1).

Successful medical treatment serves as the primary goal of medical tourism. It is the core competency of hospitals while a hospitality team has expertise in customer care. Both teams have competitive methods to reinforce their core competence and enhance their strengths. However, the greater success in medical tourism is to align these two core competencies from both parties. Productivity and efficiency can be maximised by the alignment. Also, success in medical treatment and memorable customer care are compensating each other to deliver an excellent medical tourism experience.

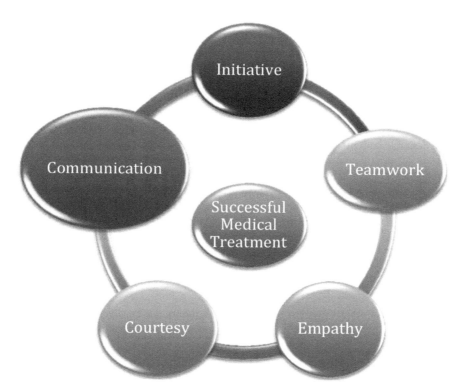

Figure 21.1   Lee's Disney model on excellent care.

For example, the majority of patients will not highly praise their healthcare experiences simply because the health institution is able to deliver successful medical treatments. It is likely that there are a handful of possible other institutions that can achieve the same result. However, H2H, composed of and complemented with medical staff, hoteliers, dining, spa staff, personal trainers and other wellbeing facilitators, can significantly differentiate the healthcare institution from conventional ones. Since the expertise of customer care can complete and strengthen the circle of true care for patients' overall wellbeing, having a strong hospitality team inside the healthcare organisation is a substantial competitive advantage. This H2H process bridges the gap between the successful medical treatment and excellent care perceived and experienced by patients. As an expert and pioneer in the field of bringing hospitality to hospitals, Dr Lee summarised the five factors that define the excellent care performed by Disney (Lee, 2004) (Table 21.1).

Table 21.1 Explanation of Disney model by Dr Lee

Initiative	Sense people's needs before they ask
Team work	Help each other out
Empathy	Acknowledge people's feelings
Courtesy	Respect the dignity and privacy of everyone
Communication	Explain what's happening

A systems model approach to H2H

A systems model approach used in manufacturing and services can be applied to the medical tourism integrated model with H2H (DeMicco, 2015). A system model is the conceptual model that describes and represents a system. A system comprises multiple views such as planning, requirement (analysis), design, implementation, deployment, structure, behaviour, input data and output data view. A systems model is required to describe and represent all these multiple views. The systems model also serves as the structure for service and provides a vantage point for these desirable patient/guest services. The Mayo Clinic systems model provides a road map or blueprint for the integration of all of the services from pre-Mayo to post-Mayo and the processes in between. The understanding of this model can lead to a very positive level of patient/guest experience which can generate loyalty and a positive health outcome.

It is important to understand the medical tourists'/patients'/guests' 'journey' as they progress in these roles through the processes of the system for planning, arrival, entry, hospitality, treatment and medical and wellness procedures. These are also referred to as human touch points. We also refer to H2H as an excellent holistic guest experience within the system. Once within the Healthcare (and Hospitality) system, many experiences take place along the journey, including transportation, arrival at the hotel and transport to the myriad of health services. In addition, the patient/guest encounters many important subsystems from dining to transportation, to medical/wellness treatments, lodging and entertainment. Finally, in the output phase of the systems model process, the patient/guest departs the system and follow-up communication should take place.

Healthcare hospitality management as a career

Healthcare includes hospitals, clinics, nursing homes, life care and continuing care facilities. It is a segment that shows no signs of slowing and there will be many career openings for hotel and restaurant management graduates. This is due to the fact that people are ageing and will therefore require more medical procedures going forward into the future. This segment is managed by contract companies and also self-operated. For example, ARAMARK has hospitals such as Hahnemann Hospital in Philadelphia and the Massachusetts General Hospital in Boston (where I completed my dietetic internship for registered dietitian certification) and is self-operated. The healthcare setting usually has several types of food service. There are the clinical patients in the hospital rooms who typically have their trays sent up from the kitchen (centralised service). There is also decentralised tray service where food is sent up in bulk in heated and refrigerated food carts with no sugar added. The trays are assembled on the guest floor. About half of all patient tray service is a special diet (such as reduced sodium or low fat). In addition, the healthcare facility will have food courts and coffee shops and today more and more are adding restaurants and branded concepts to appeal not only to visitors of patients, but also to the medical and clinical staff employed at the facility. Graduates from hospitality programmes who join this segment of the hospitality industry can look forward to solid growth for the future, stable work hours, good pay and benefits (particularly medical insurance), oftentimes day care for employee children, career growth and making a difference serving people in need. Usually graduates of 4-year hospitality programmes begin as an assistant director, work up to a director of food services and eventually can become a general manager or vice-president for patient/guest services. As more healthcare facilities grow to become 'medical campuses' and medical meccas for medical tourism, they emulate hotels in their quality and delivery of health and wellness services. In fact, in hospitals, approximately 75 per cent of the services provided to patients are hospitality/hotel-related services. For example, they may add wellness and spa operations, which hospitality school graduates should be prepared to oversee.

In addition, more food service directors are becoming general managers of the entire healthcare campus enterprise and lead not only the traditional hospital facilities but also, the hotel(s), spa and wellness, environmental services (e.g. housekeeping), transportation services, parking, the grounds, snow removal and all dining venues. This is usually a vice-president position on the healthcare campus and can provide challenge, excitement and very good pay and benefits in the six-figure salary range.

In sum, hospitality schools prepare graduates to be general managers of hotels and now graduates should think of becoming general managers/vice-presidents of healthcare (non-medical) operations and services in the future (DeMicco and Williams, 1999). This is clearly a field for hospitality graduates that provides challenge and growth opportunities well into the future.

Conclusion

In summary, since approximately 75 per cent of patient/guest healthcare services are hospitality-related services, the pre-planning of the medical journey leading up to the arrival at the medical/health/wellness destination begins a cascade of multiple H2H services to create an entire satisfying experience for the patient/guest. This understanding and the complete design of the patient/guest experience can lead to loyalty if performance in the entirety of the process is at the highest level.

This chapter looked at service elements if Disney did indeed run your hospital. It is written by a person who worked for Disney and also obtained his Ducktorate degree from Disney University and also examining some of the chapters from the popular book *If Disney Ran Your Hospital* by Fred Lee (2004). Every hospitality and healthcare manager (*hospitelity* manager) needs to reinforce the principles of service excellence and employ some of the tools and suggestions described in this chapter in order to bring about loyalty. They need to focus on why patient or guest loyalty is very important, why satisfied patients/guests do not equate to loyalty and show why each employee has a role to play in the service setting and how attitude, courtesy and compassion are the bedrock for success.

Lessons learned from Disney University use a Sleeping Beauty and the Seven Dwarfs Disney analogy which has application to H2H. Be Happy, by making eye contact and smile; be like Sneezy and greet and welcome each and every guest. Spread the spirit of hospitality, it is contagious; don't be Bashful, seek out guest contact; be like Doc and provide immediate service recovery; don't be Grumpy, always display appropriate body language at all times; be like Sleepy and create dreams and preserve the 'magical' guest experience and don't be Dopey, thank each and every guest (Cockerell, 2008). Sharing this vision with employees and providing a structure for them to serve the patient/guest while understanding their role and following the script (storyboard) leads to success.

Case study: Indego: a new technology for mobile travel and tourism?

Frederick J. DeMicco and Kristen Hickman

The purpose of this case study is to introduce the Indego technology[1] and evaluate if it can be successfully introduced into theme parks (such as Disney, Universal Studios) and for other travel where physical assisted mobility is needed (for example, medical tourism). The background of

(continued)

(continued)

the product is thoroughly discussed to explain how this technology could aid disabled guests at a large theme park. The challenges and benefits are also laid out in order to see a potential outcome for theme parks if they implemented this product.

In the USA over one million people are confined to a wheelchair. This means that 1 in every 250 people cannot walk on their own (Cetron, DeMicco and Davies, 2010). Out of these one million people, 307,000 are under the age of 44. This number grows as more and more Americans become disabled: 10,000 people significantly injure their spinal cord every year and 82 per cent of these injuries happen to the male population.

The majority of Americans who are limited to a wheelchair and are unable to participate in everyday activities are a part of the older generations. However, there is still a significant number who are young and would like to live normal lives with their friends and families. Many of these injured males probably have a wife and children that they would like to spend time with in a more ordinary way, such as going to a theme park such as Disney World.

Disney, for example, is one of the most coveted and frequently made trips for families in the USA. Disney's Magic Kingdom alone had over 17 million visitors in one year. Most young people, whether they be children or parents, visit a theme park at some point in their lives.

Disney World is much more than your average theme park. With 47 square miles of entertainment, it is one of the largest destination theme parks in the world.

For the average guest, theme parks such as Disney World and Universal Studios and other mega-theme park brands are an entertainment dream. For a disabled guest, a theme park could be a logistical nightmare. While the theme parks do have wheelchairs, both traditional and electronic, guests who require wheelchairs are still very limited in where they can go and what rides, if any, they can go on. This reveals a need in the theme park industry for a better solution for disabled guests.

History of Indego product

Information about the robotic legs known as Indego was first being published in the summer of 2012. Research has been conducted on the possibility of robotic legs since the 1990s; however, this was mainly for use in research labs and not for the public. It was not until years later that researchers thought they could produce a product strong and smart enough not only to support a human being, but also to understand what the user was telling it to do. However, since this is a new product it is still rather expensive. Each set of legs would cost $70,000 for the initial investment, but as the technology becomes more common, the price will go down.

The purpose of Indego is to increase the mobility of paraplegics by standing, walking, turning and sitting for them. Indego is a set of bionic legs that attach at the hip, the thigh and the calf. There are motors in the joints that are able to provide the correct amount of force to do the requested movements. Individuals wearing Indego are able to request to move forward by leaning slightly forward. Similarly, they can request to move backwards or stop by leaning backwards. If they want to move a specific leg, they can lean towards the opposite leg, which will inform Indego which leg it should move.

This technology totally redefines paraplegic disability. A disability that once meant confinement to a chair does not necessarily mean that any more.

Challenges and benefits

Incorporating Indego into theme parks, just like any new, cutting-edge technology, would come with both challenges and benefits. Some of the challenges would be:

- The price of Indego is still very high, so putting enough sets in the park for all disabled visitors would be an extremely expensive investment.
- Any technology, even when well tested, has the possibility of malfunction. This can create a possibility for liability on the part of a theme park.
- Indego seems fairly simple to use; however, most guests probably have not used this type of technology before. A short training period on how to use the machinery would be necessary in order to rent out the equipment. This would require an expert on the subject to be present wherever Indego is made available.
- Because this equipment is so expensive, high security measures would have to be taken to protect the investment.

Some of the benefits would be:

- No other vacation spot has implemented this technology. Theme parks would be the first to have such a desirable and unique feature.
- Eventually, this may be a requirement of the Americans with Disabilities Act, so theme parks would already be very familiar with the technology before any laws about it reach the surface.
- When word of mouth spreads that a particular theme park is giving paraplegics the freedom to walk around the park and go on rides, many more individuals with disabilities will feel comfortable going to a theme park. This could increase the park's total sales.

Key points

Bob Ingram, the current CEO of the Fun in the Sun theme park corporation, has a lot to say about the theme park brand, how it should be run and how their guests should be treated. Here are some quotes that show Mr Ingram's enthusiasm for the park:

- 'The heart and soul of the company is creativity and innovation.'
- 'I think it is incredibly important to be open and accessible and treat people fairly.'
- 'People don't like to follow pessimists.'
- 'The riskiest thing we can do is just maintain the status quo.'

Summary

As outlined above, mega theme parks are a vast entertainment world with so many things to do, things in which a paraplegic would be unable to participate. The parks are not the only unobtainable asset; the golf courses and aspects of the resorts are also difficult to utilise when in a wheelchair. However, the new technology, Indego, has been created to give 'new' legs to those who cannot use their own. These sets of bionic legs would exponentially increase the activities guests with disabilities could enjoy. While this may be a big step for any company, the CEO of the corporation not only believes in innovation, but also treating all guests fairly.

Note

1 'Indego, which weighs 26 pounds and functions as an external skeleton, could benefit an estimated 1.7 million people in the US alone, including 25,000 military veterans with spinal-cord injuries' (Tita, 2014).

References

Cetron, M., DeMicco, F. and Davies, O. (2010) *Hospitality and Travel 2015*, Orlando, FL: The American Hotel and Lodging Association Educational Institute.

Cockerell, L. (2008) *Creating Magic: 10 Common Sense Leadership Strategies from a Life at Disney*, New York: Doubleday Press.

DeMicco, F.J. (ed.) (2016) *Medical Tourism and Wellness: Hospitality Bridging Healthcare (H2H ©)*. Waretown, NJ: Apple Academic Press.

DeMicco, F.J. and Williams, J.A. (1999) 'Down-board thinking (what are our next moves?)', *J. Am. Diet. Assoc.*, 99, 285–286.

Gallup Organization (1999) http://www.gallup.com/consulting/52/employee-engagement.asp.

Lee, F. (2004) *If Disney Ran Your Hospital: 9 1/2 Things You Would Do Differently*, Bozeman, MT: Second River Healthcare Press.

Mengyu, M. L. (2015) *The Guest Experience in Healthcare*, unpublished manuscript.

Pine, B. J. and Gilmore, J. H. (1999) *The Experience Economy: Work Is Theater and Every Business a Stage*, Boston, MA: Harvard Business School Press.

—— (2011) *The Experience Economy*, Boston, MA: Harvard Business Review Press.

Press Ganey Satisfaction Report (2003) Volume VII, August, p. 1.

Tita, B. (2014) 'Robotic legs for the disabled', *Wall Street Journal*, November 11, D1.

22

Balneology and health tourism

Melanie Kay Smith and László Puczkó

Introduction

The use of water as a form of therapy has existed for thousands of years and was often connected to religious and spiritual traditions too. The Romans and Greeks were perhaps the first civilisations to emphasise the importance of cleanliness for health and sanitation and this tradition has continued ever since, especially in Europe. The Romans already differentiated baths for leisure or prevention (i.e. *thermae*) and bathing establishments for healing or medical purposes (i.e. *balnea*). Although there were times when less than sanitary conditions prevailed (e.g. medieval times), water of all kinds has for centuries been recognised as being essential for maintaining a healthy body. Indeed, in many countries, especially in Europe, water-based therapies are accepted as a legitimate form of medicine where they are supervised and supported by governments and can be a reimbursable medical expense. Although some countries do not recognise such therapies as medicine and financial support is slowly decreasing in certain countries, water still plays a central role in the healthcare and health tourism sectors. Countries regulate differently how thermal, mineral or healing waters are defined in terms of temperature of the water at source (e.g. 30 or 32°C) and the minimum expected mineral content (e.g. 1,000 mg/l). The medical quality of the hot springs has to be tested by rigorous clinical trials and in every country such processes and consequently the accreditation is undertaken by government bodies.

Early definitions of health tourism focused especially on natural resources, including water, such as the International Union of Tourist Organizations (IUOTO) (1973: 7), which stated that health tourism is 'the provision of health facilities utilising the natural resources of the country, in particular mineral water and climate'. The International Spa Association defines a mineral springs spa as 'a spa offering an on-site source of natural mineral, thermal or seawater used in hydrotherapy treatments' (ISPA, 2016). Countries in many parts of the world have mineral-rich healing waters which are used by very different segments such as leisure customers, wellness enthusiasts or medical patients as part of their leisure, prevention, therapy, treatment or rehabilitation. Erfurt-Cooper and Cooper (2009) describe in detail the way in which hot springs are used in health and wellness tourism in numerous destinations around the world. This includes Central and Eastern European countries, Baltic States, Russian-speaking countries and many countries which have hot springs which were or could be used for healing or leisure purposes, for example, New Zealand, South Korea, Japan and China. Tukamusaba (2013) writes about hot springs and healing waters in Uganda, and Boekstein (2001) about South Africa.

This chapter focuses in particular on balneology, which is the medical use of waters, as well as climate and mud, as this area has been relatively under-researched in a health tourism context compared to thermal waters, which are used for wellness, prevention or leisure purposes.

Defining balneology

Hydrotherapy is one of the basic methods of treatment widely used in the system of natural medicine, which is also called water therapy, aquatic therapy, pool therapy and balneotherapy (Mooventhan and Nivethitha, 2014). Riyaz and Riyaz Arakkal (2011) describe how hydrotherapy involves the use of water in all its forms (internally and externally) to assist in the healing process. Karagülle (2006) differentiates between hydrotherapy and balneology as follows:

- Balneotherapy employs generally natural thermal mineral water, mostly at a spa.
- Hydrotherapy, on the other hand, consists of the use of ordinary water (tap or very low mineralised), whether at a spa or not.

Spa therapy comprises a broad spectrum of therapeutic modalities, including hydrotherapy, balneotherapy, physiotherapy, mud pack therapy and exercise (Fioravanti, Cantarini, Guidelli and Galeazzi, 2011). Balneotherapy (Latin: *balneum*, bath) refers to the medical use of water as opposed to its recreational use. Therapeutic use of muds is also included in balneotherapy. Bogdanov, Kircheva, Miteva and Tsankov (2012) suggest that balneology is part of the wider therapy of climatotherapy, which includes: thalassotherapy (sea water baths), heliotherapy (exposure to sunlight), peloid therapy (mud baths) and balneotherapy (mineral water baths). The Global Wellness Institute (2011) provides an overview of some of the evidence-based therapies referred to as either spa evidence or, lately, wellness evidence.

A therapy based on balneology tends to be called balneotherapy, the most common being bathing in or drinking healing or medicinal waters, applying mud and peloid packs to the body and exposure to gases during 'gas bathing' in a mofetta or as inhalation. However, the main mode of balneotherapy is immersion in thermal water with a natural temperature of at least 20°C or mineral water with a total mineral content of at least 1 g/L (Gutenbrunner, Bender, Cantista and Karagülle, 2010), but, as stated earlier, these conditions can differ country by country. These are used to treat various conditions, such as musculoskeletal, gynaecological and dermatological disorders as well as vascular conditions, amongst others (Bender, Bálint, Prohászka, Géher and Tefner, 2014). Varga (2012) suggests that the term balneotherapy should only be used for those treatments that have a curative effect. He uses the word 'balneoprevention' for therapies that are used to prevent certain diseases or conditions. The therapeutic effects of 'taking the waters' can also be linked to leisure or wellness services.

Peloids include medicinal muds, clay, peat and similar substances which come from the sea, salt lakes and mineral or medicinal waters. Pelotherapy is currently used in southern and central European countries and is synonymous with the term mud therapy (Gomes et al., 2013). Peat and various peat preparations have been successfully used in the balneological practice of clinical medicine. Several European countries (Germany, Austria, the Czech Republic, Hungary and Latvia) have long traditions of using balneological peat. In recent decades it has also been studied and used in Finland. However, the country most widely using peat for therapeutic purposes is Germany. The peat suitable for balneology has to be well humidified (40–50 per cent). Its natural moisture content has to be at least 85 per cent and the peat layer has to be under the peat water level. Balneological peat should not contain harmful bacteria and heavy metals (Orru, Übner and Orru, 2011).

Mud, like water, has different healing (as well as beauty skin care) properties depending on where it is found in the world. Mud composition varies with the place of origin, e.g. according to the kind of rocks found in the region, the process of soil formation and the kind of flora and fauna of the region. Mud baths can commonly be found in areas where hot spring water can combine with volcanic ash. Mud baths come from many sources, e.g. lakes, sea water, hot springs and mud volcanoes. Mud contains important minerals which have positive effects on human health. Mud can absorb toxins from the human body, and therefore is very useful in preventing many diseases. It also helps in cooling and relaxing the body as it can hold moisture for a long time. It relaxes muscles and improves blood circulation. It maintains metabolism, rendering positive impact on digestion. It is useful in conditions of inflammation/swelling, relieves pain and is useful in condition of stiff joints. It is also a good hair conditioner and is beneficial for skin, therefore it is used in beauty as well as medical treatments.

Evidence for the health benefits of balneology

Global Spa Summit (GSS, 2011) research suggested that many people would be far more likely to visit spas if there were more medical evidence that treatments have health benefits. The Tourism Observatory for Health, Wellness and Spa (2013) wellness, spa and travel survey of 420 operators showed that spas which have natural healing resources are becoming one of the most popular facilities for international tourists and that therapies using natural resources with proven benefit (e.g. water, mud) are the most popular activities. Bogacheva (2012: 21) writes that most spa therapists in Russia have to have basic medical education, so are setting a good example for an evidence-based approach. More up-to-date evidence-based research is needed about the health benefits of thermal waters. As stated by Fioravanti et al. (2011: 6), 'This is the only way for Thermal Medicine to emerge from the restrictive environment of alternative or "miracle" therapies and free itself of the scepticism of many doctors and patients, gaining the scientific respect that it truly deserves'.

In terms of the evidence base for balneology, over the past 30 years several controlled research trials have tried to demonstrate the efficacy of these treatments, but they are not accepted in all parts of the world. Research is inconclusive or currently too limited to prove the medical benefits, but it seems to be beneficial for back pain as well as other ailments and afflictions according to numerous trials. For example, Fioravanti et al. (2011) note the (short-term) benefits of balneotherapy for rheumatic diseases, including immersion in mineral or thermal water or the application of mud. The aim of such therapies is to reduce pain, relieve muscle spasms and improve muscle strength and functional mobility. The following benefits may also occur:

- Mechanical effects: spa therapy may have beneficial effects on muscle tone, joint mobility and pain intensity (through immersion in hot springs).
- Thermal effects: hot stimuli (e.g. water, mud packs) may influence muscle tone and pain intensity, helping to reduce muscle spasm and to increase the pain threshold in nerve endings.
- Chemical effects: organic substances or minerals in water or mud, sometimes present in trace amounts, can be absorbed through the skin and then act at a systemic level (although evidence for this is limited).
- Immunological aspects: absorption through the skin of trace elements present in mineral water and mud packs may affect the immune system.
- Anti-inflammatory and chondroprotective aspects: reduced pain.

Karagülle and Karagülle (2015) suggest that balneotherapy is widely used by Europeans for musculoskeletal problems, especially chronic lower-back pain. A systematic review on eight trials assessing 649 patients with lower-back pain suggests short- and long-term benefits in pain reduction and improved function, but evidence is insufficient and inconclusive (Karagülle and Karagülle, 2015). An earlier meta-analysis on the effectiveness of balneotherapy and spa therapy for treating low-back pain was published ten years previously, aiming to assess the existing evidence based on very few – only five in total – published clinical trials. The analysis showed that, even though the data were scarce, the evidence was encouraging, suggesting that these modalities might be effective in pain reduction. However, balneotherapy was not included among almost 40 different therapies that were scrutinised for developing European treatment guidelines for lower-back pain or among the recommended six therapies in European guidelines for the management of chronic low-back pain (Burton et al., 2005).

Smith, Puczkó and Sziva (2015) discuss how thermal bath tourists are rarely, if ever, counted in medical tourism statistics. This is because only certain countries and medical systems recognise and believe in the healing properties of thermal waters. Gutenbrünner et al. (2010) describe why balneology, medical hydrology and climatology are not fully recognised as independent medical specialties at a global international level. First, there is a lack of internationally approved and accepted definitions. English has become the dominant scientific language but balneology developed mainly in countries where English is not the main language. There is a lack of scientific evidence for the medical benefits of balneology, although they suggest that it is no weaker than some other fields like physiotherapy or psychotherapy. Balneotherapy and climatotherapy is not used in all countries and some countries do not recognise any similar medical specialisation or qualification (e.g. UK, the Netherlands, Sweden and Denmark), since these countries have no or very limited relevant natural resources and traditions. Balneology is also increasingly being used for short-term wellness-oriented treatments rather than as prescribed medical therapies. This also undermines its acceptance as a health-enhancing therapy.

The changing nature of balneology

The growth of tourism has started to lead to tensions between the old notion of the medical bath and the new vacationer in search of pleasure (Naraindasa and Bastos, 2011). Smith et al. (2015) describe how many waters are used for multiple purposes simultaneously because many tourists are curious about traditions but have no specific or diagnosed health problems. They give the example of Hungary, where medical waters are used by local people and domestic tourists for healing purposes, whereas international tourists often use them for recreational reasons, visiting local heritage or experience seeking. Changes have also ensued as a result of the shifting priorities of governments in countries where balneology was traditionally state-subsidised (e.g. Central and Eastern Europe and the Balkan region).

In Central and Eastern Europe, until the collapse of state socialism or communism, thermal bath visits and therapies were seen as both a reward for workers as well as a way of increasing their productivity. However, in recent years, some spas are being re-invented as wellness rather than medical destinations. Naraindasa and Bastos (2011) give the example of Germany, which is the largest spa-going nation in Europe. The spa concept is captured in the three German terms of *Bad* (bath), *Therme* (a hot mineral water source or pool) and the *Kur* (cure or the regimen). Over time, the *Kur-Bad* or the *Therme* has slowly had to re-invent itself by expanding its therapeutic repertoire. This is partly due to a dwindling insurance fund and an ageing population (true for all of Europe). German therapeutic practice increasingly shows a blurring of the boundaries between medicine and (wellness) spas. The *Kur* industry even includes new therapeutic formats like Ayurveda and many healers are allowed to practise a range of therapies with minimal healing.

Speier (2011) undertook one year of ethnographic research on health tourism in Marianske Lazne, a Western Bohemian town in the Czech Republic with an abundant source of natural mineral springs. The term *lazne*, or spa, in the Czech Republic denotes a place that administers balneotherapy or treatments that use natural sources such as mineral waters, gas that comes from the earth, mud or peat bogs. In the Czech Republic, balneotherapy entails a complex range of therapeutic procedures involving mineral spring water, peloids (mud and peat) and natural gases. Mineral waters of various chemical components are professed to heal chronic diseases, some of which are diseases of the digestive tract; metabolic disorders; illnesses of the respiratory system; disorders of the locomotor system; and of the kidneys and urinary tract. Waters are the basis for the drinking cure, for which each patient drinks two cups before every meal. People visit Czech spas for an average of three weeks and undergo various treatments that are prescribed by the spa doctor.

Balneotherapy was authorised as legitimate medicine by the socialist regime and has remained a central branch of rehabilitative medicine in the Czech Republic today. Most illnesses that are indicated for balneotherapy are chronic. Traditional treatments entail four full regimented weeks of strict diet, exercise and fitness programmes, complex therapies such as hydrotherapy, gas injections, electrotherapy, inhalation and paraffin packs. Today there are approximately 30 hotels that offer treatment packages as well and new ones open annually. The majority of guests are between their 50s and their 80s. In addition to drinking cures, most patient tourists have two to three procedures a day, which last approximately 20–30 minutes each. According to the guests, procedures fall under the 'pleasant' or 'unpleasant' categories. There are pleasant procedures, such as massages, and unpleasant procedures like gas injections (98 per cent carbon dioxide) into pained areas such as the neck, the knees and the lower back.

Speier (2011) notes that there are problems of packages being shortened to two weeks with too many treatments being given in a short time, including anti-stress and beauty and not only medical procedures. It is apparent that the role of the doctor is changing and doctors are having a greater involvement in the business side of balneology. Master's-level courses in balneology at university are starting to focus more on managerial issues than medicine. Marketing directors and advertising executives are creating new spa packages for tourists that do not take into consideration indications or contraindications for certain procedures. While physicians recommend three to four weeks for an effective treatment, guests can now choose from a range of one- to two-week programmes such as 'relaxation' or 'beauty week' or 'anti-stress'. However, doctors claim that if you only visit the spa for one week, you feel worse. There is a palpable change from a public health system to a health tourism industry.

Lebe (2013) provides an overview of the changing nature of balneology in Slovenia. Slovenia has 20 thermal sources that are commercially used by thermal spas. Until 1990, 80 per cent of guests were coming automatically as direct referrals (insurance company contact). After that, thermal spas had to find the major part of their business on the free market. Between 1995 and 2010 all Slovenian spas added wellness programmes to their classical health spa (and thus medicine-based) offer. Consequently, new segments of guests joined the traditional convalescent ones; however, they did not always mix well. Today all Slovenian thermal spas have a segmented offer. The vast majority of guests (60–100 per cent) are now wellness guests. Pak and Altbauer (2014) estimate that 32 per cent of overnights in Slovenia in 2013 were taken in thermal spa resorts, 22 per cent of total international overnights and 47 per cent of total domestic overnights. The top five markets for spas come from Austria, Italy, Russia, Germany and Croatia. The average length of stay is about 3.98 days. Other countries in the Balkan region are discussed in the following section.

Balneology in the Balkan region

The Balkan Peninsula has an overwhelmingly large number of balneotherapy resources compared to most other countries in Europe (Stăncioiu, Botos and Pargaru, 2013). In the Balkan region, balneotherapy tends to include the treatment of diseases using thermal or mineral water and muds. Stăncioiu et al. (2013) give the example of Romanian balneotherapy resorts where specific diseases are treated using therapeutic use of mineral waters, hydrotherapy, application of therapeutic mud and gases, kinetotherapy, occupational and massage therapy, electrotherapy and respiratory therapy. Many of the balneotherapy treatments take place in spas or *banja* (in Slavonic languages). Karagülle (2013) suggests that a 'traditional Balkan spa' offers a combination between elements of balneology, climatology and environment. Stăncioiu et al. (2013) also suggest that an additional element for the future Balkan balneotherapy product could be gastronomy, especially the ingredients which are specific to the region.

Nearly all of the countries in the Balkans have mineral, thermal and healing waters, but they are under-used in most cases. There are also widespread problems of under-investment, lack of renovations, poor infrastructure, a need for product development and inadequate customer service. Bosnia and Herzegovina have hyper-thermal, thermo-mineral, calcic and sodic waters (Stăncioiu et al., 2013). The majority of spas are still mainly treatment and rehabilitation centres for domestic visitors. Felic (2013) suggests that most of the users of health tourism services are local, although the number of foreign tourists is growing. Although health tourism has been identified as one of the major opportunities for the development of the Bosnian economy, spas or *banja* accounted for only 5 per cent of the total overnights in Bosnia and Herzegovina in 2012, of which 14 per cent were domestic visitors.

Bulgaria has a long history of balneology and spa tourism, with over 600 mineral waters as well as curative gases, peloids and a favourable climate (Stăncioiu et al., 2013). InvestBulgaria Agency (2013) describes how Bulgaria ranks second to Iceland in terms of the number of mineral springs. However, only about 30 per cent of them are being used. There are around 65 balneological resorts, but there was a significant decline in the number of operating sanatoria after 2000 (Hall, Smith and Marciszewska, 2006).

In Croatia, although several coastal destinations offer spa and wellness hotels or resorts, most of the balneological thermal spas are in northern and eastern Croatia. Here, there is a need for private investment if the facilities are to be brought to a level which would be more desirable for international health (either wellness or medical) tourists.

Greece is one of the richest countries in the world in terms of thermal and mineral springs in more than 850 different geographical locations and many of these have therapeutic properties which have been known about since ancient times. However, Constantinides (2013) suggests that Greece has been one of the laggards in the health tourism sector and health tourism has declined in recent years (Euromonitor International, 2014a).

Macedonia is rich in geothermal waters with healing effects and there are around 64 springs with different water temperatures. However, Taleska, Gorin, Radevski and Dimitrovska (2015) suggest that, despite the rich resources, the health tourism potential of Macedonia has not been fully realised. This is partly because of their poor technical condition, inadequate and worn-out infrastructure, the scarcity of available accommodation, lack of financial resources and new investment opportunities. The spas are also not separated from the healthcare system and are not treated as tourist resorts, so although there are qualified medical personnel in the spas, there are few or no qualified tourism personnel. Taleska et al. (2015) suggest that the total international tourists who visited the spa resorts in Macedonia in 2014 was less than 1 per cent. The number of overnight stays by domestic tourists is around eight times bigger.

However, a National Strategy on Health Tourism Development 2012–2018 was launched and, according to Eurostat (cited by Kurir, 2015), revenue from health tourism, including those from the thermal baths in 2013, was significantly higher than in neighbouring countries (e.g. Serbia or Bosnia Herzegovina).

Riggins (2014) suggests that health tourism in Montenegro has increased by 20 per cent in the past five years, but mainly because of the medical tourism industry (e.g. dentistry, rheumatics, cardiac rehabilitation programmes). Romania has a long history of spa tourism which goes back to Roman times. It is estimated that there are around 70 natural spas providing treatments for many medical disorders. This includes thermal and mineral waters but also muds. However, the interest in spa resorts decreased dramatically after 1990 as it was no longer supported by local or central administration. Domestic tourists could not afford it and a research study in 2009 showed that only 3.5 per cent of tourists to Romanian spa resorts were foreigners. Therefore, there was a National Strategy of the Development of Spa Tourism in 2009 which emphasised the need for new planning, infrastructural improvements and investment (Dinu, Zbuchea and Cioacă, 2010).

Health tourism does not feature prominently in the online communication of Serbia, although there are over 1,000 cold and warm mineral water springs as well as natural mineral gases and medicinal mud. However, only around 5 per cent of these are used. There are over 53 thermal resorts as well as climatic health resorts with favourable climates and geographic locations. Wellness programmes have become more popular in Serbian spas in recent years (National Tourism Organisation of Serbia, 2015). Horwath (2013) estimated that Serbian baths and spas attract 347,000 visitors and generated two million guest nights with an average length of stay of 5.86 days. However, Berber, Gajić and Dordević (2010) suggest that Serbian spas are lacking quality, partly because there has been relatively little or no investment in the maintenance and construction of tourist infrastructure in spa towns. They note that only a very small percentage of foreign tourists go to Serbian spas.

Turkey is one of the seven main countries in the world in terms of thermal source richness, with almost 1,300 thermal springs throughout Anatolia; however, only a small percentage of these are used (GoTurkeyTourism, 2015). Euromonitor International (2014b) describes how in the previous two years the Turkish government introduced incentives to encourage growth in health and wellness tourism. These included issuing licences to a higher number of natural spas which attracted a high number of local and foreign tourists.

Case study: health tourism and balneology in Hungary

Hungary has a bathing culture that is over 2,000 years old, with many balneotherapeutic natural healing resources. Bottoni, Óvári, Záray and Caroli (2013: 770) state that:

> Hungary ranks among the countries that are richest in thermal springs: thermal waters are extremely abundant in this part of Europe and available in more than two thirds of the territory, thus making their use for balneotherapy widespread, easily accessible and increasingly important as a primary economic resource.

Bender et al. (2014) state that 1,300 springs have been registered and 800 of these are used for medical purposes. Other balneotherapy resources include five healing caves, five different types of peloid and mud and post-volcanic discharges of radon and carbon dioxide gases (mofettas).

(continued)

(continued)

Even though balneological research in Hungary began in the late nineteenth century, the results have not always been reported or accepted internationally. The majority of published papers focus on balneotherapy for musculoskeletal disorders. Bender et al. (2014) examined the evidence base for balneotherapy in Hungary, including 18 clinical trials. They concluded that thermal mineral water in Hungary alleviates pain caused by different musculoskeletal diseases, significantly reducing pain in degenerative joint and spinal disease, as well as osteoarthritis of the hand and knee, and that they also alleviate chronic low-back pain. However, they also acknowledge that 'only well-designed and implemented trials can prove or refute the efficacy of balneotherapy' (Bender et al., 2014: 321). Bottoni et al. (2013) concur with Bender et al. (2014) that effective advancement in balneotherapy is only possible if basic research is systematically undertaken on the curative potential of thermal spring waters in Hungary (and, indeed, elsewhere too).

In terms of health tourism, during the Socialist period (1945–1989) the focus in Hungary was predominantly on thermal medical tourism for domestic and intra-regional tourists. Besides tourism demand, thermal facilities (and day hospitals at such facilities) served the healthcare needs of the local population, too. After 1989, governments continued to support domestic thermal medical tourism in the form of holiday vouchers, but by the 2000s and after EU accession in 2004, policy started to focus more on surgical medical tourism (Smith et al., 2015). Hungary is often promoted as the 'Land of Spas' and Budapest (its capital city) as 'The City of Baths'. Jónás-Berki et al. (2015) refer to health tourism as the leading tourism product in Hungary. Priszinger and Formádi (2013) noted that, according to statistics, there are around 243 different spas in Hungary (that means that every 13th Hungarian settlement has some sort of spa); and every fifth room is in a medical or wellness hotel. Jónás-Berki et al. (2015) suggest that health tourism destinations tend to be highly concentrated spatially in certain settlements, even though thermal waters can be found in most of the country. Balneology-based tourism demand (based on natural healing resources) is largely determined by the composition of the waters; however, in the case of wellness tourism, competition is greater and it is harder to create unique facilities.

Jónás-Berki et al. (2015) researched the following health tourism destinations outside Budapest, all of which offer some form of balneotherapy: Bük, Egerszalók, Harkány, Hajdúszoboszló, Hévíz, Zalakaros, Gyula and Sárvár. They concluded that the foundation of health tourism in these settlements is the medicinal water; however, alongside medical hotels some wellness hotels and even aquaparks have also been developed. Settlements have to meet strict legal as well as health criteria to be awarded the designated health tourism destination status. Combined products are emerging, such as business, conferences and golf, to enhance competitiveness and potentially to attract new market segments. It remains to be seen what impact this may have on the balneological side of health tourism, but suggests a similar development to the Czech Republic, as discussed earlier.

The challenges for balneology

One of the biggest challenges for thermal baths in the future is likely to be the decline of government support for balneology for domestic and regional tourists. This is especially true of Central and Eastern Europe and Russian-speaking countries. Words like 'sanatorium' and 'rehabilitation' can also be off-putting (with many Western people associating the concept of sanatorium with mental health problems and rehabilitation with drug and alcohol addictions).

Thermal baths are often promoted as 'spas', causing confusion in the minds of foreign visitors who may then expect wellness products based on relaxation, leisure, pampering and beauty. Several other countries, such as China, Thailand, Australia, New Zealand, the USA, Argentina and Peru, have been looking at how they can use and develop hot spring or thermal water-based services. The market in Spain and Portugal has also been heavily affected by regulation and market changes. The traditional service provision at *balnearios* faces challenges, since younger segments do not seem to appreciate what old facilities can offer.

Probably the most critical situation is how to provide evidence for the beneficial effects of balneology. Different legislative measures as well as healthcare approaches limit the wider understanding or acceptance. The pharmaceutical industry applies and follows standardised clinical trial approaches and regulations. The fragmented balneological industry cannot follow similar processes. Thermal springs have different healing capacities and traditions. Themal bath operators have limited financial means to support clinical trials similar to that of the pharmaceutical industry. Individual operators of thermal springs would need to join forces both in terms of clinical trials as well as in communication to achieve better awareness, understanding and acceptance. Thermal bath operators frequently witness a lack of understanding from medical professionals, insurance policy providers and from the general public.

Medical schools' curricula rarely introduce what balneotherapy can do for patients (and for prevention). The lack of support from medical professionals in many countries limits how much interest balneotherapy services in another country can achieve. Thermal bath operators, therefore, would need to communicate both to doctors as well as to insurance companies. Insurers without sound clinical test results would not finance balneology treatments and they do not include such provision in their policies.

References

Bender, T., Bálint, G., Prohászka, Z., Géher, P. and Tefner, I. K. (2014) 'Evidence-based hydro- and balneotherapy in Hungary – a systematic review and meta-analysis', *International Journal of Biometeorology*, 58, 311–323.

Berber, N., Gajić, T. and Dordević, M. (2010) 'Management and development possibilities for spa tourism in Serbia', *Revista de Turism*, No. 9, file:///C:/Documents%20and%20Settings/ASUS/Dokumentumok/Downloads/89-278-1-SM.pdf (accessed 17 September 2015).

Boekstein, M. (2001) *The Role of Health in the Motivation to Visit Mineral Spa Resorts in the Western Cape*, Unpublished Master's dissertation, Cape Town, South Africa: University of the Western Cape.

Bogacheva, E. (2012) *Global Spa and Wellness Industry Briefing Papers 2012*, New York: Global Spa and Wellness Summit, pp. 21–22.

Bogdanov, I., Kircheva, K., Miteva, L. and Tsankov, N. (2012) 'Quality of life in patients undergoing combined climatotherapy and phototherapy', *Revista Medicala Romana*, Volume LIX, NR. 3, http://www.medica.ro/reviste_med/download/rmr/2012.3/RMR_Nr-3_2012_Art-16.pdf (accessed 20 March 2016).

Bottoni, P., Óvári, M., Záray, G. and Caroli, S. (2013) 'Characteristics of spring waters in Budapest: A short review', *Microchemical Journal*, 110, 770–774.

Burton, A. K., Balagué, F., Cardon, G., Eriksen H. R., Henrotin, Y., Lahad, A., Leclerc, A., Müller, G. and van der Beek, A. J. (2005) 'How to prevent low back pain', *Best Practice and Research in Clinical Rheumatology*, 19(4), 541–555.

Constantinides, C. (2013) 'Times are changing as Greece tries to become a major destinations', 29 November, *International Medical Travel Journal*, http://www.imtj.com/articles/times-are-changing-greece-tries-become-major-destination (accessed 15 September 2015).

Dinu, M., Zbuchea, A. and Cioacă, A. (2010) 'Health tourism in Romania: main features and trends', *Journal of Tourism Challenges and Trends*, 3(2), 9–34.

Erfurt-Cooper, P. and Cooper, M. (2009) *Health and Wellness Tourism: Spas and Hot Springs*, Clevedon, UK: Channel View.

Euromonitor International (2014a) *Health and Wellness Tourism in Greece*, http://www.euromonitor.com/health-and-wellness-in-greece/report (accessed 17 September 2015).

—— (2014b) *Health and Wellness Tourism in Turkey*, http://www.euromonitor.com/health-and-wellness-in-turkey/report (accessed 17 September 2015).

Felic, E. (2013) 'Health tourism opportunity for BiH', *Balkan Insight*, 30 July, http://www.balkaninside.com/health-tourism-opportunity-for-bih (accessed 17 September 2015).

Fioravanti, A., Cantarini, L., Guidelli, M. and Galeazzi, M. (2011) 'Mechanisms of action of spa therapies in rheumatic diseases: What scientific evidence is there?', *Rheumatology International*, 31, 1–8.

Global Spa Summit/GSS (2011) *Wellness Tourism and Medical Tourism: Where do Spas Fit?*, New York: Global Spa Summit.

Global Wellness Institute (2011) *Wellness Evidence*, http://www.wellnessevidence.com/wellnessevidence (accessed 15 April 2016).

Gomes, C., Carretero, M. I., Pozo, M., Maraver, F., Cantista, P., Armijo, F., Legido, J. L., Teixeira, F., Rautureau, M. and Delgado, M. (2013) 'Peloids and pelotherapy: Historical evolution, classification and glossary', *Applied Clay Science*, 75–76, 28–38.

GoTurkeyTourism (2015) *Thermal Springs in Turkey*, http://www.allaboutturkey.com/spa.htm (accessed 17 September 2015).

Gutenbrunner, C., Bender, T., Cantista, P. and Karagülle, Z. (2010) 'A proposal for a worldwide definition of health resort medicine, balneology, medical hydrology and climatology', *International Journal of Biometeorology*, 54, 495–507.

Hall, D. R., Smith, M. K. and Marciszewska, B. (2006) *Tourism in the New Europe: The Challenges and Opportunities of EU Enlargement*, Wallingford, UK: CABI.

Horwath (2013) *CrossSpa Study on Joint Potential of Health and Wellness Tourism Development in the Cross-border Area (Sarajevo Macro Region and Tourism Region of Western Serbia)*, Belgrade, Serbia: Horwath.

InvestBulgaria Agency (2013) 'Healthcare and medical tourism in Bulgaria', *European Identity Politics? Southeast European and Black Sea Studies*, 4(3), September, 399–418.

ISPA (2016) *Spa 101*, http://experienceispa.com/resources/spa-goers (accessed 5 May 2016).

IUOTO (1973) *Health Tourism*, Geneva, Switzerland: United Nations.

Jónás-Berki, M., Csapo, J., Palfi, A. and Aubert, A. (2015) 'A market and spatial perspective of health tourism destinations: The Hungarian experience', *International Journal of Tourism Research*, 17, 602–612.

Karagülle, M. Z. (2006) *Is Balneotherapy More Effective Than Hydrotherapy?* Presentation given at IV Turkish-Hungarian Balneological Meeting, 18–22 January, Balçova, Turkey.

—— (2013) 'Wellness at traditional Balkan spas: Innovation or authenticity?', Serbia: 3rd Balkan Spa Summit.

Karagülle, M. and Karagülle, M. Z. (2015) 'Effectiveness of balneotherapy and spa therapy for the treatment of chronic low back pain: A review on latest evidence', *Clinical Rheumatology*, 34, 207–214.

Kurir (2015) *Macedonia First in the Region for Health Tourism, 26 December*, http://kurir.mk/en/?p=40654 (accessed 15 September 2015).

Lebe, S. S. (2013) 'Wellness tourism development in Slovenia in the last two decades', in M. K. Smith and L. Puczkó (eds) *Health, Tourism and Hospitality: Spas, Wellness and Medical Travel*, London: Routledge, pp. 315–319.

Mooventhan, A. and Nivethitha, L. (2014) 'Scientific evidence-based effects of hydrotherapy on various systems of the body', *North American Journal of Medical Sciences*, 6(5), 199–209.

Naraindasa, H. and Bastos, C. (2011) 'Healing holidays? Itinerant patients, therapeutic locales and the quest for health', *Anthropology and Medicine*, 18(1), 1–6.

National Tourism Organisation of Serbia (2015) *Spas and Health Resorts*, http://www.serbia.travel/destinations/spas-and-health-resorts (accessed 17 September 2015).

Orru, M., Übner, M. and Orru, H. (2011) 'Chemical properties of peat in three peatlands with balneological potential in Estonia', *Estonian Journal of Earth Sciences*, 60(1), 43–49.

Pak, M. and Altbauer, I. (2014) 'Strategy for development and marketing of Slovenian spas', *SPACE*, October 24.

Priszinger, K. and Formádi, K. (2013) 'Comparative analysis of health tourism products and online communication of selected Hungarian spas and hotels', in M. K. Smith and L. Puczkó (eds) *Health, Tourism and Hospitality: Spas, Wellness and Medical Travel*, London: Routledge, pp. 285–290.

Riggins, N. (2014) 'Montenegro's tourism industry turns a corner', *Business Destinations*, September 17, http://www.businessdestinations.com/acte/montenegros-tourism-industry-turns-a-corner (accessed 16 September 2015).

Riyaz, N. and Riyaz Arakkal, F. (2011) 'Spa therapy in dermatology', *Indian Journal of Dermatology, Venereology and Leprology*, 77(2), 128–133.

Smith, M. K., Puczkó, L. and Sziva, I. (2015) 'Putting the thermal back into medical tourism', in N. Lunt, D. Horsfall and J. Hanefeld (eds) *Handbook on Medical Tourism and Patient Mobility*, Cheltenham, UK: Edward Elgar Publishing, pp. 393–402.

Speier, A. R. (2011) 'Health tourism in a Czech health spa', *Anthropology and Medicine*, 18(1), 55–66.

Stăncioiu, A., Botos, A. and Pargaru, I. (2013) 'The Balkan balneotherapy product – an approach from the destination marketing perspective', *Theoretical and Applied Economics*, XX, 10(587), 5–22.

Taleska, M., Gorin, S., Radevski, R. and Dimitrovska, O. (2015) 'Assessment of the conditions for the development of spa tourism in the Republic of Macedonia', http://geobalcanica.org/proceedings/2015/GBP.2015.62.pdf (accessed 1 September 2015).

Tourism Observatory for Health, Wellness and Spa/TOHWS (2013) *Global Wellness and Spa Tourism Monitor 2012–2013*, Budapest, Hungary: TOHWS.

Tukamusaba, E. (2013) 'Hot springs in Uganda', in M. K. Smith and L. Puczkó (eds) *Health, Tourism and Hospitality: Spas, Wellness and Medical Travel*, London: Routledge, p. 66.

Varga, C. (2012) 'Balneoprevention: New approaches', *International Journal of Biometeorology*, 56, 195–197.

Part VII

Health destination development and management

This part analyses the ways in which health destinations are being developed and managed. Telle Tuominen, Susanna Saari and Daniel Binder propose a model which incorporates multi-actor supply networks and emphasises the importance of strategic and long-term visioning and planning (Chapter 23). It is recognised that there are different types and levels of cooperative relationships, but that strong leadership, seamless service chains, as well as shared vision in public/private and local partnerships can be the keys to success.

Henna Konu and Melanie Kay Smith focus in Chapter 24 on collaboration, which is defined in some health and tourism destination models as being the first dimension. This can be particularly challenging across different regions when involving numerous countries. The major challenge comes from implementation, as well as limitations of time and finances, inadequate leadership, cultural and linguistic differences, variable levels of interest and commitment, mistrust and too much focus on competition rather than collaboration or 'coopetition'.

Georg Christian Steckenbauer, Stephanie Tischler, Arnulf Hartl and Christina Pichler show how evidence-based health tourism products and services can be used in health tourism destination development (Chapter 25). A combination of quality (based on regulation) and authenticity (based on evidence) is necessary to ensure the success of health tourism destinations, especially those that wish to convince tourists that they will experience measurable health benefits.

Sarah Rawlinson and Peter Wiltshier give an example of the Peak District as a wellness destination, showing how destinations can be rejuvenated or developed through product differentiation and diversification (Chapter 26). This can mean drawing on a combination of natural assets such as thermal waters, landscape, historic traditions and cultural heritage to create attractive visitor services.

All of the chapters in this part emphasise the need to collaborate and to establish partnerships across geographical and sectoral scales, to enhance destination competitiveness through the development of new products or the re-inforcement of old ones using research or more creative approaches to branding and marketing. Sustainability is also noted as an essential element in all forms of health tourism development.

23

Enhancing the competitiveness of a wellness tourism destination by coordinating the multiple actor collaboration

Telle Tuominen, Susanna Saari and Daniel Binder

Introduction

Tourism destinations compete against each other in order to attract visitors in a globalised market place. The aim of this chapter is to discuss the role of stakeholder coordination and collaboration in order to enhance the competitiveness of a wellness destination. According to the literature, controversy exists in, for example, how destination management and destination development are defined and who are or should be the actors involved at destination level. The main focus of the chapter will be to provide an overview of the WelDest model created by Saari and Tuominen during the WelDest project[1] (Dvorak, Saari and Tuominen, 2014: 27). The model incorporates the endowed resources and tourism superstructure that create the comparative advantage of a destination specialised in contributing to the health and wellbeing of tourists and residents alike, but also the role of successful management and development of these resources and structures, which may result in competitive advantage. However, the main emphasis in this chapter will be in the activities and actors needed in coordinated collaboration aiming at enhancing the destination competitiveness. Also the similarities and differences between this model and some other destination competitiveness models are discussed in more detail from this point of view.

Literature review

Entire countries, regions, cities, communities and even multinational areas are examples of destinations on different scales. Destinations marketing themselves as wellness destinations can be found on any scale (Voigt and Pforr, 2014: 9). Because of the complexity and inter-related nature of a tourism destination it must be analysed as a composite entity (Fyall, Garrod and Wang, 2012: 11). Cooper (2012: 32) defines destinations as 'loosely bounded networks of organisations that deliver the tourism experience', whereas Prideaux (2009: 8) has a more detailed approach, when he characterises destinations as 'complicated structures built from a fusion of natural resources, the intellectual capacity of its residents, investors, the workforce, political structures, governance arrangements, residents and the visitors it receives'.

Defining wellness destination

Attempts to define a health or a wellness destination are thus far scanty. Cassens (2013: 147) briefly states that if the brand created by the destination and the image the customers have about it are characterised by contributions to health, then it is a health tourism destination. Although the definitions for the core terms and classifications of the services related to health, wellness and wellbeing tourism vary in different languages and cultures, health tourism is mostly seen as an umbrella term and wellness tourism as a sub-term (Dvorak et al., 2014: 19–20). We propose the following definition: A wellness destination is a multi-actor supply network managed and marketed as a unit, which has a strong image as a destination offering services for body, mind and soul as well as special knowledge, facilities and natural resources in order to prevent disease, improve health and enhance the quality of life.

Destination management and destination development

According to Morrison (2013: 5), the concept destination management encompasses coordination and integrated management of the so-called destination mix, which consists of infrastructure, facilities, transportation, hospitality services, attractions, events, etc. He considers the term destination management also to involve strategic and long-term visioning and planning. Straightforwardly, he states that destination management is accomplished through destination management organisations (DMOs). Similarly, the rather normative and descriptive Practical Guide to Destination Management by the United Nations World Tourism Organization (UNWTO) notes that destination management covers not only the traditional role to market the destination but also to lead the strategic development of the destination (UNWTO, 2007: 2). Ritchie and Crouch (2003: 147) have a different approach, in which they emphasise the distinction between destination policy, planning and development as an intellectual visioning process linked to macro-level. According to them, destination management is the realisation of this vision on a daily basis at micro-level.

Inter-organisational collaboration in tourism destinations

Researchers paid attention to cooperation among stakeholders at destination level in the 1990s. Selin and Chavez presented their evolutionary model of tourism partnerships in 1995 based on empirical research. The term stakeholders includes organisations, groups and individuals having a direct or indirect interest in the management of a tourism destination: tourists, hospitality and tourism organisations, community and environment groups as well as multiple governance organisations at different levels (Morrison, 2013: 23).

Beritelli (2011: 613) as well as Fyall et al. (2012: 12–16) elaborate different theories explaining relationships and inter-organisational cooperation. Resource-based theories can be applied when the actors are interested in cooperation in order to gain improved access to common resources like beaches, parks or other public goods or to save costs through cooperation in procurements or marketing. Destination learning and competition between destinations instead of competition between tourism companies are emphasised in relationship-based theories. Politics-based theories highlight consensus-building practices creating social, intellectual and political capital; in other words, trust, flow of information, mutual understanding of shared challenges, joint solutions and authority. In addition, process-based theories (e.g. how collaboration evolves or declines) as well as complexity theories (how organisations try to adapt to the changing environments) enlighten the motivation for collaborative behaviour.

There are several terms used for inter-organisational relationships, e.g. the terms cooperation, collaboration and partnerships are often used as synonyms. However, Wang and Krakover (2008: 131) make a difference between four cooperative relationship types with various degrees of formalisation, integration and structural complexity: affiliation (loose, informal connections), coordination (aligning self-interests with others' interests), collaboration (joint efforts to promote joint strategies) and, at the highest level, the strategic networks (shared vision as well as strategy, a system approach to destination success). Formal, contract-based cooperation is typical in case of e.g. economic interdependencies or common institutional resources. Informal, relation-based cooperation is characterised by mutual trust, personal commitment and inter-relationships and can address a range of benefits (Beritelli, 2011: 613).

According to Fyall et al. (2012: 11), destination collaboration can be analysed along two dimensions:

1   Does the DMO facilitate the collaboration (mediated intra-destination collaboration) or is it independent of a DMO (organic collaboration)?
2   Does the collaboration take place within a destination or between destinations?

Highlighting interdependencies among stakeholders and intense communication can be used as a means to induce collaborative behaviour. The empirical research of Beritelli brought out that connections between persons explain collaborative behaviour better than connections on an organisational level (Beritelli, 2011: 623–624). Voigt and Laing refer to case studies showing the importance of strong leadership for stakeholder collaboration and innovation (Voigt and Laing, 2014: 66).

Different funding and legal forms of the DMO (e.g. publicly funded government agencies, publicly–privately funded companies, non-profit organisations like trade associations) influence the power, roles and functions the coordinating destination organisation can have in destination management and strategic development (Wang, 2011: 7–8). Volgger and Pechlaner (2014: 72) found out that high networking capability of a DMO increases its power and acceptance within a destination, which in turn had positive correlation with perceived destination success. Coordinated destination-level cooperation does not exclude organic collaboration between individual actors or sector-specific collaboration (e.g. hotel associations) because of its more simple and short-term effective character (Fyall et al., 2012: 22–23).

Haugland, Ness, Grönseth and Aarstad (2011: 280), in their framework for tourism destination development, stress the overall destination strategy, coordination at the destination level, integration of actor-level resources and competencies as well as capabilities to build services across individual actors and communicate the destination product through a brand shared by the actors. They additionally highlight the role of the so-called bridge ties between destinations as a source of innovation and imitation. Jamal and Jamrozy (2006: 165, 171–172), in their integrated destination management framework, emphasise a systems view of destination management: the role of the DMO is mostly to integrate a variety of formal and informal processes and structures responsible for destination planning, marketing and management. National health, wellness or other related tourism strategies or policies may induce cooperation between the wellness destination and respective authorities. In many countries also voluntary organisations like branch associations guide with certifications the development of the destinations and businesses there (Smith and Puczkó, 2009: 178).

Destination competitiveness

Tourism destinations face growing competition in the global marketplace (Voigt and Pforr, 2014: 8). Contrary to corporation competitiveness, collaboration between destination actors seems to be a necessary function for destination competitiveness (Fyall et al., 2012: 10). Competitiveness is a complex concept, because many factors in the internal as well as external environment of the destination seem to affect it (Dwyer and Kim, 2003: 373). According to Ritchie and Crouch (2011: 327), a competitive destination is able:

> to increase tourism expenditure, to increasingly attract visitors while providing them with satisfying, memorable experiences and to do so in a profitable way, while enhancing the wellbeing of destination residents and preserving the natural capital of the destination for future generations.

Hassan (2000: 243) introduced in addition to partnerships between private companies and public organisations also the need for cooperation with organisations like citizen groups. In long-term competitiveness a key question is if the destination has mechanisms to identify changes in demand. This presumes continual market research as well as re-evaluation of the destination supply (Prideaux, Berbigier and Thompson, 2014: 45–47).

A detailed discussion of existing models for tourism destination competitiveness falls outside the scope of this chapter. These models are explained only from the destination management and development point of view focusing on the coordination of stakeholder collaboration. Probably the most quoted generic model of destination competitiveness, the Conceptual Model of Destination Competitiveness of Ritchie and Crouch (2003: 63), identifies 36 destination competitiveness attributes clustered under the following five main groups: (1) supporting factors and resources; (2) core resources and attractions; (3) destination management; (4) destination policy, planning and development; and (5) qualifying and amplifying determinants. In the model, Ritchie and Crouch (2003: 73, 105) acknowledge a DMO as 'a somewhat recent conceptualisation of the organization function for destination management' as well as the existence of other players like industry associations, government departments and different publics involved in destination management. However, terms like destination leadership, teamwork and cooperation are mentioned only in passing without any explanations (Ritchie and Crouch, 2003: 70, 74).

Another general model, the Integrated Model of Destination Competitiveness of Dwyer and Kim (2003: 378, 386–388), contains many headings and variables identified by Ritchie and Crouch, but emphasises the multilevel character of destination management ranging from decisions and policies from the local and regional to the national and even to the international level. It acknowledges also the need for participatory planning, consensus building, conflict resolution and joint vision as well as a DMO with the primary function of coordinating the collaboration between many public and private organisations.

Besides the WelDest model, to be presented later in this chapter, there are two other models dealing with the competitiveness of wellness destinations: the Model of Sustainable Wellness Destination of Sheldon and Park (2009: 108), which is based on the previously mentioned model of Ritchie and Crouch, and the Framework of Wellness Tourism Destination Competitiveness, of Voigt and Pforr (2014: 17, 301–302), which synthesises the findings of several studies, including those of Ritchie and Crouch and Sheldon and Park. In their model Sheldon and Park (2009: 110–111) highlight collaborative policy formulation and planning between public tourism actors, private wellness service providers and host communities as well as pooling resources in order to manage, develop and monitor the specific wellness assets and quality of the destination supply. Similarly to Sheldon and Park, Voigt and Pforr (2014: 303) stress collaboration as well as resource and competence sharing between the DMO, other private and public stakeholders and the community. They also recognise the significant role of different governmental bodies at different levels as facilitators of wellness tourism. From the wellness destination competitiveness point of view, the additional contribution of the models by Sheldon and Park and Voigt and Pforr is in the recognition of specific wellness resources. Sheldon and Park (2009: 108) mention knowledge of healing practices and specific healing, therapeutic and wellness resources, whereas Voigt and Pforr (2014: 292–295) list the core resources and competencies of a wellness destination as follows: specific natural and cultural, historical and spiritual resources for body, mind and soul, complementary and alternative medicine offerings, community mind set and wellness-related lifestyle, human resources and specific wellness competencies, wellness-specific superstructure and events as well as crossover of wellness with other offerings.

The concept of comparative advantage relates to a range of physical, intellectual, financial and political resources (in a wellness destination, e.g. thermal waters, trained staff giving treatments, political decision making in land use planning for recreational use) as a basis for the destination supply. The concept of competitive advantage describes how effectively, efficiently and value adding these resources are used when creating a destination experience (Prideaux et al., 2014: 47–48). As collaboration is increasingly being identified as a valuable strategy for destinations, also the term collaborative advantage is used (Fyall et al., 2012: 23). Destination competitiveness as such is not the definitive aim, but more an intermediate goal in order to contribute to local, regional or national prosperity (Dwyer and Kim, 2003: 377).

One important element in destination competitiveness is the destination brand. The core in destination branding is to build an appealing identity that potential customers identify and which differentiates the destination from its competitors. This unique destination identity is the essence of positioning the destination (Qu, Kim and Im, 2011: 466). Many researchers see destination brand management as a multi-stakeholder collaborative decision-making process, where the often contrasting interests of different stakeholders have to be aligned under a consistent destination brand. Cox, Gyrd-Jones and Gardiner (2014: 85–86, 93) call the destination brand a network brand. There is empirical evidence that informal communication and bottom-up approach lead to better commitment of stakeholders to the brand essence than directive top-down leadership.

A framework for developing a health and wellbeing tourism destination

The WelDest framework model (Figure 23.1) for understanding and developing a health and wellbeing tourism destination was created as a result of a European Commission-funded research project during 2012–2014.[2] The model tries to answer two questions: (1) How can a tourism destination be developed towards becoming a more holistic, sustainable and competitive destination specialised in health and wellbeing? and (2) What are the key service supply, resources, staff competencies and elements of health and wellbeing appreciated by both tourists and locals in the destination?

Looking at the model, the outermost circle represents the destination's endowed resources – above all, nature, but also culture, authenticity and reputation are appreciated by customers. The key question is understanding how to manage and develop these resources that create the basis for destination competitiveness. There are multiple actors that offer their services at destination level, both private and public. According to research, consumers

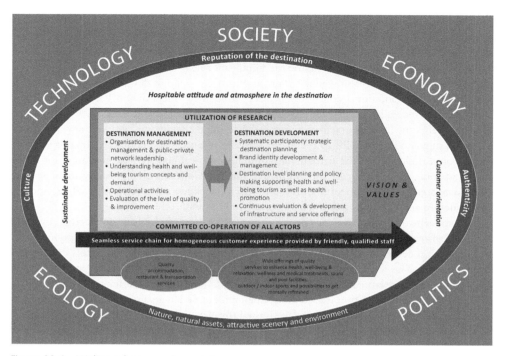

Figure 23.1 WelDest framework model.

Source: Dvorak, Saari and Tuominen (2014: 27).

are looking to the destination for relaxation, for mental refreshment and for an escape from everyday pressures. When choosing a wellness destination, visitors highly value a modern, holistic and widely specialised supply of services and facilities. What can be considered as standard tourism services are extremely important, but not usually included among the main reasons that consumers give for choosing a destination, which is why they are considered in this model as supporting tourism services.

Another management challenge at destination level is how to offer customers a seamless service chain. The guests often use services and infrastructure offered by several companies or organisations, yet expect a homogeneous overall wellness tourism experience. To answer this expectation involves a lot of scheduling, planning, coordination and collaboration. From the managerial perspective the answer is to strengthen destination-level thinking among the companies and service providers. The collaboratively created vision and values of the destination should be the driving force in all actions taken. Finally, sustainable development, creating a hospitable attitude and atmosphere and customer orientation should guide both destination and company-level actions as indicated in the light-coloured area outside the dynamic management and development arrow.

Destination management process

In the model, destination management and destination development are linked. The reason for this is the need for committed cooperation of all actors and especially a flow of information between those responsible for destination planning, development and management and service offerings. As a stakeholder said: 'developing local partnerships is the key to any future success'.

The model presents four dimensions of destination management. The first point is organisation of destination management and public–private network leadership. To begin with, a coordinating tourism body (e.g. a DMO, association or similar) is needed. How it is organised may vary, but its main role is to coordinate collaborative activities and to communicate between private and public stakeholders of the destination. This tourism body must play the role of the network leader in the management of the destination. The second management dimension is understanding health and wellbeing tourism concepts and demand in order to be successful in differentiation, targeting and destination product development. The third dimension includes operational activities such as managing and evaluating joint sales and marketing activities, visitor services management, destination product development and community relations. Finally the evaluation of the level of overall service quality and its improvement form the fourth dimension of destination-level management.

Destination development process

There are similarly four dimensions of destination development. The first point is systematic, participatory strategic destination planning. The key for success is the commitment and cooperation from private and public actors at destination level or 'a high level of public and private-sector partnership with a shared vision', as an interviewee put it. The planning process needs to have an owner who leads the work. However, organisations and individuals with an interest in the development of the destination could form a 'stakeholder working group', which acts as a destination-wide collaborative structure. This group can consist of organisations and individuals who have interests in the development of the destination and wish to be involved. The strategic planning activities need to be supported, for example, with systematic collection and utilisation of destination-level data or other relevant market analysis, monitoring of trends, participating actively in various horizontal and vertical networks and observing the changes in the macro environment.

The second dimension is brand identity development and management. The foundation of the destination tourism strategy is differentiation, positioning and destination branding with a bottom-up approach. All actors, including the community residents, should support the brand essence. A joint strategy for communicating the brand identity to external audiences is also needed. Furthermore the communicated brand needs to correspond with the service delivery systems, physical settings and their quality level. However, recent developments and the extensive use of social media have changed branding and marketing. The customers are now co-creators of the destination brand and the aim should be to get them to become ambassadors of it. According to the interview, one challenge the destinations are facing is how the brand is being developed: 'They all [companies] all develop their own businesses and that has many challenges. Of course the companies network but perhaps the development should be that big entities are done together instead of alone'.

The third dimension in development functions is destination-level planning and policy making to support health and wellbeing tourism as well as health promotion. It is very important that upper-level strategies, policies, plans and decisions are taken into consideration when developing the destination in the long run and in a sustainable manner. In addition to internal and external expertise it is advisable to involve policy makers and locals in the decision-making process when development questions are deliberated: 'It is important to develop agreement for tourism development with local residents. Advice on wise sustainable growth needs a bottom-up approach and local mechanisms to ensure the views of locals are considered.'

Finally, the fourth dimension is continuous evaluation and the development of infrastructure and service offerings. In the discussion the many forms of development were listed as follows:

'we attend exhibitions, conferences, networking events and read trade publications. We also discuss new product development with other companies. Business owners travel abroad for ideas regarding key and emerging trends'. From the managerial perspective one of the key issues is the monitoring of the implementation of strategic priorities. A clear outline of responsibilities is also needed, as well as a set of performance indicators and a time frame for the activities. A strategy also needs regular updates as a part of well-planned destination development process. Finally, the seeking of funding (private, public or a mix of these) for various development activities may also be required.

All these factors that make up the framework of a destination are of course interconnected and interdependent and, therefore, it is important to understand the significance of each of the components.

Finally, it is also important to remember that the destination does not exist in a vacuum. It has to react to advancements of other destinations, but there are also many other external factors at the macro level that must be monitored. There exists bilateral interaction of the health and wellbeing destination with its local/regional/national/international environment, dominated by many types of societal, economic, political, ecological and technological aspects.

Discussion

The starting points and applicability of different destination competitiveness models presented in this chapter are slightly different. The WelDest model is based on empirical research involving different types of stakeholders like hospitality and health service providers, DMO managers, regional developers and policy makers as well as consumers. The model and the supporting destination self-assessment tool[3] are meant to help the destinations in becoming a more holistic, sustainable and competitive destination specialised in health, wellness and wellbeing. During the research project the term health and wellbeing destination was used as an umbrella term covering the broad variety of offerings, from the reactive medical tourism services to the proactive wellness services. Despite this, we consider the model applicable for the development of wellness destinations as wellness tourism is considered as a sub-category of health and wellbeing tourism.

The tourism destination competitiveness models and indicator systems of Ritchie and Crouch (2003: xiii) as well as of Dwyer and Kim (2003: 369) were aimed to enable comparisons especially between tourism countries as they were based partly on earlier generic index systems measuring competitiveness of countries rather than destinations. As challenges with objectively measurable and subjective attributes of competitiveness have been recognised earlier (Dwyer and Kim, 2003: 406), the model presented as well as the self-assessment tool with its statements is designed to be used more as a communication tool between the stakeholders when analysing the present situation and development needs in the destination – not for measuring the relative position of the destination compared to competing destinations.

As several studies have indicated that the personal connections contribute to collaboration, we foresee the WelDest model to be most applicable in local and regional destinations where it is possible for the DMO to identify the different stakeholders and bring them together to focus on a shared vision and goals. The model of Dwyer and Kim (2003) supports our findings to a greater extent than that of Ritchie and Crouch (2003). The former emphasises the need for participatory planning, cooperation of private and public organisations on different governance levels, coordination as primary function of the DMO as well as demand conditions like level of destination awareness and customer preferences as important determinants of destination competitiveness (Dwyer and Kim, 2003: 377, 386). The explanation of the WelDest model also contains some points of resemblance with the integrated destination management model of

Jamal and Jamrozy (2006: 165) which, besides formal collaborative structures, also highlights the need for bridging organisations and open systems.

In our opinion the form of the model itself better illustrates the need to act and to react to the constantly changing internal and external environment of the destination rather than the linear form of the models of Ritchie and Crouch or Sheldon and Park. In the model the destination and its actors are imbedded in a wider macro environment. The big arrow in Figure 23.1 illustrates not only the importance but also the continuity of destination management and development as a competitiveness factor. The need for leadership and coordination of multi-level cooperation in management, planning and development is expressed with the two-way arrow between destination management and development and with the direction towards the shared vision and values. With its collaborative, multilevel approach the model supports the idea of collaborative destination governance of Voigt and Pforr (2014: 303). In other words, the DMO should be the active nexus and lobbyist in the collaborative structure and fill in the gaps between different actors involved in destination management, planning and policy making, e.g. regarding land use planning, traffic planning and environmental protection.

Our findings coincide with the wellness destination specific model of Voigt and Pforr (2014) in many ways. Both models acknowledge that the wellness supply and facilities should be developed not only for tourists, but also for the locals. We highlight the need for specific services enhancing health, wellbeing and relaxation, whereas Voigt's and Pforr's perspective is in the outcome, in other words, the health benefits created. The WelDest model and the conceptual models of Sheldon and Park or Voigt and Pforr highlight quite different fields of know-how typical for both hospitality and tourism business and destination management as well as the expertise needed in developing and delivering evidence-based health and wellness services for body, mind and soul. In our opinion cross-sectoral communication and learning between e.g. health tourism and marketing professionals can contribute to a competitive advantage for the destination. An example could be that the employees connected to sales and marketing should be able to answer questions regarding e.g. health benefits of various treatments. Similarly, destination branding is seen as a collaborative process in the model. The aim is to align the actors, their employees and also the locals to deliver a consistent brand experience.

How does the model turn into managerial reality? It seems evident that destination-level networking is one of the key issues. From the managerial perspective one of the tasks of a DMO is to recognise the actors needed in the network and to lead them. The role of a DMO is to bring together the many self-interested players. A cohesive inter-organisational supply network is necessary for seamless delivery of integrated tourism experiences. A destination network with strong ties between the actors is also important to manage the development and rejuvenation of the destination supply efficiently in times of change.

One cannot emphasise enough the importance of mutual trust and communication as full potential of collaboration is rarely tapped, e.g. because of imbalances of power, lack of trust or commitment. It is also due to cross-sectoral and co-producing characteristics of tourism that the different tourism actors have to improve their collaboration skills and define their role in the destination network.

There is also the need to encourage collective learning (e.g. on subjects like health, tourism and sustainability) at the destination level. Knowledge exchange and intensive information sharing among stakeholders are needed, so that those responsible for destination promotion, selling the services or making political decisions have adequate knowledge and deeper understanding of tourism business, health promotion and wellness services.

The real challenges posed are the ways of funding, legitimacy issues and governance structures that vary from one country to another. However, we strongly recommend the deliberations on how the DMO could be raised into a real destination leadership role instead of dealing only with the more traditional matters of destination promotion and visitor services management.

Sometimes the destination simply does not have the critical mass of actors to support the development as a network led by a DMO. Some case studies challenge the prevailing DMO-dominated approach to destination collaboration and competitiveness and emphasise the role of innovative entrepreneurs instead (Komppula, 2014; Aarstad, Ness and Haugland, 2015: 359). In the comparative case study presented in this chapter we introduce one such destination. The Finnish Vierumäki is predominantly run and developed by a single company acting as a DMO whereas at the Austrian Thermenland Steiermark the organisation's main role is multi municipality/regional marketing evolving into a deeper destination management point of view.

What then are the future directions for destination management? Looking round, the current role seems to be tourism marketing or brand managers, where DMOs are trying to build a favourable yet differentiated image to attract potential visitors. The role that follows could be that of tourism destination managers (DMO as a real decision maker), where a direct role in the planning, marketing and management of the destination has grown. Finally the pioneer future role could be to become a community brand manager, where the major role is the participation in community decision making and building a favourable image of the destination as a whole.

Putting aside the limitations of the small sample size at WelDest, we foresee that the application of the WelDest model or the self-assessment tool in wellness destination case studies could increase the validity of the model. One way of doing this could be to try to find the key factors for successful collaboration and leadership, e.g. relating structures and relationships to their effects on wellness destination coordination, collaboration and competitiveness. Also horizontal collaboration across administrative borders as well as vertical collaboration of actors on local, regional, national and international levels could be under scrutiny.

Case study: Vierumäki and Thermenland Steiermark

The aim of this comparative case study is to discuss the management and collaboration structures of two tourism destinations, namely Vierumäki in Finland and Thermenland Steiermark in Austria.

Vierumäki is a Finnish destination specialised in indoor and outdoor sports, fitness and wellness services with about 2,800 guest beds. It is located in a rural area with forests and lakes in the town of Heinola, South Finland. Vierumäki Corporation is the leading actor of the destination and has assumed a leadership role typical of a DMO.

Thermenland Styria is located in the eastern part of Austria and markets six Styrian thermal baths: Bad Radkersburg, Bad Gleichenberg, Loipersdorf, Bad Blumau, Bad Waltersdorf and Sebersdorf. The destination itself is well known for its thermal water, regional food and wine, as well as the more than 3,000-km-long bike routes which connect the main hotspots in the area. During 2013, about two million overnights were generated in the 15,200 guest beds of the area and about 6,000 people are directly working in the field of tourism in Thermenland Styria.

Background

Vierumäki has been known for its Sport Institute of Finland since the 1920s. The Sport Institute of Finland is a national coaching and training centre for sports and physical education. It operates under the auspices of the Finnish Ministry of Education and Culture and is run by an entity created to support the activities, called Suomen Urheiluopiston Kannatusosakeyhtiö.

Vierumäki Country Club was founded in the 1970s and its subsidiaries offer fitness, wellness and golf services, health-related tests, occupational health services as well as a variety of food, accommodation, conference and facilities services. The entirety forms what is called Vierumäki Corporation. It has been a trailblazer for other tourism companies in many aspects; for example, Vierumäki has had the ISO 14001 certification for environmental management since 2001. The corporation is owned by several foundations and other organisations linked to sports and by an employment pension insurance company. The size and supply of other companies in Vierumäki vary from Scandic Vierumäki Hotel to an equestrian company or from an ecological adventure park in the forest to a company offering 'smoke sauna' experiences.

Thermenland Styria is managed as a registered association and the ownership is split between a limited company Thermenland Süd and Oststeiermark Marketing (74 per cent) and Tourismusregionalverband Oststeiermark (26 per cent). The limited company employs the staff of Thermenland Styria and runs the operational management of Thermenland Styria. Strategy development and main management decisions are made by the board of the registered association Thermenland Styria. The board consists of a chairman and members who represent the six thermal baths and the biggest tourism associations in the whole region of Thermenland Styria, which is also geographically defined. The marketing activities are focussed on Austria, Germany, Italy and Switzerland.

Coordination of collaboration

Customer orientation and collaboration at destination and region level are the guiding values in Vierumäki. The visitor finds all offerings and online services as well as the destination brochures (PDF) coordinated by Vierumäki Corporation at the web portal (www.vierumaki.fi). Cooperation in sales and marketing is regulated in partnership agreements, including the commission practices. A good example of resource pooling is that the destination visitor information and the spa services offered by Vierumäki Corporation are located in Scandic Vierumäki Hotel – this type of local cooperation is exceptional for an international hotel chain. The Vierumäki actor network is cooperating at regional level, e.g. in strategic planning, in tourism trade fairs and in opening new foreign markets. Nationally and internationally, Vierumäki cooperates with the national tourism organisation Visit Finland and with the Ministry of Employment and the Economy, as well as with sports organisations like the Olympic Committee of Finland and the Vierumäki Unit of HAAGA-HELIA University of Applied Sciences. Vierumäki Corporation has coordinated several regional development projects, e.g. 'Increased internationalization through wellness tourism networks'.

As a DMO, Thermenland Styria (http://www.thermenland.at/en) is allied with many stakeholders in the destination and beyond. One example of this cooperation is the *Genusscard* (a regional tourism card) which allows guests to visit more than 120 destination hotspots free of charge, when staying a minimum of one night at one of more than 100 partnering accommodation facilities. During the first two years of its existence nearly 100,000 cards were distributed to guests. After their holiday visitors can use the card as a club card, including some specials when coming back to the destination. Thermenland Styria is not only a typical regional marketing association but also developing and leading national and international projects, e.g. Regio Vitalis,

(continued)

(continued)

aiming at creating jobs in tourism, RezeptTouren and Cycling AT-HU, a project to develop a borderless biking experience. Finally, by offering e-marketing workshops for hotels, managing art festivals and culinary events and running projects with universities, Thermenland Styria is becoming a leader in regional project development in the broad field of health tourism.

Future prospects

In order to face the growing competition and changes in demand, Vierumäki Corporation has founded a separate innovation and development unit. An investment of time and money is needed to develop further the customer databases and the seamless service chain at the destination.

As a European destination Thermenland Styria is facing severe challenges with declining length of stays and the impact of financial crises in Europe. As a consequence, efforts are being made regarding online marketing and tourism service product development to enhance the guest experience in the thermal baths and the destination.

Notes

1 Health and Wellbeing in Tourism Destination (WelDest 2012–2014) was an EU-funded research and development project in five countries across Europe (Austria, the Czech Republic, Finland, Germany and the UK) with the participation of representatives from both the supply and demand sides in health and wellbeing destinations, including visitors and tourists, managers of local health and wellbeing tourism companies, managers/experts of, e.g., destination development organisations, environmental administration and healthcare administration and policy makers. The aim of WelDest was to create a development framework to be used by public bodies, destination management organisations and private companies at tourism destinations willing to strengthen the elements influencing the wellbeing level of tourists and locals alike. Read more at: http://weldest.blogspot.com.
2 The WelDest primary research utilised a mixed-methods approach: semi-structured interviews (qualitative), consumer survey (quantitative) and focus groups (qualitative). In total, 52 interviews were conducted (10 in Finland, Germany and the UK and 11 in Austria and the Czech Republic) comprising 15 regional developers, 15 hospitality managers, 12 health managers, 8 local tourism managers and 2 policy makers. In addition 784 customers answered the survey in the five participating countries. A full WelDest research report is available at http://weldest.blogspot.com/p/weldest-media.html.
3 The link to the WelDest self-assessment tool can be found from page 2 at http://julkaisut.turkuamk.fi/isbn9789522165404.pdf.

References

Aarstad, J., Ness, H. and Haugland, S. (2015) 'Innovation, uncertainty and inter-firm shortcut ties in a tourism destination context', *Tourism Management*, 48, 354–361.

Beritelli, P. (2011) 'Cooperation among prominent actors in a tourism destination', *Annals of Tourism Research*, 38(2), pp. 607–629.

Cassens, M. (2013) *Gesundheitstourismus und touristische Destinationsentwicklung*, Munich, Germany: Oldenbourg Verlag.

Cooper, C. (2012) *Essentials of Tourism*, Harlow, UK: Prentice Hall – Pearson Education.

Cox, N., Gyrd-Jones, R. and Gardiner, S. (2014) 'Internal brand management of destination brands: Exploring the roles of destination management organisations and operators', *Journal of Destination Marketing and Management*, 3, 85–95.

Dvorak, D., Saari, S. and Tuominen, T. (eds) (2014) *Developing a Competitive Health and Wellbeing Destination*, http://julkaisut.turkuamk.fi/isbn9789522165404.pdf (accessed 7 June 2015).

Dwyer, L. and Kim, C. (2003) 'Destination competitiveness: Determinants and indicators', *Current Issues in Tourism*, 6(5), 369–414.

Fyall, A., Garrod, B. and Wang, Y. (2012) 'Destination collaboration: A critical review of theoretical approaches to a multi-dimensional phenomenon', *Journal of Destination Marketing and Management*, 1, 10–26.

Hassan, S. (2000) 'Determinants of market competitiveness in an environmentally sustainable tourism industry', *Journal of Travel Research*, 38(3), 239–245.

Haugland, S. A., Ness, H., Grönseth, B-O. and Aarstad, J. (2011) 'Development of tourism destinations, an integrated multilevel perspective', *Annals of Tourism Research*, 38(1), 268–290.

Jamal, T. and Jamrozy, U. (2006) 'Collaborative networks and partnerships for integrated destination management', in D. Buhalis and C. Costa (eds) *Tourism Management Dynamics*, Amsterdam, The Netherlands: Elsevier, pp. 164–172.

Komppula, R. (2014) 'The role of individual entrepreneurs in the development of competitiveness for a rural tourism destination – A case study', *Tourism Management*, 40, 361–371.

Morrison, A. (2013) *Marketing and Managing Tourism Destinations*, London: Routledge.

Prideaux, B. (2009) *Resort Destinations: Evolution, Management and Development*, Oxford, UK: Butterworth-Heinemann.

Prideaux, B., Berbigier, D. and Thompson, M. (2014) 'Wellness tourism and destination competitiveness', in C. Voigt and C. Pforr (eds) *Wellness Tourism, A Destination Perspective*, London: Routledge, pp. 45–60.

Qu, H, Kim, L. H. and Im, H. H. (2011) 'A model of destination branding: Integrating the concepts of the branding and destination image', *Tourism Management*, 32, 465–476.

Ritchie, J. R. B. and Crouch, G. I. (2003) *The Competitive Destination: A Sustainable Tourism Perspective*, Wallingford, UK: CABI International.

—— (2011) 'A model of destination competitiveness and sustainability', in Y. Wang and A. Pizam (eds) *Destination Marketing and Management: Theories and Applications*, Wallingford, UK: CABI, pp. 326–339.

Selin, S. and Chavez, D. (1995) 'Developing an evolutionary tourism partnership model', *Annals of Tourism Research*, 22(4), 844–856.

Sheldon, P. J. and Park, S-Y. (2009) 'Development of a sustainable wellness destination', in R. Bushell and P. J. Sheldon (eds) *Wellness and Tourism: Mind, Body, Spirit, Place*, New York: Cognizant Communication Corporation, pp. 99–113.

Smith, M. and Puczkó, L. (2009) *Health and Wellness Tourism*, Oxford, UK: Butterworth-Heinemann.

UNWTO (2007) *A Practical Guide to Tourism Destination Management*, https://pub.unwto.org/WebRoot/Store/Shops/Infoshop/4745/8BCE/AD9A/ECA8/048B/C0A8/0164/0B7A/071115_practical_guide_destination_management_excerpt.pdf (accessed 15 August 2015).

Voigt, C. and Laing, J. (2014) 'An examination of the extent of collaboration between major wellness tourism stakeholders in Australia', in C. Voigt and C. Pforr (eds) *Wellness Tourism, A Destination Perspective*, London: Routledge, pp. 63–77.

Voigt, C. and Pforr, C. (2014) 'Concluding discussion: Implications for destination development and management', in C. Voigt and C. Pforr (eds) *Wellness Tourism, A Destination Perspective*, London: Routledge, pp. 290–310.

Volgger, M. and Pechlaner, H. (2014) 'Requirements for destination organizations in destination governance: Understanding DMO success', *Tourism Management*, 41, 64–75.

Wang, Y. (2011) 'Destination marketing and management: Scope, definition and structures', in Y. Wang and A. Pizam (eds) *Destination Marketing and Management*, Wallingford, UK: CABI International, pp. 1–20.

Wang, Y. and Krakover, S. (2008) 'Destination marketing: Competition, cooperation or coopetition?', *International Journal of Contemporary Hospitality Management*, 20(2), 126–141.

24

Cross-border health tourism collaborations

Opportunities and challenges

Henna Konu and Melanie Kay Smith

Introduction

There has been a proliferation of collaborations in recent years in many countries and regions of the world, both in general business (Porter, 1990, 2003) but also specifically in tourism. This includes collaborations between different industries and stakeholders, e.g. entrepreneurs, public sector, research institutes and tourism destinations. The complex nomenclature of collaborations includes networks, clusters, cooperations, partnerships, destination management organisations (DMOs) and more besides. Collaboration refers to all of these and usually implies the conscious and willing decision to work together with other organisations, businesses and agencies towards some common goals. This does not imply renouncing all autonomy, nor does it assume that organisations compromise their individual remit(s). Jamal and Stronza (2009: 169) suggest that, 'Collaboration provides for a flexible and dynamic process that evolves over time, enabling multiple stakeholders to jointly address problems or issues' and that:

> It is important to view collaboration as spatial and temporal, activities are occurring both within and outside the collaborative space of gathering; they may involve short or medium term collaborations with a finite end . . . or may involve a longer-term collaboration with phased ownership and other development/management activities to be implemented over time.
>
> *(Jamal and Stronza, 2009: 177)*

The extent to which the collaboration develops depends on the needs and aims of the partners involved and they may be involved to varying degrees at different points in the collaboration's existence. Collaborations are dynamic rather than static entities which can change over time depending on their lifespan.

The forms and issues of collaboration have been studied from very different theoretical aspects, including resource-based theories, relationship-based theories, politics-based theories, process-based theories and chaos-based theories (Fyall, Garrod and Wang, 2012). Previous studies showed that the level of cooperation between different stakeholders at destination level is influenced by the maturity of destination marketing approaches, leadership of DMO, distance of marketing campaign and focus of strategic thinking (Wang and Krakover, 2008). However, there is a limited amount of information available about what kind of influence the scope of destination has on cooperation. Many studies of tourism collaborations focus on collaboration at destination level (national at most) and there is a limited amount of research that examines the scope of the collaboration at transnational or international level and what kind of influence it has, e.g. whether the benefits and challenges are the same, how the collaboration works and who are the stakeholders involved. Sheldon and Park (2009) suggested five stages for the development of a sustainable wellbeing destination. Stage 3 focuses on wellbeing destination policy and planning, which includes network collaborations. Tuominen, Saari and Binder (see Chapter 23, this volume) emphasise the need for committed cooperation of all actors and the development of local partnerships in successful destination planning, development and management. They suggest that collaboration forms part of the first dimension of destination development.

One of the newest trends is to develop health tourism collaborations (or variations thereof) which may focus on one or more dimensions of health, such as spas, wellness, wellbeing or medical activities. Early definitions of health tourism include the International Union of Tourist Organizations (IUOTO) in 1973, which stated that health tourism is 'the provision of health facilities utilising the natural resources of the country, in particular mineral water and climate' (7). Smith and Puczkó (2009) suggest that health tourism is the 'umbrella' term for wellness tourism and medical tourism. Wellness tourism includes spas, wellness hotels and retreats which focus on preventive healthcare. Medical tourism focuses more on curative and surgical approaches to health (e.g. hospitals, clinics). There has been a recent growth in the number of collaborations between sectors within wellness tourism and medical tourism; however they have not as yet been researched in much depth.

This chapter focuses on collaborations in health tourism in the Nordic and Baltic region. Two main case studies, the Nordic Wellbeing network and the Baltic Health Tourism Cluster, are used to exemplify the processes by which collaborations develop, the factors that affect their success or effectiveness and some of the inherent challenges of establishing and managing them. The researchers draw on past and present action research and their own experiences of being involved in the establishment and operationalisation of the collaborations explored in the case studies. This includes Delphi studies, attendance of expert meetings and project-based research.

Benefits and challenges of collaboration

Collaborations can span different planning scales and organisational levels, including local, regional, national and international level, as well as cross-border initiatives. Collaborative arrangements can operate through informal agreements and in unstructured forms (e.g. grassroots initiatives). Organisations can collaborate within and across these spatial domains (e.g. local–international, national–international). Partnership structures can also vary greatly depending on the purpose and scope of the collaboration (Jamal and Stronza, 2009). Personal connections also make an important contribution to collaboration (Beritelli, 2011; see Tuominen, Saari and Binder, Chapter 23, this volume).

Some of the purported benefits of collaborations are the enhancement of competitiveness, increased productivity and innovation and the development of entrepreneurship (Jackson and Murphy, 2002; Breda, Costa and Costa, 2004; Capone, 2004; Flowers and Easterling, 2006; Novelli, Schmitz and Spencer, 2006; Fereira and Estevão, 2009; Iordache, 2010). Inter-organisational collaborations help tourism organisations overcome individual resource deficiencies and, therefore, remain competitive (Wang and Fesenmaier, 2007). Iordache (2010) suggests that clusters can increase competitiveness in three dimensions: productivity, innovations and starting new businesses (entrepreneurship). The main aims of clusters include providing quality goods and services, carrying out a common marketing policy, coordinating the activities of local companies and creating complex and complementary tourism products which appeal to tourists and grant competitive advantage (Novelli et al., 2006; Fereira and Estevão, 2009). Collaboration can help to lever scarce resources (Selin and Chavez, 1995), as well as providing tourists with holistic and individually meaningful experiences (Woodside and Dubelaar, 2002). Collaborative relationships can afford organisations the opportunity of obtaining access to a wider stock of knowledge, more experience and additional business opportunities (Selin, 1993; Wang and Xiang, 2007). Transnational and cross-border initiatives can create additional benefits: 'Transnational cooperation projects present an element of novelty and can boost the process of value creation and collective competitive advantage' (Contò, Vrontis, Fiore and Thrassou, 2014: 1800).

Box 24.1 summarises the benefits that are connected to collaborative activities in the tourism industry.

Box 24.1   A summary of the benefits of collaborations in tourism

- Creating complementary goods and services
- Improving quality of goods and services
- Levering more resources
- Moving from competition to 'coopetition'
- Increasing productivity
- Sharing and expanding knowledge
- Developing joint marketing strategies
- Improving competitiveness
- Increasing innovation
- Fostering entrepreneurship
- Affording new business opportunities
- Creating holistic experiences of destinations for tourists

Tourism organisations often find themselves in a situation of 'coopetition' (Tsai, 2002), where they both compete with each other at the same time as collaborating to create complementary goods and services (Zach and Racherla, 2011). However, tourists tend to evaluate destinations as a single product rather than a combination of individual services (Wang and Xiang, 2007). As stated by Zach and Racherla (2011: 98), 'the success of a destination depends on the seamless coordination of the players comprising the tourism value chain to provide wholesome and memorable experiences to tourists'. A collaborative approach to destination management means that visitors can move through destinations linking together individual places (Zach, Gretzel and Fesenmaier, 2008).

Given the above apparent advantages of collaborations in tourism destinations, there have been relatively few studies which focus on the complexity of destination collaboration. Zach and Racherla (2011) cite the exceptions of Scott, Baggio and Cooper (2008), who used network analysis, and Lemmetyinen and Go (2009), who used the Value System Continuum framework. Fyall et al. (2012) state that much of the destination literature has tended to focus on competitiveness rather than collaboration, despite Pavlovich (2014: 6) suggesting that over almost a century of tourism destination development 'collaboration emerged as the central property of transformational network change'. She states that destination networks can be characterised according to three premises: non-linearity, collaboration and wholeness. She emphasises the importance of collaborative relationships in the local context, especially those which are non-linear and anti-hierarchical and which contain informal social relationships.

However, it is also common for cross-border projects to face difficulties (despite research and development funding) because of conflicts over territorial space, governance, policy making and planning (Ilbery and Saxena, 2011). Jamal and Stronza (2009) suggest that a major weakness of collaborative processes lies in the third phase (implementation and institutionalising the shared meanings that emerge), with the earlier two phases being problem setting and direction setting. Szivás (2005) quotes the example of health and spa and other forms of tourism between Hungary and neighbouring countries, where cross-border destination development was not very successful. Recognising that there are many more examples of cross-border initiatives in tourism more generally (successful or otherwise), the following section however focuses specifically on health tourism and those collaborations that span more than one border.

Collaboration in health tourism

Health, wellness or medical tourism collaborations or clusters are usually networks consisting of a combination of leading hospitals, spas, clinics, providers, hotels, tourism operators and/or government officials who are working together to promote their services and location to health tourists (Medical Tourism Association, 2013). There may also be other important objectives, such as information sharing, education and training, product and services development or research. Universities or other research institutes may also be involved, although many clusters (especially in medical tourism) are mainly industry-focused.

Several researchers have emphasised the importance of collaborations such as networks and clusters in health tourism destination development (e.g. Locher, Voigt and Pforr, 2014; Pforr, Pechlaner, Locher and Jochmann, 2014; Voigt and Laing, 2014). Pforr and Locher (2014: 266) state that 'stronger local and regional collaboration amongst various health tourism providers will become a crucial prerequisite for the future development of health tourism destinations'. Voigt and Pforr (2014) suggest that the wellness tourism sector is highly fragmented and diverse; however, quality tourism experiences need to be delivered through DMOs or networks of organisations. A resource-based approach is not enough without a strategic approach to destination management. They recommend that a health tourism cluster should aim for 'relational strategic destination management'. As discussed earlier, the term 'health tourism' incorporates elements of both wellness tourism and medical tourism. However, as noted by Voigt (2014), biomedical and wellness services seem just to co-exist without much evidence of an integrated, cooperative approach. Baum and Lockstone-Binney (2014) suggest that medical, paramedical, wellness, leisure, tourism and hospitality services do not have traditions of collaboration and sometimes operate in counter-directions. However, in some cases, so-called 'health regions' have been developed which include an active collaboration of service providers and industry sectors in a regional setting. For example, the establishment of Health Region Kneippland Unterallgau in Germany has successfully led to the development of new products and services, quality control measures and a satisfactory visitor experience (Locher et al., 2014; Pforr et al., 2014). In addition to regional collaboration, health and wellness collaboration emerges between different industries. Hjalager and Konu (2011) examined different forms of collaboration between wellness tourism businesses and cosmetic suppliers. In their study they found that collaboration may have very different forms, from stakeholders (e.g. businesses) being traditional sub-suppliers to having fully integrated activities when attempting to achieve inimitability and competitiveness.

There are several challenges when establishing and managing health tourism collaborations. Voigt and Laing (2014) discuss how stakeholder collaborations in wellness tourism often fail due to lack of time, lack of managerial capabilities, lack of leadership, unequal financial contribution, disagreements between stakeholders about goals and commitments and language barriers and mistrust. Certainly, there are several benefits of clustering but the cooperation works only if members (partners) share the same vision and they understand that every member (partner) has to participate and often contribute financially as well. It is important to establish key aims and activities from the outset. Steinhauser and Jochum (2006) suggest that wellness clusters help to build trustworthy and strong brands and quality criteria; however, Bertsch, Schobersberger, Blank and Ostermann (2011) see brands of wellness clusters as being relatively weakly anchored in people's minds. Todd (2012) sees that many medical tourism clusters are failing to be fully successful because of the lack of consideration of certain key elements such as (amongst others) how to fund the cluster, the need for cluster leadership training, long-term sustainability of the cluster, marketing of health tourism products, customer satisfaction, regulatory compliance of healthcare, accreditation and cultural sensitivities. Contò et al. (2014: 1802) state that, in order for collaborations to be successful, they need a carefully designed strategic plan, true long-term commitment to the plan by all stakeholders, communication of the plan to all concerned and securement of the necessary funds to support, implement and monitor the venture.

Certainly, forming an association or cluster is not enough to become a successful destination in health tourism. The discussion about stakeholders and scope of collaborative activities and how these influence the benefits and challenges have been missing from previous research. This chapter aims to show, with the help of case studies, how health tourism collaborations work in practice, especially those with cross-border relationships within the Nordic and Baltic regions.

Case studies of health tourism collaboration

Two case studies are used to analyse how collaborations develop in health tourism and how they can be managed. It is common in case study research to use multiple methods of data collection which triangulate (Yin, 2009). Both case studies (Nordic Wellbeing and the Baltic Health Tourism Cluster) included similar research methods (e.g. a Delphi study, workshops with expert participants, action research), but research was undertaken during different time periods and not in parallel. The authors draw on longitudinal action research that they undertook during their involvement in the establishment of the Nordic Wellbeing network and Baltic Health Tourism Cluster, including Delphi study research, participation in working group meetings during the initial phases of establishment and subsequent management. The authors analyse the importance of cross-border collaboration when establishing health tourism networks and clusters, the structure and nature of such collaborations, typical aims and activities and some of the problems and challenges.

Case 1: Nordic Wellbeing network

Aims and objectives of the collaboration

Nordic Wellbeing (Norway, Sweden, Denmark, Finland and Iceland) is a network which was established in 2009 and focused on research, product development and promotion. The network aimed to develop international and cross-border collaboration by examining shared resources and competences of the Nordic countries that can be utilised in developing Nordic wellbeing tourism. The aim was to draw a wider picture of what constitutes the wellbeing category of tourism in the transnational geographical context of the Nordic countries. To do this, potential exploitation of special and even unique Nordic resources and advantages was articulated in policy considerations for the emergence and support of development of a Nordic Wellbeing brand (Hjalager et al., 2011). Thus, the research activities aimed to gain a more profound understanding of the driving forces and resources that could lead to the successful development of coherent wellbeing tourism in the Nordic region, including increasing innovation and sharing and expanding knowledge. The activities adapted an innovation perspective to develop Nordic content of wellbeing to be offered by tourism enterprises and destinations across the five Nordic countries (Hjalager et al., 2011).

Main stakeholders and structure of the collaboration network

In the Nordic Wellbeing network the main activities were built around research activities that aimed to support new innovations, product development and promotional activities. The network was funded as an international research and development project (2009–2010) by the Nordic Innovation Centre. At international level most of the collaboration happened in the research institutes. The collaborative structure in the network was built in such a way that activities were undertaken in different scopes (Figure 24.1). All the case regions selected were interested in wellbeing tourism development in their area and they had already developed some activities related to that.

The researchers had their national collaborators who utilised the research information and transferred it to practical activities that were implemented at national and local levels. The national-level collaboration was the most active in Finland, where the research activities were undertaken in close collaboration with the Finnish Tourist Board. The more concrete activities took place in the case regions of each country. The collaboration networks in each of the case areas

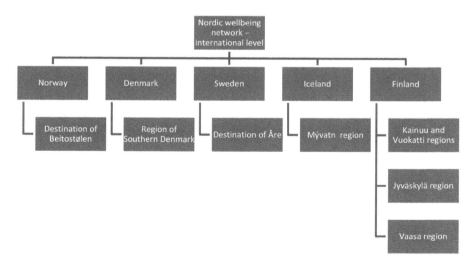

Figure 24.1   Collaborative structure of the Nordic Wellbeing network.

(continued)

(continued)

differed; in some areas the main collaborative partners were educational and research institutes, regional development companies, business networks or destination marketing and management organisations. In most of the case areas businesses were involved mainly through the regional networks by taking part in workshops and participating interviews.

The international collaboration was led by a research institute where the project coordinator was based. At national level the collaborative activities and the stakeholders involved differed from each other. Also in some countries the national-level collaborative partners were missing and the main practical activities took place in a regional context. At regional level the activities were led by the main collaborative partners, mentioned above.

Main activities

The research activities were undertaken both at international and regional levels depending on the issue in question. The research framework and communication activities were developed together with the stakeholders of the network. The project started with a wide literature review related to concept development and theories in wellbeing tourism. The selected case areas acted as platforms of empirical studies and later they implemented the research results in regional development contexts. The research activities in the case areas were organised in collaboration with researchers and regional partners. The development activities included workshops and seminars, study visits to locations and businesses offering wellbeing products and services and different discussions and consultation with the key stakeholders in case areas.

Professionals in the tourism industry were interviewed in each case area to gather information on innovation processes, product development and collaboration in wellbeing tourism. In addition, a Delphi study was conducted among tourism professionals, including researchers, marketing organisations and tourism developers. To get a wide perspective, e.g. on the concept development, the experts involved in the Delphi study also came from other European countries, from the USA and from Japan.

During the project customer surveys were conducted in some of the case areas to gain customer perspective about the essence of Nordic Wellbeing. The customer research brought information about the current perception of the Nordic Wellbeing concept among customers. The customers also gave suggestions about what Nordic Wellbeing should embody in the future to create added value for Nordic tourism businesses.

The main research activities were reported in several research reports. In addition, a final report combining results from all research activities was written. The report includes information about wellbeing tourism market trends in a Nordic context, unique selling points of Nordic Wellbeing, new wellbeing tourism niches and policies to support the development of Nordic Wellbeing tourism (Hjalager et al., 2011). As a conclusion, eight recommendations for industry and policy makers were made (Hjalager et al., 2011):

1   harvesting the benefits of the unique selling points;
2   developing new, adapted sports and leisure activities;
3   widening the food link;
4   signature products of medicine and cosmeceuticals;

5   addressing lifestyle diseases with wellbeing;
6   spiritualising the experience;
7   supporting the Nordic infrastructures;
8   creating an international media awareness.

Benefits of collaboration

The network activities support the differentiation of Nordic Wellbeing from other wellbeing tourism concepts by increasing the knowledge about the unique selling points of the Nordic Countries. In addition, the research identified new innovations and collaboration opportunities, e.g. between different industries, that can be utilised in Nordic Wellbeing tourism product development. This has led to developing complementary wellbeing (tourism) services. The concrete product development took place in different case areas building on local and regional strengths, e.g. sauna in Finland. In Finland the results of the project were also adapted and used as a starting point for regional wellbeing development projects and the content of Nordic Wellbeing has been used as starting point for new business ideas related to life and culture in the Finnish Lakeland too (e.g. http://www.saimaalife.com/).

Sharing information about diverse wellbeing tourism products and development practices across the Nordic countries and also about customer expectations supported and gave new ideas to regional development processes. The research activities addressed also the innovation structures, collaboration patterns and destination leadership in the case areas. These issues helped to identify who are the leading stakeholders in development processes at regional level (see e.g. Tuohino and Konu, 2014).

One of the aims was to develop a common brand of Nordic Wellbeing. The research activities supported this by providing recommendations for policy makers and for the tourism industry. During the project international collaboration took place mainly in the research network and the other international or cross-border activities were rather minimal. In Finland the Finnish Tourist Board was strongly supporting the project activities as the content supported the Finnish wellbeing tourism strategy 2009–2013. However, within the framework of the Nordic Wellbeing project network there was hardly any collaboration between national tourist boards which could have developed joint marketing strategies.

Problems and challenges

The network was set up in the form of a development project. Hence since the project ended at the end of 2010 there have not been any unified international activities related to the theme because no one took responsibility for managing the whole network. However, the basic guidelines, themes and suggestions have been adapted by national and regional DMOs and individual businesses.

The lack of leadership has been the main challenge. This is not just in the Nordic Wellbeing collaboration but also in collaboration in tourism in general at Scandinavian level (e.g. efficiency of national tourism organisation collaborations). There have been attempts to market the region as a whole but at the moment the impacts are rather unknown. International collaboration in enhancing cross-border tourism in Scandinavian countries should be developed

(continued)

(continued)

further. For instance, marketing international Nordic Wellbeing round tours to Asian markets might enhance the appeal of the thematic product (having the Nordic Wellbeing experience in different Nordic countries).

Future of the collaboration

There are a number of possibilities in utilising a Nordic approach to wellbeing tourism. The research activities and development practices showed that it is essential to focus on stakeholder collaboration in terms of marketing and innovation. To be able to utilise the legacy of or lessons from the project, there is a need for well-planned joint marketing of Nordic wellbeing activities and this should be developed in the context of a long-term strategy and expanding networks of collaboration. However, this will require willingness and commitment from the actors at national and international level as well as strong leadership.

Case 2: Baltic Health Tourism Cluster

Background of the collaboration

The Baltic Health Tourism Cluster was established between Estonia, Latvia and Lithuania in 2013. The logic of having a cross-border health tourism cluster in the Baltic States was based on some existing collaborations in tourism, as well as national clusters in health and medical tourism. Existing collaborations between the three countries previously consisted mainly of marketing activities between the tourist boards (e.g. Great Baltic Travel 2011–2012), joint press trips, trade shows and tourist fairs, joint publications (such as the Baltic map and brochure), information days and workshops (e.g. Baltic Connecting Event in 2013) (Kalvik, 2013; Pankova, 2013).

Main stakeholders

The Baltic Health Tourism Cluster is a partnership of existing national spa, medical, wellness, health and tourism clusters and associations with signatories from all three Baltic countries. A memorandum of understanding was signed in October 2013 representing a collaboration between the Lithuanian Medical Tourism Cluster, the Latvian Health Tourism Cluster and the Estonian Health Tourism Cluster. The members are mainly associations and industry representatives (e.g. from spas, tourist boards), although officials from central and regional government also attended some of the joint meetings.

Aims and objectives

The main purpose was to increase the global competitiveness of the region in health tourism. Secondary aims included the following:

- enhancing *trust* and *coopetition* among the partners and their members;
- improving *quality* (accessibility, safety, effectiveness, efficiency, etc.) of the services provided to clients/patients;
- joint *marketing* resources and efforts to promote Cluster's services effectively to potential and new target markets (e.g. Russia, Belarus and Ukraine).

These aims correspond closely to the main benefits of tourism collaborations, as identified earlier in Box 24.1.

Eighty per cent of the funding was to come from partnership membership fees and 20 per cent would come from national funding instruments or projects.

Main activities

Research was undertaken to support the establishment and development of the cluster using a Delphi study method to collect data about existing national and common regional resources, their potential use in product and destination development, the main areas in which partici-pants would like to collaborate and some suggestions for destination image enhancement. The Delphi study took place between autumn 2013 and spring 2014, with contacts recruited from the launch of the Health Tourism Cluster from a range of government agencies, tour-ist boards, academic institutions, health, wellness and medical clusters and associations and spas. Twenty-five respondents eventually took part in the first round of ten questions and 14 in the second round of 12 questions. Data were also gathered from presentations by experts and round-table discussions at three health tourism events in Estonia (Parnu) in May 2013, Lithuania in October 2013 and Estonia (Tallinn) in April 2014. It is not the aim of this study to focus on these results, but to extract those elements of the primary data that are relevant to cross-border health tourism collaboration.

When asked to state which words or images came to mind when the Baltic States are mentioned, more than one respondent referred to the relationship between the countries, suggesting that the number 3 should be used in marketing to emphasise 'togetherness'. Some referred to 'common his-tory' and 'cooperation', calling the countries 'sisters' and 'partners'. It is also seen as a 'post-Soviet cross-border region', with all countries therefore understanding former USSR and Eastern European mentality. The respondents also identified several health, wellness and medical resources, traditions, products and services that are common to all of the Baltic countries (Figure 24.2).

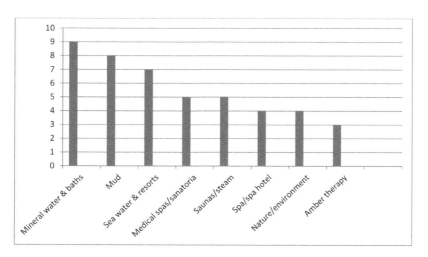

Figure 24.2 Common health tourism resources in the Baltic region.

(continued)

(continued)

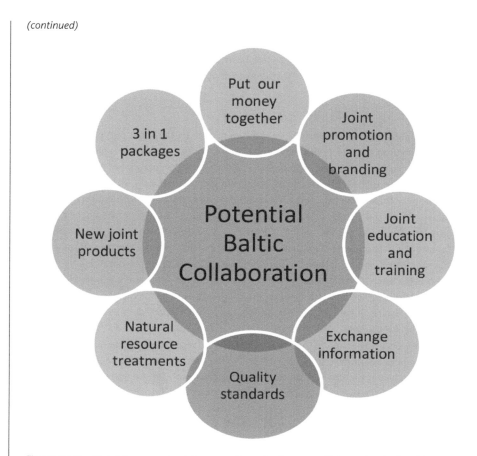

Figure 24.3 Delphi respondents' suggestions for future collaboration in health tourism.

Respondents could not identify many existing areas of collaboration in health tourism between the three countries (although they named at least four or five national ones per country), except for some of the work of the Baltic Assembly, town-twinning schemes, some collaboration between Parnu in Estonia and Jurmala in Latvia and some tour operators offering joint packages to spa hotels. When asked about potential areas of collaboration, the respondents suggested the following, as identified in Figure 24.3.

The benefits of collaboration seemed to be recognised by some respondents. For example, one (from a spa resort association) stated that:

Cooperation between the Baltic States in the area of health tourism is highly supported by our geographic location, mild climate and the fact that there are no mental and language barriers. Acknowledging the fact that our internal market is small and internal consumption is low, there is mutual understanding that it is necessary to specialize in certain areas and services and that there is a need to develop new products that could be marketed together in larger markets, such as Germany, Norway and the UK.

Other interesting and relevant suggestions are listed in the direct quotations below:

- 'Baltic countries can provide for all stages of human health: prevention; medical intervention and rehabilitation. I would suggest developing a plan or program, where each Baltic country has its exact goal of participation, so there wouldn't be competition. Each Baltic country is specialized in healing one/two/three exact conditions – through all stages mentioned'.
- 'Each medical or health institution finds their twin partner in all three countries and on bases of cooperation offers joint products to target markets'.
- 'The key focus should be to sell the region as one destination (develop joint packages) such as a 3 in 1 package that in 7–14 days a client visits all three regions'.
- 'Surgery services might be provided in one country and rehabilitation in another'.
- 'We need to identify strong fields in every country, make price comparisons in all these fields and make a strong marketing instrument. Web page, brand, stand in exhibitions, etc. Put together money and promote together medical tourism'.
- 'We are too small for foreign markets, to get higher visibility we should do co-marketing and lobby other countries – more common brand, label and marketing'.
- 'There could be better organized collaborations between all Baltic countries. For example, organizing specialized seminars for each sphere leading specialists. Information and practice exchange could be useful as well'.
- 'The Baltics are all the same in the eyes of many Russians! Joint offers for Russians especially from St Petersburg. Maybe also some collaborations with Russian spas too'.

In terms of specific product development in health tourism in the Baltic region, the respondents suggested the themes presented in Figure 24.4.

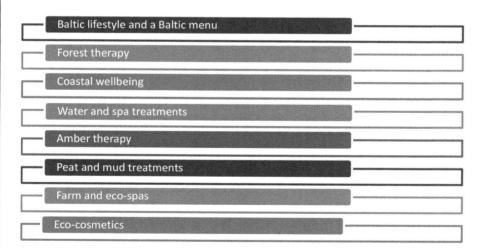

Figure 24.4   Potential joint products in Baltic health tourism as identified by Delphi study respondents.

(continued)

(continued)

Problems and challenges

It can be seen that there are a number of ideas and initiatives that emerged from the research so far. However, it seemed from the most recent Health Tourism Cluster event (April 2014) that the individual countries actually have reservations about the benefits of clustering and cross-border collaboration rather than simply engaging in national product development and marketing. It was also evident that the momentum had shifted considerably from one country to another since the Cluster was first established. Whereas one country was dynamic and enthusiastic at the beginning and another was lagging behind, this was completely reversed a year later. One of the biggest difficulties is that the individual countries see themselves as specialising in slightly different areas of health tourism. For example, Lithuania originally wanted to establish a medical tourism cluster across the Baltic region as this is their main (recent) focus. Estonia is more interested in developing wellness spas and Latvia has many seaside and mineral water resorts which still focus on rehabilitation. Although this could be an opportunity for true 'coopetition', it unfortunately does not seem to bode well for the future of the Cluster as a joint initiative.

Discussion and conclusions

The two case studies above are clearly different in terms of their scope, focus, structure and time scale. Nordic Wellbeing activities were officially funded, whereas Baltic Health Tourism activities were not. However, both had a major focus on product and service development, marketing, branding and researching what are the unique selling points of the Nordic and Baltic regions respectively. Both collaborations aimed to identify the common health and wellbeing tourism resources in the region and to establish a joint brand. Ideally, this would place both the Nordic and the Baltic regions on the world map of health tourism. The extent to which this was successful is difficult to measure, but some regional initiatives (e.g. in Finland) have shown how an international collaboration could filter down to regional and local businesses and initiatives. The main challenge to this common goal is that the individual countries may not have such a specific history of or interest in health tourism (e.g. Sweden, Norway) or they may wish to focus on different aspects of health tourism (e.g. the Baltic States).

It seems that some collaborations like these are established as a result of research funding and a specific remit which necessitates collaboration (e.g. a cross-border bid). Some collaborations function fairly well at national and sub-national level (e.g. spa associations, medical clusters) and one individual or association has the initiative of extending the collaboration to other associations in different countries. This seemed to be the case in the Baltic Health Tourism example. Their later success is dependent on the equal and continuing enthusiasm of all partners, but this appears to be rather fickle or at best fluctuating. Although collaborations can continue despite unequal efforts from all members, the results are likely to be somewhat uneven and may drift back to a national or sub-national agenda (partly the case in both of these case studies). Even if language and cultural barriers are not explicitly mentioned as barriers, transnational and cross-border working can be more difficult than operating within a national context. Policy, administration, bureaucracy and funding are always easier to understand within one's own country.

This is not to say that all national and sub-national collaborations are more effective or successful than cross-border ones, but it can be simpler to operate them.

The Nordic Wellbeing network included more partners from research and higher education institutions, whereas Baltic Health Tourism consists of mainly industry partners. Although one could try to identify the ideal or optimum number and type(s) of stakeholders needed for health tourism collaboration, the reality is that this mix will be very much dependent on funding, willingness and time to participate, perceived personal or institutional benefit. Even those who do participate may demonstrate waning levels of enthusiasm or dynamism during the course of the collaboration. Not much can be done to solve this problem but it is for certain that strong and consistent leadership is needed. Even though most of the international collaboration took place between research and higher education institutions in the Nordic Wellbeing case, the project activities and results were adapted and applied by different stakeholders at national and regional levels.

Both collaborations benefited from the results of a Delphi study, interviews and workshop data. These are rich qualitative resources which usually result in consensus. There was agreement about product development and the types of future collaboration that would be useful in the Baltic context, for example (at least in theory). Even though the content of the Nordic Wellbeing concept was integrated into different regional research and development projects and as a guiding principle for new businesses, the Nordic Wellbeing network members could (technically) use the Nordic Wellbeing concept in their product and service development at national, regional and local level more widely. In the Nordic Wellbeing case it can be said that the international collaborative activities brought benefits at national level, as the Finnish Tourist Board could adapt the information gained into its Finnish wellbeing tourism development activities.

The lessons learnt from these case studies are broadly similar to those of other collaborations, as discussed earlier. For example, implementation is the most challenging part (Jamal and Stronza, 2009) and lack of leadership is problematic (Voigt and Laing, 2014). However, there appear to have been few or no disputes over territorial space or governance (as identified by Ilbery and Saxena, 2011) and there are seemingly few language barriers (as suggested by Voigt and Laing, 2014). So far it is clear that cross-border destination development has not really happened (like in the case quoted by Szivás, 2005). As stated by Voigt and Pforr (2014), a resource-based approach is not enough without a strategic approach to destination management and Contò et al. (2014) stress the need for a strategic plan as well as necessary funds (the Baltic Health Tourism Cluster currently has neither!). It should also be added that health and wellness collaborations in the context of destinations need to include local people as well as tourists and integrate employee expertise into the creation of health benefits (Voigt and Pforr, 2014; see Tuominen, Saari and Binder, Chapter 23, this volume).

It could be said that both networks were successful in adapting a resource-based approach in identifying what is both common and unique to these regions, but less successful in the leadership and implementation of initiatives relating to concrete products and their promotion at international/cross-border level. The Nordic Wellbeing Network affords several more examples of this perhaps, especially in Finland, but it is important to establish what took place as a direct result of the network and what was happening already. Similarly, several interesting national and regional health tourism initiatives could be identified in the Baltic region, but they have so far taken place outside the remit of this Cluster. Table 24.1 summarises the main achievements and challenges of the Nordic Wellbeing network and the Baltic Health Tourism Cluster.

Table 24.1 Achievements and challenges of the collaborations

Collaboration	Achievements	Challenges
Nordic Wellbeing network	• Clear understanding of wellbeing tourism, its driving forces and resources • Collaboration with the Finnish Tourist Board and other regional DMOs • Involvement of regional and local businesses • Customer research on concepts, potential products and services • Recommendations for policy makers and tourism industry • Spin-off projects for wellbeing tourism development at regional level • New business ideas/individual business opportunities: content of Nordic Wellbeing being a core thematic guideline	• More practical activities at regional than national or international levels • Problems with leadership • No international collaborative marketing or development activities after the development project ended
Baltic Health Tourism Cluster	• Identification of common and unique health tourism resources in the region • Interesting recommendations for product development • Knowledge of existing and potential markets	• Fluctuation in interest levels and changes in leadership • Different national priorities in health tourism • Failure to see the benefits of collaboration compared to national agendas

Note: DMO, destination management organisation.

This study has several managerial implications. As a summary, several recommendations for health tourism collaboration can be suggested:

• Ensure that there is a strong leader who is willing to guide the project for at least two years.
• Set up secure funding not only for establishment and research, but also for implementation and monitoring.
• Identify what resources, products and services are common to a region or destination – are they strong enough to build a definite health tourism brand?
• Make sure consumer research is robust – is there definitely a market for health tourism and at which levels? (transnational, national, sub-national, local?)
• Are national agendas stronger than the desire for wider collaboration? If so, a strategy based on complementarity should be considered.

References

Baum, T. and Lockstone-Binney, L. (2014) 'Fit for purpose: Delivering wellness tourism through people', in Voigt, C. and Pforr, C. (eds) *Wellness Tourism*, London: Routledge, pp. 130–143.

Beritelli, P. (2011) *Tourist destination governance through local elites – looking beyond the stakeholder level*, Postdoctoral thesis, University of St Gallen.

Bertsch, G., Schobersberger, W., Blank, C. and Ostermann, H. (2011) 'Importance of wellness quality criteria and positioning of wellness cooperation brands', *International Journal of Leisure and Tourism Marketing*, 2(3), 194–208.

Breda, Z., Costa, R. and Costa, C. (2004) 'Do clustering and networks make small places beautiful? The case of Caramulo (Portugal)', in Lazzeretti, L. and Petrillo, C. (eds) *Tourism Local Systems and Networking*, Oxford: Elsevier, pp. 67–82.

Capone, F. (2004) *Regional Competitiveness in Tourism Local Systems*, 44th European Congress of the European Regional Science Association, Regions and Fiscal Federalism, University of Oporto.

Contò, F., Vrontis, D., Fiore, M. and Thrassou, A. (2014) 'Strengthening regional identities and culture through wine industry cross border collaboration', *British Food Journal*, 116(11), 1788–1807.

Fereira, J. and Estevão, C. (2009) *Regional Competitiveness of Tourism Cluster: A Conceptual Model Proposal*, http://mpra.ub.uni-muenchen.de/14853 (accessed 15 June 2015).

Flowers, J. and Easterling, K. (2006) 'Growing South Carolina's tourism cluster', *Business and Economic Review*, 52(3), 15–20.

Fyall, A., Garrod, B. and Wang, Y. (2012) 'Destination collaboration: A critical review of theoretical approaches to a multi-dimensional phenomenon', *Journal of Destination Marketing and Management*, 1, 10–26.

Hjalager, A. and Konu, H. (2011) 'Co-branding and co-creation in wellness tourism: The role of cosmeceuticals', *Journal of Hospitality Marketing and Management*, 20(8), 879–901.

Hjalager, A., Konu, H., Huijbens, E. H., Björk, P., Flagestad, A., Nordin, S. and Tuohino, A. (2011) *Innovating and re-branding Nordic wellbeing tourism*, http://www.nordicinnovation.org/Global/_Publications/Reports/2011/2011_NordicWellbeingTourism_report.pdf (accessed 10 November 2014).

Ilbery, B. and Saxena, G. (2011) 'Integrated rural tourism in the English–Welsh cross-border region: An analysis of strategic, administrative and personal challenges', *Regional Studies*, 45(8), 1139–1155.

Iordache, C. (2010) 'Clusters – tourism activity increases competiveness support', *Theoretical and Applied Economics*, XVII(5), 99–112.

IUOTO (1973) *Health Tourism*, Geneva, Switzerland: United Nations.

Jackson, J. and Murphy, P. (2002) 'Tourism destinations as clusters: Analytic experiences from the New World', *Tourism and Hospitality Research*, 4(1), 36–52.

Jamal, T. and Stronza, A. (2009) 'Collaboration theory and tourism practice in protected areas: Stakeholders, structuring and sustainability', *Journal of Sustainable Tourism*, 17(2), 169–189.

Kalvik, M. (2013) *Development of the Baltic Joint Regional Tourism Concept*, presentation at the Launch Event of the Baltic Health Tourism Cluster, Vilnius, October.

Lemmetyinen, A. and Go, F. (2009) 'The key capabilities required for managing tourism business networks', *Tourism Management*, 30(1), 31–40.

Locher, C., Voigt, C. and Pforr, C. (2014) 'The Kneipp philosophy – a "healthy" approach to destination development', in Voigt, C. and Pforr, C. (eds) *Wellness Tourism*, London: Routledge, pp. 188–199.

Medical Tourism Association (2013) *Healthcare Clusters, Medical Clusters and Healthcare Association*, http://www.medicaltourismassociation.com/en/healthcare-clusters.html (accessed 19 December 2015).

Novelli, M., Schmitz, B. and Spencer, T. (2006) 'Networks, clusters and innovation in tourism: A UK experience', *Tourism Management*, 27, 1141–1152.

Pankova, M. (2013) *Development of the Joint Regional Tourism Conception in the Baltic Region*, presentation at the Launch Event of the Baltic Health Tourism Cluster, Vilnius, October.

Pavlovich, K. (2014) 'A rhizomic approach to tourism destination evolution and transformation', *Tourism Management*, 41, 1–8.

Pforr, C. and Locher, C. (2014) 'Health tourism in the context of demography and psychographic change: A German perspective', in Voigt, C. and Pforr, C. (eds) *Wellness Tourism*, London: Routledge, pp. 255–268.

Pforr, C., Pechlaner, H., Locher, C. and Jochmann, J. (2014) 'Health regions: Building tourism destinations through networked regional core competencies', in Voigt, C. and Pforr, C. (eds) *Wellness Tourism*, London: Routledge, pp. 99–111.

Porter, M. E. (1990) *The Competitive Advantage of Nations*, New York: Free Press.

—— (2003) 'The economic performance of regions', *Regional Studies*, 37(6 and 7), 21.

Scott, N., Baggio, R. and Cooper, C. (2008) *Network Analysis and Tourism: From Theory to Practice*, Clevedon, UK: Channel View Publications.

Selin, S. W. (1993) 'Collaborative alliances: New interorganizational forms in tourism', *Journal of Travel and Tourism Marketing*, 2(2–3), 217–227.

Selin, S. and Chavez, D. (1995) 'Developing an evolutionary tourism partnership model', *Annals of Tourism Research*, 22(4), 844–856.

Sheldon, P. and Park, S.-Y. (2009) 'Development of a sustainable tourism destination', in Bushell, R. and Sheldon, P. J. (eds) *Wellness and Tourism. Mind, Body, Spirit, Place*, New York: Cognizant Communication, pp. 99–113.

Smith, M. K. and Puczkó, L. (2009) *Health and Wellness Tourism*, Oxford, UK: Butterworth Heinemann.

Steinhauser, C. and Jochum, B. (2006) 'Markenpolitik im Gesundheitstourismus am Beispiel von "Alpine Wellness" [Brand policy in health tourism using the example 'Alpine Wellness']', in Krczal, A. and Weiermair, K. (eds) *Wellness und Produktentwicklung, Erfolgreiche Gesundheitsangebote im Tourismus* [*Wellness and Product Development, Successful Health Products in Tourism*], Berlin, Germany: Erich Schmidt Verlag, pp. 131–144.

Szivás, S. E. (2005) 'European Union accession: Passport to development for the Hungarian tourism industry?', *International Journal of Tourism Research*, 7, 95–107.

Todd, M. (2012) 'Medical tourism clusters . . . beyond the hype', *International Medical Travel Journal*, http://www.imtj.com/articles/2012/medical-tourism-clusters-30138 (accessed 16 February 2015).

Tsai, W. (2002) 'Social structure of "coopetition" within a multiunit organization: Coordination, competition and intraorganizational knowledge sharing', *Organization Science*, 13(2), pp. 179–190.

Tuohino, A. and Konu, H. (2014) 'Local stakeholders' views about destination management: Who are leading tourism development?', *Tourism Review*, 69(3), 202–215.

Voigt, C. (2014) 'Towards a conceptualisation of wellness tourism', in Voigt, C. and Pforr, C. (eds) *Wellness Tourism*, London: Routledge, pp. 19–44.

Voigt, C. and Laing, J. (2014) 'An examination of the extent of collaboration between major wellness tourism stakeholders in Australia', in Voigt, C. and Pforr, C. (eds) *Wellness Tourism*, London: Routledge, pp. 63–77.

Voigt, C. and Pforr, C. (2014) *Wellness Tourism*, London: Routledge.

Wang, Y. and Fesenmaier, D. R. (2007) 'Collaborative destination marketing: A case study of Elkhart county, Indiana', *Tourism Management*, 28(3), 863–875.

Wang, Y. and Krakover, S. (2008) 'Destination marketing: Competition, cooperation or coopetition?', *International Journal of Contemporary Hospitality Management*, 20(2), 126–141.

Wang, Y. C. and Xiang, Z. (2007) 'Towards a theoretical framework of collaborative destination marketing', *Journal of Travel Research*, 46, 75–85.

Woodside, A. G. and Dubelaar, C. (2002) 'A general theory of tourism consumption systems: A conceptual framework and an experimental exploration', *Journal of Travel Research*, 41(2), 120–132.

Yin, R. K. (2009) *Case Study Research: Design and Methods*, 4th edition, Thousand Oaks, CA: Sage.

Zach, F., Gretzel, U. and Fesenmaier, D. R. (2008) 'Tourist activated networks: Implications for dynamic packaging systems in tourism', in O'Connor, P., Höpken, W. and Gretzel, U. (eds) *Information and Communication Technologies in Tourism 2008*, Vienna, Austria: Springer, pp. 198–208.

Zach, F. and Racherla, P. (2011) 'Assessing the value of collaborations in tourism networks: A case study of Elkhart County, Indiana', *Journal of Travel and Tourism Marketing*, 28(1), 97–110.

25

Destination and product development rested on evidence-based health tourism

Georg Christian Steckenbauer, Stephanie Tischler,
Arnulf Hartl and Christina Pichler

Introduction

Health tourism is often considered as a growth driver within the tourism and healthcare industry (Illing, 2008; Rulle, Hoffmann and Kraft, 2010; Peris-Ortiz and Alvarez-Garcia, 2015). Therefore, health tourism strategies are now more and more integrated in tourism strategies of several countries and tourism destinations.

In order to exploit the growth potential of health tourism, a systematic innovation process as well as a structured product and destination development approach is required. Products and service chains that are based on empirical medical evidence can be keys to success in a health tourism market where the consumer is confronted with enormous amounts of similar offers but lacking quality assurance.

Furthermore, location-bound natural resources that are geographically specific and cannot be exported are likely to develop a unique health tourism appeal (Puczkó, 2009: 256). The health tourism potential of a destination is therefore comprised of the tourism potential (economic and infrastructural background) as well as the health potential in terms of scientifically proven natural remedies. However, evidence-based health tourism product development based on local natural remedies seems to be underestimated. This chapter tries to shed light on destination and product development in health tourism using an evidence-based approach and considering a destination's resources. The case study shows a good-practice example of evidence-based health tourism product development in Austria. Thereafter, some recommendations for the industry and a model of evidence-based health tourism product development are provided and some future perspectives on evidence-based health tourism (especially with regard to destination and product development, cooperation, sustainability, target group orientation and service quality as well as service design) are presented. Finally, this chapter concludes with a discussion of the growth potential of evidence-based health tourism.

Health tourism and destination/product development

The competitiveness of a destination is, *inter alia*, defined by its core competencies and resources. The systematic collection and use of resources can serve as a base for tourism development and fosters competitiveness of and innovation in destinations (Ritchie and Crouch, 2003). Similarly, Lee and King (2006: 195) argue that resources in a destination should guide the formulation and implementation of tourism policies of the destination development strategies.

Pechlaner and Fischer (2004: 266ff) suggest a resource-oriented product development process for destinations based on core competencies. However, they claim that considerable effort is needed to derive core products and turn them into marketable offers. But this resource-oriented destination development approach can drive the competitiveness of companies and destinations and can therefore be used to develop competitive strategies based on the resources of a destination (Lee and King, 2006). Dwyer, Edwards, Mistilis, Roman and Scott (2009) claim that product and marketing development in destination management has to be increasingly targeted and theme-based. Destination managers should explore unique assets in their regions, which can serve as a basis for tourism planning, policy and marketing.

Denicolai, Cioccarelli and Zucchella (2010) recommend even expanding the resource-based approach to a networking approach of a destination. This perspective aims at using local resources as a basis of joint and integrated strategies of decision makers in the destination. Inter-operational activities and inter-organisational learning will then influence the development of core tourism competencies. This networking idea can especially drive innovation through collaborations, particularly in small and medium-sized enterprises (Pikkemaat and Weiermair, 2007).

Applied to health tourism, this means that regional resources and their inherent therapeutic potential have to be seen as a central basis of destination development and health tourism offers. These local resources are a necessary, but not sufficient condition, in product development. Equally important is regional networking to develop health tourism services chains. According to Sheldon and Park (2008), the development of health tourism in a region can foster entrepreneurship and thus create economic benefits. Health tourism can therefore be seen as an innovation driver for other sectors (such as crafts and trade, building industry). This can create substantial value chains, far beyond the actual tourism industry.

However, quite often health tourism regions are not primarily derived from the idea of tourism providers, but are initiated by other sectors such as the medical and healthcare industry. Based on this stimulus more and more destinations see health and medical tourism as an opportunity to target new customer groups and for further economic development. However, tourism providers and the medical or healthcare industry are hardly interlinked, which often leads to a lack of combination of medical and tourism expertise. The amalgamation of medicine and the healthcare industry with the tourism industry bears the potential to develop innovative and target group-specific products. This creates the chance for destinations to foster a unique selling proposition (BMWI, 2011).

Nowadays, a growing number of tourism destinations are positioning themselves as health destinations in order to attract health-conscious consumers (Erfurt-Cooper and Cooper, 2009; Chang and Beise-Zee, 2013). But, these health-promoting destinations should assure tourists that the location truly offers health benefits. Marketing these destinations involves designing the facilities and infrastructure that convince consumers of the health benefits of that location. The approach to use scientific evidence on the health benefits of a particular location can reduce rational uncertainty regarding health claims. Destination managers must identify market segments that share similar health beliefs and target those segments that can be best served by the destination. Nevertheless, the effectiveness of this approach depends on the natural attributes of the destination and its ability and competences to match certain health beliefs (Chang and Beise-Zee, 2013: 44).

Scientific evidence and cooperation of all central players within a destination are major success factors for the development of sustainable, high-quality health tourism offerings. In conjunction with medical and economic research, innovation processes can be initiated that lead to new tourism products in health tourism. An approach based on medical indications and evidence-based health effects can lead to a high product truth and product quality to address specific target groups (Hartl, Granig, Steiner, Klingbacher and Ritter, 2010; Lohmann, 2011; Winklmayr and Hartl, 2013).

Evidence-based health tourism

Quality and authenticity as well as evidence-based services with scientifically proven health benefits are seen as trends within the health and wellness tourism industry. This is also due to the fact that there is an over-supply of wellness and spa offers in many countries such as Germany and Austria (Smith and Puczkó, 2014a: 208). The rapid market development in health and wellness tourism has often led to a neglect of quality and evidence indicators. Treatments without scientifically proven health benefits dominate the market (Populorum, 2008). Customers are increasingly confused by the plethora of new treatments and is mostly not able to identify whether treatments actually foster their personal health.

There appears to be a mismatch between health tourism offerings and evidence-based medical research regarding these products. Their health outcomes have rarely been evaluated according to criteria of evidence-based medicine. Thus, the essential product truth in the sensitive field of personal health is missing (Vahrner and Strozzi, 2014). Knowledge about the effects of health tourism is therefore not only important in terms of marketing, but represents a fundamental prerequisite for a responsible relationship with the guest (Leichtfried, Möller, Raggautz and Schobersberger, 2011).

The authors therefore propose the approach of 'evidence-based health tourism' that focuses on medical standards as well as on the demands of the tourism industry. 'Evidence-based health tourism', as proposed by the authors, combines medical and business perspectives within the cornerstones of tourism, medical indication and evidence.

Tourism as a social phenomenon can be defined in various ways, focusing on different aspects. Typically, a constitutive element of these definitions is location change (Wall and Mathieson, 2006). This is also a relevant aspect of our definition in order to distinguish health tourism from the use of local healthcare infrastructure.

Another key element is the indication-based approach to health tourism. Following *Merriam Webster's Medical Dictionary* (2015), indication can be defined as 'a symptom or particular circumstance that indicates the advisability or necessity of a specific medical treatment or procedure'. Applied to health tourism, this means that product development is based on the individual need for intervention derived from a specific health condition of the clientele. Indication in the context of health tourism can therefore be defined as the basis or rationale to use a certain health tourism product. This includes reduction of symptoms and cure as well as prevention of defined health problems.

Third, the concept of evidence is integrated into our approach to health tourism. This refers to the notion of evidence-based medicine, which means that decision making on diagnosis and

Table 25.1 Levels of quality of a body of evidence in the GRADE approach

Underlying methodology	Quality rating
Randomised trials or double-upgraded observational studies	High
Downgraded randomised trials or upgraded observational studies	Moderate
Double-downgraded randomised trials or observational studies	Low
Triple-downgraded randomised trials or downgraded observational studies or case series/case reports	Very low

Note: GRADE, grading of recommendations, assessment, development and evaluation.

Source: Higgins and Green (2011).

treatment is based on the best available current research, the physician's clinical expertise and the needs and preferences of the patient (*Mosby's Medical Dictionary*, 2012).

To determine the best available current research, an evaluation of the quality of evidence has to be done. The international standard for this evaluation is the GRADE approach (grading of recommendations, assessment, development and evaluation), which specifies four levels of quality, where the highest quality rating is for a body of evidence based on randomised trials without important limitations (Table 25.1). The system has been adopted by more than 20 leading international organisations, including the World Health Organization (WHO), the American College of Physicians, BMJ Clinical Evidence and the Cochrane Collaboration (Higgins and Green, 2011; Chandler and Hopewell, 2013).

With regard to health tourism, the notion of evidence-based means that all health related interventions within a health tourism product have to be developed and evaluated on the basis of best available scientific research and integrate the clientele's interests, values and needs. Thus, the approach also reflects a high customer involvement.

Summarising, the authors define 'evidence-based health tourism' as a temporary movement of a person to a place, where he or she finds a particular intervention for a specific health condition in a holiday setting that will have beneficial effects and promote health and wellbeing based on the best available current scientific research.

This is close to a definition of Goeldner (1989: 7, cited in Hall, 2011: 5), who defined health tourism as '(1) staying away from home, (2) health [as the] most important motive and (3) done in a leisure setting'. The conceptual approach is therefore demand- and customer-oriented and not a supply-side categorisation of available products. The definition is focused on the health motive of the traveller to a place outside home with a clear underlying medical indication referring to his/her health status.

Health tourism rested on evidence-based medicine demands high quality standards. Evidence-based medicine explicitly calls for interventions based on empirically proven health effects. Therefore, a critical evaluation of the outcome of a product or offer has to be done in health tourism (Rulle et al., 2010; Leichtfried et al., 2011).

Natural resources as a basis of evidence-based health tourism

The International Union of Tourist Organizations (IUOTO) defined 'health tourism' in 1973 as 'provision of health facilities utilizing the natural resources of the country, in particular mineral water and climate' (IUOTO, 1973: 7 in Hall, 2011: 5). The availability and use of natural resources were seen as constitutive for health tourism.

Throughout societies an innate human need for contact with nature can be observed. This phenomenon was first described as biophilia by the sociobiologist Edward Wilson. His early interpretation of biophilia was based on the notion that a particular characteristic of humans was their tendency to pay attention to, affiliate with or otherwise respond positively to nature (Wilson, 1984). According to Kellert and Wilson (1993), this phenomenon can be understood through an evolutionary perspective: we humans have spent almost all of our evolutionary history in the natural environment and have only migrated to urban environments in relatively recent times. Therefore, this attraction, identification and need to connect to nature is thought to remain in our modern physiology and psychology.

The inception of the notion of biophilia has created considerable debate among scientists and there have been concerted attempts to examine empirically the human relationship with the natural world (Hanna and Coussens, 2001; Maller et al., 2009). There is growing evidence that providing access to nature plays a vital role in human health and well-being: positive health effects on green space have been observed on longevity, cardiovascular disease, people's self-reported general health, mental health, sleep patterns, recovery from illness and even social health aspects (Gladwell, Brown, Wood, Sandercock and Barton, 2013; Nieuwenhuijsen et al., 2014).

In the last few hundred years, there has been an extraordinary disengagement of humans from the natural environment: For the first time in human history, more of the world's population now lives in urban instead of rural areas (CIA, 2015; United Nations, 2015). The gap in natural exposure between our early evolutionary environments and modern life is growing tremendously. This physical disconnection from the environment in which we evolved has a diametric impact on our health and emotional wellbeing (Capaldi, Dopko and Zelenski, 2014). A growing amount of health science studies show a significant correlation between increased urbanisation and poor physiological and psychological health (Dustin, Bricker and Schwab, 2009; Cyril, Oldroyd and Renzaho, 2013). Furthermore, life satisfaction, wellbeing and happiness are significantly lower in urban and densely populated areas (MacKerron and Mourato, 2013; Schwanen and Wang, 2014).

In this way, our modern urban societies increase the need for recreation and preference for nature (Van den Berg, Hartig and Staats, 2007). Outdoor recreation in natural environments is well on the way to becoming an important element of healthy living and a remedy against the deficiencies of a modern life separated from nature (Bell, Tyrväinen, Sievänen, Pröbstl and Simpson, 2007). Health tourism built on natural resources is therefore seen as a very prosperous field for development (Peris-Ortiz and Alvarez-Garcia, 2015).

According to Cassens (2013: 151), nature holds many potentials when it comes to health tourism destination development: nature offers space for activities, observations and learning. It simultaneously provides a healthy and natural environment. Additionally it can supply local natural remedies which can be used for health tourism.

Regarding the scientific evidence of nature's positive effects on health and wellbeing, natural resources build an excellent base for the development of evidence-based health tourism. Smith and Puczkó (2009: 257) see a clear upward trend in the use of nature and natural healing assets as resources for health and wellness tourism.

Destinations with a rich heritage of natural health resources (such as Alpine regions) provide excellent prerequisites to develop evidence-based health tourism products and to integrate them into economic value chains. However, from a European point of view, the healing potential as well as the resulting health tourism potential are still underestimated.

In Japan, on the contrary, natural healing assets are becoming a staple of mainstream medicine called *shinrin-yoku* or forest therapy. *Shinrin-yoku* is a term that means 'taking the forest atmosphere' or 'forest bathing'. Since the development of the concept during the 1980s, considerable scientific research on its health effects and the mechanisms behind the healing effects has been conducted (Tsunetsugu, Park and Miyazaki, 2010). Evidence-based benefits include long-lasting impacts on humans' immune system markers, boosting natural killer cells and anticancer proteins (Li, 2010), reduced stress, improved mood, sleep and wellbeing, reduced blood pressure, accelerated recovery from illness and an increased ability to concentrate, even in children with attention-deficit hyperactivity disorder (Shin, Yeoun, Yoo and Shin, 2010; Tsunetsugu, Park, Lee, Kagawa and Miyazaki, 2011; Kamioka et al., 2012; Lee et al., 2014; Miyazaki, Ikei and Song, 2014). Based on these results, more than 50 forest therapy trails were developed in Japan with millions of annual visitors, and forest therapy has become a cornerstone of preventive healthcare and healing in Japanese medicine. The concept is rapidly spreading globally, e.g. in South Korea and the USA, and is also already offered in Europe, e.g. in Finland (HikingResearch, 2013).

The first Austrian approach to evidence-based health tourism was the Austrian Moderate Altitude Studies (AMAS). AMAS I (2000) focused on the indication of the metabolic syndrome, a combination of overweight, disturbed blood sugar and blood fat metabolism as well as elevated blood pressure, which are massive cardiovascular risk factors, whereas AMAS II (2006) focused on persons with high stress levels. The studies proved that an active sojourn (a combination of hiking and active/passive regeneration) at Alpine moderate altitudes (1,500–2,500 m) under the guidance of professional coaches has positive effects in persons with metabolic syndrome as well as in a clientele suffering from stress. These effects include reduction in blood pressure and heart rate, increased endothelial stem cell circulation, reduction of body weight without specific dietary measures as well as positive psychological effects such as improved sleep quality, wellbeing and social and physical recuperation (Schobersberger et al., 2003; Strauss-Blasche et al., 2004; Strauss-Blasche, Reithofer, Schobersberger, Ekmekcioglu and Marktl, 2005; Frick et al., 2006; Theiss et al., 2008). Based on these results, the health tourism product 'welltain' (*well*being in the moun*tain*) has been developed, which is currently offered by 13 high-quality hotels in the region of Lech Zürs Arlberg (Welltain, 2016).

Another example of evidence-based health tourism in Austria is the hotel cooperation Lifetime Hotels that focuses on improvement of cardiorespiratory fitness and wellbeing (Lifetime Hotels, 2016). Cardiorespiratory fitness is defined as the ability to deliver and use oxygen during intense and prolonged exercise or work and is an important medical health and wellbeing indicator. The benefits of good cardiorespiratory fitness include a reduced risk of heart disease, lung cancer, type 2 diabetes and stroke, which are major health challenges in today's societies (Plowman and Smith, 2014). The Hiking and Coaching Study, conducted by the Paracelsus Medical University Salzburg, showed that even one week of hiking in the mountains can improve cardiorespiratory fitness and health-related quality of life. These effects were even stronger in combination with individual health psychological coaching. On the basis of these results the hotel cooperation Lifetime Hotels was developed, offering a health tourism product that promises positive effects on cardiorespiratory fitness and health-related quality of life. These effects are being made measurable and visible for guests through a Rockport Fitness Test and a specifically developed and validated online questionnaire using comic strips (Sittenthaler, Hartl, Traut-Mattausch and Hahne, 2014; Lifetime Hotels, 2016).

Evidence-based health tourism in Austria

Case study: Hohe Tauern Health within the Alpine Health Region Salzburg

Smith and Puczkó (2014b: 184f) suggest that ideally, governments should agree on a health tourism strategy and identify regions that will focus on health tourism. Towns and resorts should then develop their health tourism offers in accordance with regional priorities.

The Austrian federal province Salzburg is currently following this approach of government-driven health tourism regional development. Within the strategy of the Alpine Health Region Salzburg (Alpine Gesundheitsregion SalzburgerLand), the province positions itself as a major health tourism destination. The strategy fosters innovative approaches in health tourism and stimulates inter-sectoral and inter-organisational cooperation to boost regional tourism development and the creation of new health tourism value chains. The high level of interaction between medical research, healthcare facilities, businesses and the tourism industry fosters quality, professionalism and specialisation. A strong focus is on the theme complex of 'nature and health'. Within this thematic field, health tourism products based on natural health resources are developed, offered and promoted, which are highly specialised and evidence-based. Regarding the prerequisites of the province in terms of its enormous nature potential, this approach is seen as clear competitive advantage (Gschwandtner, 2014).

Hohe Tauern Health: holidays for allergic and asthmatic guests

In accordance with this strategy, the National Park Hohe Tauern Salzburg (that is depicted as a good-practice example in this case study) develops and markets health tourism products for a clientele that suffers from allergies and asthma. The product core builds a location-bound natural health resource – the Krimml waterfalls. With a total height of 380 metres in three stages, they are the highest waterfalls in Europe and the fifth highest in the world. With approximately 400,000 visitors each year, they are one of the most visited tourist sites in Austria. A hiking trail allows visitors to get very close to this breath-taking nature attraction (Krimmler Wasserfälle – OeAV Sektion Warnsdorf / Krimml, 2015).

Research shows that the Krimml Waterfalls have positive health effects on allergic and asthmatic people. The healing effect lies in the specific environment with particularly fine water spray around the waterfalls. This spray is composed of negatively charged, finely atomised breathable water fragments known as waterfall aerosols. The water rushes into the valley with such great kinetic force that the water molecules shatter into tiny fragments upon impact with the rock and result in nanometre-sized waterfall aerosols. These specific nano-aerosols comprise mainly negatively charged intermediate ions, which trigger a variety of biological effects. Their minuscule size allows them to penetrate deep into the respiratory tract and to develop an immune-modulatory effect. This effect was shown in a randomised controlled trial involving 54 asthmatic children, conducted by the Paracelsus Medical University Salzburg. Children who stayed at the waterfalls for three weeks enjoyed significant improvement in the medical guiding parameters of their allergic asthma. These positive effects last up to four months (Gaisberger et al., 2012; Kolarz et al., 2012).

(continued)

(continued)

A further clinical cross-over study revealed that the major part of the charge of the negative air ions is delivered to the mucous membranes already in the nose. Negative air ions accelerate the movement of the cilia, which leads to a considerably higher cleaning effect of the nasal mucosa and the mucous membranes of the respiratory system. Therefore, the waterfalls stimulate the immune system and lead to a persistent improvement of the respiratory tract and positively affect lung function (Hartl et al., 2010; Gaisberger et al., 2012; Kolarz et al., 2012).

The results of the medical research built the basis for Hohe Tauern Health, a health initiative developed by regional tourism and medical experts in cooperation with governance and stakeholders at the federal and regional level. Within this initiative, evidence-based health tourism products for the target group of allergic and asthmatic guests are promoted.

During the waterfall therapy, participants spend an hour a day in the vicinity of the Krimml waterfalls. A course of therapy should last at least 14 days; the ideal length of stay is three weeks. During the summer months (May–October) a molecular biologist from the Paracelsus Medical University Salzburg provides professional guidance through the holidays. Guests receive a medical check-up (including pulmonary function test, respiratory gas analysis, symptoms checklist, fitness test) and an individual consultation at the beginning and the end of their stay (Hohe Tauern Health, 2015). In this way, the positive health effects are made measurable and visible for the guests, which is a critical success factor.

Besides the waterfall therapy, a diversified programme is offered within the holiday package, such as physiotherapy with breathing techniques, nutrition classes, personal health counselling and various workshops and sports activities, which are individually designed for allergic and asthmatic patients (Hohe Tauern Health, 2015).

Furthermore, Hohe Tauern Health offers the Splash Camp Krimml, which is a three-week camp for children with asthma. During their stay, which includes daily visits to the waterfall (1 hour), they are supported by specially trained pedagogues and a paediatrician specialised in pulmonology and asthma (Hohe Tauern Health, 2015).

The success of the waterfall therapy is bolstered significantly by the conditions in the Hohe Tauern Health's allergy-friendly partner hotels. In cooperation with the Paracelsus Medical University Salzburg, strict quality criteria based on scientific evidence were developed. These include the following criteria (Hohe Tauern Health, 2015):

- The concentration of fine dust and the eight most important indoor allergens is regularly monitored.
- Fine dust concentration has to be below 20 μg / m³ PM10 (recommended maximum indoor values in Austria and Germany: 80 μg / m³ PM10).
- Housekeeping has to be adapted to the needs of allergic people (e.g. special HEPA filter vacuum cleaner).

In addition, the hotel staff has to participate in regular training to be re-certified (at two-year intervals). This includes training on hygiene regulations, dietetic know-how for kitchen staff and responding to special needs of allergic and asthmatic guests. This applies to guests with food allergies and intolerances as well as to people with allergy symptoms due to house dust mites, animal hair and pollen (Hohe Tauern Health, 2015).

The Hohe Tauern Health product clearly addresses the target group of people and particular families with children suffering from allergies and asthma. This target group is large: 30 per cent of western Europeans are suffering from allergies, in Germany (the most important source market for the destination), 40–43 per cent develop an allergy throughout their lifetime (Böcking and Renz and Pfefferle, 2012).

Extensive customer surveys were carried out in the summer season of 2012 by the IMC University of Applied Sciences Krems, asking guests of the region and visitors of the Krimml waterfalls about their motivation to come to the region, their knowledge of the product, their behaviour on site and their satisfaction with offers and services. In relevant items, guests suffering from allergies or asthma showed higher satisfaction, higher willingness to return to the destination and high rates of recommendation (Steckenbauer, 2013).

Taking into consideration that 20 per cent of all visitors of the region stated that a member of their household suffers from an allergy and 59 per cent stated that they had a person suffering from allergies in their own circle of friends (Steckenbauer, 2013), one could assume that focusing on a specific target group and offering specialised services based on medical research could be very dynamic in tourism communication and marketing.

Representatives of the local tourism association in Krimml describe their experience and the current situation as follows. The health initiative has been recognised and respected nationally and internationally (e.g. Hohe Tauern Health was EU RegioStar finalist 2012[1]). Hohe Tauern Health guests are demanding, willing to spend money and critical about the offers and services provided. If the guest feels well and the waterfall therapy shows lasting effects, the guest is likely to return (P. Lemberger and E. Czerny, personal communication, 8 January 2016). Statements of guests underpin this appraisal. Krimml also faces an increase of 21 per cent in the number of overnight stays during the summer season throughout project term (2010–2015).

Following our operational definition of 'evidence-based health tourism', we can summarise that the product Hohe Tauern Health within the Alpine Health Region Salzburg fulfils all necessary conditions for this kind of offer. It is clearly offered in a leisure setting as it offers (family) holidays in adequate surroundings, it has clear product modules for the respective target group and their health condition and offers relief and health benefits based on medical evidence. The quality of the body of evidence of the product can be rated as high according to the GRADE approach, as it is based on a randomised controlled trial without important limitations.

Note

1   The RegioStars Award is initiated by the European Commission as a project in the field of regional policy: 'The objective of the RegioStars Awards is to identify good practices in regional development and to highlight original and innovative projects which could be attractive and inspiring to other regions' (European Commission (2016) RegioStars Awards. Brussels: European Commission. http://ec.europa.eu/regional_policy/de/regio-stars-awards/ (accessed 9 August 2016)).

Practical implications for the health tourism industry

An essential prerequisite for health tourism offers is medical evidence, i.e. the use of scientifically proven and effective resources and interventions. Medical evidence can act as a criterion to set offers apart from pure wellness and relaxation products. In evidence-based health tourism – both preventive and curative – medical and scientific proof of the effectiveness of a healing resource has to be in the focus and has to be communicated. There are of course

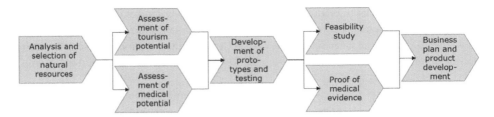

Figure 25.1 Process model to develop evidence-based health tourism products.

Source: Steckenbauer, Tischler and Hartl (2015).

natural healing resources such as thermal waters or terrain that may very well serve as a basis for wellbeing and relaxation offers. However, these resources need medical evidence in order to create a health tourism product. By the demonstration of this scientific proof, health tourism products can be differentiated from spa and wellness offers.

Ideally, local natural remedies build the basis of evidence-based health tourism. The type of resources used can vary, ranging from hot springs and thermal water to waterfalls, plants and herbs, air, altitude and terrain as a basis for health-related treatments. The use of local resources for these therapies helps to ensure uniqueness and authenticity. Most importantly, the development of health tourism offers has to be done systematically and in a structured way and it requires the involvement of key regional stakeholders. Furthermore, medical as well as tourism expertise has to be combined to ensure evidence-based and marketable health tourism products. Based on this approach, a profiling opportunity for a tourism destination can be developed. Therefore, a structural approach using a process model that follows this approach to develop evidence-based health tourism offers should be followed and serve as a work plan for health tourism product and destination development (Figure 25.1).

Outlook and future perspectives of evidence-based health tourism

Finally, future perspectives of evidence-based health tourism will be discussed. Developments in health tourism in general and in particular in evidence-based health tourism specifically seem to affect five areas: destination and product development, cooperation, sustainability, target group orientation as well as service quality and service design.

Structural approaches in destination and product development

Especially Alpine regions are characterised by an exceptional natural landscape, healthy climate and high environmental quality. They have a wide range of regional and local natural health resources, which potentially build the base for destination development. Some of the Alpine natural health resources are historically known or even already scientifically evaluated, but are insufficiently integrated in economic value chains and professional product and service development. Other natural health resources are already integrated in traditional health tourism products and services like cure and rehabilitation resorts. These products are usually offered in traditional, historically grown healing spa villages. However, this sector faces a range of challenges due to changing circumstances and new customer demands in the health market: a rapid growth of the second health market, demographic transition, changing target groups, growing importance of work–life balance, an increasing health consciousness and subjective health as well as a rising personal responsibility for health and a paradigm shift in the primary healthcare system with decreasing reimbursements of medical services and cures (Holjevac, 2003; Hartl et al., 2010; Winklmayr and Hartl, 2013). The challenges in this sector affect its realignment and the development of product and service innovations. For both reasons a structured approach in destination and product development and innovation is very much needed and provides many areas for further research.

Cooperation

Health tourism demands highly specialised knowledge on the specific target group and indication, which is mostly not available for individual hotels and health tourism providers, as they mostly act as small and mid-sized enterprises (SMEs). Furthermore, the tourism industry is traditionally weak in innovation and cross-sectoral innovation and cooperation. However, it is precisely this cooperation between businesses in the tourism sector and related sectors, universities and other research and educational institutions, administration and governance that could stimulate cross-fertilisation, especially in less-developed rural regions. New health tourism services based on local natural resources and an innovation model could therefore help to generate new business scenarios and sustainable economic value chains.

Zehrer (2009: 342f) argues that in particular SME can benefit from cooperation (horizontal, vertical or diagonal) to generate know-how and create competitive sets of services offered to meet the needs of customers. This leads to greater 'virtual size' (Zehrer, 2009: 343), better visibility and therefore better chances in the tourism market.

Sustainability

Health tourism can be a core area to establish new sustainable tourism strategies, as the use of regional natural resources as a basis makes it possible for providers in tourism to create products that are ecologically and socially sustainable, as these resources are locally available and can be used in a sustainable manner to create regional value. Health tourism using regional natural resources can therefore be a driving factor for the creation of new forms of sustainable health tourism.

The possibility of sustainable economic value generation through the utilisation of natural resources is also an important base for political argumentation against increasing development pressure (artificial leisure facilities etc.) even in protected areas. In contrast to other tourism approaches that often create a non-reversible pressure and alienation on nature and space, natural health tourism contributes to the promotion and protection of natural and cultural heritage.

Target group orientation

The trend towards a healthy lifestyle (Erfurt-Cooper and Cooper, 2009), lifestyle-factors (e.g. 'downsizing') (Smith and Puczkó, 2009) and societal changes (e.g. 'new ageing') (Barth and Werner, 2005) can act as demand drivers for health and wellness tourism. However, these changes do not lead to a growth automatism in health tourism (Lohmann, 2010, 2015; Steckenbauer and Tischler, 2015), but suggest a clearer focus on (potential) target groups.

Rather, it is necessary to analyse existing target groups and their peculiar demands depending on their specific health condition. Target groups in health tourism can partly be derived from the requirements that are directly associated with their state of health, such as a person suffering from allergies (see above) or diabetes or a guest in need of holiday dialysis.

These clear profiles on requirements for hotels and destinations help tourism providers to develop products based on the needs of the customers and thus create an environment for defined target groups that build the perfect framework for their holidays. Of course, individual needs of guests have to be considered in the context of health tourism (cf. Tuominen et al., 2014: 81), but this can be seen as a prerequisite for a tourism provider.

Service quality and service design

Service quality has been one of the key issues in tourism management for the last two decades. Particularly, tourism as a service-intensive industry depends on the quality of services and customers' service experiences. The management of service quality therefore is essential for tourism providers to achieve customer satisfaction as a precondition for market success (Zehrer, 2009: 332).

An important aspect of service quality in health tourism refers to the professionals delivering these products, as the human factor verifiably contributes to the success of tourism product offerings. Quality has to be seen in the products themselves and the personnel delivering these products. This applies not only to therapists and physicians, who come into direct contact with tourists, but also those not in direct contact with the end-consumer, such as executives and managers of health tourism-related facilities (hotels, destinations, etc.). To ensure evidence-based health tourism offerings are of high quality, professionals within this area should have a certain level of (academic) education and training (Blank and Schobersberger, 2013). The authors therefore strongly recommend the fostering of the development of academic programmes focusing on health tourism.

Guiry, Scott and Vequist (2013: 433f) have researched the service quality expectations of (US) medical tourists and conclude that only by exceeding tourist expectations will satisfaction occur and result in loyalty and positive word-of-mouth communication. Interestingly, in their study it was the case that experienced medical tourists had significantly lower expectations than potential medical tourists. Among others, items like 'Patients feel safe in interactions with employees', 'Up-to-date equipment', 'Employees tell patients exactly when services will be performed' or 'Provide services at the time promised' (Guiry et al., 2013) show large differences in the expectations of experienced and inexperienced customers, which indicates that, once facing realities of health tourism, consumers revise their expectations due to frustration – or 'customer sacrifice', as this could be called, following Pine and Gilmore (1999). However, limitations (sample size, sample population, scales) of the study (Guiry et al., 2013: 442f) must be taken into consideration and generalisability therefore is limited. Yet, it draws attention to the paramount importance of service quality to create a positive customer experience in the field of health tourism.

Improvement of customer experience can therefore be seen as a condition for companies – in particular, for SMEs – working in the segment of health tourism. The use of service design tools allows companies to create both form and function of a service from the perspective of the customer. This refers to the creation of new services as well as to the improvement of existing services (Mager and Gais, 2009: 42).

Service design can be seen as an iterative four-step process: exploration, creation, reflection and implementation (Stickdorn and Schneider, 2011: 125). In the best case, service design based on thorough evaluation (of customers' expectations and experiences, market and competitors) could lead to services exceeding customers' expectations and creating competitive advantages for providers.

Zehrer (2009: 342) thus recommends the use of service design for SME providers in tourism as it would be likely to 'reduce costs, maximise customer and employee satisfaction and support the decision-making process of management with regard to the allocation of their scarce resources'. This applies in particular to providers in health tourism: as expectations of customers are high, the market is international, competitive and fragmented, providers highly depend on customer satisfaction and loyalty of customers. The use of service design methods enables providers to analyse structurally and improve their services to become outstanding on the market.

Conclusion

In general, the growth potential for health tourism seems to remain underexploited, as the trend towards a bigger share of health tourism cannot be found in aggregated data for many countries (e.g. Germany and Austria) (Lohmann, 2010, 2015; Loh, 2014; Steckenbauer and Tischler, 2015). The non-growing segment of health tourism could be observed for several years now, although several trends could tremendously drive health tourism, such as societal and demographic changes as well as lifestyle-factors such as complementary and alternative medicine, healthy nutrition, 'downsizing' – voluntary simplicity, new spirituality, etc. (Barth and Werner, 2005; Erfurt-Cooper and Cooper, 2009; Smith and Puczkó, 2009).

Another, as yet underestimated development factor in health tourism is the growing amount of people who are willing but cannot go on holidays due to health reasons. A recent survey among EU citizens shows that health problems were the second most common reason for not going on holiday in 2014. In Germany, which is an important tourism source market, respondents even rated health problems as the main reason (24 per cent) for staying at home (European Commission, 2015). This offers a variety of chances for businesses and destinations to develop innovative indication-tailored health offers, e.g. for people with dementia or incontinence or those who need dialysis and their relatives, who would otherwise not go on vacation.

Uncertainty about the quality of health tourism products and services might have notably deterred growth in health tourism so far. Healthcare as well as health tourism providers in destinations have to demonstrate credibly that their quality of services in health tourism complies with international standards, such as those set by the International Organization for Standardization (ISO) or the Joint Commission International (JCI) (Loh, 2014).

However, the current status quo in the health and wellness tourism industry is characterised by a proliferation of general labels such as Best Health Austria (a state-approved certificate for health tourism in Austria). In a review conducted by *Stiftung Warentest*, the leading German customer safety group, only 9 out of 53 labels in the health tourism and wellness sector were rated as helpful (*Stiftung Warentest*, 2013). And even within these helpful labels, only a vague customer value regarding measurable health benefits can be observed.

Therefore, more product-specific and target group-oriented labels such as the quality certification for Hohe Tauern Health's allergy-friendly hotels accredited by Paracelsus Medical University Salzburg seem to be needed to help to identify, regulate and promote indication-tailored and evidence-based health tourism resources and services to exploit the above-mentioned growth potential fully.

To conclude, health tourism does not represent automatic growth (Lohmann, 2010), but can act as a growth driver within the tourism industry. For this, health tourism products have to be of high quality and authenticity, which could be reached by evidence-based services with scientifically proven health benefits that are also made visible and understandable for the customer. Health tourism products have to be developed following the principles of evidence-based medicine (based for instance on expertise of medical universities or the GRADE approach) on the one hand and on professional tourism know-how on the other hand. This, however, needs close cooperation and exchange of knowledge between medical research and healthcare providers as well as the tourism industry.

References

Barth, R. and Werner, C. (2005) *Der Wellness Faktor*, Vienna, Austria: Relax Guide and Magazin Verlag Christian Werner.

Bell, S., Tyrväinen, L., Sievänen, T., Pröbstl, U. and Simpson, M. (2007) 'Outdoor recreation and nature tourism: A European perspective', *Living Reviews in Landscape Research*, 1, 2–46.

Blank, C. and Schobersberger, W. (2013) 'Academic education in health tourism – knowledge about and willingness for academic training within the field of health tourism: A cross-country evaluation within the German-speaking Alpine area', *Tourism and Hospitality*, 2(1), 2–6.

BMWI (2011) *Innovativer Gesundheitstourismus in Deutschland. 'Gesundheitsregionen und Gesundheitsinitiativen' (Branchenreport)*, Berlin, Germany: BMWI.

Böcking, C., Renz, H. and Pfefferle, P. I. (2012) 'Prävalenz und sozioökonomische Bedeutung von Allergien in Deutschland', *Bundesgesundheitsblatt*, 55, 303–307.

Capaldi, C. A., Dopko, R. L. and Zelenski, J. M. (2014) 'The relationship between nature connectedness and happiness: A meta-analysis', *Frontiers in Psychology*, 5, 976.

Cassens, M. (2013) *Gesundheitstourismus und touristische Destinationsentwicklung: Ein Lehrbuch*, Munich, Germany: Oldenbourg.

Chandler, J. and Hopewell, S. (2013) 'Cochrane methods – twenty years experience in developing systematic review methods', *Systematic Reviews*, 2(1), 76.

Chang, L. and Beise-Zee, R. (2013) 'Consumer perception of healthfulness and appraisal of health-promoting tourist destinations', *Tourism Review*, 68(1), 34–47.

CIA (2015) *The World Factbook: Rate of Urbanization*, https://www.cia.gov/library/publications/the-world-factbook/fields/2212.html (accessed 13 January 2016).

Cyril, S., Oldroyd, J. and Renzaho, A. (2013) 'Urbanisation, urbanicity and health: A systematic review of the reliability and validity of urbanicity scales', *BMC Public Health*, 13, 513.

Denicolai, S., Cioccarelli, G. and Zucchella, A. (2010) 'Resource-based local development and networked core-competencies for tourism excellence', *Tourism Management*, 31(2), 260–266.

Dustin, D. L., Bricker, K. S. and Schwab, K. A. (2009) 'People and nature: Towards an ecological model of health promotion', *Leisure Sciences*, 32(1), 3–14.

Dwyer, L., Edwards, D., Mistilis, N., Roman, C. and Scott, N. (2009) 'Destination and enterprise management for a tourism future', *Tourism Management*, 30, 63–74.

Erfurt-Cooper, P. and Cooper, M. (2009) *Health and Wellness Tourism. Spas and Hot Springs*, Bristol, UK: Channel View Publications.

European Commission (2015) *Preferences of Europeans towards Tourism 2015*, Flash Eurobarometer 414, Brussels, Belgium: European Commission.

Frick, M., Rinner, A., Mair, J., Alber, H. F., Mittermayr, M., Pachinger, O., . . . Weidinger, F. (2006) 'Transient impairment of flow-mediated vasodilation in patients with metabolic syndrome at moderate altitude (1,700 m)', *International Journal of Cardiology*, 109(1), 82–87.

Gaisberger, M., Sanovic, R., Dobias, H., Kolarz, P., Moder, A., Thalhamer, J., . . . Hartl, A. (2012) 'Effects of ionized waterfall aerosol on pediatric allergic asthma', *Journal of Asthma*, 49(8), 830–838.

Gladwell, V. F., Brown, D. K., Wood, C., Sandercock, G. R. and Barton, J. L. (2013) 'The great outdoors: How a green exercise environment can benefit all', *Extreme Physiology and Medicine*, 2(1), 3.

Gschwandtner, C. (2014) *Alpine Gesundheitsregion SalzburgerLand*, presented at the Tag der Tourismuswirtschaft, 28 October 2014, Zell am See.

Guiry, M., Scott, J. J. and Vequist IV, D. G. (2013) 'Experienced and potential medical tourists' service quality expectations', *International Journal of Health Care Quality Assurance*, 26(5), 433–446.

Hall, C. M. (2011) 'Health and medical tourism: A kill or cure for global public health?', *Tourism Review*, 66(1/2), 4–15.

Hanna, K. and Coussens, C. (2001) *Rebuilding the Unity of Health and the Environment: A New Vision of Environmental Health for the 21st Century*, Washington DC: National Academy Press.

Hartl, A., Granig, P., Steiner, M., Klingbacher, M. and Ritter, M. (2010) 'Nutzung natürlicher Gesundheitsressourcen – Möglichkeiten und Grenzen', in P. Granig and L. A. Nefiodow (eds) *Gesundheitswirtschaft: Wachstumsmotor im 21. Jahrhundert*, Wiesbaden: Gabler, pp. 272–302.

Higgins, J. P. T. and Green, S. (2011) *Cochrane Handbook for Systematic Reviews of Interventions, Version 5.1.0 [updated March 2011]: The Cochrane Collaboration*, www.cochrane-handbook.org (accessed 20 January 2016).

HikingResearch (2013) *Hiking Research: Connecting People to the Restorative Power of Nature*, https://hikingresearch.wordpress.com/tag/forest-therapy/ (accessed 16 January 2016).

Hohe Tauern Health (2015) *Wasserfall-Therapie*, http://www.hohe-tauern-health.at/de/wasserfall-therapie (accessed 20 January 2016).

Holjevac, I. A. (2003) 'A vision of tourism and the hotel industry in the 21st century', *International Journal of Hospitality Management*, 22(2), 129–134.

Illing, K.-T. (2008) *Gesundheitstourismus und Spa-Management*, Munich, Germany: Oldenbourg.

Kamioka, H., Tsutani, K., Mutoh, Y., Honda, T., Shiozawa, N., Okada, S., . . . Handa, S. (2012) 'A systematic review of randomized controlled trials on curative and health enhancement effects of forest therapy', *Psychology Research and Behavior Management*, 5, 85–95.

Kellert, S. and Wilson, E. (1993) *The Biophilia Hypothesis*, Washington DC: Island Press.

Kolarz, P., Gaisberger, M., Madl, P., Hofmann, W., Ritter, M. and Hartl, A. (2012) 'Characterization of ions at Alpine waterfalls', *Atmospheric Chemistry and Physics*, 12, 3687–3697.

Krimmler Wasserfälle – OeAV Sektion Warnsdorf / Krimml (2015) *Europe's Highest Waterfalls – Experience Water*, http://www.wasserfaelle-krimml.at/html_engl/wasserfall_engl.html (accessed 20 January 2016).

Lee, C.-F. and King, B. (2006) 'Assessing destination competitiveness: An application to the hot springs tourism sector', *Tourism and Hospitality Planning and Development*, 3(3), 179–197.

Lee, J., Tsunetsugu, Y., Takayama, N., Park, B. J., Li, Q., Song, C., . . . Miyazaki, Y. (2014) 'Influence of forest therapy on cardiovascular relaxation in young adults', *Journal of Evidence-Based Complementary and Alternative Medicine*, 2014, Article ID 834360.

Leichtfried, V., Möller, C., Raggautz, M. and Schobersberger, W. (2011) 'Evidenz-basierter Gesundheitstourismus', in A. Krczal, E. Krczal and K. Weiermair (eds) *Qualitätsmanagement in Wellnesseinrichtungen*, Göttingen: Schmidt, pp. 155–168.

Li, Q. (2010) 'Effect of forest bathing trips on human immune function', *Environmental Health and Preventive Medicine*, 15(1), 9–17.

Lifetime Hotels (2016) *Die HICO Studie: die Basis eines Lifetime Urlaubs*, http://www.lifetimehotels.at/medizinische-studie (accessed 8 January 2016).

Loh, C. P. (2014) 'Health tourism on the rise? Evidence from the Balance of Payments Statistics', *European Journal of Health Economics*, 15(7), 759–766.

Lohmann, M. (2010) *Nachfragepotenziale im Gesundheitstourismus – Chancen und Herausforderungen im Quellmarkt Deutschland*, presented at the ÖGAF / ITF – Expertengespräch, 25 November 2010, Vienna.

—— (2011) *Innovativer Gesundheitstourismus in Deutschland*, Berlin, Germany: Bundesministerium für Wirtschaft und Technologie.

—— (2015) *Nachfrage nach gesundheitsorientierten Urlaubsformen in Deutschland – Von Trends, gutem Leben und Verantwortung*, presented at the 3. Gesundheitstourismus-Kongress 2015, Hochschule für Wirtschaft und Umwelt Nürtingen-Geislingen.

MacKerron, G. and Mourato, S. (2013) 'Happiness is greater in natural environments', *Global Environmental Change*, 23(5), 992–1000.

Mager, B. and Gais, M. (2009) *Service Design*, Paderborn, Germany: UTB.

Maller, C., Townsend, M., St Leger, L. H., Henderson-Wilson, C., Pryor, A. and Prosser, L. (2009) 'Healthy parks, healthy people: The health benefits of contact with nature in a park context', *The George Wright Forum*, 26(2), 51–83.

Merriam Webster's Medical Dictionary (n.d.) *Indication*, http://www.merriam-webster.com/medical/indication (accessed 30 December 2015).

Miyazaki, Y., Ikei, H. and Song, C. (2014) 'Forest medicine research in Japan', *Nippon Eiseigaku Zasshi (Japanese Journal of Hygiene)*, 69(2), 122–135.

Mosby's Medical Dictionary (2012) *Evidence-based Medicine*, 9th edition, St Louis, MO: Elsevier.

Nieuwenhuijsen, M. J., Kruize, H., Gidlow, C. Andrusaityte, S., Anto, J. M., Basagana, X., . . . Grazuleviciene, R. (2014) 'Positive health effects of the natural outdoor environment in typical populations in different regions in Europe (PHENOTYPE): A study programme protocol', *BMJ Open*, 4(4), Article ID e004951.

Pechlaner, H. and Fischer, E. (2004) 'Alpine Wellness – Auf dem Weg von der Kernkompetenz zum Produkt', in *Jahrbuch 2003/2004 Schweizerische Tourismuswirtschaft*, St Gallen, Germany: Institut für Öffentliche Dienstleistungen und Tourismus, pp. 265–283.

Peris-Ortiz, M. and Alvarez-Garcia, J. (eds) (2015) *Health and Wellness Tourism. Emergence of a New Market Segment*, Cham, Switzerland: Springer.

Pikkemaat, B. and Weiermair, K. (2007) 'Innovation through cooperation in destinations: First results of an empirical study in Austria', *Anatolia: An International Journal of Tourism and Hospitality Research*, 18(1), 67–83.

Pine, B. J. and Gilmore, J. H. (1999) *The Experience Economy. Work Is Theatre and Every Business a Stage*, Boston, MA: Harvard Business Review Press.

Plowman, S. A. and Smith, D. L. (2014) *Exercise Physiology for Health, Fitness and Performance*, Baltimore, MD: Lippincott Williams and Wilkins.

Populorum, M. A. (2008) 'Qualitätssicherung im Gesundheits- und Wellnesstourismus – Möglichkeiten und empirische Befunde', in A. Kyrer and M. A. Populorum (eds) *Trends und Beschäftigungsfelder im Gesundheits- und Wellness-Tourismus*, Berlin, Germany: Lit Verlag.

Ritchie, J. R. B. and Crouch, G. I. (2003) *The Competitive Destination*, New York: CABI.

Rulle, M., Hoffmann, W. and Kraft, K. (2010) *Erfolgsstrategien im Gesundheitstourismus: Analyse zur Erwartung und Zufriedenheit von Gästen*, Berlin, Germany: Schmidt.

Schobersberger, W., Schmid, P., Lechleitner, M., von Duvillard, S. P., Hortnagl, H., Gunga, H.C. and Humpeler, E. (2003) 'Austrian Moderate Altitude Study 2000 (AMAS 2000). The effects of moderate altitude (1,700 m) on cardiovascular and metabolic variables in patients with metabolic syndrome', *European Journal of Applied Physiology*, 88(6), 506–514.

Schwanen, T. and Wang, D. (2014) 'Well-being, context and everyday activities in space and time', *Annals of the Association of American Geographers*, 104(4), 833–851.

Sheldon, P. J. and Park, S. Y. (2008) 'Sustainable wellness tourism: Governance and entrepreneurship issues', *Acta Turis-Tica*, 20(2), 151–172.

Shin, W. S., Yeoun, P. S., Yoo, R. W. and Shin, C. S. (2010) 'Forest experience and psychological health benefits: The state of the art and future prospect in Korea', *Environmental Health and Preventive Medicine*, 15(1), 38–47.

Sittenthaler, S., Hartl, A., Traut-Mattausch, E. and Hahne, P. (2014) *Validierung des QOLC (Quality of Life Comic) - Ein neues Instrument zur Messung der gesundheitsbezogenen Lebensqualität*, presented at the 11. Tagung der Österreichischen Gesellschaft für Psychologie, Vienna.

Smith, M. and Puczkó, L. (2009) *Health and Wellness Tourism*, 2nd edition, Oxford, UK: Butterworth-Heinemann.

—— (2009) *Health and Wellness Tourism*, Burlington, MA: Elsevier.

—— (2014a) 'Future trends and predictions', in M. Smith and L. Puczkó (eds) *Health, Tourism and Hospitality. Spas, Wellness and Medical Travel*, 2nd edition, New York: Routledge, pp. 203–227.

—— (2014b) 'Planning and management', in M. Smith and L. Puczkó (eds) *Health, Tourism and Hospitality. Spas, Wellness and Medical Travel*, 2nd edition, New York: Routledge, pp. 169–201.

Steckenbauer, G. C. (2013) *Ergebnisse Befragung Hohe Tauern Health 2012*, Krems, Austria: IMC University of Applied Sciences Krems.

Steckenbauer, G. C. and Tischler, S. (2015) *Health as a Stagnating Travel Motive – The Case of Austria*, presented at the Consumer Behavior in Tourism Symposium 2015 (CBTS 2015), December 2–4, 2015, Munich.

Steckenbauer, G. C., Tischler, S. and Hartl, A. (2015) 'Entwicklung eines Prozessmodells zum Aufbau gesundheitstouristischer Produkte: Case Study "Hohe Tauern Health"', in *Wegbereiter – Karrierepfade durch ein Fachhochschulstudium*. 9. Forschungsforum der österreichischen Fachhochschulen, Tagungsband, Hagenberg.

Stickdorn, M. and Schneider, J. (2011) *This Is Service Design Thinking. Basics – Tools – Cases*, Hoboken, NJ: John Wiley.

Stiftung Warentest (2013) *Wellness-Siegel: Nur neun Siegel sind wirklich hilfreich*, https://www.test.de/Wellness-Siegel-Nur-neun-Siegel-sind-wirklich-hilfreich-4612145-0 (accessed 20 January 2016).

Strauss-Blasche, G., Riedmann, B., Schobersberger, W., Ekmekcioglu, C., Riedmann, G., Waanders, R., . . . Humpeler, E. (2004) 'Vacation at moderate and low altitude improves perceived health in individuals with metabolic syndrome', *Journal of Travel Medicine*, 11(5), 300–304.

Strauss-Blasche, G., Reithofer, B., Schobersberger, W., Ekmekcioglu, C. and Marktl, W. (2005) 'Effect of vacation on health: Moderating factors of vacation outcome', *Journal of Travel Medicine*, 12(2), 94–101.

Theiss, H. D., Adam, M., Greie, S., Schobersberger, W., Humpeler, E. and Franz, W. M. (2008) 'Increased levels of circulating progenitor cells after 1-week sojourn at moderate altitude (Austrian Moderate Altitude Study II, AMAS II)', *Respiratory Physiology and Neurobiology*, 160(2), 232–238.

Tsunetsugu, Y., Park, B. and Miyazaki, Y. (2010) 'Trends in research related to "Shinrin-yoku" (taking in the forest atmosphere or forest bathing) in Japan', *Environmental Health and Preventive Medicine*, 15(1), 27–37.

Tsunetsugu, Y., Park, B.-J., Lee, J., Kagawa, T. and Miyazaki, Y. (2011) 'Psychological relaxation effect of forest therapy – results of field experiments in 19 forests in Japan involving 228 participants', *Nippon Eiseigaku Zasshi (Japanese Journal of Hygiene)*, 66(4), 670–676.

Tuominen, T., Binder, D., Dvorak, D., Husak, C., Illing, K., Lange, S., . . . Schmidt, R. (2014) *Developing a Competitive Health and Well-being Destination*, http://julkaisut.turkuamk.fi/isbn9789522165405.pdf (accessed 20 January 2016).

United Nations (2015) *World Urbanization Prospects: The 2014 Revision*, New York: United Nations, Department of Economic and Social Affairs, Population Division.

Vahrner, A. and Strozzi, M. (2014) 'Mehr Gesundheit für Tirol-Urlauber – Expertenrunde', *Tiroler Tageszeitung*, 19 January 2014.

Van den Berg, A. E., Hartig, T. and Staats, H. (2007) 'Preference for nature in urbanized societies: Stress, restoration and the pursuit of sustainability', *Journal of Social Issues*, 63(1), 79–96.

Wall, G. and Mathieson, A. (2006) *Tourism: Change, Impacts and Opportunities*, Harlow, UK: Pearson Education.

Welltain (2016) *Welltain Destinationen*, http://www.welltain.at/_DEV/ (accessed 12 January 2016).

Wilson, E. (1984) *Biophilia*, Cambridge, MA: Harvard University Press.

Winklmayr, M. and Hartl, A. (2013) *Erfassung, Analyse und Potentialabschätzung der Wirkung natürlicher Heilvorkommen in Salzburg*, Salzburg: Land Salzburg, Abteilung für Wirtschaft und Tourismus, Salzburg.

Zehrer, A. (2009) 'Service experience and service design: Concepts and application in tourism SMEs', *Managing Service Quality: An International Journal*, 19(3), 332–349.

26

Developing a wellness destination

A case study of the Peak District

Sarah Rawlinson and Peter Wiltshier

This chapter explores the opportunity and strength of a destination management approach to identifying resources, stakeholders, consumers and the willingness to promote the concept and practices of wellness tourism in a destination case study. The case study is a destination familiar to over 50 per cent of the UK's resident population – the Peak District of the North Midlands. Our case study demonstrates the importance of a structure to the destination development model. We identify several key issues to ensure the successful outcome for the key stakeholders and the basis for ongoing developments in wellness and tourism. We consider and recommend that public-sector governance and partnership arrangements in management of operations, research and development, knowledge transfer and repository thereof, are critical and central to this success. The fundamentals are reinforced through clear brand identity and marketing built upon this from core values and beliefs to drive the community's aim and objectives in achieving success through wellness.

Before embarking on an exploration of new services to be delivered and consumed in a specific and very special UK destination we will first explain the concept and practices anticipated in wellness tourism.

Our initial exploration features a mature destination at the top of its life cycle (Butler, 2006). In the Butler model the destination can be rejuvenated through product or service expansion, differentiation, market penetration or product diversification. In this chapter we will demonstrate that the rejuvenation through product innovation and market penetration is possible with the collaboration of the stakeholders engaged in proposing a wellness tourism model designed by the community with the encouragement of central and local government; the skills and knowledge of the University of Derby; the Peak District National Park authority and a myriad of informed service sector businesses that have emerged over the six decades since the Park was first established (Glasby, 2012). The parameters and resources to establish a learning destination with a wellness and tourism welcome are demonstrated.

> A pre-requisite for innovation is the understanding of how destinations source, share and use knowledge.
>
> *(Baggio and Cooper, 2010: 2)*

We recognise that the English National Parks emerged from anxieties about communities' access to recreation in the countryside and the debate is encapsulated in the *débâcle* of the Mass Trespass of 1932 by ramblers on Kinder Scout in the Peak District. Workers and their families determined their right of access to areas of recreation and relaxation at a time of civil disturbance related to the Great Depression of 1929. Pressures on communities to survive an economic crisis 90 years ago are in effect repeated in the twenty-first century as the same communities struggle for social and economic equity and survival in a market-forces model in a geopolitical neoliberal context. The origins of National Parks are indeed traced to the Mass Trespass of 1932. Our case study highlights the importance of this assertion to recreation born in our region and living on in the conceptual 'green lungs' of the rural idyll in a new form of tourism incorporating health, wellbeing and rejuvenation and assuring a better future quality of life for all (Ritter, 2005; Steiner and Reisinger, 2006; Chen, 2007; Kelly, 2010; Pesonen and Komppula, 2010).

We are accustomed now to the practices of spa, beauty, health and wellbeing in individual enterprises; we now focus on wellness tourism as a concept, embodied in destination management objectives and driven by the communities in which wellness tourism is practised.

- 'The average three- to five-star hotels provide fairly comprehensive wellness facilities' (Mueller and Kaufmann, 2001: 1).
- 'Wellness tourism can be considered one of the most ancient forms of tourism if one considers the scrupulous attention to wellbeing of Greeks and Romans' (Smith and Kelly, 2006: 1).

Smith and Puczkó (2008) would see a broader multicultural definition of wellness tourism to include health, wellbeing, welfare and destressing for individuals as well as entire nations. Their approach is global; wellness tourism has different meanings in various countries and is largely contemporary with studies of health tourism (including surgery) and of preventive medical tourism (perhaps Ayurvedic practices) and tourism that relates to water and thermal treatment. Largely our definition falls within the internationally recognised tourism for personal, social, cultural, educative, spiritual and wellbeing improvement and enhancement through to high specific treatments largely in destinations possessed of accommodation, spa water and thalasso-therapies. This latter exploration includes reflections on wellness and water through treatments in Asia and Australia in the context of health and wellness (Erfurt-Cooper and Cooper, 2009). Water and all its possible permutations for participation therein, consumption thereof and bathing within is central to many aspects of wellness tourism over millennia. The specific benefits and enjoyment of wellness tourism through water are key to our understanding of how we can adapt or commodify wellness tourism for new markets and existing suppliers willing and wishing to rejuvenate contemporary destinations, their constituent businesses and excite new and existing consumers (see, for example, Konu et al., 2010 in Finland; Rodrigues et al., 2010 in Portugal; Ringer, 2007; Lehto et al., 2006 in the USA). Current research seeks to identify purpose of travel and recreation at specific sites in order for suppliers to provide appropriate services and respond to increasingly complex needs from more well-informed consumers. 'More and more people are seeking information for vacations at a spa' is the closing statement from research in Greece (Didascalou et al., 2009: 124).

Wellness tourism is a growing market and a number of destinations worldwide are positioning themselves as wellness tourism destinations. Destinations such as Bali, Costa Rica, Thailand, New Zealand and India are obvious wellness destinations but others are entering the market, such as South Africa, Turkey, Arizona, Madeira and Canada (for examples, see Chen et al.,

2008; Dimitrov, 2012; Voigt and Pforr, 2013; Peris-Ortiz et al., 2015). For wellness tourism destinations to be successful there need to be health and wellness assets that will help to create a unique selling proposition and distinctive brands to attract new wellness tourists who are self-aware and seek enhanced wellbeing, health and happiness. A successful wellness tourism offer focuses on the natural assets and environment of the destination and draws on local traditions to create wellness experiences (Messerli and Oyama, 2004; Mair, 2005; Laing and Weiler, 2008; Kim and Batra, 2009; Magdalini and Paris, 2009; Georgiev and Vasileva, 2010; Quintela et al., 2011; Pesonen et al., 2011). The success of any tourism destination is where its competitiveness is built on markets that best match its resources (Sheldon and Park, 2009; Prideaux et al., 2013). The wellness tourism offer is the sum of a destination's physical, psychological, spiritual and social wellbeing resources (Voigt et al., 2011).

The purpose of our exploration of a case study in a more developed destination is partly related to the proven link between tourism and cultural heritage product offers. It is also partly to do with the availability of accessible transport, infrastructure and maturity of the suppliers and services provided. Couple this maturity and ready recall of identity and brand with safety and security concerns minimised for the majority of current and potential consumers and we can evidence reasons why wellness tourism as a concept is primed for expansion and integration into the mainstream visitor economy. Much of the current research in the context of wellness has been sourced from mature spa destinations in many more-developed destinations (Weiermair and Steinhauser, 2003; Johanson, 2004; Chen et al., 2008; Hall, 2011; Hjalager and Konu, 2011; Kelly, 2012). Inevitably a link is created in the potential consumers' recall and conscious selection of destinations that has historical clarity and consistency of market message and recall. Unfortunately for suppliers there has been insufficient primary research and evidence that consumers are well informed about the choices in wellness, spa and rejuvenation in more developed destinations and a need for a clearer understanding over what motivates consumers and how we can effectively respond by delivering products and stories that meet expectations (see examples in Dryglas, 2013 in Poland; Supapol and Barrows, 2007 in Canada; Bertsch and Ostermann, 2011 in Austria). In emerging wellness destinations there is also uncertainty as to the attractiveness of the offer (Kim and Batra, 2009). There are also lessons to be learned from emerging forms of niche tourism, including adventure and outdoor-focused activity (Kulczycki and Lück, 2009). In some situations niche tourism in wellness is scarcely linked to recreation and tourism and more so towards curing illness (Mueller and Kaufmann, 2001). So the case study approach in this chapter aims to bridge the gap between knowledge of health and recreation through a deeper understanding of our motivation to consume services in the cognate areas (see, for example, Pesonen et al., 2011 in Finland). The second key story surrounding motivation to consume wellness tourism is of quality and value for money (see the examples of Peris-Ortiz et al. (2015) in Spain; Quintela et al. (2011) in Portugal; Supapol and Barrows (2007) in Canada; Johanson, 2004).

Our focus is to steer the recall and cultural legacy towards under-utilised resources in specific sites of potential spa, resort and health and wellbeing history. As well as Buxton in the centre of the region we provide insights into the relationship between knowledge of wellness and spa; heritage of wellbeing from resort status, connections between exceptional service provision in hotels, resorts and spas and the explicit and tacit calls to action already created by the famous attractions of Harrogate (some 90 minutes distance by rail or car), Chatsworth House Estate, with its focus on food and drink sourced ethically and from within the region, Buxton Spa water bottled on site in the Peak District and distributed worldwide, emerging breweries adjacent to the site (Thornbridge Hall), wineries (Renishaw Hall), craft ale festivals (Derby and Burton), and celebrated produce from pasture (oat cakes and prime beef and lamb). The sum total of these products and services, coupled with an exceptional offer of attractions and access, has created the environment for sustaining a further enhanced product destination development that featured rest, recreation, rejuvenation in the limestone and gritstone crags that comprise the Peak District. Our case study delivers to the tourist the most accessible hill country north of London and the affluent English south-east and home counties. Not only is it easily accessible by rail but there is also the potential to explore rail travel from the west of Europe, especially with Eurostar high-speed links through the Channel Tunnel to Belgium, Holland, Germany and France (Association of Leading Visitor Attractions, 2016).

Crouch and Ritchie (2012) proposed a conceptual model of destination competitiveness and sustainability which was adapted by Sheldon and Park (2009) to be more appropriate in a wellness tourism concept. Sheldon and Park's model has four stages of development before arriving at a sustainable wellbeing tourism destination. The concepts of wellness and wellbeing are closely related and therefore we argue that Sheldon and Park's model for a sustainable wellbeing tourism destination development is equally valid for developing wellness tourism destinations.

Sheldon and Park's five stages of development for a sustainable wellbeing tourism destination are:

- Stage 1: Supporting wellbeing resources and factors – this stage includes infrastructure, superstructure, hospitality and destination atmosphere (a sense of place).
- Stage 2: Core wellbeing resources and attractions – this stage includes unique wellbeing destination features: natural and cultural resources and traditional healing/therapeutic/ wellness/wellbeing resources.
- Stage 3: Wellbeing destination policy and planning – this stage includes strategic planning, vision, goals and policies, network collaborations, monitoring and evaluation.
- Stage 4: Wellbeing destination development and management – this stage includes human resources, training, education, networks of actors and quality programmes.
- Stage 5: Sustainable wellbeing tourism destination.

The characteristic of the wellness tourist is one of the key benefits to a destination in developing wellness tourism as a niche tourism product. Wellness tourists often have similar characteristics as eco-tourists, cultural tourists and sports tourists, which provides a destination with numerous opportunities to cross-market niche tourism products. They are likely to contribute more to a destination than other types of tourists because wellness tourists are more likely to be wealthier and better educated and spend more in the destination (Yeung and Johnston, 2013). Wellness tourists are also more likely to contribute to the sustainability of cultural assets and events such as local festivals and engage in sports and sporting activities, adventure and other activities (Clapham, 2015).

Case study: the Peak District

The Peak District is located in the northern Midlands of England, covering parts of the counties of Derbyshire, Staffordshire, Cheshire, Greater Manchester and South Yorkshire. It is home to the UK's first national park, established in 1951 and covering 143,830 hectares. The Peak District landscape is diverse and ranges from open moorlands and gritstone that form the Dark Peak to

(continued)

(continued)

the limestone peaks, wooded valleys, gorges and dales of the White Peak. This rich diversity of natural and cultural heritage attracts millions of visitors each year. The Peak District has a population of approximately 161,000, of which 38,000 live within the national park. The national park is surrounded by major urban conurbations, with 16.1 million people living within 40 miles, making it one of the UK's most accessible outdoor destinations.

The Peak District boasts mineral springs, rich in iron and thermal waters used for medicinal purposes since the seventeenth century. The spa towns and villages have developed during the Victorian era from centres of medical treatment to fashionable leisure and tourism destinations, including Buxton, Matlock, Matlock Bath, Bakewell, Ashbourne, Tideswell, Wirksworth and Bradwell. In the 1840s Matlock was world-famous for its hydrotherapy treatment. Visitors and patients travelled by train from London, including Queen Victoria, who visited as a child. Buxton is probably one of the best-known spa towns in the UK. The Romans were attracted to the area by the warm thermal springs, with a constant temperature of 28°C. The Romans built baths and, by Tudor times, Buxton was fairly well established as a spa. The Fifth Duke of Devonshire built the Crescent in 1780 and this was the start of a series of iconic buildings constructed in Buxton, including the Dukes stables which were converted to a hospital in the 1880s and a university campus in 1999. In 1863 the railways arrived in Buxton and the town boomed. Large hotels were constructed, including the Palace Hotel, fashionable town houses sprang up and leisure and entertainment facilities were built, including the Opera House and the Pavilion Gardens. These buildings survive today, making Buxton a delightful place to visit. Buxton was the last hydropathic centre to close in the UK in 2000.

The Peak District receives millions of visitors each year attracted by the natural beauty of its landscape, market towns, villages, historic houses and traditional events. It is one of the most accessible and inspiring visitor destinations in the UK. Visitors participate in activities such as walking, cycling, climbing, caving, horse riding, canoeing and adventure sports. For the less active the Peak District offers historic houses and castles, family fun attractions, museums, galleries, parks and gardens.

Whilst the Peak District tourism offer is strong and supported by an iconic brand, visitor spend is significantly lower than equivalent rural destinations for both day visitors and staying visits. In 2014 Derbyshire received 186,000 staying visits and generated £56 million in visitor spend whilst Hereford and Worcester attracted fewer staying visits (158,000) but generated a higher visitor spend (£66 million) (Visit England, 2015). A key factor in Derbyshire's poor performance is that the depth, range and value of the tourism products on offer in Derbyshire and the Peak District are not as strong as other destinations. This is despite the Peak District being home to Chatsworth, a stately home and one of the UK's leading tourist attractions. Chatsworth received approximately 610,000 visitors in 2014 according to the Association of Leading Visitor Attractions (2016), but there are no data that suggest that these visitors spend in the wider visitor economy of the Peak District. Destinations need quality products and visitor experiences, including food and drink, attractions, outdoor activities and unique events to entice them to stay longer in the destination and spend more.

Seventy-nine per cent of visitors to the Peak District are day visitors with an average stay of 3.4 hours. The average length of visit for those staying overnight is 3.8 days (Peak District National Park Visitor Survey, 2014). Apart from the main tourist attractions like Chatsworth and some limited but good-quality accommodation, very few visitors realise the real breadth of experiences the Peak District has to offer. There is a need to develop the Peak District's product offer so that these frequent visitors can engage in more activities to keep them in the Peak District for longer, spending more and visiting more frequently.

As the competition between destinations grows there is a need to refocus and rediscover what makes a destination distinctive and how that distinctiveness can meet the changing demands of the visitor in order to develop an effective tourism strategy (Pechlaner et al., 2012; Murphy, 2013). To attract new visitors the Peak District needs to expand its tourism offer and be clear about its distinctiveness. One of the major failings of the destination is that visitors do not get a sense of the distinctiveness of what the Peak District has to offer and struggle to make connections between the many different tourism products on offer.

An examination of the Peak District reveals a destination with a wealth of wellness resources and wellness tradition to support its development as a wellness tourism destination. It has the supporting wellbeing resources, infrastructure, superstructure, hospitality and destination atmosphere identified at stage 1 of Sheldon and Park's model of a sustainable wellbeing tourism destination and the core wellbeing resources and attractions, natural and cultural resources, traditional healing/therapeutic/wellness/wellbeing resources required of unique wellbeing resources identified at stage 2 of the model (Sheldon and Park, 2009).

According to Welcome Tourism Worldwide (2013), 'natural assets are the most critical component to a wellness tourism development'. The connection between the environment, landscape, nature and its history of spa provides the Peak District with an opportunity to meet a variety of visitor motivations related to health and wellbeing, ranging from relaxation, traditional spa breaks and specialised health treatments to energising walks, connections to nature and the great outdoors and adventure activities. The historic links to the right to roam and access to lands for the workers and their families in 1932 are thus reinforced by the concept of wellness and tourism.

The ability of the Peak District to improve its competitiveness in the marketplace requires a strong destination image, good-quality products and experiences and an effective marketing strategy. Whilst it can be argued that the Peak District has a strong destination image, good-quality products and a strong brand, there is still ample opportunity to build a strong platform for growth with existing infrastructure and product, to entice visitors to extend their stays, visit outside of the peak summer season and generate additional jobs and increase revenue from appropriately managed tourism marketing (Jardine, 2009). As we have established, the pre-conditions for a rejuvenating economy coupled to an attractive visitor destination are already in existence. Forty per cent of the resident population have education attainment at university degree level and above. The local university (University of Derby) has developed its credentials to deliver higher-level thinking and analytical skills in hospitality and tourism degree offerings for more than 20 years. The green shoots of innovation in welfare and wellbeing emerged with the New Labour contract to re-energise the post-industrial landscape and recognition at the turn of the twenty-first century of the Peak District as symbolic of England's 'green lungs' (Shoard, 1980; Matthews et al., 2000; Thompson et al., 2007; Park and Selman, 2009). We are setting the scene of an idyll and the capture of a brand and identity underpinned by social and cultural heritage and a legacy embedded by centuries of endeavour and enterprise (Elliott, 2009; Uglow, 2003).

A review of the Visit Peak District and Derbyshire's website, the destination marketing organisation (DMO) for the Peak District, highlights a marketing strategy based on promoting

(continued)

(continued)

products and suppliers. The DMO website is dominated by accommodation suppliers and visitor attractions. Many of these businesses have their own websites and can easily, and, some would argue, more effectively be found on the internet through various search engines and are rated by consumers on websites such as TripAdvisor. The DMO could be more effective in its promotion of the Peak District by targeting specific markets, concentrating on what the consumer is seeking in a destination and demonstrating how the Peak District can fulfil that need.

The Peak District is not alone in selling the destination via its products and supplies. However, products and supplies do not create a reason to visit. For example, selling a visit to Chatsworth is not a reason to visit the Peak District as a destination.

According to Jardine (2009), developing a distinctive tourism product in the Peak District:

> is about small business growth, linking businesses together to create fresh new opportunities and to deliver more joined-up, exciting and fulfilling visitor experiences and delivering economic impacts such that local communities and the businesses of tourism are more resilient, prosperous and self-sustaining.

Tourism in the Peak District is typified by a fragmentation of small independent businesses working in silos in a disjointed way. A failure to provide a collective approach to tourism marketing has led to a tendency to sell individual products rather than the destination. This had led to a lack of knowledge by visitors of the genuine product distinctiveness the Peak District has to offer. As we have already proposed, there is a need to drive collaborative tourism product development to provide visitors with a mix of different experiences by combining different products which would enhance the Peak District's visitor offer.

Developing the Peak District as a wellness destination will require a move to stage 3 of Sheldon and Park's model. This stage includes strategic planning, vision, goals, policies, network collaborations, monitoring and evaluation. This stage should be built on a strong evidence base that supports the view that the Peak District has the quantity, quality and distinctiveness of wellness resources to achieve economic growth as a wellness tourism destination. This will require an assessment of the key wellness features of the Peak District, including:

- tourism facilities: accommodation, cuisine, events, retail and other activities;
- wellness heritage and culture: historical traditions and links to wellness, arts and crafts and other aspects of living culture;
- landscape and countryside: distinctiveness of the landscape and the nature connectivity to wellness;
- built environment: spa towns and villages, parks and gardens;
- access and transport: road, rail and air links to and within the Peak District;
- visitor services: marketing, information provision, signposting, car parking accessibility of the tourism products and services.

The assessment of the wellness features should identify the potential for new product development. New product development will require closer collaborative working across the existing businesses and a focus on the distinctiveness of the wellness offer. This can be achieved through a wellness destination management plan. A management plan can help to address fragmentation and provide a framework for public, private and voluntary organisations to work together to strengthen the quality of the visitor experience, monitor impact and effectively manage resources. We have suggested that the destination has the resources, skills, will and vision to harness stakeholders and services in an integrated development of wellness and tourism.

We recommend a framework for developing the Peak District as a wellness tourism destination. This will require a steering group to work with the DMO to oversee the implementation of the wellness destination management plan. The main function of the steering group would be to work with the stakeholders in the allocation of key actions, secure funding and resources and provide access to research and technical assistance that supports the implementation of the plan. The steering group will have responsibility for communicating progress of the wellness destination management plan, providing information on the progress of individual actions, agreeing forthcoming priorities and taking any necessary management decisions. At the same time the University of Derby will provide a repository for wellness tourism research valorised by location in the beautiful and accessible Peak District. Lessons learned from niche tourism and community-based sustainable tourism activity supporting local goods and service contribute to current knowledge. The expectations of sophisticated and informed consumers can be met by the quality marks in wellness tourism emerging in Europe, North America and Australasia. These quality marks or accreditation to international standards organisations like ISO14001 can support heightened awareness to both host and guest in our destination of the benefits to all stakeholders of wellness tourism. Moreover, dual goals of improved recreation and wellness through our own interpretation at the destination will be embedded in the skills delivered through scholarship in higher education within the context of the heritage 'green lungs' of England.

Figure 26.1 illustrates a multi-level approach to destination management. There are key stakeholders critical to the successful development and implementation of a wellness destination management plan.

- The overall responsibility for implementing the plan should rest with the DMO, which has responsibility for representing tourism and the visitor economy, quality of the visitor experience and destination branding and marketing.
- The local and district councils will have a key role in transport, planning, visitor and information services.
- The Peak District National Park will have responsibility for the conservation, enhancement and visitor enjoyment of the protected environment.
- Parish councils and community groups should be engaged in the future direction and planning for the community and providing local activities and events to support the wellness product offer.
- The local enterprise partnership can provide economic and business development, investment in promotion and funding for enterprise-focused initiatives.
- Individual tourism businesses will play a critical part in the development and operation of visitor facilities, new product development and the promotion of the business linked to the wellness brand. They are also the custodians of the visitor welcome orientation and care.

(continued)

(continued)

- Local landowners provide access to wellness sites and future development opportunities.
- Local civic societies, heritage, arts and culture groups and other voluntary bodies provide a sense of place, cultural assets and events such as local festivals and niche cultural products that support the wellness product.
- The local university provides a repository of research, skills, forward thinking and creativity linking a historic landscape with people intent on embedding a political and social will to conserve and develop heritage with a purpose to build wellness tourism for the benefit of future generations in the community and its invited visitors.

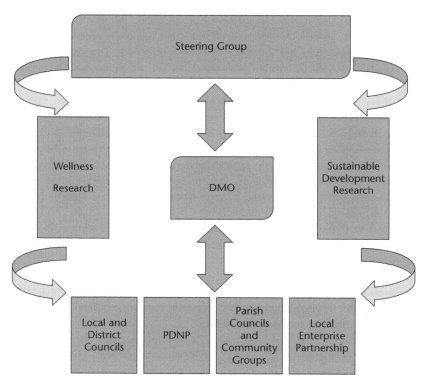

Figure 26.1 Developing a wellness destination.

Note: DMO, *destination marketing organisation*; PDNP, *Peak District National Park*.

Conclusion

Steering panels for community tourism development have been in existence for a decade or more. The University of Derby resourced and housed the first Tourism Stakeholders' Steering Panel in 2001, which led to the establishment of a tourism forum for private providers and the beginnings of the Visit Peak District and Derbyshire Destination Management Partnership. The University continues to support voluntary-sector organisations to deliver initiatives to improve the quality of life and health and wellbeing for their communities. In so doing, these volunteers are aiding the taxpayer funding and bolstering resources. The collaboration between voluntary-sector organisations and the University explores possible developments in spa and wellness and supporting community initiatives such as transport and accessibility research. The collaboration is intended to promote knowledge transfer to connect volunteers, service providers and public-sector partners to generate a wellness destination. The collaboration also encourages a relationship of trust between all sectors that becomes transparent in its focus on creating a better understanding of what wellness tourism can bring to all. We have seen this emerge over a decade of partnership working. University-led research is now beginning to be widely promulgated for the benefit of the voluntary sector and to the delivery of new initiatives. There is ample empirical and conceptual research developed through the research centres at the University, National Park and Local Enterprise Partnership that is fragmented in storage and capacity for retrieval. A steering group can bring this resource together and access the University's resources to make the data readily available to all.

References

Association of Leading Visitor Attractions (2016) http://alva.org.uk/details.cfm?p=423 (accessed October 2015).

Baggio, R. and Cooper, C. (2010) 'Knowledge transfer in a tourism destination: The effects of a network structure', *The Service Industries Journal*, 30(10), 1757–1771.

Bertsch, G. and Ostermann, H. (2011) 'The effect of wellness brand awareness on expected and perceived service quality', *Tourismos*, 6(2), 103–120.

Butler, R. (ed.) (2006) *The Tourism Area Life Cycle* (Vol. 1), Bristol, UK: Channel View Publications.

Chen, J. S. (2007, July) 'Wellness tourism: Measuring consumers' quality of life', in *Leisure: Business Advances and Applied Research Conference* (p. 32).

Chen, J. S., Prebensen, N. and Huan, T. C. (2008) 'Determining the motivation of wellness travelers', *Anatolia*, 19(1), 103–115.

Clapham, M. (2015) BRDC Continental, http://bdrc-continental.com/opinions/wellness/ (accessed 17 October 2015).

Crouch, G. I. and Ritchie, J. B. (2012) 'Destination competitiveness and its implications for host-community QOL', in Uysal, M., Perdue, R. and Sirgy, J. (eds) *Handbook of Tourism and Quality-of-Life Research: Enhancing the Lives of Tourists and Residents of Host Communities*, Dordrecht, The Netherlands: Springer Science and Business Media, pp. 491–513.

Didascalou, E., Lagos, D. and Nastos, P. (2009) 'Wellness tourism: Evaluating destination attributes for tourism planning in a competitive segment market', *Tourismos*, 4(4), 113–125.

Dimitrov, P. (2012) 'Long-term forecasting of the spa and wellness subsector of the Bulgarian tourism industry', *Tourism and Management Studies*, 7, 140–148.

Dryglas, D. (2013) 'Spa and wellness tourism as a spatially determined product of health resorts in Poland', *Current Issues of Tourism Research*, 2(2), 30–38.

Elliott, P. A. (2009) *The Derby Philosophers: Science and Culture in British Urban Society, 1700–1850*, Manchester, UK: Manchester University Press.

Erfurt-Cooper, P. and Cooper, M. (2009) *Health and Wellness Tourism: Spas and Hot Springs*, Bristol, UK: Channel View Publications.

Georgiev, G. and Vasileva, M. T. (2010) 'Conceptualization and classification of balneo, spa and wellness establishments in Bulgaria', *UTMS Journal of Economics*, 1(2), 37.

Glasby, G. (2012) *Mass Trespass on Kinder Scout in 1932: And the Founding of Our National Parks*, Philadelphia, PA: Xlibris Corporation.

Hall, C. M. (2011) 'Health and medical tourism: A kill or cure for global public health?', *Tourism Review*, 66(1/2), 4–15.

Hjalager, A. M. and Konu, H. (2011) 'Co-branding and co-creation in wellness tourism: The role of cosmeceuticals', *Journal of Hospitality Marketing and Management*, 20(8), 879–901.

Jardine, I. (2009) 'The role of natural heritage in driving tourism', in *Investing in Success, Heritage and the UK Tourism Economy*, London: Heritage Lottery Fund, pp. 23–24.

Johanson, M. M. (2004) 'Health, wellness focus within resort hotels', *Hospitality Review*, 22(1), 3.

Kelly, C. (2010) 'Analysing wellness tourism provision: A retreat operator's study', *Journal of Hospitality and Tourism Management*, 17(1), 108–116.

—— (2012) 'Wellness tourism: Retreat visitor motivations and experiences', *Tourism Recreation Research*, 37(3), 205–213.

Kim, B. H. and Batra, A. (2009) 'Healthy-living behaviour status and motivational characteristics of foreign tourists to visit wellness facilities in Bangkok', in *The 2nd Annual PSU Phuket Research Conference Proceedings*, Phuket, Prince of Songkla University, pp. 1–8.

Konu, H., Tuohino, A. and Komppula, R. (2010) 'Lake Wellness – a practical example of a new service development (NSD) concept in tourism industries', *Journal of Vacation Marketing*, 16(2), 125–139.

Kulczycki, C. and Lück, M. (2009) 'Outdoor adventure tourism, wellness and place attachment', *Wellness and Tourism: Mind, Body, Spirit, Place*, New York: Cognizant Communication Corporation, pp. 165–176.

Laing, J. and Weiler, B. (2008) 'Mind, body and spirit: Health and wellness tourism in Asia', *Asian Tourism: Growth and Change*, 379–389.

Lehto, X. Y., Brown, S., Chen, Y. and Morrison, A. M. (2006) 'Yoga tourism as a niche within the wellness tourism market', *Tourism Recreation Research*, 31(1), 25–35.

Magdalini, V. and Paris, T. (2009) 'The wellness tourism market in Greece – an interdisciplinary methodology approach', *Tourismos*, 4(4), 127–144.

Mair, H. (2005) 'Tourism, health and the pharmacy: Towards a critical understanding of health and wellness tourism', *Tourism (Zagreb)*, 53(4), 335–346.

Matthews, H., Taylor, M., Sherwood, K., Tucker, F. and Limb, M. (2000) 'Growing-up in the countryside: Children and the rural idyll', *Journal of Rural Studies*, 16(2), 141–153.

Messerli, H. R. and Oyama, Y. (2004) 'Health and wellness tourism – global', *Travel and Tourism Analyst*, (August), 1–54.

Mueller, H. and Kaufmann, E. L. (2001) 'Wellness tourism: Market analysis of a special health tourism segment and implications for the hotel industry', *Journal of Vacation Marketing*, 7(1), 5–17.

Murphy, P. E. (2013) *Tourism: A Community Approach (RLE Tourism)*, London: Routledge.

Park, J. J. and Selman, P. (2009) 'Attitudes toward rural landscape change in England', *Environment and Behavior*, 1–25.

Peak District National Park Visitor Survey (2014) and Non-Visitor Survey (2014). Research and Programme Management Team, Policy, Peak District National Park Authority.

Pechlaner, H., Herntrei, M., Pichler, S. and Volgger, M. (2012) 'From destination management towards governance of regional innovation systems – the case of South Tyrol, Italy', *Tourism Review*, 67(2), 22–33.

Peris-Ortiz, M., del Río, M. D. L. C. and Álvarez-García, J. (2015) 'Benefits of implementing a quality management system in Spanish thalassotherapy centres', in Peris-Ortiz, M., Álvarez-García, J. and Rueda-Armengot, C. (eds) *Achieving Competitive Advantage Through Quality Management*, Berlin, Germany: Springer International, pp. 1–16.

Pesonen, J. and Komppula, R. (2010) 'Rural wellbeing tourism: Motivations and expectations', *Journal of Hospitality and Tourism Management*, 17(1), 150–157.

Pesonen, J., Laukkanen, T. and Komppula, R. (2011) 'Benefit segmentation of potential wellbeing tourists', *Journal of Vacation Marketing*, 17(4), 303–314.

Prideaux, B., Berbigier, D. and Thompson, M. (2013) 'Wellness tourism and destination competitiveness', *Wellness Tourism: A Destination Perspective*, 33, 45.

Quintela, J. A., Correia, A. G. and Antunes, J. G. (2011) 'Service quality in health and wellness tourism – trends in Portugal', *International Journal of Business, Management and Social Sciences*, 2(3), 1–8.

Ringer, G. D. (2007) 'Healthy spaces, healing places – sharing experiences of wellness tourism in Oregon, USA', *Selective Tourism*, 1(1), 29–39.

Ritter, S. (2005) 'Trends and skills needed in the tourism sector: "Tourism for wellness"', *Trends and Skill Needs in Tourism*, 115, 79.

Rodrigues, Á., Kastenholz, E. and Rodrigues, A. (2010) 'Hiking as a relevant wellness activity – results of an exploratory study of hiking tourists in Portugal applied to a rural tourism project', *Journal of Vacation Marketing*, 16(4), 331–343.

Sheldon, P. and Park, S.-Y. (2009) 'Development of a sustainable tourism destination', in Bushell, R. and Sheldon, P. J. (eds) *Wellness and Tourism: Mind, Body, Spirit, Place*, New York: Cognizant Communication, pp. 99–113.

Shoard, M. (1980) 'Metropolitan escape routes', *Landscape Research*, 5(2), 8–13.

Smith, M. and Kelly, C. (2006) 'Wellness tourism', *Tourism Recreation Research*, 31(1), 1–4.

Smith, M. and Puczkó, L. (2008) *Health and Wellness Tourism*, London: Routledge.

Steiner, C. J. and Reisinger, Y. (2006) 'Ringing the fourfold: A philosophical framework for thinking about wellness tourism', *Tourism Recreation Research*, 31(1), 5–14.

Supapol, A. B. and Barrows, D. (2007) 'Canadian health and wellness tourism: Obstacles impeding international competitiveness', *The Public Sector Innovation Journal*, 12(3), 2–18.

Thompson, C. W., Aspinall, P. and Montarzino, A. (2007) 'The childhood factor: Adult visits to green places and the significance of childhood experience', *Environment and Behavior*, 1–33.

Uglow, J. (2003) *The Lunar Men: Five Friends Whose Curiosity Changed the World*, London: Macmillan.

Visit England website, https://www.visitengland.com/biz/resources/insights-and-statistics/market-size-and-value/destination-analysis (accessed 12 October 2015).

Visit Peak District website, http://www.visitpeakdistrict.com (accessed 21 October 2015).

Voigt, C. and Pforr, C. (2013) *Wellness Tourism*, New York: Routledge.

Voigt, C., Brown, G. and Howat, G. (2011) 'Wellness tourists: In search of transformation', *Tourism Review*, 66(1/2), 16–30.

Weiermair, K. and Steinhauser, C. (2003) 'New tourism clusters in the field of sports and health: The case of Alpine wellness', in *12th International Tourism and Leisure Symposium*, Barcelona, pp. 15–18.

Welcome Tourism Worldwide (2013) http://www.wellnesstourismworldwide.com/top-10-wellness-travel-trends-2013.html (accessed 14 October 2015).

Yeung, O. and Johnston, K. (2013) *Global Spa and Wellness Monitor*, New York: SRI International, Global Wellness Institute.

Part VIII

Therapeutic and healing landscapes

This part reflects on the ways in which landscapes can provide refuge from the pressures of the modern world, its increasing speed and the monopolisation of attention by technological devices. Harald A. Friedl refers in Chapter 27 to 'places of power' as extraordinary sites of scenic beauty or spiritual significance which are usually located in nature and provide a shelter and escape from everyday life. Although the confrontation of the totality of the self may be over-whelming at first, it can also lead to the (re)discovery of one's autonomy and can ultimately lead to transcendence.

Edward H. Huijbens also elaborates on the restorative effects of nature and landscape which enable visitors to attune to natural cycles and rhythms which enhance wellbeing (Chapter 28). This can entail an elementary and primitive connection to the universe itself and a return to the essence of life through an attunement to aesthetics, quality of experience and spirituality. Like Friedl, he highlights the development of those forms of tourism that are starting to break the rhythms of a hectic life such as slow tourism or spiritual tourism and emphasises the value of spontaneous experiences which are less organised, structured and measured. Visiting landscapes can help with the restoration of the self as well as fostering ecological sensibilities that may also benefit nature itself.

Timothy J. Lee and Jinok Susanna Kim analyse the extent to which certain types of landscape and healing programmes can help to improve the relationship between emotion regulation, attention restoration and life satisfaction (Chapter 29). Forest therapy and healing programmes are given as an example to illustrate the positive effects of nature on modern people. Peter Kruizinga focuses in Chapter 30 rather on the healing power of the seaside or coast as a health-enhancing space or therapeutic landscape. Research shows that living beside or visiting the seaside can have measurable restorative effects, such as improvement of sleep, stimulation of exercise, mood enhancement and stress reduction. Although there is little evidence that thalassotherapy is an effective treatment, there is increasing research that so-called 'blue spaces', especially those by the sea, are the healthiest types of landscape to spend time in. The latter part of the chapter considers whether a whole health region could be developed in a coastal destination.

This part overall re-emphasises concerns expressed in earlier chapters that modern living conditions are not conducive to optimum health and wellbeing and that re-connection to both green and blue spaces may be one of the best ways to return to the essence of self and one's inextricable connection to the universe.

27

'Places of power': can individual 'sacred space' help regain orientation in a confusing world?

A discussion of mental health tourism to extraordinary natural sites in the context of Antonovsky's 'sense of coherence' and Maslow's 'hierarchy of needs'

Harald A. Friedl

In this chapter, the phenomenon of 'places of power' is discussed from a cultural, cognitive and psychophysical perspective in order to understand the mental state of people who sense the existence of 'places of power' as well as the specific circumstances of their perception. Therefore, characteristics of modern life such as commercialisation, consumption and permanent connectedness are examined in order to explain widespread mental complaints such as burnout or diverse forms of addiction. In this context, calming 'places of power' are conceptualised as offering shelter from the pressures of the modern world. In the framework of Antonovsky's concept of a 'sense of coherence', such places protect people temporarily against irritations arising from daily life, allowing them to re-establish inner peace and orientation. To explain better the important social effects of distancing oneself from peer groups in order to 'transcend' social constraints, the tradition of pilgrimage is discussed. This traditional collective visitation of officially recognised 'places of power' is explained using Maslow's concept of the 'hierarchy of needs'. Finally, this concept is adapted to natural places that could serve as individual 'power places' and the fundamental requirements needed to promote such places in the context of mental health tourism are discussed.

Introduction

Across the globe, there are 'extraordinary' places, such as Uluru (Ayers Rock) in the heart of Australia, the Meteora monasteries in northern Greece (Dora, 2012), Mount Kailash in the

Himalayas or the Cathedral of Santiago di Compostela in Spain which play a key role in tourist culture as 'outstanding' landmarks (Schultz, 2011). In contrast, Indigenous inhabitants typically refer to such places as 'sacred places', i.e. places inhabited by gods, spirits or other invisible powers and thus recognised as religious or spiritual centres (Engels, 2010: 6). In addition, most of these mythical places are highly regarded for having healing 'powers' to promote and strengthen emotional, cognitive or psychological health (Curtis, 2010: 161).

However, members of modern societies are increasingly chronicling landmark places with positive healing effects that may manifest themselves in the body, soul and spirit. Places such as these, which are often located in nature, are referred to as 'places of power'. They are characterised by attributes such as a 'special aura', which, according to Purner (2008: 53), is 'associated with certain effects'. These may be 'positive' or 'negative' and can manifest themselves in psychological, emotional and mental outlets (Purner, 2008: 53). For the present chapter, the decisive characteristic of such places of power is that they may contribute to a form of change in persons (Kraft, 2015: 236) in the ways explained below.

Diverse cultures of perception

People who subscribe strongly to the natural sciences tend to refuse to acknowledge that places of power have this potential. They essentially argue that, since currently available instruments have never detected any significant, unusual physical powers (e.g. 'earth rays') in such places that could be the physical cause of alleged benefits, from a scientific standpoint the term 'place of power' is misleading (Brönnle, 2009: 38–39). Jordan (2008: 113) interprets this rejection as the expression of a perception culture that is oriented towards naïve objectivism, whereby the only things that are recognised as 'real' are those that can be directly perceived using the five senses. However, as Hamlet observed: 'There are more things in heaven and earth, Horatio, than are dreamt of in your philosophy' (Shakespeare, 2014: 167–168). Thus, it could be assumed that a more in-depth, mindful level of perception is required to perceive, much less recognise, the greater meaning of existence in all its facets.

The nature and substance of perception are always an expression of the particular perceiving culture, which is characterised by cultural patterns for constructing meaning and inter-relationships (Denora, 2014; Hinton, 2015). Thus, physicists perceive the world differently (Hawking and Mlodinow, 2010) than biologists (Maturana and Varela, 1992), psychologists, psychotherapists (Rosenhan, 2006; Gruen, 2007: 10) or members of Indigenous cultures (Pert et al., 2015). They 'see' the world differently, in that they ascribe different relevance to objectively perceivable objects and thus claim to recognise different causalities. 'World views' of this sort are clearly expressed in the different theoretical constructs of the various scientific disciplines that explain the world as perceived by each of them (DeWitt, 2010; Kuhn, 2012).

According to Brönnle (2009: 40), in order first to understand the experiences of people at a place of power and, eventually, to be able to relate to those experiences personally, it is necessary to move beyond a 'realistic' world view geared towards causality and causation and explore a world view of 'identity', whereby the perception of the 'external world' is conceived of as an expression of self-awareness (Brönnle, 2009: 40). This world view is found in numerous cultures, including the philosophy of Buddhism (Ricard, 2001: 275–279), but also in the epistemology of constructivism (Glasersfeld, 2007), as explained below. This view assumes that the perception of the external world, the perception of the perceiving person by that individual and the perception of one's own physical condition are inter-related (Jarrett et al., 2015: 40).

In this context, it is worth noting that the 'power' perceived by some people in certain places must primarily be understood as a cognitive phenomenon. In terms of the epistemology of constructivism, the only thing that is 'real' to the perceiving person is what that person personally and actually perceives. Here, it is assumed that 'all cognitive activity occurs within the experience of goal-directed consciousness' (Glasersfeld, 2006: 31). Accordingly, the only thing that the perceiving person can perceive is what has already been experienced and learned as being 'perceivable' and 'worthy of perceiving'. In this sense, the scientist Purner, invoking his own experiences and research, holds the view that the 'perceived' effects in places of power essentially depend on the perceiving individuals (Purner, 2008: 66). Does this mean, as a consequence, that the special perception in places of power is solely reserved for the 'initiated'? If this were the case, the phenomenon of places of power would ultimately be rejected as an esoteric phenomenon, as a pure figment of the imagination. However, this is not the issue, for several reasons.

First, the physical change perceived in the environment of places of power appears in the form of a falling pulse rate and other measurable parameters. Therefore, it is real and not pure imagination. What is more, this physical change is the consequence of a special technique of perception, 'mindfulness', which anyone can learn. According to Kabat-Zinn (2013: IXII), the internationally recognised meditation instructor and founder of the Stress Reduction Clinic in Massachusetts, 'Mindfulness . . . [is] . . . basically just a particular way of paying attention and the awareness that arises from paying attention in that way. It is a way of deeply looking into oneself in the spirit of self-inquiry and self-understanding'. This perception technique can be learned and practised on the basis of all cultures, but particularly within the realm of meditation. The inter-relationships between mindfulness training, physical reactions and neuronal processes have now been sufficiently documented (Ricard et al., 2014; Barnby et al., 2015; van der Velden and Roepstorff, 2015). The beneficial efficacy of mindfulness training is recognised in the fields of stress therapy (Mayor, 2015), addiction prevention (Witkiewitz et al., 2014; Nallet et al., 2015), psychotherapy (Fennell et al., 2015), organisational development (Hergesell, 2013; Apple, 2015) and others.

Consequently, instruments for physical measurement would be inadequate for trying to comprehend the 'effect' of places of power and, by extension, for using such places for health tourism purposes. On the contrary, what is needed here is a cultural anthropological or natural psychological approach that poses the following questions: (1) What are the special characteristics of people who perceive 'places of power'? (2) What special attributes are exhibited by the places perceived as being 'places of power'? (3) What conclusions can be derived from both of these insights? Only when these three questions have been resolved can there be meaningful considerations as to the ways in which places of power can be utilised for health tourism.

The culture of perception of the modern world

Life in the modern Western world is subject to a variety of changing needs. The multi-optional society (Gross, 2005), with its endless variety of lifestyles and consumption choices, requires high expertise at filtering and organising the incoming flood of desired stimuli, as well as undesired or even annoying influences, such as traffic noise (Łowicki and Piotrowska, 2015), if individuals are to select helpful information meaningfully for daily life. Here, technical means, such as smartphones and navigation devices, play an increasingly important role for daily life by decisively influencing and partially replacing the task of interpreting the world or giving it meaning through specific filtering programmes. This is clearly evident from the growing phenomenon of people in public places and especially in tourism areas (Pesonen and Horster, 2012), who devote their attention primarily to their smartphones instead of to their environment. In this manner, devices such as these provide their users with an initial impression of helping them cope with their complex surroundings by claiming to make the growing demands of modern society more manageable (Rodriguez-Sancheza et al., 2013).

At the same time, however, devices such as these, with their function of recording and managing complexity by means of linking with global networks via the internet, also contribute to the increasing complexity of the world around us. Therefore, they exacerbate the problem of stimulus overload they purportedly claim to solve by increasingly making demands on the user's attention through the provision of innovations. The essential problem of news feeds received from social networks via smartphones, which are available around the clock (Adachi-Mejia et al., 2014), is their individual coding, as they originate from an identifiable and emotionally meaningful person. As a result, for users who are considered unstable or in a developmental phase, social media takes on the increasingly significant role of a feedback system with identifiable emotions. This means that social media are bound to become a central source for satisfying the need for belonging and recognition and thus a source of value orientation. Expressed in simple terms, the thesis can be formulated that, for heavy users of these networks, the only things that can be perceived as good, important and truly perceivable are those communicated via the network. What does not exist in the network also does not exist in the reality of the user. This seemingly banal circumstance is associated with highly problematic consequences. Smartphone and social media addiction, which has been well documented and is increasing in intensity in all industrialised societies (Yen et al., 2009; Chóliz, 2010; Gautier, 2010; Halayem et al., 2010; Lopez-Fernandez et al., 2014; Travasso, 2014), may be interpreted as a validation of the thesis concerning the monopolisation of attention by the smartphone.

Individuals who break away from this network or perhaps even shut off their smartphones inevitably detach themselves from this virtual source of emotional attention and enter into a completely new perception situation, since the attention resources that are deprived of the information flood from the network are now available in a concentrated form for the perception of a place and its effects on the body. Anyone not accustomed to confrontation with the totality of self may experience this the first time as deeply estranging and overwhelming. The high stress factor of this experience of losing contact with the social frame of reference, combined with the simultaneous experience of new, initially unexplainable stimuli (Ward et al., 2001: 71–75), can be aptly explained by the theory of culture shock (Pedersen, 1995). As a result, in terms of 'fight or flight', this experience can only be managed through 'withdrawal' into the social network, paralysis or by confronting these strange stimuli.

Taking the step of independently subjecting oneself to this alien world and thereby temporarily releasing the emotional frame of reference and forgoing received orientation and self-affirmation initially requires great effort and courage. The significance of this challenge also explains the high addiction potential of heavily used social networks. However, it is precisely this act of giving up intimacy and reassurance through commitment to a strange or estranging experience that is the fundamental prerequisite for achieving autonomy. It is the act of weaning oneself from the social frame of reference in the form of a 'rite of passage' (van Gennep, 1960; Leneveu, 2013) which is indispensable to each individual's personality development and enables the formation of independent decision making and the capacity for action.

Yet this 'off-line condition' *vis-à-vis* the main peer group is increasingly becoming the exception in the post-modern world in which we live, which appears to have serious health repercussions. Thus, there are myriad indicators for the rapid spread of adverse mental effects among juveniles (Heritier, 2001: 511; Forgeron et al., 2010; Keel and Forney, 2013; Luthar et al., 2013; Platt et al., 2013; García-Fernández et al., 2014; Freisleder and Hordych, 2014; Whiting et al., 2014; Bowes et al., 2015) from stress syndromes among all age groups (Alarcon et al., 2011; Pas et al., 2012; Pagnin et al., 2013; Kogoj et al., 2014; Schulte-Markwort, 2015), as well as the ubiquitous general feeling of being overwhelmed (Bertram and Deuflhard, 2014; Miegel, 2014; Abeles, 2015; Frenkel et al., 2015).

As a common denominator, all of these studies and analyses suggest that, under currently prevailing conditions, people unquestioningly measure the 'rectitude' of their actions in terms of the reactions of their peer group, such that they appear to sacrifice the satisfaction of their other needs in order to satisfy their need to belong. This process of submitting to the addiction to recognition for the price of repressing their own needs is amplified within the system, as the persons affected forget how to perceive their own needs. This process of dehumanisation as a consequence of submitting to an authority was described by several authors, such as Erich Fromm (1994, 2010, 2013) or Hannah Arendt (1973), in the years following the German National Socialist catastrophe. Can indicators of these structures of disenfranchisement also be found in the present day?

Commercial displacement of realms of transcendence

According to the view presented here, the aforementioned societal phenomena can be understood on the basis of their internal systemic principles as an unavoidable consequence of capitalist growth processes. This results exclusively from the commercial appropriation and integration of previously untapped areas, be it in the form of subsistent ethnic groups or inner-societal spheres. In this integration process, social networks play a special role in that their specific structure suggests to their users a feeling of intimacy in the form of supposedly direct communication with 'friends', with whom sometimes highly intimate 'news' is exchanged. The growing size of the network is necessarily accompanied by an increase in the frequency of news exchange. As a result, the user feels 'integrated' and informed in real time and at the same time personally 'on the ball'. This feeling of integration, however, comes at a high price in terms of attention and time, as well as the disclosure of private details, which are made available for extensive commercial utilisation by harnessing consumer patterns. Users become increasingly transparent and thus more subject to manipulation, although they perceive this manipulation subjectively as the successful satisfaction of the need to belong. At this point, the behaviour of social media users already follows the basic pattern of addictive behaviour, according to which the users require ever-higher 'doses' of reassurance and, as a result, increasingly lose control over their user behaviour (Pedrero Pérez et al., 2012).

This behaviour pattern is considered desirable in our commercial culture, considering the fact that our entire economic system is based on the principle of continuous growth as a condition of maintaining prosperity. Over the course of the twentieth century, the growth ethos became the paradigmatic response to solve all societal and individual problems, while traditional transcendent models for explaining the world and the institutions representing them (i.e. religions) lost influence. The 'old' recipes of traditional religions increasingly appeared to be unsatisfactory answers to the questions of modern life. As a consequence, the enlightened, secular human being was compelled to find a substitute for this lost faith in paradise in the afterlife by pursuing happiness in this life (Sharpley and Jepson, 2011: 52–54). However, since, in the context of a growth culture, merely perceiving the feeling of happiness is no longer sufficient to provide meaning, here, too, human beings require a numerical yardstick to assess whether they are on the 'sure path' to 'salvation' that leads to a 'meaningful' life.

According to Schulze (2005), this purpose is also accomplished by the principle of experience maximisation, which is why people in the Western world are always striving for ever-greater quantity and ever-more intensive quality and more extraordinary 'experiences'. As a result, the classic 'Seven Deadly Sins' have been transposed into their opposites: whereas in the

Middle Ages, the greedy satisfaction of all the senses was considered despicable, in the context of the current secular experience society, a constant successful maximisation of sensual experiences is understood as the sign of a meaningful life on earth (Schulze, 2008). In this context, one can interpret rampant destructive civilisation phenomena as expressions of this maximisation culture that are inherent in the system. Thus, obesity (Flegal et al., 2010; Wietlisbach et al., 2013) is the consequence of gluttony, burnout is the consequence of addiction to work and fame, the worldwide leading illegal economic factor of woman trafficking (Méndez, 2015) and pornography (Hald, 2015) is the consequence of commercialised sexual addiction to hedonism and the financial crisis (Zanalda, 2015) is a result of institutionalised greed.

If, in fact, the continuous increase of attractive stimuli is considered the only path to earthly happiness, then it is understandable why tourism, as an expansion of familiar territory for the purpose of pleasure and self-actualisation (Freyer, 2009: 73), has advanced as the ideal path to happiness. This is also reflected in a panoply of book titles, all of which tout travel as the direct 'path to happiness' (Weiner, 2009; Lelord, 2010; Leaming, 2014) or even directly to 'Paradise' (Baker, 2006; Alderson, 2015). Considering this widespread 'secular-religious' connotation of travel, Hennig (1997: 78–85), who defines travel as a secular ritual of modern pilgrimage in search of salvation on earth, appears to be vindicated. The combination of travel as a means of experience maximisation and a path to happiness on earth explains the unabated growth of the tourism industry from a psychological perspective. At the same time, however, the ecological, economic and social consequences of this unchecked growth for littoral destinations are obvious, while frequent travellers' search for salvation is doomed to fail in the dead end of the paradox principle of 'more of the same' (Watzlawick et al., 1974: 31–39), as the experience of 'meaning', understood as the long-term satisfaction of human transcendence or the need for self-fulfilment, cannot generally be achieved by commercial means. This is perhaps an essential reason for the vast proliferation of consumer patterns for artificial satisfaction of sensory needs in modern societies and at the same time the cause of their necessary failure.

Market strategies for satisfying transcendence needs

Transcendence essentially means crossing the threshold of what is familiar in order to find orientation and meaning within one's own life. According to Reed, within this concept we can distinguish between three aspects of intrapersonal, interpersonal and transpersonal transcendence. Reflecting on intrapersonal transcendence essentially focuses on one's own life, interpersonal transcendence focuses on the personal relationships with other people and the rest of the world and transpersonal transcendence encompasses the unfathomable relationships of existence or higher powers (Reed, 1991).

In the pre-modern societies and especially in segmental societies, the need for transcendence was satisfied by collective rites and customs, which were carried out within the scope of collectively regulated, cyclically recurring 'sacred' times, such as Sunday in Christianity, the Sabbath in Judaism or Ramadan in Islam. These 'timeouts' sought to structure time by remaining separated from the time dedicated to life's everyday concerns and were therefore considered special. At the core of these times of transcendence stood the collective repetition and assurance by recognised 'certainties' for explaining and interpreting the world, which provided the community with a sense of meaning and orientation (Obrecht, 2014: 267–269). Drugs and other mind-expanding substances were used exclusively in this context in such societies. Thus, their handling was strictly regulated and controlled by older members of the tribe, who in turn imparted 'expertise in drug use' to their younger members within the bounds of spiritual rituals, thereby simultaneously preventing abuse (Obrecht, 1995).

These framework conditions for satisfying transcendence needs, as well as the rules of learning how to satisfy transcendence needs, existed in all pre-modern cultures. However, due to modernisation processes, these types of collective orientation patterns are increasingly being lost in a differentiated society marked by individual lifestyles. Since this means that the transcendence needs are at risk of remaining unsatisfied, there is an increasing need for alternative, commercially driven services for conveying meaning and orientation. One good example of the consumer search for timeouts of this nature is the wellness boom between the years of 1990 and 2010, which led to a 'wellness label' being applied to every conceivable product, in order to convey to the consumer the impression that the particular products were extremely effective (Friedl, 2006: 7). In this sense, in the context of the criticism of the acceleration of the modern consumer culture (Romeiss-Stracke, 2003), all waves of demand for purportedly meaningful products can be understood as strategies of transcendence, e.g. the organic and regionalisation wave (Friedl, 2013a: 21–22), the trend toward slow food (Lee et al., 2015; Williams et al., 2015) and slow tourism (Fullagar et al., 2012; Georgica, 2015), especially with respect to holidays in monasteries (Kriechbaum, 2008: 8; Drule et al., 2012), spiritual trekking (Hartmann, 2013) or other forms of pilgrimage tourism, which is experiencing a veritable renaissance in Europe (Štefko et al., 2015). All these trends share the primary need for 'timeouts' and 'protected areas' as a condition for discovering meaning, but beyond the formalised, structured and ritualised circumstances offered in traditional religious contexts (Sharpley and Jepson, 2011: 55–58).

However, with respect to their success in regard to the long-term satisfaction of transcendent needs, all these products 'suffer' from the aforementioned inherent laws of the capitalist system and the growing commercialisation of all areas of life. As part of this integration process, the above-mentioned spheres of healing are inevitably being integrated into the commercialised exchange relationship and thus into the sphere of the mundane, whereby they risk losing their transcendence-enabling potential. Examples of this regularity include the mounting widespread disappointment over industrially produced organic foods as an expression of the 'organic lie' (Arvay, 2012) or the increasing failure of love relationships, which is seen as the result of choosing the wrong partner (Friedl, 2013b: 107–108) or having an insufficient mastery of 'romantic' cultural techniques (Illouz, 2007). In this sense, the relative success of a monastery holiday is reduced to the result of a deficient product instead of a problematic relationship to transcendence.

As transcendence is something that cannot be 'bought', its experience also cannot be won in a lawsuit. This fact is shared by all areas of life where success depends on the ability of spontaneous emotional reactions, which always presupposes a high degree of trust amongst human beings and thus a setting for protective intimacy. Yet it is precisely these conditions that run contrary to the principles of a service industry, where meeting economic demands relies on cost reduction through serial production and therefore on a maximum degree of control. Spontaneity, in contrast, is unpredictable and necessarily defies economic and contractual control. This is why, up to now, the problem of 'authenticity' in tourism – despite any argumentative contortions – has not been convincingly resolved (Rickly-Boyd, 2012; Zenga, Go and de Vries, 2012; Shepherd, 2015). Interpersonal phenomena linked to feelings such as courage, love and warmth can indeed be successfully simulated, but cannot be forced and are therefore also not for sale. They are the fundamental expression of autonomy of human existence, following its own strict internal system of rules: all human beings have their own, highly individual needs shaped by specific life experiences and thus their own individual boundaries of what is allowed concerning the experience of intimacy. Transcendence, however, is possibly one of the strongest forms of intimacy.

If attempts to satisfy the need for meaning via commercialised solutions fail, people necessarily respond in our consumer culture by searching for 'innovative', 'better' products. One expression of this strategy is the rapidly growing demand for self-help literature, various forms of coaching and psychotherapy (Remele, 2001; Bergmann, 2015). Although coaching and systemic forms of therapy apply helpful methods for overcoming perception and thought patterns, there is still the danger that extremely successful economic approaches in these segments will fail for this very reason when it comes to the quest for meaning. A coach who provides successful help will in turn be in high demand, whereby forms of dependency could arise at the expense of the desired autonomy. Success defined as the satisfaction of transcendent needs, however, occurs precisely when the coach, consultant, teacher or therapist becomes superfluous to the 'client', who has learned how to solve problems independently or simply to accept them (Aguinis et al., 2011; Milyavskaya and Koestner, 2011; Fazel, 2013; Steckelberg, 2015). This is where the principle of the Montessori teaching approach (Montessori, 1964) and neurodidactics (Herrmann, 2006) comes into play: 'Teach me to do it myself!' (Mooney, 2013: 48–50). This paradigm of enlightenment and autonomy contradicts the ideal of long-term customer loyalty, however, by which a satisfied customer should book additional coaching sessions wherever possible.

Transcendence: the restitution of the sense of coherence according to Antonovsky

Satisfying the need for transcendence or self-actualisation requires regaining and strengthening one's autonomy, which is facing increasing pressure in a society with a compulsion towards consumption, achievement and recognition. Yet recognising this very pressure for what it is and overcoming it, or at least coping with it, requires a protected realm in which subjects can examine, question and assess the circumstances and compulsions of their daily lives, freed from those very compulsions. It requires sufficient distance from the system to learn how to unmask and control it, free from the root anxieties, rather than being unmasked and controlled by the system. Each form of criticism, whether it be of one's own behaviour, of one's immediate social environment or of the fundamental motivating values of one's own surroundings, requires distance to precisely this social environment or one's own surroundings. Transcendence without distance is a contradiction in terms.

In traditional societies, enabling this realm of distance was the purpose of sacred places such as caves, temples or other forms of protected areas (Curtis, 2010: 167; Engels, 2010: 6–8), within which special rules always prevailed. That is why, from ancient times, it was considered a particular act of sacrilege for earthly powers to ignore the inviolability of such areas. In this way, we can also interpret the outrage of Jesus Christ over the abuse of the temple area by merchants, moneychangers and prostitutes (Matthew, 21: 12; Mark, 11: 15). In this manner, by vehemently demanding the inviolability of places of refuge from commercial interests, Jesus was also the first radical critic of consumerism. It is precisely the 'purity' of these spheres from everyday life that creates an indispensable condition to enable self-discovery and transcendence by confronting the meta-system face to face in the form of a 'higher power' (Holl, 1998: 109–110).

But what exactly occurs in the process of transcendence? If we seek to understand the process of life basically as the successful management of challenges of the particular world around us, then healthy people are defined, according to the salutogenic model (Antonovsky, 1987; Lindström and Eriksson, 2005), as having the feeling that they can successfully cope with their environment with their available resources and skills. Thus, health is concerned with the subjective perception of not only the world, but also one's own skills adapted to the world. As long as the perceived 'images' or concepts are coherent, a human being feels 'healthy'. Antonovsky refers to this perception as a 'sense of coherence' (Antonovsky, 1993). It is characteristic of the subjective impression of 'meaningfulness' if subjects are able to understand the 'world' and its inter-relationships and thus consider themselves capable of responding 'meaningfully' in order to maintain their own existence successfully. To this extent, the sense of coherence can also be understood as the expression of sufficient confidence in one's ability to cope with the challenges of daily life now and in the future (Antonovsky, 1987: 19).

Naturally, the world around us is frequently in flux, which is why modern people are forced to engage in lifelong learning in order to adapt to new, unfolding challenges. Here, learning is understood as a reinforcement of existing skills or the development of new ones, to enable the individual to cope with newly recognised challenges. If experiences of failing in the face of perceived challenges accumulate in a human being (e.g. successfully and sustainably coping with the growing mountain of career responsibilities, providing all of one's Facebook friends with news or remaining up to date in all key areas of research), people can begin to feel overwhelmed and stressed. If this condition persists, physical damage resulting from this burden may increase due to chronic stress. That is, the person becomes ill (Torsheim et al., 2001; Love et al., 2011).

Being overwhelmed for a short period is a well-known phenomenon in tourism. If people are subjected to a cultural environment to which they have had little previous exposure, all of their perception channels will inevitably be exclusively confronted with stimuli that are identified by the limbic system of the brain as being 'alien', due to the continuous failure to reconcile incoming stimulus patterns with stored, familiar perception patterns. This phenomenon, known as culture shock (Ward et al., 2001), manifests as apathy, loss of appetite and the need for darkness. From a neurobiological perspective, the brain is signalling that it is overwhelmed and thus desperately requires a retreat in order first to 'restore' order in the chaos of the perceived stimuli by integrating them into existing, familiar perception patterns. In fact, the brain must first regenerate 'coherence' in the area of sanctuary. Only after this phase of retreat will a subject regain enough confidence to cope with the exotic stimuli or even interpret them as enjoyable inspiration (Shaules, 2015: 71–77).

From a systems perspective, this regeneration process can be explained as the restoration of the homeostasis of the perception system in the aftermath of an excessive perturbation. The key element here, however, is that the integration of new perturbation patterns into the familiar pattern of the perception system alters or expands these patterns as well. People thus alter their perception capability and, as a logical consequence, their assessment of reality, although the external reality may well have remained the same.

The decisive effect of the retreat of an overloaded system into a protected area lies in this enabling of a new systemic configuration of the personal perception pattern as a result of the relief of stress. From a safe distance, this retreat allows for the undisturbed and therefore relaxed integration of new stimuli and the evaluation of irritations. Continuing along this path, a modified, more helpful 'image' of the world develops and a situation previously perceived as a threat is now reassessed as an 'exciting challenge'. This opens up new options for response and creativity and, in doing so, enables a restoration of the sense of coherence.

Based on this understanding, the satisfaction of the transcendence need can be described as the restitution of the sense of coherence. Subjects can bring their world views or their meta-views of the world back into equilibrium, once again experiencing themselves as being autonomous, capable of decisions and actions and, as a result, viewing their actions as being meaningful again. The decisive prerequisite for this restitution of full autonomy is the opportunity to retreat from overwhelming everyday life into a sphere perceived as a sanctuary. Individuals must perceive this 'place' as being secure, pleasant and inspiring in order to deal critically with their own perspectives of things, as well as their own actions and to seek long-term, effective solutions and devise autonomous decisions. Wherever this successfully occurs, the place in question could basically be perceived by the subject as a 'place of power'.

It becomes evident that, when the sense of coherence is lost, the purchase of a wellness product can merely combat the symptom (i.e. a feeling of being overwhelmed), but can never address the actual challenge of developing a modified view of the world. Although the strategy of combating symptoms is the preferred methodology of the wellness and health market, this suppresses the root cause of the problem behind the symptom, thereby increasing the long-term risk of the subject's total breakdown. Probably due to the growing number of people who constantly feel overwhelmed and seek to escape from this market system of combating symptoms, there is growing demand for forms of tourism that appear to address the restitution of the sense of coherence more effectively: individual forms of pilgrimage, whose social-psychological dynamics, according to the viewpoint expressed here, represent the key to understanding places of power.

Pilgrimage as a collective cultural technique from the viewpoint of Maslow's hierarchy of needs

From ancient times, pilgrimage has been seen as a search for spiritual experience, which is equally valid for modern pilgrims (Collins-Kreiner, 2010a: 445), even if 'secular' tourists increasingly visit religious centres due to their significance to art history. However, this was also true of traditional pilgrims, as Forster demonstrated in his research on Christian pilgrim culture (2008: 129–138). To this extent, one might argue that, from a tourism sociological perspective, there is a functional congruence between religious pilgrims to 'sacred places' and secular travel to tourism sites of worldly pilgrimage (Hennig, 1997: 84; Collins-Kreiner, 2010b; Willson et al., 2013). All of these pilgrimages therefore fulfil the function of 'places of power' by serving as recognised places of retreat to visitors, where they experience special feelings of being uplifted and, from this viewpoint, are allowed to experience transcendence, connectedness and a new perspective on life (Curtis, 2010: 162–165). In order for this to succeed, however, a pilgrimage must follow a certain structural routine. Here, we can use Maslow's 'hierarchy of needs' (2014: 141) as a guide to distinguish between various developmental phases, over the course of which each of the five different basic needs must be satisfied.

- A pilgrimage begins with a departure from a familiar environment, which, however, is no longer perceived as coherent, into the unknown. In fact, people frequently embark on pilgrimages when they no longer feel at ease with themselves and the world to which they are accustomed, due to internal and external changes. In order to gain a perspective on this familiar world, pilgrims are required to leave their social frame of reference and subject themselves to a foreign environment.
- In order to cope successfully with this journey away from familiar environs and towards personal discovery, the satisfaction of the pilgrim's basic physiological needs for food, shelter and sleep must be guaranteed. For this purpose, there is an established network of hostels and places of refreshment along collectively recognised pilgrimage routes. Once relieved of this worry, pilgrims can thus more effectively concentrate on coping with their 'journey as the destination'. According to Gatrell (2013), significant therapeutic effects are ascribed to the mere act of being on a journey by foot.
- To be able to concentrate on the 'journey to oneself', the pilgrim is required to be relieved of the worry of being hijacked or the risk of getting lost. On the other hand, a minimum level of travel safety allows the traveller to experience and cope with unusual emotions. This is enabled by an established system of guideposts, as well as numerous other pilgrims along the way, who also provide a sense of orientation and safety.

- Eventually, pilgrims who remain alone on their journey will be burdened by feelings of loneliness. By contrast, the pilgrim's satisfaction of the need of belonging to a group of like-minded individuals with comparable needs and experiences serves as an important emotional support. Comparable to a group-dynamic process within self-help groups, pilgrims can exchange news and views and, in this manner, develop a feeling of profound solidarity and community identity. At the same time, the pilgrims' newly developed frame of reference reinforces the process of distancing themselves from the old frame of reference left behind (Hennig, 1997: 79–80).
- Once the pilgrims have jointly overcome all the obstacles of travelling and reaching their destination, this success reinforces the collective, newfound identity through mutual respect (Buzindea et al., 2014). Above all, however, pilgrims also experience their success in terms of increased recognition *vis-à-vis* those who stayed at home. Equipped with this gain of symbolic capital (Bourdieu, 1985), pilgrims acquire a different social status in their old frame of reference and consequently – after their return – find new ways of shaping their old environments, precisely because, from the perspective of those who remained at home, they have indeed become 'a different person'. In Islam, this status transformation of the successful Mecca pilgrim is manifest in the acquired title of *Hajji* (Friedl, 2008: 87; Jafari and Scott, 2014).
- Before arriving at the 'sacred area', the pilgrims have already progressed through several phases of social change. Yet only upon entering this 'pristine' sphere, which is completely protected and free of all distractions and needs and thus freed of all mundane things, does the pilgrim enter into the aura of the 'extraordinary'. This awareness is reinforced by the respect shown to this sacred site by key peer groups. In this context, the equipping of the pilgrimage site with clear direction signs as a means of reassurance plays a major role (Hughes et al., 2013: 216–219). In this manner, the pilgrims can devote themselves entirely to contemplation, free of worry about their belonging and respect, in that the pilgrimage site becomes a 'meta-sphere' for the pilgrims, which stands 'above all mundane things'. Mentally and physically far away from home, pilgrims are liberated in their perspective of understanding and assessing their lives up to that time and the world associated with them, yet they do not feel far away from that world, but rather 'connected'.

Under these circumstances it is much easier for pilgrims to gain autonomy from their old frame of reference by searching inside themselves, feeling their own 'truth' and on this basis, autonomously taking forward-looking decisions for their future. This process is the essence of restoring the sense of coherence and thus of hope and confidence in being able to cope successfully in an appropriate way with one's own living environment upon returning. With this feeling of discovering a new path, pilgrims fulfil their need to find themselves.

- The pilgrimage is made complete with the return to the original social frame of reference. Because the pilgrims have changed on the inside through the personal experience of gaining distance and changing their perspective and they are also perceived by loved ones at home as being new persons with the new social status gained by what they have 'accomplished', there is a need to adjust to the social frame of reference. For returnees, this opens up significant new opportunities to shape their old but newly perceived environment in meaningful ways. Of course, this was, in fact, the precise objective of the journey: to regain the complete life-coping and creative capacity and thus to restore the feeling that life has meaning.

Places of power as individual pilgrimage destinations?

From a social psychology perspective, both the act of identification and the active use of the place of power exhibit key parallels to a pilgrimage. Thus, it is said that all four basic needs of a visitor to a place of power must be fulfilled before the visitor can commit to meeting the need for transcendence.

- First, users must leave their frame of reference, as places of power are normally found far removed from centres of everyday culture.
- However, a place of power can only be perceived if the visitor's senses are receptive and not totally distracted by hunger and thirst, for example.
- One key aspect is that places of power must be free from distractions and societal, commercial and time constraints. Users must also be shielded from disturbances by undesired visitors in order to commit completely to sensing the 'proper' place that is 'just right' for them.
- For people to notice a place of power, it is helpful for it to be recognised by important peer groups because this can serve as a 'self-fulfilling prophecy' (Eden, 1992; Smith et al., 1998; Rosenthal, 2012) for visitors. 'Authorities' or experts, such as priests or geomantists, can contribute to this recognition, as can earlier civilisations. This is why historical places for ceremonial gatherings and religious sites (e.g. churches and chapels) are often considered places of power. In this regard, Hughes et al. (2013) recommend that an appropriate description with a balanced mix of spiritual and sacred information can help a sacred place become more well known.

Places of power are generally marked by a special scenic characteristic. What is considered 'extraordinary', however, depends on individual perception patterns. These could include striking cliff formations, outstanding scenic elevations, majestic clearings, gnarled trees or lovely bodies of water. People may also identify completely foreign places as places of power as soon as they exhibit scenic elements that they recall from home (Cheng and Kuo, 2015). It must be noted that it depends on the particular background of the visitor as to which specific scenic shapes are perceived as spiritually stimulating places (Petina et al., 2015). In this context, the sounds of nature may also play a significant role, depending upon the particular cultural influences of the visitors (Schwarz, 2013). However, manmade areas (e.g. gardens, specially appointed rooms) or even certain corners in a building (e.g. so-called devotional corners) may be recognised as places of power.

- Ultimately, a decisive factor for the identification of a place of power is its staying power as a place of transcendence, a place where visitors can tune out everyday thoughts and mindfully listen initially to the charms of nature and soon thereafter to the signals of their own bodies. The ensuing tranquillity transforms the place of power into a 'meta-sphere', which enables the perception of a lucid, serene and detached perspective on one's own life. At this moment, the Delphic principle of 'knowing thyself' takes over as a catalyst for regaining the sense of coherence. For, when people look closely into a mirror, they can recognise what they are afraid of, what is good for them, what they can and cannot do and what they don't want to do. In the process, people can recognise how to decide and how to act in the future.
- Through this act of liberating recognition, visitors to the place of power regain hope and the ability to act and thus more 'power' to cope with everyday life once again with success and satisfaction.

Conclusions: using places of power for health tourism

Given the heavy burdens of modern everyday life, the need for areas of retreat is growing, in order to satisfy the transcendence needs that go above and beyond typical tourism needs as well. 'Places of power' that offer both extraordinary scenery and protection from the influences of civilisation can fulfil these needs. Removed from the complex world with its many perceived contradictions, such places can help people regain their personal sense of coherence as defined in terms of successfully coping with their environment. If these places of power are adequately designated and made sufficiently accessible by means of an unobtrusive infrastructure, this will enable peripheral tourism regions, in particular, to provide interesting impetus for the development of mental health tourism. Over the medium term, the challenge is to attract an adequate number of visitors. However, if a place of power develops too great an attraction, it can indeed become an economically interesting secular 'pilgrimage site' in the sense of a new tourist attraction, but it may lose its value as a 'metasphere' for regaining inner tranquillity power and thus its relevance as an oasis for mental health tourism.

References

Abeles, V. (2015) *Beyond Measure: Rescuing an Overscheduled, Overtested, Underestimated Generation*, New York: Simon and Schuster.

Adachi-Mejia, A.M., Edwards, P.M., Gilbert-Diamond, D., Greenough, G.P. and Olson, A.L. (2014) 'TXT me I'm only sleeping: Adolescents with mobile phones in their bedroom', *Family and Community Health* 37(4), 252–257.

Aguinis, H., Joo, H. and Gottfredson, R.K. (2011) 'Human performance. Why we hate performance management – and why we should love it', *Business Horizons* 54(6), 503–507.

Alarcon, G.M., Edwards, J.M. and Menke, L.E. (2011) 'Student burnout and engagement: A test of the conservation of resources theory', *Journal of Psychology* 145(3), 211–227.

Alderson, S. (2015) *Can We Live Here? Finding a Home in Paradise*, London: Blink.

Antonovsky, A. (1987) *Unraveling the Mystery of Health: How People Manage Stress and Stay Well*, San Francisco, CA: Jossey-Bass.

—— (1993) 'The structure and properties of the sense of coherence scale', *Social Science and Medicine* 36(6), 725–733.

Apple, R. (2015) 'Mindfulness matters: A powerful resource for over-stressed physician leaders', *Physician Leadership Journal* 2(3), 42–44.

Arendt, H. (1973) *The Origins of Totalitarianism*, San Diego, CA: Harcourt, Brace, Jovanovich.

Arvay, C.G. (2012) *Der grosse Bio-Schmäh: wie uns die Lebensmittelkonzerne an der Nase herumführen*, Berlin, Germany: Ueberreuter.

Baker, I. (2006) *The Heart of the World: A Journey to Tibet's Lost Paradise*, London: Penguin Books.

Barnby, J.M., Bailey, N.W., Chambers, R. and Fitzgerald, P. (2015) 'How similar are the changes in neural activity resulting from mindfulness practice in contrast to spiritual practice?', *Consciousness and Cognition* 36, 219–232.

Bergmann, J. (2015) *Der Tanz ums Ich: Risiken und Nebenwirkungen der Psychologie*, Munich, Germany: Pantheon Verlag.

Bertram, H. and Deuflhard, C. (2014) *Die überforderte Generation: Arbeit und Familie in der Wissensgesellschaft*, Opladen, Germany: Verlag Barbara Budrich.

Bourdieu, P. (1985) 'The market of symbolic goods', *Poetics* 14(1–2), 13–44.

Bowes, L., Joinson, C., Wolke, D. and Lewis, G. (2015) 'Peer victimisation during adolescence and its impact on depression in early adulthood: Prospective cohort study in the United Kingdom', *British Medical Journal* 350, h2469.

Brönnle, S. (2009) *Die Kraft des Ortes. Die Energien der Erde erspüren, erkennen und nutzen*, Saarbrücken, Germany: Neue Erde.

Buzindea, C.N., Kalavarb, J.M., Kohlic, N. and Manuel-Navarretea, D. (2014) 'Emic understandings of Kumbh Mela pilgrimage experiences', *Annals of Tourism Research* 49, 1–18.

Cheng, C.-K. and Kuo, H.-Y. (2015) 'Bonding to a new place never visited: Exploring the relationship between landscape elements and place bonding', *Tourism Management* 46, 546–560.

Chóliz, M. (2010) 'Mobile phone addiction: A point of issue', *Addiction* 105(2), 373–374.

Collins-Kreiner, N. (2010a) 'Researching pilgrimage. Continuity and transformations', *Annals of Tourism Research* 37(2), 440–456.

—— (2010b) 'The geography of pilgrimage and tourism: Transformations and implications for applied geography', *Applied Geography* 30(1), 153–164.

Curtis, S. (2010) *Space, Place and Mental Health*, Burlington, VT: Ashgate.

Denora, T. (2014) *Making Sense of Reality: Culture and Perception in Everyday Life*, Thousand Oaks, CA: SAGE.

DeWitt, R. (2010) *Worldviews: An Introduction to the History and Philosophy of Science* (2nd edn), Chichester, UK: Wiley-Blackwell.

Dora, V. (2012) 'Setting and blurring boundaries: Pilgrims, tourists and landscape in Mount Athos and Meteora', *Annals of Tourism Research* 39(2), 951–974.

Drule, A.M., Chiş, A., Băcilă, M.F. and Ciornea, R. (2012) 'A new perspective of non-religious motivations of visitors to sacred sites: Evidence from Romania', *Procedia – Social and Behavioral Sciences* 62, 431–435.

Eden, D. (1992) 'Leadership and expectations: Pygmalion effects and other self-fulfilling prophecies in organizations', *The Leadership Quarterly* 3(4), 271–305.

Engels, C. (2010) *1000 heilige Orte. Die Lebensliste für eine spirituelle Weltreise*, Potsdam, Germany: Ullmann.

Fazel, P. (2013) 'Teacher-coach-student coaching model: A vehicle to improve efficiency of adult institution', *Procedia – Social and Behavioral Sciences* 97, 384–391.

Fennell, M., Sumbundu, A. and Perczel, J. (2015) 'Mindfulness-based cognitive therapy', *Psychiatria Hungarica* 30(1), 100–103.

Flegal, K.M., Ogden, C.L., Yanovski, J.A., Freedman, D.S., Shepherd, J.A., Graubard, B.I. and Borrud, L.G. (2010) 'High adiposity and high body mass index-for-age in US children and adolescents overall and by race-ethnic group', *American Journal of Clinical Nutrition* 91(4), 1020–1026.

Forgeron, P.A., King, S., Stinson, J.N., McGrath, P.J., MacDonald, A.J. and Chambers, C.T. (2010) 'Social functioning and peer relationships in children and adolescents with chronic pain: A systematic review', *Pain Research and Management* 15(1), 27–41.

Forster, N. (2008) *Die Pilger. Reiselust in Gottes Namen*, Erftstadt, Germany: Area.

Freisleder, F.J. and Hordych, H. (2014) *Anders als die anderen: Was die Seele unserer Kinder krank macht*, Munich, Germany: Piper.

Frenkel, B., Randerath, A. and Brodbeck, N. (2015) *Die Kinderkrankmacher: Zwischen Leistungsdruck und Perfektion. Das Geschäft mit unseren Kindern*, Freiburg im Breisgau, Germany: Verlag Herder.

Freyer, W. (2009) *Tourismus: Einführung in die Fremdenverkehrsökonomie* (9th edn), Munich, Germany: Oldenbourg Wissenschaftsverlag.

Friedl, H.A. (2006) 'Wer braucht Wellness – und warum gerade jetzt? Über die gesellschaftlichen Hintergründe des Wellness-Booms', *Integra* 4(6), 6–10.

—— (2008) *KulturSchock Tuareg*, Bielefeld, Germany: Reise Know-How.

—— (2013a) 'Recht auf Erlösung? Der Anspruch aufs Paradies als postmoderne Paradoxie', in Russ, G. (ed.) *Steiermark: Innovation: 2013 Recht haben*, Graz, Austria: Leykam, pp. 19–23.

—— (2013b) 'Über die Unmöglichkeit der "richtigen" Partnerwahl', in Russ, G. (ed.) *Steiermark: Innovation: 2010*, Graz, Austria: Leykam, pp. 103–108.

Fromm, E. (1994) *Escape from Freedom*, New York: Henry Holt.

—— (2010) *On Disobedience: Why Freedom Means Saying 'No' to Power*, New York: Harper Perennial Modern Classics.

—— (2013) *To Have or To Be?* New York: Bloomsbury Academic.

Fullagar, S., Markwell K. and Wilson, E. (eds) (2012) *Slow Tourism: Experiences and Mobilities*, Bristol, UK: Channel View.

García-Fernández, J.M., Inglés, C.J., Marzo, J.C. and Martínez-Monteagudo, M.C. (2014) 'Psychometric properties of the School Anxiety Inventory-Short Version in Spanish secondary education students', *Psicothema* 26(2), 286–292.

Gatrell, A.C. (2013) 'Therapeutic mobilities: Walking and "steps" to wellbeing and health', *Health and Place* 22, 98–106.

Gautier, J. (2010) 'Addiction and new forms of virtual communication', *Revue de l'Infirmière* 162, 24–25.

Georgica, G. (2015) 'The tourist's perception about slow travel – a Romanian perspective', *Procedia Economics and Finance* 23, 1596–1601.

Glasersfeld, E. v. (2006) 'Einführung in den radikalen Konstruktivismus', in Watzlawick, P. (ed.) *Die erfundene Wirklichkeit. Wie wir wissen, was wir zu wissen glauben? Beiträge zum Konstruktivismus*, Munich, Germany: Piper, pp. 16–38.

Glasersfeld, E. v. (2007) *Key Works in Radical Constructivism*, Rotterdam, The Netherlands: Sense.

Gross, P. (2005) *Die Multioptionsgesellschaft*, Berlin, Germany: Suhrkamp.

Gruen, A. (2007) *The Insanity of Normality: Toward Understanding Human Destructiveness*, Berkeley, CA: Human Development Books.

Halayem, S., Nouira, O., Bourgou, S., Bouden, A., Othman, S. and Halayem, M. (2010) 'The mobile: A new addiction upon adolescents', *La Tunisie Médicale* 88(8), 593–596.

Hald, G.M. (2015) 'Pornography', in Wright, J.D. (ed.) *International Encyclopedia of the Social and Behavioral Sciences* (2nd edn), Amsterdam, The Netherlands: Elsevier, pp. 613–618.

Hartmann, S. (2013) *SpiriTrekking. Theoretische Grundlagen und deren praktische Umsetzung für Reiseveranstalter*, Master's thesis, Institute of Health and Tourism Management, University of Applied Sciences, Bad Gleichenberg, Austria.

Hawking, S. and Mlodinow, L. (2010) *The Grand Design*, New York: Bantam.

Hennig, C. (1997) *Reiselust: Touristen, Tourismus und Urlaubskultur*, Frankfurt am Main, Germany: Insel Verlag.

Hergesell, H.J. (2013) *Mindful Leadership and Corporate Culture – Achtsamkeit als Hilfestellung für Unternehmensleiter in Führungsstil und Unternehmenskultur*, Master's thesis, Institute of Health and Tourism Management, University of Applied Sciences, Bad Gleichenberg, Austria.

Heritier, F. (2001) 'L'idée de crise adolescente: est-elle universelle?', *Neuropsychiatrie de l'Enfance et de l'Adolescence* 49(8), 502–511.

Herrmann, U. (2006) 'Neurodidaktik – neue Wege des Lehrens und Lernens', in Hermann, U. (ed.) *Neurodidaktik. Grundlagen und Vorschläge für gehirngerechtes Lehren und Lernen*, Weinheim, Germany: Beltz, pp. 9–19.

Hinton, P.R. (2015) *The Perception of People: Integrating Cognition and Culture* (2nd edn), London: Routledge.

Holl, A. (1998) *Jesus in schlechter Gesellschaft*, Vienna, Austria: Libro.

Hughes, K., Bond, N. and Ballantyne, R. (2013) 'Designing and managing interpretive experiences at religious sites: Visitors' perceptions of Canterbury Cathedral', *Tourism Management* 36, 210–220.

Illouz, E. (2007) *Der Konsum der Romantik: Liebe und die kulturellen Widersprüche des Kapitalismus*, Berlin, Germany: Suhrkamp-Taschenbuch Wissenschaft.

Jafari, J. and Scott, N. (2014) 'Muslim world and its tourisms', *Annals of Tourism Research* 44, 1–19.

Jarrett, E.S., Gower, A.L. and Borowsky, I.W. (2015) 'The relationship between adolescent self-perception of weight, mental health and social-protective factors', *Minnesota Medicine* 98(5), 40.

Jordan, H. (2008) *Orte heilen. Die energetische Beziehung zwischen dem Menschen und seinem Wohnort*, Baden, Germany: AT.

Kabat-Zinn, J. (2013) *Full Catastrophe Living: Using the Wisdom of Your Body and Mind to Face Stress, Pain and Illness* (2nd edn), New York: Bantam.

Keel, P.K. and Forney, K.J. (2013) 'Psychosocial risk factors for eating disorders', *International Journal of Eating Disorders* 46(5), 433–439.

Kogoj, T.K., Cebašek-Travnik, Z. and Zaletel-Kragelj, L. (2014) 'Role of stress in burnout among students of medicine and dentistry – a study in Ljubljana, Slovenia, Faculty of Medicine', *Collegium Antropologicum* 38(3), 879–887.

Kraft, E. (2015) 'Kraftplätze als emotionale Aneignung von Orten. Gesundheitstourismus am Weg vom Erlebniskonsum in Wellnesstempeln zur mentalen Selbststärkung in Naturräumen', in Egger, R. and Luger, K. (eds) *Tourismus und mobile Freizeit. Lebensformen, Trends, Herausforderungen*, Norderstedt, Germany: BoD, pp. 235–245.

Kriechbaum, R. (2008) *Klöster in Österreich*, Rosenheim, Germany: Weltbild.

Kuhn, T.S. (2012) *The Structure of Scientific Revolutions: 50th Anniversary Edition* (4th edn), Chicago, IL: University of Chicago Press.

Leaming, L. (2014) *A Field Guide to Happiness: What I Learned in Bhutan about Living, Loving and Waking Up*, London: Hay House.

Lee, K.-H., Packer, J. and Scott, N. (2015) 'Travel lifestyle preferences and destination activity choices of Slow Food members and non-members', *Tourism Management* 46, 1–10.

Lelord, F. (2010) *Hector and the Search for Happiness*, London: Penguin Books.

Leneveu, M.-C. (2013) 'Définition d'un concept: approche anthropologique du rite de passage', *Éthique and Santé* 10(2), 66–69.

Lindström, B. and Eriksson, M. (2005) 'Salutogenesis', *Journal of Epidemiological Community Health* 59, 440–442.

Lopez-Fernandez, O., Honrubia-Serrano, L., Freixa-Blanxart, M. and Gibson, W. (2014) 'Prevalence of problematic mobile phone use in British adolescents', *Cyberpsychology, Behavior and Social Networking* 17(2), 91–98.

Love, P.E.D., Goh, Y.M., Hogg, K., Robson, S. and Irani, Z. (2011) 'Burnout and sense of coherence among residential real estate brokers', *Safety Science* 49(10), 1297–1308.

Łowicki, D. and Piotrowska, S. (2015) 'Monetary valuation of road noise. Residential property prices as an indicator of the acoustic climate quality', *Ecological Indicators* 52, 472–479.

Luthar, S.S., Barkin, S.H. and Crossman, E.J. (2013) '"I can, therefore I must": Fragility in the upper-middle classes', *Development and Psychopathology* 25(4), 1529–1549.

Maslow, A.H. (2014) *Towards a Psychology of Being*, Floyd, VA: Sublime Books.

Maturana, H.R. and Varela, F.J. (1992) *The Tree of Knowledge: The Biological Roots of Human Understanding*, Boston, MA: Shambhala.

Mayor, S. (2015) 'Mindfulness based therapy is as effective as antidepressants in preventing depression relapse, study shows', *British Medical Journal* 350, h2107. doi: 10.1136/bmj.h2107.

Méndez, M. (2015) 'Globalization and human trafficking', in Wright, J.D. (ed.) *International Encyclopedia of the Social and Behavioral Sciences* (2nd edn), Amsterdam, The Netherlands: Elsevier, pp. 206–212.

Miegel, M. (2014) *Hybris: Die überforderte Gesellschaft*, Berlin, Germany: Propyläen Verlag.

Milyavskaya, M. and Koestner, R. (2011) 'Psychological needs, motivation and well-being: A test of self-determination theory across multiple domains', *Personality and Individual Differences* 50(3), 387–391.

Montessori, M. (1964) *The Montessori Method*, New York: Schocken.

Mooney, C.G. (2013) *Carol Garhart Theories of Childhood: An Introduction to Dewey, Montessori, Erikson, Piaget and Vygotsky* (2nd edn), St Paul, MN: Redleaf Press.

Nallet, A, Briefer, J.F. and Perret, I. (2015) 'Mindfulness in addiction therapy', *Revue Médicale Suisse* 11(480), 1407–1409.

Obrecht, A.J. (1995) *Panoptismus in Papua Neuguinea. Akkulturation und sozialer Wandel in ehemals segmentären Gesellschaften*, Frankfurt am Main, Germany: Europäischer Verlag der Wissenschaften.

—— (2014) *Wozu wissen wollen? Wissen – Herrschaft – Welterfahrung. Ein Beitrag zur Wissensdiskussion aus kultur- und wissenssoziologischer Perspektive*, Vienna, Austria: Edition Ausblick.

Pagnin, D., De Queiroz, V., De Oliveira Filho, M.A., Gonzalez, N.V., Salgado, A.E., Cordeiro e Oliveira, B., Lodi, C.S. and Melo, R.M. (2013) 'Burnout and career choice motivation in medical students', *Medical Teacher* 35(5), 388–394.

Pas, E.T., Bradshaw, C.P. and Hershfeldt, P.A. (2012) 'Teacher- and school-level predictors of teacher efficacy and burnout: Identifying potential areas for support', *Journal of School Psychology* 50(1), 129–145.

Pedersen, P. (1995) *The Five Stages of Culture Shock: Critical Incidents Around the World*, Westwood, CT: Greenwood Press.

Pedrero Pérez, E.J., Rodríguez Monje, M.T. and Ruiz Sánchez De León, J.M. (2012) 'Mobile phone abuse or addiction. A review of the literature', *Adicciones* 24(2), 139–152.

Pert, P. L., Hill, R., Maclean, K., Dalej, A., Rist, P., Schmider, J., Talbota, L. and Tawalee. L. (2015) 'Mapping cultural ecosystem services with rainforest aboriginal peoples: Integrating biocultural diversity, governance and social variation', *Ecosystem Services* 13, 41–56.

Pesonen, J. and Horster, E. (2012) 'Near field communication technology in tourism', *Tourism Management Perspectives* 4, 11–18.

Platt, B., Cohen Kadosh, K. and Lau, J.Y. (2013) 'The role of peer rejection in adolescent depression', *Depression and Anxiety* 30(9), 809–821.

Purner, J. (2008) *Im Zeichen der Wandlung. Über Forschungen und Erfahrungen auf dem Weg in eine andere Wirklichkeit* (2nd edn) Schaffhausen, Switzerland: Novalis.

Reed, P.G. (1991) 'Toward a nursing theory of self-transcendence: Deductive reformulation using developmental theories', *Advances in Nursing Science* 13, 64–77.

Remele, K. (2001) *Tanz um das goldene Selbst?. Therapiegesellschaft, Selbstverwirklichung und Gemeinwohl*, Graz, Austria: Styria.

Ricard, M. (2001) *The Quantum and the Lotus. A Journey to the Frontiers where Science and Buddhism meet*, New York: River Press.

Ricard, M., Lutz, A. and Davidson, R.J. (2014) 'Mind of the meditator', *Scientific American* 311(5), 38–45.

Rickly-Boyd, J.M. (2012) 'Authenticity and aura: A Benjaminian approach to tourism', *Annals of Tourism Research* 39(1), 269–289.

Rodriguez-Sancheza, M.C., Martinez-Romob, J., Borromeoa, S. and Hernandez-Tamamesa, J.A. (2013) 'GAT: Platform for automatic context-aware mobile services for m-tourism', *Expert Systems with Applications* 40(10), 4154–4163.

Romeiss-Stracke, F. (2003) *Abschied von der Spassgesellschaft: Freizeit und Tourismus im 21. Jahrhundert*, Amberg: Büro Wilhelm Verlag.

Rosenhan, D.L. (2006) 'Gesund in kranker Umgebung', in Watzlawick, P. (ed.) *Die erfundene Wirklichkeit. Wie wir wissen, was wir zu wissen glauben? Beiträge zum Konstruktivismus*, Munich, Germany: Piper, pp. 111–137.

Rosenthal, R. (2012) 'Self-fulfilling prophecy', in Ramachandran, V.S. (ed.) *Encyclopedia of Human Behavior* (2nd edn), London: Academic Press, pp. 328–335.

Schulte-Markwort, M. (2015) *Burnout-Kids: Wie das Prinzip Leistung unsere Kinder überfordert*, Munich, Germany: Pattloch.

Schultz, P. (2011) *1,000 Places to See Before You Die. A Traveller's Life List* (2nd edn), New York: Workman.

Schulze, G. (2005) *Die Erlebnisgesellschaft: Kultursoziologie der Gegenwart*, Frankfurt am Main, Germany: Campus.

—— (2008) *Die Sünde: Das schöne Leben und seine Feinde*, Frankfurt am Main, Germany: Fischer.

Schwarz, O. (2013) 'What should nature sound like? Techniques of engagement with nature sites and sonic preferences of Israeli visitors', *Annals of Tourism Research* 42, 382–401.

Shakespeare, W. (2014) *Hamlet*, Act 1, Scene 5. http://www.shakespeare-online.com/plays/hamlet_1_5.html (accessed 1 October 2015).

Sharpley, R. and Jepson, D. (2011) 'Rural tourism: A spiritual experience?', *Annals of Tourism Research* 38(1), 52–71.

Shaules, J. (2015) *The Intercultural Mind: Connecting Culture, Cognition and Global Living*, Boston, MA: Interculutral Press.

Shepherd, R.J. (2015) 'Why Heidegger did not travel: Existential angst, authenticity and tourist experiences', *Annals of Tourism Research* 52, 60–71.

Smith, A.E., Jussim, L., Eccles, J., VanNoy, M., Madon, S. and Palumbo, P. (1998) 'Self-fulfilling prophecies, perceptual biases and accuracy at the individual and group levels', *Journal of Experimental Social Psychology* 34(6), 530–561.

Steckelberg, A.V. (2015) 'Orchestrating a creative learning environment: Design and scenario work as a coaching experience – how educational science and psychology can help design and scenario work', *Futures*, http://dx.doi.org/10.1016/j.futures.2015.05.005 (accessed 10 June 2015).

Štefko, R., Kiráľová, A. and Mudrik, M. (2015) 'Strategic marketing communication in pilgrimage tourism', *Procedia – Social and Behavioral Sciences* 175, 423–430.

Torsheim, T., Aaroe, L.E. and Wold, B. (2001) 'Sense of coherence and school-related stress as predictors of subjective health complaints in early adolescence: Interactive, indirect or direct relationships?', *Social Science and Medicine* 53(5), 603–614.

Travasso, C. (2014) 'India opens clinic to help people "addicted" to mobile phones and video games', *British Medical Journa* 4(349), 4439. doi: 10.1136/bmj.g4439.

van der Velden, A.M. and Roepstorff, A. (2015) 'Neural mechanisms of mindfulness meditation: Bridging clinical and neuroscience investigations', *Nature Reviews. Neuroscience* 16(7), 439. doi: 10.1038/nrn3916-c1.

van Gennep, A. (1960) *The Rites of Passage. A Classic Study of Cultural Celebrations*, Chicago, IL: University of Chicago Press.

Ward, C., Bochner, S. and Furnham, A. (2001) *The Psychology of Culture Shock* (2nd edn), Philadelphia, PA: Routledge.

Watzlawick, P., Weakland, J. and Fisch, R. (1974) *Change: Principles of Problem Formation and Problem Resolution*, New York: W.W. Norton.

Weiner, E.W. (2009) *The Geography of Bliss: One Grump's Search for the Happiest Places in the World*, New York: Twelve Books.

Whiting, S.E., Jenkins, W.S., May, A.C., Rudy, B.M., Davis, T.E. and Reuther, E.T. (2014) 'The role of intolerance of uncertainty in social anxiety subtypes', *Journal of Clinical Psychology* 70(3), 260–272.

Wietlisbach, V., Marques-Vidal, P., Kuulasmaa, K., Karvanen, J. and Paccaud, F. (2013) 'The relation of body mass index and abdominal adiposity with dyslipidemia in 27 general populations of the WHO MONICA project', *Nutrition, Metabolism and Cardiovascular Diseases* 23(5), 432–442.

Williams, L.T., Germov, J., Fuller, S. and Freij, M. (2015) 'A taste of ethical consumption at a slow food festival', *Appetite* 91(1), 321–328.

Willson, G.B., McIntosh, A.J. and Zahra, A.L. (2013) 'Tourism and spirituality. A phenomenological analysis', *Annals of Tourism Research* 42, 150–168.

Witkiewitz, K., Bowen, S., Harrop, E.N., Douglas, H., Enkema, M. and Sedgwick, C. (2014) 'Mindfulness-based treatment to prevent addictive behavior relapse: Theoretical models and hypothesised mechanisms of change', *Substance Use and Misuse* 49(5), 513–524.

Yen, C.F., Tang, T.C., Yen, J.Y., Lin, H.C., Huang, C.F., Liu, S.C. and Ko, C.H. (2009) 'Symptoms of problematic cellular phone use, functional impairment and its association with depression among adolescents in Southern Taiwan', *Journal of Adolescence* 32(4), 863–873.

Zanalda, G. (2015) 'Financial crises, history of', in Wright, J.D. (ed.) *International Encyclopedia of the Social and Behavioral Sciences* (2nd edn), Amsterdam, The Netherlands: Elsevier, pp. 183–190.

Zenga, G., Go, F. and de Vries, H. J. (2012) 'Paradox of authenticity versus standardization: Expansion strategies of restaurant groups in China', *International Journal of Hospitality Management* 31/4, 1090–1100.

28

Rhythmic revitalisations

Attuning to nature for health and wellbeing

Edward H. Huijbens

Introduction

Nature and natural landscapes can afford a therapeutic and healing connection that can be promoted at tourism destinations set within such environments. The potential therapeutic effect of nature and natural settings is well documented (Hartig et al., 2014). Simply viewing natural landscapes has shown to help with short-term recovery from stress or mental fatigue (Pearson and Craig, 2014: 3), enable faster physical recovery from illness and contribute to long-term overall improvement of people's health and wellbeing (Velarde et al., 2007). Experimental approaches in the medical literature gauging physiological and psychological benefits abound. Bowler et al. (2010) synthesise the findings from 25 studies on physical health benefits of nature, demonstrating the ways in which natural environments may have direct and positive impacts on wellbeing. Haluza et al. (2014: 5454), in their review of the medical literature on natural health, found that '[s]hort-term restorative effects of outdoor Nature could be found for almost all measured physiological parameters'. These tentative indications of nature's restorative capacities have also been the focus of environmental psychology grasping individual perceptions and experiences of the healing and wellbeing benefits of the environment. This is exemplified in the work of Kaplan (1995), who frames the restorative capacities of nature through its role in focusing attention and integrally reducing stress.

In this chapter more emphasis will be placed on the setting itself, nature and its materiality and how it is imbricated with us in a continual unfolding of our being and our surroundings. What I would like to argue, following Conradson (2005, 2010), is how places emerge through a host of interactions between people, things and the relational self, carefully distinguishing between a 'therapeutic landscape' and a 'therapeutic landscape experience', as Gesler (2005: 296) explains Conradson's work. Relating to the environment and others is not a volitional one-directional reaching out of the individual, but a matter of affect. As Anderson (2014: 6) argues, the theorisation of affect is manifest in Conradson's (2005, 2010) therapeutic landscapes as two-sided, 'consist[ing] of bodily capacities to affect and to be affected that emerge and develop in concert' (Anderson, 2014: 9). This concert needs to be attended to and how the potential restoration of not only the individual but also the landscape emerges through the relational configurations of self and the landscape.

A therapeutic landscape thus is not only about the restoration of self, but can foster ecological sensibilities to the benefit of nature itself. We, as part of each ecological system, 'must be understood as the ongoing exploration of and experimentation with the forms of bodily activity that living things are capable of undertaking' (Grosz, 2011: 22). Through exploration and experimentation we unlock matter in its vibrancy.

> my hunch is that the image of dead or thoroughly instrumentalized matter feeds human hubris and our earth-destroying fantasies of conquest and consumption . . . if a set of moral principles is actually to be lived out, the right mood or landscape of affect has to be in place . . . [and] we have to be perceptually open to it.
>
> *(Bennett, 2010: ix, xii and 14)*

As Bennett (2010: xi) argues, 'human decency and the decent politics are fostered if we tune in to the strange logic of turbulence'. Turbulent and unpredictable, nature untamed can intimidate some, but once attuned to through an open-ended comportment, what emerges is an ecological sensibility promoting health and happiness through raising the status of the materiality of which we are composed (Bennett, 2010: 12).

This chapter will follow up on these thoughts and argue for ways of conceptualising nature's restorative capacities. Previously I have made sense of this through the role of wellbeing and water in destination promotion (Huijbens, 2011) and the role of wilderness landscape vistas (Huijbens and Benediktsson, 2013; Huijbens, 2014). For the conceptualisation presented in this chapter I will draw on Henri Lefebvre's rhythm analysis, wherein he lays the foundation for understanding how bodily rhythms relate to natural cycles and rhythms. The chapter will argue for the necessity of attuning to the latter for wellbeing benefits. This attuning is exemplified with a short case vignette from Icelandic waterfalls and an outline of how coupling the rhythms of nature and ourselves can afford a healing connection. The chapter will unfold in three sections. First, the idea of rhythms will be fleshed out and how these open an understanding of the production of space and how rhythms have been used as an analytical tool in terms of tourism. Second, the idea of attuning will be discussed and how this links to rhythm. Third, a case study will be presented, exemplifying how attuning to rhythms can be facilitated in tourism practices.

Rhythms

> My sense of being 'in' a time and of inhabiting a 'place' depends on forms of regularity.
>
> *(Morton, 2013: 69)*

> Crucially, these are rhythms of concern which present themselves to us and demand we rethink our assumptions, habits, taken-for-granteds and unthought embodiments.
>
> *(Jackson and Fannin, 2011: 435)*

Rhythm analysis is a conceptual tool, albeit not the most rigorous one, developed by the French theorist of geography and society Henri Lefebvre to grasp how the world discloses itself through rhythm. According to him, rhythms are the ultimate 'exposition of the production of space' (Lefebvre, 1991: 404), making spaces and places 'a garland of rhythms, [or] one could say a bouquet' (Lefebvre, 2004: 20). In formulating rhythm analysis Lefebvre outlines the constitutive parts of rhythms, referring to these as 'elements' of rhythm analysis. The 'first element' of rhythm analysis is repetition, i.e. all rhythms entail repetition. But Lefebvre argues that there can be no pure repetition, i.e. no absolute, unchanging repetition. An absolute, unchanging rhythm is a pure logical abstraction, a kind of eternal machine, and does not exist in reality. With this argument he states further that repetition, as it cannot be absolute, gives rise to difference. The differentiating power of rhythms is the 'second element' of his analysis, i.e. that difference is inherent in the repetition and it will sooner or later give rise to it.

At the same time, though, the abstracted or pure repetition also has a role to play. Much as Lefebvre had before postulated in terms of the production of space (Lefebvre, 1968, 1991), the transcendental conceived (abstract) spaces had real concrete manifestations playing a role in people's everyday lives. In the same way implicit with all notion of rhythm there is measure, i.e. an abstraction through making it 'law, calculated and expected obligation, a project' (Lefebvre, 2004: 8) that has concrete manifestations. The manifest examples of measured rhythms he cites through his book are of music, language and media, bodily training in terms of dressage and acquired gestures, dance and work. As he makes very clear, the examples can be understood as abstractions or pure measure, but they are nonetheless all intricately bound with difference since, although 'rhythm appears as regulated time, governed by rational laws, [it is] in contact with what is least rational in human being: the lived, the carnal, the body' (Lefebvre, 2004: 9). With these two constitutive elements of rhythm, i.e. as difference and measure, Lefebvre can claim that rhythm has logic although it inherently escapes logic. This interaction of the cyclical (difference producing repetition) and linear (measure) folds component rhythms into a poly-rhythmic ensemble that constitutes spaces and places.

With the notion of polyrhythmia it becomes clear what Lefebvre means when he states that space can be viewed as 'a garland of rhythms, [or] one could say a bouquet'. This symphony of rhythms, to pick up on another metaphor (Lefebvre, 2004: 31) is the ultimate expression of the production of space and through rhythm Lefebvre shows 'the interrelation of understand-ings of space and time in the comprehension of everyday life' (Elden, 2004: vii). In this sense rhythms are everywhere, in everything we do and every place we see. These rhythms however are of varying speeds and intensities. To make sense of this Lefebvre presents a tentative typol-ogy of rhythms starting with what he calls 'secret rhythms', those that are physiological and also psychological or those circadian rhythms of the body and in living things and those of the functioning mind, e.g. in memory. Second, there are 'public rhythms' – those found on calen-dars, work routine, ceremonies and those of the body rhythms one can express, e.g. tiredness or hunger. Third, there are 'fictional rhythms' or the imaginary rhythms of the learning person, those rhythms one picks up and appropriates, e.g. dispositions. Fourth, there are 'dominating-dominated rhythms' or those that are completely made up and aim for effect that is beyond that which can be found in themselves. Lastly, once confronted with rhythms weaving non-anthropogenic material, he cites 'cosmic rhythms' of all kinds.

For Lefebvre it is for the attentive ear of the rhythm analysist to discern those rhythms, using their own bodies as a metronome. For Lefebvre, space 'is always now and formerly, a present space, given as an immediate whole, complete with its associations and connections in their actuality' (Lefebvre, 1991: 37). For him space 'isn't just the staging of reproductive require-ments, but part of the cast and a vital, productive member of the cast at that' (Merrifield, 2000: 173). Lefebvre passed away before further being able to flesh out the details of his rhythm analy-sis, but many have followed in his wake. Grosz (2008) uses rhythms to explicate how we can connect to our surroundings:

> Rhythm is what connects the most elementary and primitive bodily structures of even the most simple organisms to the implacable movements of the universe itself . . . The refrain is how rhythm stakes out a territory from chaos that resonates with and intensifies the body.
>
> *(19)*

> Both rhythm and milieu are the slowing down, the provisional formalization of elements of chaos: the milieu, the congealing of a block of space-time and a rhythm, the emergence of a periodicity, are not separable from the block of emergent territoriality.
>
> *(47)*

Rhythms thus stake out territory, they entail the slowing down and formalisation of the vibrant material chaos that is the earth and our surroundings and afford us a connection to this very territory. These are not measured rhythms or pure repetitions, but a sense of regularity and stability that creates the conditions for life, as Grosz (2011) further elaborates on:

> It is this relative stability and orderliness, predictability, that is the very foundation or condition for a life of invention and novelty, a life in which pure repetition is never possible.
>
> *(Grosz, 2011: 30)*

Life on earth is conditioned by regularity, an orderliness that allows for predictability. As Jackson and Fannin (2011: 435) explained with reference to Sarah Whatmore, 'earthlife' unfolds 'through nexuses, assemblages, hybrids and networks of a return to matter, but under different rhythms of repetition'.

> Nature itself is musical, composed of material notes which each play their own melody, a melody complicated, augmented, syncopated and transformed through the melodies of the other living and nonliving things with which it engages . . . Each living creature is a series of 'tonal' responses to various 'melodies' played by its Umwelt, through various performances it undertakes.
>
> *(Grosz, 2011: 174 and 176)*

Through repetition we connect to our surroundings, we respond to the rhythms around us, attune to these and make sense of our selves.

Travelling rhythms

In tourism studies, especially through tourism geographies, rhythm has featured as the point of departure for the analysis of travel and tourism. Table 28.1 pulls together the existing literature dealing with rhythms from a travelling perspective and highlights distinctive themes and focus areas being scrutinised.

As Table 28.1 demonstrates, six distinctive themes can be identified in a review of the 28 articles that dealt with rhythm and tourism explicitly. Three of those 28 deal explicitly with health and wellbeing thereof, with two moreover tying health and wellbeing with slow travel and mobility (Doughty, 2011; Rantala and Valtonen, 2014). The latter argue through a case study amongst nature-based tourists in Finnish Lapland and their sleeping behaviour how 'holidays provide[s] evidence as to the importance of the natural changes in luminosity, activeness and affectiveness' (Rantala and Valtonen, 2014: 28, see also Krause, 2013). Rantala and Valtonen (2014) claim that acknowledging the constancy and multiplicity of rhythms can capture the specific features involved in nature holidays, especially those related to the inner aspects of the body. The former is more directly related to the topic of this chapter from an individual health and wellbeing perspective. The doctoral thesis of Doughty (2011) demonstrates through an investigation into walkers in the UK Hampshire

Table 28.1 Summary of literature on tourism, travel and rhythm

Key themes on rhythm and tourism	Studies
Health and wellbeing	Tamarozzi (2002); Doughty (2011); Rantala and Valtonen (2014)
Slow travel	Gelter (2000); Knox (2005); Edensor and Holloway (2008); Germann-Molz (2009, 2010); Sverrisdóttir (2011); Edensor (2012); Kaaristo and Järv (2012); Jayne et al. (2012); Dickinson et al. (2013); Rantala and Valtonen (2014)
Music/performance	Duffy et al. (2007, 2011); Waitt and Duffy (2010); Edensor (2012); Simpson (2012)
Mobility	Gelter (2000); Zillinger (2007); Edensor and Holloway (2008); Huijbens (2008); Germann-Molz (2009, 2010); Cresswell (2010); Doughty (2011); Edensor (2012); Jayne et al. (2012); Dickinson et al. (2013); Falconer (2013); Lagerkvist (2013); Rantala and Valtonen (2014); Rogers (2015); Vannini (2012)
Food/drinks	Bishop (2011); Jayne et al. (2012); Falconer (2013)
Urban rhythms	Knox (2005); Bishop (2011); Prior (2011); Rogers (2015)
Other	Huang and Ma (2011); Birenboim et al. (2013); Krause (2013)

landscape how it is experienced as a therapeutic landscape. The experience was highlighted through the number of intersecting rhythms in nature impacting the degree to which the walk was experienced as restorative.

Dominating the studies recounted in Table 28.1 is the measured notion of rhythm, i.e. how rhythm structures time through a social management regime people seek to escape from in their travelling practices, e.g. the overwhelming rhythms of urban life. As Edensor (2010: 1) makes clear:

> In this context, rhythm analysis is particularly useful in investigating the patterning of a range of multiscalar temporalities – calendrical, diurnal and lunar, lifecycle, somatic and mechanical – whose rhythms provide an important constituent of the experience and organisation of social time.

But the studies in Table 28.1 also offer a departure from this social time. Rhythms of music and performance arts, food, e.g. through meal times offer an escape and breaking away from the rigours of measured rhythm. The measured rhythms and organisation of social time, not least in our hyper-productive day and age, are seen as opposed to or something to break in order to facilitate slow tourism. Sverrisdóttir (2011: 83) describes the measured abstracted rhythms, the ones dictated by social schedules and argues for a slowing down.

> In my capacity as a guide, I found that the most treasured moments of the tours were often completely unorganized, unforeseen everydayish happenings in the extraordinary setting offered by a random place in nature, when time had the opportunity to win over space and ambiance, mood or chance 'appropriated' a certain moment.

The patterning and range of temporalities manifest in different rhythms have to do with speed and intensities. Allowing time to win over space and appropriating the moment is about moving beyond the illusion of rhythmic order, as Edensor (2010: 13) calls it. But, following Edensor (2010), I argue that:

consistencies, repetitions and reproductions, moments of quietitude, notwithstanding the furious work that goes into the sustenance of stable arrangements, [and] is open to moments of chaos, dissonance and breakdown; moments of arrhythmia.

(Edensor, 2010: 18)

Through consistencies, repetitions and reproductions we need to be attentive to the moments which allow the other in, be it our surroundings, matter or other people. Attuning to the 'secret', 'public', 'fictional', 'dominating-dominated' or 'cosmic rhythms', to use Lefebvre's typology, rhythms open the door to becoming different, e.g. restored or feeling better.

Attuning

The key to understanding and sensing rhythms is attunement and, as made clear with reference to Bennett (2010), this attunement is to be directed at matter's vibrancy through and with us. Attunement affects in the way Anderson (2014: 163) describes it:

First, affective life is always-already 'in the midst of' relations and processes and inseparable from those relations and processes. Second, processes of mediation are active in the sense that affective life differs as it is mediated.

We are continually preoccupied by an exposure to what is other; a corporeality that is driven by inhuman forces (Grosz, 2011) and can develop creative ways of attuning to this wider conception of nature and space as a garland of rhythms. 'They are resources that must be attuned to by bodies' (Anderson, 2014: 45). The sense we make of ourselves and each other shapes who we become and influences our wellbeing.

Attunement implies that nature is not out there to be made sense of but interlaces and interacts with us through perceptions and conceptions of spaces. Thus we need to distinguish carefully between a 'therapeutic landscape' and a 'therapeutic landscape experience'. The perceptions and conceptions are the 'processes of the production of things, processes that transform states of matter, processes that enable and complicate life . . . an impersonal force of contraction and dilation that characterizes events' (Grosz, 2011: 2 and 27). A therapeutic landscape is not because it is subjective experiences as such, but objectively produced and maintained as such through our attentiveness to it.

John Wood (2007: 196) quotes Francisco Varela's notion of autopoiesis when arguing that 'by suspending our habit of objectifying or particularising our experiences . . . [we should] broaden our focus in order to perceive the whole . . . [and] "see" what is happening from inside it'. Through broadening our focus we could get more sensitively attuned to the natural world and our earthly entanglements, better grasping what for us is information and inspiration. Attuning means experimental living and allowing space for matter and that which composes the environment. The co-generation of matter and human beings through a rhythmic ensemble allows us to rethink our relationship to time, place and the agency of matter that shape new ways of thinking and feeling.

Elucidating ways in which nature and the earth can be made sensible through tourism practices and development amounts to a new individual and social ethos, an environmental morality tied with new modes of knowledge production, where our collective force is entangled with the forces of the earth (Gren and Huijbens, 2016). It is imperative that we invent new ways of granting authority to more-than-human forms of life and matter in times of global environmental change (Bennett, 2010). Developing a particular kind of sensitivity based on reciprocity should allow for hospitality that can facilitate wellbeing and nature's restorative capacities, be it for physiological or psychological benefits.

Attuning is thus about intimacy with more-than-human worlds, the world of nature, matter and that which seemingly surrounds us, but is constitutive of us. It requires an active distancing from the intimacy of the organic body and its lived experiences and affects. The scale of rhythmic attunement can vary enormously, ranging from the 'secret' personal rhythms of our bodies to the 'cosmic' rhythms of the lunar cycle or even the earth's axial tilt. On the most general level, however, being receptive to more-than-human forces is about exceeding the spaces and times of human experience bringing us into contact with what might have been and could be. With this we re-inscribe futurality 'into the present, ending the metaphysics of presence' (Morton, 2013: 94). Reorienting causality in this way, we make room for aesthetics. The ways in which we apprehend the future bears directly upon our present and our presence. Practices of attunement thus share affinity with aesthetics, the quality of experience and spirituality, all of which feature in studies of health and wellbeing tourism.

In what follows I would like to explore practices of attunement to more-than-human temporalities and material processes in terms of Icelandic waterfalls.

Case study: Icelandic waterfalls

On 16 May 2015 I partook in a daylong workshop organised by the Icelandic Environment Association (IEA) and the Iceland Nature Conservation Association (INCA), both of which collaborate on the Icelandic Highland Project meant to promote events and advertise the need to conserve this largest wilderness area in Europe. The title of the workshop and day of talks was: why protect the central highlands? The talk portrayed this wilderness area of Iceland in a range of terms from a typography of ecosystems there to poetic apprehensions of being there at various times of year. The way of envisioning the future of this wilderness area is part of an unfolding land-use debate. The aims of the IEA and the INCA clash foremost with the question of taming the rivers and hot springs found in abundance in this wilderness area in order to generate energy for the heavy industry sector, comprising one of the three pillars of the Icelandic economy. The IEA and the INCA levy against this the interests of tourism, another of the three economic pillars (see Sæþórsdóttir and Saarinen, 2015).

Taming a river entails mediating its flow through reservoirs in order to harmonise it, so that hydro-power plant generators can be kept humming at an even pace all through the year, through spring floods and winter draughts. Some of the most popular and iconic features of the wilderness landscapes in the central highlands are its waterfalls, often adorning tourism promotional material from Iceland. Foreign visitors do indeed come to the island primarily for its natural attractions and prominent amongst those are the waterfalls. Visitors sighing on the road in Europe 'yet another castle' are known to say in Iceland after spending a few days on the road there; 'yet another waterfall'. Europe's most powerful waterfall is in the north-east of the island: Dettifoss, close to the iconic and picturesque Goðafoss. Both are in glacial rivers coming from Europe's largest icecap, the Vatnajökull icecap. Both waterfalls and a number of lesser-known waterfalls along the length of the rivers feeding them and their contributories have not been harnessed. Their flow rate follows the seasons and diurnal rhythms, their periodical floods and ebbs offer an experience of their waterfalls that is never the same. The measured rhythm of the mediated river in the service

(continued)

(continued)

of industrialisation sits in stark contrast with the natural rhythms of an untamed river, one holding the promise of being ever different, ever differentiating, as is the second element of rhythms as outlined by Lefebvre.

Simply viewing natural landscapes has been shown to help with short-term recovery from stress or mental fatigue induced by ever more sedentary and motile livelihoods in the urbanised Western world. Under these conditions, slowing down becomes imperative in order to detach from stress inducement, as commonly recognised in studies of health. Attuning to the flow of the water and recognising its diurnal and seasonal variations can function as a catalyst to this slowing. Indeed,

> 'Time' is inevitably an important experiential component and the awareness of time passing during the outdoor journeys is felt during the 'passage' of the journey itself and via natural change such as light and dark, tides and weather.
>
> *(Varley and Semple, 2015: 82)*

A waterfall can afford this connection to time and slowing down or any other feature of the natural landscape. The key is to highlight and promote its seasonality, 'rhythmicity' and natural cycles and allowing the tourist to feel its effect through the journey. These affordances of nature can perhaps be called 'slow adventure tourism', which is the notion Varley and Semple (2015) use to capture this, and can be contrasted against travel practices that come pre-packaged and in ever more strictly managed time regimes.

Concluding remarks

Simply viewing landscapes can have an effect on short-term recovery from stress or mental fatigue, enable faster physical recovery from illness and contribute to long-term overall improvement of people's health and wellbeing. What I have argued for in this chapter is that connecting to the 'rhythmicity' of natural phenomena can afford this effect. This occurs through recognition of our imbrication with the natural world and its materiality. For a landscape to become therapeutic, bodily capacities to affect and to be affected have to emerge and develop in concert with its surroundings. Attuning to this concert is key and tourism products and practices should figure ways of enabling this attunement for the betterment of us and ecology more generally. My example of the waterfalls of Iceland and the unfolding land-use controversies surrounding them should indicate some of the stakes involved. For tourism to be sustainable and health tourism to live up to its potential, more attuned sensibilities are required to nature's rhythms and ours.

Acknowledgements

I would like to acknowledge the help of Iris Homan, an intern at the Icelandic Tourism Research Centre from Wageningen University in the Netherlands, in constructing the review of the literature on tourism and rhythms. Also I thank the European fund for cooperation in science and technology (COST) for facilitating some of the encounters that have allowed these thoughts to take shape through funding Tourism, Wellbeing and Ecosystem Services (COST IS 1204).

References

Anderson, B. (2014) *Encountering Affect: Capacities, Apparatuses, Conditions*, Surrey, UK: Ashgate Publishing.

Bennett, J. (2010) *Vibrant Matter. A Political Ecology of Things*, Durham, NC: Duke University Press.

Birenboim, A., Anton-Clavé, S., Russo, A.P. and Shoval, N. (2013) 'Temporal activity patterns of theme park visitors', *Tourism Geographies*, 15(4), 601–619.

Bishop, P. (2011) 'Eating in the contact zone: Singapore foodscape and cosmopolitan timespace', *Continuum*, 25(5), 637–652.

Bowler, D.E., Buyung-Ali, L.M., Knight, T.M. and Pullin, A.S. (2010) 'A systematic review of evidence for the added benefits to health of exposure to natural environments', *BMC Public Health*, 10(456), 1–10.

Conradson, D. (2005) 'Landscape, care and the relational self: Therapeutic encounters in rural England', *Health and Place*, 11, 337–348.

—— (2010) 'The orchestration of feeling: stillness, spirituality and places of retreat', in Bissell, D. and Fuller, G. (eds) *Stillness in a Mobile World*, London: Routledge, pp. 71–86.

Cresswell, T. (2010) 'Towards a politics of mobility', *Environment and Planning D: Society and Space*, 28(1), 17–31.

Dickinson, J.E., Filimonau, V., Cherrett, T., Davies, N., Norgate, S., Speed, C. and Winstanley, C. (2013) 'Understanding temporal rhythms and travel behaviour at destinations: Potential ways to achieve more sustainable travel', *Journal of Sustainable Tourism*, 21(7), 1070–1090.

Doughty, K.S.E.R. (2011) 'Walking and well-being: Landscape, affect, rhythm', University of Southampton, School of Geography and Environment, Doctoral Thesis.

Duffy, M., Waitt, G.R. and Gibson, C.R. (2007) 'Get into the groove: The role of sound in generating a sense of belonging in street parades', *Altitude: A Journal of Emerging Humanities Work*, 8, 1–32.

Duffy, M., Waitt, G., Gorman-Murray, A. and Gibson, C. (2011) 'Bodily rhythms: Corporeal capacities to engage with festival spaces', *Emotion, Space and Society*, 4(1), 17–24.

Edensor, T. (2010) *Geographies of Rhythm. Nature, Place, Mobilities and Bodies*, Farnham, UK: Ashgate.

—— (2012) 'The rhythms of tourism', in Minca, C. and Oakes, T. (eds) *Real Tourism: Practice, Care and Politics in Contemporary Travel Culture*, New York: Routledge, pp. 54–71.

Edensor, T. and Holloway, J. (2008) 'Rhythmanalysing the coach tour: The Ring of Kerry, Ireland', *Transactions of The Institute of British Geographers*, 33(4), 483–501.

Elden, S. (2004) *Understanding Henri Lefebvre*, London: Continuum.

Falconer, E. (2013) 'Transformations of the backpacking food tourist: Emotions and conflicts', *Tourist Studies*, 13(1), 21–35.

Gelter, H. (2000) 'Friluftsliv: The Scandinavian philosophy of outdoor life', *Canadian Journal of Environmental Education*, 5(1), 77–92.

Germann-Molz, J. (2009) 'Representing pace in tourism mobilities: Staycations, Slow Travel and *The Amazing Race*', *Journal of Tourism and Cultural Change*, 7(4), 270–286.

—— (2010) 'Performing global geographies: Time, space, place and pace in narratives of round-the-world travel', *Tourism Geographies*, 12(3), 329–348.

Gesler, W. (2005) 'Theraputic landscapes: An evolving theme', *Health and Place*, 11, 295–297.

Gren, M.G. and Huijbens, E.H. (eds) (2016) *Tourism and the Anthropocene*, London: Routledge.

Grosz, E. (2008) *Chaos, Territory, Art. Deleuze and the Framing of the Earth*, New York: Columbia University Press.

—— (2011) *Becoming Undone. Darwinian Reflections on Life, Politics and Art*, Durham, NC: Duke University Press.

Haluza, D., Schönbauer, R. and Cervinka, R. (2014) 'Green perspectives for public health: A narrative review on the physiological effects of experiencing outdoor nature', *International Journal of Environmental Research and Public Health*, 11, 5445–5461.

Hartig, T., Mitchell, R., de Vries, S. and Frumkin, H. (2014) 'Nature and health', *Annual Review of Public Health*, 35, 211–222.

Huang, X.T. and Ma, X.J. (2011) 'Study on tourists rhythm of activities based on GPS data', *Tourism Tribune*, 26(12), 26–29.

Huijbens, E.H. (2008) 'Destination weaving: The rhythms of Goðafoss as a tourist attraction', in Backhaus, G., Heikkinen, V.A., Huijbens, H., Itkonen, M., Majkut, P. and Varmola, J. (eds) *The Illuminating Traveller: Expressions of the Ineffability of the Sublime*, Jyväskylä: University of Jyväskylä, Icelandic Tourism Research Centre and University of Lapland, pp. 147–176.

—— (2011) 'Developing wellness in Iceland – theming wellness destinations the Nordic way', *Scandinavian Journal of Hospitality and Tourism*, 11(1), 20–41.

—— (2014) 'Natural wellness. The case of Icelandic wilderness landscapes for health and wellness tourism', in Smith, M.K. and Puczkó, L. (eds) *Health, Tourism and Hospitality: Spas, Wellness and Medical Travel*, London: Routledge, pp. 413–416.

Huijbens, E. and Benediktsson, K. (2013) 'Inspiring the visitor? Landscapes and horizons of hospitality', *Tourist Studies*, 13(2), 189–208.

Jackson, M. and Fannin, M. (2011) 'Letting geography fall where it may – aerographies address the elemental', *Environment and Planning D: Society and Space*, 29, 435–444.

Jayne, M., Gibson, C., Waitt, G. and Valentine, G. (2012) 'Drunken mobilities, backpackers, alcohol, "doing place"', *Tourist Studies*, 12(3), 211–231.

Kaaristo, M. and Järv, R. (2012) 'Our clock moves at a different pace: The timescapes of identity in Estonian rural tourism', *Electronic Journal of Folklore*, 51, 109–132.

Kaplan, S. (1995) 'The restorative benefits of nature – toward an integrative framework', *Journal of Environmental Psychology*, 15, 169–182.

Knox, P.L. (2005) 'Creating ordinary places: Slow cities in a fast world', *Journal of Urban Design*, 10(1), 1–11.

Krause, F. (2013) 'Seasons as rhythms on the Kemi River in Finnish Lapland', *Ethnos*, 78(1), 23–46.

Lagerkvist, A. (2013) 'Communicating the rhythms of retromodernity: "Confused and mixed Shanghai"', *Urban Rhythms*, 61(1), 144–161.

Lefebvre, H. (1968) *Dialectical Materialism*, London: Jonathan Cape.

—— (1991) *The Production of Space*, Oxford, UK: Blackwell.

—— (2004) *Rhythmanalysis. Space, Time and Everyday Life*, London: Continuum.

Merrifield, A. (2000) 'Henri Lefebvre. A socialist in space', in Crang, M. and Thrift, N. (eds) *Thinking Space*, London: Routledge, pp. 167–182.

Morton, T. (2013) *Hyperobjects: Philosophy and Ecology after the End of the World*, Minneapolis, MN: University of Minnesota Press.

Pearson, D.G. and Craig, T. (2014) 'The great outdoors? Exploring the mental health benefits of natural environments', *Frontiers in Psychology*, 5(1178), 1–4.

Prior, N. (2011) 'Speed, rhythm and time-space: Museums and cities', *Space and Culture*, 14(2), 197–213.

Rantala, O. and Valtonen A. (2014) 'A rhythmanalysis of touristic sleep in nature', *Annals of Tourism Research*, 47, 18–30.

Rogers, L. (2015) 'The rhythm of non-places: Marooning the embodied self in depthless space', *Humanities*, 4, 569–599.

Simpson, P. (2012) 'Apprehending everyday rhythms: Rhythm analysis, time-lapse photography and the space-times of street performance', *Cultural Geographies*, 19(4), 423–445.

Sæþórsdóttir, A.D. and Saarinen J. (2015) 'Challenges due to changing ideas of natural resources: Tourism and power plant development in the Icelandic wilderness', *Polar Record*, DOI: 10.1017/S00322474150002731.

Sverrisdóttir, H. (2011) 'The destination within', *Landabréfið Journal of the Association of Icelandic Geographers*, 25, 77–84.

Tamarozzi, F. (2002) 'Return to basics ebb and flow of tourists taking the waters in Salsomaggior', *Ethnologie Française*, 32(3), 415–427.

Vannini, P. (2012) 'In time, out of time. Rhythmanalyzing ferry mobilities', *Time and Society*, 21(2), 241–269.

Varley, P. and Semple, T. (2015) 'Nordic slow adventure: Explorations in time and nature', *Scandinavian Journal of Hospitality and Tourism*, 15(1), 73–90.

Velarde, M.D., Fry, G. and Tveit, M. (2007) 'Health effects of viewing landscapes – landscape types in environmental psychology', *Urban Forestry and Urban Greening*, 6, 199–212.

Waitt, G. and Duffy, M. (2010) 'Listening and tourism studies', *Annals of Tourism Research*, 37(2), 457–477.

Wood, J. (2007) *Design for Micro Utopias*, Aldershot, UK: Gower.

Zillinger, M. (2007) 'Tourist routes: A time-geographical approach on German car-tourists in Sweden', *Tourism Geographies*, 9(1), 64–83.

29

Relationships between emotion regulation seeking, programme satisfaction, attention restoration and life satisfaction

Healing programme participants

Timothy J. Lee and Jinok Susanna Kim

Introduction

Recently, as general interest in health has been increasing all over the world, health tourism has rapidly increased. In Korea, health-related travel activities are drastically increasing and the Korea Forest Service and local governments are implementing healing programmes using forests. The purpose of this study was to examine the structural relationships between the impact of healing tourists' emotion regulation seeking, attention restoration, programme satisfaction and life satisfaction. The study subject was 311 forest healing programme participants from the healing forest programme managed by the Korea Forest Service. The results suggest that emotion regulation seeking has a positive effect on healing programme satisfaction. Also, emotion regulation seeking has a positive effect on life satisfaction through attention restoration rather than directly. In addition, healing programme satisfaction has a positive effect on life satisfaction through attention restoration, but healing programmes do not directly influence life satisfaction. The findings of this study imply that attention restoration plays an important role in mediating between healing programme satisfaction and life satisfaction.

With a growing interest in health and wellbeing, health-related industries have rapidly grown across the world. As a result, the focus of medicine has transitioned from treating diseases to pursuing improved quality of life by promoting health, preventing disease and seeking health (Song et al., 2014). In the same way, health tourism with the purpose of seeking health has significantly grown within the broader health tourism industry. Health tourism is largely divided into medical tourism with the purpose of treating diseases and wellness tourism with the aim of seeking health (Smith and Puczkó, 2014). In recent years, wellness tourism (seeking health and wellbeing) has continued to grow (Allen, Rivkin and Lopez, 2014; Hall, 2013; Vork and Lombarts, 2014). Due to the socio-cultural factors currently present in Korea, health-related industries as well as health-seeking tourism activities are growing in Korea as well. Consequently, the government is operating healing programmes by creating paths and trails in national parks and building forests for the purpose of promoting public health (Kim, Lee and Kim, 2014).

The increased tourism activities related to health are attributable to the fact that modern people have an increased need for physical and emotional stability because of mental fatigue from urban life, stress and work (Baur and Tynon, 2010; Heintzman, 2014). Nature-based tourism activities have been found to have a positive effect on psychological healing of modern people, including relief from stress, reduction of depression, decrease of anxiety and improved sleep quality, along with restoration of attention (Bowler, Buyung-Ali, Knight and Pullin, 2010; Korpela, Borodulin, Neuvonen, Paronen and Tyrväinen, 2014; Song et al., 2014).

Beginning with the psychological wellbeing from natural scenes as described by Ulrich (1979), psychological healing has been continuously studied ever since, based on the restoration of attention that nature gives human beings. The field is known as environmental psychology (Berto, 2005; Hartig, 2004; Irvine, Warber, Devine-Wright and Gaston, 2013; Kaplan, 1995; Kaplan and Kaplan, 1989; Korpela et al., 2014; Wolsko and Lindberg, 2013). Recently, studies on the healing effects of nature have been carried out in Northern Europe, Japan and Korea, focusing on forest healing in the fields of psychology and forest science, psychology and psychology-physiology (Park, Tsunetsugu, Kasetani, Kagawa and Miyazaki, 2010; Song, Ikei and Miyazaki, 2014; Tsunetsugu, Park, Lee, Kagawa and Miyazaki, 2011; Tyrväinen et al., 2014). However, few studies have been conducted to investigate the healing effect of health-seeking tourism activities in the field of tourism. Therefore, it is thought that such studies on the healing effect of health-seeking tourism activities are needed.

Accordingly, this chapter aims to investigate the effect of a nature-based healing programme on emotion regulation, satisfaction with the healing programme, attention restoration and life satisfaction. In other words, it attempts to examine how health-seeking tourism activities affect the psychological restoration and eventually, the quality of life of tourists.

Literature review

Emotion regulation

Emotion is a person's perception of the combination of the image, thought and memory felt by the body (Hochschild, 1979). Emotion is defined within two dimensions: positivity and negativity and activeness and passiveness (Cowie, Douglas-Cowie and Romano, 1999). Emotion regulation is the process by which a person expresses what is being experienced (Gross, 1998).

Dividing the characteristics of adjustment and maladjustment in emotion regulation, Cole, Michel and Teti (1994) referred to emotion regulation as socially acceptable voluntary responses, as well as emotional abilities to defer voluntary responses smoothly and continuously when needed. Thompson (1994) suggested that emotion regulation is the act of modifying, assessing and searching emotional responses and consists of internal and external processes. Since emotion regulation has complexity where multiple situations, not just a single situation, are considered, it has multi-dimensional constructs (Gross, 1998; Walden and Smith, 1997). In general, people try to regulate their emotions in a negative situation and not in a positive situation (John and Gross, 2007). They regulate their emotions in multi-dimensional ways, including cognitive, emotional and behavioural methods (Denham, 1993; Walden and Smith, 1997). Many studies have documented that nature reduces negative emotions and increases positive emotions (Berman, Jonides and Kaplan, 2008; Sung, Woo, Kim, Lim and Chung 2012; Tyrväinen et al., 2014). Therefore, nature can be used as a tool to regulate emotions and people can live with nature to regulate their emotions (Johnsen, 2013).

Attention restoration theory

Attention restoration theory (ART) is a theory that proposes an alternative explanation for the psychological effect of nature (Kaplan and Kaplan, 1989). In daily life, tasks that require mental effort require directed attention which, when used for periods of time, can lead to mental fatigue (Kaplan, 1995). Tired directed attention can be restored through the use of involuntary attention, which can be achieved with an attractive restorative environment such as nature (Kaplan, 1995; Wells, 2014). The necessary conditions for the restorative environment for attention restoration include being away, fascination, extent and compatibility (Berto, 2005; Hartig, Korpela, Evans and Gärling, 1997; Kaplan and Kaplan, 1989).

Today, with accumulated mental fatigue from living in an urban environment and having to carry out endless routine work, people search for health-seeking tourism activities in the natural environment. Exposure to the natural environment was found to lead to attention restoration, psychological stabilisation and emotional stability (Ratcliffe, Gatersleben and Sowden, 2013; Tyrväinen et al., 2014; Wolsko and Lindberg, 2013). Therefore, studies on nature-based activities that can provide psychological healing and help restore directed attention have continued based on ART (Kim et al., 2014; Pasanen, Tyrväinen and Korpela, 2014; Sahlin, Ahlborg, Matuszczyk and Grahn, 2014; Shin, Shin and Yeoun, 2012).

For example, Kim et al. (2014) investigated the effect of the restorative environment and pursuing wellness on the positive decision-making process in mountain hikers visiting national parks. Pasanen et al. (2014) examined the positive effect of nature-based activities on emotional wellbeing, quality of sleep and health in terms of benefits from nature. In addition, Shin et al. (2012) found that depression in alcoholics who participated in forest healing programmes significantly improved. With the increasing prevalence of mental diseases in Sweden, Sahlin and colleagues (2014) developed a nature-based rehabilitation programme and found that the programme decreased depression and anxiety. These studies based on ART suggest that nature-based health-seeking activities can facilitate psychological healing.

Programme satisfaction

Satisfaction is the result of pleasure that a person feels from the perception of and expectation for certain objects (Human and Naude, 2014). It is the final result of the process of consuming products and includes both cognitive and emotional aspects (del Bosque and San Martín, 2008; Omar, Alam, Aziz and Nazri, 2011). Since satisfaction is an essential factor for a sustainable business (Lee, Lee, Lee and Babin, 2008) and significantly affects behavioural intention and the loyalty of consumers, it is an important variable in marketing. A number of previous studies suggest that satisfaction with experience-based tourism activities significantly affects behavioural intention and loyalty. Yoon, Lee and Lee (2010) found that quality and value positively affect loyalty through satisfaction in festival participants and Choi, Kim, Lee and Hickerson (2015) showed that wellness value significantly affects behavioural intention through satisfaction in red ginseng spa tourists. Kim and Kim (2015) found that pursuing wellness and emotion greatly affects loyalty through satisfaction in the participants of healing programmes.

Life satisfaction

Life satisfaction is a comprehensive evaluation of a life and an instant judgement of that life (Diener, Inglehart and Tay, 2013; Horley, 1984; Shin and Johnson, 1978). Life satisfaction is related to the subjective satisfaction of a person with work, health, family and leisure (Fernández-Ballesteros,

Zamarrón and Ruiz, 2001). In social science, life satisfaction is used as a similar concept to quality of life, including subjective wellbeing, subjective happiness and emotional wellbeing. The satisfaction with life scale consisting of five items, including the source of happiness, influence and life satisfaction, is widely used (Pavot and Diener, 1993). It was found that various tourism activities can make people happy (Nawijn, 2011) and that satisfaction with tourism activities is an important determinant of life satisfaction (Chen, Huang and Petrick, 2016). For that reason, studies are continuously conducted to investigate the relationship between tourism activities and life satisfaction (Chen et al., 2016; Kim, Woo and Uysal, 2015; Pagán, 2015).

Chen and colleagues (2016) found a significant association between vacation recovery experience, tourism satisfaction and life satisfaction through an online survey. Kim et al. (2015) showed a positive association in the structural relationship between quality of life and re-visit intention through involvement, value, travel experience and satisfaction with leisure life in elderly tourists. Pagán (2015) compared the effect of holiday trips on life satisfaction in people with disabilities and non-disabled people and found that the effect was more significant in people with disabilities. Since satisfaction with tourism significantly affects quality of life, it is thought to be desirable to encourage tourism activities to improve quality of life.

Methods

Measurement

This study aimed to reveal how emotion regulation affects attention restoration, programme satisfaction and life satisfaction. Therefore, emotion regulation is divided into three different elements according to Johnsen's (2013) scale. Attention restoration was assessed by using six items adapted from studies by Korpela, Ylén, Tyrväinen and Silvennoinen (2008). Programme satisfaction was measured through a scale used in previous research (Choi et al., 2015; Kim, Lee, Chung and Kim, 2013). Life satisfaction was assessed using five items adapted from studies by Diener, Emmons, Larsen and Griffin (1985). All measurement elements used a five-point Likert scale (where 1 = strongly disagree, 2 = disagree, 3 = neutral, 4 = agree and 5 = strongly agree).

Data collection and analysis

The data were collected from 22 October 2014 to 30 November 2014 at the Healing Forest of Saneum in Korea Forest Service in Yangpyeong. A total of 964 questionnaires were distributed, with 338 returned. Based on this, the rate of response was 35.06 per cent. Twenty-seven questionnaires included unanswered items, leaving 311 questionnaires to be used for empirical analysis. SPSS 21.0 was used for data analysis, for frequency analysis and exploratory factor analysis. Also, in this study, the two-stage testing procedure was adopted using AMOS 21.0. In the first stage, confirmatory factor analysis was executed to identify the reliability and validity of underlying structure of factors and systematically purify measured indicators of constructs.

Results

Respondents' demographic characteristics

The general characteristics of respondents are shown in Table 29.1. There were 41.2 per cent female respondents and 58.8 per cent male. In terms of marital status, 17.0 per cent were single, 82.0 per cent married, and 1.0 per cent unknown. According to age of respondents,

Table 29.1 Demographic characteristics of the respondents

Characteristics		Sample	%
Gender	Male	128	41.2
	Female	183	58.8
Marital status	Single	53	17.0
	Married	255	82.0
	Other	3	1.0
Age	19–29	22	7.1
	30–39	81	26.0
	40–49	98	31.5
	50–59	70	22.5
	Over 60	40	12.9
Education	High school or less	16	5.1
	Junior college	44	14.1
	University	192	61.7
	Graduate school	59	18.9
Occupation	Professional	78	25.1
	Business	32	10.3
	Service	42	13.5
	Clerical	61	19.6
	Official	19	6.1
	Housewife	29	9.3
	Student	16	5.1
	Unemployed	12	3.9
	Others	22	7.1
Monthly household	Less than 1,000	23	7.4
income in US dollar	1,000–2,999	66	21.2
(1 US$=1,000 Korean won)	3,000–4,999	113	36.3
	5,000–6,999	78	25.1
	7,000 or more	31	10.0
Total		311	100

7.1 per cent were 19–29 years of age, 26.0 per cent 30–39, 31.5 per cent 40–49, 22.5 per cent 50–59 and 12.9 per cent over 60 years of age. The level of education of respondents varied between 5.1 per cent for high school or less, 14.1 per cent for junior college, 61.7 per cent for university and 18.9 per cent for graduate school or more. For occupation, professionals represented 25.1 per cent, 10.3 per cent business people, 13.5 per cent service-related employees, 19.6 per cent clerical staff, 6.1 per cent official workers, 9.3 per cent housewives, 5.1 per cent students, 3.9 per cent unemployed and 7.1 per cent others. In terms of monthly household income, 7.4 per cent of respondents earn less than US$1,000, 21.2 per cent US$1,000–2,999, 36.3 per cent US$3,000–4,999 and 25.1 per cent US$5,000–6,999.

Measurement model

This study used confirmatory factor analysis to analyse structural relationships and the structure model as the two-stage testing procedure (Anderson and Gerbing, 1988). Measurement model and structural model in this study are found to be suitable as compatibility was higher than average, as shown in Table 29.2. The measurement model indicates a good fit to the data: normed

Table 29.2 Results of confirmatory factor analysis

Constructs and items	Convergent validity			
	λ	C.R.	AVE	CR
Emotion regulation			0.567	0.791
I go out into nature to experience positive feelings	0.870			
I go out into nature to experience joy	0.806	21.646		
Whenever I am outdoors in nature I feel happy	0.543	15.934		
Attention restoration			.666	.923
I feel calmer after being here	0.756			
After visiting this place I always feel restored and relaxed	0.823	21.646		
I get new enthusiasm and energy for my everyday routines from here	0.861	15.934		
My concentration and alertness clearly increase here	0.863	15.971		
I can forget everyday worries here	0.759	13.798		
Visiting here is a way of clearing and clarifying my thoughts	0.826	15.189		
Programme satisfaction			0.693	0.900
Healing satisfies my expectation	0.876			
I am satisfied with my decision to participate in the healing programme	0.887	20.659		
I feel very good with the healing programme	0.788	16.991		
Overall, I am satisfied with the healing programme	0.772	16.425		
Life satisfaction			0.651	0.903
I am satisfied with my life	0.773			
The conditions of my life are excellent	0.739	16.705		
In most ways my life is close to my ideal	0.886	16.497		
So far I have gotten the important things I want in life	0.802	14.785		
If I could live my life over, I would change almost nothing	0.826	15.315		

Goodness-of fit	x^2	df	Normed x^2	GFI	NFI	TLI	CFI	RMSEA
	228.754	126	1.816	0.923	0.945	0.969	0.974	0.051

Notes: λ, factor loading; C.R., critical ratio; AVE, average variance extracted; CR, construct reliability; α, Cronbach's alpha; GFI, goodness-of-fit index; NFI, normed fit index; TLI, Tucker–Lewis index; CFI, comparative fit index; RMSEA, root mean square error of approximation.
Parameter fixed at 1.0 for the maximum-likelihood estimation and thus, t-values were not available (Back, Lee and Abbott, 2011).

$x^2 = 1.816$, goodness-of-fit index (GFI) = 0.923, normed fit index (NFI) = 0.945, Tucker–Lewis index (TLI) = 0.969, comparative fit index (CFI) = 0.974 and root mean square error of approximation (RMSEA) = 0.051, which were higher than the cut-off values (Hair, Black, Babin and Anderson, 2010). The convergent validity was confirmed because factor loadings ranged from 0.543 to 0.887, average variance extracted ranged from 0.567 to 0.693 and construct reliability ranged from 0.791 to 0.923, which is relatively higher than the average (Hair et al., 2010). Therefore, convergent validity of this study is found to be suitable.

Discriminatory validity was verified by comparing squared correlations with average variance extracted (Hair, Sarstedt, Hopkins and Kuppelwieser, 2014). There are three kinds of method used to test discriminant validity which shows the difference among latent variables (Anderson and Gerbing, 1988; Fornell and Larcker, 1981). Table 29.3 indicates that generally average variance extracted values were higher than squared correlations, which confirms discriminatory validity.

Table 29.3 Measure correlations, squared correlations and average variance extracted

	ER	AR	PS	LS
ER	**0.567**			
AR	0.501***	**0.666**		
	(0.251)			
PS	0.438***	0.804***	**0.693**	
	(0.191)	(0.646)		
LS	0.443***	0.538***	0.462***	**0.651**
	(0.196)	(0.289)	(0.213)	

Notes: ER, emotion regulation; AR, attention restoration; PS, programme satisfaction; LS, life satisfaction. Numbers in parentheses indicate R squared (R^2), diagonal bold text is average variance extracted. All correlations were significant at ***$p < 0.001$.

Structural model

Figure 29.1 shows the results of the proposed research model in this study. Maxim-likelihood estimates for the various parameters of the overall fit of the model are given. Structural model fits the data well: x^2 = 228.754, df = 126, x^2/df = 1.816, GFI = 0.923, NFI = 0.945, TLI = 0.969, CFI = 0.969 and RMSEA = 0.051. The explained variance in endogenous constructs was 68.4 per cent for attention restoration, 20.1 per cent for programme satisfaction and 31.9 per cent for life satisfaction. Results show that emotion regulation (ER) had a significant positive effect on programme satisfaction (PS) (γER $\rightarrow$ PS = 0.449, t = 5.932, $p < 0.001$), (PS) (γER $\rightarrow$ AR = 0.178, t = 3.503, $p < 0.001$) (where AR = attention restoration), life satisfaction (LS) (γER $\rightarrow$ LS = 0.236, t = 3.257, $p < 0.01$). PS has a significant positive effect on AR (βPS $\rightarrow$ AR = 0.732, t = 11.525, $p < 0.001$), but no effect on life satisfaction (LS). AR has a significant positive effect on LS (βAR $\rightarrow$ LS = 0.379, t = 3.410, $p < 0.001$).

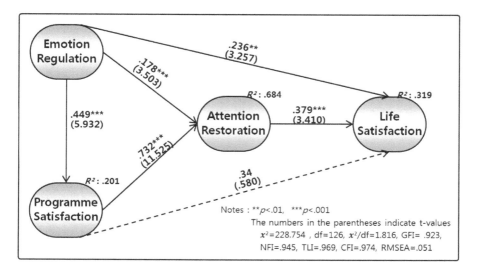

Figure 29.1 Results of the research model.

Conclusions and implication

The purpose of this study was to investigate the effect of a healing programme on emotion regulation, satisfaction with the healing programme, attention restoration and life satisfaction in tourists who participated in the healing programme. Therefore, this study intended to enhance knowledge of the psychological restoration of healing tourists who participated in the healing programme with the purpose of seeking health.

The results of the study were positively significant in most areas, but it was found that satisfaction with the healing programme did not directly affect life satisfaction. Therefore, satisfaction of the tourists participating in the healing programme with the purpose of seeking health enhances attention restoration, which in turn affects their quality of life, indicating that attention restoration plays an important mediating role. These results support previous studies suggesting that modern people who have a large consumption of directed attention try to obtain emotional stabilisation through nature-based activities based on ART (Ratcliffe et al., 2013; Tyrväinen et al., 2014; Wolsko and Lindberg, 2013). They are also consistent with previous studies showing that nature-based activities improve quality of life (Bimonte and Faralla, 2014; Ray and Jakubec, 2014; Sung et al., 2012). In conclusion, this study supports previous studies stating that tourism activities ultimately improve quality of life (Chen, Petrick and Shahvali, 2014; Pearce, 2012).

The academic implication of this study is that it represents an exploratory study that applied environmental psychology on tourists who have experienced healing programmes in health-seeking tourist destinations, within the broader situation of the recent increase of health-seeking tourism activities across the world. More specifically, the study investigated the effect of a healing programme and attention restoration on the quality of life by applying ART. This study is also of significance as it presents practical implications to activate healing programmes by presenting the importance of healing programmes. Attention restoration is significantly affected by satisfaction with healing programmes. More specifically, healing programmes need to allow participants to feel positive emotions by improving psychological stability through nature.

In other words, related businesses need to strengthen the programmes that stabilise both body and mind through nature, rather than promoting artificial facilities and unnecessary programmes designed only for entertainment. Since satisfaction with healing programmes affects attention restoration in a significant manner, it is crucial for the success of healing tourist destinations. In addition, as nature-based healing tourist destinations improve the current life satisfaction through attention restoration, the government needs to implement policies to support health-seeking tourism activities as an effort to promote public health. In other words, national parks, the Korea Forest Service and local governments should provide healing tourist destinations to promote public health using national forests. This can ultimately improve the health of the citizens through tourism activities.

The limitation of this study is that it is not reasonable to generalise the results to health-seeking tourism activities more generally because the survey was limited and only conducted with tourists who have experienced the healing programme. There are many tourists who did not participate in this healing programme but participated with the purpose of psychological health therapy in the nature-based environment. It is thought that future studies can conduct a comparative analysis between participants and non-participants of certain programmes in health-seeking tourism activities and a comparative analysis of healing effects through various health-seeking tourism activities.

References

Allen, J., Rivkin, I. D. and Lopez, E. D. (2014) 'Health and wellbeing', in Leong, F. T. L, Comas-Díaz, L., Nagayama, H., Gordon, C., McLoyd, V. C. and Trimble, J. E. (eds) *APA Handbook of Multicultural Psychology, Vol. 1: Theory and Research*. Washington, DC: American Psychological Association, pp. 299–311.

Anderson, J. C. and Gerbing, D. W. (1988) 'Structural equation modeling in practice: A review and recommended two-step approach', *Psychological Bulletin*, 103(3), 411–423.

Back, K. J., Lee, C. K. and Abbott, J. (2011) 'Internal relationship marketing: Korean casino employees' job satisfaction and organizational commitment', *Cornell Hospitality Quarterly*, 52(2), 111–124.

Baur, J. W. and Tynon, J. F. (2010) 'Small-scale urban nature parks: Why should we care?', *Leisure Sciences*, 32(2), 195–200.

Berman, M. G., Jonides, J. and Kaplan, S. (2008) 'The cognitive benefits of interacting with nature', *Psychological Science*, 19(12), 1207–1212.

Berto, R. (2005) 'Exposure to restorative environments helps restore attentional capacity', *Journal of Environmental Psychology*, 25(3), 249–259.

Bimonte, S. and Faralla, V. (2014) 'Happiness and nature-based vacations', *Annals of Tourism Research*, 46, 176–178.

Bowler, D. E., Buyung-Ali, L. M., Knight, T. M. and Pullin, A. S. (2010) 'A systematic review of evidence for the added benefits to health of exposure to natural environments', *BMC Public Health*, 10(1), 456–466.

Chen, C. C., Huang, W. J. and Petrick, J. F. (2016) 'Holiday recovery experiences, tourism satisfaction and life satisfaction – Is there a relationship?', *Tourism Management*, 53, 140–147.

Chen, C. C., Petrick, J. F. and Shahvali, M. (2014) 'Tourism experiences as a stress reliever examining the effects of tourism recovery experiences on life satisfaction', *Journal of Travel Research*, doi: 10.1177/0047287514546223.

Choi, Y., Kim, J., Lee, C. K. and Hickerson, B. (2015) 'The role of functional and wellness values in visitors' evaluation of spa experiences', *Asia Pacific Journal of Tourism Research*, 20(3), 263–279.

Cole, P. M., Michel, M. K. and Teti, L. O. D. (1994) 'The development of emotion regulation and dysregulation: A clinical perspective', *Monographs of the Society for Research in Child Development*, 59(2–3), 73–102.

Cowie, R., Douglas-Cowie, E. and Romano, A. (1999) 'Changing emotional tone in dialogue and its prosodic correlates, in *ESCA Tutorial and Research Workshop (ETRW) on Dialogue and Prosody*. Veldhoven, The Netherlands, 1–3 September.

del Bosque, I. R. and San Martín, H. (2008) 'Tourist satisfaction: A cognitive-affective model', *Annals of Tourism Research*, 35(2), 551–573.

Denham, S. A. (1993) 'Maternal emotional responsiveness and toddlers' social emotional competence', *Journal of Child Psychology and Psychiatry*, 34(5), 715–728.

Diener, E. D., Emmons, R. A., Larsen, R. J. and Griffin, S. (1985) 'The satisfaction with life scale', *Journal of Personality Assessment*, 49(1), 71–75.

Diener, E., Inglehart, R. and Tay, L. (2013) 'Theory and validity of life satisfaction scales', *Social Indicators Research*, 112(3), 497–527.

Fernández-Ballesteros, R., Zamarrón, M. D. and Ruiz, M. Á. (2001) 'The contribution of socio-demographic and psychosocial factors to life satisfaction', *Ageing and Society*, 21(1), 25–43.

Fornell, C. and Larcker, D. F. (1981) 'Evaluating structural equation models with unobservable variables and measurement error', *Journal of Marketing Research*, 18(1), 39–50.

Gross, J. J. (1998) 'The emerging field of emotion regulation: An integrative review', *Review of General Psychology*, 2(3), 271–299.

Hair, J. F., Black, W. C., Babin, B. J. and Anderson, R. E. (2010) *Multivariate Data Analysis: A Global Perspective* (7th edn), New Jersey, NJ: Pearson Education.

Hair Jr., J. F., Sarstedt, M., Hopkins, L. and Kuppelwieser, V. G. (2014) 'Partial least squares structural equation modeling (PLS-SEM): An emerging tool in business research', *European Business Review*, 26(2), 106–121.

Hall, C. M. (2013) *Medical Tourism: The Ethics, Regulation and Marketing of Health Mobility*, New York: Routledge.

Hartig, T. (2004) 'Toward understanding the restorative environment as a health resource', in *Open Space: People Space. Engaging with the Environment. Conference Proceedings*. Openspace research centre, Edinburgh. Available from: http://www.openspace.eca.uk/conference/proceedings/summary/Hartig.htm (accessed 29 June 2007).

Hartig, T., Korpela, K., Evans, G. W. and Gärling, T. (1997) 'A measure of restorative quality in environments', *Scandinavian Housing and Planning Research*, 14, 175–194.

Heintzman, P. (2014) 'Nature-based recreation, spirituality and persons with disabilities', *Journal of Disability and Religion*, 18(1), 97–116.

Hochschild, A. R. (1979) 'Emotion work, feeling rules and social structure', *American Journal of Sociology*, 85(3), 551–575.

Horley, J. (1984) 'Life satisfaction, happiness and morale: Two problems with the use of subjective wellbeing indicators', *The Gerontologist*, 24(2), 124–127.

Human, G. and Naude, P. (2014) 'Heterogeneity in the quality–satisfaction–loyalty framework', *Industrial Marketing Management*, 43(6), 920–928.

Irvine, K. N., Warber, S. L., Devine-Wright, P. and Gaston, K. J. (2013) 'Understanding urban green space as a health resource: A qualitative comparison of visit motivation and derived effects among park users in Sheffield, UK', *International Journal of Environmental Research and Public Health*, 10(1), 417–442.

John, O. P. and Gross, J. J. (2007) 'Individual differences in emotion regulation', in Gross J. J. (ed.) *Handbook of Emotion Regulation*, New York: The Guilford Press, pp. 351–372.

Johnsen, S. Å. K. (2013) 'Exploring the use of nature for emotion regulation: Associations with personality, perceived stress and restorative outcomes', *Nordic Psychology*, 65(4), 306–321.

Kaplan, S. (1995) 'The restorative benefits of nature: Toward an integrative framework', *Journal of Environmental Psychology*, 15(3), 169–182.

Kaplan, R. and Kaplan, S. (1989) *The Experience of Nature: A Psychological Perspective*, New York: Cambridge University Press.

Kim, H., Woo, E. and Uysal, M. (2015) 'Tourism experience and quality of life among elderly tourists', *Tourism Management*, 46, 465–476.

Kim, J. O. and Kim, D. Y. (2015) 'The effect of healing tourism participants' attention restoration and emotion for healing programs on satisfaction with life and loyalty', *Korean Journal of Hospitality and Tourism*, 24(4), 161–178.

Kim, J. O., Lee, J. E. and Kim, N. J. (2014) 'An influence of outdoor recreation participants' perceived restorative environment on wellness effect, satisfaction and loyalty', in *SHS Web of Conferences*, 12(7), http://dx.doi.org/10.1051/shsconf/20141201082.

Kim, M. J., Lee, C. K., Chung, N. and Kim, W. G. (2013) 'Factors affecting online tourism group buying and the moderating role of loyalty', *Journal of Travel Research*, doi: 10.1177/0047287513497837.

Korpela, K. M., Borodulin, K., Neuvonen, M., Paronen, O. and Tyrväinen, L. (2014) 'Analyzing the mediators between nature-based outdoor recreation and emotional wellbeing', *Journal of Environmental Psychology*, 37, 1–7.

Korpela, K. M., Ylén, M., Tyrväinen, L. and Silvennoinen, H. (2008) 'Determinants of restorative experiences in everyday favorite places', *Health and Place*, 14(4), 636–652.

Lee, Y. K., Lee, C. K., Lee, S. K. and Babin, B. J. (2008) 'Festivalscapes and patrons' emotions, satisfaction and loyalty', *Journal of Business Research*, 61(1), 56–64.

Nawijn, J. (2011) 'Determinants of daily happiness on vacation', *Journal of Travel Research*, 50(5), 559–566.

Omar, N. A., Alam, S. S., Aziz, N. A. and Nazri, M. A. (2011) 'Retail loyalty programs in Malaysia: The relationship of equity, value, satisfaction, trust and loyalty among cardholders', *Journal of Business Economics and Management*, 12(2), 332–352.

Pagán, R. (2015) 'The contribution of holiday trips to life satisfaction: The case of people with disabilities', *Current Issues in Tourism*, 18(6), 524–538.

Park, B. J., Tsunetsugu, Y., Kasetani, T., Kagawa, T. and Miyazaki, Y. (2010) 'The physiological effects of Shinrin-yoku (taking in the forest atmosphere or forest bathing): Evidence from field experiments in 24 forests across Japan', *Environmental Health and Preventive Medicine*, 15(1), 18–26.

Pasanen, T. P., Tyrväinen, L. and Korpela, K. M. (2014) 'The relationship between perceived health and physical activity indoors, outdoors in built environments and outdoors in nature', *Applied Psychology: Health and Wellbeing*, 6(3), 324–346.

Pavot, W. and Diener, E. (1993) 'Review of the satisfaction with life scale', *Psychological Assessment*, 5(2), 164–172.

Pearce, P. L. (2012) 'Relationships and the tourism experience: Challenges for quality-of-life assessments', in Uysal, M., Perdue, R. and Sirgy, J. (eds) *Handbook of Tourism and Quality-of-Life Research*, Dordrecht, The Netherlands: Springer, pp. 9–29.

Ratcliffe, E., Gatersleben, B. and Sowden, P. T. (2013) 'Bird sounds and their contributions to perceived attention restoration and stress recovery', *Journal of Environmental Psychology*, 36, 221–228.

Ray, H. and Jakubec, S. L. (2014) 'Nature-based experiences and health of cancer survivors', *Complementary Therapies in Clinical Practice*, 20(4), 188–192.

Sahlin, E., Ahlborg, G., Matuszczyk, J. V. and Grahn, P. (2014) 'Nature-based stress management course for individuals at risk of adverse health effects from work-related stress-effects on stress related symptoms, workability and sick leave', *International Journal of Environmental Research and Public Health*, 11(6), 6586–6611.

Shin, D. C. and Johnson, D. M. (1978) 'Avowed happiness as an overall assessment of the quality of life', *Social Indicators Research*, 5(1–4), 475–492.

Shin, W. S., Shin, C. S. and Yeoun, P. S. (2012) 'The influence of forest therapy camp on depression in alcoholics', *Environmental Health and Preventive Medicine*, 17(1), 73–76.

Smith, M. and Puczkó, L. (2014) *Health Tourism and Hospitality: Spas, Wellness and Medical Travel*, New York: Routledge.

Song, C., Ikei, H., Igarashi, M., Miwa, M., Takagaki, M. and Miyazaki, Y. (2014) 'Physiological and psychological responses of young males during spring-time walks in urban parks', *Journal of Physiological Anthropology*, 33(8), 1–7.

Song, C., Ikei, H. and Miyazaki, Y. (2014) 'Elucidation of the physiological adjustment effect of forest therapy', *Japanese Journal of Hygiene*, 69(2), 111–116.

Sung, J., Woo, J. M., Kim, W., Lim, S. K. and Chung, E. J. (2012) 'The effect of cognitive behavior therapy-based "forest therapy" program on blood pressure, salivary cortisol level and quality of life in elderly hypertensive patients', *Clinical and Experimental Hypertension*, 34(1), 1–7.

Thompson, R. A. (1994) 'Emotion regulation: A theme in search of definition', *Monographs of the Society for Research in Child Development*, 59(2–3), 25–52.

Tsunetsugu, Y., Park, B. J., Lee, J., Kagawa, T. and Miyazaki, Y. (2011) 'Psychological relaxation effect of forest therapy: Results of field experiments in 19 forests in Japan involving 228 participants', *Japanese Journal of Hygiene*, 66(4), 670–676.

Tyrväinen, L., Ojala, A., Korpela, K., Lanki, T., Tsunetsugu, Y. and Kagawa, T. (2014) 'The influence of urban green environments on stress relief measures: A field experiment', *Journal of Environmental Psychology*, 38, 1–9.

Ulrich, R. S. (1979) 'Visual landscapes and psychological wellbeing', *Landscape Research*, 4(1), 17–23.

Vork, J. and Lombarts, A. (2014) 'Research on preventive wellness in the Netherlands', in Smith, M. K. and Puczkó, L. (eds) *Health Tourism and Hospitality: Spas, Wellness and Medical Travel*, New York: Routledge, pp. 407–411.

Walden, T. A. and Smith, M. C. (1997) 'Emotion regulation', *Motivation and Emotion*, 21(1), 7–25.

Wells, N. M. (2014) 'The role of nature in children's resilience: Cognitive and social processes', in Tidball, K. G. and Krasny, M. E. (eds) *Greening in the Red Zone*, Dordrecht, The Netherlands: Springer, pp. 95–109.

Wolsko, C. and Lindberg, K. (2013) 'Experiencing connection with nature: The matrix of psychological wellbeing, mindfulness and outdoor recreation', *Ecopsychology*, 5(2), 80–91.

Yoon, Y. S., Lee, J. S. and Lee, C. K. (2010) 'Measuring festival quality and value affecting visitors' satisfaction and loyalty using a structural approach', *International Journal of Hospitality Management*, 29(2), 335–342.

30

Health tourism and health promotion at the coast

Peter Kruizinga

The role of nature and landscape in health tourism

In this chapter we discuss the role of the coast in health tourism and for health promotion. In the first section an overview is given of the recent literature regarding the coast as a therapeutic landscape and health effects of the coast; in the second section a short genealogy is given on the developments of coastal health tourism; in the third section coastal health tourism is framed in the broader debate on medicalisation, lifestyle and consumerism and the growing body culture. In the next section a case study is presented of the construction of the province of Zeeland in the Netherlands into a 'healthy region', in which health tourism is an essential part. We conclude with some recommendations, both for further research and for the tourist industry.

The coast and health: theoretical framework

The coast as a therapeutic landscape

Seashores are immensely popular and there is evidence that vacations at the seaside have gained enormously growing attention in the last 50 years. In the early 1960s approximately 36 per cent of French vacationers spent their holidays at the seaside, in 1970 this surpassed 45 per cent and in 1994 this was 50.4 per cent (Urbain, 2003). In the Netherlands the coast in 2014 was the most popular holiday destination, both for inland and foreign tourists (NBTC, 2015). Also many fortunate people choose to live at the coast, while many less fortunate people choose to spend their holidays in coastal resorts (Depledge and Bird, 2009). The coast creates a strong sense of place in residents (Bell et al., 2015) and in regular guests, who may have been visiting the coast for decades, like German families from North Rhineland-Westphalia (Tesdorff, 2013). The social-historic and economic development of many coastal towns is deeply interwoven with the development of tourism (Andrews and Kearns, 2005; Borsay and Walton, 2011; Derrics, 2014; Green, 2010; Walton, 1983; Wesley and Pforr, 2009).

An important element in its popularity is the character of the coast as a therapeutic landscape (Bell et al., 2015). Therapeutic landscapes can be defined as places, settings, situations, locales and milieus that encompass both the physical and psychological environments associated with treatment or healing and the maintenance of health and wellbeing (Williams, 1998). In the concept of therapeutic landscape, environmental, individual and societal factors can be explored that come together in the healing process in both traditional and non-traditional landscapes (Kearns, 1997). The concept of therapeutic landscape has proven to be very fruitful in exploring new fields in health geography (Parr, 2004). It was first used to investigate places that achieved lasting reputations for healing and over time this was extended to places associated with the maintenance of health and wellness and everyday pursuits of health and wellbeing (Gesler, 2009), such as coastal towns (Andrews and Kearns, 2005). As a 'container metaphor', therapeutic landscape can be applied to entire places such as Epidauros or Bath (Geores, 1998; Gesler, 1992) as well as 'non-traditional' and more tightly defined healthcare settings, both 'natural' surroundings and manmade landscapes, such as green space in cities (Hartig et al., 2014) or riverside promenades (Völker and Kistemann, 2011, 2013) or can be used on a national scale (Ormond, 2013).

Health effects of the coast

The coast became popular in the eighteenth and nineteenth century because of its health effects, which were then specifically attributed to the curative effects of sea water and climate (Charlier and Chaineux, 2009). Recently these effects became a subject for scientific studies as part of the growing interest in the relationship between nature and health and the increasing adaptation of personal responsibility for health (Crawford, 1980). The main health effects promoted by a visit to the coast appear to be the restorative effects of the coast on improvement of sleep and mood, enhancement of subjective wellbeing, as expressed in better reported health, stimulation of exercise and the possibilities for therapy.

According to Bennett (2011), coasts are so popular because of the fact that 'they are visually complex, offer the premise of perceived tranquillity and escape opportunities' (III). Her research among Utah students indicates that especially pastoral coastal landscapes, representing a peaceful rural life, devoid of urban or societal influences, are perceived as restorative. Visiting the coast thus helps to restore from fatigue and to focus on difficult mental activities, which is in line with attention restoration theory (Bennett, 2011). Families visiting the beach in the south-west of England reported that the key health benefits they perceived were psychological, including experiencing fun, stress relief and engagement with nature (Ashbullby et al., 2013).

The growing popularity of the beach is superbly described and interpreted by Urbain (2003). He describes the beach as a place where from the beginning of the twentieth century a 'hedonistic morality took hold of practices that had initially been subjected to medical standards; a morality of pleasure placed happiness above even health and made way for the physical expression of passions' (Urbain, 2003: 107). With the start of paid holidays in the 1930s all social layers in society started to head for the shore, which since then has grown and is almost completely focused on the discovery or re-appropriation of elementary contacts, on the individual level of the own body and interpersonally, as a couple or a group (Urbain, 2003).

A study by Wyles et al. (2011) at a rocky coast showed that visitors to the coast already arrive in a positive state of mind, but that they leave the coast with significantly heightened positive mood. Marine awareness towards the biology and ecology of a rocky shore increases with this simple leisurely visit to the coast. The specific activities carried out on the coast were also seen to have different impacts on affect, showing that blue space may be a key ingredient in the beneficial effects of nature (Wyles et al., 2011). Their results are in line with two studies by Völker and Kistemann (2011 and 2013) into the effects of water as a blue space, showing that water has a strong perception and preference, brings emotional benefits, is stress reducing and mood enhancing and thus has direct health effects (Völker and Kistemann, 2011, 2013).

Radcliffe's comparison (Radcliffe, 2015) of walkers by the British coast with walkers inland showed a significantly higher improvement in sleep, in length, sleep quality and alertness among coastal walkers. Also coastal workers reported more 'place memory associations relating to family, childhood and holidays as well as opportunities for introspection and reflective thought' (Radcliffe, 2015: 4), which could be explained by associations with holidays and escape to a special destination.

Proximity to the coast as an indicator for health

Researchers of the European Centre for Environment and Human Health (ECEHH) in Exeter (UK) did relevant studies on the relationship between the coast and health. Using the 2001 census data for England (n = 48.2 million), they identified a strong association between reported good health and coastal proximity, strongest in urban and town/fringe areas, weaker in rural areas, with a stronger effect when green space also increased. They also found that the effects of deprivation decreased when closer to the coast. Their conclusion was that coastal proximity has positive impacts on perceived health of residents, but this could also be due to the fact that residents select themselves by choosing to live near the coast (Wheeler et al., 2012). However, a following panel data study of ECEHH, using longitudinal data of households, confirmed the effect: proximity to the coast is an indicator of both generic and mental health. In support of cross-sectional analysis, individuals reported significantly better general health and mental health when living closer to the coast (White et al., 2013).

Outdoor activity

A coastal effect on activities was shown by Bauman et al. (1999), for residents of New South Wales (Australia). People in coastal areas showed higher levels of physical activity: they were found to be 23 per cent less sedentary, showed 27 per cent more adequate activity and reported 38 per cent higher levels of physical activity than overall. This may be due to the fact that a coastal environment nurtures mediating factors that are related to exercise participation, such as higher self-efficacy for physical activity, fewer perceived barriers and greater exercise enjoyment, or that coastal locations are the preferred living environment of people who place higher value upon physical activity and have cultural norms regarding activity, that may be inter-related with geographical location (Bauman et al., 1999), but the fact remains that apparently the coast encourages people to do exercise. An example of the encouragement of a coastal landscape to become physically active is given in the study of Ashbullby et al. (2013). Their findings indicated that a beach visit encouraged families to be physically active.

The presence of water, as part of nature, plays a substantial role here. There is a vast amount of literature on the relation between nature and health (Hartig et al., 2014), but far less on the specific effects of types of landscapes like the coast and specifically the effect of water. Barton and Pretty (2010) did a multi-study analysis from ten UK studies, indicating that engagement in green exercise showed considerable physical benefits. Green environment improves self-esteem and mood, but striking was that the presence of water in nature generated greater effects, especially in the age group of 30 years and younger and in the mentally ill (Barton and Pretty, 2010).

Wyles et al. (2014) researched the effects of activities at the coast, both in visitors and on the environment. For a rocky shore they found that different activities had different effects on both. All activities improved mood, but the level of arousal varied: snorkelling was seen as most exciting, while sunbathing/relaxing was the most calming. Rock pooling was perceived as most detrimental to the environment. Their study shows that it is important not to look at nature and activities too generally (Wyles et al., 2014).

The presence of the sea apparently motivates people to do outdoor activity, sporting or recreational (Hospers, 2014). According to Depledge and Bird (2009), this reminds us of our intimate relationship with natural ecosystems.

Therapy

The coast can also be a place for therapy, of which the most well known is thalassotherapy, in which water plays an important, but not the only, role. Water in itself has meaning for health, illness and wellbeing. In nearly all societies water has a twofold meaning. In the first place it represents notions such as purity, life, fertility and beauty, although it can also represent mysterious, chaotic and potentially dangerous experiences. Water is also involved in social processes and ritual practices of washing and bathing (Verouden and Meijman, 2010).

Next to physical effects the coast is applied for mental therapies, such as yoga, tai chi, meditation and mindfulness, as part of wellness-oriented preventive health (Lombarts, 2013) or for recovery from mental problems (Timmermans et al., 2016), like burnout.

Genealogy of the coast and health: from bathing resort to magnet for tourists

The therapeutic use of sea water was already known in ancient Egypt, France, Italy and Greece as far back as 300 BC. What we now would call 'thalassotherapy' was part of the medical arsenal (Charlier and Chaineux, 2009). The Greek poet Euripides (480–460 BC) wrote: 'The sea restores man's health' (Kiel, 1982) and the philosopher Plato (428–437) held that 'The sea washes all man's ailments' (Charlier and Chaineux, 2009). In the following centuries the use of sea water therapy faded away in the Western world. Verouden and Meijman (2010) suggest this was caused by stricter scientific viewpoints and rational reasoning by Renaissance thinkers. Also the sea was seen as a dark and sinister force, the domain of monsters and associated with catastrophe and fear by many Europeans (Corbin, 1989). This changed in the early eighteenth century, when ideas rose that water held health-enhancing properties. Its medical application was promoted by French and English physicians, who widely agreed that cold water was beneficial for health (Verouden and Meijman, 2010). It was a period in which all kinds of new medical ideas were circulating and standards were lacking (Lintsen et al., 1993). Disease was still largely seen as the product of the dynamic inter-relationship of the individual organism with the environment. Many doctors emphasised the importance of restoring harmony between nature and the body, in which water had a major role. Therapies with water fitted perfectly into the context of the evolving health culture in this period among English and French upper classes and led to a growing interest in the seaside and the curative properties of its waters (Verouden and Meijman, 2010). According to Corbin (1989), medical ideas played a pivotal role in the development of seaside resorts. Physicians actively encouraged visitors to follow therapeutic regimes in order to 'steel' their bodies. From specially designed sea bathing carriages, visitors could plunge unseen into the sea water. The therapy was supposed to enhance bathers' strength and vitality by restoring the balance between their body and nature (Corbin, 1989).

The growing appeal of the sea reflected a cultural change in the meaning of the sea, whose negative image was gradually replaced by a more positive view, emphasising health-enhancing properties (Verouden and Meijman, 2010). Curing at the seaside became a new fashion, which meant a journey to a cure station to improve or restore one's health. This can be seen as the genesis of tourism (Pforr and Locher, 2012), linking the medical quality of cures and the tourists' and curists' quality of life (Charlier and Chaineux, 2009).

Sea water cures could imply drinking sea water daily, bathing in the (cold or heated) sea water, in combination with exercise in the open air and rest. Bathing in sea water was recommended for recovery from depression and nervous diseases, but also from respiratory problems, like asthma and pulmonary illnesses. The first care centres emerged in England from the eighteenth century, from where in the nineteenth century they spread along west European coasts.

In 1865 the term thalassotherapy was coined by Professor Joseph de la Bonnardière, from the College of Medicine of the University of Montpellier, France (Charlier and Chaineux, 2009). The French physiologist Quinton by the end of the nineteenth century disclosed the similarity between sea water and human blood plasma (Quinton, 1912: 2), which laid the basis for further development of thalassotherapy, especially in France and Germany. After the First World War sea water therapy was practically abandoned, although seaside sanatoria remained part of respiratory and pulmonary therapies. In 1964 the first modern thalassotherapy centre in France was opened in Quiberon, Brittany, by the champion bicycle racer Louis Bobet, who was treated by Dr Bagot after a severe car accident (Charlier and Chaineux, 2009). Thalasso centres nowadays can be found throughout the world, but especially at the European Atlantic and Baltic coasts and in the Mediterranean (Smith and Puczkó, 2014).

Modern thalassotherapy is categorised in different ways: medical, traditional medicine, wellness, preventive, curative or just as an authentic experience. The European Spas Association, an interest group of the traditional spa industry, promotes the medical approach and established the following criteria for the use of the word thalassotherapy (ESPA, 2008):

- therapeutic concept for defined indications under medical control;
- situated directly by the sea under the direct influence of sea climate;
- sea water for inhalation and/or bathing, for example, in tubs or in pools or in the sea;
- products of the sea such as mud or algae for different treatments;
- helio therapy – primary use of natural sunbeams and, if weather conditions are unfavourable, sunlight can be replaced by artificial ultraviolet rays;
- sea air containing a low level of harmful substances and allergens to be used for long stays in the fresh air;
- regulated stays in the fresh air and training near the seaside;
- measures accompanying the main health point: healthy food and activity of the body.

The World Health Organization considers thalassotherapy to be a traditional medicine and places it in the same category as the use of mineral waters (Charlier and Chaineux, 2009). Johnston et al. (Global Spa Summit, 2011) categorise thalassotherapy as an authentic, location-based experience. The Global Spa and Wellness Summit (2013) places it in the same range as spas, salons, baths and springs, but also considers it to overlap between wellness tourism (preventive) and medical tourism (curative), as part of a process in which conventional medicine is beginning to embrace preventive and alternative approaches to care (SRI/Global Wellness Summit, 2013). It thus attracts both travellers seeking for care and cure and visitors who want a check-up or to relax.

Although claims on medical results are increasingly being made, there is far from agreement on the effectiveness of the therapy. With the increasing popularity of thalassotherapy, due to the growth of health tourism, a number of studies have been published in the last decades. Climatic and thalassotherapeutic medicine is included in the curricula of some colleges of medicine in Europe, as a constituting part of thermalism (Charlier and Chaineux, 2009). Studies of patient cohorts show a lowering of pharmaceutical consumption, fewer hospitalisations of patients treated and a decline in ailment recurrence compared with patients who had not followed such therapy (Charlier and Chaineux, 2009). There is evidence on the application for rheumatism, fibromyalgia (de Andrade et al., 2008; Zijlstra, 2007; Zijlstra et al., 2005) and psoriasis (Zlatkov et al., 1973). Claims are also made regarding dermatological problems, osteoarticular pathologies, psychological and psychosomatic problems, oncological diseases, hyperactivity, autism, Down's syndrome for children, Parkinson's disease and multiple sclerosis (Cerrada, 2014). In most European Union countries thalassotherapy cures, prescribed by medical practitioners, are reimbursable expenses (Charlier and Chaineux, 2009).

Coastal health tourism in the light of medicalisation, lifestyle and consumerism and the growing body culture

The development of (coastal) health tourism can be attributed to the development of the medicalisation of society that started in the eighteenth century. Foucault (1973) described medicalisation as a process in which human bodies are increasingly brought under medical gaze. This process was reinforced by the centralisation and modernisation of governments, which, in close cooperation with medical professionals, took on 'the task of the management of life in the name of the well-being of the population' (Rose, 2001: 1). A strong influence in the medicalisation of society was asserted by the movement of so-called hygienists, medical professionals in the nineteenth century, who made strong pleas for hygienic measures and sanitation by governments, in order to improve the health situation in the cities and in the countryside (Lintsen et al., 1993). Through the process of medicalisation medical and health precepts were embodied in individuals. By processes of disciplining through schools, bathing houses, health education and vaccination, but also by health legislation and provision, people were taught to take responsibility for their health. Currently internet and social media play an important role in the dissemination of health issues, including 'self-diagnosis' and 'disciplining' of the body (Parr, 2002). Due to the rise of the information society we can speak of an 'informed' body (Chrysanthou, 2002). Western society is quickly moving in a direction in which people can monitor their health 24 hours a day, with the aid of electronic devices (Meskó, 2013). This process can be described as 'de-medicalisation' as in a direct sense no physician is involved, but may also be interpreted as a growing penetration of the medical gaze into everyday life, including people's emotional states, the nature of their interpersonal relationships, their management of stress and their lifestyle choices (Parr, 2002).

The preoccupation with personal health and the body in the last decades has led to a boom in diets and fitness. Health has become a focus for the definition and achievement of wellbeing, a goal obtained primarily through the modification of lifestyles, which can be defined as: increased physical activity, abstention from smoking, eating healthier, losing weight and reducing alcohol intake (Cheek, 2008). These characteristics of present health consciousness fit within the concept of 'healthism', which situates the problem of health and disease at the level of the individual (Crawford, 1980). The desire for health is a crucial aspect of modern consumer culture. Self-identity and consumption have become ever more closely entwined (Brown and Duncan, 2000) and the individual cultivation of a healthy body is exalted as an ideal (Nye, 2003). The process of disciplining the body can also be interpreted as a new form of patriarchal power, governing thoughts of women and to an increasing degree also men, by which free choice concerning body practices is an illusion (Rysst, 2010), as individuals produce the space of their bodies in accordance with the disciplinary gaze of others rather than their own desires (Valentine, 1999). Due to the growing popularity of wellness and lifestyle, the growing importance of health and individual responsibility, the coast has gained interest for health seeking over the past decades.

The features of (natural) coastal landscapes make it an ideal place to recover from the stress of modern society, to work on the body (or to display it) and to (re)gain health. At the coast the three most sought elements can be found: nature, as a place for recovery and to destress, the beach as the pre-eminent place to show the body and as a setting for health promotion (Ashbullby et al., 2013), to gaze at the other's body and to do sport (Urbain, 2003) and water to bathe in, be it for joy, sports or to cure (Charlier and Chaineux, 2009).

Case study: Zeeland – health and health tourism as a motor for development

The Vital Revolution

The authorities of the province of Zeeland, in the south-west of the Netherlands, want to develop the province into a healthy region, which is attractive both for residents and for tourists. The aim is to reach a higher level of health and healthcare for citizens by starting a 'Vital Revolution', which will make the province attractive to live in. The Vital Revolution should lead to lower levels of illness leave and higher productivity (GGD Zeeland, 2015b). A programme has been developed, based on the ideas of the Blue Zones projects, as developed in the USA. Blue Zones projects are based on the research and publications of Dan Buettner, a *National Geographic* journalist, who played a major role in identifying five geographic regions throughout the world (Okinawa, Japan; Loma Linda, California; Sardinia, Italy; Ikaria, Greece and Nikoya Island, Costa Rica) with high percentages of centenarians (Buettner, 2008). By comparing the lifestyles in these regions he developed what he called the key lessons for healthy living, the so-called 'Power 9', which are taken as a blueprint for health promotion in communities in the USA, e.g. Albert Lea, Minnesota and the state of Iowa (Carter, 2015). In the approach of Blue Zones projects the premise is that regional lifestyle and 'natural' life habits of inhabitants, together with the characteristics of the region, are decisive for health and longevity (Buettner, 2005).

This idea inspired the health authorities of Zeeland in 2013 to start a Blue Zones project in Zeeland, aimed at a considerable improvement of health indicators by 2025. The idea was adapted by the provincial government and several municipalities (Meij, 2015). However, the cooperation with Healthways Inc., the company that licenses Blue Zones projects, failed due to financial and juridical obstacles (Popma, 2016), so the health authorities decided to create their own project, which started in 2015. The ambition of the programme is to develop the region into one which people live longer, feel vital and where everybody participates (GGD Zeeland, 2015a). Achieving this would lead to higher productivity and considerable decrease in costs of healthcare (GGD Zeeland, 2015b). It is found that there is every reason for this. Despite the alleged 'healthy coast effect' (Hospers, 2014), Zeeland residents in 2010 only had a slightly higher life expectancy than Dutch people in general – 81.3 vs. 80.5 years (Bijl et al., 2013). In 2012 20 per cent of adults (19–64 years of age) in Zeeland perceived their health as 'reasonably good', 'bad' or 'very bad', whereas in the Netherlands as a whole this was 19 per cent (GGD Zeeland, 2013a). For elderly people (65 and older) this was 39 per cent, which is the same as the Dutch average (GGD Zeeland, 2013b). Moreover, between 2009 and 2013 the perception of good health by people living in the province declined substantially, from 81 to 77 per cent (male) and from 77 to 74 per cent (female) (Scoop, 2014). This could be attributed to the economic crisis, leading to loss of jobs, income deprivation and feelings of uncertainty, but this is speculation, as the relationship is not straightforward (Catalano, 2009).

The GGD health monitor of 2012 shows that residents in Zeeland have about the same lifestyle as Dutch people in general. On the indicators of smoking, drinking, physical activity and overweight, adults (19 years and older) in Zeeland score the same as the rest of the Dutch population, with the exception of physical activity. Older people (65 or more) score somewhat better in this respect: 72 per cent in 2012 met the 'healthy exercise norm' (exercise five times a week for half an hour or more), whereas in the Netherlands as a whole this is 69 per cent (GGD Zeeland, 2013c).

Health tourism in Zeeland

At the same time health tourism is being developed in the province, as this is considered to be an opportunity to stimulate the economy and to give an answer to current challenges: a rapidly ageing population, decreasing numbers of young people, a shrinking population and rising costs of healthcare (Zeeland, 2012; GGD Zeeland, 2014). As a coastal region, with 490 kilometres of coast, of which 60 kilometres are dunes (Omroep Zeeland, 2014), pure sea air, a natural environment, clean beaches, dunes and forests, the province is popular among Dutch, German and Flemish tourists. With the increasing interest in health the focus of the tourist industry is increasingly on health tourism. In 2008 a project was started to define the potential for health tourism, leading to new products and forms of cooperation between entrepreneurs and local authorities. At the end of the project the municipalities of Veere and Sluis decided to concentrate on health tourism and started the procedure to obtain the official 'bath status' for the villages Domburg and Cadzand (Gemeente Sluis, 2014; Gemeente Veere, 2014), two of the most popular resorts in the province. Acquiring the bath status, which was granted in May 2014, meant that these sites meet the criteria of the European Spas Association and the Deutscher Heilbäder Verband as a healing resort because of the quality of the sea water, the climate, the environment and the availability of natural products for treatments.

The bath status recognition enhances the special character as a seaside resort, where treatments are offered to preserve, improve or regain health. It also gives the possibility for reimbursement of treatments by health insurance, especially the German *Krankenkassen*. The bath status also works as a quality label to get more visitors to come outside peak season.

The claim by health authorities and governments that Zeeland can become an attractive province for health tourism is based on two premises. The first is that the environment has considerable influence on health. The second is that health is of growing importance as a motive within tourism in general and in Zeeland especially (Roos, 2013). Research among German visitors to Zeeland does not confirm this in a strict sense. It was found that the main reason to visit the province was relaxing, by walking on the beach and cycling (Tesdorff, 2013). These activities are popular for foreign visitors of Zeeland throughout (Kenniscentrum Kusttoerisme, 2012). Recent research by the Research Centre Coastal Tourism among a panel of visitors confirms that the natural environment is the main reason to visit the province. But the research also showed that a vast majority (97 per cent) consider Zeeland as a suitable environment to relax and that around 50 per cent see the province as a region for rehabilitation after medical surgery. Also 76 per cent claim to pay attention to an active lifestyle to prevent illness and do more exercise during holidays than at home (Timmermans et al., 2016).

(continued)

(continued)

Both wellness and medical tourism can be developed in Zeeland. The origins of both can be located in the nineteenth century, when Domburg attracted guests from the Dutch and European elite because of the beneficial effects of sea water and the healthy sea air, but especially because of the treatments, provided by the famous Dr Georg Mezger (Warners, 1984), who laid the basis for Western massage (Benjamin, 2010) and can be considered as one of the first physiotherapists. The guests visited the bath houses, where they were treated and bathed in the sea. The bathing culture, including the bath houses, came to a demise after the First World War, together with the nobility. The economic crisis of the 1930s gave the final blow (Warners, 1984). From the middle of the twentieth century the coast became a popular mass tourism destination, which changed the character of the destinations in Zeeland. Next to hotels, campsites and holiday parks were built, attracting growing masses of tourists from the Netherlands, Germany and Belgium, attracted by sun, sea and sand.

There is some experience in Zeeland with medical tourism. The leading provider in the Dutch holiday market, Roompot Holidays, began dialysis in one of her holiday parks in Kamperland, to give people with kidney failure the opportunity to go on vacation (Brooker and Go). Because of the success that ensued, RP Care was founded, with the goal of combining health and a Dutch sea and beach holiday. In 2011 RP Care became part of Zeeland Care, a new private healthcare organisation in Zeeland, which offers private and public healthcare, for both residents and for medical tourists, such as ear, nose and throat, plastic surgery, dialysis and orthopaedics. Other healthcare organisations followed this example and started rehabilitation programmes in a four-star hotel or care hotels. These care hotels offer short stays, for both those with care needs and their partners or other family members.

Zeeland as a unique case

The case of Zeeland is a unique one, as there are no examples yet of regions or places where health promotion aimed at residents and the development of health tourism are used for economic development at the same time. The idea of developing a health(y) region can be placed in an international context. In EU policy regions and regionalisation are important features, aimed at stimulation of the economy and the quality of life of residents (Brand et al., 2008; EU, 2016; South Denmark European Office, 2010). The World Health Organization stimulates Regional Health Networks (WHO, 2014), but there are few examples yet. Bavaria is one, as it promotes itself as a healthy region and has introduced a quality seal for medical tourism (Gesundheitsregion Bayreuth, 2016). The region promotes itself for its touristic characteristics, involving spa and wellness (Mainil, 2012; Pforr et al., 2012), which of course are also of great value for residents. Another example is the region of Bournemouth and Poole in the UK, where the project Destination Feel Good is aimed at the promotion of wellbeing as a destination resource (Bournemouth University, 2015). In all these cases, however, the focus is either on residents or on the tourism industry. The connecting factor in Zeeland is the environment, which is seen as a positive asset for both residents and visitors. Health authorities and governments use the attractiveness of the province's natural assets to influence the lifestyle of residents to give an answer to the challenges they face. Touristic entrepreneurs and municipal governments, supported by the provincial government, do the same to develop health tourism. Being a region with higher life expectancy and favourable health indicators would make the region attractive, both for visitors and for residents (Roos, 2013).

Some recommendations

The coast is an excellent place for health tourism. Myriads of possibilities can be found at the coast for developing both wellbeing and medical tourism, from luxury resorts to basic facilities. The coast, as a specific therapeutic landscape, has extreme strongpoints both for health tourists and for residents. Essential here however are the natural assets of the coast. For further development of health tourism at the coast the starting point thus always needs to be respect for the natural characteristics, as these are the most powerful pull factors.

As it can be expected that the importance of health and lifestyle issues will grow in future years, health prevention and thus wellness-oriented facilities will offer the best opportunities. Exercise and relaxation are the most obvious in this respect, but programmes aimed at mental health or nutrition (not discussed here) would also respond to growing needs. When it comes to therapy, information on the possibilities and proven effects is strongly needed, as this is still an obscure domain, where knowledge is mainly shared in academic circles. This would mean cooperation of entrepreneurs and authorities with academics in the field.

The coast also offers plenty of possibilities for lifestyle interventions for residents. Combining this with developing facilities for visitors can bring economies of scale, but also create possibilities to maintain facilities in peripheral regions with low population density and ageing population. Residents in Zeeland are aware of the economic impact of tourism and – to a certain degree – of the positive effects on liveability, but their commitment will be stronger when they see a direct impact on their health and on the health facilities offered.

However, little is known yet on the relationship between the health of residents and health tourism. Some questions for further research could be: Does the presence of medical and wellness facilities have an impact on the health or wellbeing of residents and if so, how? Or how could the development of health tourism help to improve wellbeing of residents?

References

Andrews, G. J. and Kearns, R. A. (2005) 'Everyday health histories and the making of place: The case of an English coastal town', *Social Science and Medicine*, 60, 2697–2713.

Ashbullby, K. J., Pahl, S., White, M. P. and Webley, P. (2013) 'The beach as a setting for families' health promotion: A qualitative study with parents and children living in coastal regions in Southwest England', *Health and Place*, 23.

Barton, J. and Pretty, J. (2010) 'What is the best dose of nature and green exercise for improving mental health? A multi-study analysis', *Environmental Science Technology*, 44, 3947–3955.

Bauman, A., Smith, B., Stoker, L. B. B. and Booth, M. (1999) 'Geographical influences upon physical activity participation: Evidence of a "coastal effect"', *Australian and New Zealand Journal of Public Health*, 23, 322–324.

Bell, S. L., Phoenix, C., Lovell, R. and Wheeler, B. W. (2015) 'Seeking everyday wellbeing: The coast as a therapeutic landscape', *Social Science and Medicine*, 142, 56–67.

Benjamin, P. J. (2010) *Tappan's Handbook of Healing Massage Techniques*, fifth edition, Boston, MA: Pearson.

Bennett, M. L. (2011) *The Relation Between Landscape Type and Perceived Restorative Character of Coastal Landscapes*, PhD Doctoral, University of Utah.

Bijl, R., Boelhouwer, J., Pommer, E. and Sonck, N. (2013) *De Sociale Staat van Nederland 2013*, The Hague, The Netherlands: Sociaal en Cultureel Planbureau.

Borsay, P. and Walton, J. K. (2011) *Resorts and Ports: European Seaside Towns Since 1700*, Bristol, UK: Channel View.

Bournemouth University (2015) *Destination Feel Good*, Bournemouth, https://microsites.bournemouth. ac.uk/destinationfeelgood/ (accessed 29 January 2016).

Brand, H., Hollederer, A.,Wolf, U., Brand, A. (2008) 'Cross-border health activities in the Euregios: Good practice for better health', *Health Policy*, 86(2–3), 254.

Brooker, E. and Go, F. M. (2006) *Health Care Tourism – A Classic Example of Disruptive Innovation*. Paper presented at Travel and Tourism Research Association Canada Chapter Conference, 15–17 October 2006, Montebello, Quebec.

Brown, T. and Duncan, C. (2000) 'London's burning: recovering other geographies of health', *Health and Place*, 6, 363–375.

Buettner, D. (2005) 'The secrets of longevity', *National Geographic*, November.

Buettner, D. (2008) *The Blue Zones: Lessons for Living Longer from the People Who've Lived the Longest*, Washington, National Geographic Society.

Carter, E. D. (2015) 'Making the blue zones: Neoliberalism and nudges in public health promotion', *Social Science and Medicine*, 133, 374–382.

Catalano, R. (2009) 'Health, medical care and economic crisis', *New England Journal of Medicine*, 360, 749–751.

Cerrada, A. (2014) 'New approach to water treatments: Hydrology, balneotherapy and thalassotherapy – the new health tourism', *Journal of the Japanese Society of Balneology, Climatology and Physical Medicine*, 77, 490–491.

Charlier, R. H. and Chaineux, M. C. P. (2009) 'The healing sea: A sustainable coastal ocean resource: Thalassotherapy', *Journal of Coastal Research*, 25, 838–856.

Cheek, J. (2008) 'Healthism: A new conservatism?', *Qualitative Health Research*, 18, 974–982.

Chrysanthou, M. (2002) 'Transparency and selfhood: Utopia and the informed body', *Social Science and Medicine*, 54, 469–479.

Corbin, A. (1989) *Het Verlangen naar de Kust*, Nijmegen, The Netherlands: Sun.

Crawford, R. (1980) 'Healthism and the medicalization of everyday life', *International Journal of Health Services*, 10.

De Andrade, S. C., De Carvalho, R. F. P. P., Soares, A. S., De Abreu Freitas, R. P., De Medeiros Guerra, L. M. and Vilar, M. J. (2008) 'Thalassotherapy for fibromyalgia: A randomized controlled trial comparing aquatic exercises in sea water and water pool', *Rheumatology International*, 29, 147–152.

Depledge, M. H. and Bird, W. J. (2009) 'The blue gym: Health and wellbeing from our coasts', *Marine Pollution Bulletin*, 58, 947–948.

Derrics, T. (2014) *Reinventing the Seaside? Insights in Coastal Tourism Destination Development in North-western Europe*, Vlissengen, The Netherlands: Research Centre for Coastal Tourism.

ESPA (2008) *Thalasso*, http://www.espa-ehv.eu/thalasso (accessed 27 January 2016).

EU, Directoraat-Generaal Regionaal Beleid en Stadsontwikkeling (2016) *Regionaal Beleid*, http://ec.europa.eu/dgs/regional_policy/index_nl.htm (accessed 31 July 2016).

Foucault, M. (1973) *The Birth of the Clinic*, London, Routledge.

Gemeente Sluis (2014) *Bidbook Cadzand-Bad, Stijlvolle Zeebadplaats*, Oostburg, The Netherlands: Gemeente Sluis.

Gemeente Veere (2014) *Bidbook Domburg Heilzame Zeebadplaats*, Domburg, The Netherlands: Gemeente Veere.

Geores, M. (1998) 'Surviving on metaphor: How "health = hot springs" created and sustained a town', in Kearns, R. A. and Gesler, W. M. (eds) *Putting Health Into Place: Landscape, Identity and Wellbeing*, Syracuse, NY: Syracuse University Press.

Gesler, W. M. (1992) 'Therapeutic landscapes: Medical issues in light of the new cultural geography', *Social Science and Medicine*, 34, 735–746.

—— (2009) 'Therapeutic landscapes', in Thrift, R. K. (ed.) *International Encyclopedia of Human Geography*, Oxford, UK: Elsevier.

Gesundheitsregion Bayreuth (2016) *Health Care Regions in Bavaria*, http://www.gesundheitsregion-bayreuth.de/en/profile/bavarian-health-care-region.php (accessed 31 July 2016).

GGD Zeeland (2013a) *Gezondheidsmonitor 2012*, Volwassenen, Tabellenboek: GGD Zeeland.

—— (2013b) *Gezondheidsmonitor 2012*, Ouderen. Tabellenboek: GGD Zeeland.

—— (2013c) *Gezondheidsmonitor 2012*, Samenvatting: GGD Zeeland.

—— (2014) 'Zeeland wordt de gezondste provincie van Nederland', *Zeeland samen gezond*, http://www.zeelandsamengezond.nl/magazine/thema:lente-editie/bericht:zeeland-wordt-de-gezondste-provincie-van-nederland.htm#.U5Q4Yyjm6Es (accessed 8 June 2014).

—— (2015a) *'De Vitale Revolutie'*, in Zeeland, G. (ed.), Goes: GGD Zeeland.

—— (2015b) *Strategisch Plan De Vitale Revolutie*, Goes: GGD Zeeland.

Global Spa Summit (2011) *Wellness Tourism and Medical Tourism: Where Do Spas Fit?* New York, Global Spa Summit.

Green, R. (2010) *Coastal Towns in Transition: Local Perceptions of Landscape Change*, Dordrecht, The Netherlands and CSIRO Publishing, Collingwood, Australia, Springer Science Business Media.

Hartig, T., Mitchell, R., De Vries, S. and Frumkin, H. (2014) 'Nature and health', *Annual Review of Public Health*, 35, 207–228.

Hospers, G. J. (2014) *Zee + Land. De Kracht van Kustregio's*, Vlissingen: Den Boer/De Ruiter.

Kearns, R. A. (1997) 'Narrative and metaphor in health geographies', *Progress in Human Geography*, 21, 269–277.

Kenniscentrum Kusttoerisme (2012) *Kerncijfers Toerisme Zeeland 2012*, http://pretwerk.nl/wp-content/uploads/Leaflet-zeelAND-2013.pdf (accessed 11 February 2014).

Kiel, G. R. (1982) 'Zwei Beiträge zur Geschichte der Balneologie', *Die kulturgeschichtlichen und medizinischen Wurzeln des Bäderwesens. 100 Jahre wissenschatliche Balneologie*, 45 edn. Kassel: Verlag Hans Meister.

Lintsen, H. W., Bakker, M. S. C. and Bosch, A. (1993) *Geschiedenis van de techniek in Nederland: de wording van een moderne samenleving 1800–1890: gezondheid en openbare hygiëne, waterstaat en infrastructuur, papier, druk en communicatie*, 's-Gravenhage: Stichting Historie der Techniek.

Lombarts, A. E. (2013) *Preventieve Wellness, ook in Nederland, Een onderzoek naar trends, kansen en uitdagingen op het gebied van preventieve wellness*, Hogeschool Inholland, http://www.aloaconsultancy.nl/publicaties-angelique-lombarts/preventieve-wellness-ook-in-nederland/ (accessed 31 July 2016).

Mainil, T. (2012) *Transnational Health Care and Medical Tourism. Towards a Rationale of Transnational Health Region Development*, PhD thesis, University of Antwerp, NRIT Media, Nieuwegein.

Meij, R. D. (2015) *Interview Ronald de Meij*, 14 January 2015.

Meskó, B. (2013) *Social Media in Clinical Practice*, London: Springer.

NBTC (2015) *Kerncijfers 2014*, http://kerncijfers.nbtc.nl/nl/magazine/8374/764309/binnenlandse_vakanties.html (accessed 28 January 2016).

Nye, R. A. (2003) 'The evolution of the concept of medicalization in the late twentieth century', *Journal of History of the Behavioral Sciences*, 39, 115–129.

Omroep Zeeland (2014) *Hoeveel kilometer kust heeft Zeeland?* Oost Souburg: Omroep Zeeland, http://www.omroepzeeland.nl/nieuws/014-08-11/721888/hoeveel-kilometer-kust-heeft-zeeland#.VqtA-VjoD4U (accessed 29 January 2016).

Ormond, M. (2013) *Neoliberal Governance and International Medical Travel in Malaysia*, Abingdon, UK: Routledge.

Parr, H. (2002) 'Medical geography: Diagnosing the body in medical and health geography, 1999–2000', *Progress in Human Geography*, 26, 240–251.

—— (2004) 'Medical geography: Critical medical and health geography?', *Progress in Human Geography*, 28, 246–257.

Pforr, C. and Locher, C. (2012) 'The German spa and health resort industry in the light of health care systems reform', *Journal of Travel and Tourism Marketing*, 29, 298–312.

Pforr, C., Pechlaner, H., Locher, C. and Jochmann, J. (2012) 'Health regions as tourism destination: A new approach to regional development?', *International Conference on Tourism (ICOT)*, Rhodes Island, Greece, IATOUR.

Popma, B. (2016) *Interview Barry Popma*, 28 January 2016.

Quinton, R. (1912: 2) *L'eau de mer, milieu organique: constance du milieu marin originel, comme milieu vital*, Paris, Masson.

Radcliffe, E. (2015) *Sleep, Mood and Coastal Walking*, Rotherham, UK: National Trust.

Roos, A. (2013) *Zeeland als gezondheidsregio*, Economische Impuls Zeeland and Santé Zeeland.

Rose, N. (2001) 'The politics of life itself', *Theory, Culture and Society*, 18, 1–30.

Rysst, M. (2010) '"Healthism" and looking good: Body ideals and body practices in Norway', *Scandinavian Journal of Public Health*, 38(5 suppl), 71–80.

Scoop (2014) *Staat van Zeeland. Zeeland in tijden van crisis*, Middelburg, The Netherlands: Scoop.

Smith, M. and Puczkó, L. (2014) *Health, Tourism and Hospitality, Wellness, Spas and Medical Travel*, 2nd edition, Abingdon, UK: Routledge.

South Denmark European Office (2010) *Healthy Regions. When Well-being Creates Economic Growth*, http://www.healthyregions.eu/ (accessed 31 July 2016).

SRI/Global Wellness Summit (2013) *The Global Wellness Tourism Economy, Executive Summary*, New-York, Global Wellness Summit, http://www.globalspaandwellnesssummit.org/images/stories/pdf/wellness_tourism_economy_exec_sum_final_10022013.pdf (accessed 31 July 2016).

Tesdorff, J. (2013) *The Distinctiveness of Zeeland, Compared to Its Competitive Destinations, A Research Study into the Image Perceptions of German Visitors*, Bachelor thesis, NHTV, Breda: Breda University of Applied Sciences.

Timmermans, O., Marijs, J., Bijl, J. and Tempelman, M. (2016) *Gezondheidstoerisme in Zeeland*, Vlissingen, The Netherlands: Kenniscentrum Kusttoerisme/Lectoraat Healthy Region.

Urbain, D. (2003) *At the Beach*, Minneapolis, MN: University of Minnesota Press.

Valentine, G. (1999) 'A corporeal geography of consumption', *Environment and Planning D: Society and Space*, 17, 329–351.

Verouden, N. W. and Meijman, F. J. (2010) 'Water, health and the body: The tide, undercurrent and surge of meanings', *Water History*, 2, 19–33.

Völker, S. and Kistemann, T. (2011) 'The impact of blue space on human health and wellbeing – salutogenetic health effects of inland surface waters: A review', *International Journal of Hygiene and Environmental Health*, 214, 449–460.

Völker, S. and Kistemann, T. (2013) 'Reprint of: "I'm always entirely happy when I'm here!" Urban blue enhancing human health and wellbeing in Cologne and Düsseldorf, Germany', *Social Science and Medicine*, 91, 141–152.

Walton, J. K. (1983) *The English Seaside Resort: A Social History 1750–1914*, Leicester, UK: Leicester University Press.

Warners, J. (1984) *Domburg, 150 jaar badplaats*, Middelburg, The Netherlands: Den Boer.

Wesley, A. and Pforr, C. (2009) 'Historical dimensions of coastal tourism', in Dowling, R. and Pforr, C. (eds) *Coastal Tourism Development*, New York: Cognizant Communication Corporation.

Wheeler, B. W., White, M., Stahl-Timmins, W. and Depledge, M. H. (2012) 'Does living by the coast improve health and wellbeing?', *Health and Place*, 18, 1198–2001.

White, M. P., Alcock, I., Wheeler, B. W., Depledge, M. H. and Bird, W. J. (2013) 'Coastal proximity, health and wellbeing: Results from a longitudinal panel survey', *Health and Place*, 23, 97–103.

Williams, A. (1998) 'Therapeutic landscapes in holistic medicine', *Social Science and Medicine*, 46, 1193–1203.

Wyles, K. J., Pahl, S. and Thompson, R. (2011) '"Oh I do like to be beside the seaside": A field study on the psychological benefits of going to the coast', *9th Biennial Conference on Environmental Psychology*, Eindhoven.

—— (2014) 'Perceived risks and benefits of recreational visits to the marine environment: Integrating impacts on the environment and impacts on the visitor', *Ocean and Coastal Management*, 88, 53–63.

Zeeland, P. (2012) *Economische Agenda 2013–2015*, Middelburg, The Netherlands: Provincie Zeeland.

Zijlstra, T. R. (2007) *No Pain, No Gain: Measuring Treatment Effects in Fibromyalgia*, Twente, The Netherlands: University of Twente.

Zijlstra, T., Van de Laar, M., Moens, H. B., Taal, E., Zakraoui, L. and Rasker, J. (2005) 'Spa treatment for primary fibromyalgia syndrome: A combination of thalassotherapy, exercise and patient education improves symptoms and quality of life', *Rheumatology*, 44, 539–546.

Zlatkov, N., Bozhkov, B. and Genov, D. (1973) 'Serum copper and ceruloplasmin in patients with psoriasis after helio- and thalassotherapy', *Archiv für dermatologische Forschung*, 247, 289–294.

Part IX

Nature, health and tourism

This final part builds on the previous one, which emphasised the benefits of nature and certain types of landscape for enhancing health and wellbeing. Here, the focus is more on the types of products and services that can be developed within natural environments such as national parks in order to create the most beneficial and enjoyable forms of nature-based, wellbeing tourism. In Chapter 32 Sonia Ferrari and Monica Gilli discuss how natural parks should add to their services in order to create restorative environments based on environmental psychology and principles of 'eco-wellness'. This includes historical and cultural sites as well as wellness and medical tourism resources such as thermal baths. Similar to the earlier case study by Sarah Rawlinson and Peter Wiltshier (Chapter 26), it is argued that destinations offering multiple services can become more competitive and appealing and offer a truly restorative experience.

In Chapter 31 Juho Pesonen and Anja Tuohino fill a gap in the demand side of rural wellbeing tourism showing which factors motivate visitors to rural landscapes. One of the most important elements, which is also emphasised by Ferrari and Gilli in Chapter 32, as well as Friedl and Huijbens in Chapters 27 and 28, is the escape from everyday life which is afforded by nature-based experiences. Visitors also noted peacefulness and tranquillity which act as a counterbalance to the noise and crowds of modern life, as well as the pure air, which is very different from that of polluted cities, for example. Like Ferrari and Gilli, Pesonen and Tuohino argue that rural wellbeing destinations need to focus on connecting both nature and communities to offer the optimum experience. Some of the most popular activities include simply walking in nature (accessible to all) as well as outdoor sports; however, more traditional wellbeing services such as treatments and spa were also popular.

Finally, in Chapter 33 John S. Hull and Courtney Mason provide interesting examples of national parks in Canada which combine spas, wellness, health, natural landscape and Indigenous culture in a tourism product. Once again, nature and landscape are described as being attractive to those seeking a healthy lifestyle and, for many decades, have also represented an escape from urban living. As stressed by the previous authors in this part, community should be central to rural wellbeing development. In this case, although Indigenous people were originally displaced and exploited by tourism developers, they have gradually gained ownership of health and wellness tourism facilities, programmes and marketing and their traditions and stories feature in the tourism experience. Such experiences reflect an innovative fusion of Indigenous and modern spa modalities.

This final part demonstrates the importance of combining nature and culture, local people's traditions and modern lifestyles, as well as other services (e.g. outdoor recreation, sports) to create the optimum rural wellbeing environment. Pesonen and Tuohino's detailed analysis of demand suggests that more sophisticated service and activity development may be needed to take into consideration the diverse needs of different segments of visitors. By offering a wide range of services, as advocated by Ferrari and Gilli, this issue can be partially addressed, assuming that the geographical area in question is not too vast.

31

Rural wellbeing tourism destinations

Demand side viewpoint

Juho Pesonen and Anja Tuohino

Introduction

Tourism destination is a central feature of tourism research (Pearce, 2014) due to its significant constructs for the examination of tourism with a geographically bounded locality, in which both economic and social interactions occur (Tinsley and Lynch, 2007). The attractiveness of a destination as a marketing resource can be considered from different angles, such as those of nature and landscape, the climate, culture, history, the possibility of engaging in various hobbies and activities and accessibility. However, the resource itself is not a product. Rather, existing resources are the necessary preconditions for the creation of a travel experience that can be turned into a saleable tourism product (Middleton and Clarke, 2001; see also Bærenholdt et al., 2004; Tuohino, 2015).

On one hand, the literature on tourism destination management has been the focus of interest in recent years among both academics and practitioners (Laesser and Beritelli, 2013; Pearce and Schänzel, 2015). On the other hand, destination management requires a comprehensive and multifaceted approach, which among others provides greater insights and understanding of demand side issues, e.g. information about different types of customers (Fyall and Garrod, 2012).

The importance of marketing, which probes the wishes and likings of tourists, has long played an essential role in the development of customer-oriented tourism destinations. From the marketing management viewpoint destinations are considered a traditional commodity product and therefore agglomerations of both public and private facilities and services designed to meet the needs of tourists (e.g. Dredge and Jenkins, 2003; Pavlovich, 2003; Cooper et al., 2005; Saraniemi and Kylänen, 2011). Further, destinations are geographically disconnected actors on the demand and supply side, but on the other hand, consumption (demand) and production (supply) occur in the same place (Vanhove, 2011).

Destinations can also be examined from the viewpoint of activities. Reinhold et al. (2015) identify a gap in the destination definition regarding the demand side as definitions typically focus on institutional and supply-oriented perspectives. Also, when tourists choose a destination, they are interested in what they can do there while they are on holiday

(Pesonen and Tuohino, 2015). In this study, the concept of a rural wellbeing destination is examined through a demand side survey with a focus on the activities a rural destination potentially provides for tourists.

Literature review

Tourism destinations

Destination is by nature a challenging concept because its spatial angle of approach is often from a technical and static viewpoint (Saarinen, 2004). Destinations are traditionally defined as geographic areas such as a country, an island or a town (Davidson and Maitland, 1997). Destinations are also defined as a unit of action, where different private and public stakeholders, e.g. companies and public organisations, interact and provide all those facilities, infrastructures and services that are needed during the holiday distinct from visitors' usual place (Pechlaner et al., 2009; Jenkins et al., 2011; Saraniemi and Kylänen, 2011; Vanhove, 2011; Bregoli and Del Chiappa, 2013), albeit Pearce (2014) argued that destination is a commonly used term without definition. Tuohino and Konu (2014) correspondingly defined destination as a geographical area including various tourism products and services and the prerequisites needed for realising them. Buhalis (2000: 97) in turn highlights that 'it is increasingly recognized that a destination can also be a perceptual concept, which can be interpreted subjectively by consumers, depending on their travel itinerary, cultural background, purpose of visit, educational level and past experience'. Bærenholdt et al. (2004) approached tourism as social and cultural practice by stating that places receive the meaning only through concrete production and consumption processes that connect people to the realm by contextualising their experiences (see also Saraniemi and Kylänen, 2011) while Ritchie and Crouch (2000) stated that destination experience is the fundamental product of tourism.

According to Reinhold et al. (2015), issues in five domains of destination management preoccupy the discourse of scholars and practitioners, including the definition of the destination, the purpose and legitimacy of destination management organisations (DMOs), governance and leadership in destination networks, destination branding and sustainability. Reinhold et al. (2015) suggest that scholars and practitioners think about the ways in which decision makers in destinations can make destinations and DMOs fit for the new needs that changing customers have. Indeed, Murphy et al. (2000) consider that the destination is a construct driven by tourists. Beritelli et al. (2014) and Reinhold et al. (2015) also argue that networks and the networking capabilities of destinations are becoming critical for the success of the destination.

The built-up and natural physical environment of a destination, its local culture and community spirit can be considered as the core resources in tourism. From the resource point of view, the attractions have vital importance, as without attractions there is no tourism (Ritchie and Crouch, 2000, 2003/2005, 2011; Sheldon and Park, 2009; Vanhove, 2011). From the tourism point of view, the built-up and natural environment forms a physical framework for the detection and experience setting manifest as a visual experience and a sensory-based landscape experience. As a functional resource, the built-up and natural environment provides opportunities for versatile recreational and leisure activities. It also provides a comprehensive frame for a variety of independent or guided activities and tourism products or services built by local tourism entrepreneurs. As a symbolic resource built-up and natural environment has many meanings experienced subjectively, e.g. as a rural landscape (Tuohino, 2015).

Recently in the literature a demand-based view of a destination has received increased attention (Beritelli et al., 2014; Reinhold et al., 2015). Beritelli et al. (2014) argue that a destination is actually a network of suppliers activated by demand. Fine (1999) sees a destination as a demand-caused supply network where different actors respond to the developments in the market place to produce tourism goods. DMOs should not focus just on geographical areas but tourism destinations are overlapping spaces that consist of dynamic flows (Beritelli et al., 2014).

Tourists frequently seek locations and activities that are transcendent (Smith and Kelly, 2006) – places that influence the quality of experience (Sheldon and Park, 2009). De Botton (2002) described how travellers are attracted to landscapes that benefit their soul by making them feel small, yet part of an infinite and universal cycle (see Smith and Kelly, 2006). Therefore, destinations with unique natural features have been attracting tourists seeking increased health in various forms for centuries and tourism destinations have developed naturally around special features (e.g. Sheldon and Park, 2009; Smith and Puczkó, 2009; Konu et al., 2010). Rodrigues et al. (2010) on the other hand state that successful tourism destinations must offer new tourism products and address special-interest niches, too. They continue that wellbeing is a relevant motive and should be considered in tourism strategies. Rural areas can be seen as examples of this type of destination just as rural places can be seen as a refuge from urban life and a place to engage (Rodrigues et al., 2010).

Rural wellbeing

Rural wellbeing tourism is related to wellness and health tourism, for example as defined by Sheldon and Bushell (2009), but it has a broader stance and it might be seen as a further development of historical trends (Connell, 2006; Erfurt-Cooper and Cooper, 2009; Müller and Lanz Kaufmann, 2001; Smith and Puczkó, 2009, 2014).

The development of the traditional spa and wellness resorts towards a more holistic paradigm is widespread. According to García-Altés (2005), diverse demographic, economic and lifestyle-related factors have enhanced this. Many people are stressed by living in work-obsessed, time-pressed, materialistic and over-individualistic societies (Laing and Weiler, 2008; Sheldon and Bushell, 2009; Smith and Puczkó, 2009, 2014). Where experienced travellers seek new experiences (Konu and Laukkanen, 2010), this adds to the increased emphasis on more holistically oriented wellness products (Lehto et al., 2006; Mak et al., 2009; Koh et al., 2010).

The main motivations in the wellbeing and wellness tourism sector seem to be relaxation, escape, pampering, physical activity, avoiding burnout and mental wellbeing. Relaxation in many cases is connected to 'rest' and 'physical relaxation'. Escape is in many studies seen as one of the most important motivations. Pampering seems to be a motivation that is characteristic of wellness and spa tourism (Mak et al., 2009; Laesser, 2011). Pampering is also connected to the enjoyment of comfort (Laesser, 2011). Physical activity includes sports and multiple activities and similarly physical health and appearance. Mental wellbeing is likewise a motivation that can be seen to be specific to wellness tourism. It includes motivations such as 'to seek mental peacefulness' (Mak et al., 2009) and 'to help me gain a sense of balance' (Lehto et al., 2006).

Concerning the interpretative way, it is relevant to seek inspiration in ideas set out by Woods (2011) and Halfacree (2006, 2007). The rural can be approached from different, but intermeshing, facets: those of spatial practices (rural localities), representations of space (formal representations of the rural) and lived spaces (everyday rural lives). In short, these ideas refer to the production, reproduction and employment of rurality and rural space (Woods, 2011).

In a tourism context and particularly in relation to wellbeing tourism, the attributes of the rural are, however, more interesting as they are of significance not only for the provision of the products but also for marketing and branding.

The rural is also often approached as an opposite to the urban. When referring to tourism, it can be a highly valuable way of definition. Both rural and urban attributes can be structured via opposing adjectives linked to them: e.g. clean–polluted, tranquil–turbulent, natural–artificial, authentic–staged, silent–noisy, spacious–crowded, safe–dangerous (Bell et al., 2009). The Finrelax study (Tuohino et al., 2015) analyses Finnish wellbeing tourism in rural areas and identifies the following attributes, most of which are not compatible with the urban image: lakes, watersheds, coasts, the archipelago, the sea, forests, hills, fields, meadows, tundra, wilderness, natural phenomena (northern lights, seasons), landscapes, cleanliness, clean air, water, resources (berries, mushrooms), topography and unbuilt-up countryside. These give the most 'authentic' nature: food (game, wild food, countryside food, traditional food), peace and quiet, safety, freedom, uncrowdedness, non-violence, the diversity of activities (ice swimming, rowing, cruises, courses, familiarisation with forms of agriculture), traditions and cultural experiences.

Moreover, as Sharpley and Sharpley (1997: 14) state: 'it [rural] is the comparison between the tourist's home (and usually urban) environment and the characteristics of the destination that mark it as rural'. Approaching the term in this way gives an idea about the potential of the rural to contribute to wellbeing, especially when taking into account the central motivation factor of wellbeing tourists, namely escape. In addition, as Jepson and Sharpley (2015: 2) note, the 'fundamental attraction of the countryside as a tourist destination' is greatly woven into a sense of rurality. It is not only the physical attributes and intrinsic elements of the countryside but the idea of what the rural space represents to them. In addition, the size of the settlement may be an important marker for rurality, economy and the presence of traditional social structures or a certain backwardness and physical isolation from economic, social and cultural networks (Bramwell and Lane, 1994; Sharpley and Sharpley, 1997; Butler et al., 1998; Juska, 2007). There is a high level of ambiguity in such interpretations and the fine-tuning of these definitions is always made on an individual level by the tourist and by the stakeholders at the destination.

The viewpoints discussed above indicate the most interesting potential resources for rural wellbeing tourism. Rural wellbeing tourism could indeed be implemented based on the resources and needs of the local community, therefore benefitting mostly the locals. For an emerging number of tourists, rural areas also provide access to nature, local food and local ingredients. The rural is a playground not yet fully explored from a tourism development perspective.

In marketing research trend studies have often been applied (Naisbitt and Aburdene, 1990; Aburdene, 2007; Varey, 2013; von Groddeck and Schwarz, 2013) to identify new customer segments and understand customer behaviour to a significant extent. This has also been witnessed in tourism research (Leigh et al., 2013). Wellbeing travel activities (and particularly wellness and spa tourism) have also received considerable attention in academic and trade trend studies (Smith and Puczkó, 2013, 2014).

Previous studies have shown that rural tourists are likely to consider rural areas as places to escape the overcrowded and stressful urban life (Urry, 2002) and rural settings appear to be ideal places which reflect peacefulness, relaxation, authenticity, tranquillity and pure air (Dong et al., 2013). Further, Rodrigues et al. (2010) suggested that health and wellness tourism should be integrated into rural tourism destination marketing.

The landscape, space and place refer correspondingly to 'an environment felt to be important in human life, which is loved, admired and rejected, an environment which is interpreted and "read"' (Porteus, 1990, cited by Häkli, 1999: 82). In the tourism context, this implies the examination of a place as a social space and from the perspective of the offering of tourist destinations (the production of space) and tourist demand (the consumption of space) (Gottdiener, 2000; Saarinen, 2004; Williams, 2009, see also Vanhove, 2011). Therefore, this study aims to increase the understanding of a rural tourism destination as a provider of wellbeing service and activities and the understanding about the perceptions of tourists and their landscape preferences and their needs in experiencing rural nature. Thus, this study has three research questions:

1   What kind of rural wellbeing services are provided in Northern Europe?
2   What kind of rural wellbeing tourism products can be created from these services?
3   How can rural tourism destinations utilise the wellbeing products identified?

Data and methods

To gather a comprehensive list of rural wellbeing activities, members of five rural tourism destinations or DMOs, located in Norway, Finland, Lithuania, Latvia and Denmark, were gathered for a group interview. Also members of two tourism departments focusing on rural tourism from Finland and Denmark were present, as well as representatives of VisitFinland. Thus, altogether ten rural wellbeing tourism experts were present in the group interview. In the presented case, the goal of the group interview was to gather a comprehensive list of rural wellbeing services provided in Northern Europe currently or in the near future. Based on the group interview we identified altogether 63 possible rural tourism services.

To understand what kind of wellbeing tourism products can be created from these 63 identified services we designed a survey that studied how interesting these rural tourism services are for rural tourists in Northern Europe. The goal of the survey was to identify which services the rural tourists regard as similar to each other. This could be used to group rural tourism services into complete rural tourism products in which each service would be interesting to rural tourists.

In the survey, respondents were asked to rate how important are the possibilities of enjoying various wellbeing services during their rural holiday. Answer options ranged from 0 to 4 (0: not important at all, 1: slightly important, 2: moderately important, 3: important, 4: very important), with the possibility of choosing the option: No opinion. 'No opinion' choices were coded as missing values.

The survey was distributed on five rural tourism websites and in social media in Finland, Norway, Latvia, Lithuania and Denmark. Banner advertising was used, with a lottery of a gift certificate of €500 for one respondent. The gift certificate could be used to purchase rural tourism products in five aforementioned countries.

We obtained altogether 550 usable responses. The profile of the respondents is presented in Table 31.1. Most of the respondents came from Latvia, with Lithuania and Finland in second and third place. Most respondents were female, which was to be expected as the main target group for rural wellbeing services is women (Pesonen and Tuohino, 2015).

To identify the underlying dimensions among rural wellbeing services, principal component analysis with Varimax rotation was conducted on 63 rural wellbeing services. Communalities

Table 31.1 Comparing differences in socio-demographics between clusters

Age	% (n = 550)
18–25 years	6.7%
26–35 years	28.2%
36–45 years	33.1%
46–55 years	23.6%
56–65 years	7.6%
More than 65 years	0.7%
Mean age	40.34 years
Gender	
Male	21.5%
Female	78.5%
Nationality	
Finnish	10.2%
Norwegian	0.7%
Latvian	63.6%
Lithuanian	18.8%
Danish	1.3%
Russian	2.6%
Estonian	0.2%
German	0.5%
Other	2.2%

were higher than 0.5, Kaiser–Mayer–Olkin (KMO) test value was 0.937 with Bartlett's test of sphericity significance less than 0.001. Fourteen principal components explained 69.408 per cent of total variance.

According to Hair et al. (2010), the primary purpose of factor analysis is to define the underlying structure among the variables in the analysis. Factor analysis provides tools for analysing the structure of the inter-relationships among a large number of variables – in this case tourists' interest in rural wellbeing services and activities. As we do not have any information on how rural wellbeing services are inter-related, an exploratory approach with principal component analysis was applied. The principal components identified in this study have different loadings from different variables. A factor loading is the correlation between the variable and the factor (Hair et al., 2010), meaning that a 0.30 loading translates to approximately 10 per cent explanation and 0.50 loading to 25 per cent explanation. Thus, the larger the loading, the more important the loading is in interpreting the factor matrix. To confirm the results correlation analysis among principal components was conducted and no significant correlations were found. This means that the principal components identified are not connected to each other but form independent constructs, just as they should.

As presented in Table 31.1, there are many different nationalities among the respondents. There might be response-style effects (Dolnicar and Grün, 2007) that affect the results of different nationalities. Comparing median scores of different activities between nationalities shows us that there are national differences among respondents in interest in wellbeing activities. To check the validity of the principal components identified in this study, nation-specific correlation analysis among variables was conducted. Presenting these results in detail is out of the scope of this chapter but correlation analysis shows statistically significant ($p < 0.05$) correlations among variables in each principal component among respondents from each main nationality (Latvian, Lithuanian, Finnish) in the study. In particular, items with high loadings are correlated among all nationalities, increasing the validity of the results.

Case study: ProWell – promoting and enhancing sustainable rural wellbeing tourism in Northern Europe

The ProWell project – towards a new understanding of rural wellbeing tourism – aims at enhancing, developing and promoting sustainable thematic rural wellbeing tourism products in Europe. This objective is pursued through a transnational cooperation between different tourism stakeholders: small and micro tourism enterprises (SMTEs), DMOs, tourism development organisations and research institutes. In a wider perspective, the project aims at profiling and adding competitiveness to Northern Europe as a rural wellbeing tourism destination.

More specifically the project activities were:

1   Definition of the concept of sustainable rural wellbeing for marketing and further development purposes (e.g. related to the Finrelax concept in Finland, WellCome in Denmark and other national or regional products and product lines). Rural wellbeing was defined as follows:

> Rural wellbeing tourism is a form of tourism that takes place in rural settings and that interconnects actively with local nature and community resources. Based on the rural tangible and intangible, openly accessible and commercial ingredients, wellbeing tourism is a holistic mode of travel that integrates physical and mental wellness and/or health and contributes to wider positive social and individual life experiences.

2   Identification of products and product lines of rural wellbeing, including the identification of the service components that focus on or arise from the specialties of the natural and cultural heritage of Northern Europe.
3   Developing the guidelines for sustainable thematic rural wellbeing tourism product development.
4   Forming the transnational Rural Wellbeing Tourism Network of organisations for the promotion of rural wellbeing tourism products and sustainable practices and to increase the competitiveness and development of such tourism products. This includes sharing best practices in marketing and sustainability activities.
5   Providing settings that encourage SMTEs and other stakeholders, including local authorities, to participate in promotional activities and enhance their own product developments and other activities related to the theme.
6   Promoting rural wellbeing at a European level by using a range of methods, including interactive marketing methods that innovatively activate service providers and customers.

The participating countries were Denmark, Finland, Latvia, Lithuania and Norway, with an emphasis on actors in regions that are dominated by natural and rural resources.

(continued)

(continued)

Figure 31.1 ProWell partnership.

Source: Prowell project owned by UEF. The ProWell project addressed transnational thematic tourism products contributing to more sustainable tourism and is co-funded by the EU, awarded under the 2013 call for proposals 'supporting the enhancement and promotion of transnational thematic tourism products'. ProWell also receives significant support in kind and crucial information and knowledge from its project partners in all five countries. Read more here: http://www2.uef.fi/fi/mot/prowell. http://www.uef.fi/en/web/mot/paattyneet-hankkeet.

Results

The results of the principal component analysis are presented in Tables 31.2–31.16 (see below). We identified altogether 14 dimensions of rural wellbeing services. KMO value for principal component analysis was 0.937 and Bartlett's test of sphericity has significance value less than 0.001. All values for communalities were greater than 0.5.

Most important services were outdoor sports and walking in nature when the median score of the highest loading item is examined (Table 31.2). Most of the Cronbach alpha values are higher than 0.7 recommendation (Nunnally, 1967), but some principal components are clearly less reliable than required. The last component, sleeping, had only one item with significant loading. The alpha values of all principal components were maximised by removing items that reduced the value. We allowed an item to load on more than one principal component as it is only logical that a single wellbeing service can be connected to several themes or products.

The principal component with the largest variance explained and greatest number of items was treatments and spa (Table 31.3). The items that loaded most strongly on this principal component were visiting spa with relaxation focus, special saunas, yoga and treatments, massages and traditional and alternative treatments. Other services loading on treatments and spa mostly belong to the aforementioned categories, but fitness exercises, tests and seminars are similar to treatments and spas.

Table 31.4 contains items connected with slow living. People interested in slow living also prefer growing their own food in the destination, doing charity work, events and volunteering for the local community and having a digital detox. However, as they are the opposites of each other, it is interesting to notice that technology-enhanced tourism experiences also load to this principal with digital detox. This could either be a reliability issue in the data or mean that tourists do not want the whole holiday to be a digital detox, just a part of it. The data from the study do not provide more details on the matter.

Table 31.2 Principal component analysis results

Principal component	Variance explained	Eigenvalue	Median score of the highest loading item	Cronbach alpha
1 Treatments and spa	32.275	20.333	2	0.964
2 Slow living	6.582	4.146	1	0.937
3 Exercises	4.723	2.975	0	0.933
4 Alternative medicine	4.544	2.863	1	0.944
5 Local life	3.125	1.969	1	0.816
6 Wilderness	2.620	1.651	2	0.678
7 Outdoor adventure	2.428	1.529	1	0.880
8 Meditation	2.181	1.374	1	0.864
9 Eco-village	2.026	1.276	2	0.869
10 Outdoor sports	1.945	1.225	3	0.608
11 Learning about nature	1.831	1.153	2	0.742
12 Walking in nature	1.786	1.125	3	0.560
13 Museums	1.696	1.068	2	0.628
14 Sleeping	1.648	1.038	1	N/A

Table 31.3 First principal component: treatments and spa

Items	Loadings
Visiting spa (relaxation, special saunas, yoga, treatments, etc.)	0.836
Massage	0.823
Taking traditional treatments (e.g. foot care, facial treatments, cupping therapy)	0.723
Taking alternative treatments (e.g. sauna therapy, reiki, peat therapy)	0.717
Hot stone massage	0.664
Visiting recreational spa (swimming, hot tubs, slides, etc.)	0.647
Muscle therapies	0.627
Sauna treatments	0.608
Thalassotherapy	0.596
Finnish sauna	0.595
Physical research or fitness test	0.595
Balance exercises	0.573
Participating in fitness and wellbeing seminars	0.567
Fitness exercise	0.552
Exercise with personal trainer	0.548
Local fruit-based treatments	0.546
Acupuncture	0.464
Reflexology	0.431
Chiropractic care	0.420
Stress coaching	0.416
Folk medicine	0.376
Forest therapy	0.367
Taking part in personal development course (for example, mindfulness)	0.304

Table 31.4 Second principal component: slow living

Items	Loadings
Slow-living studies	0.725
Participating in growing your own food	0.716
Charity work/events	0.699
Volunteer work for local community	0.678
Silence tour	0.666
Protection of local resources	0.659
Digital detox	0.648
Collect your own herbs	0.612
Visiting an eco-village	0.446
Staying in an eco-village	0.443
Photography tours	0.401
Forest therapy	0.400
Spiritual training	0.385
Technology-enhanced tourism experiences	0.383
Doing handicrafts	0.355
Meditating	0.353
Local fruit-based treatments	0.306

Table 31.5 Third principal component: exercises

Items	Loadings
Indoor group exercises	0.811
Outdoor group exercises	0.699
Nordic walking	0.650
Going to a gym	0.638
Jogging	0.474
Doing yoga	0.455
Fitness exercise	0.450
Physical research or fitness test	0.383
Taking part in personal development course (for example, mindfulness)	0.374
Participating in fitness and wellbeing seminars	0.356
Balance exercises	0.340
Muscle therapies	0.337
Meditating	0.335

Table 31.6 Fourth principal component: alternative medicine

Items	Loadings
Reflexology	0.723
Chiropractic care	0.723
Acupuncture	0.692
Folk medicine	0.537
Spiritual training	0.410
Hot stone massage	0.409
Thalassotherapy	0.407
Stress coaching	0.403
Muscle therapies	0.381
Balance exercises	0.376

In Exercises (Table 31.5), the main services are group exercises, Nordic walking and going to a gym. Also fitness exercises, tests and seminars belong to this principal component. It is interesting to note that doing yoga and meditating are also regarded as exercises. Logically also muscle therapies and balance exercises load into this principal component.

Alternative medicine is focused on alternative medicine such as reflexology, chiropractic care, acupuncture and folk medicine (Table 31.6).

The fifth principal component was labelled as local life (Table 31.7). Rural tourists interested in doing handicrafts are also interested in buying local products and studying local traditions, cooking classes and local food.

Wilderness contains items that relate to foraging and being in nature, especially close to water (Table 31.8). Going boating and fishing, picking berries and mushrooms and swimming load strongly into this principal component.

Outdoor adventure items kayaking and canoeing load into their own principal component instead of being connected to wilderness items, as some might presume

(Table 31.9). This means that kayaking and canoeing are separate activities different from all other services.

Meditation contains services such as meditating, a personal development course, yoga and spiritual training, all focused on increasing and maintaining mental wellbeing (Table 31.10).

Besides being part of Slow living, eco-village items load strongly on their own principal component, Eco-village (Table 31.11). The results define the concept of eco-village and the services tourists are interested in enjoying in the village. These include sauna, forest therapy and local fruit-based treatments.

Table 31.7 Fifth principal component: local life

Items	Loadings
Doing handicrafts	0.694
Buying local handicrafts and other local products	0.678
Studying local traditions (like weaving, embroidery)	0.562
Cooking classes	0.553
Traditional local food	0.543
Collecting your own herbs	0.372

Table 31.8 Sixth principal component: wilderness

Items	Loadings
Going boating	0.744
Fishing	0.679
Berry or mushroom picking	0.625
Swimming	0.581

Table 31.9 Seventh principal component: outdoor adventure

Items	Loadings
Kayaking	0.859
Canoeing	0.846

Table 31.10 Eighth principal component: meditation

Items	Loadings
Meditating	0.628
Taking part in personal development course (for example, mindfulness)	0.596
Doing yoga	0.556
Spiritual training	0.412
Stress coaching	0.331
Folk medicine	0.315

Table 31.11 Ninth principal component: eco-village

Items	Loadings
Staying in an eco-village	0.617
Visiting an eco-village	0.569
Sauna treatments	0.451
Finnish sauna	0.422
Local fruit-based treatments	0.395
Forest therapy	0.367

Table 31.12 Tenth principal component: outdoor activities

Items	Loadings
Hiking	0.716
Cycling	0.563
Riding therapy	0.394
Jogging	0.338

Table 31.13 Eleventh principal component: learning about nature

Items	Loadings
Study local flora/fauna	0.699
Study local traditions (like weaving, embroidery)	0.449
Protection of local resources	0.424
Silence tour	0.325
Walking in nature trails	0.306

Table 31.14 Twelfth principal component: walking in nature

Items	Loadings
Walk in nature trails	0.532
Traditional local food	0.527
Trekking	0.489

Outdoor activities are connected to moving around in nature (Table 31.12). Hiking and cycling load strongly into this principal component. Riding therapy and jogging have minor loadings.

Studying local flora and fauna loads the strongest into the Learning about nature component (Table 31.13). This belongs together with items such as studying local traditions, protection of local resources, silence tours and walking in nature trails.

Walk in nature trails also loads strongly to the twelfth principal component together with traditional local food (Table 31.14). Also trekking loads quite strongly into this component. Thus this principal component was labelled as Walking in nature.

Table 31.15 Thirteenth principal component: museums

Items	Loadings
Visiting museums	0.664
Technology-enhanced tourism experiences	0.517
Photography tours	0.452
Visiting recreational spa (swimming, hot tubs, slides, etc.)	0.353

Table 31.16 Fourteenth principal component: sleeping

Items	Loadings
Sleep more than at home	0.828

The second to last component contains items such as visiting museums, technology-enhanced tourism experiences and photography tours (Table 31.15). It seems that technology, museums and photography are connected to each other, but also recreational spa has a minor loading in this component. This could provide a novel approach to designing a museum and spa products.

The last component, Sleeping, has only one item (Table 31.16). Sleeping more than at home seems to be special for rural tourists

Conclusions

Based on a group interview, this study identified altogether 63 different rural wellbeing activities. These various activities provide an overview of how rural areas can be used to increase the wellbeing of tourists and travellers. Rural areas have numerous different opportunities to maintain and increase wellbeing as well as profile themselves among different travellers.

The results provide quite an interesting overview of rural wellbeing activities and products that can be created based on those. There are 14 different categories of rural wellbeing services that can be considered as rural wellbeing product families. There is some overlap between the components, meaning that some activities can be a part of different products. The 14 principal components of this study do not correlate with each other, meaning that they represent 14 different dimensions of rural wellbeing activities. The results show what kind of activities rural wellbeing destinations should provide together. People interested in one activity in a product category are likely to be interested in other activities in the same category. Thus, it is reasonable for tourism providers to build rural wellbeing activity packages based on the results of this study. The most interesting rural wellbeing tourism goods were walking in nature and outdoor sports, which emphasise active rural wellbeing tourism. After those come the more traditional pampering-focused wellbeing services such as treatments and spa.

The study provides interesting insights for rural destinations to utilise the results in designing their services and marketing. Especially activities that load strongly into the same component should be marketed together and customer experiences built around them. Activities with lower loadings could be regarded as supporting activities that some tourists interested in higher loading items could potentially be interested in. Activities with loadings above 0.6 and especially above 0.7 in the same component are likely to attract the same kind of customers and should be provided together as frequently as possible. The principal components identified can be directly used to create product packages, for example containing a boat trip to an island to pick berries or mushrooms, going for a swim and fishing on the way back (sixth principal component, wilderness).

Theoretically, this study increases our understanding in utilising activities in rural destination management and design. Not all activities should be marketed together but destinations should focus on activities and services that have synergy from the customer point of view. The results of this study demonstrate, for example, how people who enjoy kayaking also like canoeing, but do not necessarily like boating, fishing or swimming.

This study contributes to the demand-based management of a destination and presents a demand-based viewpoint of rural wellbeing tourism destinations. The results support the notions presented by Beritelli et al. (2014) that destinations are not geographically based constructs but are based on tourism flows. Tourists go after the services and activities that they like and these might not necessarily be geographically in the same location. Destination managers and businesses operating in rural wellbeing should understand, based on these results, what tourists want and identify the possibilities for creating tourism goods that rural wellbeing tourists prefer. DMO is able to create added value for visitors and suppliers in need of specific services (Beritelli et al., 2014). This indeed requires destinations to be networks of actors that enable creation of services that the rural tourists value (Reinhold et al., 2015).

While interpreting the results more closely, we also have to take into account the fact that Latvian and Lithuanian respondents represent over 82 per cent of the total and their understanding about wellness or wellbeing may differ from those in Nordic countries due to their long history of thermal water use and rehabilitation spas. As Smith (2015) states, in the Baltic States spas are an important part of both wellness and medical tourism. Also healing and rehabilitation aspect of spas are important. In this study there are differences among nationalities regarding how much they prefer certain activities. However, the data analysis methods used were not focused on differences in answering patterns but aimed to find similarities between the respondents.

The results of this study also provide important insights into understanding what rural wellbeing constitutes for different tourists. There are a variety of ways in which wellbeing can be created, both active as well as passive. This study has discovered the main dimensions of rural wellbeing and also what kind of activities support these rural wellbeing experiences.

The sample obtained in this study is similar to earlier studies (Pesonen and Tuohino, 2015). People interested in rural wellbeing tourism products seem to be middle-aged females. Online surveys on the topic with a lottery as a reward seem to work well for this group of rural tourists. The study also has primary limitations. Even though the sample size is adequate according to Hair et al. (2010), more data would have increased the reliability of the results.

References

Aburdene, P. (2007) *Megatrends 2010: The Rise of Conscious Capitalism*, Charlottesville, VA: Hampton Roads Publishing.

Bærenholdt, J.O., Haldrup, M., Larsen, J. and Urry, J. (2004) *Performing Tourist Places*, Aldershot/Burlington, VT: Ashgate.

Bell, S., Simpson, M., Tyrväinen, L., Sievänen, T. and Pröbstl, U. (2009) *European Forest Recreation and Tourism: A Handbook*, Abingdon, UK: Taylor and Francis.

Beritelli, P., Bieger, T. and Laesser, C. (2014) 'The new frontiers of destination management applying variable geometry as a function-based approach', *Journal of Travel Research*, 53(4), 403–417.

Bramwell, B. and Lane, B. (1994) *Rural Tourism and Sustainable Rural Development*, Clevedon, UK: Channel View Publications.

Bregoli, I. and Del Chiappa, G. (2013) 'Coordinating relationships among destination stakeholders: Evidence from Edinburgh (UK)', *Tourism Analysis*, 18(2), 145–155.

Buhalis, D. (2000) 'Marketing the competitive destination of the future', *Tourism Management*, 21(1), 97–116.

Butler, R., Hall, C.M. and Jenkins, J. (eds) (1998) *Tourism and Recreation in Rural Areas*, Chichester, UK: John Wiley.

Connell, J. (2006) 'Medical tourism: Sea, sun, sand and surgery', *Tourism Management*, 27(6), 1093–1100.

Cooper, C., Fletcher, J., Wanhill, S., Gilbert, D. and Shepherd, R. (2005) *Tourism: Principles and Practice*, Harlow, UK: Pearson Education.

Davidson, R. and Maitland, R. (1997) *Tourism Destinations*, London: Hodder and Stoughton.

de Botton, A. (2002) *The Art of Travel*, London: Penguin.

Dolnicar, S. and Grün, B. (2007) 'Cross-cultural differences in survey response patterns', *International Marketing Review*, 24(2), 127–143.

Dong, E., Wang, Y., Morais, D. and Brooks, D. (2013) 'Segmenting the rural tourism market: The case of Potter Country, Pennsylvania, USA', *Journal of Vacation Marketing*, 19(2), 181–193.

Dredge, D. and Jenkins, J. (2003) 'Destination place identity and regional tourism policy', *Tourism Geographies*, 5(4), 383–407.

Erfurt-Cooper, P. and Cooper, M. (2009) *Health and Wellness Tourism, Spas and Hot Springs*, Bristol, UK: Channel View Publications.

Fine, C.H. (1999) *Clockspeed: Winning Industry Control in the Age of Temporary Advantage*, New York: Basic Books.

Fyall, A. and Garrod, B. (2012) Editorial. *Journal of Destination Marketing and Management*, 1, 1–3.

García-Altés, A. (2005) 'The development of health tourism services', *Annals of Tourism Research*, 32(1), 262–266.

Gottdiener, M. (2000) 'The consumption of space and the spaces of consumption', in Gottdiener, M. (ed.) *New Forms of Consumption. Consumers, Culture and Commodification*, Lanham, MD: Rowman and Littlefield, pp. 265–285.

Hair, J., Black, W., Babin, B. and Anderson, R. (2010) *Multivariate Data Analysis* (7th ed.), Upper Saddle River, NJ: Prentice Hall.

Halfacree, K. (2006) 'Rural space: Constructing a three-fold architecture', in Cloke, P., Marsden, T. and Mooney, P. (eds) *Handbook of Rural Studies*, London: Sage Publications, pp. 44–62.

—— (2007) 'Trial by space for a "radical rural": Introducing alternative localities, representations and lives', *Journal of Rural Studies*, 23(2), 125–141.

Häkli, J. (1999) *Meta Hodos. Johdatus ihmismaantieteeseen*, Tampere, Finland: Vastapaino.

Jenkins, J., Dredge, D. and Taplin, J. (2011) 'Destination planning and policy: Process and practice', in Wang, Y. and Pizam. A. (eds) *Destination Marketing and Management: Theories and Applications*, Wallingford: CABI International, pp. 21–38.

Jepson, D. and Sharpley, R. (2015) 'More than sense of place? Exploring the emotional dimension of rural tourism experiences', *Journal of Sustainable Tourism*, 23(8–9), 1157–1178.

Juska, A. (2007) 'Discourses on rurality in post-socialist news media: The case of Lithuania's leading daily "lietuvos rytas" (1991–2004)', *Journal of Rural Studies*, 23(2), 238–253.

Koh, S., Yoo, J.J.E. and Boeger, C.A. (2010) 'Importance performance analysis with benefit segmentation of spa goers', *International Journal of Contemporary Hospitality Management*, 22(5), 718–735.

Konu, H. and Laukkanen, T. (2010) 'Predictors of tourists' wellbeing holiday intentions in Finland', *Journal of Hospitality and Tourism Management*, 17(1), 144–149.

Konu, H., Tuohino, A. and Komppula, R. (2010) 'Lake Wellness – a practical example of a new service development (NSD) concept in tourism industries', *Journal of Vacation Marketing*, 16(2), 125–139.

Laesser, C. (2011) 'Health travel motivation and activities: Insights from a mature market – Switzerland', *Tourism Review*, 66(1/2), 83–89.

Laesser, C. and Beritelli, P. (2013) 'St. Gallen consensus on destination management', *Journal of Destination Marketing and Management*, 2(1), 46–49.

Laing, J. and Weiler, B. (2008) 'Mind, body and spirit: Health and wellness tourism', in Asia, in Cochrane, J. (ed.) *Asian Tourism: Growth and Change*, Amsterdam, The Netherlands: Elsevier, pp. 379–389.

Lehto, X.Y., Brown, S., Chen, Y. and Morrison, A.M. (2006) 'Yoga tourism as a niche within the wellness tourism market', *Tourism Recreation Research*, 31(1), 5–14.

Leigh, J., Webster, C. and Ivanov, S. (eds) (2013) *Future Tourism: Political, Social and Economic Challenges*, Abingdon, UK: Routledge.

Mak, A., Wong, K.K. and Chang, R.C. (2009) 'Health or self-indulgence? The motivations and characteristics of spa-goers', *International Journal of Tourism Research*, 11(2), 185–199.

Middleton, V.T.C. and Clarke, J. (2001) *Marketing in Travel and Tourism*, Oxford, UK: Butterworth Heinemann.

Müller, H. and Lanz Kauffman, E. (2001) 'Wellness tourism: Market analysis of a special health tourism segment and implications for the hotel industry', *Journal of Vacation Marketing*, 7(1), 5–17.

Murphy, P., Pritchard, M.P. and Smith, B. (2000) 'The destination product and its impact on traveller perceptions', *Tourism Management*, 21(1), 43–52.

Naisbitt, J. and Aburdene, P. (1990) *Megatrends 2000*, New York: William Morrow.

Nunnally, J.C. (1967) *Psychometric Theory*, New York: McGraw-Hill.

Pavlovich, K. (2003) 'The evolution and transformation of a tourist destination network: The Waitomo Caves, New Zealand', *Tourism Management*, 24(2), 203–216.

Pearce, D.G. (2014) 'Toward an integrative conceptual framework of destinations', *Journal of Travel Research*, 53, 141–153.

Pearce, D.G. and Schänzel, A. (2015) 'Destinations: Tourists' perspectives from New Zealand', *International Joural of Tourism Research*, 17(1), 4–12.

Pechlaner, H., Herntrei, M. and Kofink, L. (2009) 'Growth strategies in mature destinations: Linking spatial planning with product development', *Tourism Review*, 57(3), 285–307.

Pesonen, J.A. and Tuohino, A. (2015) 'Activity-based market segmentation of rural wellbeing tourists: Comparing online information search', *Journal of Vacation Marketing*, October 28, doi: 10.1177/1356766715610163.

Reinhold, S., Laesser, C. and Beritelli, P. (2015) '2014 St. Gallen Consensus on destination management', *Journal of Destination Marketing and Management*, 4(2), 137–142.

Ritchie, J.R. and Crouch, G.I. (2000) 'The competitive destination: A sustainability perspective', *Tourism Management*, 21(1), 1–7.

—— (2003/2005) *The Competitive Destination: A Sustainable Tourism Perspective*, Wallingford, UK: CABI Publishing.

Ritchie, J.R. and Crouch, G.I. (2011) 'A model of destination competitiveness and sustainability', in Wang, Y. and Pizam, A. (eds) *Destination Marketing and Management. Theories and Applications*, Wallingford, UK: CABI.

Rodrigues, Á., Kastenholz, E. and Rodriques, A. (2010) 'Hiking as wellness activity, an exploratory study of hiking tourists in Portugal', *Journal of Vacation Marketing*, 16(4), 331–343.

Saarinen, J. (2004) '"Destinations in change". The transformation process of tourist destinations', *Tourist Studies*, 4(2), 161–179.

Saraniemi, S. and Kylänen, M. (2011) 'Problematizing the concept of tourism destination: An analysis of different theoretical approaches', *Journal of Travel Research*, 50(2), 133–143.

Sharpley, R. and Sharpley, J. (1997) *Rural Tourism. An Introduction*, London: Thompson.

Sheldon, P. and Bushell, R. (2009) 'Introduction to wellness and tourism', in Bushell, R. and Sheldon, P.J. (eds) *Wellness and Tourism. Mind, Body, Spirit, Place*, New York: Cognizant Communication, pp. 3–18.

Sheldon, P.J. and Park, S.-Y. (2009) 'Development of sustainable wellness destination', in Bushell, R. and Sheldon, P. J. (eds) *Wellness and Tourism – Mind, Body, Spirit, Place*, New York: Cognizant Communication Corporation, pp. 99–113.

Smith, M. (2015) 'Baltic health tourism: Uniqueness and commonalities', *Scandinavian Journal of Hospitality and Tourism*, 15(4), 357–379, DOI: 10.1080/15022250.2015.1024819.

Smith, M. and Kelly, C. (2006) 'Wellness tourism', *Tourism Recreation Research*, 31(1), 1–4.

Smith, M. and Puzckó, L. (2009) *Health and Wellness Tourism*, Oxford, UK: Butterworth-Heinemann.

—— (2013) 'Regional trends and predictions for global health tourism', in Voigt, C. and Pforr, C. (eds) *Wellness Tourism: A Destination Perspective*, Abingdon, UK: Routledge.

—— (2014) *Health Tourism and Hospitality: Spas, Wellness and Medical Travel*, Abingdon, UK: Routledge.

Tinsley, R. and Lynch, P. (2007) 'Small business networking and tourism destination development: A comparative perspective', *Entrepreneurship and Innovation*, 8(1), 15–27.

Tuohino, A. (2015) *In Search of the Sense of Finnish Lakes. A Geographical Approach to Lake Tourism Marketing*, vol. 44, issue 5, Oulu, Finland: Nordia Geographical Publications.

Tuohino, A., Eronen, R. and Konu, H. (2015) '*Suomalainen maaseutu hyvinvointimatkailun sisältönä*', http://epublications.uef.fi/pub/urn_nbn_fi_uef-20150169/urn_nbn_fi_uef-20150169.pdf (accessed 8 April 2016).

Tuohino, A. and Konu, H. (2014) 'Local stakeholders' views about destination management: Who are leading tourism development?', *Tourism Review*, 69(3), 202–215.

Urry, J. (2002) *The Tourist Gaze*, London: Sage Publications.

Vanhove, N. (2011) *The Economics of Tourism Destinations*, New York: Routledge.

Varey, R.J. (2013) 'Marketing in the flourishing society megatrend', *Journal of Macromarketing*, 33(4), 354–368.

von Groddeck, V. and Schwarz, J.O. (2013) 'Perceiving megatrends as empty signifiers: A discourse-theoretical interpretation of trend management', *Futures*, 47, 28–37.

Williams, S. (2009). *Tourism Geography: A New Synthesis*, Abingdon, UK: Routledge.

Woods, M. (2011) *Rural*, Abingdon, UK: Routledge.

32

Protected natural areas as innovative health tourism destinations

Sonia Ferrari and Monica Gilli

Introduction

Today stressful lifestyles often push people towards the search for relaxing holidays in natural environments not affected by pollution or altered by human intervention. The positive impact of nature on wellness and health is well known and it is directly linked to levels of biodiversity.

In this chapter we will describe the effects of nature on human health and the role that natural parks could play in the improvement of public health and wellness levels, meanwhile positioning themselves as innovative tourist destinations. We will present an Italian case study, that of Trentino, an area that has invested in becoming a successful nature and wellness tourism destination.

Wellness and medical tourism

Reaching higher levels of health and wellbeing has always been one of the main aims of tourists, who in ancient times chose thermal centres and later sea bathing and who are today often looking for nature, sports, meditation and spiritual holidays (Connell, 2006). Nowadays the sectors of wellness, medical and health tourism are growing significantly, at the same time changing rapidly and profoundly, thus creating space for new and innovative types of products and destinations (Smith and Puczkó, 2009, 2014; Voigt and Pforr, 2013; Voigt et al., 2011). It is not our intention to offer definitions of the concepts of health, medical and wellness tourism. In fact, it is not easy to do so and the different definitions of the various types of tourism reflect heterogeneous ways of observing, describing and studying these phenomena and their evolution over time.

It is however important to make a distinction. First, 'health tourism' can be considered the main category which comprises many subcategories, such as spa tourism, medical tourism, new age tourism (Garcia-Altes, 2005; Hall, 2011; Smith and Puczkó, 2009). It should also be clarified that, while 'health tourists' are looking for cures to improve their health status, the main aim of 'wellness tourists' is prevention of illness. The latter are healthy people mainly interested in preserving and promoting their condition by means of various products and services such as diet, fitness, beauty care and relaxation (Mueller and Kaufmann, 2001). For this reason, wellness tourism can be considered as a sub-segment of the sector of health tourism.

In the last few years a new niche in the tourism industry emerged, which is 'medical tourism'. Medical tourism can be divided into two segments: surgical and therapeutic (Smith and Puczkó, 2009). It is related to the offer of specific medical interventions, such as dental and surgical care, during a holiday in a tourism and sometimes exotic destination (Connell, 2006; Ruspini, 2010). More and more frequently operators in the destinations as well as organisations are creating and promoting packages that are bundles of mixed health, wellness, fitness and aesthetic services combined with leisure and tourist activities. This market segment is rapidly growing. The reasons for this are linked to the higher costs of the services (especially in rich countries) and the long waiting lists for public healthcare in tourists' motherlands compared to the privacy and good services offered in certain locations. In addition, important factors include favourable exchange rates, good airline prices and the ageing of the baby-boomer generation, as well as the experience of being on vacation in a pleasant destination during the treatment.

Protected natural areas as tourist destinations

'Nature tourism' has been defined as 'tourism in which the main aim of the holiday is the observation and enjoyment of nature and traditional culture' (Osservatorio Permanente sul Turismo Natura, 2007: 6). Protected natural areas are today important tourist destinations with an increasing role in the tourist market and a growing demand. Parks are promoted domestically and internationally as must-see attractions and, in many cases, have become real 'tourist markers', namely key elements of the tourism offer which provide information and evoke mental images in current and potential visitors' minds (Ferrari and Pratesi, 2012; Frost and Hall, 2010; Haukeland et al., 2011; Leiper, 1990; MacCannell, 1976; Wall Reinius and Fredman, 2007).

According to the United Nations World Tourism Organization (2008), rarely do tourists move for just one purpose. Those whose only interest is nature, the so-called 'hard ecotourists' (Blamey, 1995), are a small niche in the market and they are looking solely for a deep immersion in nature. On the other hand, much more numerous are the 'soft ecotourists', who combine other interests, linked for example to the local culture, food and wine and to sporting activities (Fredman and Tyrvainen, 2011). Soft ecotourists look for a complete holiday experience, which includes authentic elements of the area visited (Ferrari, 2006). Tourists looking for authenticity (MacCannell, 1976), in fact, particularly appreciate contact with local culture, which allows them to immerse themselves in the lifestyle of the place they are visiting through events, social gatherings and contact with residents. Frequently tourist destinations can differentiate their images through local unique resources and the offer related to their culture and tradition. In this way it is possible to create a successful tourist brand emphasising local specialisms and traditional ancient healing practices (Smith and Puczkó, 2014), especially immersing the visitor in natural resources such as thermal waters, forests and waterways.

From this viewpoint, a natural park should complete its offer adding services related not only to the enjoyment of the natural environment, but also to other aspects of the holiday, such as visits to historic and cultural sites, artistic, handicraft and culinary resources, traditions and folklore. Besides, the holiday in a natural destination can also include elements related to wellness and medical tourism, i.e. thermal baths, medical treatments, relaxation and sport activities, health and wellness education programmes.

Thus, the market of natural tourist destinations must include quite a varied range of offers, which are connected in different ways to the philosophy of 'slow travel' and wellness tourism. They are, in other words, connected to the chance of improving visitors' psycho-physical health state, while enjoying real contact with nature, hosting places and local people. There is a strong link between a slow tourism approach and the new attitude of consumers towards wellness. In fact, the term slow tourism:

> is a holistic and wide-ranging concept which covers everything from a literal slowing down of activity (spending more time in each location), to the promotion of alternative non-aviation transport methods (reducing carbon emissions), to spatial escape, to the pursuit of well-being and an enhanced quality of life for the tourist and receiving communities.
>
> *(Cater et al., 2016: 460)*

It comprises four different main themes: slowness and the value of time; locality and activities at the destination; mode of transport and travel experience; and environmental consciousness (Lumsdon and McGrath, 2011). Of course, sustainability is one the basic concepts of this approach to travel.

Positive impact of nature on wellness and health

Natural elements, such as animals, trees and water, have always symbolised powerful forces and, for this reason, have been staged as myths (Gesler, 1993). In fact, 'nature's goods and services are "the ultimate foundations of life and health"' (World Health Organization, 2005: 1). In our society it has been intuitively clear since the birth of the first big cities, in the ancient Rome era, that nature has a positive impact on wellbeing and health, reducing stress and offering restoration (Ulrich, 1991). Women and men require nature for their psychological, emotional and spiritual needs (Maller et al., 2005). These are the basis of the creation of urban and suburban parks and protected natural areas, that in the nineteenth century the Landscape Architecture and American Parks Movement considered important instruments to regain physical and mental health. Natural protected areas offer mental and physical relaxation, together with spaces and services for physical and sporting activities (hiking, trekking, walking, cycling, skiing, swimming, etc.) in wonderful surroundings, with optimal effects in physical and emotional terms. As Smith and Puczkó (2009: 252) state:

> nature plays a significant role in health and wellness in many countries, especially those which have a sea coast and can offer products like thalassotherapy (common in Europe). Mountains are another feature which have always attracted health visitors, especially the Alps in Europe. Jungles and national parks (e.g. in Central and South America, Africa) make ideal locations for adventure and ecospas, which is a growing trend. To a lesser (but increasing) extent deserts (e.g. in the Middle East or North Africa) are being used as locations for yoga and meditation holidays.

In past decades many studies have shown that the natural environment has a strong positive physical and psychological impact on human health and wellness for both individuals and communities. The new trend towards the return to nature and spirituality plus a greater interest in sustainability and eco-friendly experiences have made a natural setting become a way to be more inviting and competitive, also thanks to the search for unspoiled environments and centres offering wellness and healthcare (Cohen and Bodeker, 2008). One of the main fields of study into the effects of nature on health and wellness is that of 'health geography', specialised in the research on the relationship between health and places (Fleuret and Atkinson, 2007; Milligan and Wiles, 2010). However, most of these studies are concentrated on the impact of urban and suburban parks, neglecting the importance of natural protected areas (Romagosa et al., 2015). The major effects of contact with nature, flora, fauna, landscapes and wilderness on health can be described in terms of relaxation and easing minor stress with the possibility of participating in outdoor and sporting activities. They also concern the prevention and reduction of hypertension problems and difficulties in concentrating, faster recovery from surgery, better pain control as well as improvement of children's attention and behavioural disorders, plus positive effects on depression and anxiety (De Oliveira et al., 2013; Kaplan, 1995; Kaplan and Kaplan, 1989; Lemieux et al., 2012; Maller et al., 2005; Ulrich, 1991). These effects are more evident in natural protected areas than in urban and suburban parks, caused by the levels of biodiversity which have a direct effect on visitors' wellness and capacity of recovery from illness (Fuller et al., 2007).

But how does nature help us in improving wellness and health? The exposure to everyday nature (sometimes just to pictures of natural landscape or to views of nature from out of the window) has positive effects on psychological, physiological and behaviour components of stress (Godbey, 2009; Ulrich, 1991; Ulrich et al., 1991).

The effects of natural elements on psychological wellbeing are the object of 'environmental psychology' (Hartig et al., 2003; Mehrabian and Russell, 1974). It asserts that nature favours positive feelings, reducing negative emotions and stressful thoughts, besides having a positive impact on paying attention. In fact, as stated by Kaplan and Kaplan (1989), people respond to a natural environment with involuntary attention (they called it 'fascination'), obtaining as a consequence restoration from stress and mental fatigue. They spoke of 'restorative environments' referring to the effects on concentration of being in and viewing nature which increases happiness (Lemieux et al., 2012; Reese and Myers, 2012). The distance from natural environments leads to many negative effects that have been described as nature-deficit disorder (Louv, 2008). Nature also has a physiological positive impact, reducing blood pressure, cholesterol and muscular tension, producing vitamin D, managing weight and improving emotions. Besides, outdoor recreation contributes to human health mostly in prevention terms, especially helping to face stress and obesity problems and reducing the risk of cardiovascular diseases (Godbey, 2009).

Parks offer not only a setting in which people feel better in psychological and physical terms, but also opportunities to live unique personal experiences for young people and children first of all. Such experiences can lead to improvements in self-esteem (thanks to challenging activities), learning how to adopt healthier lifestyles and better nutritional habits, to play sport and practise outdoor activities also with friends, family and other people (Europarc – España, 2013). In fact, many parks organise health education programmes in order to promote healthy lifestyles, local and natural food and sports. One of the first and most important of such programmes is the Australian 'Healthy Parks, Healthy People'. Promoted in 1999, it was later followed by 'Healthy Parks, Healthy People US' in the USA, 'Equilibri Naturali' in Italy, and many others.

Studies on the positive impact of exposure to natural settings on health are mainly focused on viewing, but in the future it would be interesting to analyse all sensory effects. The first study on the connection between natural sounds and health was carried out in 2014 and demonstrated the positive influence of natural soundscape on cognition, stress and other health and wellness components (Benfield et al., 2014). Many scholars think that all these results are linked to the human genetic need to be connected with nature (Keller and Wilson, 1993), while others attribute them to our 'ecological unconscious' (the core of the mind, that is the living record of cosmic evolution) (Roszak, 1992). For all the reasons described, a natural setting, thanks to its psychological supportive and relaxing effects, appears to be the best environment for healing, especially for long-term care patients (Olmsted, 1865). Natural elements are a tangible distraction in the physical setting that positively stimulate patients. In hospitalisation it reduces levels of pain and the need for drugs, shortening the period of illness and obtaining better evaluation by nurses (Maller et al., 2005; Ulrich, 1991; Ulrich et al., 1991).

The importance of nature in healing and wellness is also shown by the frequent use of natural materials, such as stone or woods, in the architecture of spas and wellness centres or in the choice of using themes recalling natural environments in the interior design of these buildings, such as rainforests, jungles and beaches. Also in the treatments natural raw materials are often used, such as water (thermal or non-thermal), oil, fruit, hay, milk and leafs (Ferrari et al., 2014).

A concept which is useful when summarising what has been described in this chapter is that of 'ecowellness', defined by Reese and Myers (2012: 400) as 'a sense of appreciation, respect for and awe of nature that results in feelings of connectedness with the natural environment and the enhancement of holistic wellness'. Ecowellness has three dimensions. The first is access to nature: it can have a great positive impact on health in the case of the absence of pollution and a good overall quality of the environment. The second component is environmental identity. The personalities who present a strong and positive environmental identity are more connected with nature and experience better effects on their wellness and health through contact with a natural environment. The last dimension is transcendence. Many people if immersed in nature can feel a sense of transcendence, living 'peak experiences' (Maslow, 1976).[1] Besides, being in natural settings increases generosity, interest in promoting the wellbeing of others and social connections, so that individuals can feel themselves safer and less isolated. To conclude this section, we can say that parks contribute, in terms of prevention, promotion and recovery, to five components of wellbeing and health: physical, mental, spiritual, social and environmental dimensions (Maller et al., 2005).

Natural areas as tourist destinations that offer health and wellbeing benefits

Frequently protected natural areas host therapeutic services, spas and medical centres. Since 1800 natural protected areas have hosted healing activities such as sanatoria, thalassotherapies and thermal baths, also thanks to famous hot springs. The origins of nature-based wellness and health tourism are in 'climate tourism'. This refers to the habit of Western populations to move seasonally towards more salubrious places, mostly during summer, in search of warmer or cooler destinations. But the birth of this type of tourism and its link to both nature and wellbeing could also be traced back to different traditions, for example, Romanticism and the search for the sublime in nature; the 'taking the waters' habit; the love of the sea; the love of outdoor recreation, sports, fishing and hunting; the attraction for the exotic; and spiritual aspects of nature (Meyer-Arendt, 2004).

Many spa and thermal centres which were developed inside natural parks in the past have now added rehabilitation departments to their offer. The nineteenth-century sanatoria, constructed to fight diseases such as tuberculosis, are antecedents of modern wellness centres and clinics. Many were built in what are today natural protected areas, mostly in mountain zones, and some are still operating, for example the Sanatorium Energetik in Tunkinsky National Park in Siberia and the Sanatorium Amber Shore in Kemeri National Park in Latvia (WWF and Equilibrium Research, 2010).

Today in many countries, especially in Northern and Balkan Europe, the wellness offer is focused on landscape and wilderness, e.g. in Finland and Iceland (Huijbens, 2014; Konu et al., 2014; Nordic Council of Ministers, 2005). The search for the sublime which can recover the soul and the mind is always alive, therefore wellness, holistic and medical centres are often positioned in wonderful and unspoiled natural areas. Spiritual and new age tourism should also be taken into consideration. They comprise natural settings, ecotherapy, greenery, agoraphilia[2] and other aspects of health tourism related to nature (Huijbens, 2010; Smith and Puczkó, 2014).

For all these reasons, nowadays, in protected natural areas it is possible to find innovative health and medical centres, together with wellness resorts, thermal baths and spas, offering tourists various kinds of health, medical, aesthetic, wellness and holistic services, also in direct contact with natural resources (thermal, mineral and marine waters, forests, landscapes, plants, animals and wilderness). They provide visitors not only more effective therapies and fast recoveries from diseases and surgery, but also unique and enriching experiences in unspoiled and wonderful natural settings.

In fact, natural parks have the four characteristics of a 'restorative environment', that are: fascination; a sense of being away (a temporary escape from everyday life); extent or scope (the idea of being part of a larger whole); and compatibility with personal inclinations (thanks to the possibility of satisfying different needs and expectations). So parks can be considered as ideal restorative environments which also offer social benefits in terms of the possibility of socialisation and increased community cohesion (Maller et al., 2005).

Protected areas contribute to improving human health in different ways (Moyle et al., 2014; Thomsen et al., 2013). First of all, they provide direct benefits in terms of the protection of ecosystems; furthermore, nature is a source of local and global medicines; additionally, parks are environments in which it is possible to provide mental care, for example, playing sports (Romagosa et al., 2015; WWF and Equilibrium Research, 2010). Protected areas are really useful in wellness, because of their unspoiled environment, easy accessibility and services and infrastructure for visitors. They offer different types of values that can be linked with their intrinsic components (flora, fauna, ecosystems) or with products and services offered (education, guided tours, plan products, health education programmes). These values can be community-oriented (with cultural and/or spiritual meanings) or individual-oriented (towards physical and/or psychological health, or spiritual wellbeing) (Lockwood et al., 2006).

Italian situation and the case of Trentino

What is the Italian situation with regard to the offer of nature and wellness destinations? Despite having undertaken a survey on Italian natural parks, we did not find major examples of wellness tourism in protected natural areas, with the exception of wellness centres, thermal baths, spas and minor examples of psychiatric rehabilitation, such as the cases of horticultural therapy in Montemarcello-Magra Regional Park and hippotherapy in Monte San Giorgio Natural Park. These do not represent cases of wellbeing-oriented tourism and the park's management is never directly involved.

Today many Italian parks have invested in health education activities, especially designed for schoolchildren, and prevention programmes and in some cases they offer services and infrastructure for disabled visitors. For example, Sila National Park has invested in limiting architectural barriers with initiatives such as providing Braille signs in its visitor centres, trails for the disabled and a promotional video of the park in deaf sign language. However, there are not many cases of well-organised and structured offers targeted at segments of health tourists. More frequent is the offer of autonomous tourism products oriented to wellness that improve their image thanks to their location inside protected natural areas.

Therefore, the case of Trentino seems to be an exception in Italian parks overall, in which the role of natural protected areas as instruments for the treatment and prevention of physical and mental illnesses is as yet underestimated.

Case study: Trentino: a green wellness tourist destination in Italy

Trentino is the area surrounding Trento province, an important mountain tourism destination in the Italian Alps. In 2014 it attracted 3.5 million tourists (41 per cent of them arriving from foreign countries) for a total of 15.4 million nights (4 per cent of the total in Italy). It is interesting to note that the average length of stay in Trentino is longer than the Italian average: 4.39 in Trentino and 3.54[3] in the whole country.

Trentino was one of the first Italian areas to create its own tourism marketing strategy and to launch a tourist brand, investing in the integration of local resources, products and services.

Its image is strongly linked with nature and biodiversity. In fact, it hosts three protected areas: Stelvio National Park and the natural parks of Adamello Brenta and Paneveggio. The destination is also famous for its ski areas and routes. A total of 800 km of tracks are gathered into two separate ski systems served by 237 lifts. The region is also rich in thermal baths and wellness centres in natural contexts of great beauty. In addition to the benefits of the thermal waters, Trentino promotes a rich variety of medicinal herbs and flowers. Today the destination has two peak seasons with a high seasonality, especially considering Italian tourist flows: the summer and winter periods (the latter focused on snow tourism). This could represent a major problem in the future, considering climate change and the risk of suffering a decrease in winter tourism.

In a research study carried out in 2012,[4] the quality of the natural environment was found to be the most important element of Trentino's tourist image for Italians. Another survey confirms this result: the natural setting is the first element considered as a value for the area by Italian and foreign tourists coming to the destination all year round (Provincia Autonoma Trento, 2014). Other values include wellness and sporting activities. In this survey the most relevant motivation for Italian and foreign visitors, during both summer and winter, turned out to be 'rest and relaxation' (winter: 48 per cent of Italians and 31 per cent of foreigners; summer: 66 per cent of Italians and 41 per cent of foreigners). The majority of visitors are loyal tourists; in fact, more than 60 per cent of foreign and 70 per cent of Italian visitors repeat their holiday experiences in Trentino. However, there is also an increasingly high percentage of newcomers (29 per cent of the total during winter and 23 per cent during summer). In a survey carried out in 2011 (Provincia Autonoma Trento, 2012), wellness treatments are one of the activities in which tourists visiting parks in the area are interested, with an increasing percentage (7 per cent).

Taking into consideration such a situation and the evolution of tourism demand, visiting Trentino tourist website (www.visittrentino.it), it seems that tourism marketing strategies have been focused on some thematic products, by means of specific positioning choices. The aim is to attract different market segments, differentiating the offer in experiential terms and creating unique proposals based on local resources and authenticity. One of the proposals is that of wellness in a natural unspoiled environment. The website offers Italian visitors (Italian pages are slightly different from non-Italian ones) ten different holiday themes: outdoor; happy family; wellness in nature; taste; biodiversity tours; thermal spas and health; culture and events; the Great War; gastronomy and wine; I love skiing. It is interesting that 'wellness in nature' offers different packages, including innovative bundles of experiences in natural settings and wellness services.

(continued)

(continued)

Product clubs have also been created. The first one, Vita Nova – Trentino Wellness, is dedicated to wellness. It was developed at the beginning of 2000 and it has also had a brand since 2009 and a consortium of about 50 hoteliers. The club groups the best wellness hotels in the area.

The idea is to develop local resources which have been forgotten or are relatively unknown by visitors, gathering them in an offer that comprises traditional local components. The names of the offers are fascinating. They include: 'flower of pine forest' (in which local natural products are used as raw materials for treatments such as apple scrubs, calendula and chamomile flower baths, massage with currants, hay baths; these are combined with meditation and wellness centres); 'pampering and wellness in the top of the mountain'; 'nature and shiatsu' (in the natural oasis of Nembia); 'nature, yoga and wellness' (including a guided tour of natural parks); 'thermal baths and nature' (which offers a night excursion in Stelvio National Park and deer and roe deer sighting in fauna centres).

This case shows us that using traditional local elements as components of a tourist package is possible in order to create an innovative, differentiated and competitive offer, also taking into account trends in demand. Such a strategy is based on the main elements of the image of the destination: nature, biodiversity, wellness and relaxation.

Conclusions

The reasons for the lack of an Italian offer of natural parks as wellness tourist destinations could be the object of future research. It is evident that today the situation is the result of an insufficient capacity to programme strategically the position of parks in the tourist market, without doubt due to their scarcely market-oriented public governance. But the source of this scarce attention to the great potential of natural protected areas in Italy is also to be found on the demand side. In fact, there is little interest, attention, awareness and knowledge of public opinion and policy makers about this subject, that is not studied and discussed in mass media.

In the future, also in Italy, where there is a limited tradition in this field in comparison with Nordic countries, natural parks could position themselves as out-and-out green health tourist destinations, attracting flows of wellness visitors but also people with health problems and patients for rehabilitation programmes. It will be possible to invest in this area by means of careful plans and partnerships with other subjects, stimulating outdoor and sports activities and addressing specific actions to younger generations, likewise giving greater weight to the function of prevention and health, nutrition and lifestyle education, in which parks are already engaged.

Thus various important results may be obtained – first of all, that of becoming a medical and wellness nature tourist destination for visitors afflicted by serious problems who would find relief and recovery in an unspoiled natural environment. These initiatives, that have a great weight in a socio-sanitary sphere, would also attract resources and investments for the conservation of habitats and biodiversity, enhancing local production, resources, culture, traditions and natural products, besides reinforcing the role of parks as instruments to improve public health in the future.

In order to achieve these aims the basic ideas of such strategies have to be shared by stakeholders, policy makers and public opinion; indicators of places' health levels are needed, together with specific investments in services and infrastructure. Finally, marketing strategies have to be focused on the promotion of this new image and role of the protected areas, identifying specific market segments and specialising the offer of protected natural areas in the larger segment of wellness and health tourism.

The conclusion is that the enhancement of this innovative role of Italian parks requires a great effort in the areas of research, communication and testing of new management models, together with experiences of public–private governance, which today are still in an embryonic stage.

Notes

1 Peak experiences are self-transformation experiences, episodes of inner change that can help to achieve moments of intense satisfaction, especially related to experiences called extraordinary or 'flow' (Arnould and Price, 1993; Csikszentmihalyi, 1990).
2 Agoraphilia is a form of tourism based on gazing at wilderness (Huijbens, 2010).
3 Source: ISTAT and Trentino APT, Year 2014.
4 In 2012 the School of Tourism Management commissioned Sociometric, a market research firm, to undertake a survey on Trentino's image.

References

Arnould, E. and Price, L. (1993) 'River magic: Extraordinary experience and the extended service encounter', *Journal of Consumer Research*, 20(1), 24–45.
Benfield, J.A., Taff, B.D., Newman, P. and Smyth, J. (2014) 'Natural sound facilitates mood recovery', *Ecopsychology*, 6(3), 183–188.
Blamey, R. K. (1995) 'The nature of ecotourism', *Occasional Paper*, 21, Canberra, Australia: Bureau of Tourism Research.
Cater, C., Garrod, B. and Low, F. (2016) *Encyclopedia of Sustainable Tourism*, Wallingford, UK: CABI.
Cohen, M. and Bodeker, G. (eds) (2008) *Understanding the Global Spa Industry. Spa Management*, Oxford, UK: Butterworth-Heinemann.
Connell, J. (2006) 'Medical tourism: Sea, sun, sand and . . . surgery', *Tourism Management*, 27, 1093–1100.
Csikszentmihalyi, M. (1990) *Flow: The Psychology of Optimal Experience*, New York: Harper and Row.
De Oliveira, E.S., Aspinall, P., Briggs, A., Cummins, S., Leyland, A.H., Mitchell, R., Roe, J. and Thompson, C.W. (2013) 'Scotland's woodland improvement programme – "Woods In and Around Towns" (WIAT) – at improving psychological well-being in deprived urban communities? A quasi-experimental study', *BMJ Open*, 8(3), 3:e003648.
Europarc – España (2013) *Salud y áreas protegidas en España. Identificación de los beneficios de las áreas protegidas sobre la salud y el bienestar social*, Madrid, Spain: Europarc – España.
Ferrari, S. (2006) *Modelli gestionali per il turismo come esperienza. Emozioni e polisensorialità nel marketing delle imprese turistiche*, Padua, Italy: Cedam.
Ferrari, S. and Pratesi, C.A. (2012) 'National parks in Italy: Sustainable tourism marketing strategies', *Finnish Journal of Tourism Research*, 8(1), 7–25.
Ferrari, S., Puczkó, L. and Smith, M. (2014) 'Co-creating spa customer experience', in Kandampully, J. (ed.) *Customer Experience Management: Enhancing Experience and Value through Service Management*, Dubuque, USA: Kendall Hunt, pp. 187–203.
Fleuret, S. and Atkinson, S. (2007) 'Wellbeing, health and geography: A critical review and research agenda', *New Zealand Geographer*, 63, 106–1118.
Fredman, P. and Tyrvainen, L. (eds) (2011) *Frontiers in Nature-based Tourism*, Abingdon, UK: Routledge.
Frost, W. and Hall, C.M. (2010) 'National parks, national identity and tourism', in *Tourism and National Parks*, Abingdon, UK: Routledge, pp. 63–78.
Fuller, R.A., Irvine, K.N., Devine-Wright, P., Warren, Ph. and Gaston, K.J. (2007) 'Psychological benefits of greenspace increase with biodiversity', *Biology Letters*, 3, 390–394.
Garcia-Altes, M. (2005) 'The development of health tourism services', *Annals of Tourism Research*, 33(1), 262–266.
Gesler, W.M. (1993) 'Therapeutic landscapes: Theory and a case study of Epidauros, Greece', *Environment and Planning D: Society and Space*, 11(2), 171–189.

Godbey, G. (2009) *Outdoor Recreation, Health and Wellness. Understanding and Enhancing the Relationship*, Discussion Paper, May, Washington, DC: Resource for the Future, pp. 9–21.

Hall, C.M. (2011) 'Health and medical tourism: A kill or cure for global public health?', *Tourism Review*, 66(1/2), 4–15.

Hartig, T., Evans, G., Jamner, L.D., Davis, D.S. and Garling, T. (2003) 'Tracking restoration in natural and urban field settings', *Journal of Environmental Psychology*, 23(2), 109–123.

Haukeland, J.V., Grue, B. and Veisten, K. (2011) 'Turning national parks into tourist attractions: Nature orientation and quest for facilities', in Fredman, P. and Tyrvainen, L. (eds) *Frontiers in Nature-based Tourism*, Abingdon, UK: Routledge, pp. 76–99.

Huijbens, E.H. (2010) *Iceland Country Report. The Myvatn Region as a Possible Nordic Wellbeing Destination*, Borgum v/ Norðursló: Iceland Tourism Research Center.

—— (2014) 'Natural wellness. The case of Icelandic wilderness landscapes for health and wellness tourism', in Smith, M. and Puczkó, L. (eds) *Health, Tourism and Hospitality. Spas, Wellness and Medical Travel*, 2nd edition, Abindgon, UK: Routledge, pp. 413–416.

Kaplan, S. (1995) 'The restorative benefits of nature: Toward an integrative framework', *Journal of Environmental Psychology*, 15, 169–182.

Kaplan, R. and Kaplan, S. (1989) *The Experience of Nature*, Cambridge, UK: Cambridge University Press.

Keller, S.R. and Wilson, E.O. (1993) *The Biophilia Hypothesis*, Washington, DC: Island Press.

Konu, H., Tuohino, A. and Bjork, P. (2014) 'Well-being tourism in Finland', in Smith, M. and Puczkó, L. (eds) *Health, Tourism and Hospitality. Spas, Wellness and Medical Travel*, 2nd edition, Abingdon, UK: Routledge, pp. 345–349.

Leiper, N. (1990) 'Tourist attraction systems', *Annals of Tourism Research*, 17(3), 367–384.

Lemieux, C.J., Eagles, P.F.J., Slocombe, D.S., Doherty, S.T., Elliot, S.J. and Mock, S.E. (2012) 'Human health and well-being motivations and benefits associated with protected area experiences: An opportunity for transforming policy and management in Canada', *Parks*, 18(1), 71–84.

Lockwood, M., Worboys, G.L. and Kothary, A. (2006) *Managing Protected Areas: A Global Guide*, London: IUCN, Earthscan.

Louv, R. (2008) *The Last Child in the Woods. Saving Our Children from Nature-Deficit Disorder*, Chapel Hill, NC: Algonquin Books.

Lumsdon, H. and McGrath, G. (2011) 'Developing a conceptual framework for slow travel: A grounded theory approach', *Journal of Sustainable Tourism*, 19(3), 265–279.

MacCannell, D. (1976) *The Tourist Gaze: A New Theory of the Leisure Class*, New York: Schocken Books.

Maller, C., Townsend, M., Pryor A., Brown, P. and St Leger, L. (2005) 'Healthy nature, healthy people: "Contact with nature" as an upstream health promotion intervention for populations', *Health Promotion International*, 21(1): doi:10.1093/heapro/dai032.

Maslow, A.H. (1976) *Religions, Values and Peak-Experiences*, New York: Penguin Compass.

Mehrabian, A. and Russell, J.A. (1974) *An Approach to Environmental Psychology*, Cambridge, MA: MIT Press.

Meyer-Arendt, K. (2004) 'Tourism and the natural environment', in Lew, A.A., Hall, C.M. and Williams, A.M. (eds) *A Companion to Tourism*, Victoria, Australia: Blackwell Publishing, pp. 425–437.

Milligan, C. and Wiles, J. (2010) 'Landscapes of care', *Progress in Human Geography*, 34(6), 736–754.

Moyle, B.D., Weiler, B. and Moore, S.A. (2014) 'Benefits that matter to managers: An exploratory study of three national park management agencies', *Managing Leisure*, 19(6), 400–419.

Mueller, H. and Kaufmann, E.L. (2001) 'Wellness tourism: Market analysis of a special health tourism segment and implications for the hotel industry', *Journal of Vacation Marketing*, 7(1), 5–17.

Nordic Council of Ministers (2005) *National Parks, Outdoor Life and Health*, Nordic Conference, Freynes, Iceland, 5–7 May.

Olmsted, F.L. (1865) *The Value and Care of Parks. Report to the Congress of the State of California*. [Reprinted in Nash, R. (ed.) (1976) *The American Environment*, Reading, MA: Addison-Wesley, pp. 18–24.]

Osservatorio Permanente sul Turismo Natura (2007) *5° Rapporto Ecotur sul Turismo Natura*, Milan, Italy: Il Sole 24 Ore.

Provincia Autonoma Trento (2012) *Turisti nei parchi del Trentino*, Trento, Italy: Provincia Autonoma Trento.

—— (2014) *Turismo in Trentino. Rapporto 2014*, Trento, Italy: Provincia Autonoma Trento.

Reese, R.F. and Myers, J.E. (2012) 'EcoWellness: The missing factor in holistic wellness models', *Journal of Counselling and Development*, 90, 400–406.

Romagosa, F., Eagles, P.F.J. and Lemieux, C.J. (2015) 'From the inside out to the outside in: Exploring the role of parks and protected areas as providers of human health and well-being', *Journal of Outdoor Recreation and Tourism*, 10, 70–77.

Roszak, T. (1992) *The Voice of the Hearth: An Exploration of Ecopsychology*, Grand Rapids, MI: Phanes Press.

Ruspini, E. (2010) 'Salute e bellezza "tutto compreso". Domanda e offerta di turismo medico-estetico', in Marra, E. and Ruspini, E. (eds) *Altri turismi. Viaggi, esperienze, emozioni*. Milan, Italy: Franco Angeli, pp. 149–163.

Smith, M. and Puczkó, L. (2009) *Health and Wellness Tourism*, Oxford, UK: Butterworth-Heinemann.

—— (2014) *Health, Tourism and Hospitality. Spas, Wellness and Medical Travel*, 2nd edition, Abingdon, UK: Routledge.

Thomsen, J.M., Powell, E.B. and Allen D. (2013) 'Designing parks for human health and development', *Park Science*, 3(2), 30–36.

Ulrich, R.S. (1991) 'Effects of interior design on wellness: Theory and recent scientific research', *Journal of Healthcare Interior Design*, 97–109.

Ulrich, R.S., Simons, R.T., Losito, B.D., Fiorito, E., Miles, M.A. and Zelson, M. (1991) 'Stress recovery during exposure to natural and urban environments', *Journal of Environmental Psychology*, 11, 201–230.

United Nations World Tourism Organization (2008) *International Recommendations for Tourism Statistics 2008*, retrieved 18 August 2011, from statistics.unwto.org.

Voigt, C. and Pforr, C. (2013) *Wellness Tourism. A Destination Perspective*, Abingdon, UK: Routledge.

Voigt, C., Brown, G. and Howat, G. (2011) 'Wellness tourism: In search of transformation', *Tourism Review*, 66(1/2), 16–30.

Wall Reinius, S. and Fredman, P. (2007) 'Protected areas as tourism attractions', *Annals of Tourism Research*, 34(4), 839–854.

World Health Organization (2005) *Ecosystems and Human Well-being: Health Synthesis. A Report of the Millennium Ecosystem Assessment*, Geneva, Switzerland: World Health Organization.

WWF and Equilibrium Research (2010) *Vital Sites. The Contribution of Protected Areas to Human Health*, Gland, Switzerland: WWF.

33

Understanding the links between wellness and Indigenous tourism in western Canada

Critical sites of cultural exchange

John S. Hull and Courtney W. Mason

Introduction

This chapter offers an overview of how wellness and Indigenous tourism are related in western Canadian contexts. By examining the historical foundations and contemporary linkages between the industries, this chapter centres on why these two distinct economies have been developed in tandem. At the beginning of the twentieth century, tourism capital and expanding markets facilitated the reimagining of the Canadian Rockies as a 'natural' environment with particular appeal to affluent tourists with a desire to escape urban centres and to pursue the health benefits of spending time in the mountains. The tourism economies of the period jointly marketed wellness and health tourism with Indigenous cultural tourism. Banff, Alberta has a storied history of both wellness and Indigenous tourism. These tourism industries relied on a selective inclusion of local Indigenous peoples (Nakoda, Cree, Ktunaxa, Blackfoot and Secwepemc) even while they were increasingly refused access to the protected areas that were appropriated in the formation of Banff National Park.[1]

Primarily since the 1960s, Indigenous communities in western Canada have been heavily investing in tourism sectors as a strategy for sustainable economic development. This chapter also introduces a contemporary case study of the Quaaout Lodge and Spa, located in the British Columbia (BC) interior. The Secwepemc-owned spa promotes health and wellness as well as Indigenous cultural tourism. The main objective of this chapter is to explore the historical and contemporary connections between Indigenous tourism and health/wellness tourism to understand its significance to broader tourism industries and Indigenous communities. We rely on analyses of archival documents and literature, personal interviews with staff members at Quaaout Lodge and Spa and tourism promotional materials from websites for primary data. Our findings suggest that combining wellness and cultural tourism have been productive ventures for Indigenous communities with notable economic and cultural opportunities as this sector continues to see growth in western Canada.

In order to gain an understanding of the origins of health and wellness and Indigenous visitor experiences in the Canadian Rockies, the following literature review is divided into three sections: (1) early tourism economies in Canada's west; (2) the development of health and wellness industries in Banff; and (3) the relations between health, wellness and Indigenous tourism.

Early tourism economies in the Canadian Rockies

Increasing significantly with the package travel business in the 1860s and the creation of the British travel firm Thomas Cook, western elites toured mountain ranges like the European Alps and later more 'exotic' destinations such as the Canadian Rockies. The touring of these environments emerged as these landscapes began to offer recreational and relaxation experiences for elite tourists. Urban-elite conceptions of these environments also arrived with the affluent tourists and the flow of economic capital that facilitated the development of the tourism industry. Although it was established two decades after Thomas Cook, the Canadian Pacific Railway (CPR) became one of the world's largest travel companies by the turn of the twentieth century.[2]

The 1887 formation of Rocky Mountains Park (RMP), the precursor to Banff, was the beginning of tourism infrastructure development in the Canadian Rocky Mountains. As a joint venture between the Canadian federal government and the CPR, the national park was the first of its kind in Canada and was originally established as a means of generating railway tourism with few conservation or preservation objectives considered. As was the case for much of Canada's early history and especially in the development of the west, public and private interests were strongly linked in the formation and development of RMP (Hart, 1983). The construction of the national railway and the building of a new nation brought about severe financial challenges. Through the creation of the park, the federal government and private corporations sought to develop the tourism industry to recover some of the mounting costs of completing the east–west railway that linked central Canada to the emergent west (Nicol, 1970).[3] As William Cornelius Van Horne, the president of the CPR, stated in 1888: 'If we cannot export the scenery, we will import the tourists' (Hart, 1999: 114). The park solidified a symbiotic relationship between the CPR and the federal government that would prosper throughout much of the twentieth century. This protected area became a convenient way to establish a monopoly on transportation access to the region, which effectively controlled development. The establishment of the national park designated governmental control of natural resource management and the leasing of property.

The majority of evidence suggests that even though the federal government did claim that they were securing land to be 'set apart as a public park and pleasure ground for the benefit, advantage and enjoyment of the people of Canada',[4] they were initially motivated by natural resource and tourism development opportunities. It is indicative that the legislation actually endorsed the growth of the tourism industry and permitted, under government direction, the development of mining sites, timber interests and grazing lands. Park leadership also reflected the government's development intentions. In his annual report, the commissioner of Dominion Parks, J.B. Harkin, stated that 'Nothing attracts tourists like National Parks. National Parks provide the chief means of bringing to Canada a stream of tourists and a stream of tourist gold' (Marty, 1984: 98). In reviewing early government policy and practice it is clear that tourism and natural resource development were the primary rationale in the formation of RMP.

Tourism at Banff townsite began as a spa, wellness and health tourism destination for elite guests of considerable financial standing. The luxurious facilities built by the CPR, like the Banff Springs Hotel, completed in 1888, were designed to meet the needs of its affluent clientele and were some of the continent's most opulent accommodations during the period. As Canada's first Prime Minister, Sir John A. MacDonald, stated during the development of the townsite, 'the doubtful classes of people will probably not find an overly gracious welcome at Banff' (Brown, 1970: 46). The MacDonald administration advocated developing the townsite in the style of an elite European health resort community and only leasing the land to affluent individuals who could afford to erect buildings that would complement the local environment and reflect the government's vision of the townsite. While the initial promotional campaigns of the park concentrated on the wealthy clientele that had the leisure time to undertake such an extended sojourn and the capital to facilitate it, tourism producers soon expanded the tourism market.

Access to Banff townsite and RMP was rapidly increasing with the 1914 creation of the Calgary–Banff coach road and the proliferation of the automobile. After the road was completed, the CPR monopoly on transportation access to the region ended and individual entrepreneurs began to expand the tourism market by providing cheaper accommodation and alternative forms of recreation. While access to the region was opening up, this did not signify the end of the CPR's dominant influence in Banff, as the company developed strategies to capitalise on new forms of automobile tourism (Bella, 1987). Facilitated by transportation infrastructure and marketing campaigns, the attraction of middle-class tourists to Banff and the consequent expansion of accommodation and recreation opportunities to meet these visitors' needs led to a distinct shift in the orientation of the townsite. Although initially established as an elite wellness or health tourism destination, with the introduction of the automobile, it was transformed into a place that also catered to middle-class tourists with an infrastructure that would accommodate the mass tourism of the coming decades (Mason, 2014).

The development of health and wellness tourism industries in Banff

In response to international travel trends of the late nineteenth century, 'natural' environments were positioned as prime tourist destinations throughout the Western world. Seizing upon the growth of interest in especially foreign travel to regions conceptualised as 'natural', competing travel firms promoted the health benefits of visiting these locations. The tourists who travelled to places like the Canadian Rocky Mountains were partly in pursuit of a healthy lifestyle. This is reflected in the tourism advertising campaigns that emphasise the health benefits of being surrounded by Banff's pristine mountain air and glacier-fed rivers (Williams, 1922). The healing and curative potential of visiting the hot springs was particularly promoted in marketing campaigns. In the 1880s, the CPR employed Dr Robert G. Brett to help establish and promote the healing values of the waters of the hot springs (Hart, 1999). The health and wellness benefits of the region made Banff an attractive place to visit for tourists of the period. Banff was sold as a location that provided not only curative properties, but also an escape from urban life. In this regard, tourism campaigns endorsed the properties of health and wellness in the region.

Despite the efforts of the CPR and government to sell Banff as a health destination, the rejuvenating value of mountains and rivers for the ills of industrial capitalism were as much a product of prevailing discourse as was the 'naturalness' of the environments themselves. At the turn of the twentieth century, tourism materials suggest that Banff was advertised as a place that offered urban tourists an escape from the complexities of modernity as well as leisure opportunities that would rejuvenate the mind, body and soul (Williams, 1922); however, this escape had to be carefully constructed by the producers. Motivated by capitalist objectives that facilitated the (re)imagining of the region to align with mass tourism markets, the federal government, the CPR and local tourism entrepreneurs produced holiday experiences that sold Banff as an outdoor recreation paradise that had various health or wellness benefits while intentionally hiding the evidence of productive sites of labour and subsistence land use practices. This often meant concealing the presence and history of the resource extraction industry, some technology such as hydro-electric power infrastructure and local Indigenous and non-Indigenous communities, as well as the work that sustained them, including mining, railway construction, hunting, trapping, gathering and fishing (Mason, 2008).

With the creation of the park, access to the region for local Nakoda peoples was greatly reduced as their subsistence land uses were redefined as intolerable or illegal. As a consequence, Nakoda communities were actively excluded from the park because their hunting, fishing and gathering practices did not align with tourism entrepreneurs' expectations and subsequent marketing of the region. However, pre-colonial representations of Indigenous peoples were frequently utilised in tourism marketing campaigns to promote Banff townsite and the park (Mason, 2012). These representations were critical as Indigenous peoples were imagined by many tourists to be embedded within the 'natural' environment and as a result a significant component of tourists' experiences.

For the urban elite tourists who arrived from Europe and North America, conceptions of Indigenous peoples were heavily influenced by their exposure to Wild West literature, live performances and film (Kasson, 2000). At the beginning of the nineteenth century, this imagery captured significant portions of popular culture markets. The Wild West genre re-enacted colonial narratives and celebrated pre-colonial representations of Indigenous cultures (Deloria, 2004). Exemplified by the mass appeal of Buffalo Bill Cody's Wild West live theatre in the USA and Western Europe in the 1870s (Moses, 1996) and the incredible success of Karl Friedrich May's Wild West-themed novels in Germany in the 1890s (Bugmann, 2008), these pre-colonial representations were highly visible in Western culture prior to the turn of the twentieth century. Later, Wild West films, which were widespread by 1910, solidified the entrance of the Wild West genre into mainstream popular culture in both Europe and North America. The conceptions of Indigenous peoples that the Wild West genres helped manufacture greatly influenced the urban elite that travelled throughout western Canada during this period. The tourists who visited Banff during this period arrived with specific expectations of Indigenous peoples.

The relations between health, wellness and Indigenous tourism in Canada's West

As noted above, as a consequence of the mass interest in Indigenous cultural tourism during this period, the park heavily marketed Banff as a location that could offer both forms of health/ wellness and Indigenous cultural tourism (Mason, 2008). However, even though official park policy in the USA and Canada attempted increasingly to restrict Indigenous use of park lands during this period (Keller and Turek, 1999; Binnema and Niemi, 2006), certain types of representations of Indigenous peoples were highly valued by tourism producers in Banff because they helped meet tourists' expectations. The developing tourism industries would not only encourage the use of representations of Indigenous peoples in the marketing of the region, but also their employment in expanding tourism industries.

The primary example of mass tourism participation of Indigenous peoples in Banff's tourism economies is the Banff Indian Days tourism festivals, which ran annually from 1894 to 1978. The festivals mainly consisted of all-Indigenous rodeo and sporting competitions and Indigenous musical and cultural performances (Meijer-Drees, 1993). Over the many decades the festivals were celebrated, the Indian Days became one of the most influential tourism events in the history of the Banff-Bow Valley. The festivals originally involved only local Nakoda peoples, but by the 1920s, several other Indigenous groups, including Secwepemc (Shuswap)

Cree, Ktunaxa (Kootenay), Tsuu T'ina (Sarcee), Pikunni (Peigan), Siksika (Blackfoot) and Kainai (Blood) also participated as guests of the Nakoda (Snow, 2005). Some years there were over 1,000 Indigenous participants, with a record high of 1,200 in 1959. At some festivals, all American states and Canadian provinces were represented in the audiences and over 30 nationalities were noted in attendance (Mason, 2015). At its peak, the Indian Days were attracting over 70,000 tourists to the region, which facilitated substantial growth of the local tourism economy. Along with considerable economic impacts, the Indian Days were influential events that shaped regional, national and international perceptions of Indigenous peoples and the Banff-Bow Valley (Mason, 2014).

At the turn of the twentieth century, very few Indigenous peoples lived in Banff townsite as they were effectively displaced in the formation of the national park. Moreover, as there were few spaces during this period which afforded extensive interaction between local Indigenous peoples, urban Canadians and international tourists, the Indian Days became an essential space for the exchange of intercultural knowledge (Snow, 2005). The festivals had an incredible appeal to audiences, as they were the region's most successful tourist draw throughout the first half of the twentieth century. To examine comprehensively the impact of the festivals within a broader historical context, one must understand how they provided atypical socio-economic, political and cultural opportunities for participating Indigenous communities. Important aspects of these opportunities included financial gain, establishing critical spaces of interaction and reasserting links to significant cultural sites. Some scholars have identified that Indigenous participants were at times exploited through the festivals and tourism entrepreneurs also tried to control some of the representations of Indigenous participants (Parker, 1990; Meijer-Drees, 1993). Despite these negative impacts on Indigenous participants, due to their resilience and continued efforts to assert their cultural representations in ways that they saw fit, the tourism industry and the festivals themselves became a dynamic space for cultural exchange. Through the Indian Days, local Indigenous peoples also regained access to the region and responded to the colonial structures that at times were designed to repress and assimilate their cultures (Mason, 2015). While this literature review has served to document the links between health and wellness tourism and Indigenous tourism and representations of Indigenous peoples during the early stages of tourism development in Canada's West, the next section outlines the methods used to investigate these links in a contemporary context through a case study of the Secwepemc First Nation's Quaaout Lodge and Spa.

Methodology

This research adopts a case study approach using mixed methods. Case studies provide flexibility when using multiple data collection methods (Veal, 2006; Singh et al., 2012). They also provide a social and historical context for understanding peoples, events, experiences and organisations. In the first phase of data collection, a review of secondary literature and in-depth interviews with key informants at Quaaout Lodge and Spa in 2013 helped identify a number of focal themes and content categories linking Indigenous tourism and health/ wellness tourism to provide a context for analysing the websites. Four 40-minute interviews were conducted in 2013 at the Quaaout Lodge and Spa in October with the lodge manager, the spa manager, the cultural programme manager and one of the cultural guides who led the Salmon Run Canoe Excursion. These results have served to gain a better understanding of the contemporary case study and the linkages between Indigenous and health/wellness tourism at the Quaaout Lodge and Spa in comparison to earlier Indigenous and health/wellness tourism development in the late nineteenth and early twentieth centuries.

The second phase of the research involved a content analysis of two key tourism websites (Quaaout Lodge and Spa, Aboriginal Tourism BC) that are promoting the Quaaout Lodge and Spa. Content analysis is defined as an observational research method used to make valid inferences from the actual and symbolic content of all forms of recorded communication in a systematic and replicable manner (Hall and Valentin, 2005; Bryman, 2012). This phase of the research focused on investigating the actual representation of images and texts used by the websites from the region. The analysis reflects the interpretations of the researchers coding images to identify specific patterns and frequency of specific images and subjects as well as key focal themes from phase one supported in the website texts. Themes were identified in phase one of the research. The categories were then used to assist with interpreting how Indigenous tourism and health/wellness tourism is being represented and conveyed to potential customers on two promotional websites.

Tourism websites present images of places, cultures and ethnicities that reflect the desires and interests of the cultures in which they are created. They also contribute to shaping tourists' experiences of people and place (Rakić and Chambers, 2011). There have been numerous studies by tourism researchers applying the use of content analysis of website images and textual analysis in a cultural context (Albers and James, 1988; Echtner and Prasad, 2003; Caton and Santos, 2008). The next section provides a summary of the secondary literature review of the case study and interviews, followed by the results of the content analysis.

Case study: Secwepemc Peoples: Quaaout Lodge and Spa

The Secwepemc are the Indigenous peoples who inhabit the south central interior of BC (Figure 33.1). Representing a nation of 17 bands, their territory extends from the Columbia River Valley on the eastern slopes of the Rocky Mountains to the Fraser River on the west and from the upper Fraser River in the north to the Arrow Lakes in the south. The region is approximately 180,000 square kilometres. The ancestors of the Secwepemc people have lived in the interior of BC for at least 10,000 years. They were semi-nomadic and their lifestyles were based on fishing, hunting and gathering. They travelled great distances to secure food and other technological needs. The various landscapes they used provided everything the Secwepemc needed to survive and flourish. With intimate knowledge of their environments, the Secwepemc based their subsistence economy on a balance of resource use and management of regional ecosystems. The Secwepemc maintained a vast storehouse of ecological and cultural knowledge gathered from years of experience and observations on the land (Manuel and Posluns, 1974).

At the time of contact with the first Europeans in the late eighteenth century, the Secwepemc occupied a significant territory. The nation was a political alliance that managed land and resource use as well as ensured protection of their territories. Although the bands were independent, similar cultures, belief systems and a common language united them (Manuel and Posluns, 1974). Their territory was an extensive and varied environment, even though it has been greatly changed by forestry, mining, mass-scale tourism and other commercial developments throughout the twentieth century (Furniss, 1995). Since colonisation, most of the old growth forests of Secwepemc territory have been destroyed by the transnational logging industry. Railway and highway construction in Secwepemc territory has drastically altered their lands and ecosystems (Palmer, 2005). Another threat to Secwepemc territory is the destructive impact of mass tourism. The province's development stance in the twenty-first century is to support numerous expansions

(continued)

(continued)

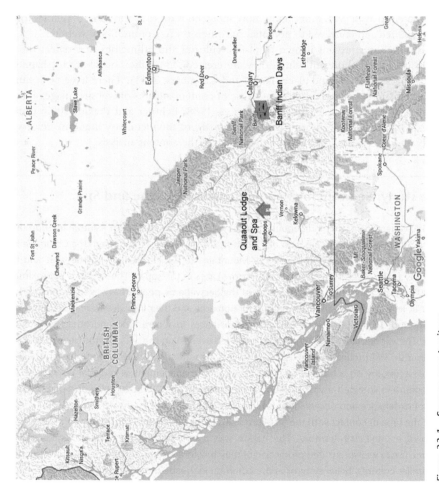

Figure 33.1 Secwepemc territory.

of recreation resorts as part of the 2003 Heartlands Economic Strategy aimed at investing $2–3 billion (CDN) over ten years to promote resort development in the mountainous BC interior (Nepal and Jamal, 2011).[5] Ski and golf resort development in the eastern part of Secwepemc territory in the communities of Revelstoke and Golden, BC, have led to rapid growth over the last decade. Resorts in BC profit greatly from the government's selling or leasing of Crown land, which is often contested Secwepemc land.

As a result of the new economic development strategies, Secwepemc communities have begun to assert control over their lands and resources. Part of this process has been to participate in various provincial and regional development plans to foster Indigenous ownership and operation of local businesses and increase employment opportunities for their peoples. In 1989, the Little Shuswap Indian Band's Chief, Felix Arnouse, working with band councillors and band members, decided to retire a substantial number of leases on Little Shuswap Lake as part of a vision to develop a world-class, four-star destination lodge, conference centre and golf course and wellness centre (Cooperman, 2015). The lodge design is inspired by the traditional round pit house and includes massive log beams; animal carvings and rock pictographs are etched into walkways and outdoor patios on the ground-floor rooms (Monforton, 2013). The lodge was named Quaaout Lodge, meaning where the sun's rays first touch the water. It is located on the banks of the Little Shuswap Lake (Cooperman, 2015).

In 2013, the Lodge Manager of the Quaaout Lodge and Spa spoke of the importance of their membership in Aboriginal Tourism BC, the Thompson Okanagan Tourism Association and the Shuswap Tourism Development Plan as a means of promoting and marketing Indigenous people's stories, to provide visitors with learning opportunities about their culture and heritage, to include authentic experiences in packaging and to facilitate emotional connections that visitors seek. In addition to the conference centre and golf course, the lodge manager mentioned the lodge's Le7ke spa (pronounced Lah-(pause)-kah). Le7ke means: I am well. The spa manager described the facility as providing treatment rooms named after local animals and having a mandate to provide holistic wellness programmes for visitors that offer a full range of modern treatments, including massage, facials, body wraps, manicures/pedicures, a Vichy shower and hydrotherapy treatments in addition to Indigenous healing practices. They have also created a product line of natural anti-ageing lotions, health-based wellness packages and weekend holistic retreats. Treatments are linked to healthy eating and nutrition, hormone balancing, detox, weight loss, anti-ageing and fitness. The spa manager also spoke of the importance of providing a sense of wellbeing for both guests and residents by infusing Indigenous healing with plants, hot stones and water with today's spa modalities. A traditional sweat lodge[6] located on the shores of Little Shuswap Lake provides one authentic experience available by invitation only.

There is also a cultural education element on the property with a replica pithouse, sweat lodge and smoke house where Secwepemc guides provide cultural programming for interested guests throughout the year (Scott, 2012). The cultural programme manager mentioned the importance of cultural walks, storytelling in the *kekuli* and at the campfire, as well as guided canoe trips.[7] The cultural guide for the Salute to the Salmon Run Celebration explained the Secwepemc people have been celebrating the salmon run for years. As one of the elders on the trip explained, 'we know the creator still loves us, because we're getting the salmon back' (Allford, 2014). In 2014 over 250,000 people came to the Adams River to witness the famous salmon run (Allford, 2014).

In 2010 the lodge underwent a $2 million renovation to bring the standards of the rooms and amenities up to par with the golf experience (Scott, 2012; Monforton, 2013). The lodge is known

(continued)

(continued)

for its spectacular waterfront setting, award-winning golf course, 70 comfortable rooms with balconies, spa/wellness centre, relaxed and spiritual atmosphere and sophisticated dining experience as well as for showcasing a display of Indigenous art, culture and history. Forty per cent of the workforce is Indigenous (Scott, 2012).

The province of BC is known for its spectacular natural environment and diverse Indigenous heritage (Williams and O'Neill, 2007). Aboriginal Tourism BC reported in 2013 that this tourism sector in the province earned $45 million, up from $20 million in 2012 (Dyck, 2014). The key development strategies from 2012 to 2017 are to: push for market readiness; build and strengthen partnerships; focus on online marketing, emerging markets and authenticity and quality assurance; as well as to adopt a regional approach through an investment of $10 million over the five-year strategy (ATBC, 2012).

In summarising the focal themes of the secondary literature review and informant interviews linking Indigenous tourism and health/wellness tourism, it is evident that Quaaout Lodge is helping to promote the growth of Indigenous ownership and strategic planning aimed at expanding both Indigenous and health/wellness tourism facilities in the province and across Canada. Partnerships with provincial and regional tourism agencies also illustrate the efforts of Quaaout Lodge to improve competitiveness and online marketing. The construction of Quaaout Lodge speaks to the importance of integrating Indigenous design into physical infrastructure and resort development. The host/guest relations identify the importance of offering Indigenous and health/wellness programmes for domestic and international markets. The wellness programmes, retreats and products for sale at the Le7ke spa indicate the importance of the fusion of Indigenous traditions such as healing through the use of plant-based lotions, hot stones and water treatment along with modern spa modalities such as massage and exfoliation. The wellness offerings at the lodge also provide holistic health products and services that focus on both mental and physical health. Finally, cultural programming and storytelling are integral aspects of the Indigenous tourism offering that is bridging Indigenous heritage with health/wellness.

Box 33.1   Focal themes linking Indigenous and health/wellness tourism

---

Indigenous ownership
Partnerships
Indigenous design
Host/guest relations
Fusion
Holistic health products and services
Cultural programming/storytelling

Web audit of Quaaout Lodge using content analysis

This next section will now explore the themes linking Indigenous tourism and health/wellness tourism through a content analysis of the Quaaout Lodge and Spa and the Aboriginal Tourism BC websites.

Indigenous ownership

In evaluating evidence of ownership on the two sites, the Quaaout Lodge and Spa website states that it is owned and operated by the Little Shuswap Indian Band, providing the following statement on its home page:

> The Quaaout Lodge and Spa at Talking Rock Golf Course with Jack Sam's Restaurant, the pride of the Little Shuswap Indian Band, is situated on the north shore of Little Shuswap Lake.

The Aboriginal Tourism BC (ATBC) homepage features a statement about the Association at the bottom of the page.

> The Aboriginal Tourism Association of British Columbia is a non-profit, membership-based organization that is committed to growing and promoting a sustainable, culturally rich Aboriginal tourism industry.

There is no specific mention of health and wellness services as part of the ownership statements. Emphasis is placed generally on organisational structure, vision, culture, recreational activities, cuisine and geographic location. However, Quaaout Lodge does use the word 'Spa' on the homepage of its website: Quaaout Lodge and Spa at Talking Rock Resort.

Partnerships

When evaluating evidence of partnerships on the two websites, on the Quaaout Lodge and Spa home page, the following links are provided: to the Green Key Eco-rating programme featuring its three-key rating; to TripAdvisor, the world's largest travel planning and booking site; to six social media platforms, including Facebook, Twitter, Google+, Share, Pinterest and Linkedin; and to various corporate sponsors through online advertisements. The lodge also links to 23 regional partners that include 17 local suppliers and six tourism/business associations from the region, including the home page of the Little Shuswap Lake Indian Band. Of these suppliers there are three health/wellness links for massage therapy, a naturopathic clinic and the Spas of America.

In contrast, the ATBC website includes a direct link to the Quaaout Lodge and Spa website as well as to six social media platforms – Facebook, Twitter, YouTube, Google+, Instagram and Pinterest – reflecting its mandate to promote and grow the Indigenous tourism industry in the province. Linkages to Indigenous health/wellness tourism providers are included as part of the Resorts and Spa menu that features six Indigenous businesses and the Traditional Lodgings and Sweat Lodges menu that features five Indigenous businesses.

Both websites demonstrate linkages to local suppliers, tourism and business associations, corporate sponsors and social media platforms that reflect a focus on cooperative marketing and working with private businesses and local Indigenous and community organisations. Health and wellness is an important product offering, with both websites integrating this sector across various menus (i.e. Resorts and Spa, Restaurant) on their websites that reflect traditional (i.e. sweat lodge) and modern (i.e. spa, nutrition) modalities.

Indigenous design

In reviewing the Quaaout Lodge and Spa website for evidence of Indigenous design in physical infrastructure at the resort, 10 per cent of the images on the website ($n = 12$) feature Indigenous designs. The majority of these photographic images are of pictographs, Secwepemc traditional means of communication, which are used as a design element.

Aboriginal motifs are found all around the property, like the animal carvings beneath the eaves of the lodge's periphery and on the treatment room doors in the Le7ke Spa on the premises. Red pictographs are etched into the walkways and outdoor patios on the ground-floor rooms (Monforton, 2013).

These designs are also used in the restaurant on the menus that feature authentic Indigenous gourmet meals, as well as on the promotional materials highlighting the golf course, conference and banquet facilities and the spa. Indigenous designs based on physical structures such as teepees and *kekulis* located on site are also highlighted as cultural interpretive areas. The text on the website specifically mentions the use of Indigenous design elements in the construction of the Conference Centre:

> Quaaout Lodge offers a uniquely designed Conference Centre using the native kekuli (native winter house) as architectural inspiration.
>
> *(Quaaout Lodge and Spa at Talking Rock Golf Resort, 2016)*

There were no Indigenous health and wellness photographic images of facilities from Quaaout Lodge and Spa (i.e. sweat lodge) featured on their website. However, the ATBC website contains an extensive collection of 593 photographic images as part of the Things To Do Menu. This is the most extensive menu on the website and includes the following categories: arts and culture, food and wine, wildlife tours, accommodation, golf and spa and outdoor adventures.

In conducting an inventory of images that reflect Indigenous design as part of the physical infrastructure at BC resorts, 42 per cent of the images ($n = 247$) included Indigenous design elements (i.e. artistic images on buildings, totems, teepees, *kekulis*). Seven per cent of the images ($n = 40$) reflected Indigenous transport infrastructure in the form of cultural boat excursions (i.e. ocean-going canoes, canoes and kayaks). One per cent of the images ($n = 6$) feature traditional Indigenous health/wellness facilities (i.e. sweat lodges). Modern photographic images of spa/wellness facilities on the ATBC website do not integrate Indigenous design.

Both the Quaaout Lodge and Spa and the ATBC website use Indigenous design images, as reflected in physical infrastructure at resorts as a means of presenting their cultural heritage. These images reflect the diversity of Indigenous communication (i.e. pictographs), transport (i.e. canoes, kayaks), structural design (i.e. *kekuli*, teepee, sweat lodge), cuisine and heritage structures (i.e. totems) that are present across the province. Health and wellness products and services integrate Indigenous design elements through structures linked to the physical space where health and wellness activities are administered (i.e. sweat lodge) as well as in decorative design elements on products and services at the resorts (i.e. spa doors with animal symbols, restaurant menus).

Host–guest relations

The summary of hosts and guests in images from the Quaaout Lodge and Spa revealed that the highest representation was of guests engaging in an activity such as eating or golfing ($n = 22$) followed by hosts presenting an activity such as a dancing or storytelling ($n = 7$). The lowest representation was of hosts and guests 'co-producing' an activity at the resort such as a wedding ceremony ($n = 4$). On the ATBC website, the majority of results were representative of hosts and guests 'co-producing' an activity at the resort ($n = 222$), followed by guests engaging in an activity ($n = 146$) as the second most frequently represented images. Hosts demonstrating or engaging in activities was the third most frequently represented image ($n = 99$).

The issue of the 'co-production' of activities at Indigenous resorts was also an important aspect mentioned in the text on both the Quaaout Lodge and Spa and the ATBC websites, as follows:

> At Quaaout Lodge Resort our cultural coordinator will be happy to take you on a tour of the grounds or answer questions you may have about the area.
>
> *(Quaaout Lodge and Spa at Talking Rock Golf Resort, 2016)*

On the ATBC website visitors are also invited to:

> Come face to face with the fascinating stories, legends and myths of British Columbia's Aboriginal peoples through educational and unique interpretive exhibits and activities.
>
> *(ATBC, 2016)*

The results from both websites reflect the importance of guests and their direct participation in Indigenous tourism activities and experiences.

The co-production of the health and wellness experience at Quaaout Lodge and Spa is reflected in photographic images ($n = 3$) featuring modern spa modalities and wellness activities. On the ATBC website there are ten photographic images featuring traditional and modern spa modalities. Of these images, five present the co-production of a health and wellness experience through examples such as a neck and foot massage, a sweat lodge demonstration and participation in yoga and aquafit classes.

Fusion

One of the important considerations of Indigenous tourism and its links with health/wellness tourism is the evidence of fusion of Indigenous traditions with modern spa modalities. Even though both websites lacked specific photographic images of Indigenous wellness traditions and modern spa modalities visually together, the text on the websites details some of the progress that is being made to offer new integrated opportunities for visitors. The Quaaout Lodge and Spa is addressing this opportunity through its treatments rooms, therapies and skincare:

> The spa director has put a lot of thought into the calming space [of the treatment rooms]. A smooth, dark wood table shaped like a boat is used for water, colour and sound therapy, using aboriginal chants. Each treatment room is named for an animal, such as the bear – meaning strength or hummingbird, meaning beauty. Four treatment rooms are used for an array of treatments, such as scrubs, massages and facials. The spa's vibe is aboriginal-meets-European. Staff members use some Indigenous herbs, such as sage and sweet grass or cedar in various therapies. The spa also carries its own line of all-natural skincare.
>
> *(Monforton, 2013)*

On the ATBC website, resorts make specific mention of the use of Indigenous hot stone massage and its links to modern treatments:

> Our full service spa offers wellness treatments ranging from Hot Stone Massages to desert inspired body wraps to massages and aesthetics to a special gentlemen's menu.
>
> *(ATBC, 2016)*

The fusion of Indigenous tourism and health/wellness tourism integrates the local Indigenous cultural heritage and natural environment with new health/wellness therapies and treatments.

Holistic health products/services

Holistic health products/services, reflecting body, mind and spirit, are represented on both websites. The Quaaout Lodge and Spa website reinforces the importance of holistic health by referencing the visitor's wellbeing:

> Le7ke spa professionals know how to relax our clients' senses and activate your well-being.
> *(Quaaout Lodge and Spa at Talking Rock Golf Resort, 2016)*

The media has also highlighted the holistic health benefits of the Quaaout Lodge's sweat lodge:

> Nearby is the sweat lodge, which [the director] describes as "our church". It's used regularly and guests are welcome to experience its powers of cleansing mind, spirit and body.
> *(Monforton, 2013)*

Under their Spa and Resorts menu of ATBC website, they list six Indigenous-owned full-service resorts that offer a suite of holistic health products and services, including:

> first class treatment, while sharing the treasures of our traditional lands and taking you on memorable adventures, excursions and activities that explore our rich history and heritage.
> *(ATBC, 2016)*

The Solterra Desert Spa, at the Spirit Ridge Vineyard Resort and Spa in Osoyoos, offers:

> an experience of wellness to clear your mind, to relax and rejuvenate your body and release your spirit. Our treatments are designed to connect with your energy and bring you to a place of balance.
> *(ATBC, 2016)*

The Traditional Lodgings and Sweat Lodges offer visitors the opportunity to:

> Step into a sweat lodge and experience true spiritual and sacred Aboriginal culture as you commune with the past to cleanse your mind, body and spirit and become renewed through one of the oldest ceremonies handed down from time immemorial and countless generations.
> *(ATBC, 2016)*

Holistic health products and services are an important aspect of the health/wellness message at Quaaout Lodge and Spa and on the ATBC website. They provide visitors with opportunities for relaxation, cleansing, memorable adventures, rejuvenation, release and balance as part of long-standing Indigenous traditions.

Cultural programming/storytelling

Cultural programming is also an integral part of both websites. The Little Shuswap Indian Band has built a link to the Quaaout Lodge and Spa website, stating that:

> Preserving and passing on our native culture is one of the most important pillars of our band.
> *(Little Shuswap Indian Band, 2016)*

The website highlights cultural programming through photographic images and written descriptions focused on annual Band events and Indigenous cuisine. There are four photographic images and three videos of cultural programming, all linked to the annual Skwlax Pow Wow held in July. The photographic images feature Band members conducting traditional dance performances while the videos present traditional drumming at the Pow Wow. As demonstrated below, text on the website also highlights Indigenous cuisine and cultural activities:

> Guests will find delicacies on the seasonal dinner and catering menus which honour the First Nations traditions of the region such as Venison, Salmon, Bison or Elk and our traditional "Chicken or Salmon" in Clay (48hrs notice required) to name just a few.
> *(Quaaout Lodge and Spa at Talking Rock Golf Resort, 2016)*

> Cultural activities include an Aboriginal Arts Festival in April and the Skwlax Pow Wow in July.
> *(Quaaout Lodge and Spa at Talking Rock Golf Resort, 2016)*

Cultural interpretive areas, including a *kekuli* and traditional sweat lodge, are featured in articles published by travel writers listed on the media pages.

On the ATBC website, cultural programming is reflected through 290 photographic images. The Our Cultures menu of the website offers visitors opportunities to:

> Learn and share in the traditions of our land, water and our people. Get front row seats to an amazing show, featuring landscapes that will capture your imagination. Be a patron of the arts and see how BC's Aboriginal peoples have used ancient art forms for storytelling since time immemorial. Meet our local legends, the wildlife that also call this land their home.
> *(ATBC, 2016)*

The photographic images feature artifacts and handicrafts ($n = 105$), traditional clothing and textiles ($n = 59$), festivals, performances and storytelling ($n = 54$) and cuisine ($n = 72$). In addition there is an invitation to visitors to participate in hands-on cultural workshops:

> Experience the enchantment of authentic Aboriginal demonstrations through cultural workshops. Immerse yourself in our crafts through hands-on workshops and discover how honoured traditions and methods, staples of the first nations culture, are being used and adapted for a modern world.
> *(ATBC, 2016)*

The ATBC website also features nine unique and authentic blog posts of storytelling, dancing, knitting, festivals and cultures from BC First Nations and Métis. Cultural programming on the websites highlights the diversity of both the tangible (i.e. artifacts, handicrafts) and intangible heritage (i.e. dance, drumming, storytelling) of over 200 First Nations and Métis groups in BC. Visitors are invited and encouraged to engage with and actively participate in Indigenous cultural programming.

Discussion

In reviewing the focal themes analysed in the web audit, the authors have chosen four themes for critical analysis and further discussion as they relate to the changes in Indigenous cultural tourism and health/wellness tourism in western Canada: Indigenous ownership, partnerships, host/guest relations and cultural programming

Indigenous ownership

Indigenous cultural tourism is defined by Butler and Hinch (2007) as the tourism activities in which Indigenous people are directly involved either through control and/or by having their cultures serve as the essence of the attraction. Whoever has control or exercises power generally determines such critical factors as the scale, pace, nature and, indeed, the outcomes of development. Researchers (Williams and O'Neill, 2007; Hull et al., in press) point out that the recent growth of Indigenous tourism in Canada has been dependent upon shifts in government policies that have devolved rights and responsibilities to Indigenous groups and organisations. As a result, Indigenous communities have advanced economic development strategies that have ensured their involvement in marketing strategies that promote Indigenous cultural tourism that incorporates health/wellness products and services.

Results of the research point out that, historically, Indigenous cultural tourism and health/wellness tourism in western Canada served as 'the essence of the attraction' for visitors to Banff in the late nineteenth and early twentieth centuries. However, control of the two sectors was in the hands of large corporations (i.e. the CPR) and government agencies (i.e. National Parks) that were targeting initially a luxury market linked to the railway and then a mass travel market with the advent of the automobile through staged events such as the Banff Indian Days tourism festivals.

In the twenty-first century, the review of the Quaaout Lodge and Spa and the ATBC websites illustrates a distinct shift to Indigenous ownership with full control of Indigenous cultural tourism and the health and wellness products and services tied directly to Indigenous tourism associations and businesses. These services and products are promoted on their websites, which target both an Indigenous cultural tourism as well as a health/wellness market through authentic experiences and customised services.

Partnerships and collaboration

Collaboration is a process of joint decision making among key stakeholders to resolve planning problems. Voigt and Laing (2014) argue that stakeholder collaboration evolves over time and can take many forms: relatively simple or complex; temporary or long-lasting; and with or without formal rules. There are two types of collaboration: specialised collaboration, where the same type of tourism firms collaborate (i.e. accommodations) and complementary collaboration, where organisations collaborate across different sectors (i.e. Indigenous, health/wellness). Collaboration is recognised as a key factor for destination competitiveness, innovation and long-term survival (Pechlaner et al., 2008). The key players collaborating in the tourism sector are tourists and hosts, travel agents, transportation companies, outbound and inbound tour operators, government agencies and the media (Butler and Hinch, 2007). By working together, a number of benefits from collaboration include: increased cost savings; higher-quality products; product innovation and diversification; and enhanced market visibility through cross-marketing (Bramwell and Lane, 2004). Barriers to collaboration include mistrust, rivalry and competition, lack of strategic vision and leadership in development of wellness tourism, language barriers, hostile political systems, strongly varying expectations and unequal financial participation (Hjalager et al., 2011).

For the Banff Springs Resort at the turn of the twentieth century, the federal government, the CPR and local tourism entrepreneurs collaborated on packages that promoted Banff as an outdoor recreation paradise with health/wellness benefits for urban elite tourists from Europe and North America. Pre-colonial representations of Indigenous peoples were utilised in tourism marketing campaigns that re-enacted colonial narratives (Mason, 2014). Issues of mistrust, hostile political systems and unequal financial participation are evident. The 1885 creation of the Banff Hot Springs Reserve, the precursor to Banff National Park (1930), reduced the Nakoda people's access to the region, as their subsistence practices directly conflicted with sport hunting and fishing businesses and they did not support tourist expectations of a 'natural' environment. Indigenous use of parkland was also increasingly restricted and researchers point out that Indigenous participants in the Banff Indian Days were at times exploited through the festival and tourism entrepreneurs (Meijer-Drees, 1993; Mason, 2008).

The website audit reveals that the numerous partners on the Quaaout Lodge and Spa and ATBC websites represent key players in the provincial Indigenous cultural tourism industry and the health/wellness sectors. Land claim settlements and the devolution of powers to local groups have resulted in greater collaboration, more supportive political systems and increased financial benefit for Indigenous peoples, with the Indigenous tourism sector in BC earning $45 million in 2013 (Dyck, 2014). There is collaboration across both the Indigenous cultural tourism and health/wellness sectors, reflecting complementary collaborations that are resulting in high-quality products, product diversification and greater cross-marketing efforts.

Host/guest relations

Bruner (2005) refers to cultural tourism as a 'borderzone' between consumers and producers where tourists and locals meet. Creativity is a practice that unites consumers and producers in the construction of space based on the co-creation or co-production of experiences (Richards, 2011; Hull et al., in press). Music, dance, visual arts, storytelling, ceremonies, rituals and folklore are all traditions of Indigenous communities that are enhancing place making and place marketing through creative tourism development (Gibson, 2012).

The Banff Indian Days are recognised as an influential event that shaped visitor perceptions of Indigenous peoples and the Banff-Bow Valley (Mason, 2014). The festival was an essential and dynamic space for the exchange of intercultural knowledge, the co-creation of experiences, as well as a space for regaining access to the region and responding to colonial structures designed to repress and assimilate Indigenous cultures (Snow, 2005; Mason, 2015).

The web audit of the Quaaout Lodge and Spa and the ATBC websites both use photographic images and text to present hosts and guests co-producing Indigenous cultural activities such as drumming and storytelling and health/wellness experiences, such as participating in a sweat lodge ceremony. Text indicates that hosts and guests are 'learning and sharing' and 'immersing' themselves in guided tours with local elders through educational and interpretive exhibits with local guides and arts and crafts workshops. The websites illustrate that Indigenous cultural tourism and health/wellness tourism in western Canada are increasingly offering visitors direct participation in unique, hands-on, authentic Indigenous activities.

Cultural programming

When summarising the profile of travellers to Canada interested in cultural programming, results show that these types of visitors also have interests in both health/wellness tourism and Indigenous tourism. In 2006 the Canadian Tourism Commission (Destination Canada, 2006) released a study of health/wellness travellers that indicated that many of them were motivated by various factors that included culture, history, cuisine, sightseeing, education and shopping as popular leisure pursuits while on vacation. The Global Spa Summit (2011) adds further that wellness tourism involves people who are looking for local, traditional and unique experiences that acknowledge location, geography and people. Williams and O'Neill's research (2007) of Indigenous tourism in BC also found that travellers to BC were most satisfied with Indigenous tourism experiences that involved viewing and purchasing authentic crafts, touring museums and art galleries. Their most positive impressions were linked to opportunities to learn from the region's Indigenous cultures, the friendliness/receptiveness of Indigenous peoples and to view/ purchase Indigenous arts and crafts.

The evolution of the Indigenous and health/wellness tourism sectors in western Canada illustrates how the region initially focused on attracting an international luxury tourism market from cities in Europe and North America through package trips organised with CPR, hoteliers and the National Parks. As access improved to western Canada with the advent of the automobile, cultural programming featured Indigenous festivals and events focused on marketing the Wild West genre to mass markets. In the twenty-first century, online marketing through a variety of Indigenous websites and social media is targeting domestic and international niche markets interested in a diverse offering of tangible (i.e. artifacts, built environment) and intangible (i.e. drumming, storytelling) Indigenous heritage that is increasingly incorporating authentic health/wellness experiences.

Conclusion

Over the last three centuries, western Canada has benefitted from the growth of Indigenous tourism and health/wellness tourism. The region's initial development with the construction of the CPR, the founding of Canada's Mountain Parks and the discovery of the Banff Hot Springs offered luxury urban markets an escape from the city and leisure opportunities to rejuvenate the body, mind and soul at an elite health/wellness destination in the Canadian Rockies (Williams, 1922). For Indigenous communities residing in the region the main outcome of development was exclusion from traditional lands due to land use conflicts with tourism entrepreneurs and park agencies.

With the opening of the Calgary–Banff coach road, individual entrepreneurs opened up the region to mass tourism markets, providing greater access, cheaper accommodation and alternative forms of recreation. By the early twentieth century, Wild West films and literature created colonial narratives and pre-colonial representations of Indigenous cultures that were manifested through the Banff Indian Days tourism festivals (Deloria, 2004). Banff was marketed as a destination offering both health/wellness tourism and Indigenous cultural tourism (Mason, 2008), attracting thousands of tourists to the region. For many Indigenous participants, the festival provided financial gain and intercultural exchange, but also resulted in exploitation of Indigenous communities (Meijer-Drees, 1993).

By the twenty-first century, shifts in government policies devolving rights and responsibilities to Indigenous groups and organisations have resulted in greater Indigenous ownership in the tourism industry in the region through economic development strategies that are promoting both Indigenous cultural tourism and health/wellness tourism, as exemplified through the Quaaout Lodge and Spa case study. As a result of these regulatory changes there has been an increase in partnerships and complementary collaboration across the two sectors that is providing numerous benefits to Indigenous tourism entrepreneurs through cost savings, higher-quality products and product diversification. Support from a regional Indigenous tourism association, ATBC, is also providing benefits from cross-marketing. In addition, host/ guest experiences are increasingly focused on the co-production of the visitor experience through hands-on, experiential, authentic, cultural programming. Indigenous communities are not only integrating traditional health/wellness traditions into tourist offerings but also linking traditional and modern spa/wellness modalities. Finally, market studies also point to an increasing convergence of visitors interested in both Indigenous tourism and health/wellness tourism experiences that acknowledge location, geography and people.

Notes

1 In Canada, the term 'Indigenous' has been established as one of the most useful to refer collectively to First Nations, Métis and Inuit peoples. For this reason, throughout this chapter we have chosen the term when describing general Canadian contexts. However, it is critical to invoke an Indigenous nation's own self-appellation whenever possible and we do this throughout, for example, by referring to Nakoda or Secwepemc peoples. Attention to such terminological specificity prevents a homogenisation of distinct cultures and recognises the heterogeneity and diversity of Indigenous languages and cultural groups.
2 The CPR was formed in 1881 with the intention of building a railway that would unite central Canada with BC and the Pacific coast. From the 1880s until the beginning of the Second World War, the CPR diversified into tourism ventures, including hotel and infrastructure construction. For more, see Choko and Jones (2004).
3 The railway was completed at Craigellachie, BC, on 7 November 1885. The completion of the railway fulfilled the 1871 commitment that the Canadian federal government made to connect BC to central Canada. The promise of a transcontinental railway was a significant factor in securing the western province in Canadian Confederation (Nicol, 1970: 23–25).
4 Rocky Mountains National Park Act, 23 June 1887 (Statutes of Canada, 50–51 Victoria, Chapter 32).
5 Unless otherwise specified, all monetary figures are in Canadian dollars.
6 Although there are diverse experiences and regional variations associated with sweat lodges, they can be considered spiritual purification ceremonies. They usually consist of several rounds that include ritualised forms of various cultural practices. As guests to these ceremonies, we are not qualified or permitted to speak specifically about sweat-lodge experiences. In 1885, through introducing legislation, the federal government began to repress directly the cultural practices of Indigenous peoples in Western Canada. In an effort to assimilate Indigenous communities into broader Euro-Canadian society, the sweat lodge, along with Sun Dance ceremonies, was made illegal. During this period these practices continued, but simply moved outside the gaze of missionaries, the police, Indian agents and other members of the colonial bureaucracy who enforced this assimilatory legislation.
7 A *kekuli* pit is a traditional winter home built by the interior Indigenous peoples of BC. Built underground with log flooring, *kekuli* pit roofs were made of grass, pine needles, cedar bark and earth.

References

Albers, P. and James, W. (1988) 'Travel photography: A methodological approach', *Annals of Tourism Research*, 15, 134–158.
Allford, J. (2014) *Shuswap BC, on the Adams River: Marvelling at the Miraculous Adams River Sockeye Salmon Run*, Toronto, ON: Toronto Star.
ATBC (2012) *AtBC Launches New Five Year Plan – Forecasts Significant Growth to 2017*, https://www.aboriginal bc.com/corporate/news/atbc-launches-new-five-year-plan-forecasts-significant-growth-to-2017 (accessed 8 February 2016).
ATBC (2016) *Things to Do*, 1 January, https://www.aboriginalbc.com/ (accessed 8 February 2016).
Bella, L. (1987) *Parks for Profit*, Montreal, QC: Harvest House.
Binnema, T. and Niemi, M. (2006) 'Let the line be drawn now: Wilderness, conservation and the exclusion of Aboriginal people from Banff National Park in Canada', *Environmental History*, 11(2006), 724–750.
Bramwell, B. and Lane, B. (2004) 'Collaboration and partnerships in tourism planning', in *Tourism Collaboration and Partnerships: Politics, Practices and Sustainability*, Clevedon, UK: Channelview Publications.
Brown, R.C. (1970) 'The doctrine of usefulness: Natural resources and the National Park Policy in Canada, 1887–1914', in Nelson, J.G. (ed.) *Canadian Parks in Perspective*, Montreal, QC: Harvest House.
Bruner, E.M. (2005) *Culture on Tour: Ethnographies of Reality*, Chicago, IL: University of Chicago Press.
Bryman, A. (2012) *Social Research Methods*, Oxford, UK: Oxford University Press.

Bugmann, M. (2008) *Savage to Saint: The Karl May Story*, New York: Book Surge Publishing.

Butler, R. and Hinch, T. (2007) *Tourism and Indigenous Peoples: Issues and Implications*, Oxford, UK: Elsevier.

Caton, K. and Santos, C.A. (2008) 'Closing the hermenutic circle? Photographic encounters with the other', *Annals of Tourism Research*, 35(1), 7–26.

Choko, M.H. and Jones, D.L. (2004) *Posters of the Canadian Pacific*, Toronto, ON: Firefly Books.

Cooperman, J. (2015) *Quaaout – A Community Enhanced by Tourism*, 30 April, http://shuswappassion.ca/culture/quaaout-a-community-enhanced-by-tourism/ (accessed 15 February 2016).

Deloria, P.J. (2004) *Indians in Unexpected Places*, Lawrence, KS: University of Kansas.

Destination Canada (2006) *2006 Canadian Spa Sector Profile*, Vancouver, BC: Destination Canada Destination Canada.

Dyck, D. (2014) *Aboriginal Cultural Tourism 'Booming' in B.C.*, 18 March, http://www.cbc.ca/news/aboriginal/aboriginal-cultural-tourism-booming-in-b-c-1.2576971 (accessed 15 February 2016).

Echtner, C. and Prasad, P. (2003) 'The context of third world tourism marketing', *Annals of Tourism Research*, 30(3), 660–682.

Furniss, E. (1995) *Victims of Benevolence: The Dark Legacy of the Williams Lake Residential School*, Vancouver, BC: Arsenal Pulp Press.

Gibson, C. (2012) 'Cultural economy: Achievements, divergences, future prospects', *Geographical Research*, 50(3), 282–290.

Global Spa Summit 2011 (2011) 'Wellness tourism and medical tourism: Where do spas fit?', Global Spa Summit 2011, Miami, FL: Global Wellness Summit Headquarters.

Hall, C.M. and Valentin, A. (2005) 'Content analysis', in Ritchie, B., Burns, P. and Palmer, C. (eds) *Tourism Research Methods: Integrating Theory with Practice*, Wallingford, UK: CABI International.

Hart, E.J. (1983) *The Selling of Canada: The CPR and the Beginning of Canadian Tourism*, Banff, AB: Altitude Publishing.

—— (1999) *The Place of Bows: Exploring the Heritage of the Banff-Bow Valley*, Banff, AB: EJH Literary Enterprises.

Hjalager, A.-M., Konu, H., Huijbens, E., Bjork, P., Flagestad, A., Nordin, S. and Tuohino, A. (2011) *Innovating and Re-branding Nordic Wellbeing Tourism*, Oslo, Norway: Nordic Innovation Centre.

Hull, J.S., de la Barre, S. and Maher, P. (in press) 'Peripheral geographies of creativity: The case for Indigenous tourism and community economic development in the western Canadian Arctic', in Viken, A. and Muller, D.K. (eds) *Tourism and Indigeneity in the Arctic*. Bristol, UK: Channel View.

Kasson, J.S. (2000) *Buffalo Bill's Wild West: Celebrity, Memory and Popular History*, New York: Hill and Wang.

Keller, R.H. and Turek, M.F. (1999) *American Indians and National Parks*, Tucson, AZ: University of Arizona Press.

Little Shuswap Indian Band (2016) *Cultural Activities*, 1 January, http://www.lslib.com/ (accessed 15 January 2016).

Manuel, G. and Posluns, M. (1974) *The Fourth World: An Indian Reality*, Toronto, ON: Collier-Macmillan.

Marty, S. (1984) *A Grand and Fabulous Notion: The First Century of Canada's National Parks*, Toronto, ON: NCP.

Mason, C. (2008) 'The construction of Banff as a natural environment: Sporting festivals, tourism and representations of Aboriginal peoples', *Journal of Sport History*, 35(2), 221–239.

—— (2012) 'Consuming the physical and cultural practices of aboriginal peoples: Spaces of exchange, conflict and (post) colonial power relations', in Hughson, J. (ed.) *The Role of Sports in the Formation of Personal Identities: Studies in Community Loyalties*, London: Edwin Mellen Press.

—— (2014) *Spirits of the Rockies: Reasserting an Indigenous Presence in Banff National Park*, Toronto, ON: University of Toronto Press.

—— (2015) 'The Banff Indian Days tourism festivals', *Annals of Tourism Research*, 53(2015), 77–95.

Meijer-Drees, L. (1993) 'Indians' bygone past: The Banff Indian days, 1902–1945', *Past Imperfect*, 2(1993), 7–28.

Monforton, L. (2013) *Gathering Place for R & R Seekers – and Golfers*, http://www.festivalseekers.com/okanaganinteriorfestivals/quaaoutlodge (accessed 15 January 2016).

Moses, L.G. (1996) *Wild West Shows and the Images of American Indians, 1883–1933*, Albuquerque, NM: University of New Mexico Press.

Nepal, S. and Jamal, T.B. (2011) 'Resort-induced changes in small mountain communities in British Columbia, Canada', *Mountain Research and Development*, 31(2), 89–101.

Nicol, J.I. (1970) 'The national parks movement in Canada', in Nelson, J.G. (ed.) *Canadian Parks in Perspective*, Montreal, QC: Harvest House.

Palmer, A.D. (2005) *Maps of Experience: The Anchoring of Land to Story in Secwepemc Discourse*, Toronto, ON: University of Toronto Press.

Parker, P. (1990) *The Feather and the Drum: The History of Banff Indian Days, 1889–1978*, Calgary, AB: Consolidated Communications.

Pechlaner, H., Fisher, E. and Hamman, E.M. (2008) 'Leadership and innovation processes: Development of products and services based on core competencies', *Journal of Quality Assurance in Hospitality and Tourism*, 6, 31–57.

Quaaout Lodge and Spa at Talking Rock Golf Resort (2016) *Welcome*, 1 January, http://quaaoutlodge. com/ (accessed 15 February 2016).

Rakić, T. and Chambers, D. (2011) *An Introduction of Visual Research Methods in Tourism*, London: Routledge.

Richards, G. (2011) 'Creativity and tourism: The state of the art', *Annals of Tourism Research*, 38(4), 1225–1253.

Scott, G. (2012) *First Nations Resort Redefines Relaxation*, 23 July, http://www.canada.com/business/First+ Nations+resort+redefines+relaxation/6975934/story.html (accessed 15 January 2016).

Singh, E., Milne, S.S. and Hull, J.S. (2012) 'Use of mixed methods case study to research sustainable tourism development in South Pacific SIDs', in Hyde, K., Ryan, C. and Woodside, A.G. (eds) *Field Guide to Case Study Research in Tourism, Hospitality and Leisure, volume 6*, Bingley, UK: Emerald.

Snow, J. (2005) *These Mountains Are Our Sacred Places: The Story of the Stoney Indians*, Toronto, ON: Fifth House Publishing.

Veal, A.J. (2006) *Research Methods for Leisure and Tourism: A Practical Guide*, London: Pearson Education.

Voigt, C. and Laing, J. (2014) 'An examination of the extent of collaboration between major wellness tourism stakeholders in Australia', in Voigt, C. and Pforr, C. (eds) *Wellness Tourism*, London: Routledge.

Williams, M.B. (1922) *The Heart of the Rockies*, Hamilton, NJ: H.R. Larson Publishing.

Williams, P. and O'Neill, B. (2007) 'Building a triangulated research foundation for Indigenous tourism in BC, Canada', in Butler, R. and Hinch, T. (eds) *Tourism and Indigenous Peoples: Issues and Implications*, Oxford, UK: Elsevier.

34

Conclusion

Melanie Kay Smith and László Puczkó

The authors in this handbook have reflected on a number of the most significant themes relating to health tourism. Not all of the chapters focus on 'health tourism' *per se*, but instead on the complex inter-relationships between health, tourism and wellbeing. It can be (and has been) argued that all forms of tourism can contribute to wellbeing or health, but the question is, how long-lasting can the health or wellbeing effects of tourism be? This question is still open for debate, but one of the foundations of a healthier form of tourism is that it benefits the local people and the place as much as it benefits the tourists visiting that destination. This point is made especially prominently by Robyn Bushell in Chapter 8, and again by Colin Michael Hall in Chapter 16 (but the latter more specifically in the context of medical tourism). Health tourism clearly needs to follow the now well-established principles of sustainable development; however, many authors also argue that there is an inextricable link between wellbeing, health and sustainable development. For example, Edward H. Huijbens (Chapter 28) suggests that, along with the restoration of the self, visiting therapeutic landscapes can help to foster ecological sensibilities which may lead to higher levels of sustainable behaviour. Indeed, the emphasis on nature in this book is quite considerable. It is perhaps not surprising given that many of the authors have recently been exploring the relationship between tourism, wellbeing and ecosystem services in the context of an EU-funded COST project. However, others besides those authors seem to subscribe to Richard Louv's (2005) notion that nature deficit disorder could be a real threat to human beings' health and wellbeing. Harald A. Friedl in Chapter 27, for example, posits natural landscapes as an antedote to modern lifestyles within which attention is often wholly monopolised by digital devices. Both he and Edward H. Huijbens advocate forms of tourism that can attune human beings to different rhythms, such as those espoused by slow tourism or spiritual tourism. The rediscovery of one's autonomy and sense of self away from the ordered, measured, hectic and stressful nature of modern life can be one of the rewards of spending more time in nature.

Indeed, the loss of the self in modern lifestyles is a recurrent theme in some of chapters in this book. Kelly and Smith discuss how retreat experiences can lead to a re-connection to the true or 'authentic' self rather than the 'ideal' or 'social' self (Chapter 12). This is especially important for those people whose lives may have been taken over not only by work or technology, but also by caring for others (e.g. mothers of small children, people with ageing or sick relatives). The need to retreat from modern life into more serene environments with like-minded people is a major motivation for many tourists. The presence of sublime natural landscapes can afford certain benefits, but the presence of like-minded others may also be of considerable importance in terms of emotional support and development. Glouberman and Cloutier, for example, emphasise the importance of community and social support in the context of retreats to counterbalance the growing epidemic of isolation in many societies (Chapter 13). Smith's chapter looks at some of the most important elements of a happy and healthy life (Chapter 3), and one of the most significant dimensions is the connection to or relationship with others.

One of the fundamental questions addressed in this handbook is actually what constitutes a healthy life and how can tourism contribute to this (if at all)? There is some consensus about what healthy means, but it is also contested over time and research studies can be contradictory. It is essential when talking about health tourism that we have a clear sense of what health means in this context. Authors in this handbook take a somewhat broad view of health, which concurs with that of the World Health Organization, but with slightly more emphasis also on the spiritual dimensions of health. These are discussed, for example, not only in the context of landscape, as mentioned above (e.g. Huijbens, Friedl), but also in the contexts of retreats (e.g. Kelly and Smith; Glouberman and Cloutier) as well as in the chapter about yoga by Smith and Sziva (Chapter 14). Spirituality is not always counted in the domains of life satisfaction, therefore it may or may not be included in studies of tourism and wellbeing.

Wellbeing is defined fairly broadly in this handbook and those authors who consider how far tourism can contribute to wellbeing or life satisfaction (e.g. Mitas et al. [Chapter 5]; Uysal et al. [Chapter 6]) tend to incorporate many different domains. Research is inconclusive on this issue, but it seems that tourism can have at least a short-term impact on wellbeing; it can depend on life stage, importance of tourism for individuals or cultures, types of tourism and the activities undertaken on holiday. For example, Coffey and Csikszentmihályi (Chapter 7) suggest that flow-inducing activities can improve health and psychological wellbeing but also the propensity to feel positive about and return to destinations. Lee and Kim (Chapter 29) discuss the benefits of forest landscapes and healing programmes on emotion regulation, attention restoration and life satisfaction. Pesonen and Tuohino (Chapter 31) analyse a wide range of activities in the context of rural wellbeing tourism; simple pleasures like walking in nature as well as outdoor sports are the most popular. Types of landscape can also affect health differently, with blue spaces and especially seaside considered to be one of the healthiest landscapes and the most conducive to wellbeing, as discussed by Peter Kruizinga (Chapter 30).

In terms of developing landscapes which benefit visitors' health and wellbeing even more, certain approaches to destination development or management can be seen to be optimum. Most of these involve multi-level and multi-sectoral partnerships as well as holistic and integrated approches. Tuominen, Saari and Binder propose in Chapter 23 a particularly comprehensive model for health destinations. Konu and Smith (Chapter 24) give examples of collaborations in health tourism which have had varying degrees of success and make recommendations for facilitating networks and partnerships. Some of the most important elements for the future of health tourism destinations are likely to be the extent to which there are proven benefits for the products and services offered, as discussed by Steckenbauer and his co-authors (Chapter 25). Other important aspects noted by these authors include quality and authenticity of experience. Smith and Puczkó note in Chapter 22 that, even though many destinations are based around balneology or healing water traditions, the evidence base for these is globally not yet strong enough to convince international tourists and the medical profession to accept them. Pesonen and Tuohino make the important point that not all visitors will be attracted to the same activities or clusters of activities and that differentiations may need to be made (Chapter 31). Rawlinson and Wiltshier (Chapter 26) as well as Ferrari and Gilli (Chapter 32) recommend product and service developments across landscapes like national or natural parks which offer visitors a wide range of experiences, such as nature, culture and spas in combination. Kruizinga (Chapter 30) even gives a case study which suggests that developing whole health regions which are also visited by tourists may become a reality in the future.

The relationship between the local and tourism is fundamental to the success of all health tourism developments and destinations. All of the authors mentioned in the previous part also emphasise the importance of local communities and cultures in the context of health destination development and management. John S. Hull and Courtney Mason (Chapter 33) provide a detailed analysis of the importance of local and Indigenous people in the development of wellness and cultural services for visitors to national parks. Going back to Robyn Bushell's chapter (Chapter 8), the health and wellbeing of the local people and host populations are absolutely essential to all forms of tourism, but especially to health tourism. There is no greater irony than a form of health tourism that impacts negatively on the wellbeing of local people and places, and in extreme cases, as noted by Colin Michael Hall (Chapter 16), can even contribute to health problems and illnesses. Another important issue is ensuring that the most deprived people in a society have access to the health benefits of tourism, for example, poor families, disabled people, the elderly, as discussed in more detail by McCabe and Diekmann (Chapter 9) in the context of social tourism.

However, it also needs to be recognised that people's needs may change over time and that we are not dealing with uniform groups of tourists. Pesonen and Tuohino made this point in the context of rural wellbeing tourism (Chapter 31). Gareth Shaw and his co-authors (Chapter 10) demonstrate through life course analysis that tourists' interests, preferences and needs tend to change over the course of their lifetime depending on different stages and levels of health and mobility. Their emphasis is on older tourists, but Kelly and Smith (Chapter 12) focus more on middle-aged women. The main target market for all forms of health tourism tends to be middle-aged women. Mid-life crisis has perhaps turned out to be less of an 'urban myth' than it was often thought to be, with happiness levels generally reaching their nadir by mid-life. Women may have the additional transition phases of childbirth or menopause to contend with. It is also important to consider the preferences of different nationalities. Although few of the authors have done so, Pesonen and Tuohino's research focuses more on Baltic State visitors and Smith's chapter includes a case study of residents of 11 Balkan countries. Individual case studies within the chapters also give some insights into national and cultural differences, but more research is clearly needed on this as well as life stage or life course.

This handbook does not provide numerous chapters on the different sub-sectors of health tourism (e.g. spas, wellness hotels), as it was felt that this had been covered quite extensively elsewhere (e.g. Smith and Puczkó, 2013). However, many authors provided specific examples of broader themes in contexts such as spas, retreats, hospitals or clinics, as well as natural landscapes, as already discussed. For example, Jeremy McCarthy (Chapter 11) uses spas as an example of spaces that are considered to be sanctuaries away from increasingly stressful and technologically driven modern lives in much the same way as Friedl's 'places of power', Huijben's 'therapeutic landscapes' and Kelly and Smith's or Glouberman and Cloutier's holistic retreats. Frost and Laing (Chapter 2) also trace the importance of spas and spa resorts in the history of health tourism and the various ways in which trends have been influenced by cultures, religion, social fashions and individual celebrities. Although spas have often been, and still are, to an extent, associated more with the leisure, wellness and hedonic sides of tourism, McCarthy makes an important point that there are few such places left where one can retreat from the modern world. Human touch in the form of massage and therapies may also help to alleviate the symptoms of loneliness or isolation, an 'epidemic' noted by Glouberman and Cloutier.

Several authors focus on medical tourism, which is perhaps the fastest-growing sector of health tourism. All forms of tourism ideally require sustainable and ethical approaches, but nowhere is this more true than in medical tourism. David Reisman (Chapter 15) provides an incredibly powerful analysis of ethics, arguing that medical tourism does not exist independently from wider systems of morals and social justice. Colin Michael Hall (Chapter 16) also makes the point that, in an increasingly global and mobile world, medical tourism does not concern just individual and personal issues of ethics and equity. Regulation is a central issue in the context of medical tourism, unlike in spas and wellness sectors, where many of the therapies and treatments may simply offer placebo effect (as discussed by McCarthy in Chapter 11). On the other hand, Gallagher and Joppe (Chapter 18) suggest that increased regulation may be needed in some domains of spa therapy where medical procedures are administered, i.e. by aestheticians. Markus Frischhut (Chapter 17) adds to these debates by emphasising the legal dimension of health tourism, especially in some of the most sensitive areas of healthcare, such as cross-border reproductive care.

Ethical, legal and regulatory issues aside, patients or medical tourists have an increasingly diverse choice of destinations and hospitals to choose from when they are electing treatments. It was originally thought that proximity and price might be the most important factors, but several more subtle and complex factors may also come into play. Medical tourism is not so different from other forms of tourism in that tourists would like to be treated to a positive experience in terms of service and hospitality. Sharon Kleefield (Chapter 19) mentions that accreditation, safety and a hospital's good reputation might be important; however, quality and service might also influence decision making. In Chapter 21 DeMicco takes this a stage further, even suggesting that hospitals could or should be run more like visitor attractions which place a strong emphasis on hospitality, service quality and a wide range of other 'soft' factors which impact significantly on tourists' experiences. Medical and healthcare services are not always as customer-orientated as they could be. For local residents who have no other choice, this may be sufficient. For international medical tourists who have a large number of choices, it may not. Kai Illing in Chapter 20 refers to the idea of 'guest patients' in the context of medical hotels, but actually, in medical tourism all patients become guests. There are still considerable debates about whether the term 'medical tourist' should even be used when the tourists 'only' use the services and facilities of a hospital and no other attraction. They should nevertheless be treated as guests, especially as research shows that the psychological dimensions of healing can be as strong as, or even stronger than, the physical ones. A good bedside manner, kindness, a culture of caring and respect should be fundamental to medical tourism and, indeed, all forms of healthcare.

Not all health tourists are unwell and strict regulations and legal frameworks may not be necessary for all forms of health tourism. However, all health tourists are looking for enhanced health and all tourists are hoping for improved levels of wellbeing. Healthy destinations or regions which are based on principles of sustainability and ethics where local people have a high quality of life are in a better position to offer this. Health regions or whole destinations may become the norm in the future. Whether they are health tourists or wellbeing-seeking tourists, all tourists want to gain positive experiences, to be offered high-quality hospitality and services, and to feel welcomed by their hosts. This is especially true of tourists who are not well and are seeking medical services. The choice of locations and destinations for improving health and wellbeing is now vast. It may happen in a specially designated centre like a spa or holistic retreat; it may happen in a hospital or clinic; it may happen in a landscape or national park. The desire to encounter green and blue spaces is growing in popularity as urban dwellers start to recognise their nature deprivation and technology addictions. Spas and retreats can offer sanctuaries or refuges from which to escape or take a deep breath away from the increasingly stressful and crisis-ridden world we live in. Some tourists are trying to regain a sense of self, others are seeking like-minded communities. Some need nothing more than a rest, while others are hoping for self-development, transformation, even transcendence. The expanding and diversifying world of health tourism can offer all of this and more to world-weary tourists of all ages and in all life stages. It is the job of providers to anticipate, meet and ideally exceed their needs in this increasingly competitive field of tourism.

References

Louv, R. (2005) *Last Child in the Woods: Saving Our Children from Nature Deficit Disorder*, Chapel Hill, NC: Algonquin Books.

Smith, M.K. and Puczkó, L. (2013) *Health, Tourism and Hospitality: Spas, Wellness and Medical Travel*, London: Routledge.

Index

For Product Safety Concerns and Information please contact our
EU representative GPSR@taylorandfrancis.com Taylor & Francis
Verlag GmbH, Kaufingerstraße 24, 80331 München, Germany